THE INTERNATIONAL ENCYCLOPEDIA OF COMMUNICATION

At Blackwell Publishing

Commissioning editor:	Elizabeth Swayze
In-house project managers:	Ken Provencher and Tiffany Mok
Production manager:	Simon Eckley
Production editor and text designer:	Jenny Phillips
Marketers:	Alex Robinson, Desirée Zicko, Louise Cooper
Freelance project manager:	Fiona Sewell
Copyeditors:	Jean Ashford, Mary Franklin, Jacqueline Harvey, Jane Kerr, Pandora Kerr Frost, Leah Morin, and Fiona Sewell
Proofreaders:	Helen Kemp, Marie Lorimer, Mary Malin, and Colin Owens
Indexers:	Philip Aslett and Marie Lorimer

VOLUME IX

THE INTERNATIONAL ENCYCLOPEDIA OF COMMUNICATION

EDITED BY | WOLFGANG DONSBACH

PRECISION JOURNALISM –
RHETORIC IN WESTERN EUROPE: BRITAIN

© 2008 by Blackwell Publishing Ltd

BLACKWELL PUBLISHING
350 Main Street, Malden, MA 02148-5020, USA
9600 Garsington Road, Oxford OX4 2DQ, UK
550 Swanston Street, Carlton, Victoria 3053, Australia

The right of Wolfgang Donsbach to be identified as the author of the editorial material in this work has been asserted in accordance with the Copyright, Designs and Patents Act 1988.

First published 2008 by Blackwell Publishing Ltd

1   2008

Library of Congress Cataloguing-in-Publication Data

The international encyclopedia of communication/edited by Wolfgang Donsbach.
   p. cm.
Includes bibliographical references and index.
ISBN 978-1-4051-3199-5 (hardcover : alk. paper)
1. Communication—Encyclopedias.   I. Donsbach, Wolfgang, 1949–

P87.5.158   2008
302.203—dc22

                                                                    2007047271

A catalogue record for this book is available from the British Library.

Set in 10/13pt Minion
by Graphicraft Limited, Hong Kong
Printed in Singapore
by C.O.S. Printers Pte Ltd

The publisher's policy is to use permanent paper from mills that operate a sustainable forestry policy, and which has been manufactured from pulp processed using acid-free and elementary chlorine-free practices. Furthermore, the publisher ensures that the text paper and cover board used have met acceptable environmental accreditation standards.

For further information on
Blackwell Publishing, visit our website at
www.blackwellpublishing.com

Editors

Editorial Areas

Communication as a Field and Discipline
Communication and Media Law and Policy
Communication and Social/Behavioral Change
Communication and Technology
Communication Theory and Philosophy
Development Communication
Developmental Communication
Exposure to Communication Content
Feminist and Gender Studies
Information Processing and Cognitions
Instructional/Educational Communication
Intercultural and Intergroup Communication
International Communication
Interpersonal Communication
Journalism
Language and Social Interaction
Media Economy
Media Effects
Media History
Media Production and Content
Media Systems in the World
Organizational Communication
Political Communication
Popular Communication
Reality Perception through the Media
Research Methods
Rhetorical Studies
Strategic Communication, Public Relations, Advertisement
Visual Communication

Contents

Precision Journalism

Stephen K. Doig

Arizona State University

Precision journalism is the use of social and behavioral science → research methods to gather and analyze data, bringing a level of rigor to journalistic work beyond anecdotal evidence. Although it can be practiced without computers, precision journalism is usually a subset of "computer-assisted reporting," the catch-all term for anything from using the Internet for gathering information to developing newsroom intranets for sharing information among reporters. Another common term is "database journalism," which focuses on gathering and analyzing large collections of government data.

Precision journalism may expand most in places with high concentrations of computers, where public records exist in electronic form, but internationally journalists practice it using any available techniques if they can get access to information and have sufficient training to carry out an analysis.

ORIGINS

The term "precision journalism," and the central idea behind it, were popularized by the 1973 book of the same name written by Knight-Ridder reporter Philip Meyer. He had discovered the journalistic potential of using public opinion research (→ Survey) and other social science methods during a sabbatical year at Harvard University in 1966–1967. He applied what he learned shortly thereafter by doing groundbreaking surveys of participants in race riots in Detroit and Miami. He credits journalism educator Everette Dennis with creating the term precision journalism (Meyer 1991).

Perhaps the earliest precursor to precision journalism occurred on the US presidential election night of 1952. Walter Cronkite, then the Washington correspondent for CBS News (→ Broadcast Journalism; Election Polls and Forecasts; Political Journalists), used a Univac I computer analysis of early returns to predict correctly that Dwight Eisenhower would easily win the presidency.

A pioneering use of the techniques was a 1969 *Miami Herald* study of the Dade County, Florida, criminal justice system. In 1972, the *New York Times* analyzed how arrest statistics differed across New York police precincts. A year later, the *Philadelphia Inquirer* investigative team worked with Meyer to quantify racial bias in criminal sentencing (→ Investigative Reporting). In 1978, Meyer assisted *Miami Herald* reporters (one of whom, Rich Morin, later became survey research editor for the *Washington Post*) in an analysis of property tax records that revealed the undervaluation of expensive homes compared to more modest homes in the Miami area (Cox 2000). These US examples illustrate the initial pattern of major newspapers using advanced computing in a media system that fostered journalistic independence.

Despite a widely read book and successful models, precision journalism was slow to spread in its country of origin or elsewhere during the 1970s for two reasons. First, it required access to large mainframe computers like the Univac or IBM 360, expensive "big iron" hardware typically available only at large corporations or major universities. Second, most datasets interesting to journalists, such as court records, existed only on paper, requiring tedious hand-entry into a computer before analysis.

In the early 1980s, the spread of microcomputers started with hobbyist machines and then entered small businesses. Microcomputers also began to appear in government offices, leading to increased availability of machine-readable data that did not need keypunch data entry. Precision journalism then had the possibility of international diffusion but lagged behind the spread of its instrumental technologies (→ Information and Communication Technology, Development of).

DIFFUSION

A tiny scattering of US reporters began using early microcomputers, including machines like the Apple, Atari, Kaypro, and IBM PC, for newsroom work. Some had purchased computers for home hobby use, but then began to realize how the machines could help with their reporting. For instance, a reporter in the *Miami Herald* state capital bureau in 1983 wrote, for his IBM PC in the computer language BASIC, a vote analysis program that would take in a legislative roll-call vote and produce cross-tabulations of the data (→ Statistics, Descriptive) based on political demographics of law-makers (party, race, gender, leadership role, region, campaign funds from special interests, and the like).

The profile of database reporting grew in the mid-1980s when Elliot Jaspin, a reporter for the *Providence Journal*, matched Rhode Island databases of school bus drivers, traffic violators, and drug arrests, finding bus drivers with histories of bad driving records or drug dealing. On another occasion, he used a computer to analyze 35,000 mortgages meant to help lower-income home buyers and discovered many of the best loans going to the children of senior state officials. His stories prompted changes in state licensing procedures for bus drivers and indictments for those who had abused the mortgage program, attracting the attention of investigative reporters around the country (Cox 2000).

Interest in precision journalism skills exploded in 1989 when a young *Atlanta Journal-Constitution* reporter named Bill Dedman won a Pulitzer Prize for an investigative project called "The Color of Money." Computer analysis of mortgage applications showed how banks in the Atlanta area were shunning predominantly African-American neighborhoods, refusing to approve home loans there even for families with good incomes. The stories forced Atlanta banks to stop the practice and prompted US newspapers to do similar analyses in their own areas.

Later that year, Jaspin joined the University of Missouri journalism school and created what became the National Institute of Computer-Assisted Reporting (NICAR), under the wing of Investigative Reporters and Editors (IRE), an organization based there (→ Journalism Education; Journalists: Professional Associations). NICAR began training reporters in the techniques of using computers and database software to extract government data from magnetic tapes and analyze it for patterns. At about the same time, the first national conference of reporters focused on precision journalism took place at Indiana University. Centers at other universities followed.

Interest in and application of precision journalism grew rapidly in the United States during the 1990s. In 1992, IRE began computer-assisted reporting training sessions and panels at its annual conferences. The next year, NICAR held the first of what have become annual conferences that hundreds of reporters now attend. More than a thousand reporters now subscribe to the NICAR-L email listserv.

METHODS AND APPLICATIONS

Notable precision journalism stories include topics such as natural disasters, school performance, and crime, and apply a range of methods, including surveys (→ Public Opinion Polling), geographic information software (GIS), financial data analysis, and cross-tabulations. Most of these applications of information technologies to → news originated in the United States.

Precision journalism techniques have enhanced the coverage of *natural and human-produced disasters*. The *Miami Herald* won a Pulitzer in 1993 for a computer-aided analysis of the destruction patterns from Hurricane Andrew. Even more extensive computer work went into tracking the diaspora of victims of Hurricane Katrina in New Orleans in 2005, mapping the debris field from the 2003 loss of the space shuttle *Columbia*, and cataloguing the devastation of the September 11, 2001, attacks on New York City and Washington, DC.

To cover *school performance*, reporters have used statistical software like SPSS to create linear regression models that account for the effect of students' poverty on standardized test scores (→ Test Theory). The same statistical techniques also have uncovered significant cases of teachers and administrators fraudulently inflating classroom test scores in order to qualify for salary bonuses.

To cover the *criminal justice system*, one striking example was the use by the *Dallas Morning News* of logistic regression models to examine racial bias in jury selection by prosecutors and defense attorneys. Curiously, the paper found that both sides were biased in opposite directions, thereby canceling out the effects of the bias. In Brazil, *O Globo* did a computer-aided study of the incarcerations of more than 700 violent criminals, revealing that most had been quietly released long before their sentences were up. Newspapers and their network news partners in major cities around the world regularly do national public opinion polls using scientifically drawn random samples of respondents (→ Sampling, Random). Papers and networks such as the *New York Times*, the → BBC World Service, *Le Monde* in Paris, *El País* in Madrid, *Yomiuri Shinbun* in Japan, and *Folha de Sao Paulo* in Brazil practice this type of precision journalism. Geographic information systems software allows newspapers and television stations to reveal crime patterns, show the impact of toxic waste sites on the poor, and examine overbuilding in areas prone to floods or fires, among other topics. Dutch papers, for instance, used GIS to map the results of the referendum on the European Union constitution.

Financial data can uncover scandals involving the dates of stock transactions and trades favorable to insiders. Social → network analysis software can show, for example, the relationships of those who make large donations to the political candidates they support. Other examples include the creation of a database of the personal finances of Brazilian legislators, and analyses of the uncounted votes in Florida's controversial presidential election returns in 2000.

Precision journalism is not only for major investigative projects. Examples of lighter topics include cross-tabulation of pet licenses for most popular breeds and names; the different traits men and women seek when placing personal ads, the pattern of parking tickets on college campuses, sports ratings for the performance of players and teams, and a study of the profits of Mexican soccer teams.

INTERNATIONAL SPREAD

Precision journalism may have started in the United States, but the practice is spreading around the world. In 1997, IRE trainers held their first computer-assisted reporting workshops in Europe. The Danish International Center for Analytical Reporting (DICAR) then became an early proselytizer for precision journalism among international reporters. Since then, Global Investigative Journalism conferences in Copenhagen, Amsterdam, and Toronto have provided training in the use of spreadsheets, database programs, mapping, and statistics. *Precision journalism trainers* have conducted workshops in South Korea, China, and Nigeria, as well as in other countries in Latin America and Europe, including Bosnia. After attending the training sessions, reporters have gone on to do important stories despite the difficulty of getting public records in many countries. In a 2006 example, DICAR founder Nils Mulvad organized an international team of reporters to gather and publish a database revealing country-by-country details of the European Union 55-billion-euro farm subsidy program for the first time.

By the beginning of the twenty-first century, precision journalism had evolved from an exotic newsroom specialty into mainstream practice among some reporters in all but the smallest US newspapers as well as television stations. Journalism schools have begun teaching the basics to students. Although institutions and practitioners have emerged slowly in other countries, precision journalism has become widespread. The use of precision journalism techniques can grow as more countries put their census, courts, economic, election, and other data online. Ambitious international reporters can easily discover how the power of precision journalism is being used elsewhere and learn to use those tools in their own work.

SEE ALSO: ▶ BBC ▶ Broadcast Journalism ▶ Election Polls and Forecasts ▶ Information and Communication Technology, Development of ▶ Investigative Reporting ▶ Journalism Education ▶ Journalists: Professional Associations ▶ Network Analysis ▶ News ▶ Political Journalists ▶ Professionalization of Journalism ▶ Public Opinion Polling ▶ Research Methods ▶ Sampling, Random ▶ Statistics, Descriptive ▶ Survey ▶ Test Theory

References and Suggested Readings

Cox, M. (2000). The development of computer-assisted reporting. Paper presented to the Newspaper Division, AEJMC Southeast Colloquium, March 17, University of North Carolina, Chapel Hill. At www.com.miami.edu/car/cox00.htm.

Houston, B. (2004). *Computer-assisted reporting: A practical guide*, 3rd edn. Boston: Bedford and St. Martin's.

Meyer, P. (1973). *Precision journalism*. Bloomington, IN: Indiana University Press.

Meyer, P. (1991). *The new precision journalism*. Bloomington, IN: Indiana University Press.

Prejudiced and Discriminatory Communication

Janet B. Ruscher

Tulane University

Devin L. Wallace

Towson University

Prejudiced and discriminatory communication is studied in a wide range of social science disciplines, including communication, sociology, anthropology, and social psychology. Some forms, such as hate speech, are explicit, and they are recognized easily by an audience as reflecting prejudiced viewpoints. Other forms are more implicit: neither the speaker nor the audience may be aware that the speaker holds prejudiced views, even though independent evidence demonstrates that such views indeed are held. The conditions under which prejudiced views are expressed, as well as the forms that these communications take, are the subject of this entry ($\rightarrow$ Social Stereotyping and Communication; Stereotypes).

FUNCTIONS OF DISCRIMINATORY LANGUAGE

Discriminatory language is insidious because of the myriad functions that it serves. Drawing upon the extant literature on prejudice, Ruscher (2001) identifies *five types of functions*: economy of expression, group enhancement/ego defense, social functions, ingroup dominance, and impression management. These functions are not mutually exclusive, and can have similar surface features. For instance, two individuals may have similar stereotypes of lower income individuals and both call them "trailer trash," but one may use the term when his or her own middle income group is threatened (i.e., ego defense) and the other simply may use the term as a quickly understood social reference (i.e., economy of expression). Specific illustrations of these functions appear below in the discussion of explicitly and implicitly prejudiced language.

The five functions are important to consider because they provide insight into *why* speakers use prejudiced and discriminatory language. For example, *economical expression*, often seen in the short or symbolic labels used for outgroups, helps individuals preserve mental resources. As cognitive misers, social perceivers utilize shortcuts or heuristics whenever possible. Using stereotypes to group people is economical because attention is freed to focus elsewhere. Reliance upon the perceptual shortcuts of stereotypes – and shorthand expressions to reference the stereotyped group – proves both functional and practical. Speakers should use economical expressions when they would use stereotypes: when they are not motivated to think carefully about the targeted group or when they are under time pressure ($\rightarrow$ Elaboration Likelihood Model; Information Processing: Stereotypes; Limited Capacity Model).

Discriminatory language also serves as an *ego protector* and as a way to enhance the social status of the ingroup. In many cases, people derive self-esteem from comparing their own status to that of others. When downward social comparisons are made, people feel good about their status relative to others, and self-esteem can be maintained or even increased. As Thompson and Crocker (1990) demonstrated, social comparisons at the group level may engender intergroup bias, which tends to increase as presumed group threats also increase. Thus, certain forms of discriminatory and prejudiced language emerge when people feel threatened.

Prejudiced language also serves three social functions: avoiding contact, detachment, and delegitimization. By *avoiding interactions* with groups who may be the subject of prejudice or discrimination, people convince themselves that they are nonprejudiced. When people selectively avoid contact with disparaged outgroups, they reduce their opportunities to behave in a discriminatory fashion. Ironically, rather than recognizing their avoidance as discriminatory, individuals who have limited their own opportunities for further discrimination instead boast of their exemplary record in not discriminating in daily interactions.

If contact is inevitable, people may become *verbally and emotionally detached* from certain outgroups, and reference them in sterile ways, if they mention them at all. For example, rather than referencing outgroups in ways that might evoke emotion or action (e.g., "Women are raped in Dafur refugee camps"), detached speakers avoid emotional descriptions (e.g., "There's unrest in Sudan"). Finally, *delegitimization* is the most severe social function of prejudiced language. Bar-Tal (1989) notes that this process involves rejection based on the perceived "less than human" status of a group or individual. People use language to communicate these perceived differences to others, which in turn justifies an outgroup's low status and mistreatment. Discriminatory and prejudiced language that serves social functions appears most when a group benefits from social distinctions, such as during wartime or periods of scarce resources.

A fourth function served by discriminatory language is *dominance maintenance*. In order to maintain power hierarchies, privileged groups attempt to guard other groups' access to certain resources. Privileged groups may blatantly prevent or subtly interfere with certain ethnic minority groups and women acquiring or maintaining high-status positions. By blocking avenues to access, the ingroup protects and maintains its power. The more powerful ingroup may, for example, control the news media or determine which dialects and languages are appropriate for formal discourse. A more subtle example in interpersonal communication involves the use of "tags" to imply what positions are descriptively or prescriptively normal. Unless otherwise specified, listeners often assume "doctor" references a white man, and speakers' use of terms such as "lady doctor" emphasize this assumption. Such tags implicitly can communicate both how speakers believe the world is and how it should be.

Finally, using discriminatory language allows people to *maintain their nonprejudiced self-perceptions*. Social sanctions discourage people from openly expressing prejudiced ideals; consequently, people use language to deny or mask their prejudice. To this end, people may use bifurcations (verbally distinguishing between acceptable and unacceptable subgroups of the outgroup) or concessions (disparaging qualities about the outgroup that are acknowledged in the occasional ingroup member). Alternatively, prejudiced language can serve → impression-management functions by playing to the audience's presumed opinions: a speaker who wishes to be viewed favorably will adjust his or her degree of explicitly prejudiced language to match the audience's presumed views of the outgroup.

EXPLICITLY PREJUDICED AND DISCRIMINATORY LANGUAGE

Explicitly prejudiced and discriminatory communication often involves derogatory comments about an outgroup or outgroup member. Sometimes these comments comprise brief group epithets, whereas sometimes they are lengthy narratives about an outgroup's alleged negative behavior.

Group epithets comprise short, usually negative, labels applied to outgroups and individual outgroup members. Sometimes called ethnophaulisms (from *ethnos* for "nationality" or "a people" and *phaulizo* "to disparage"), these slurs provide economical expressions for outgroups. Historical examples include "frogs" for Frenchmen, "iron maidens" for professional women, "pickaninnies" for African-Americans, and "crackers" for lower income rural whites. Derogatory labels provide insight into how the speaker – and his or her own group – views members of an outgroup. First and foremost, the use of a label implies that the speaker views the target as an outgroup member rather than as an individual. Second, the speaker views the target negatively, and is willing to let listeners infer that negativity; even speakers ignorant of a label's meaning will use it in order to convey negativity.

Derogatory labels also serve a *social function*, insofar as they can indicate social roles or delegitimize group members from the larger society. The speaker essentially tells listeners to stay away from labeled outgroup members. The most extreme form of delegitimization involves the reconstruction of outgroup members into less-than-human outcasts. In wartime or during periods of "ethnic cleansing," for example, outgroup members are referenced with dehumanizing terms such as "gooks," "social diseases," "savages," and "animals." Bar-Tal (1989) notes that extreme delegitimization helps justify atrocities such as slavery, internment, and extermination.

Derogatory labels for outgroups may be used when ingroup members are communicating among themselves, or they may be used in communications intended for outgroup members to overhear or inadvertently read. Most people recognize derogatory labels as being intentionally expressed and potentially harmful; such labels epitomize the subjective understanding of hate speech. From a *legal standpoint*, however, derogatory labels may not meet stringent criteria for hate speech. In the United States, for example, the first constitutional amendment protects freedom of speech; hate speech is an exception, but is not simply hateful language. The criteria for hate speech are that the words threaten an immediate breach of the peace, are intended to hurt message recipients, and that exposure to these words is inescapable to their target (i.e., "fighting words"). Scrawling derogatory labels in public locations (e.g., graffiti) is unlikely to meet these stringent criteria, although obfuscating the source and potentially affecting more recipients actually may be more destructive than "fighting words" (→ Hate Speech and Ethnophaulisms).

Although few objective truths about outgroups are easily proven, social scientists regularly find that people prefer to believe that their own viewpoints are veridical. With respect to views of outgroups, validation can be provided through a wide variety of storytelling methods. In both casual and formal communication settings, speakers provide alleged evidence for why certain outgroups deserve to be viewed negatively; speakers may be indoctrinating new group members or may be validating the views of veteran group members. For example, van Dijk (1988) reports a storytelling session by a Dutch couple who relay a tale about their Turkish neighbor. The story details the slaughtering of a sheep in a bathtub during Ramadan, pieces of the sheep becoming lodged in the drain, and the eventual arrival of the police. In recounting this explicitly prejudiced communication, the couple clearly is aware that their impression of the outgroup is negative. But because they have presented factual disparaging evidence, they also presumably expect the listener to share their view, or at least to appreciate why they have the right to hold it.

In recent years, stories about outgroup members have circulated on weblogs (→ Blogger) and → electronic mail. Occasionally, the stories include digitally manipulated photographs or are attributed to an expert. Although these stories share a similar purpose – demonstrating an outgroup's abominable behavior – the → Internet medium allows communication to be rapid and widespread. Prejudiced communication over the Internet also has ideal features for impression management. Bloggers can post anonymously or through a pseudonym. Alternatively, individuals who forward stories through electronic mail can include comments that mask their own opinion (e.g., "I didn't write this . . . just passing it along"). Electronically shared stories quickly can develop into urban legends. One example – which has been falsified – provides a detailed testimonial about unsanitary and aggressive behavior of a busload of New Orleans evacuees at a Texas rest stop following Hurricane Katrina. Like the interpersonally communicated story of the Turkish neighbor, the electronic story of evacuees helps ease guilt about the Hurricane Katrina catastrophe and justifies social distance (→ Online Media).

Discriminatory language also may be couched in terms of *jokes or purportedly humorous emails*. In a sense, prejudiced jokes are a type of storytelling about disparaged outgroups. Prejudiced humor serves many roles, including entertainment, promoting ingroup camaraderie, and expressing shared attitudes and values. Depending on the particulars of the joke, this form of prejudiced communication may serve group enhancement functions (e.g., disparaging the outgroup), social functions (e.g., prescriptions for social interaction), dominance maintenance (e.g., proving why the outgroup deserves its inferior social status), or impression management (e.g., the audience will think more favorably of the person who sent it). Outgroup-disparaging humor also serves economical expression in the sense that it can bolster the stereotypes held by recipients, rendering them stronger and more easily retrieved for use.

IMPLICITLY PREJUDICED AND DISCRIMINATORY LANGUAGE

Prejudiced and discriminatory communication also can assume more subtle implicit forms; speakers of these communication patterns may not even recognize that they are betraying their own prejudices and listeners also may not realize that the language is discriminatory.

Several types of implicit discriminatory communication patterns serve the *ego-defensive/group enhancement function*. For example, researchers find that first person plural pronouns (e.g., we) are associated quickly with positive feelings about the ingroup, and are used when referencing the ingroup. Cialdini et al. (1976) found that when the home sports team won a game, people used expressions such as "we won," thereby enhancing themselves through connection to the team. Conversely, people used expressions such as "they lost" when the home team lost a game, thereby protecting self-esteem by distancing themselves. Thus, consistent with the ego-defensive/group enhancement function of discriminatory language, people desire to see their own group in a favorable light; when they cannot easily do so, they find a way to distance themselves from it.

The general preference to view the ingroup in a favorable fashion in part underlies intergroup bias. Consistent with intergroup bias, people tend to see their own groups as possessing more favorable characteristics and producing more superior work than other groups. In communication, intergroup bias is seen clearly in the *linguistic intergroup bias* (LIB), initially investigated by Maass (1999) and her colleagues. Generally speaking, the LIB reflects a communication pattern in which the behaviors of the ingroup are portrayed more favorably than the behaviors of an outgroup. When an ingroup member performs a positive behavior, the speaker characterizes the behavior abstractly, as though the behavior is indicative of the actor's personality.

For example, if an ingroup member donates money to charity, the speaker might say, "she is generous." Using this adjective implies that the actor performs similar actions across time and different situations. In contrast, if an outgroup member performs the same behavior, however, the speaker concretely might say, "she gave some money today," which fails to imply generosity across time and situations. For negative behaviors, the LIB shows the converse: negative behavior performed by an ingroup member is characterized concretely (e.g., "He did not tell the truth about Paul") whereas negative behavior performed by an outgroup member is characterized abstractly (e.g., "He is dishonest"). Because so many of the stereotypic qualities that people believe about outgroups are negative, abstract characterizations often serve to bolster and preserve stereotypes.

Among the most researched indicators of intergroup bias in communication settings, the LIB shows considerable generalizability across languages, communication mediums, and type of intergroup relationship. The pattern has been demonstrated in multiple languages in various countries, including Italy, Spain, the United States, and China. It also emerges orally, in writing, and when people select among written descriptions. Finally, the pattern emerges in a variety of intergroup settings, such as with ethnic, regional, and political outgroups, age cohorts, personal relationships (e.g., enemies vs. friends), and rival teams. Perhaps most interesting, the bias can be exacerbated or mitigated by motivational and dispositional factors. Threats to self-esteem or high levels of dispositional prejudice can exacerbate the LIB, whereas the motivation to be accurate can mitigate the bias. Research suggests that most people do not realize that they are displaying any bias in their communication patterns.

Besides the degree of linguistic abstraction for specific behaviors, implicitly prejudiced communication also emerges in *how speakers characterize events*. For example, in their delineation of how powerful people camouflage the control that they wield, Ng & Bradac (1993) proposed how speakers rely upon a number of linguistic masking devices; these non-mutually exclusive devices include generalization and permutation. Generalizations can include the use of adjectives to characterize behaviors (i.e., as in the LIB), but also comprise generalizations to entire groups (e.g., "People on welfare don't want to work") or to unspecified events (e.g., "Immigrants cause a lot of problems"). Permutation relies upon the fact that listeners typically assign greater responsibility to the subject of the sentence than to factors later in the sentence. A statement such as "The defendant lied to the judge" implicitly assigns more blame to the defendant than a statement such as "The judge was lied to by the defendant." As with the LIB, the groups to which speakers belong and their prejudices can influence their use of linguistic masking devices (→ Power in Intergroup Settings).

Implicitly discriminatory language also emerges in whether language is inclusive or prescribes what is normal. Organizations that address invitations for social events to "employees and their wives" send a subtle message to female employees, unmarried individuals, same-sex couples, and couples in unformalized relationships: although diversity may be tolerated, it is not expected or celebrated. Gender-biased language also sends messages about what is normal. The tags (e.g., lady doctor) discussed earlier are one example. Another example involves use and perceptions of gender-biased terms such as stewardess instead of flight attendant or chairman instead of chair. Research shows that individual differences in sexist attitudes are linked to the use and perceptions of gender-biased language, suggesting that it can serve a group-dominance function. Finally, subtle discrimination in language can be found in what is *not* said. For instance, men may ask a female co-worker her opinion on a tie or retail store, but may fail to include her in discussions of football (→ Gender and Discourse).

Although most widely considered with respect to gender, language that prescribes normalcy extends to bias toward other groups. For example, speakers may include an ethnic tag for historically white male positions (e.g., black doctor). Whites may solicit computer advice from an Asian colleague. Job recruitment websites may be devoid of photographs depicting applicants over 45, suggesting older adults are unwelcome and consequently deterring applications. Implicitly prejudiced communication therefore can be subtle, barely noticed, and far-reaching.

SEE ALSO: ▶ Blogger ▶ Elaboration Likelihood Model ▶ Electronic Mail ▶ Gender and Discourse ▶ Hate Speech and Ethnophaulisms ▶ Impression Management ▶ Information Processing: Stereotypes ▶ Internet ▶ Limited Capacity Model ▶ Online Media ▶ Power in Intergroup Settings ▶ Social Stereotyping and Communication ▶ Stereotypes

References and Suggested Readings

Allport, G. W. (1989). *The nature of prejudice.* Reading, MA: Addison Wesley. (Original work published 1954).

Bar-Tal, D. (1989). Delegitimization: The extreme case of stereotyping and prejudice. In D. Bar-Tal, C. F. Graumann, A. Kruglanski, & W. Stroebe (eds.), *Stereotyping and prejudice: Changing conceptions.* New York: Springer, pp. 169–182.

Cialdini, R. B., Borden, R. J., Thorne, A., Walker, M. R., Freeman, S., & Sloan, L. R. (1976). Basking in reflected glory: Three (football) field studies. *Journal of Personality and Social Psychology*, 34, 366–375.

Maass, A. (1999). Linguistic intergroup bias: Stereotype perpetuation through language. In M. P. Zanna (ed.), *Advances in experimental social psychology*, vol. 31. San Diego, CA: Academic Press, pp. 79–121.

Ng, S. H., & Bradac, J. J. (1993). *Power in language.* Newbury Park, CA: Sage.

Ruscher, J. B. (2001). *Prejudiced communication: A social psychological perspective.* New York: Guilford.

Thompson, L. L., & Crocker, J. (1990). Downward social comparison in the minimal group situation: A test of a self-enhancement interpretation. *Journal of Applied Social Psychology*, 20, 1166–1184.

van Dijk, T. A. (1988). How "they" hit the headlines: Ethnic minorities in the press. In G. Smitherman-Donaldson & T. A. van Dijk (eds.), *Discourses and discrimination.* Detroit, MI: Wayne State University Press, pp. 221–262.

Presence

Tilo Hartmann

Free University Amsterdam

Presence, in its broadest sense, is a media user's state that is characterized by the illusion of nonmediation. If present, media users are temporarily unaware of the mediated origin of their experience. Their thoughts, feelings, and behavior tend to react to the media content as if the portrayed scenery, persons, or objects were real, because the general artificiality of media imitation produced by human-made technology is not recognized (International Society for Presence Research 2001; → Media Equation Theory).

As a psychological state, presence is determined by the interplay of both situational or enduring individual factors, and environmental factors, which include qualities of the media technology and aspects of the content. The potential of the media technology to evoke illusions of nonmediation is addressed as its "immersive quality" (Slater & Steed 2000). The greater the likelihood that technological aspects or content factors foster the formation of presence, the more immersive is a medium. As any kind of media experience builds on subjective → perceptions, however, low-immersive media might also initiate a state of presence if users are susceptible to forget about the illusory origins of their experiences (for relevant individual factors, like a person's willingness to suspend disbelief, see Wirth et al. 2007; → Suspension of Disbelief).

The umbrella term "presence" has been picked up in diverse fields of communication and related disciplines. As a result of the diverse perspectives that have applied the term, presence has been understood in different ways. A review by Lombard and Ditton (1997) lists six different meanings, ranging from "presence as social richness" to "presence as transportation" (→ Transportation Theory) to "presence as medium as social actor." In general, a state of presence can occur in two distinct ways (Lombard & Ditton 1997): (1) "the medium can appear to be ... transparent ... as a large open window, with the user and the medium content (objects and entities) sharing the same physical environment" (invisible medium) or "the medium can appear to be transformed into something other than a medium" (transformed medium). In the context of presence that builds on an invisible medium, a popular classification is to distinguish *spatial presence* (sometimes addressed as physical presence or telepresence) from *social presence*.

SPATIAL PRESENCE

Spatial presence can be defined as "a binary experience, during which perceived self-location and, in most cases, perceived action possibilities are connected to a mediated spatial environment, and mental capacities are bound by the mediated environment instead of reality" (Wirth et al. 2007, 497). In short, spatial presence refers to a user's *"feeling of being there"* in the mediated environment (Biocca 1997; Riva et al. 2003; Lee 2004). Research on spatial presence evolved in technology-oriented disciplines like computer science and engineering. The term was first coined by Minsky (1980). Particularly, researchers concerned with interactive teleworking applications and sophisticated virtual reality systems applied the construct to their studies (Steuer 1992; → Computer–User Interaction; Virtual Reality). Spatial presence was deemed relevant as it was thought to affect a user's task performance (Barfield et al. 1995). Some definitions that originated from this perspective characterized spatial presence solely on the basis of technological determinants. Among the most often cited factors are the degree of interactivity provided by a medium, and the number and balance of human sensory channels addressed by a medium (Steuer 1992; Biocca 1997).

More recently, the construct of spatial presence has also received the attention of researchers who are concerned with the description and explanation of experiential phenomena of media exposure and → media effects (→ Exposure to Communication Content). In this way, the perspective changed from rather technology-driven approaches to rather psychological interpretations (Ijsselsteijn et al. 2000). With the shift to a psychological perspective, the user's → attention to media content emerged as one of the central determinants of spatial presence (Draper et al. 1998). More recently, → emotions and arousal have been addressed as important determinants of the formation of spatial presence as well (Baumgartner et al. 2006; → Excitation and Arousal). With researchers from more diverse backgrounds starting to work on the construct, not only highly immersive media like virtual reality systems were deemed capable of evoking spatial presence, but also low-immersive media, for example, books (the so-called "book problem"). In sum, in the past the concept of spatial presence has been studied in the context of quite different media, like virtual reality environments, → video games, the → Internet, → television, and → books (→ Computer Games and Reality Perception).

Throughout the past two decades, related approaches to nonmediation phenomena that emerged in other disciplines were continuously incorporated in research on spatial presence, particularly the study of transportation, which originated in literature research, conceptualizations of a user's → involvement with media content (Schubert et al. 2001), flow experiences (Draper et al. 1998), and explications about the perceived reality of authentic or fictional media content (Lee 2004; → Media and Perceptions of Reality). Today, the existing conceptualizations still differ in the way they define spatial presence as psychological state, for example, in terms of the dimensionality of the construct. Accordingly, they also highlight different determinants. For example, Schubert et al. (2001) argue that a user's experience of self-location, his or her involvement, and the perceived realness of the media content resemble three dimensions of spatial presence. In a more recent conceptualization, Wirth et al. (2007) argue that involvement and realness resemble determinants, while they regard the user's self-location and perceived action possibilities as actual dimensions of the construct. As the concept of spatial presence has been addressed from very heterogeneous areas of research, an interdisciplinary shared theoretical understanding that clearly distinguishes determinants, dimensions, and outcomes is still a major challenge of this line of research.

A broad range of measurements to assess spatial presence have been developed in the past (see www.presence-research.org for an overview; Laarni et al. in press). Certainly, the variety of theoretical approaches to spatial presence also accounts in part for the diversity of existing measurements (Schuemie et al. 2001). Post-test questionnaires are applied immediately after the exposure to a medium and have been the most common way to measure spatial presence in the past. The most popular questionnaires include the Presence Questionnaire, the ITC Sense of Presence Inventory, and the I-Group Presence Questionnaire. Recent methodological issues were concerned with the → validity of existing questionnaires to assess spatial presence (Schuemie et al. 2001; Insko 2003), as well as with the different factor structures underlying existing paper-and-pencil measurements (→ Factor Analysis). Next to questionnaires, other subjective methods like think-aloud have been applied to study spatial presence as well. Also, a multitude of objective measurements have been introduced in the past, like psychophysiological measures, postural responses, and functional magnetic resonance imaging.

SOCIAL PRESENCE

Social presence can be defined as a "sense of being together" with one or more other social beings, although the others are fictional (like characters in a science-fiction movie) or mediated appearances of real counterparts (e.g., through camera recordings or as avatars; Biocca et al. 2003; → Avatars and Agents). The conceptualization of the term is still a little bit vague and the construct combines different aspects and outcomes of interpersonal encounters (Schroeder 2002).

The term was first introduced to the realm of media technologies by Short et al. (1976) in the context of mediated interpersonal communication. Social presence was defined as "the salience of the other in a mediated communication and the consequent salience of [the] interpersonal interactions" (Short et al. 1976, 65). The authors used the term for the users' evaluation of the extent to which different communication media convey social cues. Accordingly, social presence was not conceptualized as an experience but rather as an attitude toward a medium that guides → selective exposure behavior. Similar notions of social presence have been pursued in successive theoretical conceptualizations of interpersonal communication media, like the media richness theory.

In the context of virtual reality research, the term has been applied to describe the sense of being together in collaborative environments. Thus, the term changed to describe rather an experience than an attitude. For example, Biocca et al. (2003) construe social presence as a multidimensional experience that involves the feeling of sharing a space with another social being, being emotionally and cognitively connected to another person, and feeling reciprocally engaged in an interaction. Bente et al. (2005) argue that social presence builds on shared meaning and develops as intimateness, awareness, understanding, and contingency throughout the interaction. Still other researchers regard social presence as an experience, but argue for a distinction between feeling present with another entity and feeling connected to another entity.

So far only a few measurements have been developed for the study of social presence. Short et al. (1976) simply applied four semantic differential scales to assess the social qualities of a communication medium perceived by users (insensitive–sensitive, cold–warm, impersonal–personal, unsociable–sociable). Other recent paper-and-pencil tools have been introduced by Biocca et al. (2003) and others.

AUGMENTED REALITY

A reality is augmented, if in a real surrounding one or more objects or social entities are perceived as real that actually are displayed or imitated by human-made technology (Azuma 1997). Thus, in contrast to states of presence that build on an "invisible medium" (see above), in augmented reality it is not the media that create the illusion of an environment. Rather, the real environment of the user is enhanced by the mediated illusion of an object or social entity. Lombard and Ditton (1997) speak of a medium that is transformed into an object or social entity that is erroneously perceived as real. If nonmediated sensations occur this way, they are addressed as "presence as augmented reality." For example, a hologram imitating a shelf in a real living-room could create an augmented reality. Another example would be glasses that enrich the perception of the real world by adding simulated objects or social beings to the perceived scenery.

SEE ALSO: ► Attention ► Avatars and Agents ► Book ► Computer Games and Reality Perception ► Computer–User Interaction ► Emotion ► Escapism ► Excitation and Arousal ► Exposure to Communication Content ► Factor Analysis ► Identification ► Internet ► Involvement with Media Content ► Media Effects ► Media Equation Theory ► Media and Perceptions of Reality ► Parasocial Interactions and Relationships ► Perception ► Selective Exposure ► Suspension of Disbelief ► Television ► Transportation Theory ► Validity ► Video Games ► Virtual Reality

References and Suggested Readings

Azuma, R. (1997). A survey of augmented reality. *Presence*, 6(4), 355–385.

Barfield, W., Zeltzer, D., Sheridan, T., & Slater, M. (1995). Presence and performance within virtual environments. In W. Barfield & T. Furness (eds.), *Virtual environments and advanced interface design*. Oxford: Oxford University Press, pp. 473–513.

Baumgartner, T., Valco, L., Esslen, M., & Jancke, L. (2006). Neural correlate of spatial presence in an arousing and non-interactive virtual reality: An EEG and psychophysiology study. *Cyberpsychology and Behavior*, 9, 30–45.

Bente, G., Rüggeberg, S., & Krämer, N. C. (2005). Virtual encounters: Creating social presence in net-based collaborations. In M. Slater (ed.), *Proceedings of the 8th International Workshop on Presence*. London: University College London, pp. 97–102.

Biocca, F. (1997). The cyborg's dilemma: Progressive embodiment in virtual environments. *Journal of Computer-Mediated Communications*, 3(2). At http://jcmc.indiana.edu/vol3/issue2/biocca2.html, accessed April 9, 2007.

Biocca, F., Harms, C., & Burgoon, J. (2003). Toward a more robust theory and measure of social presence: Review and suggested criteria. *Presence*, 12(5), 456–480.

Draper, J. V., Kaber, D. B., & Usher, J. M. (1998). Telepresence. *Human Factors*, 40(3), 354–375.

Ijsselsteijn, W. A., de Ridder, H., Freeman, J., & Avons, S. E. (2000). Presence: Concept, determinants and measurement. In B. E. Rogowitz & T. N. Pappas (eds.), *Proceedings of SPIE, Human vision and electronic imaging V*, vol. 3959. Bellingham, WA: SPIE, pp. 520–529.

Insko, B. E. (2003). Measuring presence: Subjective, behavioral and physiological methods. In G. Riva, F. Davide, & W. A. Ijsselsteijn (eds.), *Being there: Concepts, effects and measurements of user presence in synthetic environments*. Amsterdam: IOS Press, pp. 110–118.

International Society for Presence Research (2001). The concept of presence: Explication statement. At http://www.temple.edu/ispr, accessed June 1, 2006.

Laarni, J., Ravaja, N., Saari, T., Böcking, S., Hartmann, T., & Schramm, H. (in press). Ways to measure presence: Review and future directions. In F. Biocca, W. A. Ijsselsteijn, & J. Freeman (eds.), *Handbook of presence research: Cognition, measurement, and interface design*. Mahwah, NJ: Lawrence Erlbaum.

Lee, K. M. (2004). Presence, explicated. *Communication Theory*, 14, 27–50.

Lombard, M., & Ditton, T. (1997). At the heart of it all: The concept of presence. *Journal of Computer-Mediated Communication*, 3(2). At http://jcmc.indiana.edu/vol3/issue2/lombard.html, accessed September 25, 2007.

Minsky, M. (1980). Telepresence. *Omni*, 2, 45–51.

Riva, G., Davide, F., & Ijsselsteijn, W. A. (eds.) (2003). *Being there: Concepts, effects and measurement of user presence in synthetic environments*. Amsterdam: IOS Press.

Schroeder, R. (2002). Social interaction in virtual environments: Key issues, common themes, and a framework for research. In R. Schroeder (ed.), *The social life of avatars: Presence and interaction in shared virtual environments*. London: Springer, pp. 1–18.

Schubert, T., Friedmann, F., & Regenbrecht, H. (2001). The experience of presence: Factor analytic insights. *Presence: Teleoperators and Virtual Environments*, 10(3), 266–281.

Schuemie, M. J., van der Straaten, P., Krijn, M., & van der Mast, C. A. P. G. (2001). Research on presence in virtual reality: A survey. *Cyberpsychology and Behavior*, 4(2), 183–202.

Short, J. A., Williams, E., & Christie, B. (1976). *The social psychology of telecommunications*. New York: John Wiley.

Slater, M., & Steed, A. (2000). A virtual presence counter. *Presence: Teleoperators and Virtual Environments*, 9(5), 413–434.

Steuer, J. (1992). Defining virtual reality: Dimensions determining telepresence. *Journal of Communication*, 42(4), 73–93.

Wirth, W., Hartmann, T., Boecking, S., et al. (2007). A process model of the formation of spatial presence experiences. *Media Psychology*, 9, 493–525.

Press Conference

Craig Allen
Arizona State University

Newsmakers arrange a *press conference* to announce news to groups of reporters. The meetings vary in size, setting, and subject. Some detail plans and decisions. Others promise surprise revelations. A common feature distinguishes all press conferences: the opportunity for reporters to question a newsmaker.

The most familiar are those of presidents, prime ministers, and crisis managers during key events, but smaller press conferences supply much of the information the public receives as news. The thousands of briefings, councils, and exchanges that the public seldom sees generate the daily flow of news. In most countries, the press conferences of government officials, dignitaries, business leaders, activists, scientists, politicians, and entertainers shape national news (→ News Sources). In local communities, the same is true of the press conferences that civic leaders, police and emergency personnel, arriving celebrities, and sports figures hold.

For their sponsors, as well as for those obliged or impelled to become newsmakers, press conferences are opportunities to reach the public. Not all the information they provide is urgent and vital. Press conferences are first and foremost a public relations device that fails unless it supplies news (→ Public Relations: Media Influence). Except for those conferences broadcast live, the public knows about press conferences only through reporters' later news accounts. Newsmakers cannot control what unfolds in a press conference, given the uncertainty of reporters' questions, which can foul the messages newsmakers seek to convey.

For reporters, press conferences are essential but not without constraints. Research shows that reporters dislike press conferences for forcing them to share information with competitors, but appreciate them for allowing direct access to those making news (Bantz 1985). Alert reporters watch for angles and leads that might later inspire a story that will scoop the competition or win an award.

Press conferences are characteristic of older democratic countries, notably the United States, where governments do not control the press. Only in societies with many news organizations are press conferences needed. Press conferences are rare in authoritarian societies where press systems are monolithic and run by the state (Frederick 1993). The *first press conferences* were convened around the beginning of the twentieth century when newspapers first gave regular assignments to writers and correspondents (→ Newspaper, History of). In the United States, President Theodore Roosevelt popularized press sessions. His famed pulpit for Progressive Era reforms was the talks he gave to the reporters assigned the White House beat (McKerns 1990). US president Franklin Roosevelt developed the *modern press conference* format during the New Deal programs in 1933. Seeking favorable publicity, Roosevelt invited question-and-answer sessions (Winfield 1990). Even so, by mid-century, when Harry Truman was US president, only newspaper and wire service reporters could attend. Microphones were prohibited, and reporters had to crowd around the president's Oval Office desk (Startt 1990).

Dramatic changes came with the *arrival of television* in the 1950s (→ Television News). Under US president Dwight Eisenhower, press conferences became public events. The rules changed, and reporters sat in large auditoriums. The first televised press conference, with Eisenhower, was broadcast in 1954. Early TV press conferences were recorded on film. Finally in 1961, US president John Kennedy permitted live cameras. His appearances captivated the public, and every succeeding president followed his example by doing press conferences on live TV (Allen 1993).

A major *criticism of press conferences* – that newsmakers arrange media events for the cameras – emerged because of television. US president Ronald Reagan, a former actor, staged press conferences with Hollywood-like effects. Engaging TV communication, directed not at reporters but at opinion leaders and home viewers, contributed to Reagan's popularity. News reporters could not question him effectively (Donaldson

1987). Other leaders including Canadian prime minister Pierre Trudeau, British prime minister Margaret Thatcher, and Russian president Boris Yeltsin were known for staging press conferences with popular and charismatic appeal.

The presence of cameras influences even the most routine press sessions. Only major press conferences attract live TV coverage, but almost all aim for televised accounts and recaps on the evening news. Research shows that reporters and their editors reduce and frequently eliminate coverage of press conferences they perceive as media events (Berkowitz 1993; Harmon 1989). Studies further suggest that the largest news organizations most often compress or dismiss press events (Carroll 1986). To help insure coverage, newsmakers answer reporters with rehearsed statements appropriate for TV sound bites. They also attend to the needs that Reagan instilled, for staging and for looking at the camera so that they appear to speak to the viewer (Hilton 1990).

Around the world, press conferences are spurred by policies that seek privatization and media multiplicity (→ Privatization of the Media). In Japan and many Asian countries, and particularly in western Europe, monolithic state-operated public broadcasters are joined by numerous private networks and channels (Dragomir & Reljic 2005). In the UK, televised press conferences were not common until the 1980s and 1990s, when newsmakers needed to gather reporters not only from the BBC but from Sky-TV, newly expanded independent channels, and other private TV news providers.

Changes within the US media stemming from the fragmentation and decline of newspaper and broadcast audiences have encouraged *alternatives to press conferences*. When print, broadcast, and online news providers employ a common newsroom, newsmakers can give announcements to the one reporter that several media share (Quinn & Filak 2005). In another trend, the media have divided news staffs into specialty teams, with the aim of targeting particular demographic groups. Instead of convening a mass gathering of reporters, newsmakers now channel information to appropriate specialists.

Changes in *media technology* have accompanied the evolution of press conferences. Little research has been conducted on the impact of recent technology. Yet from the Internet, reporters can acquire information with superior detail to that packaged in press sessions. Compelling questions for scholars relate to newsmakers' uses of new technology. Newsmakers can avoid the ordeal of convening reporters in some situations, communicating directly to the public through websites, weblogs, streaming audio and video, and other innovations, many of them incorporating interactivity (→ Technology and Communication; Interactivity, Concept of).

Despite changing arrangements and newer techniques, press conferences are still useful. They remain the standard means for news exchange, because of their convenience, expedience, and success at disseminating information widely. Press conferences can enlarge the esteem of organizations and leaders, and so newsmakers continue to meet the press. Reporters continue to attend for the volume of news and the interaction that the meetings provide.

SEE ALSO: ▶ Interactivity, Concept of ▶ Journalism ▶ News Sources ▶ Newspaper, History of ▶ Political Communication ▶ Privatization of the Media ▶ Public Relations: Media Influence ▶ Technology and Communication ▶ Television News

References and Suggested Readings

Allen, C. (1993). News conference on TV. *Journalism Quarterly*, 70, 13–25.
Bantz, C. (1985). News organizations: Conflict as a crafted cultural norm. *Communication*, 8, 225–244.
Berkowitz, D. (1993). Work roles and news selection in local TV. *Journal of Broadcasting and Electronic Media*, 37, 67–81.
Carroll, R. L. (1986). Content values in TV news programs in small and large markets. *Journalism Quarterly*, 62, 877–883.
Donaldson, S. (1987). *Hold on, Mr. President*. New York: Random House.
Dragomir, M., & Reljic, D. (2005). *Television across Europe*. Budapest: Open Society Institute.
Frederick, H. (1993). *Global communication and international relations*. New York: Harcourt Brace.
Harmon, M. (1989). Mr. Gates goes electronic: The what and why questions. *Journalism Quarterly*, 66, 857–863.
Hilton, J. (1990). *How to meet the press*. Champaign, IL: Sagamore.
McKerns, J. (1990). The emergence of modern media. In D. Sloan & J. Startt (eds.), *The media in America*. Worthington, OH: Publishing Horizons, pp. 243–261.
Quinn, S., & Filak, V. (2005). *Convergence journalism*. Boston: Focal.
Startt, J. (1990). The media and modern crises. In D. Sloan & J. Startt (eds.), *The media in America*. Worthington, OH: Publishing Horizons, pp. 281–308.
Winfield, B. (1990). *FDR and the news media*. Urbana, IL: University of Illinois Press.

Prevention and Communication

Claudia Lampert
University of Hamburg

The main objective of prevention is to avoid diseases by reducing risks that may negatively affect health (→ Health Communication). The prevention approach complements the health promotion approach. While prevention intends to avoid disease and reduce risks, health promotion focuses on resources that sustain the opportunity of healthy living. Even though the two concepts are sometimes used synonymously, lately the prevention approach has been proffered as independent of the health promotion concept. Both prevention and health promotion aim at a modification of attitudes and behavior by specific communication strategies to raise the empowerment of individuals. The problem is that not all individuals are interested in health-related topics per se. In most cases, information is sought when people are directly or indirectly (e.g., through a family member or friend) concerned with a disease.

TYPES OF PREVENTION

There exist different typologies of prevention classified by either stages of health or illness or by target audience. For example, some have differentiated between *behavioral and/or environmental prevention.* While behavioral prevention concentrates on personal factors that influence health-related behaviors of an individual, environmental prevention focuses on factors that are external to the individual, such as living conditions and the opportunities to enact health behaviors such as legislation (e.g., with regard to drug use), economic and ecological preconditions for healthy living and so forth.

Another popular and often cited typology is the trichotomy of *primary, secondary, and tertiary prevention,* which considers different stages of health and/or illness. Primary prevention aims at people who are not yet affected by a disease and encompasses broad population-wide communication strategies. Secondary prevention strategies address people in a very early stage of a disease to minimize and/or avoid health risks. Tertiary prevention measures are as a general rule targeted at those who already have established diseases to avoid aggravation and complications.

In 1994, a similar classification system was proposed by the Institute of Medicine (IOM) in the United States. This classification makes the distinction between *universal, selective, and indicated prevention interventions.* In comparison to the former classification, the IOM classification focuses on the general target group of a prevention intervention, not on the underlying objective. Universal prevention concentrates on the broad population to prevent risky and unhealthy behavior. The main objective is to provide information and improve the individual skills for healthy living. Selective prevention addresses special risk groups. Indicated prevention aims at individuals with existing risky and/or unhealthy behavior, e.g., drug abuse.

MEDIA IN HEALTH CONTEXT

Apart from different typologies of prevention, different levels of communication strategies can be differentiated: → interpersonal communication, communication in and/or from health organizations, and communication via mass media. Most people talk about health-related issues with their doctor and/or family members and have the highest confidence in personal advisers (Identity Foundation 2001; → Patient–Provider Communication). But also the media have become a very important source of health-related information and a communication platform for health-related problems and support. In particular, health-related information TV programs are of high interest and are attributed with a high level of trust, followed by the pharmacist and health-related books (Identity Foundation 2001). Even health organizations (e.g., hospitals) are important for preventive strategies.

The role of media in health has been a subject of controversy. Media are an important source of information on health, and casual or incidental use of media is associated with people's knowledge, attitudes, and behavior (Finnegan & Viswanath 2002, 328). On the other hand, some have focused on the harmful effects of media, such as the effects of → video games and media violence on aggressive behavior in children (→ Computer Games and Child Development; Violence as Media Content, Effects on Children of). The role of media in health promotion through health campaigns has also been widely studied (→ Health Campaigns, Communication in; Health Campaigns for Development).

One important problem in connection with health communication strategies is that health information is often not sought until a health-related problem has occurred

($\rightarrow$ Information Scanning; Information Seeking). Some media, such as the $\rightarrow$ Internet, assist in active seeking of health information ($\rightarrow$ Health Communication and the Internet), while others, such as $\rightarrow$ television and $\rightarrow$ radio, may expose people to health information through routine use (Dutta-Bergman 2004). Media that lead to passive or casual use, nonetheless, are useful in reaching individuals who may be either uninterested in or not actively seeking health information. A major goal and challenge of prevention is to reach individuals with preventive or health-related information before a disease has developed. Media, with their broad reach and appeal, can draw attention, arouse interest, and provide alternative ways of enacting behaviors.

In recent times, the amount and range of health information has increased enormously in a variety of media, such as television and the Internet, and in different genres, such as $\rightarrow$ soap operas, telenovelas, comedy programs, music videos, talk shows, and public service advertisements, among others ($\rightarrow$ Broadcast Talk). These programs address a variety of topics, such as nutrition and eating disorders, cancer, HIV/AIDS, and alcohol and tobacco, among others. But the presence of health-related information in the media is no guarantee that individuals will change their attitudes or behaviors. A number of individual and situational characteristic influence media effects.

EXAMPLES FOR COMMUNICATION STRATEGIES

Different preventive communication strategies can be distinguished: public information campaigns, health journalism, and entertainment education, among others.

Information campaigns encompass different communicative activities to influence individual knowledge, $\rightarrow$ attitude, $\rightarrow$ meaning, and/or behavior. Social marketing is an example of an activity that promotes social or health messages in the same way as commercial marketing ($\rightarrow$ Social Marketing). Different promotional activities and media channels are combined to reach the target audience. Typical vehicles are posters at public places, public service announcements in different media, as well as hotlines and events. Information campaigns offer the opportunity to reach a broad target group, but it is difficult to communicate complex and sophisticated information. To get the attention of the audience, it is necessary to promote consonant and creative messages in a cumulative way. A related strategy is "media advocacy," which addresses not individuals but decision-makers such as legislators, policymakers, and media personnel, among others ($\rightarrow$ Media Advocacy in Health Communication). For example, the *Harvard Alcohol Project*, which promoted the concept of the designated driver, is often cited as a successful example of media advocacy.

Health journalism has an important role with regard to the communication of health-related or preventive messages ($\rightarrow$ Health Communication and Journalism). Journalists "translate" relevant scientific information for a broad audience under an enormous time pressure (Viswanath 2005, 833). They also influence the agenda concerning health-related and preventive topics ($\rightarrow$ Agenda-Setting Effects). Media coverage of health is often criticized by scientists as superficial or inaccurate and often suffers from the disadvantage of reaching only the educated and those who are already interested in the topic ($\rightarrow$ Communication Inequality).

Entertainment education (E-E) combines entertainment and education to promote prosocial messages drawing from such theories as → social cognitive theory (→ Entertainment Education). Using long-running entertainment programs, the E-E approach uses positive and negative role models to promote the desired and/or the undesired attitudes and/or behavior. Transitional characters represent the viewer's perspective, which changes over time in the desired direction. In E-E programs the health relative message is mediated in an indirect, almost subtle way. Parasocial interaction and identification with the positive or transitional character might raise the viewer's sense of self-efficacy to solve problems or to change individual behavior. Several evaluation studies have shown that the implementation of health relative, preventive messages is successful and might change attitudes under certain circumstances (Singhal et al. 2004). The idea is to encourage interpersonal discussion and reflection about the presented topics and positions as a precondition for attitude change and behavior modification. The E-E strategy offers the opportunity to reach especially those who are not interested in health-related topics and who are often hard to reach with preventive messages, e.g., adolescents or persons with a lower level of education, who are generally less information oriented. Relevant factors for the success of an E-E project are the viewer preferences (preferred medium, format, and genre) and the accurate implementation of the intended message. Media offer many opportunities for preventive purposes (Papa et al. 2000). As yet, there is no evidence that the integration of pro-social or health-related messages in entertainment generates negative reactions among the audience.

CHALLENGES

Success in prevention requires several considerations. First, the access to valid health information for different social groups has to be assured. There still exist both health and information disparities with regard to socio-economic status (→ Knowledge Gap Effects). Therefore, special communication strategies are needed to reach the different groups and to close the gap between them (Viswanath 2005).

Second, the perception of the message as the most important precondition for following cognitive processes has to be considered: age, gender, socio-economic status, educational background, and health conditions are relevant factors which have influence on media use, and access to and perception of health-related messages (Viswanath 2005). Third, individual understanding and interpretation of a message have to be taken into account. There has been a shift to an individual perspective and qualitative studies that give important hints for the construction of preventive messages. Even participative approaches offer great potential and should be regarded in the future (Singhal et al. 2004).

Communication strategies have to be seen in a context of a varied media landscape, which consists of different and sometimes inconsistent, contradictory messages (Sherry 2002; Viswanath 2005). The success of a strategy might increase if the program is embedded in a media environment that is hospitable to the communicated message. Apart from intentional communication measures, also the unintended effects of media programs have to be considered. The resonance they generate can only be investigated in long-term media effect studies.

SEE ALSO: ▶ Agenda-Setting Effects ▶ Attitudes ▶ Broadcast Talk ▶ Communication Inequality ▶ Computer Games and Child Development ▶ Entertainment Education ▶ Health Campaigns, Communication in ▶ Health Campaigns for Development ▶ Health Communication ▶ Health Communication and the Internet ▶ Health Communication and Journalism ▶ Information Scanning ▶ Information Seeking ▶ Internet ▶ Interpersonal Communication ▶ Knowledge Gap Effects ▶ Meaning ▶ Media Advocacy in Health Communication ▶ Patient–Provider Communication ▶ Radio ▶ Soap Operas ▶ Social Cognitive Theory ▶ Social Marketing ▶ Television ▶ Video Games ▶ Violence as Media Content, Effects on Children of

References and Suggested Readings

Dutta-Bergman, M. (2004). Primary sources of health information: Comparisons in the domain of health attitudes, health cognitions, and health behaviors. *Health Communication*, 16(3), 273–288.

Finnegan, J. R., & Viswanath, K. (2002). Communication theory and health behavior change. In K. Glanz, B. K. Rimer, & F. M. Lewis (eds.), *Health behavior and health education: Theory, research, and practice*, 3rd edn. San Francisco, CA: Jossey-Bass, pp. 313–341.

Greenberg, B. S., Salmon, C. T., Patel, D., Beck, V., & Cole, G. (2004). Evolution in an E-E research agenda. In A. Singhal, M. Cody, E. Rogers, & M. Sabido (eds.), *Entertainment-education and social change: History, research, and practice*. Mahwah, NJ: Lawrence Erlbaum, pp. 191–206.

Identity Foundation (2001). Gesundheitsstudie: Die Deutschen und ihre Einstellung zu Gesundheit und Krankheit. At www.identityfoundation.de/fileadmin/templates_identityfoundation/downloads/presse/Gesundheits_Studie.pdf, accessed September 26, 2007.

Papa, M. J., Singhal, A., Law, S., et al. (2000). Entertainment-education and social change: An analysis of parasocial interaction, social learning, collective efficacy, and paradoxical communication. *Journal of Communication*, 50, 4, 31–55.

Sherry, J. L. (2002). Media saturation and entertainment-education. *Communication Theory*, 12(2), 206–224.

Singhal, A., Cody, M., Rogers, E., & Sabido, M. (eds.) (2004). *Entertainment-education and social change: History, research, and practice*. Mahwah, NJ: Lawrence Erlbaum.

Thomson, T. L., Dorsey, A. M., Miller, K. I., & Parrott, R. (eds.) (2003). *Handbook of health communication*. Mahwah, NJ: Lawrence Erlbaum.

Tufte, T. (2003). Entertainment-education in HIV-AIDS communication: Beyond marketing, towards power. In C. von Feilitzen & U. Carlsson (eds.), *Promote or protect? Perspectives on media literacy and media regulations*, yearbook 2003, International Clearinghouse on Children, Youth and Media. Göteborg: Nordicom, pp. 85–97.

Viswanath, K. (2005). The communications revolution and cancer control. *Nature Reviews Cancer*, 5(10), 828–835.

Wallack, L., & DeJong, W. (1995). Mass media and public health: Moving the focus from the individual to the environment. In S. E. Martin (ed.), *The effects of the mass media on the use and abuse of alcohol*, NIAAA research monograph no. 28, NIH publication no. 95-3743. Rockville, MD: National Institutes of Health, pp. 253–268.

Priming Theory

Shanto Iyengar
Stanford University

The priming effect refers to media-induced changes in voters' reliance on particular issues as criteria for evaluating government officials. The more prominent any given issue in the news, the greater the impact of voters' opinions about that issue on their evaluations of government. The priming effect creates volatility in public opinion, especially during election campaigns (→ Public Opinion, Media Effects on; Election Campaign Communication). As casual observers of the political scene, ordinary citizens only notice events and issues that are in the news; those not covered by the media might as well not exist. What is noticed becomes the principal basis for the public's beliefs about the state of the country. Thus, the relative prominence of issues in the news is the major determinant of the public's perceptions of the problems facing the nation (see, e.g., Iyengar and Kinder 1987).

The relationship between news coverage and public concern has come to be known as the → agenda-setting effect. Over the past four decades, agenda-setting effects have been replicated in numerous studies. Cross-sectional → surveys, panel surveys, aggregate-level → time-series analyses of public opinion, and laboratory experiments (→ Experiment, Laboratory) all converge on the finding that issues in the news are the issues that people care about.

PRIMING AS AN EXTENSION OF AGENDA SETTING

Beyond merely affecting the salience of issues, news coverage influences the criteria the public uses to evaluate political candidates and institutions. A simple extension of agenda setting, priming describes a process by which individuals assign weights to their opinions on particular issues when they make summary political evaluations. In general, the evidence indicates that when asked to appraise politicians and public figures, voters weight opinions on particular policy issues in proportion to the perceived salience of these issues: the more salient the issue, the greater the impact of opinions about that issue on the appraisal (→ Issue Voting; for reviews of priming research, see Miller & Krosnick 2000; Druckman 2004).

Their dynamic nature make priming effects especially important during election campaigns. Consider the case of the 1980 American presidential campaign. Less than a week before the election, polls showed Jimmy Carter and Ronald Reagan to be dead even. Suddenly, the Iranian government offered a last-minute proposal for releasing the Americans held hostage for over a year. President Carter suspended his campaign to devote his full attention to these negotiations. The hostage story became the major news item of the day. The prominence of the hostage story caused voters to seize upon the candidates' ability to control terrorism as a basis for their vote choice (Iyengar & Kinder 1987). Given his unimpressive record on this issue while in office, the effect proved disastrous for President Carter.

Similar volatility in the state of the public agenda bedeviled President George H. Bush in the 1992 election. One year previously, he had presided over the successful liberation

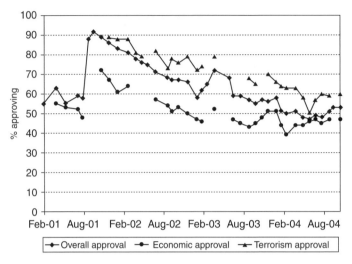

Figure 1   Ingredients of President Bush's popularity
Source: Gallup CBS News Polls and Gallup polls, 2001–2004

of Kuwait from Iraqi occupation and his popularity ratings reached 90 percent. But as news coverage of the economy gradually drowned out news about the Gulf conflict, voters came to prefer Clinton over Bush. Had the media played up military or security issues, of course, the tables would have been turned.

The most recent instance of priming comes from the post-9/11 era. Prior to September 11, President George W. Bush's overall popularity was closely tied to perceptions of his performance on economic issues (see Fig. 1). After September 11 and extending through 2003, however, Bush's popularity was more closely tied to assessments of his performance on terrorism. Terrorism and national security had replaced the economy as the yardstick for judging Bush's performance. It was only in 2004, after the onset of the presidential campaign, that economic performance and overall performance were again linked. This finding is reinforced by a time-series analysis of Bush's popularity (see Iyengar & McGrady 2007), which demonstrates that following the 9/11 attacks, news coverage of terrorism became the single most important determinant of Bush's public approval.

ANCILLARY CONDITIONS FOR PRIMING EFFECTS

Media priming effects have been documented in a series of experiments and surveys, with respect to evaluations of presidents, legislators, and lesser officials, and with respect to a variety of attitudes ranging from voting preferences, assessments of incumbents' performance in office, and ratings of candidates' personal attributes to racial and gender identities. In recent years, the study of priming has been extended to arenas other than the United States, including a series of elections in Israel (Sheafer & Weimann 2005), Germany (Schoen 2004), and Denmark (de Vreese 2004).

Typically, news coverage of issues elicits stronger priming effects in the area of *performance assessments* than in the area of personality assessments (Iyengar & Kinder

1987). In one noteworthy exception – involving "personality priming" – voters who watched the famous 1960 debate between John Kennedy and Richard Nixon on television were more likely to rely on image factors (such as integrity) when considering the candidates' performance in the debate (see Druckman 2003; → Televised Debates) than were voters who listened to the debate on the radio. The radio group, on the other hand, took into account both image and the candidates' positions on the issues. This study suggests that the visual imagery provided by television encourages voters to focus on personality-related rather than issue-related considerations when evaluating the candidates.

A special case of priming concerns the phenomenon of *momentum* in primary elections. Because news coverage during the early primaries tends to focus exclusively on the state of the "horse race," primary voters are likely to rely heavily on information about the candidates' electoral viability when making their choices (Brady & Johnston 1987). In a study of the 2004 primary campaign, researchers found that the single most important determinant of Democrats' primary vote preference between senators John Kerry and John Edwards was the voters' perceptions of the two candidates' personalities. The second-most powerful predictor of vote choice was the candidates' electoral viability (Iyengar et al. 2004). Viability was more important to voters than the candidates' positions on major issues, including the war in Iraq and outsourcing of American jobs.

The ability of the news media to prime political evaluations depends on both media content and the *predispositions of the audience*. Unsurprisingly, priming effects peak when news reports explicitly suggest that politicians are responsible for the state of national affairs, or when they clearly link politicians' actions with national problems. Thus, evaluations of President Reagan's performance were more strongly influenced by news stories when the coverage suggested that "Reaganomics" was responsible for rising American unemployment than when the coverage was directed at alternative causes of unemployment (Iyengar & Kinder 1987, ch. 9).

In a further parallel with agenda-setting research, individuals differ in their susceptibility to media priming effects. Miller and Krosnick (2000) found that priming effects occurred only among people who were highly knowledgeable about political affairs and had high levels of trust in the media (→ Credibility of Content). Iyengar and Kinder (1987) found that partisanship affected the issues on which people could be primed: Democrats tended to be most susceptible to priming when the news focused on issues that favor Democrats, such as unemployment and civil rights, while Republicans were influenced most when the news focused on traditional Republican issues like national defense (→ Exposure to Communication Content).

In sum, issues and events in the news are deemed important and weigh heavily in evaluations of incumbent officials and political candidates. As is clear from the way in which President George H. Bush benefited from media coverage of the 1991 Gulf War and then suffered from coverage of the economy, priming results equally from news of political successes and news of political failures. Priming is a double-edged sword.

SEE ALSO: ▶ Agenda-Setting Effects ▶ Credibility of Content ▶ Election Campaign Communication ▶ Experiment, Laboratory ▶ Exposure to Communication Content ▶ Issue Voting ▶ Public Opinion, Media Effects on ▶ Social Capital, Media Effects on ▶ Survey ▶ Televised Debates ▶ Time-Series Analysis

References and Suggested Readings

Brady, H. E., & Johnston, R. (1987). What's the primary message: Horse race or issue journalism? In G. R. Orren & N. W. Polsby (eds.), *Media and momentum: The New Hampshire primary and nomination politics*. Chatham, NJ: Chatham House, pp. 127–186.

de Vreese, C. H. (2004). Primed by the euro: The impact of a referendum campaign on public opinion and evaluations of government and political leaders. *Scandinavian Political Studies*, 27(1), 45–64.

Druckman, J. N. (2003). The power of television images: The first Kennedy–Nixon debate revisited. *Journal of Politics*, 65, 559–571.

Druckman, J. N. (2004). Priming the vote: Campaign effects in a U.S. Senate election. *Political Psychology*, 25, 577–594.

Druckman, J. N., & Holmes, J. W. (2004). Does presidential rhetoric matter? Priming and presidential approval. *Presidential Studies Quarterly*, 34, 755–778.

Iyengar, S., & Kinder, D. R. (1987). *News that matters: Television and American opinion*. Chicago: University of Chicago Press.

Iyengar, S., & McGrady, J. (2007). *Media politics: A citizen's guide*. New York: W. W. Norton.

Iyengar, S., Luskin, R., & Fishkin, J. (2004). Deliberative public opinion: Evidence from presidential primaries. Presented at the Annual Meeting of the American Political Science Association.

Miller, J. M., & Krosnick, J. A. (2000). News media impact on the ingredients of presidential evaluations: Politically knowledgeable citizens are guided by a trusted source. *American Journal of Political Science*, 44, 295–309.

Schoen, H. (2004). Candidate orientations in election campaigns. An analysis of the German federal election campaigns 1980–1998. *Politische Vierteljahresschrift*, 45(3), 321–345.

Sheafer, T., & Weimann, G. (2005). Agenda building, agenda setting, priming, individual voting intentions, and the aggregate results: An analysis of four Israeli elections. *Journal of Communication*, 55(2), 347–365.

Printer-Editors

Stephen J. A. Ward

University of British Columbia

Printers acted as editors from the origin of printing in eastern and western society. But Gutenberg's press in the mid-fifteenth century gave birth to journalistic printer-editors who published news regularly and informed a wide public (→ Journalism, History of). These early journalists used book production techniques to generate broadsheets, pamphlets, mercuries, intelligencers, gazettes, and newsbooks (Boyce et al. 1978). Under the eye of monarchs and their censors (→ Censorship), they disseminated reports on war, discoveries, and omens, and campaigned for or against political and religious movements across Europe in the sixteenth and seventeenth centuries as part of an emerging western print culture (Eisenstein 1979).

These printer-editors emerged in two stages (Briggs & Burke 2002). From the second half of the 1500s to the early 1600s, before the establishment of a periodic press, printer-editors were relatively obscure, were scattered widely, and operated small presses under strict censorship. Their occasional publications tended to focus on one topic or event.

The second stage extended to the eighteenth century, when printer-editors became periodic journalists, publishing well-known weekly or biweekly papers in major cities.

Printer-editors gleaned their material from many sources: officials for court gossip, soldiers for accounts of battles, alleged eyewitnesses for marvels, and correspondents for foreign news. Printer-editors operated on both sides of the law. Some were used by monarchs to defend their claims or actions, and others operated secret presses for religious dissent, much of it propaganda inspired by the upheavals of the Reformation, including Luther's 95 theses. In Mexico City, during the early 1500s, newsbooks called *hojas volantes* (flying pages) appeared in the streets, well before the first press in North America.

A periodic news press took root in the seventeenth century, encouraged – at different rates in different countries – by a more tolerant political climate, a literate public in growing cities, a network of publishers and correspondents linked by a postal service, and the stimulus of print capitalism. In England, the evolution of a Parliament-restrained monarchy allowed for periods of greater press freedom (→ Freedom of the Press, Concept of) than in France or Germany. In the colonies of North America, printer-editors labored at first under old-world governors.

Conflicts such as the Thirty Years War fueled readership and encouraged periodic publication, but news of commerce also mattered. In the freer political climate of trading centers such as Amsterdam, printer-editors published brusque *corantos* or newssheets on business and politics (Shaaber 1967). In England, under the censorious Stuarts, a cautious weekly news press took root in the London of the 1620s, imitating the Amsterdam newssheets. A vigorous periodic press arose during the Civil War (→ Partisan Press), as royalist and anti-royalist printer-editors quarreled (Smith 1994), but the Restoration brought back censorship. The English periodic press could not grow beyond a few official papers until the restrictive Printing Act expired in the late 1600s. Outside of England, authoritarian governments licensed a small periodic press while struggling to contain an illegal *underground* press. German principalities imposed strict regulations on printers. In France, Cardinal Richelieu, wary of inflammatory newsbooks, granted a monopoly on news publication to Théophraste Renaudot and his *Gazette de France*.

Printer-editors had a dubious social status well into the eighteenth century (→ Journalism). They did not fit existing social categories: part craftsperson, part entrepreneur, part bookseller, part printer, part editor, and part writer. Their ephemeral papers were neither serious books on history nor crude broadsides. Conservative clergymen and officials regarded them as crass opportunists or dangerous voices of criticism and immoral ideas.

In the eighteenth century, the role of the printer-editor changed, divided, and declined. The growth of periodic news to serve the many sites of the Enlightenment public sphere – the English coffee house, the French salon, the German scientific association – required a division of labor (Habermas 1989). By the late 1700s, daily newspapers such as the London *Times* were expanding newsrooms for thousands of readers (Rea 1963). The newspaper was a corporate product, requiring separate contributions from printers, publishers, editors, and news writers (→ Commercialization of the Media). The printer-editor, as author of many forms of journalism, was replaced by specialists – the essayist, the factual reporter, the reforming editor, the revolutionary polemist. Nineteenth-century newspapers became large commercial enterprises. The printer-editor of a small, personalized paper had receded into history.

SEE ALSO: ▶ Censorship ▶ Commercialization of the Media ▶ Ethics in Journalism
▶ Freedom of the Press, Concept of ▶ Habermas, Jürgen ▶ Journalism ▶ Journalism,
History of ▶ Partisan Press

References and Suggested Readings

Boyce, G., Curren, J., & Wingate P. (eds.) (1978). *Newspaper history from the seventeenth century to the present*. London: Constable.

Briggs, A., & Burke, P. (2002). *A social history of the media*. Cambridge: Polity.

Eisenstein, E. (1979). *The printing press as an agent of change*, 2 vols. Cambridge: Cambridge University Press.

Frank, J. (1961). *The beginnings of the English newspaper, 1620–1660*. Cambridge, MA: Harvard University Press.

Habermas, J. (1989). *The structural transformation of the public sphere: An inquiry into a category of bourgeois society* (trans. T. Burger). Cambridge: Polity.

Rea, R. (1963). *The English press in politics, 1760–1774*. Lincoln, NE: University of Nebraska Press.

Shaaber, M. A. (1967). *Some forerunners of the newspapers in England, 1476–1622*. London: Frank Cass.

Smith, N. (1994). *Literature and revolution in England, 1640–1660*. New Haven, CT: Yale University Press.

Stephens, M. (1988). *A history of news*. New York: Viking.

Printing, History of

Paul Arblaster

Catholic University of Leuven

In the broadest sense, printing is any means by which a pattern, text, or image is impressed on another surface. The creation of an impression in clay or wax with a seal, or in metal with a punch, and the printing of patterns on textiles are all ancient arts that bear some similarity to printing proper. Paper money, wallpaper, official forms, tickets, texts, images, and many other things have been and are printed with ink on paper. The concern here will be with the printing of texts on paper.

EARLY ASIAN PRINTING

By the ninth century, printing texts in ink on paper by means of relief-carved wooden blocks was a widespread practice in East Asia. The paper to be printed on was laid face down upon the inked block and rubbed over with a hand-held implement to transfer the ink. The earliest use of printing was for the reproduction of texts from the Buddhist scriptures, a ritualized pious deed not necessarily implying that such texts would be read. Some of the oldest examples of printing to survive were deposited in stupas (monuments housing Buddhist relics) in such a way as to be inaccessible to readers. Printing was, however, rapidly applied to many different forms of textual and pictorial reproduction.

China was not only the place where woodblock printing (xylography) was invented, but also the first place where movable type was cast in clay or carved as individual hardwood blocks. The first recorded use of movable metal type, probably cast in bronze, took place in Korea in 1234.

Woodblock printing remained the preferred method in East Asia for all but long print runs of important texts – often texts of a scriptural, ceremonial, administrative, or encyclopedic nature, printed by government commission or under the aegis of a wealthy private patron. The number of characters needed even for simple printing jobs entailed far more complicated systems of storage and retrieval than were required for movable type with alphabetic scripts. Even in Korea, where an alphabetic script had been invented in the fifteenth century, the continuing cultural prestige of Chinese script limited the use of the Korean alphabet until well into the nineteenth century.

Joan Nieuhof, chamberlain of a Dutch trade mission to China in the mid-seventeenth century, included in his report a passage on Chinese printing, based on personal observation and the writings of Jesuit missionaries. He considered skilled Chinese workmen capable of producing woodblock impressions at as quick a rate as European compositors and pressmen with movable type and a printing press, while Chinese methods were better adapted to East Asian scripts and had the further advantage that the publisher could store hardwood blocks, and print off from them as the occasion arose (a form of print-on-demand), rather than having to print a run all at once, perhaps underestimating or overestimating its selling potential. One advantage of metal type that Nieuhof fails to consider is that for long runs it was more durable, and damaged parts more easily replaced.

THE GUTENBERG PRESS

Since parchment copies could not be economically produced on a large scale, printing only became a feasible proposition in Europe from the early fifteenth century, when the use of paper had become common. Woodblock printing, primarily of religious images and playing cards, began in Europe around 1400. Some have postulated an Asian inspiration for this, but the issue remains open. By the 1460s, block-books were being printed, combining text and image in a manner that was impossible to achieve with movable type.

Gutenberg's Inventions

The dominant form of printing in early modern Europe, however, was the printing press invented by Johannes Gutenberg, in Mainz, around 1450. Gutenberg's invention of a means of "mechanical writing" was shrouded in a commercial secrecy that even the surviving legal records of disputes with his business partners have failed to disperse. The technical details of his invention have to be inferred from later presses. The upshot of Gutenberg's falling-out with his backers was the establishment of rival presses, making it impossible to retain a monopoly on the technology; thereafter, the initiation of new individuals into the mystery of printing in some cases seems to have been on condition that they not set up shop in the immediate locality. As a result, Gutenberg's technology spread rapidly, and within a century of its invention was in use throughout western Europe and in European settlements in Mexico and Goa.

The "forme," a locked frame of metal type ready to be inked and printed from, was known to thirteenth-century Korea; one of Gutenberg's innovations was the press itself, probably based on a wine press. What resulted was a device by which a printer, working a screw-mounted platen by means of a hand-operated bar, evenly pressed the paper against an inked forme. Two sturdy columns, the "cheeks," not only served as the central support of the press, but held the platen straight during its movement up and down. For the same purpose, the size of the platen was restricted, and each side of a full sheet of paper had to be printed one half at a time. The forme was secured face up in the bed of the press, or "coffin," and then inked with hand-held inking balls or tampons. The paper, lightly dampened to take the oil-based ink that metal type required, was secured in a light fold-over frame, a "tympan," attached to one end of the coffin. The tympan was folded down over the coffin, the whole was slid under the platen, the bar was pulled one way to apply pressure, then the other to release the platen; the coffin was then moved along and the exercise repeated for the second half of the sheet. The coffin was then slid out again and the tympan opened to remove the printed sheet, which was hung up to dry. The forme of type was prepared by a compositor before being secured in the coffin, from racks of different individual pieces of type. These pieces of type had been cast in a mold that had to be of variable width for different letters, but of a standard height in order to give an even impression. The metal type was an alloy of lead, tin, and antimony; the mold was made with a punch. This method of textual reproduction provided greater standardization and considerable savings in time when compared to scribal copying, and for reproducibility of long runs or large texts also offered distinct advantages over woodblock printing.

Consequences of Gutenberg's Printing Press

Much debate has surrounded the historical importance of the printing press, which Eisenstein (1979) has viewed as an invention so revolutionary as to mark a clear break with pre-typographical culture, but Chartier (1989) more simply as an important stimulus to the dissemination of cultural practices already inherent in alphabetic script and the codex book. Consideration of non-European history suggests that any technological determinism would be misplaced. Late Ming China, without any new technology, saw a tremendous growth in publishing, and the emergence of a literary class of professional authors, editors, commentators, and anthologists that only partially overlapped with the state-authorized aristocracy of learning established by the imperial examination system. At the same time, awareness of the printing press did not lead to any immediate changes in the book culture of Russia or of the Muslim world, until figures in authority decided that it should. In these cases the printing press was much more an instrument of change than its agent.

The cultural impact of the shift from scribal publication to print may have been only an acceleration of existing trends, certainly in the first decades when printing was simply a mechanical means of producing books otherwise identical to those already being produced by scribes or stationers. But the impact of printing on the technical and economic organization of → book production and the book trade was without doubt revolutionary. The physical reproduction of texts on paper came to rely on three skilled technical jobs: casting type (technologically the hardest nut for Gutenberg to crack), composing type with speed and exactness, and pulling the press, which itself demanded great skill to produce a clean impression. The compositors and pressmen worked in the master printer's shop; most punch-cutters and type-founders set up in business independently, selling type to numerous different printing shops, but some big printing houses cast their own type on the premises. Publishing and bookselling could be independent commercial functions, but in the first two centuries of printing it was usually a single individual who owned the press and bookshop, and decided what to print and sell. Over the course of time, mechanical and commercial activities became increasingly specialized, with separation of the roles of printer and bookseller, and the dividing of type-casting, compositing, and working the press into multiple sub-specialties. Printing workers were among the most skilled and best paid of the time, and their "chapels" were early precursors of unionization. The uniquely well-preserved print shop and archive of the Plantin Office in Antwerp (now the Plantin-Moretus Museum) illuminates every aspect of the trade in the late sixteenth and seventeenth centuries.

The first decades of printing saw a series of minor but crucial developments in book design: the diversification of Latin types (Blackletter, Roman, Italic, etc.) and the creation of types for printing in Greek, Hebrew, and other scripts; the creation of decorative type and borders, and of methods of combining woodcut illustrations with letterpress text, making the work of illuminators redundant; the perfection of methods of printing in color, particularly in red and black on the same page; and the invention of the title page, first as a means of identifying printed texts and then as a means of advertising them.

The rapid dissemination of the technology, and the imperative to produce books in previously unheard of numbers, and then sell them as quickly as possible, led to new commercial interactions and marketing strategies. Although most printers initially combined the roles of publisher and bookseller, they would also happily act as printer for another bookseller, and vice versa, so that any given bookshop would contain works from many different print shops. Book trade contacts, and especially the great book fairs, initially in Lyons and later in Frankfurt and Leipzig, created new forms of commercial and intellectual networking that linked centers of printing and book-buying across western Christendom.

The very first products of the Gutenberg press were Latin Bibles, printed indulgences, and calendars, all of which required standardized reproduction in relatively large numbers. These were soon followed by Latin grammars, the works of Cicero, and then those of other classical authors read in large numbers, major works of medieval scholarship in theology, canon and civil law, natural philosophy, and medicine, and vernacular books and booklets of all sorts: devotional, educational, self-help, romantic, and sensationalist. By 1600 every type of printed work had seen the light of day, from lottery tickets and flysheets advertising wonder drugs to the great polyglot Bibles that presented parallel texts in three or four different scripts on the same page. There were ever more editions of ancient texts (classical, scriptural, or patristic), even of the more obscure ancient writers, constant reprints of late medieval romances for a popular readership, but also an increasing range of new discoveries, opinions, and arguments made available to the general public (→ Newspaper, Antecedents of).

The controversies of the Reformation greatly stimulated the growth of the press, which presented a new means of disseminating religious → propaganda, but also led to stricter regulation, on confessional grounds, of what could be published (→ Censorship; Censorship, History of). The contact that ordinary folk had with texts was increased greatly by the printing of almanacs and catechisms. In the seventeenth century, the interlocking developments in scientific experiment and the publication of results, whether in books, pamphlets, or learned journals (→ Magazine; Magazine, History of), owed a great deal to the printing press as a means of disseminating knowledge.

THE MECHANIZATION OF PRINTING IN THE NINETEENTH CENTURY

For 350 years the Gutenberg press in use in Europe, and increasingly throughout lands of European settlement overseas, saw constant minor improvements but no major modifications. Little had changed between Gutenberg's own day and the description of printing provided in Diderot's *Encyclopedia*, itself a major printing achievement. The last improvement of the handpress era, and the first that considerably increased press output, was Charles Stanhope's press. Built entirely of iron, this was a much harder-wearing machine than earlier wood-frame presses, saving on repairs and replacement; the platen was large enough to print one side of a full sheet at a single impression, and it was moved by a system of levers and counterweights rather than a screw, so that it required less force to operate. The Stanhope press, brought on to the market in 1802, was greeted by the British and Foreign Bible Society (founded 1804) as a providential invention that made it economically feasible to envisage putting a Bible in every home.

In 1812 the first steam-powered printing machine was built in London by Frederick König. The forme was secured in the flat bed of the machine, as in a Gutenberg press, but inking and impression were both carried out automatically by rollers. König's machine could produce 800 impressions per hour, as against 250 on a Stanhope press. Within two years König had developed a double-cylinder machine, first taken into use by *The Times*, that could produce over 1,000 impressions per hour. As with Gutenberg, disputes between König and his backers led to him leaving London, thus speeding the adoption of the new technology elsewhere. The König and Bauer machine works, which he co-founded, exported printing machines across Europe.

In 1844, in New York, Richard Hoe built the first practical rotary printing press – abandoning the flat bed just as König had abandoned the flat platen, so that the paper ran between an impression cylinder and a type cylinder. His machine could produce 8,000 impressions per hour. The Bullock press of 1865 added a continuous roll of paper, boosting the speed of production still further. These developments were of particular interest to newspaper publishers, who throughout the nineteenth century faced the need to print ever larger runs at ever greater speeds.

In parallel with the mechanization of printing itself, machines for making paper, for casting type, and for compositing were developed and refined, patent following patent. From the mid-nineteenth century onward newspapers, cheap novels, and other ephemera were increasingly printed on high-acid wood-pulp paper, made in Fourdrinier machines, as a cheap alternative to traditional rag- or linen-based papers. By the end of the nineteenth century, linotype, photogravure, and offset lithography all provided means of printing without traditional movable type or engraved plates. Lithography was the first European technology to offer undoubted advantages over traditional East Asian methods of reproducing nonalphabetic scripts, and was rapidly adopted in China and Japan, as were later developments. At the same time, the use of western printing technology had been spread beyond areas of European settlement by missionary societies and colonial governments, and as a tool of administrative and religious reformers was making considerable inroads into the traditional book culture of Muslim lands.

Nineteenth-century mechanization was followed in the twentieth century by a profusion of chemical printing processes, electrification, and most recently computerization. Offset filmsetting, or photocomposition, and now computer-to-plate offset printing, have made cast-metal type itself, like the woodblock, obsolete for all but bibliophile editions and quality bespoke printing.

SEE ALSO: ▶ Book ▶ Censorship ▶ Censorship, History of ▶ Labor Unions in the Media ▶ Magazine ▶ Magazine, History of ▶ McLuhan, Marshall ▶ Newspaper ▶ Newspaper, Antecedents of ▶ Newspaper, History of ▶ Printer-Editors ▶ Prints ▶ Propaganda ▶ Stereotypes ▶ Typography ▶ Underground Press

References and Suggested Reading

Annual Bibliography of the History of the Printed Book and Libraries (1970–). The Hague: Nijhoff. From 1989 online at www.kb.nl/bho.

Chartier, R. (ed.) (1989). *The culture of print: Power and the uses of print in early modern Europe* (trans. L. G. Cochrane). Cambridge: Polity.

Chow, K. (2004). *Publishing, culture, and power in early modern China*. Stanford, CA: Stanford University Press.

Darnton, R. (1979). *The business of enlightenment: A publishing history of the Encyclopédie 1775–1800*. Cambridge, MA: Belknap Press.

Eisenstein, E. L. (1979). *The printing press as an agent of change: Communications and cultural transformations in early-modern Europe*. 2 vols. Cambridge: Cambridge University Press.

Febvre, L., and Martin, H-J. (1976). *The coming of the book: The impact of printing 1450–1800* (trans. D. Gerard). London and New York: Verso.

Gaskell, P. (1985). *A new introduction to bibliography*. Oxford: Clarendon.

McKenzie, D. F. (1986). *Bibliography and the sociology of texts: The Panizzi Lectures 1985*. London: British Library.

Nieuhof, J. (1665). *Het gezantschap der Neêrlandtsche Oost-Indische compagnie, aan den grooten Tartarischen cham, den tegenwoordigen keizer van China*. Amsterdam: Jacob van Meurs.

Robinson, F. (1993). Technology and religious change: Islam and the impact of print. *Modern Asian Studies*, 27(1), 229–251.

Voet, L. (1969–1972). *The golden compasses: A history and evaluation of the printing and publishing activities of the Officina Plantiniana at Antwerp*. 2 vols. Amsterdam: Vangendt.

Prints

Lisa Pon

Southern Methodist University

Printing, strictly defined, is the process by which ink is transferred from a prepared matrix to another surface; prints are the material objects that bear the ink transferred by this process (→ Printing, History of). From the mid-fifteenth century until the early nineteenth century in the west, a printing press powered by hand was most commonly used to effect the transfer. As a result, the surface receiving the ink, often a sheet of paper, was usually relatively small in scale in order to fit into the press. The matrix was routinely inked and printed repeatedly, producing hundreds or thousands of prints that were identical in content. Although, by the late sixteenth century, collectors were able to discern qualitative differences between prints made from a new or much used matrix, and were willing to pay substantially more for the former, print scholar William Ivins was correct to point out that the fundamental importance of printed images was their status as "exactly repeatable pictorial statements" (1953).

Physical portability, existence in large numbers, and low cost in comparison to drawn or painted pictures have made prints a powerful means of bringing largely identical images to many people in many places (→ Painting). By the end of the fifteenth century, some thousand years after printing on paper began in China, printing in Europe was producing pictures faster and in greater numbers than had ever been possible previously. Since then, prints have had profound effects on how the socio-cultural world has been constituted and understood. Like printed texts (Eisenstein 1979), printed pictures led to a stabilization of certain → codes, such as a shared vocabulary of classical architecture (Carpo 2001) or a common legal tender in the form of engraved bank notes. Prints have also offered a flexible medium through which civic, national, or religious identities around the Mediterranean basin, Europe, the Americas, and Asia could be constructed and contested (San Juan 2001; van den Boogaart 2003; Wilson 2004; → Socialization by the Media). For example, the chromolithographs produced in the 1880s by the Chitrashala Press in Poona, India, emphasized the martial prowess of Hindu deities such as Khandoba and Bhavani as a call to action to a wide and politically sensitized viewership then under colonial rule (Pinney 2004).

Prints could also be presented as a means to universal knowledge. The most extensively illustrated printed → book of the fifteenth century, the *Nuremberg chronicle* (*Liber chronicarum*) compiled by Hermann Schedel, was organized as a year-by-year account of notable historical events in all the world then known to Europeans from Creation through the years just before its publication in 1493. More than 600 woodcuts from the workshop of Michael Wolgemut and Wilhelm Pleydenwurff, many printed more than once in the book to produce almost 1,900 illustrations, depicted biblical scenes, subjects from classical and medieval history, and a series of city views. Some of these views were distinct, recognizable representations (for example, Nuremberg, Venice, and Jerusalem), whereas others used the same image repeatedly to denote various cities (for example, a single woodcut was used to indicate the land of the Amazons, Alexandria, Athens, Pavia, and Prussia).

MATERIAL MANIPULATIONS

Another publication from Nuremberg demonstrates how the physical nature of prints allowed and even sometimes explicitly invited manipulation by its viewers. The *Picture academy for the young* (*Bilder-Akademie für die Jugend*) was published between 1780 and 1784 by Johann Siegmund Stoy as a volume of 52 engravings for children and two volumes of text for their teachers (Heesen 2002). Each engraving contained nine pictures, related thematically but drawn from different orders of knowledge, from biblical history to everyday life. Teachers were to start by presenting only one picture at a time, covering the others with a paper mask; alternatively, the nine pictures were to be cut apart, mounted on cardboard for durability, and stored in a specially constructed box, whose compartments mimicked the placement of each picture on its original uncut sheet. By taking the printed pictures from compartments, comparing them and replacing them to their proper places, children were prompted both to learn about the world and to organize that learning according to Stoy's framework (→ Media Use and Child Development; Media Use by Children).

The arrival of Japanese woodblock prints in Europe in the early nineteenth century offers an example of the manipulation of printed material without such explicit authorial direction. Prints by Utamaro, Hokusai, and others were first brought to the Netherlands from Nagasaki, a Dutch trading center, as wrapping for parcels and stuffing for bales of merchandise being transported to Europe. Early Dutch officials stationed in Japan did collect woodblock prints as "native illustrations . . . of passing scenes" (Captain Sherard Osborn, cited in Stewart 1979), but a European recognition of Japanese woodblock prints as objects that communicated aesthetically rather than packing material flourished only in the second half of the nineteenth century, with the 1862 International Exhibition in London. Subsequently, these prints had a profound impact on many European painters including Vincent Van Gogh, Paul Gauguin, and Claude Monet.

While the early Dutch merchandise packers in Japan and the children who used Stoy's *Picture academy* remain anonymous, there is information about other individuals who materially manipulated the prints they collected, a practice that reached a high point in the sumptuously bound, multi-volume print albums compiled by the great connoisseurs of the eighteenth century (Griffiths 1994). Jacopo Rubieri, a fifteenth-century notary in northern Italy, collected prints during his travels, cut out or painted over parts of them, and glued them into his juridical notes. Anna Jäck, prioress of the Augustinian convent in Inzigkofen, collected prints along with hand-drawn pictures to paste into a manuscript book she completed in 1449. The German text, *Sister Regula's life of Jesus* (*Leben Jesu der Schwester Regula*), was a manual intended to teach its readers to meditate by envisioning in the fullest possible detail scenes from Christ's life and passion. As an external aid to this contemplation, Jäck collected 45 small images to paste beside the relevant passages. She began writing the manuscript only after obtaining all the pictures, which fit neatly into the blank spaces she had left in the columns of text. Jäck was concerned with neither the pictures' makers nor the techniques used; rather she gathered pictures from different sources to communicate to her readers the types of images they could bring to mind during their devotions.

INTERPELLATING PUBLICS

Stoy's *Picture academy* and Anna Jäck's meditation manual were aimed at specific groups of viewers. The *Picture academy* targeted children seeking to learn about history and the world around them, while Jäck's manuscript was directed toward pious people in her community who sought instruction in devotional meditation (→ Religion and Popular

Communication). Prints were effective at mobilizing these and other types of knowledge for visual consumption by many different individuals; having interpellated these disparate viewers, prints could coalesce them into cultivated publics that could confront, contest, or accept a shared body of knowledge (→ Social Movements and Communication). In this way, they are a prime example of what Bruno Latour (1988) called "immutable mobiles," things that allow one member of a community to make a claim that can be entertained by the community at large. Prints are especially effective at communicating visual information in order to bring together a public then able to make further cultural claims (→ Art as Communication; Visual Communication). For example, Marcantonio Raimondi's print, *Parnassus* (c.1517), was not intended to reproduce the exact composition of Raphael's fresco in the Vatican. Rather, the print's message was that Raphael had made the picture: as the engraved inscription states, "Raphael depicted this in the Vatican" (RAPHAEL PINXIT IN VATICANO). The print's sixteenth-century viewers were mobilized to form a public accepting that message and crediting Raphael with both the painted and printed Parnassus. That new public, brought together by print, established Raphael's place in the history of sixteenth-century art (Pon 2005).

Marcantonio Raimondi's print was an engraving, a particularly labor-intensive technique that involved cutting into the surface of the matrix with a sharp implement called a burin. As Walter Benjamin pointed out, the development of the technique of lithography at the end of the eighteenth century allowed the production of regular, eventually daily, → news images in virtually unlimited numbers; this newly enriched traffic in printed images was a key factor the emergence of a → public sphere. Photography and digital print production, developed in the nineteenth and twentieth centuries, further accelerated the traffic in images available to the public and its various counterpublics. Whether → Jürgen Habermas's classic formulation of a well-informed, rational, and democratic bourgeois public sphere was ever actually achieved is debatable (→ Public Sphere, Fragmentation of). But the power of prints to interpellate publics is clear from the struggles to control print production during the decades in which lithographs became widespread. In Paris in the autumn of 1830, Charles Philipon began publishing a weekly paper, *La Caricature*; this was soon followed by a daily journal, *Le Charivari* (Cuno 1983; Kerr 2000; → Caricature). Both publications contained collectible lithographs about contemporaneous events, often political in nature. The political caricatures, including a biting series on the recently installed constitutional monarch, Louis-Philippe, had by 1832 led to 20 seizures by government censors, some 6,000 francs in fines, and 13 months in prison for Philipon himself as well as the arrests of his publisher, his printer, and one of his artists, Honoré Daumier.

In response, Philipon used prints to bring together a politically engaged public as the Association for the Freedom of the Press (Association pour la Liberté de la Presse), which became better known as the Association Mensuelle Lithographique. Subscribers paid a monthly fee, and in return received a lithograph exclusively commissioned for them; the fees were to be used to offset any further court costs Philipon and his journals might incur. One of Daumier's best-known lithographs, *Rue Transnonain: 15 April 1834*, was published in the last issue of *L'Association Mensuelle*. The print depicts victims of a massacre during the Paris riots of that month, killed in their homes at close range by French soldiers who believed a fatal sniper's bullet had come from the building. By bringing this single, politically potent image to the subscribers of the *Association Mensuelle* in a detachable format suitable for framing, Daumier's lithograph demonstrates how prints can be valued simultaneously for their aesthetic qualities and their power to form and inform communities.

SEE ALSO: ▶ Art as Communication ▶ Book ▶ Caricature ▶ Code ▶ Habermas, Jürgen ▶ Media History ▶ Media Use and Child Development ▶ Media Use by Children ▶ News ▶ Painting ▶ Printing, History of ▶ Public Sphere ▶ Public Sphere, Fragmentation of ▶ Religion and Popular Communication ▶ Social Movements and Communication ▶ Socialization by the Media ▶ Visual Communication

References and Suggested Readings

Boogaart, E. van den (2003). *Civil and corrupt Asia: Image and text in the 'Itinerario' and the 'Icones' of Jan Huygen van Linschoten*. Chicago: University of Chicago Press.

Carpo, M. (2001). *Architecture in the age of printing: Orality, writing, typography, and printed images in the history of architectural theory* (trans. S. Benson). Cambridge, MA: MIT Press.

Cuno, J. (1983). Charles Philipon and La Maison Aubert: The business of caricature in Paris 1829–1841. *Art Journal*, 43, 347–354.

Eisenstein, E. (1979). *The printing press as an agent of change: Communications and cultural transformations in early-modern Europe*. Cambridge: Cambridge University Press.

Griffiths, A. (1994). Print collecting in Rome, Paris, and London in the early eighteenth century. *Harvard University Art Museum Bulletin*, 2, 37–59.

Heesen, A. te (2002). *The world in a box: The story of an eighteenth-century picture encyclopedia* (trans. A. Hentschl). Chicago: University of Chicago Press. (Originally published in 1997 as *Der Weltkasten: Die Geschichte einer Bildenzyklopädie aus dem 18. Jahrhundert*.)

Ivins, W. (1953). *Prints and visual communication*. New York: Da Capo.

Kerr, D. (2000). *Caricature and French political culture 1830–1848: Charles Philipon and the illustrated press*. Oxford: Clarendon.

Larkin, G., & Pon, L. (2001). Introduction: The materiality of printed words and images. *Word and Image*, 17, 1–6.

Latour, B. (1988). Drawing things together. In M. Lynch & S. Woolgar (eds.), *Representation in scientific practice*. Cambridge, MA: MIT Press, pp. 19–68.

Ledderose, Lothar (2000). *Ten thousand things: Module and mass production in Chinese art*. Princeton: Princton University Press.

Mayor, A. H. (1971). *Prints and people: A social history of printed pictures*. New York: Metropolitan Museum of Art.

Parshall, P., & Schoch, R. (2005). *Origins of European printmaking: Fifteenth-century woodcuts and their public*. Washington, DC: National Gallery of Art/Yale University Press.

Pinney, C. (2004). *Photos of the gods: The printed image and political struggle in India*. London: Reaktion.

Pon, L. (2005). Paint/print/public. In P. Weibel & B. Latour (eds.), *Making things public: Atmospheres of democracy*. Cambridge, MA: MIT Press, pp. 686–693.

San Juan, R. M. (2001). *Rome: A city out of print*. Minneapolis: University of Minnesota Press.

Stewart, Basil (1979). *A guide to Japanese prints and their subject matter*. New York: Dover. At www.hiroshige.org.uk/hiroshige/stewart/stewart.htm, accessed on July 4, 2007.

Wilson, B. (2004). *The world in Venice: Print, the city, and early modern identity*. Toronto: University of Toronto Press.

Privacy

Fred H. Cate

Indiana University

Brooke Barnett

Elon University

"Privacy" is widely recognized as a legal right, but with a range of different meanings. These include restraints on intrusion into the home, confidentiality of correspondence, freedom to make certain fundamental decisions, control of personal data, anonymity, and many others. Countries differ as to the specific understandings of privacy their laws protect and whether those understandings apply equally against the government and private sector entities.

Since the end of World War II, *international legal agreements* have recognized privacy as a human right because "laws protecting privacy are the means through which the collective acknowledges rules of civility that are designed to affirm human autonomy and dignity" (Smolla 1992, 119). The Universal Declaration of Human Rights provides that "no one shall be subject to arbitrary interference with his privacy, family, home, or correspondence." The International Covenant on Civil and Political Rights and the European Convention on Human Rights contain identical provisions. The "Right to Privacy" clause of the → American Convention on Human Rights likewise provides that "no one may be the object of arbitrary or abusive interference with his private life, his family, his home, or his correspondence."

COMPARATIVE LAW: CONSTITUTIONS, STATUTES, AND COMMON LAW

A number of countries recognize privacy in their constitutions. For example, the South Korean Constitution states: "The privacy of no citizen shall be infringed." Similarly, the Basic Law of Germany protects privacy as part of "human dignity," "inviolability of the home," and the "privacy of correspondence, posts and telecommunications." Other countries in which privacy emanates from constitutions include Brazil, Ireland, India, Japan, the Netherlands, Russia, and the United States.

In addition to the constitutional guarantee of privacy, many nations regulate privacy as a civil or criminal offense through statutes. This is true in the 27 member countries of the European Union, which are required by the 1995 EU Data Protection Directive to adopt omnibus data protection laws applicable to both the government and the private sector (→ European Union: Communication Law). Although many European nations had adopted privacy laws prior to the Directive taking effect in 1998, the Directive significantly increased the scope and burden of privacy law throughout Europe. Argentina, Australia, Canada, Hong Kong, Japan, Singapore, South Korea, Switzerland, Taiwan, and other nations have also adopted broad data protection statutes. Common law has also played a significant role in evolving privacy requirements, especially in the United States and New Zealand.

US Constitutional Provisions

"Privacy," as a distinct set of legal rights, originated in the United States with the 1890 publication of Samuel Warren and Louis Brandeis's *Harvard Law Review* article, "The right to privacy." Warren and Brandeis proposed the creation of a tort action for invasion of privacy by the news media. In the century since, privacy law has expanded to exist in all of the forms discussed above, with the exception so far of an omnibus data protection law. This exception is increasingly bringing the United States into conflict with other nations.

The US Supreme Court has found three *privacy rights implicit in the US Constitution.* The *first* is based in the Fourth Amendment "right of the people to be secure in their persons, houses, papers, and effects, against unreasonable searches and seizures." The Court has held that the protected zone of Fourth Amendment privacy is defined by the individual's "actual," subjective expectation of privacy and the extent to which that expectation is "one that society was prepared to recognize as 'reasonable.'" The protection afforded by the Fourth Amendment is subject to many exceptions. For example, there can be no reasonable expectation of privacy in information held by a third party. Hence, the US government can collect even the most sensitive information from a third party without a warrant and without risk that the search may be found unreasonable under the Fourth Amendment.

The *second* of the constitutional privacy protections is a more general constitutional right against government-compelled "disclosure of personal matters." This right has proved quite weak, and in fact has never been used by the Supreme Court to block any government demand for personal data. The *third* constitutional privacy provision is an amorphous but controversial right of individuals to make certain fundamental decisions concerning themselves or their families. This right has been the source of considerable controversy in debates over abortion, reproduction, education, and childrearing, and seems unlikely to survive the appointment of more conservative Supreme Court justices.

The contours of the Fourth Amendment and of the right against nondisclosure of personal matters are of great importance to journalists, because they define the constitutional protection against the government seizing or searching journalists' papers, files, photographs, and outtakes. As many journalists have learned to their consternation, there are today few, if any, limits, and those that there are can always be overcome by the government applying to a court for a warrant.

US Tort Privacy Law

US common law, and later statutes, have also provided for four types of privacy torts over the years. First, the tort of unreasonable intrusion requires that it involve one's invasion of the solitude of another or his private affairs and that it be "highly offensive to a reasonable person." Second, the tort of disclosure of embarrassing facts applies to publication of private information that would be "highly offensive to a reasonable person" and is not of "legitimate public concern."

The third privacy tort is publicity that places a person in a false light before the public. To be actionable under the false light tort, the publication must be both false and highly offensive to a reasonable person. The final privacy tort is for commercial appropriation of an individual's name, likeness, or other personal characteristic without permission. Most state laws require that the appropriation be for "direct commercial gain"; the activities of the press rarely are found to satisfy this requirement. Because the torts restrict expression and therefore must withstand First Amendment review, they are rarely successful. To date, only a few awards to privacy tort plaintiffs have ever survived the Supreme Court's First Amendment scrutiny.

DATA PROTECTION AS RIGHT OF PRIVACY

Euro-American Experience

Privacy concerns almost always respond to new technologies. The latter third of the twentieth century witnessed the creation of a new and different form of privacy protection – data protection – in response to the development of computers since the 1960s. These data protection laws have evolved over the past three decades, and they have taken widely varying forms in different countries (→ Information and Communication Technology, Development of).

Data protection laws generally focus on investing individuals with control over the collection and use of information about themselves. Earlier data protection laws tended to lay less stress on individual control. Later data protection laws have become almost wholly preoccupied with this goal. The first data protection laws emerged in the United States and applied primarily to industry sectors (such as credit reporting and higher education) far removed from the activities of most journalists.

Perhaps the high point of data protection law focused on individual control is the *European Union Data Protection Directive*. The Directive reflects the European experience with personal data being misused by the Gestapo and by the East German Stasi and other national police and intelligence organizations during and after World War II. Thus, European nations have pursued a broader approach to privacy and one that regards it as a basic human right.

Europe was the site of the first national omnibus privacy legislation (Sweden, 1973). Today, all 27 members of the EU have broad-based laws, adopted in compliance with the EU Data Protection Directive of 1995. The Directive requires each member state to enact laws governing the processing of personal data. Personal data are defined as "any information relating to an identified or identifiable natural person." This would include not only textual information, but also photographs, audiovisual images, and sound recordings of an identified or identifiable person, whether dead or alive. As a practical matter, the Directive does not apply in only two contexts: activities outside of the scope of Community law, such as national security and criminal law, and the processing of personal data that is performed by a "natural person in the course of a purely private and personal activity."

The EU Data Protection Directive is noteworthy for its broad scope, its sweeping requirements, and its singular focus on privacy, often to the exclusion of other values. The national laws adopted under the EU Directive vary widely, thus largely undermining the value of the Directive in facilitating pan-European data flows. Even though member states are permitted, but not required, to carve out exceptions to most of the Directive's provisions for journalistic purposes, because national governments and individuals have broad rights to block the collection, use, and transfer of personal data, national data protection laws reduce the store of personal data on which journalists may draw.

Other National Data Protection Laws

Article 25 of the EU Data Protection Directive restricts the flow of data to countries found by European officials to lack "adequate" data protection, and this has added considerable pressure to the existing incentives for other nations to adopt new data protection laws and to model those on the Directive. To date, Switzerland, Canada, Argentina, Guernsey, and the Isle of Man have all adopted restrictive data protection laws that have been found "adequate" under the Directive. Many other nations (including Australia, Hong Kong, Japan, South Korea, and Taiwan) have adopted such laws but have not applied for adequacy determinations or have been turned down because the provisions were not considered adequate under the Directive. The United States negotiated a "safe harbor" agreement that allows US companies in many industries, on a case-by-case basis, to agree to be bound by the Directive's "principles" and to be subject to enforcement by the US Federal Trade Commission (or other federal authorities) if they fail to. In exchange for a publicly acknowledged agreement to do so, the companies may then import personal data from the EU.

Later US Data Protection Laws

The US Congress and many state legislatures have adopted more restrictive data protection laws. These laws reflect considerable movement toward investing individuals with control over information about them, irrespective of whether the information is, or could be, used to cause harm.

The Children's Online Privacy Protection Act of 1998 requires operators of websites directed to children under 13, or who knowingly collect personal information from children under 13 on the Internet, to provide parents with notice of their information practices, and obtain prior, verifiable opt-in parental consent for the collection, use, and/ or disclosure of personal information from children (with certain limited exceptions). The Driver's Privacy Protection Act of 1994 bars states and their employees from releasing information from motor vehicle records, including names, addresses, photographs, and telephone and social security numbers. The law has many exemptions, but none for the news media.

These laws apply to the press directly. The result has been quite pronounced in terms of *restricting press access* to traditionally accessible sources of information. A study by Brooke Barnett (2001) found that journalists routinely use public records not merely to check facts or find specific information, but to actually generate stories in the first place ($\rightarrow$ Freedom of Information; Journalism: Legal Situation). Other laws do not directly regulate the activities of journalists, but have limited their ability to obtain important information. For example, the privacy rules under the Health Insurance Portability and Accountability Act address the privacy of personal health information and thus severely restrict the ability of hospitals and other health-care providers to comment on the medical condition of their patients. Thus, journalists are often unable to discover even the most basic information concerning public officials and victims of crimes and natural disasters.

While more recently adopted data protection laws increasingly restrict journalists' access to personal data, in the United States they continue to impose few restraints on the use of data once obtained because of the powerful role of the First Amendment. The US Supreme Court held in *Bartnicki v. Vopper* (2001) that the broadcast of an illegally intercepted cellular telephone conversation concerning labor negotiations over public school teacher salaries was protected by the First Amendment.

SEE ALSO: ▶ American Convention on Human Rights ▶ Communication and Law ▶ European Union: Communication Law ▶ Freedom of Information ▶ Freedom of the Press, Concept of ▶ Information and Communication Technology, Development of ▶ Journalism: Legal Situation

References and Suggested Readings

Barnett, B. (2001). Use of public record databases in newspaper and television newsrooms. *Federal Communications Law Journal*, 53, 557–572.
Bartnicki v. Vopper, 532 US 514 (2001).
Cantrell v. Forest City Publishing Co., 419 US 245 (1974).
Cate, F. (1997). *Privacy in the information age*. Washington, DC: Brookings Institution Press.
Edelman, P. B. (1990). Free press v. privacy: Haunted by the ghost of Justice Black. *Texas Law Review*, 68, 1195–1198.
European Convention for the Protection of Human Rights and Fundamental Freedoms, art. 8, Nov. 4, 1950, 213 UNTS 221.
Glasser, C., Jr (ed.) (2006). *International libel and privacy handbook*. New York: Bloomberg.
Katz v. United States, 389 US 347 (1967).
McCarthy, J. (2007). *The rights of publicity and privacy*, 2nd edn. Eagan, MN: Thomson/West.
Olmstead v. United States, 277 US 438 (1928).
Paraschos, E. (1998). *Media law and regulation in the European Union*. Ames, IA: Iowa State University Press.
Rosen, J. (2000). *The unwanted gaze: The destruction of privacy in America*. New York: Random House.
Rotenberg, M. (ed.) (2006). *Privacy law sourcebook: United States law, international law, and recent developments*. Washington, DC: Electronic Privacy Information Center.
Smolla, R. (1992). *Free speech in an open society*. New York: Alfred A. Knopf.
Tugendhat, M., & Christie, I. (2002). *The law of privacy and the media*. Oxford: Oxford University Press.
United States v. Miller, 425 US 435 (1976).

Privatization of the Media

Andrew Calabrese
University of Colorado at Boulder

The term "privatization" refers to the transfer of property and/or operations from state or public ownership and control into private hands. Among the principal reasons given to justify privatization is that private ownership and operation make a company perform more efficiently because its managers will be financially obligated to make the company accountable to shareholders. By contrast, government operations are often criticized for being inefficient, corrupt, and insufficiently responsive to the interests of the taxpayers who fund them. Advocates of privatization argue that the competitive environment of private industry fosters greater technological innovation, and that it pressures companies to introduce more stringent cost-cutting measures.

Privatizations of vital public services have become a lightning-rod topic in recent decades, most notably in countries where economic and political institutions have undergone radical structural transformations, for example in central and eastern Europe and in Latin America. Following the collapse of the Soviet Union, gas and oil industries were privatized and then became the focus of corruption scandals and civic unrest as former government officials and communist party leaders became wealthy "oligarchs" through massive stock acquisitions. Elsewhere, recent attempts to privatize water services have led to public outrage and riots, most notably in Bolivia in 2000. Government efforts to privatize universal health-care services, education, and other social services have also led to significant debate and protest in several countries throughout the world. In many poor countries, privatizations have taken place as a form of "structural adjustment" in response to pressures from the International Monetary Fund and the World Bank in exchange for loans.

The government of the United States has been in the global vanguard in promoting a political economic ideology that favors the privatization of state and public services (→ Political Economy of the Media). In its foreign policy initiatives, in bilateral and multilateral agreements, and as an influential model for other governments, the US government premises its global policy agenda on firm beliefs in the value of market self-regulation, liberalization, and privatization. The US government sub-contracts with private companies for the performance of sensitive government functions. Hundreds of prisons are run by large for-profit corporations, and the US military is supported by many private enterprises, from defense contractors who design and build high-technology weapon systems, to "private military companies" (PMCs) who provide such support services as security forces, interrogation of prisoners, and training. The nature and extent to which private enterprise can be made to supplant state and public services seems to be unlimited, and the rationales and processes of privatization are especially relevant for understanding the economic and political history of the telecommunications and mass media industries. Many of the basic infrastructures and vital services in the United States are built and/or owned by private corporations, including telecommunications. US domestic policy historically has favored private ownership of media and telecommunications companies, and has tended to define the → "public interest" according to shareholder interest, a view that is increasingly embraced on a global basis.

PRIVATIZATION OF BROADCASTING

Because media industries and related policies are widely considered vital to sustaining public life, there is strong and widespread opposition to regulating them as any other industry, such as steel, coffee, or coal. Instead, the governments of most countries in the world view media and culture as exceptional because of the role they play in sustaining public life and culture (→ Culture: Definitions and Concepts). For example, the argument in favor of a "cultural exception" by signatories of the → UNESCO Convention on Cultural Diversity is in part a response to the actual or perceived threats to the sustainability of nationally based media industries that are dwarfed by global media empires (→ Globalization of the Media; Media Conglomerates). Although media privatization is on the rise worldwide, many governments tend to intervene by attempting to sustain the viability of their national media industries through import quotas and subsidies. Such policies are generally opposed by economists, and by governments and intergovernmental organizations that actively promote privatization and market liberalization.

Media industries have been privatized in many countries throughout the world for the past several decades, but the pace accelerated significantly in the 1980s and 1990s, particularly in post-socialist central and eastern Europe, throughout Latin America and much of Africa, and in India and selected East Asian economies. As well, liberal democratic welfare states in western Europe and other parts of the world have embraced media privatization. In the United States, the radio and television broadcasting system as a whole is overwhelmingly commercial, and the US system of public broadcasting, especially television, generally lacks stable and sufficient funding, or influence and importance as a vital stage for American culture and politics.

Historic resistance to socialism in the United States has provided an ideological framework for severely limiting government funding of media and cultural industries. By comparison, in many other countries, public service broadcasting has been articulated through government interventions, with reference to liberal democratic ideals, affirming a role for public leaders to develop and sustain political and cultural discourse through the media. Such systems have been well funded and insulated from political pressure (for example, through license fees rather than direct government appropriations), and have been much more central to national public life. The United Kingdom's → BBC, Germany's ARD, Japan's NHK, Canada's CBC, and Australia's ABC are among the systems that serve as public service models, particularly because of their commitments to innovative quality programming, and to the insulation of programming from direct government and market influence (→ Public Service Broadcasting: Law and Policy).

However, due to pressures from global competition and the rapid increase in the availability of new media sources, even where they are well established and relatively successful, public service broadcasters (PSBs) have found themselves having to compete for audiences in an unfamiliar commercial and multichannel media landscape. One result has been that PSBs have had to adapt at a faster pace to technological change, and to develop business models that enable them to compete with commercial networks. Such changes have led to concerns about the demise of the distinct identity and mission of public service broadcasting. Although not technically privatized, numerous PSBs have taken on more characteristics of private, commercial broadcasters, including paid advertising (→ United States of America: Media System).

PRIVATIZATION OF TELECOMMUNICATIONS

Perhaps even more dramatic than the changes to broadcasting have been the trends in privatizations of telecommunications infrastructures and the convergence of mass media and telecommunications infrastructure ownership (→ Telecommunications: Law and Policy). In the past 20 years, many governments around the world have privatized their postal, telegraph, and telephone companies (PTTs), resulting in numerous subsequent mergers with and acquisitions by larger foreign companies. As well, foreign telecommunications firms have entered new markets in which privatizations and market liberalization occurred. For example, foreign direct investment poured into post-socialist central and eastern Europe to construct new landline and wireless infrastructures, sometimes in partnership with PTTs and also through new, private companies. Telecommunications infrastructures are viewed widely as vital tools for developing the economies of the global south, which is why key intergovernmental organizations, such as the Organization for Economic Cooperation and Development (OECD), the International Telecommunications Union (ITU), and the World Bank have been active in promoting this sector. The World Bank in particular has been an advocate of telecommunications privatization, which it has advanced through a "toolkit" developed expressly for this industry sector. Given the limits of public funds in many poor countries, privatization initiatives are geared mainly toward attracting foreign direct investment.

Although it would be an exaggeration to attribute global trends in telecommunications privatization to the influence of the United States, many patterns and controversies related to deregulation, liberalization, and privatization throughout the world reflect *pre-existing patterns of policymaking in the United States* (→ Media Policy; Communication Law and Policy: North America). The US telegraph and telephone industries historically have been privately owned, with little exception of note, whereas PTTs throughout most of the world have functioned as government-owned and operated agencies. Despite the fact of private ownership, under heavy government regulation to control prices and insure quality of service, AT&T, the national telephone monopoly, functioned in many ways like a PTT. When a federal court decided in 1982 that AT&T should be broken down into several smaller companies, the results were very much like a privatization. The break-up was intended to promote a more competitive, innovative, and open network environment. The breakup contributed to the destabilization of familiar distinctions between telecommunications and the mass media, and since then, US telecommunications policy has moved in the direction of encouraging the "convergence" of previously separate industries and technologies, and the promotion of cross-industry "synergies." Also since that time, the US telephone industry has undergone a process of reconsolidation, resulting in new vertically integrated firms that combine media content production and distribution systems.

As in the case of → *cable television systems*, US telephone companies now have a conflict of interest in that their own content providers compete with other content providers needing access to the same infrastructure. Today, public interest advocates worry about the possibility that the telephone/telecommunications industry in the United States is losing its historic neutrality as a "common carrier" by having a vested interest in the success of its own content subsidiaries, which are in competition with other content providers on the same system, potentially resulting in discriminatory pricing and lower quality of service provided to competitors needing access to the same infrastructure. Whereas an original goal of the breakup of AT&T was to promote a more "open network," subsequent vertical integration of content and infrastructure has introduced a disincentive for telecommunications carriers to keep their networks open and accessible to all content providers.

Not surprisingly, similar concerns have emerged in Europe and elsewhere over the question of whether privately owned networks can serve as neutral carriers of the content of their competitors. Another important development in media privatization has been the growth of the Internet. A significant global policy concern has been the disproportionate de facto control the United States has over Internet governance through the US-based Internet Corporation for Assigned Names and Numbers (ICANN), which is self-described as being "responsible for the global coordination of the Internet's system of unique identifiers." By having control over these identifiers, ICANN possesses the capacity to shut down a country's access to the global Internet. In the wake of the UN World Summit on the Information Society, governments around the world have begun to take steps to increase multilateral control over Internet governance, particularly in response to ICANN.

QUESTIONS OF THE FUTURE

In the twenty-first century, distinctions between *ownership of media content and infrastructure* are completely blurred, and a new wave of privatization has emerged. While in the 1980s and 1990s, privatization was typically undertaken by public trading in the stock market, a new pattern of private equity investment in media and telecommunications has emerged. Through speculative forms of investment, private equity firms and majority shareholders have managed to take some of the world's leading media and telecommunications companies off the publicly traded stock market, resulting in the removal of these companies from regulatory reach or public scrutiny. This new airtight form of privatization has raised concerns about the lack of transparency in how companies operate, and the weakening of any form of public interest regulatory oversight (Noam 2007).

Beyond the question of whether media are privately or publicly owned is the matter of the *changing relationship between media and the state*. As telecommunications firms develop increasingly sophisticated capacities for surveillance and data mining, they are able to use that information not only to place their services at a competitive advantage compared with content provided by other firms on their networks. Telecommunications firms now provide surveillance services to governments through the use of data gathered about the communication patterns and information-seeking behavior of average citizens. These developments illustrate that media privatization does not necessarily signal an absence of government control or abuse of powers, nor does it insure greater public accountability.

SEE ALSO: ▶ BBC ▶ Cable Television ▶ Communication Law and Policy: North America ▶ Culture: Definitions and Concepts ▶ Globalization of the Media ▶ Media Conglomerates ▶ Media Policy ▶ Political Economy of the Media ▶ Public Interest ▶ Public Service Broadcasting: Law and Policy ▶ Telecommunications: Law and Policy ▶ UNESCO ▶ United States of America: Media System

References and Suggested Readings

Bortolotti, B., & Siniscalco, D. (2004). *The challenges of privatization: An international analysis* (Oxford: Oxford University Press).

Kessides, I. N. (2006). *Reforming infrastructure: Privatization, regulation and competition*. Washington, DC: World Bank.

Noam, E. (2007). Private equity is a problem for public media. *Financial Times*. At www.ft.com (February 19), accessed September 20, 2007.

Petrazzini, B. A. (1995). *The political economy of telecommunications reform in developing countries: Privatization and liberalization in comparative perspective*. Westport, CT: Praeger.

Rhodes, S. (2006). *Social movements and free-market capitalism in Latin America: Telecommunications privatization and the rise of consumer protest*. Albany, NY: SUNY Press.

Professionalization of Journalism

Chris Anderson

Columbia University

The professionalization of journalism refers to the process by which a category of workers engaged in reporting and commentary in the public media on current events and ideas achieves the status of the occupational professional. Key issues in understanding the professionalization of journalism center on the difficulties in defining "professionalization" itself; the historical differences between US and non-American trajectories of professionalization; the relationship between journalistic objectivity (→ Objectivity in Reporting) and professionalism, especially in the American case; and the current economic, technological, and political challenges to the professional status of → journalism.

DEFINITIONS

The difficulty most media scholars face in determining whether to consider journalism a profession links partly to the social and cultural practices of journalism and partly to difficulties in the study of the professions in general. Although the scholarly criteria for considering whether or not an occupation is a profession has remained largely stable since Durkheim – professions control their own recruitment, claim an exclusive area of competence, and postulate various normative benefits generated by their occupational autonomy – the method of analysis has moved from seeing professions as the bearers of functional traits to viewing them as interested social actors.

An older *trait approach* to the sociology of professions engaged in a → functional analysis of professional systems, a research program whose openly normative tendencies define a profession as a model of occupational autonomy and responsible self-management that everyone should imitate. Trait theories continue to manifest themselves within much of the literature on journalism, primarily in attempts to determine whether or not journalism is a profession. Most scholars working in the sociology of the professions have abandoned the trait approach and its functionalism. Many sociologists care less about answering the question "Is this occupation a profession?" and more about analyzing the circumstances in which workers attempt to turn an occupation into a profession and themselves into professionals (Hughes 1965). The study of "the profession" as an idealized functionalist category has been replaced by the more Weberian study of "professionalization" and the "professional project" (Larson 1977).

The *theory of the professional project* has remained at the center of much of the most important work in the sociology of the professions for the past several decades (MacDonald 1995). For scholars in this tradition, professions are neither naturally existing occupational categories nor the bearers of socially functional traits. Instead they are collective social actors that attempt to translate one order of scarce resources – special knowledge and skills – into social and economic rewards. Within the studies of journalism, this Weberian analysis is seen in studies that trace the rise of journalistic professionalism over the course of history.

Key to the success or failure of an occupation's professional project is its ability to achieve a regulative bargain with the state. Professional groups must also do more to secure their monopoly than simply petition state elites; they must engage in a competitive struggle with other occupational groups that offer similar knowledge-based services, a process of *struggle over jurisdiction* (Abbott 1988). Finally, the fundamental aim of a profession is less a strict monopoly than a looser form of social closure: a process that allows the professional group itself to define the criteria for judging its own competence, by promulgating abstract standards of conduct and controlling the selection and training of its members.

In the study of journalism, scholarship has moved along a similar track. Much recent research analyzes the means and methods that the journalist has employed to seize control of both the abstract knowledge base and the occupational autonomy needed to establish professional dominance. For instance, cross-national empirical evidence demonstrates that journalists see themselves as a professional ingroup (Donsbach 1981). Rather than attempting to shoehorn journalists into traditional professional criteria, a more interesting approach is to *determine categories of professional journalistic competence* and analyze how much the practice of actual journalists reflects these categories.

CROSS-NATIONAL DIMENSIONS

Many cross-national studies of professionalism and journalism adopt some or all of the sociological perspectives on professionalization, though not always explicitly. Three important cross-national studies of journalistic professionalism are "Professionalization in the media world?" (Kepplinger & Köcher 1990), *Comparing media systems* (Hallin & Mancini 2004) and *Making journalists* (deBurgh 2005). These three join others that probe professionalization and journalism (Frohlich & Holtz-Bacha 2003). The benefits of cross-national comparisons are that they call into question some of the basic assumptions of a professionalization model grounded solely in the historical experience of American or British journalism.

Hallin and Mancini (2004) includes professionalization as one of the four axes (along with media market development, political parallelism, and state intervention; → Party–Press Parallelism) along which to analyze the three major media systems of North America and Europe (the polarized pluralist, the democratic corporatist, and the North Atlantic liberal; → Political Communication Systems). The three media systems vary in their approximation to the abstract model of professionalism that Hallin and Mancini propose. *Polarized pluralist journalism* as practiced in Mediterranean countries possesses a weaker level of professionalism and closer ties to the perspectives and activities of other political and social actors. *Democratic corporatist journalism* within the northern and central European countries is a highly professionalized endeavor; journalists often join press organizations and subscribe to overt, written codes of enforceable conduct. "Professional" does not translate into either objective or "free from ties to political parties," but rather defines journalistic autonomy as a form of active political intervention in the political world. The overview of the *North Atlantic model*, finally, largely parallels analysis of the development of professionalism in the United States: high levels of professionalism of a noninstitutionalized sort, primarily dependent upon claims to journalistic objectivity and an overt abstention from political life.

Other cross-national studies have also addressed issues of journalistic professionalism. The main limitation of many of these comprehensive and theoretically sophisticated overviews of major journalism systems and global variations in professionalism and professionalization is their focus on the west: North America, Britain, and Europe. Other scholars have launched moves toward expanding the comparative frame, exploring global issues related to journalism education, training, and practice and, secondarily, professionalization (Waisbord 2000).

DISCUSSION IN THE UNITED STATES

Despite moving toward a deeper understanding of cross-national professionalism, most journalistic analyses of professionalism still use the *United States as a typical case*, either in comparison to other countries or as the definition in need of conceptual adjustment. A review of how journalistic professionalism developed in the United States must therefore precede any analysis of current challenges to journalistic professionalism (→ United States of America: Media System).

A factor complicating an overview of the American case is that few historical studies tracing the development of journalism see professionalism as the primary object of study (→ Journalism, History of). Some of the most historically detailed overviews trace the growth of the occupation of journalism in general, colorful terms (Summers 1994), and many of the most useful case studies see the emergence of objectivity as synonymous with the growth of professionalism (Kaplan 2002; Mindich 1998). As a result, journalism scholarship regularly conflates "journalistic objectivity" with "journalistic professionalism," even though the correlation does not necessarily hold true on the comparative level.

In any case, most sociologists and historians of journalism point to the *emergence of paid, full-time reporters* (coinciding with the birth of the inexpensive popular newspapers in major American urban areas, especially New York City; → Penny Press) as marking the first step toward journalistic professionalization. Originally considered a disreputable or marginal activity, reporting would, in the decades after the Civil War, yoke itself to the largely middle-class professionalization project. Journalists began to shed their so-called bohemian ways (Tucher 2004) in favor of an adopted image of solid respectability. By the early twentieth century, the Progressive Movement developed a growing emphasis on, even a mania for, democratic professionalism, and journalism moved in tandem, organizing its first professional schools, adopting its first codes of ethics, launching its first trade publications, and organizing industry and trade groups such as the American Society of Newspaper Editors (ASNE; Banning 1999).

Even more important than the adoption of these formal markers of professionalism, however, was the decoupling of the newspaper from the political party machine (Kaplan 2002) and the growth of an explicitly *commercial model of news reporting* that seized upon "objectivity" as its primarily narrative marker (Schudson 1978; → Commercialization of the Media). Scholars dispute the exact timing of this shift, as well as its sociological backdrop, but in the decades between the turn of the century and World War II, North American journalism institutionalized the current, familiar model of professionalism on a national scale.

Over the next half century, this dominant narrative fusing objectivity and professionalism would not go unchallenged. In reaction to widespread social unrest and the collapse of the postwar liberal consensus, *critical professionalism* grew in the late 1960s (Hallin & Mancini 2004), fusing a professional reportorial style with a more aggressive and power-challenging approach to the craft. Several decades later, a widespread disgust with a process of politics seen as trivial and relentlessly negative gave rise to the public journalism movement, a similarly anti-professional response among a small faction of journalists (Carey 1999). In sociology, the description of journalistic objectivity as a strategic ritual (Tuchman 1978), the detailed analysis of the daily processes for making news decisions (Gans 1979), and the critique of how the national media shaped the image and social behavior of the new left (Gitlin 1980) challenged the epistemological foundations underlying journalists' self-image (→ Journalists' Role Perceptions). Still, the success of the narrative that the North American professional model proposed has been remarkable, especially considering that journalistic professionalism rests upon shaky foundations.

CURRENT CHALLENGES

How great a challenge journalistic professionalism faces varies from country to country, depending on national factors and how institutionalized professionalized journalism has become. Several long-term social trends threaten the still weak status of journalism as a profession: growing corporatization (and its counterpart, politicization); the diffusion of digital communicative tools (→ Internet); and, at least in the United States, the collapse of the three-decades-old modus vivendi between news organizations and the government on using journalists as witnesses in legal proceedings.

Sociologists have long had theoretical and empirical concerns about the process of educated labor becoming increasingly proletarian (Larson 1977), and a few American media scholars have drawn an explicit link between the growth of centralized, profit-driven media systems (Bagdikian 2000) and a decline in journalistic professionalism. In the European context, where the tradition of mixing state and private media enterprises faces increasing pressure to Americanize, scholars have drawn a far more forceful link between professional decline and a media system grounded in a capitalistic communications environment. Bourdieu (1998) was especially polemical in this regard. To complicate matters further, *increased corporate control and consolidation* find their apparent opposite in a second trend that also could affect the status of journalism as a profession (→ Consolidation of Media Markets): the explosive growth of digital communications via the Internet, which futurists, online entrepreneurs, and scholars say has the potential to democratize the current journalistic system. Most commentators doubt that → online media forms like weblogs (→ Blogger), podcasts, videoblogs, one-woman media start-ups, or radical media enterprises like Indymedia will replace the professional journalist (→ Alternative Journalism; Citizen Journalism), but nearly all argue that the profession will not emerge from the Internet era unscathed. Scholars have so far done little to no research on how the impact of the Internet on professional journalism varies across national boundaries, leaving to speculation whether its effects have been universal.

In a sociological and cultural sense, these technological, regulatory, and economic trends are in their early stages and difficult to assess, but they are the likely terrain where the professional project of journalism will unfold. In the coming years, research should include an examination of technological challenges to journalism and journalistic expertise, a comparative analysis of legal-political culture in the relative failure of journalism professionalization; and the cross-national study of institutions of journalism education. Finally, the professional project of journalism manifests itself as much in practice as in theory or education. In the so-called "distributed newsroom" of the twenty-first century, research should assess how the organizational structures, work routines, staff interactions, and ethical decision-making processes of journalists are changing.

SEE ALSO: ▶ Alternative Journalism ▶ Blogger ▶ Citizen Journalism ▶ Commercialization of the Media ▶ Consolidation of Media Markets ▶ Functional Analysis ▶ Internet ▶ Journalism ▶ Journalism, History of ▶ Journalists' Role Perceptions ▶ Objectivity in Reporting ▶ Online Media ▶ Party–Press Parallelism ▶ Penny Press ▶ Political Communication Systems ▶ United States of America: Media System

References and Suggested Readings

Abbott, A. D. (1988). *The system of professions: An essay on the division of expert labor*. Chicago: University of Chicago Press.

Anderson, C., & Schudson, M. (forthcoming). Professionalism, objectivity, and truth-seeking. In T. Hanitzsch & K. Wahl-Jorgensen (eds.), *The handbook of journalism studies*. Englewood, NJ: Lawrence Erlbaum.

Bagdikian, B. (2000). *The media monopoly*, 6th edn. Boston: Beacon.

Banning, S. A. (1999). The professionalization of journalism: A nineteenth-century beginning. *Journalism History*, 24(4), 157–160.

Bourdieu, P. (1998). *On television*. New York: New Press.

Carey, J. (1999). In defense of public journalism. In T. Glasser (ed.), *The idea of public journalism*. New York: Guilford, pp. 49–66.

deBurgh, H. (2005). *Making journalists: Diverse models, global issues*. New York: Routledge.

Donsbach, W. (1981). Legitimacy through competence rather than value judgments: The concept of professionalization re-considered. *Gazette*, 27, 47–67.

Frohlich, R., & Holtz-Bacha, C. (2003). *Journalism education in Europe and North America: An international comparison*. Cresskill, NJ: Hampton Press.

Gans, H. J. (1979). *Deciding what's news: A study of CBS Evening News, NBC Nightly News, Newsweek, and Time*. New York, Pantheon Books.

Gitlin, T. (1980). *The whole world is watching: Media in the making and unmaking of the New Left*. Berkeley, CA: University of California Press.

Hallin, D., & Mancini, P. (2004). *Comparing media systems: Three models of media and politics*. Cambridge: Cambridge University Press.

Hughes, E. C. (1965). Professions. In K. S. Lynn & Editors of Daedalus (eds.), *The professions in America*. Boston: Houghton Mifflin, pp. 1–14.

Kaplan, R. (2002). *Politics and the American press: The rise of objectivity, 1865–1920*. Cambridge: Cambridge University Press.

Kepplinger, H. M., & Köcher, R. (1990). Professionalization in the media world? *European Journal of Communication*, 5, 285–311.

Larson, M. S. (1977). *The rise of professionalism: A sociological analysis*. Berkeley, CA: University of California Press.

MacDonald, K. (1995). *The sociology of the professions*. London: Sage.

Mindich, D. T. Z. (1998). *Just the facts: How objectivity came to define American journalism*. New York: New York University Press.

Rosen, J. (2005). Bloggers versus journalists is over. At http://journalism.nyu.edu/pubzone/weblogs/pressthink/2005/01/15/berk_pprd.html, accessed August 16, 2006.

Schudson, M. (1978). *Discovering the news: A social history of American newspapers*. New York: Basic Books.

Summers, M. W. (1994). *The press gang: Newspapers and politics (1865–1878)*. Chapel Hill, NC: University of North Carolina Press.

Tucher, A. (2004). Reporting for duty: The Bohemian Brigade, the Civil War, and the social construction of the reporter. Revised version of a paper presented to the Organization of American Historians, Boston, March.

Tuchman, G. (1978). *Making news: A study in the construction of social reality*. New York: Free Press.

Waisbord, S. (2000). *Watchdog journalism in South America*. New York: Columbia University Press.

Weaver, D. H., & Wilhoit, G. C. (1996). *The American journalist in the 1990s: U.S. newspeople at the end of an era*. Mahwah, NJ: Lawrence Erlbaum.

Professionalization of Public Relations

Magda Pieczka

Queen Margaret University

The term "professionalization" refers to the way in which occupations become recognized as professions, usually explained by a range of factors related to the improvement of services offered and status enjoyed. The precise meaning of the term depends on the approach taken to defining the concept of "profession." Three theoretical perspectives are in evidence in sociological literature: the functionalist approach, as articulated by Parsons (1954) and indebted to Durkheim, sees professions as key to maintaining social order;

the critical approach, initiated in the 1970s (Freidson 1970, Johnson 1972), which views professions as centers of monopoly power and elitism; and the Foucauldian perspective, which defines the profession as characterized on the one hand by high status and power, and on the other hand by subjugation resulting from the exercise of *self-discipline*. Professionalization, therefore, can be understood respectively as: a process of improvement of services, knowledge, and standards; a process of social closure and exploitation of a monopoly position; and finally, a "soft" technology of control of expert labor (→ Professionalization of Journalism).

In → public relations, professionalization has been discussed predominantly within the functionalist framework, and with specific reference to the dimensions established by Wilensky's seminal article "The professionalization of everyone?" (1964): emergence of a full-time occupation; establishment of formal training; formation of a professional association; agitation to achieve legal protection for the occupation; and establishment of a formal code of ethics (→ Functional Analysis). Public relations in the USA is an important case in point: it offers a good illustration of this *professionalization discourse* as well as of its influence worldwide (see Pieczka & L'Etang 2001). The critical approach to the question of professionalization of public relations has been championed mainly by media sociologists and cultural historians whose disapproval of the practice is rooted in Marxist critiques of capitalism and in the Habermasian preoccupation with the → public sphere (L'Etang, 2004; → Habermas, Jürgen). Consequently, public relations is treated here as a profession whose increasing power is seen as a corrupting influence in terms of social justice and the existence of the public sphere. This critical stance is best summed up by Wernick's verdict on promotional professions, public relations included, as "deficient in good faith" (Wernick 1991, 194). The third, Foucauldian approach to professionalization has so far not been developed in public relations.

The *history of the professionalization of public relations* post-World War II can be structured around two key moments: the emergence of professional associations at the national level in the late 1940s, significantly in the USA (Public Relations Society of America in 1947) and UK (Institute of Public Relations in 1948), and the publication of Grunig's *Excellence in public relations and communication management* in 1992. National professional associations are important because they focus efforts given to defining and representing the best interests of the occupational group, which tend to be pursued through programs of professional education, public statements and campaigns, and the drafting of codes of ethics. *Excellence in public relations* is noteworthy because, as a publication resulting from a research project conducted by an academic team and funded by a professional association, the International Association of Business Communicators, it makes a point about the value attached by the profession to abstract knowledge, while simultaneously harnessing academic interests to the professional agenda.

The set of ideas contained in the *Excellence* project became the reference point in the 1990s for the *profession's search for its modern identity*, which came to be anchored in liberal pluralism and the "empirical-administrative" approach (Dozier & Lauzen 2000). Thus the public relations profession described itself as instrumental to the existence of democracy, transparency, and order in public life through the practice of two-way-symmetrical communication, while at the same time being attentive to the worldview of corporate actors. The popularity of these ideas as represented in published research and public relations textbooks throughout the 1990s can be at least partly attributed to their usefulness to the professional project.

An important strand of research relevant to professionalization, and included in the *Excellence* project, is based on the concept of → *public relations roles*, which stratifies the profession into two layers, technicians and managers, defined with reference to tasks, competences, autonomy, and access to power. This scheme, originally developed in researching American practitioners, was subsequently applied to other countries, proposing, as its critics pointed out, the idea of the uniformity of public relations practice and professional standards globally (→ Public Relations, Intercultural). Roles research also turned out to be important in identifying gender differences within the profession and contributing to the development of the feminist theory of public relations (Grunig et al. 2001).

SEE ALSO: ▶ Functional Analysis ▶ Habermas, Jürgen ▶ Professionalization of Journalism ▶ Public Relations ▶ Public Relations, Intercultural ▶ Public Relations Roles ▶ Public Sphere

References and Suggested Readings

Dozier, D., & Lauzen, N. (2000). Liberating the intellectual domain from the practice. *Journal of Public Relations Research*, 12(1), 3–22.

Ehling, W. P. (1992). Public relations education and professionalism. In J. Grunig (ed.), *Excellence in public relations and communication management*. Hillsdale, NJ: Lawrence Erlbaum, pp. 439–464.

Ewen, S. (1996). *PR! A social history of spin*. New York: Basic Books.

Freidson, E. (1970). *Profession of medicine: A study of the sociology of applied knowledge*. New York: Dodd, Mead.

Grunig, J. (ed.) (1992). *Excellence in public relations and communication management*. Hillsdale, NJ: Lawrence Erlbaum.

Grunig, L., Toth, E., & Hon, L. (2001). *Women in public relations: How gender influences practice*. New York: Guilford.

Johnson, T. J. (1972). *Professions and power*. London: Macmillan.

L'Etang, J. (2004). *Public relations in Britain: A history of the professional practice in the twentieth century*. Mahwah, NJ: Lawrence Erlbaum.

Parsons, Talcott (1954). *Essays in sociological theory*. Glencoe, IL: Free Press.

Pieczka, M. (2006). "Chemistry" and the public relations industry: An exploration of the concept of jurisdiction and issues arising. In J. L'Etang & M. Pieczka (eds.), *Public relations: Critical debates and contemporary practice*. Mahwah, NJ: Lawrence Erlbaum, pp. 303–327.

Pieczka, M., & L'Etang, J. (2001). Public relations and the question of professionalism. In R. Heath (ed.), *Handbook of public relations*. Thousand Oaks, CA: Sage, pp. 223–235.

Sriramesh, K., & Verčič, D. (eds.) (2003). *The global public relations handbook: Theory, research and practice*. Mahwah, NJ: Lawrence Erlbaum.

Van Ruler, B., Verčič, D., Bütschi, G., & Flodin, B. (2004). A first look for parameters of public relations in Europe. *Journal of Public Relations Research*, 16(1), 35–63.

Wernick, A. (1991). *Promotional culture: Advertising, ideology and symbolic expression*. London: Sage.

Wilensky, H. L. (1964). The professionalization of everyone? *American Journal of Sociology*, 70(2), 137–158.

Propaganda

Jürgen Wilke

Johannes Gutenberg University of Mainz

The term "propaganda" is of Latin origin, meaning spreading, extending, or propagating with the help of the laity. It was first used by the Catholic church to denominate its mission. In 1622, the Sacra Congregatio de Propaganda Fide, a council of cardinals responsible for the spread of the Catholic faith, was established in Rome under Pope Gregory XV. During the Age of Enlightenment the term assumed a polemic connotation. In the course of the French Revolution "propaganda" lost its ecclesiastic meaning in favor of a political one. The term then stood for the proclamation of an ideological expansion program hitherto unknown. Propaganda was adapted in a positive sense by the European labor movement in the nineteenth century and consequently also became a central concept of communist ideology. Lenin adopted propaganda, agitation, and organization as core terms of his press theory. The term also gained ground in commerce and became partly a synonym for → advertising. While the latter term, however, referred to economic goods, propaganda took on a more psychological meaning. It was also taken on favorably in the twentieth century by the National Socialist (Nazi) movement in Germany and the fascist movement in Italy. This has always been typical of totalitarian and authoritarian states. As a consequence, the term aroused highly negative associations in western democracies and was replaced there by the term → public relations.

DEFINITIONS

There are numerous definitions of the term propaganda in the literature. It is variably interpreted in a narrow or broad sense and as rather neutral or connoted. One of the earliest scientific definitions was introduced by → Harold D. Lasswell, who wrote: "Propaganda is the management of collective attitudes by the manipulation of significant symbols" (1927a, 627). Edward L. Bernays, one of the fathers of public relations (PR), wrote at around the same time: "Modern propaganda is a consistent, enduring effort to create or shape events to influence the relations of the public to the enterprise, idea or group" (1928, 25). Jacques Ellul, a French sociologist, defined propaganda even more broadly, as the pervasive process of influencing social values (1973).

HISTORY

Although the term propaganda was only shaped ideologically and institutionally in the early seventeenth century, the phenomena it refers to are much older and may be traced back to antiquity. Thus the Athenian statesmen Solon and Pericles were characterized as early protagonists of propaganda (Sturminger 1960). Propaganda was also used in the medieval conflicts between state and church. Propaganda also flourished during the schism of the different Christian confessions of the Reformation and the subsequent political conflicts in central Europe. Propaganda was no longer limited to the religious sphere but encroached upon the state sphere too.

World War I (1914–1918) led to a hitherto unprecedented expansion especially of military propaganda. All parties were convinced that the fight by psychological means was as important as the one with military weapons. All belligerent parties created their own institutions for this purpose: Wellington House and Crewe House in the UK, the Maison de la Presse in France, the Central Office for Foreign Services in Germany, the Committee on Public Information (CPI) in the USA. Therefore, it is justified to speak of a major propaganda campaign in which even drastic means were used ("atrocity propaganda").

After World War I, the western democratic states at first demobilized their propaganda, while twentieth-century totalitarian movements drew upon massive propaganda to enforce their ideologies and claims to power. This was first the case in the Soviet Union, where a department of agitation and propaganda of the Central Committee of the Communist Party was established in 1920. The other communist countries followed this example later. In the rightist ideologies, propaganda played a no less important role. In the 1920s, the National Socialists in Germany created a propaganda apparatus at party level, which they applied to state level after 1933. Adolf Hitler was convinced that Germany's defeat in World War I had to be assigned to deficient propaganda. He followed an eclectic propaganda theory, taking up elements of mass psychology (e.g., the work of Le Bon and McDougall). A propaganda ministry under the direction of Joseph Goebbels was responsible for central control. In fascist Italy, propaganda was pursued in a similar way.

Even more than in World War I, national and international propaganda reached a climax in World War II (1939–1945; → Propaganda in World War II). This was again true of all warring countries. While the totalitarian regimes abused propaganda to mislead their peoples, the western democracies, bound to the ideals of freedom of opinion and freedom of the press, wanted to abstain from such propaganda after the war. Instead, they tended to speak of information or educational work. In military contexts, the term "psychological warfare" had been introduced. The western countries believed it necessary to defend themselves against the threat of Soviet totalitarianism even by informing and undeceiving attempts at manipulation. Therefore, the means of propaganda ruled again during the Cold War. Even after the end of the east/west conflict, propaganda has been revived in recent conflicts such as the Gulf War, Afghanistan, the Balkans, and Iraq (MacArthur 1993; → War Propaganda). Propagandists, such as groups of Islamic terrorists, now even use the Internet (→ Mediated Terrorism).

FORMS AND MEANS OF PROPAGANDA

There are three different forms of propaganda: (1) white propaganda, i.e., the open distribution of information regarded as truth; (2) gray propaganda, consisting of statements of doubtful quality, which systematically avoid identification of the source of the information; and (3) black propaganda, consisting of lies whose source is concealed, with the aim of embarking upon deception.

Propaganda may be directed inwards (national propaganda) or outwards (foreign propaganda). In the first case, the national population or parts of it are addressed by the propaganda. In the second case, propaganda is directed toward people in other countries. The form and content of such propaganda depends on whether these countries are neutral, allied, or adversary (→ International Communication).

All sorts of communication means may be employed for propaganda. In the time before modern mass media were available, symbols, coins, heraldic signs, architecture, sculptures, and paintings were used. Speeches and the theatre have also been applied. The invention of printing offered greater possibilities for distribution in more recent times. This applied especially to propaganda writings (leaflets, pamphlets). With the help of new graphic techniques visual propaganda became more diverse (→ Propaganda, Visual Communication of). With the help of lithography, caricatures as well as posters became means of propaganda. Photography and film were also very soon adopted for purposes of propaganda. The → radio, which appeared in the 1920s, served the warring parties in World War II to broadcast messages across country borders and front lines. Because of this advantage, radio transmissions were also a favored medium during the Cold War and still are established where free distribution of information within a country is not possible: → Radio Free Europe and Radio Liberty broadcast their programs to the Soviet Union and eastern Europe until 1989, and Radio Martí addresses the Cuban population from the US. In this case, television is also used (TV Martí; → Cuba: Media System). During recent years, terrorist groups have been trying to conduct propaganda to promote their aims with the help of video tapes; for this purpose the same groups make use of the Internet. Beyond the propaganda communicated through the media, it is common to speak of "propaganda of action" (demonstrations, hunger strikes, terrorist attacks).

RESEARCH

The effect of the massive impact of propaganda during World War I stimulated an intensive preoccupation with the subject. The beginning of scientific research about propaganda in the field of communication was marked by Harold D. Lasswell's study *Propaganda technique in the World War* (1927b). Lasswell not only described the organization of propaganda, but also distinguished four major aims: "(1) To mobilize hatred against the enemy; (2) To preserve the friendship of allies; (3) To preserve the friendship and, if possible, to procure the co-operation of neutrals; (4) To demoralize the enemy" (1927b, 195). Important elements of propaganda were the war objectives, the question of war guilt, the demonization of the enemy (above all by "atrocity propaganda"), and the belief in victory.

The necessity for research on and countering of propaganda increased in the US again in the late 1930s. In 1937 the Institute for Propaganda Analysis was founded, with the communication scientist Hadley Cantril as the first president. The institute was designed to detect National Socialist propaganda in the United States and to counteract it. The most important publication of the institute laid down and illustrated seven general rules of propaganda: (1) name calling, i.e., giving an idea a bad label; (2) glittering generality, i.e., associating something with a "virtue" word; (3) transfer of authority, sanction, and prestige; (4) testimonial, i.e., having someone respected say that something is good or bad; (5) plain folks, i.e., convincing by referring to other people or the majority; (6) card stacking, i.e., giving the best or worst possible case; (7) bandwagon, i.e., following the majority (Lee & Lee 1939).

Apart from the Institute for Propaganda Analysis, which above all wished to serve education, further institutions for propaganda research were founded in the US. They became the basis of empirical communication science. It was again Harold D. Lasswell who conducted a research project on National Socialist and allied propaganda, financed by the Rockefeller Foundation (Rogers 1994, 203ff.). This project became a laboratory of method development, where Lasswell systematically refined the process of → quantitative content analysis. By using this method – in quasi-diagnostic investigations – undisclosed intentions and plans of the adversary side were to be uncovered. This was based on the assumption that verbal statements were "representational" of attitudes and intentions. Several other scientists who established empirical communication research were involved in the US war propaganda research: emigrants such as Hans Speier and → Paul F. Lazarsfeld at the Columbia Bureau for Applied Social Research (New York), but also the group of researchers conducting the "American soldier" studies, including → Carl I. Hovland, who had a significant influence on the social psychological analysis of persuasion (Rogers 1994, 362ff.).

Lasswell expanded his propaganda studies after World War II in comprehensive, broadly based historical panoramas (Lasswell et al. 1979/1980). On the other hand, however, propaganda research lost its significance. The experiences with propaganda had fostered a belief in the great power of mass media. However, this conviction seemed to be jeopardized by the survey-based studies of Paul F. Lazarsfeld and his colleagues. On the basis of these studies, the *minimal effects theory* in fact became accepted (→ Media Effects; Media Effects, History of). The effects of propaganda seemed to have been overrated. This was the reason for criticizing propaganda research (Lazarsfeld & Merton 1943). Propaganda research almost disappeared from the scientific stage.

Historical and scientific reasons have again caused a revival of propaganda research. The age of propaganda by no means ended with World War II. In the east/west confrontation, propaganda remained a proven agent on both sides, all the more so as the balance of the atomic threat could avoid a "hot" war between the great powers. Above all, within the confrontation of these powers, further propaganda campaigns were launched. And also the new local wars in the world are supported by propaganda. On the other hand, the boom in public relations has led to a rediscovery of propaganda as a phenomenon representing, to a certain extent, a precursor. Additionally, the minimal effects theory has been questioned, if not abandoned. With the return of the assumption of more powerful mass media, propaganda has in turn regained attention. As a result, interest in historical propaganda research has been revived too.

SEE ALSO: ▶ Advertising ▶ Content Analysis, Quantitative ▶ Cuba: Media System ▶ Hovland, Carl I. ▶ International Communication ▶ Lasswell, Harold D. ▶ Lazarsfeld, Paul F. ▶ Media Effects ▶ Media Effects, History of ▶ Mediated Terrorism ▶ Propaganda, Visual Communication of ▶ Propaganda in World War II ▶ Public Relations ▶ Radio ▶ Radio Free Europe/Radio Liberty ▶ War Propaganda

References and Suggested Readings

Bernays, E. L. (1928). *Propaganda*. New York: Horace Liveright.
Doob, L. W. (1935). *Propaganda: Its psychology and technique*. New York: Henry Holt.
Ebon, M. (1987). *The Soviet propaganda machine*. New York: McGraw-Hill.
Ellul, J. (1973). *Propaganda: The formation of men's attitudes*. New York: Vintage. (Original work published 1963).
Jowett, G. S., & O'Donnell, V. (1986). *Propaganda and persuasion*. Newbury Park, CA: Sage.

Lasswell, H. D. (1927a). The theory of political propaganda. *American Political Science Review*, 21, 627–631.

Lasswell, H. D. (1927b). *Propaganda technique in the World War*. London: Kegan Paul.

Lasswell, H. D., Lerner, D., & Speier, H. (eds.) (1979/1980). *Propaganda and communication in world history*, 3 vols. Honolulu, HI: University Press of Hawaii.

Lazarsfeld, P. F., & Merton, R. K. (1943). Studies in radio and film propaganda. *Transactions of the New York Academy of Sciences*, series II, 6, 58–79.

Lee, E. B., & Lee, A. M. (1939). *The fine art of propaganda: A study of Father Coughlin's speeches*. New York: Harcourt Brace.

MacArthur, J. R. (1993). *Second front: Censorship and propaganda in the Gulf War*, 2nd edn. Berkeley, CA: University of California Press.

Rogers, E. (1994). *A history of communication study: A biographical approach*. New York: Free Press.

Sturminger A. (1960). *3000 Jahre politische Propaganda* [3000 years of political propaganda]. Vienna: Herold.

Welch, D. (ed.) (1983). *Nazi propaganda*. London: Croom Helm.

Wilke, J. (ed.) (1998). *Propaganda in the 20th century: Contributions to its history*. Cresskill. NJ: Hampton Press.

Propaganda, Visual Communication of

Garth Jowett

University of Houston

There is no more difficult concept to clearly define than that of → propaganda. Countless books and learned essays have grappled with a definition of this persuasive practice that would encompass all of its many manifestations. The difficulty in arriving at a definition that satisfies all aspects of this particular type of persuasive behavior is compounded by the historical shift in the acceptance of those activities that today might be labeled as propaganda. Propaganda, in its most neutral sense, means to disseminate or promote particular ideas. A working definition of propaganda which focuses on the communication process is as follows: "Propaganda is the deliberate, systematic attempt to shape perceptions, manipulate cognitions, and direct behavior to achieve a response that furthers the desired intent of the propagandist" (Jowett & O'Donnell 2006).

The concept of persuasion is an integral part of human nature and the use of specific techniques to bring about large-scale shifts in ideas and beliefs can be traced back to the ancient world (→ Persuasion; Rhetoric, Argument, and Persuasion). While propaganda activities utilize a wide range of media and virtually every form of human social interaction, the utilization of visual media has been particularly effective throughout human history (→ Rhetoric and Visuality; Visual Communication). The psychological effect attained through the visual sense is particularly powerful, and tends to lend a sense of credibility and veracity, as well as providing a strong emotional response. From the earliest periods of recorded history we have numerous examples of visual stimuli used as propaganda devices to convey a sense of power, control the flow of → information, or manipulate the → emotions and → cognitions of the → public (→ Affects and Media Exposure; Cognitive Dissonance Theory; Emotions, Media Effects on; Visuals, Cognitive Processing of).

THE EARLY HISTORY OF VISUAL PROPAGANDA

Ancient Days

The development of visual propaganda throughout history moves along two basic trajectories. The first is the desire to disseminate the message to an ever-wider public; the second is to disseminate this message as quickly and effectively as possible. In the ancient world, where communications were severely limited by distance, visual propaganda was initially confined to monumental displays associated with official sites of power such as palaces and temples, where large architectural structures, statues, obelisks, wall engravings, and other visual devices were used as a means of establishing a sense of power, social order, and hierarchy. As transportation and communications improved in the ancient world, new methods of visual propaganda emerged as a means of creating and maintaining a sense of unity and stability across far-flung regions. In particular, the use of coins, circulated widely and embossed with the visual images of rulers and symbols of state, were extremely effective as a means of conveying the importance and centrality of the state in the lives of people (Fig. 1).

Julius Caesar (100–44 BCE) was particularly adept at using sophisticated propaganda techniques. He used coins to advertise his victories or display himself in various guises, such as warlord, god, or protector of the empire. Caesar also made maximum use of the public spectacle, spending lavishly on massive triumphal processions to celebrate military victories (→ Spectacle).

The Emergence of Print

Until the fifteenth century, aside from coins, there was no means of duplicating imagery on any large scale in the west. Pictures were made for palaces, churches, and monasteries and did not travel. With the development of printing, it was possible to produce visual

Figure 1   One of Julius Caesar's coins. Coins such as this were the first genuine form of mass visual propaganda in the ancient world

Figure 2   *The leaflet seller*, an etching by Amman from 1588. Illustrated leaflets have been a staple
form of visual propaganda since the development of printing in the fifteenth century

imagery as well as textual material in large quantities and transportable forms. In many
ways, printing can be seen as the first mass production industry, and the modern age
begins with the negation of the uniqueness found in the previous forms of handwritten
communication.

The eventual development of woodblock prints, and later engravings on metal, was a
significant breakthrough in the development of visual propaganda. Now the visceral
power of the image, often accompanied by written text, could be widely disseminated in
the form of broadsheets or pamphlets. These visual prints were intended to elucidate
current events for the common man, and were focused to a large extent on religious or
political themes. This new form of visual communication fostered a new profession, that
of the engraver-artist. Lucas Cranach (1472–1553) was a master engraver whose work was
of enormous assistance to Martin Luther's propaganda campaign against the Roman
Catholic Church. His portraits celebrated the reformers and supporting Protestant princes
as heroes, and his caricatures satirized the pope and the Roman Church. These early
propaganda prints were sold on the streets, and widely circulated, and were the forerunner
of the extensive use of printed material in the development of propaganda techniques in
the modern age (Fig. 2).

The emergence of printed propaganda signaled a major shift away from the feudal power structure of the Middle Ages into a modern "bourgeois" mentality. It was at this point that propaganda as a deliberate, systematic strategy to alter perceptions, beliefs, and actions of politically engaged publics begins to emerge, fueled by new forms of communication capable of reaching a wide → audience within a relatively short period of time (→ Public Sphere). Propaganda, especially in the form of visual stimuli, enters the structure of the modern political state as a powerful weapon both of groups opposed to authority and those in power, and → prints and other forms of visual propaganda such as flags, → heraldry, medals, regalia, and all manner of art and architecture were used to legitimize authority and symbolize the inherent power of the state.

New forms of printing accelerated this development (→ Printing, History of). Lithographic printing was invented in 1798 by Alois Senefelder, and by 1848, could produce 10,000 sheets per hour. In 1856, the element of color was added, leading to the emergence of the "golden age of posters" in the late nineteenth century. While → posters had been around for centuries, the new printing techniques now available precipitated and encouraged the emergence of the poster as the foremost medium of visual propaganda in the pre-motion picture and television ages. In both of the great wars of the twentieth century the poster became a major propaganda weapon, especially in creating morale and civic motivation on the home front with slogans like "Loose lips sink ships" and "Is your journey really necessary?"

MODERN DAYS

Photography and Motion Pictures

The emergence of → *photography* in the 1830s created an entirely new possibility for increasing the effectiveness and emotional impact of visual propaganda. By the 1860s the use of photography as a dramatic illustration of the horrors of war or the plight of the poor in slum living conditions had become a major weapon for the propagandist, despite the fact that such photographs were often deliberately staged by the propagandist as a means of influencing public opinion. By the turn of the century photographs could be mechanically reproduced in newspapers and magazines, and between the world wars, → picture magazines such as the *Berliner Illustrirte Zeitung* and the *Münchner Illustrierte Presse* in Germany, *Vu* in France, the *Picture Post* in the UK, and *Life* and *Look* in the US provided the major visual news experience for a mass public (→ Photojournalism).

Photography proved to be a particularly powerful propaganda tool in the hands of skilled photographers such as Robert Capra, with his famous "Moment of death" picture from the Spanish Civil War, or Dorothea Lange, and her work in Appalachia for the New Deal administration of Franklin Delano Roosevelt. Heinrich Hoffman's carefully crafted pictures of Adolf Hitler contributed greatly to the Nazi → iconography, and were found in almost every home in Germany during that period.

The use of photographs continues to be a major weapon in the propaganda arsenal, but the digitization of photography and the potential for the manipulation of the image has both created the potential for greater "agitative creativity" and caused a growing distrust of the pictorial image as an indication of "reality" (→ Digital Imagery).

Figure 3   Part of the crowd of 151,000 who attended Party Day celebrations in the Nuremberg Stadium in 1933 to listen to Adolf Hitler's speech

The *motion picture* has always been an enigma when it comes to its use as a propaganda weapon (→ Cinema). Even as early as the 1890s, films taken of the Boer War (many of these were faked) were shown in British and American cinemas for propaganda purposes. By the time of World War I, the cinema was so popular with the international public that motion pictures became an integral part of the "official" propaganda activities of most governments. However, through its long history as an important and successful entertainment medium, the motion picture has had a checkered history of success as a vehicle for disseminating propaganda. There are, of course, individual films such as director Leni Riefenstahl's *Triumph of the will* (1935), a brilliant cinematic paean to Hitler's 1934 Nazi Party rally in Nuremberg (see Fig. 3), or current controversial documentaries, such as Michael Moore's *Fahrenheit 9/11* (2005), which can be seen as successfully communicating their propaganda objectives, but there are far more films that have failed to achieve the desired result of their propagandist creators (→ Documentary Film). It appears that over time movie audiences have come to expect entertainment, and resent being confronted with explicitly political content. The most successful forms of motion picture propaganda have always come in the guise of entertainment. The depiction of "the American way of life" in countless Hollywood films, for example, seems to have had a greater impact on foreign audiences (→ Cultural Products as Tradable Services) than a myriad of propaganda documentaries turned out by the US government.

Television

Television was first introduced to the world in the 1930s, when it was broadcast to small, elite audiences in Britain and Germany (→ Television). The Nazis immediately attempted to exploit both their scientific breakthrough and their athletic prowess by televising the 1936 Berlin Olympic Games, but this demonstration was available only to a small number of the Nazi Party elite and to the general public in tiny viewing rooms. Nevertheless, this exhibition established television's potential as a propaganda medium. The British used their early experiments with television to broadcast entertainment, thus setting a precedent for an entirely different model of how television would be used. In the United States, television was introduced in the late 1940s, largely as a visual extension of highly popular commercial → radio networks, and there was never any real question of its "power to persuade" being usurped by governmental or other potential agencies of propaganda (→ Television as Popular Culture). Of course, if we include → advertising as a form of propaganda, then television has indeed succeeded in becoming the largest propaganda medium in the world (→ Advertising as Persuasion). Even the use of television for formal educational purposes, a role for which it was ideally suited, never achieved the potential that had been part of its promise for so long (→ Educational Communication; Educational Media; Educational Media Content; Television: Social History).

Because of the technological barriers to broadcasting television signals across oceans and borders, it has only been in the past 25 years that the development of → satellite television has created the potential for global television propaganda (→ Global Media, History of; Globalization of the Media; Technology and Globalization). However, here too the public has shown a marked preference for entertainment programming, but in very recent years, particularly with growing international conflicts in the former Soviet Union, the Balkans, and the Middle East, satellite television news channels such as Fox News, → CNN, and Al Jazeera have begun to emerge as significant sources for delivering propaganda messages (→ Arab Satellite TV News; Newscast, 24-Hour). The continuous broadcasting of images of conflict, many "live" as they are unfolding, has made these satellite channels, as well as the traditional broadcast networks, among the most powerful propaganda agencies now in existence (→ International Communication; International Television).

New communication technologies, including hand-held mobile phone devices, digital cameras, and palm-sized computer interfaces, all linked to the → Internet, promise to facilitate the dissemination of imagery which could be used for a wide variety of propaganda purposes. Government attempts to regulate such widespread use of visual devices have proven to be rather futile, and there is little doubt that in the future the free flow of imagery will only increase, providing an even greater potential for diverse expression, but also for manipulation and the creation of more powerful visual propaganda.

SEE ALSO: ▶ Advertising   ▶ Advertising as Persuasion   ▶ Affects and Media Exposure ▶ Arab Satellite TV News   ▶ Audience   ▶ Cinema   ▶ CNN   ▶ Cognition   ▶ Cognitive Dissonance Theory   ▶ Cultural Products as Tradable Services   ▶ Digital Imagery   ▶ Documentary Film   ▶ Educational Communication   ▶ Educational Media   ▶ Educational Media Content   ▶ Emotion   ▶ Emotions, Media Effects on   ▶ Global Media, History of

▶ Globalization of the Media   ▶ Heraldry   ▶ Iconography   ▶ Information   ▶ International Communication   ▶ International Television   ▶ Internet   ▶ Newscast, 24-Hour
▶ Persuasion   ▶ Photography   ▶ Photojournalism   ▶ Picture Magazines   ▶ Poster   ▶ Printing, History of   ▶ Prints   ▶ Propaganda   ▶ Public   ▶ Public Sphere   ▶ Radio Networks
▶ Rhetoric, Argument, and Persuasion   ▶ Rhetoric and Visuality   ▶ Satellite Television
▶ Spectacle   ▶ Technology and Globalization   ▶ Television   ▶ Television as Popular Culture
▶ Television: Social History   ▶ Visual Communication   ▶ Visuals, Cognitive Processing of

References and Suggested Readings

Clark, T. (1997). *Art and propaganda in the twentieth century: The political image in the age of mass culture*. New York: Harry N. Abrams.
Jowett, G. S., & O'Donnell, V. (2006). *Propaganda and persuasion*, 4th edn. Thousand Oaks, CA: Sage.
Lehmann-Haupt, H. (1954). *Art under a dictatorship*. New York: Oxford University Press.
Lindey, C. (1990). *Art in the Cold War: From Vladivostok to Kalamazoo, 1945–1962*. London: Herbert Press.
McQuiston, L. (1993). *Graphic agitation: Social and political graphics since the sixties*. London: Phaidon.
Phillippe, R. (1980). *Political graphics: Art as a weapon*. New York: Abbeville.
Schnapp, J. T. (2005). *Revolutionary tides: The art of the political poster 1914–1989*. Torino: Skira.
Stone, M. S. (1998). *The patron state: Culture and politics in fascist Italy*. Princeton, NJ: Princeton University Press.
Taylor, P. M. (2003). *Munitions of the mind: A history of propaganda from the ancient world to the present day*. Manchester: Manchester University Press.
Thompson, O. (1997). *Easily led: A history of propaganda*. Phoenix Mill: Sutton.

Propaganda in World War II

Philip M. Taylor
University of Leeds

World War II witnessed the greatest propaganda campaigns in history. Often referred to as the "Fourth Arm" after the army, navy, and air force, → propaganda was conducted by all belligerents and was essentially designed to sustain domestic civilian morale during a long war at home while undermining enemy civilian *and* military confidence in the ability to achieve victory. Although propaganda was becoming a characteristic of peacetime politics in the first half of the twentieth century, it was still seen largely as a weapon of war, especially in democracies.

Dictatorships in the Soviet Union, Fascist Italy, and Nazi Germany more readily embraced its peacetime use as a form of coercion of mass populations instead of the individualistic democratic predisposition toward → persuasion and consensus-building. These different ideologies eventually went to war against each other in 1939, in a conflict that began with a cavalry charge in Poland and ended, six years later, with atomic explosions over Hiroshima and Nagasaki. It became a war of national survival – total war

– in which propaganda was used by all sides as a psychological weapon to supplement, reinforce, or counter the destructive power of military force. Ultimately, however, World War II was won by military power – which prompts the question of what role propaganda actually played in determining the final outcome (→ War Propaganda).

TOTAL WAR, TOTAL PROPAGANDA

Propaganda was highly organized from the outset, although most sides found it difficult to centralize its various functions. The Nazi Propaganda Ministry had several rival voices from within the "divide and rule" bureaucracy created by Adolf Hitler (Welch 1994). The British set up a Ministry of Information that stumbled its way through the early wartime years (including the "Phony War" or "Bore War") fighting other Whitehall departments like the Foreign Office and Service Ministries. It eventually settled down after 1941 when Brendan Bracken was appointed minister and a Political Warfare Executive was created to conduct overseas propaganda (Taylor 1999). Once the Americans entered the war in late 1941, sufficient lessons had been learned to separate out domestic and overseas propaganda functions through the Office of War Information and the Office of Special Services. For all sides, fighting the war was the major priority, but who was responsible for publicly chronicling or interpreting its progress – image rather than reality – was also important.

The idea of a *home front* or of a "nation at arms," of mobilizing entire populations for sustained conflict, first emerged during the 1914–1918 war. It came into sharper focus in the 1930s with the arrival of the bombing aircraft and its indiscriminate impact on the civilian populations of cities, first witnessed during the Sino–Japanese War (1931–1933 and from 1937 onward) and especially the Spanish Civil War (1936–1939) through newsreel footage of the bombing of Guernica. The mass bombing of cities between 1939 and 1945 was to substantially narrow the gap between soldier and civilian both physically and psychologically; all were now combatants in a people's war where the home front became as much the front line as far away battlefields. In such an environment, morale became a critical factor and one that might determine the eventual outcome. That environment was also media-rich compared to wars of the past – traditional print media were now supplemented by the arrival of broadcast → radio and sound → cinema. Although television was technically available, all belligerents decided largely to suspend its development for the duration and use the facilities for radio or jamming purposes.

Propaganda was also a weapon that could be *deployed against the enemy* when no other means of attacking them were available, especially in the form of electronic broadcasting. This was true of Britain following its retreat at Dunkirk in 1940. Until Britain could launch a "strategic" bombing offensive against the all-conquering Nazis, the → BBC played a major role in sustaining resistance movements, challenging the Nazi version of events as they unfolded and sowing seeds of doubt throughout occupied Europe about the eventual outcome. Radio broadcasts were supplemented by the dropping of millions of leaflets.

At home, the British came to blend self-knowing mockery with propaganda through the popular BBC radio show *ITMA* ("it's that man again"), whose host, Tommy Handley, lampooned the Ministry of Information (MoI) as the "Ministry of Aggravation." George

Orwell, who was to satirize the MoI as the "Ministry of Truth" in his postwar novel *Nineteen Eighty-Four*, was himself an effective wartime broadcaster, along with J. B. Priestley, whose "postscript" broadcasts from the summer of 1940 were credited with the biggest regular listening broadcasts in the world. The BBC decided not to jam German broadcasts to Britain led by William Joyce ("Lord Haw Haw") on the grounds that only → news and not views should be censored, although the views about plucky Londoners "taking it" during the 1940 Blitz espoused by such North American broadcasters as Quentin Reynolds and Edward R. Murrow did much to persuade American listeners which side they should sympathize with (Cull 1995; → Censorship, History of; Censorship).

Propaganda flourishes most effectively in the wake of victories. Until 1943, despite a decade-long existence for Josef Goebbels's Ministry of Popular Enlightenment and Propaganda, the *Nazi propaganda machine* never really shifted into top gear because it had no real need to (Balfour 1979). Hitler, who had devoted two chapters of his *Mein Kampf* to the subject, had regarded propaganda as an essential instrument of achieving, and sustaining, political power. Nazi propaganda, however, did not export successfully – except among those who wanted to believe it. For the first years of the war, Nazi propaganda flourished in the wake of military success. But after defeat at Stalingrad, Goebbels rallied the nation to "total war" with slogans such as "victory or death." This theme was partly prompted by the Allied call for "unconditional surrender" made following the Casablanca Conference of 1942 – the first real Anglo-American declaration of war aims following the USA's entry into the war after the Japanese attack on Pearl Harbor in December 1941. The British had survived their "finest hour" in the Battle of Britain of 1940 – just. They had even managed to transform the military humiliation of Dunkirk into a patriotic rallying cry – the "Dunkirk Spirit" – that is still evoked by nationalists today. In 1942, Prime Minister Winston Churchill secured one of his greatest achievements by persuading the American president, Franklin Roosevelt, to deploy the sheer weight of American military power against the Germans and Italians in a "Europe first" strategy rather than go for full-out revenge against the Japanese.

PROPAGANDA MEDIA

This was a significant development in the aftermath of Pearl Harbor, and the American film industry was mobilized to reinforce the policy decisions (→ Film Production). Hollywood movies brought the distant war beyond the Atlantic and Pacific oceans to the only home front that did not have to endure bombing. Hollywood professionals like Frank Capra were likewise enlisted to make "indoctrination films" explaining to recruits from Iowa why they should fight Germans rather than just the Japanese (→ Hollywood). Capra's *Why We Fight* series of seven films became compulsory viewing for all US armed forces personnel. The major theme of these films was that Japan, Germany, and Italy had formed an "axis" that had conspired to turn the "free world" into a "slave world" and, if they were not stopped, the "four freedoms" espoused by Roosevelt (freedom of speech and religion and freedom from want and fear), and adapted in 1941 to the Atlantic Charter with Churchill, would see the triumph of the "man-machine" over the individual.

Movies were so thoroughly infused with wartime propaganda themes that it was difficult for audiences to stand back and say "That is just a propaganda film." So all-pervading was propaganda that the experience of being propagandized could almost be defined as having lived at the time. Propaganda not only manifested itself in films and radio broadcasts, it also took the form of posters, picture postcards, china plates and ornaments, biscuit tins, cigarette cards, songs, and music. It proved capable of almost infinite applications, as with the British (and later American) "V for victory" campaign.

The effectiveness of much propaganda depended not only upon events at the fighting fronts but also upon media access to them. It took the British more than a year for the military authorities to appreciate the need for war reporters and camera men to be allowed to accompany the troops (→ War Correspondents). Operational security issues and a military predisposition toward censorship overrode any propaganda benefits. For the Nazis, it was the reverse. Their front line propaganda company units were able to capture spectacular images of the German army's initial successes in Belgium and France, which were duly incorporated into the official newsreels. Once the Americans entered the war, they allowed camera crews to accompany bombing raids over Germany, and William Wyler's documentary *The Memphis Belle* (1943) was testimony to the success of such decisions. The American influence on the British became evident with the later wartime release of major documentaries such as *Desert Victory* (1943) and the Anglo-American collaboration *The True Glory* (1945).

Almost without exception, propagandists on all sides, including journalists, saw themselves as patriotic members of the war effort (Collier 1989). Propaganda was a pejorative word; it was something that the enemy did "to us" or that "we" did "to them." The democracies had Ministries or Offices of War Information that told "the truth" whereas the dictatorships engaged in the "big lie." Although this was itself part of the propaganda war, it does highlight differences of approach toward the manipulation of opinion. Democracies understood that, in a long war of national survival, a "strategy of truth" was required to sustain credibility in a war between "good" and "evil." Goebbels famously remarked that if you repeated something over and over again – whether it was true or not – people would believe it. One of the tragedies of World War II was that when stories began to emerge from 1943 onward of the death camps built for the "final solution" they were dismissed by many people as being "atrocity propaganda" such as that used to demonize the Germans during World War I.

The *war in the Pacific* also saw major propaganda campaigns that were strikingly racist in tone. The Japanese saw themselves as the superior race in their drive for a Greater East Asian Co-Prosperity Sphere. "Tokyo Rose" (in fact several female broadcasters) tried to undermine the morale of Allied troops as island after island fell with high American casualties. Hollywood films depicted the "yellow peril" as "buck-toothed" fanatics who would rather commit suicide than be captured. The American troops, especially segregated black soldiers, were depicted by Axis propaganda as decadent, cowardly, and racially inferior. The Nazi depiction of Soviet peasant soldiers as "Untermenschen" ("subhumans") was only countered by military defeats after Stalingrad. And, of course, Nazi anti-Semitic propaganda in such films as *The Eternal Jew* (1940) exploited historical stereotypes as a method of inducing support for, or acquiescence in, the final solution. Even in Britain, the popularity of concepts like "Vansittartism" (the doctrine that the German people are innately belligerent) evoked comments that "the only good German is a dead German," while, at one point, the Americans devised the Morgenthau Plan, which would have seen the postwar pastoralization of German society. So deeply rooted were some of these prejudices that they survived long after the war had ended.

Intelligence historians have been able to make a good case that the Enigma machine that cracked the "Ultra secret" probably helped the allies to knock two years off the war. Propaganda historians can make no equivalent claims. If anything, propaganda most likely lengthened the war through instilling hatred of the enemy and bolstering domestic support for the war effort. We need only recall the 14-year-old boys defending the streets of Berlin as the Russians advanced on the city in 1945.

SEE ALSO: ► BBC ► Censorship ► Censorship, History of ► Cinema ► Film Production ► Hollywood ► News ► Persuasion ► Propaganda ► Radio ► War Correspondents ► War Propaganda

References and Suggested Readings

Balfour, M. (1979). *Propaganda in war 1939–45*. London: Routledge and Kegan Paul.

Collier, R. (1989). *The warcos: The war correspondent in World War II*. London: Weidenfeld and Nicholson.

Cull, N. J. (1995). *Selling war: The British propaganda campaign against American "neutrality" in World War II*. Oxford: Oxford University Press.

Taylor, P. M. (1999). *British propaganda in the twentieth century: Selling democracy*. Edinburgh: Edinburgh University Press.

Welch, D. (1994). *The Third Reich: Politics and propaganda*. London: Routledge.

Proxemics

Laura K. Guerrero

Arizona State University

Proxemics is the study of how humans perceive, structure, and use space as communication. Space helps people manage the dual needs for privacy and closeness in social and personal relationships. Early work on proxemics focused on classifying territory and conversational distance. Contemporary research has examined how proxemics is related to messages such as liking and dominance.

A *territory* is a fixed geographic space that is occupied, controlled, and defended by a person or group. Scholars have identified *four basic types of territory* (Altman 1975; Lyman & Scott 1967). "Body territory" includes a person's physical body as well as the invisible, adjustable, and portable bubble of personal space surrounding one's body. Personal space insulates people against physical and emotional threats from the external environment, including other people. "Primary or home territories" are private spaces that clearly belong to a person or group and provide a physical and psychological retreat from the public world. People can let their guard down in primary territories such as homes, cars, and private offices. "Secondary or interactional territories" are semi-public territories that are inhabited and temporarily "owned" by particular people at different times. Examples include university classrooms, country clubs, and gyms. Finally, "public territory" is open for use by anyone. Public beaches, shopping malls, and sidewalks are all examples of public territory, although public places are sometimes claimed as primary territories (e.g., a gang's turf).

Research has examined how *crowding* affects humans and other animals. Studies of deer and rats showed that crowding leads to stress, hyperactivity, infertility, and even death. College students are healthier and earn better grades when they live in less crowded dormitories. Crime, juvenile delinquency, and neighborhood violence go up in crowded conditions. Yet people can experience positive affect when they are part of a unified crowd, such as fans at a football game. Altman (1975) distinguished between *density* (the number of people per square foot or mile) and *psychological crowding* (discomfort and anxiety due to having one's personal space violated). Although these two terms are related, some people may experience psychological crowding in an environment characterized by low density; conversely, densely populated environments may not be experienced as crowded.

People actively identify and protect their territories. *Boundary markers* such as doorways, fences, and walls demarcate where a territory begins and ends. *Central markers*, such as draping a sweater over a chair, are used to reserve a territory. *Ear markers* are placed directly on possessions (e.g., "This book belongs to Maria") or boundary markers ("Steve's room"). When a person's territory is invaded, people often become aroused and defensive, leading to a flight or fight response. Research by Judee Burgoon suggests that violations of personal space lead to aversive reactions when they are committed by an unattractive or unrewarding communicator (Burgoon et al. 1996; → Expectancy Violation). People are more lenient when proxemic violations are committed by a highly regarded person. In fact, such violations sometimes lead to increased liking.

Like territory, conversational distance is an important component of proxemics. Edward Hall's classic work identified *four perceptual categories of conversational distance*: "intimate" (0 to 18 inches), "personal" (18 inches to 4 feet), "social" (4 to 10 feet), and "public" (over 10 feet; Hall 1966, 1968). Conversation at closer distances is defined by more sensory stimulation and a perceptual focus on the face and upper body. At farther distances, people have an overall rather than close-up view of each other and are more easily distracted. These specific distances are most applicable to North America and central/northern Europe. The intimate zone is smaller in places such as South America and the Mediterranean region and larger in most of Asia (Andersen 1999). Yet, across various cultures, people generally use smaller conversational distances with people whom they like and trust. Couples are more likely to sit close together when they are satisfied rather than dissatisfied with their relationship. People also use closer distances when they discuss personal topics and expect to have a positive interaction with someone. In the US, romantic partners and women friends generally sit closer together and in more face-to-face positions than men friends.

Contemporary communication research has investigated how other proxemic cues relate to liking. Leaning forward, communicating on the same physical plane (or at the same level), and using a face-to-face position all help reduce physical distance between people. These three cues, along with close distancing, are part of a larger cluster of *immediacy* behaviors that communicate intimacy, liking, and social support (→ Teacher Immediacy). However, proxemic immediacy only leads to liking if the receiver is comfortable with increased physical closeness.

Proxemic cues also communicate dominance and regulate interaction. Leaning in close to someone can be intimidating, as can towering over someone rather than communicating on the same physical plane. Powerful people also have more control of space; they have larger and more private territories, display more territorial markers, and have gatekeepers such as secretaries who prevent intrusion into their private quarters. In terms of regulating interaction, people lean forward when they want a speaking turn, lean back when they wish to relinquish their turn, and step away when trying to end a conversation. As these examples illustrate, proxemics play a subtle yet powerful role in people's everyday interactions.

SEE ALSO: ▶ Expectancy Violation ▶ Interpersonal Attraction ▶ Nonverbal Communication and Culture ▶ Power, Dominance, and Social Interaction ▶ Teacher Immediacy

References and Suggested Readings

Altman, I. (1975). *The environment and social behavior*. Monterey, CA: Brooks/Cole.

Andersen, P. A. (1999). *Nonverbal communication: Forms and functions*. Mountain View, CA: Mayfield.

Burgoon, J. K., Buller, D. W., & Woodall, W. G. (1996). *Nonverbal communication: The unspoken dialogue*, 2nd edn. New York: McGraw-Hill.

Guerrero, L. K., Hecht, M. L., & DeVito, J. A. (eds.) (1999). *The nonverbal communication reader: Classic and contemporary readings*, 2nd edn. Prospect Heights, IL: Waveland Press.

Hall, E. T. (1966). *The hidden dimension*. New York: Doubleday.

Hall, E. T. (1968). Proxemics. *Current Anthropology*, 9, 83–108.

Knapp, M. L., & Hall, J. A. (2005). *Nonverbal communication in human interaction*, 6th edn. Belmont, CA: Wadsworth.

Lyman, S. M., & Scott, M. B. (1967). Territoriality: A neglected sociological dimension. *Social Problems*, 15, 236–249.

Psychology in Communication Processes

Jeremy N. Bailenson

Stanford University

Nick Yee

Stanford University

Psychology is generally concerned with studying the mind, the brain, and human behavior. While popular media often focus on clinical psychology (the study and treatment of mental illness), there are many other forms of psychology, ranging from neuropsychology to cultural psychology to sports psychology. This entry largely focuses on experimental psychology, an overarching branch that includes all areas of psychology in which researchers manipulate variables in order to perform empirical tests of how people think and behave (→ Experimental Design). Examples of experimental psychology areas include cognitive, cultural, developmental, perceptual, and social psychology, all of which hold implications for communication research (→ Cognitive Science).

HUMAN COGNITIVE ARCHITECTURE

The framework of human cognitive architecture is helpful in discussing how different types of thought, as well as the corresponding areas of psychology, relate to each other along a continuum, and how this continuum, in turn, relates to communication processes. Alan Newell (1990), in his landmark text *Unified theories of cognition*, established a hierarchical structure that is based on the processing time which goes into organizing different types of human behaviors. At the very bottom level, taking fractions of seconds, are biological events, such as neurons firing. These biological events combine into *cognitive actions*, such as retrieving a memory, which typically take between 10 milliseconds and 10 seconds. Cognitive actions, next, are joined in rational actions, such as solving a math problem, which may take from minutes to hours. All of these behaviors enter into social actions, such as forming an identity, which takes months or years, and further mold historical actions such as the forming of a racial stereotype within a culture, which takes decades. Finally, at the evolutionary level, over millennia, the mind, body, and behavior of a species will change. A crucial aspect of Newell's framework is that "lower level" processes, such as neurological and perceptual events, combine and emerge as "higher level" processes, such as making decisions, forming social impressions, and communicating.

There are, of course, a number of non-experimental sub-fields within psychology that do not employ a "bottom-up" methodology. For example, one of the earliest and perhaps most controversial theories is *psychodynamics*, which posits that significant parts of our emotional or motivational forces operate at a subconscious level, and are strongly influenced by early childhood experiences and development. These latent traumas or motivations may remain in the mind and emerge on a conscious level as neuroses or psychoses. The role of psychoanalytic therapists is to identify the underlying subconscious reasons for the surface problems. The two scholars most associated with this tradition are Sigmund Freud and Carl Jung, who utilized clinical interviews with patients as the basis for formulating their theories.

COMMUNICATION PROCESSES

The relationship between psychology and communication research can be specified with reference to *three key types of communication processes* in the context of the human cognitive architecture framework introduced above. The three processes are face-to face interpersonal interaction, mediated interpersonal interaction, and communication via mass media. This framing is not intended as a historical account of these different communicative practices, nor as an exhaustive description of communication, but serves to highlight some general similarities and differences between the two fields of inquiry.

Face-to-Face Interpersonal Interaction

Consider an everyday conversation between two people sitting in a restaurant. As these people interact, they exchange information via both verbal and nonverbal cues ($\rightarrow$ Interaction; Interpersonal Communication; Nonverbal Communication and Culture). Understanding what processes govern such social interaction, and how verbal and nonverbal cues interact in providing meaning and structure to social interaction, has been one of the cornerstones of communication research since the field took shape in the 1950s.

An early theoretical framework by Adam Kendon (1970) discussed the notion of *interactional synchrony*, i.e., the idea that verbal and nonverbal behaviors are intricately tied to one another, both within a person (i.e., person A's verbal behaviors match her nonverbal behaviors) and across several individuals (i.e., person A's verbal behaviors match person B's nonverbal behaviors). By rigorously observing people as they interacted with one another in experimental settings, Kendon uncovered a number of fundamental aspects of how social interaction proceeds, establishing just how closely tied verbal and nonverbal behaviors are in what he metaphorically termed a "complex dance." Since Kendon's groundbreaking work, other researchers have elaborated theoretical frameworks covering various relationships between verbal and nonverbal behaviors.

Burgoon's $\rightarrow$ expectancy violations theory addressed how people's expectations of one another guide the ways in which they exchange verbal and nonverbal information (Burgoon 1978). When individuals violate each other's expectations in terms of how the interaction should proceed, either verbally or nonverbally, they can be seen to follow specific patterns of social interaction. For example, if a person violates a social norm, such as touching a stranger, then the stranger will react to that violation of his or her expectations, based on an assessment of the potential subsequent outcomes of his or her reaction to the unexpected touch.

Patterson (1983) expanded these previous theoretical frameworks concerning face-to-face interaction through a sequential functional model of nonverbal exchange. It allowed for more specific predictions of verbal and nonverbal behavior with reference to different parameters and relational structures of social interaction. In particular, the model incorporated long-term personal history as an antecedent to a given exchange, short-term contextual information that conditions the interaction at its outset, as well as various types of processes that occur during the exchange itself. In the scenario described above in which a person touches a stranger, the approach would consider the arousal levels or psychological states of both individuals before the event occurred, their personal characteristics such as degree of extroversion and introversion, and historical circumstances, including events that may have occurred during previous and perhaps similar meetings.

In sum, psychological frameworks and models have allowed communication researchers to produce detailed descriptions and to form specific predictions of how people exchange both verbal and nonverbal information with one another. When similar exchanges of information occur through some mediating technology, it becomes relevant to examine additional psychological processes.

Mediated Interpersonal Interaction

When small groups of people interact with one another in real time, using different types of media (e.g., telephones, computers, and video conferencing), the processes that unfold during face-to-face interaction are combined with and complicated by various factors that are unique to mediation (→ Mediated Social Interaction). One prominent example of research on this topic examines the kind of *computer-mediated communication* (CMC) in which two individuals rely on computer-based technology to conduct an interaction (→ Personal Communication by CMC).

The literature on face-to-face interactions provided the foundation for studying CMC, in which different qualities of face-to-face interaction appeared to be degraded or missing altogether. For example, in an online message board, users interact asynchronously via typed messages in a pseudonymous setting. How might the lack of visual cues or synchronicity affect such interactions? Early research in CMC hypothesized and found that the lack of social cues in CMC led to less personal forms of interaction than in face-to-face contexts (Sproull & Kiesler 1986).

But as online communities emerged, it became clear that CMC could support relationship formation and even intimate interactions (Parks & Floyd 1996; → Virtual Communities). In an attempt to reconcile experimental findings concerning the poorness of CMC with his own field observations, Walther proposed the social information processing theory, arguing that the more limited bandwidth or sensory richness of CMC, relative to face-to-face communication, meant that it would take longer for individuals to exchange information (Walther et al. 1994). Over time, however, the two types of social interaction may achieve comparable interpersonal effects and intimacy levels. One methodological lesson was that even if CMC may appear less personal in short-term experimental settings, CMC compares to other types of interaction that are typically deemed more intimate when it comes to naturalistic settings, as examined in observational studies.

Later work by Walther suggested that certain unique features of CMC enable interactions that actually can be more personal or intimate than comparable situations in face-to-face settings (Walther 1996). According to Walther, CMC creates a feedback loop of positive impression management, idealization, and reciprocity that leads to more intense interactions, which he referred to as hyperpersonal interactions. Furthermore, studies by Bailenson et al. (2005) extended the notion of hyperpersonal CMC by simulating unique communication processes that could not occur in real-life face-to-face interaction. For example, a specially designed CMC system that allowed a speaker to make eye contact with several audience members simultaneously, provided the participants with "conversational superpowers." In CMC, a speaker thus may transform his or her actions strategically to maximize intimacy or social influence.

One of the most renowned lines of research within CMC has explored how people interact with *media interfaces*. Reeves and Nass (1996) showed via a series of experiments that people have a tendency to treat media interfaces (e.g., televisions and computers) as if they were social actors (→ Media Equation Theory). For example, people become polite to computers under certain conditions in order to conform to a social norm. In one study, participants performed a learning task on a computer. They then filled out an evaluation of the event, either on the same computer or a different computer. Participants gave more positive ratings if they filled out the evaluation on the same computer that had administered the learning task than if they were assigned to a different computer. Reeves and Nass concluded that this pattern is analogous to the social norm of being polite to individuals asking for an evaluation of themselves.

To sum up, when people use media to conduct interpersonal interactions, they are combining processes that occur within face-to-face interpersonal interactions with new processes that are unique to utilizing various kinds of technology. Thus, the additive model of psychological processing, outlined in the introduction, can work as a framework for understanding mediated forms of interpersonal communication. In a further, metaphorical, sense, mass communication can be viewed as combining processes of face-to-face as well as mediated group interaction with additional processes that are inherent to the large-scale dissemination of information, even if historically, the use of mass media predates CMC.

Mass Communication

Mass communication has typically been understood as organizations (e.g., newspapers, film production companies, or television studios) using some media technology to distribute information to large audiences (→ Media Effects). With the rise of digital technology, the contrast between large organizations and large audiences has been blurred, as it is now possible for any individual to send an email to websites and listservs, which, in turn, send this message to thousands of other people (→ Media Effects, History of). As John Durham Peters has noted (1999), mass communication technologies have changed how we think about communication in general – as dialogue, dissemination, and combinations of the two. From the perspective of psychological processes, one way to approach mass communication is as a combination of face-to-face and mediated interpersonal interactions.

In the 1970s and 1980s, → George Gerbner provided some compelling evidence for his → *cultivation theory*, which is a macroscopic theory of how interpersonal interaction and mass media use may be shown to combine in predictable ways. The basic argument is that, after much exposure to various forms of mass media, people will change their patterns of interpersonal behavior because they have acquired an altered mental representation or worldview. For example, people who watched large amounts of television, which often features violence, were more likely to begin avoiding going out late at night. The theory illustrates the combinatorial aspect of the psychological processes entering into communication. In order to create a model of how a worldview is cultivated, it is necessary to understand how people perceive and attend to stimuli (e.g., watch television), how they interact with mediated versions of people, and how, as a consequence, their interpersonal interaction with actual people changes. While some of the methods employed by Gerbner and colleagues have been called into question, his approach suggested the importance of examining the connections between interpersonal communication and mass communication.

CROSS-CULTURAL RESEARCH AS A COMMON GROUND

One area which is common to psychology and communication is the study of *cultural influences* on identity formation and social interaction. Psychology has a well-respected tradition of examining cultural differences in how the mind functions. For example, work by Hazel Markus and her colleagues has demonstrated that culture is rooted so deeply within the mind that the way in which people construe the self – how we relate to other people, how interdependent social relationships are, and how cognition, emotion, and motivations are formed – vary drastically between eastern and western cultures (Markus & Kitayama 1991).

These differences are so pervasive that they extend down to the "low level" cognitive actions discussed above. For example, work by Douglas Medin and colleagues has examined biological concepts among various groups: from Petan, Guatemala, and from Native American, Amish, and majority culture groups in Wisconsin, USA. The data from these different cultures exhibit systematic differences regarding very basic and supposedly "universal" aspects of cognition – how people form categories about objects, as well as how people draw inferences based on what category an object belongs to. A methodological lesson is that when data is collected from American undergraduates, as is common practice, the findings, models, and theories may not generalize to the world at large. Even at the level of how people perceive physical objects visually ($\rightarrow$ Visuals, Cognitive Processing of), there are differences across cultures (Kitayama et al. 2003).

Also, communication scholars have argued that message production and social interaction should be studied outside the laboratory and with regard to the cultures in which those processes are entrenched ($\rightarrow$ Intercultural and Intergroup Communication). In a wider sense, James Carey (1989) has argued that communication is not simply a transmission of information, but a *ritualistic process* that creates and sustains social reality. In a ritualistic view, reading a newspaper is not so much a way of gaining new information as a communal affirmation of a shared worldview. All types of human expression – from architecture to dance to news broadcasts – confirm and propagate a symbolic order that governs social processes. In sum, psychologists have focused on how culture shapes thought by directly comparing people from different cultures. Communication scholars, in turn, have theorized and examined the very acts of expression and interaction as inherently cultural processes.

A CONTINUING INTERDISCIPLINARY RELATIONSHIP

The fields of psychology and communication are closely related, to the extent that the line differentiating the two is often quite blurry. In terms of historical roots, some of the studies that are considered landmarks in the field of communication originally were carried out in psychology departments, and/or published in psychological journals; for example, work by $\rightarrow$ Bandura, $\rightarrow$ Hovland, $\rightarrow$ Lasswell, and Lewin.

Even now, there is continuing cross-over between the two fields in terms of publication venues, collaborations among scholars, and even migration across departments for faculty and students trained in either of the two disciplines. Given the historical development of the two areas of inquiry, psychology is more of an established discipline than communication, so communication may benefit from the relatively consolidated approaches of psychology. In the future, the fields will be entering into shifting configurations as each develops further. The relationship between psychology and communication has been productive in the past, and communication scholars will continue to both learn from and inform psychologists.

SEE ALSO: ► Bandura, Albert ► Cognition ► Cognitive Science ► Cultivation Theory ► Expectancy Violation ► Experimental Design ► Gerbner, George ► Hovland, Carl I. ► Information Processing ► Interaction ► Intercultural and Intergroup Communication ► Interpersonal Communication ► Lasswell, Harold D. ► Media Effects ► Media Effects, History of ► Media Equation Theory ► Mediated Social Interaction ► Nonverbal Communication and Culture ► Objectivity in Science ► Paradigm ► Personal Communication by CMC ► Virtual Communities ► Visuals, Cognitive Processing of

References and Suggested Readings

Bailenson, J. N., Beall, A. C., Blascovich, J., Loomis, J., & Turk, M. (2005). Transformed social interaction, augmented gaze, and social influence in immersive virtual environments. *Human Communication Research*, 31, 511–537.

Burgoon, J. K. (1978). A communications model of personal space violations: Explications and an initial test. *Human Communications Research*, 4, 129–142.

Carey, J. W. (1989). *Communication as culture: Essays on media and society.* Winchester, MA: Unwin Hyman.

Gerbner, G., Gross, L., Morgan, M., & Signorielli, N. (1980). The "mainstreaming" of America: Violence profile no. 11. *Journal of Communication*, 30, 10–29.

Kendon, A. (1970). Movement coordination in social interaction: Some examples described. *Acta Psychologica*, 32(2), 101–125.

Kitayama, S., Duffy, S., Kawamura, T., & Larsen, J. T. (2003). Perceiving an object and its context in different cultures: A cultural look at new look. *Psychological Science*, 14(3), 201–206.

Markus, H. R., & Kitayama, S. (1991). Culture and the self: Implications for cognition, emotion, and motivation. *Psychological Review*, 98, 224–253.

Medin, D. L. & Atran, S. (2004). The native mind: Biological categorization, reasoning and decision making in development across cultures. *Psychological Review*, 111(4), 960–983.

Newell, A. (1990). *Unified theories of cognition.* Cambridge, MA: Harvard University Press.

Parks, M. R., & Floyd, K. (1996). Making friends in cyberspace. *Journal of Communication*, 46(1), 80–97.

Patterson, M. L. (1983). *Nonverbal behavior: A functional perspective.* New York: Springer.

Peters, J. D. (1999). *Speaking into the air: A history of the idea of communication.* Chicago, IL: University of Chicago Press.

Reeves, B., & Nass, C. (1996). *The media equation: How people treat computers, television, and new media like real people and places.* Cambridge: Cambridge University Press.

Sproull, L., & Kiesler, S. (1986). Reducing social context cues: electronic mail in organizational communication. *Management Science*, 32(11), 1492–1512.

Walther, J. B. (1996). Computer-mediated communication: Impersonal, interpersonal and hyperpersonal interaction. *Communication Research*, 23(1), 3–43.

Walther, J. B., Anderson, J. F., & Park, D. (1994). Interpersonal effects in computer-mediated interaction: A meta-analysis of social and anti-social communication. *Communication Research*, 21, 460–487.

Public

Nikolaus Jackob

Johannes Gutenberg University of Mainz

Few concepts in the social sciences have attracted more attention and caused more confusion than the concept of the "public." The dispute concerning the nature of the public is at least as old as Greek democracy. Since that time, one of the most divisive questions has been whether the public is characterized by an everyman, holding common opinions (*doxa*), or by an intellectual elite, endowed with deeper insight, knowledge, and wisdom (*episteme*). This controversy is the starting point for the following considerations. After a summary of different theoretical concepts, the relationship between the individual and the public is reviewed. The question of exposure to communication content is then addressed.

Since its beginnings in ancient times, the term "public" has bred a multiplicity of *competing meanings* (Habermas 1962; Childs 1965), which continue to shape scientific discourse today. Three major theoretical schools of thought can be identified: a normative or qualitative concept, an operationalist or quantitative concept, and a functionalist concept.

The *normative or qualitative concept* defines the public as a social elite comprising well-informed, responsible, and interested citizens. These pursue the common good and participate in an enlightened and rational discourse on societal affairs. In a democratic system, the public forms a critical counterpart to the government, acting as an imaginary parliament and engaging in political deliberation. Moreover, the public discussion of political ideas and the free exchange of arguments are regarded as the heart of the democratic process, as they make the best, wisest solutions possible (Berelson 1952; Hennis 1957; Habermas 1962; → Political Discourse; Public Opinion).

In the *operationalist or quantitative concept*, the public is regarded as a collective of diverse individuals whose views on a particular issue can be measured by opinion polls. According to this quantitative concept, the public is a certain cross-section of society, an "issue public," as defined by survey research (Converse 1987). The *functionalist concept* defines the public as a system of social monitoring, enabling a society to observe itself and to react to issues which are or may become relevant to its members. The public has the function of monitoring trends and developments in society. It identifies and brings up important issues, reduces the complexity of social and political matters, and thus reaches a consensus on social conflicts (Luhmann 1970).

In addition, according to → Noelle-Neumann (1993), the public can be understood as an institution of social control: its purpose is to enforce social conformity, stabilizing society as a whole. In contrast to the normative concept, in this view the public is concerned with political and nonpolitical issues, and includes not only the intellectual elite but every single individual within a social collective. Furthermore, the existence of the public is restricted neither to democratic systems nor to societies familiar with survey research or modern mass media (→ Spiral of Silence; Climate of Opinion).

The functionalist approach is the oldest concept: single thoughts, fragments of theory, and even comprehensive analyses can be found in every period of history (e.g., in the works of Cicero, Michel de Montaigne, or John Locke). In contrast, the normative concept did not emerge until the eve of modern democracies, during the age of Enlightenment in the seventeenth and eighteenth centuries. Finally, the operationalist concept, which is closely connected to the advent of empirical social research, appeared in the first half of the twentieth century.

An examination of the public's exposure to communication content must concentrate on the *relationship between the individual and the public*. The public is frequently viewed metaphorically as an organic being with a collective mind, yet this is an intangible generalization. Accordingly, all three concepts make statements about the relationship between the individual and the public. They share the view that the public consists of individuals who are both members of social groups and parts of specific media → audiences. In the functionalist concept, these individuals, groups – including the elite – and audiences are pooled to form a single public. According to this understanding, the mass media are also social units and components of the public. Their function is to confer publicity, to set important issues on the public agenda (→ Agenda-Setting Effects), and to serve as a general communication forum and source of information for the public. The media give attention to specific topics and problems, thereby influencing public awareness of these issues. Additionally, their coverage serves as a frame of reference in public discourse (→ Framing Effects).

The relationship between the individual and the public is determined by a *mechanism of symbolic representation* in the mind of every individual (Lippmann 1922; Mead 1934; Goffman 1963): virtually all people continuously form views of the public – it represents the generalized others in the individual's imagination, even if nobody is physically present. As the individual's perception or imagination of the public sentiment affects his or her own decisions (e.g., on voting) and opinions, it also contributes to the shaping of public opinion. Consequently, the public can also be defined as both a state of being exposed to others and an awareness of being (potentially) watched by the anonymous "public eye." Individuals rely on two sources of information in order to assess public attitudes and behavior: interpersonal communication and the mass media (Noelle-Neumann 1993). Media statements regarding public sentiment pervade interpersonal communication along several steps of the flow of communication (→ Two-Step Flow of Communication; Diffusion of Information and Innovation). In this manner, the media exert influence on the way the public is perceived; they shape the individual's understanding of the proportion of opinions, i.e., of the size of minorities and majorities (→ Media Effects). Although individuals arrive in many cases at correct estimates of the opinion of others, erroneous judgments are possible (→ Pluralistic Ignorance).

The circulation of communication content among the public takes place via intervening psychological and social processes: on the one hand, people's exposure is framed by interpersonal relations; on the other hand, individuals expose themselves selectively to communication content, i.e., they actively seek information that is consonant with their initial attitudes and that is likely to satisfy their needs (→ Selective Exposure). Exposure thus varies according to personality and social factors (→ Media Use by Social Variable; Personality and Exposure to Communication). Members of the intellectual elite, for example, usually gain greater exposure to information content in the media than does the general population (Fig. 1).

In summary, it can be concluded that the public consists of individuals who seek exposure to communication content. This content derives either from interpersonal

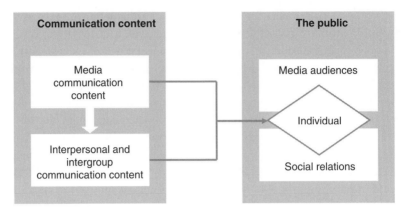

Figure 1   Exposure to communication content: the individual and the public

(intergroup) communication or from the mass media – which themselves in many cases influence interpersonal communication through their coverage. The public can be understood as a large collective of partially interconnected individuals, groups, and audiences through which (mass) communication is channeled.

SEE ALSO: ▶ Agenda-Setting Effects   ▶ Audience   ▶ Climate of Opinion   ▶ Diffusion of Information and Innovation   ▶ Exposure to Communication Content   ▶ Framing Effects   ▶ Habermas, Jürgen   ▶ Media Effects   ▶ Media Use by Social Variable   ▶ News Audience   ▶ Noelle-Neumann, Elisabeth   ▶ Personality and Exposure to Communication   ▶ Pluralistic Ignorance   ▶ Political Discourse   ▶ Public Opinion   ▶ Selective Exposure   ▶ Spiral of Silence   ▶ Two-Step Flow of Communication

References and Suggested Readings

Berelson, B. (1952). Democratic theory and public opinion. *Public Opinion Quarterly*, 16, 313–330.
Childs, H. L. (1965). *Public opinion: Nature, formation, and role.* Princeton, NJ: Princeton University Press.
Converse, P. E. (1987). Changing conceptions of public opinion in the political process. *Public Opinion Quarterly*, 51, 12–24.
Goffman, E. (1963). *Behavior in public places: Notes on the social organization of gatherings.* New York: Free Press.
Habermas, J. (1962). *Strukturwandel der Öffentlichkeit: Untersuchungen zu einer Kategorie der bürgerlichen Gesellschaft* [The structural transformation of the public sphere: An inquiry into a category of bourgeois society]. Neuwied: Luchterhand.
Hennis, W. (1957). *Meinungsforschung und repräsentative Demokratie* [Opinion polls and representative democracy]. Tübingen: Mohr.
Lippmann, W. (1922). *Public opinion.* New York: Macmillan.
Luhmann, N. (1970). Öffentliche Meinung [Public opinion]. *Politische Vierteljahresschrift*, 11, 2–28.
Mead, G. H. (1934). *Mind, self, and society: From the standpoint of a social behaviorist.* Chicago: University of Chicago Press.
Noelle-Neumann, E. (1993). *The spiral of silence: Public opinion – our social skin.* Chicago: University of Chicago Press.

Public Access Television

John S. Armstrong

Furman University

Public access television – also known as community television or open channels (→ Community Media) – is a form of → television in which citizens produce programs and bypass corporations, governments, journalists, and other gatekeepers to transmit their programs directly to audiences (→ Access to the Media). Proponents of public access television promote it as a remedy to commercialism, centralization, and lack of diversity in television systems around the world (→ Commercialization of the Media; Plurality). As a systematic alternative to commercial or government-supported television, public access television first emerged in Canada and the United States in the late 1960s and early 1970s. Public access channels have since appeared in hundreds of communities in North America, Europe, Asia, Latin America, and Oceania, although public access outlets have never attracted audiences large enough to rival those of professional television systems.

The emergence of public access television in *Canada* and the *United States* was closely associated with three developments: the appearance of media-activist movements (→ Activist Media) that promoted public access television as a means to nurture democracy and localism; the development of lightweight and relatively inexpensive equipment that facilitated video production (→ Video) by amateurs; and the construction of urban cable systems with channels available for public access programming (→ Cable Television). Beginning in 1966, the Canadian National Film Board sponsored documentaries in which citizens voiced their opinions about social and economic issues. The concept of public access was wedded to cable television in 1970 when a citizens' organization in Thunder Bay, Ontario, persuaded the local government to negotiate for community access on the local cable system. In 1971, the Thunder Bay model was adopted nationally when the Canadian Radio and Television Board stipulated that public access be a part of the country's burgeoning cable system (→ Community Video).

In the United States, media activists campaigned for similar access to cable systems (→ Citizens' Media; Citizen Journalism). Because the country's young cable industry needed allies in its regulatory battles with over-the-air broadcasters, it formed an alliance with public access advocates. When private companies negotiated the rights to wire local communities for cable, the agreement often included the reservation of channels for local public access, as well as channels for local governmental and educational programs. Frequently, the companies also agreed to provide public access producers with facilities and video equipment. In 1972, the Federal Communications Commission began requiring access channels in most local cable systems.

Produced largely on scant budgets, Canadian and US public access programs vary widely in format, content, and production quality, as do many public access programs around the world. Many address political or social issues, while others are purely entertainment. The most successful programs have attracted viewers with their originality and their willingness to address subjects ignored by other television outlets.

By the beginning of the twenty-first century, some of the world's most robust public access channels were in the Federal Republic of *Germany*. Again, they took root with the widespread advent of cable, in this case in West Germany in the 1980s. Germany's public access channels grant nondiscriminatory access to citizens and provide free production facilities. Unlike the cash-strapped systems in North America, the Federal Republic's "open channels" receive a portion of the subscription fees that Germans pay for television services. These funds support studios, technicians, and equipment for public access productions. Open channel services have also been established on local cable systems in *Sweden* and the *Netherlands*, and, to a lesser extent, in other European countries.

Although public access television is often associated with local communities, there have also been attempts to reach national audiences. In *South Korea*, the Broadcast Law of 2000 requires KBS 1, a national broadcast network, to set aside a small portion of its schedule for programs produced by the public. In 2002, South Korea's RTV network inaugurated the world's first satellite television channel devoted to public access programming (→ South Korea: Media System). In 2006, *Australia*'s Satellite Community Television (SCTV) began beaming multiethnic, multilanguage public access programs nationwide. Previously, SCTV had been limited to local broadcasts on an over-the-air channel in Sydney.

In the first decade of the twenty-first century, the future of public access television is uncertain. With over 1,000 local cable channels devoted to public access, the United States had the most extensive system in the world in 2006. However, US cable channels remain chronically underfunded and face regulatory challenges. In 1979, in the case of *FCC vs. Midwest Video*, the US Supreme Court ruled that the Federal Communications Commission could no longer require cable companies to include public access channels in local cable systems. Since that decision, local governments have had to choose whether to negotiate for public access channels and production facilities in their franchise agreements with private cable companies. The now entrenched cable industry continues to lobby the US Congress to eliminate local governments' authority to negotiate such concessions. Public access television faces similar regulatory and economic threats in many nations, and also faces the challenge of adapting to new media such as satellite television and the world wide web (→ Satellite Television; Internet). Nonetheless, the notion of unfiltered citizen access to television is likely to remain attractive to critics of professional media.

SEE ALSO: ▶ Access to the Media ▶ Activist Media ▶ Cable Television ▶ Citizen Journalism ▶ Citizens' Media ▶ Commercialization of the Media ▶ Community Media ▶ Community Video ▶ Internet ▶ South Korea: Media System ▶ Plurality ▶ Satellite Television ▶ Television ▶ Video

References and Suggested Readings

Carpentier, N., Lie, R., & Servaes, J. (2003). Community media: Muting the democratic media discourse? *Continuum: Journal of Media and Cultural Studies*, 1, 51–68.

Engelman, R. (1990). The origins of public access cable television, 1966–1972. *Journalism Monographs*, October, 1–47.

Engelman, R. (1996). *Public radio and television in America: A political history*. Thousand Oaks, CA: Sage.

Kwak, K. (2003). Civil society as the fifth estate: Civil society, media reform, and democracy in Korea. In P. Kitley (ed.), *Television, regulation, and civil society in Asia*. New York: Routledge, pp. 226–245.

Linder, L. R. (1999). *Public access television: America's electronic soapbox*. Westport, CT: Praeger.

Streeter, T. (1987). The cable fable revisited: Discourse, policy and the making of cable television. *Critical Studies in Mass Communication*, 2, 174–200.

Public Affairs

Robert L. Heath

University of Houston

Public affairs is both a generic term for the trends and conditions that define and result from socio-economic–socio-political trends, and the corporate management function that works to position each organization comfortably and cooperatively in its non-marketplace context. Focusing on the latter meaning, Madden (2005, 665) defined public affairs as "the management function responsible for interpreting an organization's external environment, or in the case of a corporation, its noncommercial environment, and managing an effective and appropriate response to that environment." Its primary connection with society centers on governmental relations, the factors in the public policy (non-marketplace) arena that can lead government to influence (support or oppose) management decisions and organizational operations and policies (→ Organizational Communication; Corporate Communication; Corporate Reputation; Organizational Image).

ORGANIZATIONAL ROLE OF PUBLIC AFFAIRS

Its corporate role, and hence its definition, depends on whose eye is seeing the beauty. Some define it as a management function that subsumes public relations and other communication functions. Especially in companies with a primary emphasis on product marketing, the public relations function is likely to be dominant. For some observers, it is often confused with or used interchangeably with → public relations. Those who see public relations as the dominant discipline feature public affairs as a sub-function devoted to government relations in the broad sense and → lobbying more narrowly. In many large organizations, especially national and international or multinational corporations, public affairs is the dominant discipline. In such organizations, public relations is a marketing, product promotion, publicity, and image-management function that reports to public affairs. In non-profits that feature public affairs, it is the planning function, whereas public relations often is designed to implement the public affairs plans. To further obscure the differences or similarities, some organizations name these kinds of functions corporate communications, external affairs, and even community affairs.

Public affairs, as a department and function, is not limited to businesses. Many non-profit organizations, especially if they are large and approach the discipline as an integration of many specialties, feature their public affair department, which often also has a public relations function. However defined and positioned, proponents of these disciplines – public relations and public affairs – prefer that they are integrated and interconnected (→ Integrated Marketing Communications). Organizations that feature public relations as the dominant discipline tend to see it as implementing marketing and advertising promotion. In such organizations, public affairs is merely government relations, if it is a part of the organization chart at all. When public affairs is the dominant discipline, marketing may reside beneath public affairs and be part of or even report to public relations. So the definition is like a kaleidoscope. As it turns, it gives different perspectives on the subject at hand, namely the nature of public affairs as an organizational discipline.

DIMENSIONS IN PUBLIC AFFAIRS RESEARCH

Dennis's (1996) book is one of the few devoted to public affairs. It was published by the Public Relations Society of America and openly vowed to not attempt to fully reconcile the specific definitions of public relations and public affairs. This work featured public relations as a broader function: "Public relations helps an organization develop and maintain quality relationships with the various groups of people ('publics') who can influence its future ... Public affairs is the public relations practice that addresses public policy and the publics who influence such policy" (1996, xviii).

Viewed this way, public affairs is the discipline that centers its attention, management counseling, and communication efforts on the dynamic factors and conditions specific to the ways in which organizations can affect public policy and the manner in which public policy can affect organizations. Public affairs, from its seminal days, has been more than publicity and promotion. It has developed to bring large organizations into the *societal dialogue* that shapes the socio-economic, socio-political arena. Public affairs became a vital topic under that rubric in the 1950s in the United States. From the start, the term "public affairs" seemed more comfortable to executives and politicians because "public relations" carried a lot of semantic baggage, which today is reflected in the editorial comment "just public relations," or the pejorative appellation "spin." As public relations seemed to lack substance and respectability, something was needed to define how this important function could be made credible and functional in the public policy arena. Continuing this tradition today, many companies and other large organizations see public affairs as being central to their efforts to manage risks, whereas public relations is more likely to be associated with revenue generation through sales or fundraising. Although experts disagree on the best methodology and independent variables (Hillman 2002; Schuler 2002), the central academic and corporate assumption is that effective public affairs performance helps overall management and organizational performance.

EMERGENCE OF PUBLIC AFFAIRS

President Dwight D. Eisenhower played a major role in the inception of public affairs when he brought a group of leading business executives together to give a bipartisan forum for Democrats and Republicans. Following World War II, many forces seemed imminently about to define and shape business interests. Eisenhower was keenly aware of the potential of international socio-economic collisions that would define the political and commercial arrangements and approach in the United States. In a spirit of citizen participation, he fostered the naming of the group as the Effective Citizens Organization. This group eventually changed its name to the Public Affairs Council (PAC) in 1965.

Many felt that public affairs was the new face of public relations practice. The 1960s and 1970s were a period of ferment, activism, reflection, combat, and self-examination in all of the institutions in the United States. Corporations and other large organizations were increasingly convinced that to ignore the public policy arena would leave them out of many decisions and allow others to define them and write their organizational missions. Whereas public relations had developed a reputation among many as featuring promotion, publicity, and image management, the tumult of the time called for a more basic and encompassing approach to positioning organizations and policies. The goal increasingly came to be to adjust organizations to the public policy arena and to adjust public policy to the needs and interests of large organizations. These organizations had increasingly become the voices that needed to be heard and needed to listen to one another, as the United States and other countries forged a postwar understanding of economics, finance, regulation, legislation, and standards of corporate citizenry.

PUBLIC AFFAIRS IN PRACTICE

Public affairs departments perform many functions. One of the most crucial is serving in the *management council* of each organization. Using monitoring and issue analysis, public affairs specialists bring ethical and public policy issues to management-level decision-making. Specialists continually assess how comfortably the organization's policies fit with those of other key organizations working to shape public affairs. As a communication function, public affairs fosters public relations, corporate communications, media relations, employee relations, and strategic philanthropy, and may participate in investor relations. Additional points of strategic response include lobbying, grassroots organization, campaign finance, management consulting, and benchmarking. In addition, public affairs specialists often play a vital role in meeting the management challenge to know and achieve the level of performance that fosters rather than diminishes the organization's social capital (→ Strategic Communication).

From the inception of modern issues management in the 1970s, public affairs has adopted that approach to its public policy challenges. It defines issues management as "the process of prioritizing and proactively addressing public policy and reputation issues that can affect an organization's success. Many large companies, in particular, use issues management techniques to keep all of their external relations activities focused on high-priority challenges and opportunities" (Public Affairs Council 2006). Public affairs and → *issue management*, perhaps the offspring of public affairs, are viewed as being necessary for companies because of the keen abilities of their adversaries to shape public opinion and therefore drive public policy. It is not coincidental that public affairs and issues management started and became mature during a period of socio-political ferment.

The *Public Affairs Council*, located in Washington, DC, has been a driving force in supporting and promoting a public affairs approach to relationship building and non-commercial positioning of organizations and their stakeholder publics (→ Stakeholder

Theory). One of the stellar accomplishments of the public affairs movement, the Council performs research to understand and refine the discipline, produces cutting-edge publications, and conducts workshops for executives and public affairs specialists. It believes that the discipline stays vital and refines its practice through continuing education. Its membership consists of major companies, associations, and consulting groups. It was one of the first organizations to innovate in, define, and give substance to issues management. "Born of a marriage between lobbying and communications and schooled in the techniques of community organizing, public affairs has grown up to be a credible participant in the formation of public policy" (Duke & Hart 1996, 14).

The public affairs movement has focused considerable attention on the *challenges facing large organizations* operating in an environment made ever more complex to management because of the tangles and challenges of public policy advocacy. If we accept that public relations failed to satisfactorily meet this challenge starting in the 1950s in the United States, then its mantle shifted to the shoulders of public affairs. Public relations seemed to lack the character and respectability to weigh in on the matters of regulatory and legislative shifts and twists. One of the failings was its historic connection with fabrication, spin, and smoke and mirrors. Some believe it came to rely on cleverly worded press releases to the extent that it lacked proactive participation in public dialogue. If an organization, industry, or other sector of society waits for other forces to shape public opinion, that body may have the conditions of its operation made more difficult. Public relations needed to act less reactively and more proactively.

Public affairs departments, and the discipline as such, developed to engage organizations earlier in the dialogues that lead to public policy formation. Some saw the advantage of working early when opinions are not well formed. Such a view can lead critics to surmise that public affairs can and will seek to undercut legitimate change in the public policy arena not by debating issues but by manipulating how those issues are debated.

In an era when public relations/public affairs scholars are again addressing responsible advocacy, one can imagine that the challenge to public affairs as a professional practice and academic discipline will be to refine its theory, ethics, practice, and management impact so that the larger interests of all legitimate voices are heard and respected. It seems that the challenge is not to know how to make an organization effective, but to learn the ways for the organization to work with other interested parties in a reflective manner to make society better, more fully functioning. Thus, public affairs as a discipline and employer of best practices is challenged to understand, appreciate, and proactively participate in the creation of effective public affairs, the socio-economic, socio-political dynamics that affect the organization's ability to function in the interest of its various stakeholders.

SEE ALSO: ▶ Corporate Communication   ▶ Corporate Reputation   ▶ Integrated Marketing Communications   ▶ Issue Management   ▶ Lobbying   ▶ Organizational Communication   ▶ Organizational Image   ▶ Public Relations   ▶ Stakeholder Theory   ▶ Strategic Communication

References and Suggested Readings

Dennis, L. B. (ed.) (1996). *Practical public affairs in an era of change.* Lanham, MD: Public Relations Society of America and University Press of America.

Duke, W. E., & Hart, M. A. (1996). Public affairs: From understudy to center stage. In L. B. Dennis (ed.), *Practical public affairs in an era of change*. Lanham, MD: Public Relations Society of America and University Press of America, pp. 3–15.

Foundation for Public Affairs (2002). *The state of corporate public affairs*. Washington, DC: Foundation for Public Affairs.

Hillman, A. J. (2002). Public affairs, issue management and political strategy: Methodological issues that count – a different view. *Journal of Public Affairs*, 1/2, 356–361.

Madden, W. (2005). Public affairs. In Robert L. Heath (ed.), *Encyclopedia of public relations*. Thousand Oaks, CA: Sage, pp. 665–666.

Pederson, W. (2005). Public Affairs Council. In Robert L. Heath (ed.), *Encyclopedia of public relations*. Thousand Oaks, CA: Sage, pp. 666–669.

Public Affairs Council (1998). *Effective public affairs organizational structures*. Washington, DC: Public Affairs Council.

Public Affairs Council (2006). Issues management. At www.pac.org, accessed August 9, 2006.

Schuler, D. A. (2002). Public affairs, issues management and political strategy: Methodological approaches that count. *Journal of Public Affairs*, 1/2, 336–355.

Public Broadcasting, History of

Jamie Medhurst

Aberystwyth University

Public broadcasting is notoriously difficult to define, and yet it has been at the center of debates in → media policy for decades in those countries where it exists. Proponents of public broadcasting argue that at its heart is the notion of providing the "best" in programming for all, while detractors would argue that it is a form of state control over what we can listen to or watch (→ Public Service Broadcasting: Law and Policy).

Public broadcasting can also be defined in economic terms (funding from the state or public taxation), cultural terms (maintaining and supporting a minority culture), social terms (broadcasting for the "social good"; → Public Goods), → audience terms (the listener/viewer as citizen) and, finally, as "that which is not commercial broadcasting." In relation to the final statement, Tracey (1998) has suggested a simple epigram for defining public broadcasting as opposed to broadcasting funded by commercial means: the former gets money to make programs while the latter makes programs to get money. However simplistic, this is what public broadcasting is about in essence (→ Media Economics; Cost and Revenue Structures in the Media).

A history of public broadcasting can usefully be divided into three periods: the early history from the 1920s until World War II, the immediate postwar period, and the 1960s onwards.

EARLY HISTORY

Scannell (2000) has argued that a historical understanding of public broadcasting needs to take into account two factors: public broadcasting as defined by the state and public broadcasting as interpreted by the broadcaster. In the *UK* for instance, the government decided upon a broadcasting service that would operate via a license granted by the Post Office. As the service had to share the airwaves with the military and emergency services, a shortage of frequencies meant that the scarce resources had to be utilized in the national interest. A similar rationale was behind the broadcasting services in Belgium and Denmark, for example. Broadcasting was viewed as a public utility, and the mandate to develop it as a national service in the public interest came from the state (→ United Kingdom: Media System).

This was in contrast to the model in the *United States*. Although the broadcaster David Sarnoff had referred to broadcasting as a public service in a speech in 1922, drawing attention to its potential to inform, educate, and entertain the nation, broadcasting development took the commercial as opposed to the state-controlled, public service path (→ United States of America: Media System). Although it would be unfair to argue that the broadcast media in the US developed in a completely chaotic and unregulated manner, there were fewer restrictions than in the UK (Hilmes & Jacobs 2003).

Monopoly Days

Once established, the British Broadcasting Company (which became a Corporation in 1927), or → BBC, was soon fashioned under the watchful eye of its first managing director, then director-general, Sir John Reith. Reith interpreted public broadcasting by developing a set of principles which were to dominate British broadcasting for decades. This Reithian approach to public broadcasting in the early days of radio broadcasting was based on four tenets. First, the need to protect broadcasting from commercial pressures was safeguarded by creating an assured source of funding (a license fee for all those who owned wireless sets). Second, the service was to be provided for the whole nation regardless of the geographical location of the listener. This policy of a universal service was achieved, third, by the establishment of a national program (broadcast from London) and, fourth, by a regional program from selected cities across the UK (including Cardiff and Birmingham).

Broadcasting had a duty to bring the "best" of British culture to every household in the UK, and this reflected the director-general's almost missionary zeal for the task in hand. It also allied Reith with the Victorian essayist, Matthew Arnold, who argued that culture was the "best" that had been thought and written in the world. Therefore, the early years of broadcasting in the UK were forged by a combination of a notion of public service and an Arnoldian vision of culture (→ Culture: Definitions and Concepts).

Meanwhile, the period of the Weimar Republic (1918–33) in *Germany* witnessed an emergent public broadcasting system, one which was state-governed and -controlled. The *Reichpost*, the state regulatory authority covering postal services, telegraphy, and the telephone service, allocated broadcasting licenses and controlled transmission facilities, and the state's hold over broadcasting was further tightened by the establishment of the Imperial Broadcasting Company in 1925. As Humphreys (1996) has argued, "the state's grip on the medium had become almost absolute by the time Hitler came to power." By the early 1930s, the service had incorporated clear elements of public broadcasting and broadcast a range of music, drama, documentary (→ Documentary Film), talk (→ Broadcast Talk), → news, and current affairs programs. When Hitler came to power in 1933, the radio service was instantly commandeered by the Nazis and exploited as a → propaganda tool under the watchful eye of the chief propagandist, Joseph Goebbels. By the mid-1930s the Nazis had turned their attention to the new medium of television, and they soon established the world's first high-definition television service. The service was distributed to public spaces as opposed to domestic receivers, however, and so the BBC receives credit for the creation of the first public television service for the home (→ Television; Television Technology; Television: Social History).

THE POSTWAR PERIOD

The world's first regular domestic television service began on November 2, 1936, when the BBC broadcast from Alexandra Palace in north London. However, the outbreak of World War II brought the service to an abrupt halt in September 1939. By the time the service resumed on June 7, 1946, it was clear that television in the UK was to be developed along the same public service principles that governed radio (→ Television Broadcasting, Regulation of; Radio Broadcasting, Regulation of). Although John Reith had left the BBC in 1938, his legacy remained and was to dominate broadcasting policy for at least another 20 years. The high moral enterprise, achieved by a policy of mixed programming on radio and television and a refusal not to pander to audience tastes alone, nevertheless alienated sections of the audience who felt that the tone and content did not reflect their interests or needs. Indeed, one member of the UK government-appointed 1949 committee of enquiry into broadcasting (the Beveridge Committee) referred to the policy as "compulsory uplift."

Reith's concept of public broadcasting nevertheless influenced the development of radio and television services in many European countries after the end of World War II and formed a key part of the → political economy of the media in these countries. For many, the adoption of this model allowed for a degree of state control and nation-building following a period of upheaval and turmoil. With nations eager to redevelop, rebuild or rediscover a sense of national consciousness in a new Europe, a model of broadcasting which catered for a national service in the national interest was seen as the way forward. Programming in which nations could reflect their own identity within and without the outside world, free from commercial pressures, would flourish under the public broadcasting model.

As television services emerged in postwar Europe, some variation in the "degree" of public service appeared. In France, for example, the state had a closer hold on broadcasters than in Spain, where the television service (which began in 1956) was funded by → advertising but controlled by the state (→ France: Media System; Spain: Media System). The main aim of the Allies' postwar broadcasting policy in Germany was to ensure that party political influence on broadcasting as a social good remained minimal. To this end, the BBC's Hugh Carleton Greene (later to become the corporation's director-general in 1960) was deployed to run the BBC-inspired *Nordwestdeutscher Rundfunk* in the British zone of occupied Germany. As a result, the overwhelming influence on German broadcasting up until the 1980s was a public broadcasting ethos. Further afield, Japan's NHK television service, introduced in 1953, drew closely on the BBC's public service model and was funded by a license fee. The Japanese public broadcasting model, whilst carrying a comprehensive diet of news and current affairs, placed its prime emphasis on entertainment (→ Japan: Media System).

Chinese broadcasting history is one of unprecedented growth and expansion after a small, relatively inauspicious start. The Communist Party which came to power in 1949 established broadcasting as a state propaganda tool. Television was introduced in 1958 in Beijing alone and spread across the country at a very slow pace. The rapid expansion took place after 1976, and by today Chinese viewers have access to a wide range of channels, some of them still closely monitored by the state (→ China: Media System). These examples highlight how political and cultural contexts impact upon the development of public broadcasting in different countries.

COMMERCIAL COMPETITION

Despite the dominance of the public broadcasting model in Europe, the postwar years saw a gradual shift towards commercialism (→ Commercialization of the Media). In the UK, the debate over a rival television service to compete with the BBC began in the years immediately after the war. The debate was fuelled by the publication of the Beveridge Report on broadcasting which, although supporting the maintenance of the BBC's monopoly over broadcasting, accused the corporation of a London-centric bias at the expense of the nations and regions of the UK. A minority report by one of the committee's members, the Conservative MP Selwyn Lloyd, went so far as to advocate the establishment of a commercially funded television service. It was this impetus, together with the activity of backbench Conservative MPs and external pressure groups, that led to the passing of the 1954 Television Act, which introduced a television service funded by advertising revenue to the UK for the first time (→ Advertising, Economics of). The 1960s and 1970s saw the continued abandonment of the Reithian model of public broadcasting across Europe. In the US, however, there was a concerted attempt to "ringfence" public broadcasting by the establishment of the *Public Broadcasting Service* (PBS) in 1969. This network of nonprofit-making stations was launched in October 1970 and drew (and continues to draw) its programming from a variety of sources offering programming in news and current affairs, children's programming, entertainment, science, and the arts. After initial success, however, the service soon declined in the face of stiff commercial competition. The 1960s saw an increasingly liberal approach to broadcasting (particularly in terms of content) and in the UK the matter came to a head in 1977 with the publication of the *Annan Report* on broadcasting. For the first time, the appropriateness of a paternalistic mode of public broadcasting in a pluralistic society was questioned, and the concerns voiced in the report reflected the changing nature of British society during the 1960s and 1970s.

A further shift took place during the 1980s when citizens were being increasingly defined as consumers. The neo-liberalist stance of the *Peacock Report* in the United Kingdom, published in 1986, referred to the now-famous notion of "consumer sovereignty," a sign for many that the death knell for public broadcasting had been rung. Across Europe, technological advances and changes in regulatory legislation made it easier to establish networks. Throughout the 1990s, increasing de-regularization, globalization, and the international marketplace placed public broadcasting systems under threat (→ Competition in Media Systems; Globalization of the Media). The notion of the "national" territory or boundary with which much of the public broadcasting ideal was bound up was eroding. At a global level, the market was considered to be the most appropriate mechanism for satisfying audience demand for broadcasting services, and the basic tenets of public broadcasting were gradually eroded.

The future of public broadcasting is uncertain. In the UK, for example, the communications regulatory body, Ofcom (Office of Communications), undertook a wholesale review of public service broadcasting during 2004–2005. The aim of the review was "to set out a new framework for public service broadcasting . . . designed for the future and sufficiently adaptable to respond to and reflect changing technologies, markets, and the needs of citizens and consumers" (Ofcom 2005). An indication of how the notion of public broadcasting has changed since the mid-1920s can be seen clearly in the inclusion of two terms that would be anathema to John Reith – "markets" and "consumers" (→ Audience Commodity). The impulse to inform, educate, and entertain remains, but it also remains to be seen whether or not the market can deliver or whether there will still be a role for the public broadcasting ideal.

SEE ALSO: ▶ Advertising ▶ Advertising, Economics of ▶ Audience ▶ Audience Commodity ▶ BBC ▶ Broadcast Talk ▶ China: Media System ▶ Commercialization of the Media ▶ Competition in Media Systems ▶ Cost and Revenue Structures in the Media ▶ Culture: Definitions and Concepts ▶ Documentary Film ▶ France: Media System ▶ Globalization of the Media ▶ Japan: Media System ▶ Media Economics ▶ Media Policy ▶ News ▶ Political Economy of the Media ▶ Privatization of the Media ▶ Propaganda ▶ Public Broadcasting Systems ▶ Public Goods ▶ Public Service Broadcasting: Law and Policy ▶ Radio Broadcasting, Regulation of ▶ Radio: Social History ▶ Spain: Media System ▶ Television ▶ Television Broadcasting, Regulation of ▶ Television: Social History ▶ Television Technology ▶ United Kingdom: Media System ▶ United States of America: Media System

References and Suggested Readings

Barnouw, E. (1966–70). *A history of broadcasting in the United States*. New York: Oxford University Press.
Briggs, A. (1961–95). *The history of British broadcasting in the United Kingdom*, vols. 1–5. Oxford: Oxford University Press.
Hilmes, M. (2001). *Only connect: a cultural history of broadcasting in the United States*. Belmont, CA: Wadsworth/Thomson Learning.
Hilmes, M., & Jacobs, J. (eds.) (2003). *The television history book*. London: British Film Institute.
Humphreys, P. (1996). *Mass media and media policy in western Europe*. Manchester: Manchester University Press.
McDonnell, J. (1991). *Public service broadcasting: A reader*. London: Routledge.
Ofcom (2005). Ofcom review of public service television broadcasting. Phase 3: Competition for quality. At www.ofcom.org.uk/consult/condocs/psb3, accessed October 29, 2007.
Scannell, P. (2000). Public service broadcasting: The history of a concept. In E. Buscombe (ed.), *British television: A reader*. Oxford: Oxford University Press, pp. 45–61.
Sendall, B. (1982). *Independent television in Britain*, vol. 1, *Origin and foundation, 1946–62*. London: Macmillan.
Sendall, B. (1983). *Independent television in Britain*, vol. 2, *Expansion and change, 1958–68*. London: Macmillan.
Smith, A. (ed.) (1995). *Television: An international history*. Oxford: Oxford University Press.
Tracey, M. (1998). *The decline and fall of public service broadcasting*. Oxford: Oxford University Press.
Williams, K. (1998). *Get me a murder a day: A history of mass communications in Britain*. London: Arnold.

Public Broadcasting Systems

Jo Bardoel

University of Amsterdam and Radboud University Nijmegen

Public service broadcasting (PSB), according to McQuail (2005, 179), refers to "a system that is set up by law and generally financed by public funds (often a compulsory license fee paid by households) and given a large degree of editorial and operating independence." Public service broadcasting is supposed to function independently of both the market and the state, and therefore differs from the alternative systems of commercial broadcasting on the one hand and authoritarian or state-operated broadcasting on the other (→ Communication and Law; Media Policy; Radio Broadcasting, Regulation of; Television Broadcasting, Regulation of).

Until the 1980s public service broadcasting was dominant, or even held a monopoly, in most countries of the western world. During that decade public broadcasters lost their dominant position because of liberalizing policies following the advent of new distribution technologies and the eroding legitimacy of the argument of spectrum scarcity as well as growing political and public criticism of the privileged position of PSBs (→ Satellite Television; Cable Television). In the 1990s commercial stations became the dominant actors in most broadcasting markets, and public service broadcasters had to adapt to a new, "dual" broadcasting context in which they are the exception rather than the rule. At the beginning of the third millennium new multimedia platforms represent yet another challenge for public broadcasters.

ORIGINS AND PHILOSOPHICAL TRACES

There is no clear definition or coherent theory of public broadcasting. When → radio was invented at the beginning of the twentieth century and → television by the middle of the same century, national governments had to regulate → access to the media – unlike the situation with the press – because of the scarcity of frequencies and a widespread concern about the impact of these new, electronic media on people and society (→ Media Effects). In this context public, noncommercial corporations were set up that presented a comprehensive program, consisting of information, education, culture, and entertainment that would raise the level of political awareness and cultural taste of citizens, not consumers. The first director general of the British Broadcasting Corporation (→ BBC), John Reith, had already put these ideals on paper in the 1920s, and his BBC became a trusted source amidst the → propaganda of authoritarian regimes in those days and indeed a model for the world (→ United Kingdom: Media System).

The philosophical traces of the concept of PSB lie in humanistic Enlightenment ideals and in normative notions on the social responsibility and public interest of media in modern societies (→ Freedom of the Press, Concept of; Journalism: Normative Theories). These notions stem from policy advisory commissions like the Hutchins commission in the US (1947), the British Royal Commission on the Press (1949 and 1977) and successive committees on broadcasting in the UK (Scannell 1980). As such this is a negotiated concept that results from a process of political struggle, social debate, and academic reflection and differs from country to country and from period to period, reflecting national media policies and research traditions.

In a situation of channel scarcity for broadcasting, where government interference was considered inevitable, explicit legitimization for a public broadcasting policy was not really necessary. But from the 1970s, interfering in public broadcasting and giving the organizations a financial prerogative and a specific role "in the → public interest" began to require legitimizing. The public monopoly, originally of a more ritualistic nature, was not seriously contested but an open government had to legitimize its prescriptive regulations. With the introduction of commercial television and, in the European context, the changed policy environment following the EC directive "Television without Frontiers," interference and preferential treatment required a more deliberate strategic policy and legitimacy (→ European Union: Communication Law).

GOALS AND DISTRIBUTION

In spite of all the differences mentioned, the goals of public broadcasting across cultures show a striking resemblance (see Broadcasting Research Unit 1985; Council of Europe 1994; McQuail 2005): (1) universality of geographic coverage and audience reach, and a common reference point and forum for all members of the → public; (2) pluralistic, innovative, and varied programming, independent of both government and market forces; (3) concern for national culture, language, and identity as well as a reflection of ideas and beliefs in a multiethnic and multicultural society; (4) accountability toward society and the audience (→ Accountability of the Media).

At present public broadcasting systems exist all over the world, but are most frequently found in European countries and in countries that have historical or colonial ties with these European countries (→ Communication Law and Policy: Europe). The example and model of PSB worldwide is the BBC, but within Europe the BBC's position is in many respects the exception rather than the rule. In fact, the position and organization of PSBs, as national institutions, reflects the history of the respective nation-states.

The American public broadcasting system, PBS, has quite a different tradition and position (Avery 1993). The United States Radio Act of 1927 enabled the commercial, advertiser-funded broadcasting system for which the US is known. In 1945 the Federal Communications Commission created licenses for noncommercial educational radio stations with a public service ideal. Educational television officially began by 1952, but it was only with the Public Broadcasting Act of 1967, following the report of the Carnegie Commission on Educational Television, that more (although limited) funding for both educational radio and television became available. Since then public radio and television gained a fixed but, compared to public broadcasters in Europe and elsewhere in the world, rather marginal position in the media landscape (→ United States of America: Media System).

PUBLIC BROADCASTING IN QUESTION

The reflection on the concept of public broadcasting has considerably increased since its existence is not self-evident any more, due to the advent of new media technologies and a liberalization of media policies all over the world. The new context of PSB has raised continual criticism on almost every aspect of its operations: its mission and its realization, its programming, organization, control, its funding and expenditure.

The question of the *mission* of public service broadcasters is greater than ever. It shows that an explicit legitimization in terms of PSB's role in society has become imperative, and serves as a battleground for different interests and insights. Traditionally, the political function of PSB in relation to democracy, pluralism, and public debate was emphasized, but more recently socio-cultural goals, such as serving social integration and cohesion, have become more prominent (Bardoel & Brants 2003). At a more practical, nonrhetorical level the independence of public broadcasting, from both the state and the market, is constantly at stake. For public broadcasters the relation to politics is most crucial, and Hallin & Mancini's seminal book *Comparing media systems* (2004) demonstrates that the relation between politics and the media and media freedom across western countries varies greatly according to their political history and culture and the room it leaves for a vivid → public sphere, including public broadcasting. In this respect, the countries of North America and western Europe are ahead of the European countries of the south and the east that have a relatively young democratic tradition.

Public broadcasters also have to redefine their relation to the public. Although the public should be the primary frame of reference, many PSBs have kept the people and civil society at a distance, while politics and the government proved to be the preferred partner. This is also a result of a tradition of paternalism, which is more or less inherent in the peda-gogical imperative practised by public broadcasters in the past. Although public broadcasters have a problem of redefining their mission in the context of the new "dual" broadcasting market and a changing, multicultural society, many believe that basic functions such as a low-cost and universally available reliable provision of information, education, and culture and the catering for minority tastes and interests cannot or will not be sufficiently served by the commercial market ("market failure").

Closely related to the mission is the *program* assignment of public broadcasting. The recent debate on this issue can be summarized by the catchwords "comprehensive or complementary": should PSB still present a full-scale program offering or should it just supplement programs that its commercial counterpart does not offer? Despite accusations of copycat strategies and a convergence between public and commercial broadcasters, research shows that most public broadcasters have chosen, principally or pragmatically, the middle way of compensation. Although there is much debate on the mission of public service broadcasting, almost no country has made the choice to really narrow the program task of PSB (→ Public Service Broadcasting: Law and Policy). In response to this critical debate, most public broadcasters look for arguments in favor of the full-scale model and try to stress their distinctiveness more than ever. The alternative option of de-institutionalizing PSB by introducing public program funds comparable with policies vis-à-vis culture and the arts ("distributed public service") has been proposed in countries that reconsidered their public broadcasting system, but no country has dared to take that far-reaching step, with the notable exception of New Zealand, where a drastic reorganization of PSB took place in 1988. Open competition via an "arts council of the air" model was meant to lead to greater value for money and add to the quality of PSB programming, but in practice it did not work out that way.

Looking further into the *organizational* aspects, the rapid rise of commercial television from the 1980s, leading to the majority of stations being private by the middle of the 1990s, has also changed the structure and culture of public broadcasting institutions considerably (→ Convergence of Media Systems). Already in the 1980s quasi-commercial elements were introduced within public service broadcasting, such as the popularization of programming in peak time in order to maximize → audiences and advertising revenues, the increasing cost-consciousness and efficiency in its activities and the adaptation of management practices from the commercial sector (→ Cost and Revenue Structures in the Media). Although there is still considerable support for the maintenance of strong PSB institutions in most countries, there is also a growing need for continual monitoring of its overall efficiency and effectiveness.

The main source of *finance* for most PSBs remains the license fee, but most countries have mixed systems. There are countries in which at least three-quarters of the budget of public television comes from license fees or public subsidies, as opposed to countries where → advertising is the major part of a channel's income. In addition, the overall financial position of public television channels differs considerably from country to country. The BBC budget is about seven times higher than the total budget of the 22 public broadcasting organizations that make up the public broadcasting service in the Netherlands. The comparative "poverty" or "wealth" of PSBs is of course closely related to the size of the population (or market) to be served. Although there is strong criticism of advertising as a partial but important source of income for public broadcasters, mixed funding has been defended as a proper tool to minimize unilateral dependence on politics and to strengthen the programming freedom of broadcasters. On the other hand, income from advertisements may motivate even PBSs to conform to tuning-in quota.

PUBLIC SERVICE BROADCASTING IN A NEW MEDIA CONTEXT

In 10 years' time TV households will devote much less of their viewing time to linear, generalist channels. Audiences will use more distribution platforms and channels alongside the currently available open broadcast channels. In order to maintain a reasonable level of audience reach public broadcasters may decide to extend their portfolio of platforms and channels. The first step will involve thematic channels, which will, to the extent that they prove successful, change the function of the present open channels to showrooms for program offerings on thematic channels and "on demand" platforms. Gradually these media and platforms will be linked as part of deliberate cross-media strategies that try to keep the viewer and the listener in their network for as long as possible. In general, brand building across media and platforms will become more important for public broadcasters. In the new media context the raison d'être of PSBs, more than ever, will lie in offering quality programming and setting the standard as well as serving as a trusted brand or as an "anchor" for citizens in the new flood of information.

SEE ALSO: ▶ Access to the Media ▶ Accountability of the Media ▶ Advertising ▶ Audience ▶ BBC ▶ Cable Television ▶ Communication and Law ▶ Communication Law and Policy: Europe ▶ Convergence of Media Systems ▶ Cost and Revenue Structures in the Media ▶ European Union: Communication Law ▶ Freedom of the Press, Concept of ▶ Journalism: Normative Theories ▶ Media Effects ▶ Media Policy ▶ Propaganda

▶ Public ▶ Public Broadcasting, History of ▶ Public Interest ▶ Public Service Broad-casting: Law and Policy ▶ Public Sphere ▶ Radio ▶ Radio Broadcasting, Regulation of ▶ Satellite Television ▶ Television ▶ Television Broadcasting, Regulation of ▶ United Kingdom: Media System ▶ United States of America: Media System

References and Suggested Readings

Avery, R. K. (ed.) (1993). *Public service broadcasting in a multichannel environment: The history and survival of an ideal*. White Plains, NY: Longman.

Bardoel, J., & Brants, K. (2003). From ritual to reality: Public broadcasters and social responsibility in the Netherlands. In G. F. Lowe and T. Hujanen (eds.), *Broadcasting and convergence: New articulations of the public service remit*. Gothenburg: Nordicom, pp. 167–187.

Broadcasting Research Unit (1985). *The public service idea in British broadcasting*. London: BRU.

Council of Europe (1994). The media in a democratic society. Political Declaration, Resolutions and Statement, 4th European Ministerial Conference on Mass Media Policy, Prague, December 7–8, MCM(94)20. At www.coe.int/T/E/Com/Files/Events/2002-09-Media/ConfMedia1994.asp, accessed September 21, 2007.

Hallin, D. C., & Mancini, P. (2004). *Comparing media systems: Three models of media and politics*. Cambridge and New York: Cambridge University Press.

McQuail, D. (2005). *McQuail's mass communication theory*. London: Sage.

Scannell, P. (1980). Public service: The history of a concept. In A. Goodwin & G. Whannel (eds.), *Understanding television*. London: Routledge, pp. 11–29.

Public Diplomacy

Beata Ociepka

University of Wroclaw

The notion of public diplomacy has been used in international relations and in international communication studies since about the mid-1960s. It originates from US foreign policy from the period of the Cold War. Public diplomacy is understood as a dialogical communication between governments and other actors on the stage of international relations via the mass communication media and non-mediated channels of contact with the foreign countries' mass audience. The aim of public diplomacy is to create or reinforce a positive → image of the country and its society, and by influencing → public opinion to shape positive attitudes toward the country, and in consequence to make the achievement of international policy goals easier.

At the beginning of the twenty-first century the notion was widely discussed, as a result of the campaigns undertaken by the USA and European countries after the September 11, 2001, attacks and the employment of public diplomacy tools by many governments in order to rebrand their country or reposition it in the new international environment. The new campaigns adjusted the images of countries in relation to political, economic, and cultural changes, acknowledging the impact the rise of global communications has had on international relations (→ Globalization Theories; Globalization of the Media).

Nowadays public diplomacy is still understood as a supplementary means of American international policy, and often taken for a new version of international → propaganda. In the past this approach was supported by the activities of the United States Information Agency (1953–1999), which was frequently cited as a model institution for public diplomacy. Nevertheless, public diplomacy understood as the long-term, symmetric, dialogical communication of governments and NGOs with broad foreign audiences differs from propaganda, but may still use the same means and apply these to the same audience as propaganda. According to Leonard et al. (2002), public diplomacy is played out in three spheres: political/military, economic (promoting products and businesses), and societal/cultural.

Public diplomacy differs from traditional forms of diplomacy in the means used, the channels the messages are sent through, and the target groups that should be reached. Traditional diplomacy was characterized by the flow of messages from government (diplomats) to government (g2g), whereas public diplomacy implies the direction governments (diplomats) to foreign public (g2p). Thus public diplomacy is understood in the countries where it has been conducted for a relatively short time as a means of supplementing traditional government-to-government diplomacy. The third form of public diplomacy nowadays is characterized by the people-to-people (p2p) flow of information. In the third case the messages are sent and received between members of the public in different countries without the mediation of governments.

THREE DIMENSIONS OF PUBLIC DIPLOMACY

According to Leonard et al. (2002), there are three dimensions of public diplomacy: news management, strategic communication, and relationship building. *News management* is seen as a short-term, reactive activity, having a long tradition in the classic form of diplomacy. It relies very much on cooperation with → foreign correspondents (→ Framing of the News; Spin Doctor).

Strategic communication covers cooperation with the mass media of communication in a longer-term and proactive way. The mass media are still seen as important tools of public diplomacy. Also, public relations agencies hired by governments have an enormous impact on strategic communication (→ Public Relations). In the media field nowadays, public diplomacy implements → advertising, as in the case of the US "Shared Values Initiative" campaign in 2003. This consisted of television spots targeted at the public in Muslim countries. The aim of the campaign was to improve the attitudes of Muslim societies toward the USA.

Relationship building, perceived as a long-term activity, relies on winning support in foreign countries by cultural and educational programs targeted at students, artists, academics, and journalists (people exchange). The practice of public diplomacy might here originate from traditional cultural diplomacy (social/cultural level). In this case, public diplomacy is understood as a "*soft power*" (Nye 2004) in international relations, focusing on the image and reputation of the country. The concept of public diplomacy as a soft power builds on the difference between public diplomacy and propaganda, and puts the stress on "attractive" power rooted in culture, typical of public diplomacy in contrast to propaganda.

Public diplomacy as a concept and a practice is rooted in international studies, the theory and practice of diplomacy, international and intercultural communication, and international public relations. The approach rooting public diplomacy in international studies and international communication is well illustrated by the writings of Gilboa and, recently, Melissen. According to Gilboa (2001), public diplomacy is one of the ways in which the mass media of communication are used as an instrument of foreign policy and international negotiations. The core of this activity lies in influencing a foreign government by influencing their citizens. This model applies to the g2p level of public diplomacy. Melissen (2005, xxi) argues that it would be a simplification to view public diplomacy as only another instrument of foreign policy. He analyzes the notion in a framework of propaganda, national branding, and cultural relations, and understands it as "part of the fabric of world politics."

The last dimension of public diplomacy according to Leonard et al., i.e., relationship building, is often equated with governmental public relations.

PUBLIC DIPLOMACY AND INTERNATIONAL PUBLIC RELATIONS

In some interpretations, public diplomacy is a part of public relations, or both notions are used interchangeably (Hiebert 2003). In the latter case public diplomacy is understood as *international public relations*. According to Signitzer and Coombs, public diplomacy and international public relations are in "a natural process of convergence" (1992, 137). Depending on the approach and the country, the theory and practice of public diplomacy might stem from public relations, meaning promotion of products and businesses (economic level of public diplomacy), and concentrate on → branding, or relate to cultural and educational exchange (social/cultural level).

Practitioners of place *branding* use the term "public diplomacy" only with reluctance, or perceive it as a core element of national branding (Anholt & Hildreth 2004). They reject the parallel use of both terms as they claim that public diplomacy is more limited to the proliferation of governmental policy. According to this approach, public diplomacy is included as a tool, part of a broader campaign of building the country's brand, understood as "the most important channel of transmitting national identities to consumers" (Leonard et al. 2002). Public relations specialists argue that branding aims at upgrading the country-of-origin effect, whereas public diplomacy concentrates mainly on the political/military level. Building a positive image of the country is much easier if its products are widely perceived as being of high quality. On the one hand, the country-of-origin effect may help to build a positive image; on the other hand, it might also become the main obstacle to rebranding the country if the place of origin is perceived in a negative way. Still, public diplomacy should be seen as wider than branding in defining its goals. Whereas branding builds on the differences between countries, and seeks for products that would be typical only of the one country, public diplomacy might also stress the similarities if it is required to support any act of international policy. Also, the target group definition in public diplomacy is wider than "consumers" only.

Images of countries are also influenced by the *image of their leaders*. In heads-of-states public diplomacy, leaders or other famous personalities are perceived as a country's products and contribute to the image of the country. The same must be said about diasporas, members of the public living abroad, and domestic institutions such as parliaments and political parties. The performance of the institutions, and contacts with elites and the general public abroad, have a significant impact on the perception of the country.

STRATEGY

Public diplomacy is implemented by governments, especially by ministries of foreign affairs but, in accordance with the logic of contemporary international politics, also by NGOs. The *main actors* of public diplomacy nowadays are still governments, coordinating the campaigns. One of the key problems of public diplomacy with the government as the main actor is how to manage perceptions of the country as a whole and coordinate such differentiated fields as politics, trade, tourism, investment, and cultural and educational relations. In the p2p type of public diplomacy, NGOs or informal groups play the main role. As public diplomacy includes promotion of products and businesses, companies might also be seen as important actors.

Because one of the main goals of public diplomacy campaigns is to foster positive attitudes among the audience abroad, the campaigns are usually *long-term activities*. Before launching the campaign a SWOT (strengths, weaknesses, opportunities, and threats) analysis is done, the country profile is analyzed, and target groups are defined. The most effective tactic, according to Leonard et al. (2002), is careful selection of foreign publics and target groups among them. Campaigns targeted at too large a community of different countries are not effective. The next step is the selection of means and tools, including the choice of channels through which to communicate the message. Key messages of the country are elaborated, often in combination with a selection of leading products and services that will be promoted. At this stage of preparation the coordination of campaigns is essential.

Many public diplomacy campaigns are run by public relations agencies in the target countries (Gilboa [2001, 6] calls such campaigns "the domestic public relations variant"). *In practice*, an agency in the target country is better accustomed to local specifics. Governments also hire well-known public relations firms to maintain favorable attitudes abroad, as was the case during Iraq's war against Kuwait in 1991, when the Kuwaiti government hired Hill and Knowlton. In the process of branding or rebranding the country, foreign specialists are employed also in order to throw fresh light on the country in question; this hiring of foreign specialists applies especially to the key messages elaboration stage. The last stage of public diplomacy campaigns is evaluation. Evaluating the effects of public diplomacy campaigns is rather difficult. First, they are long-term activities, especially if they aim at changing negative stereotypes. Second, changing attitudes are difficult to measure. The tools that are used after the campaigns are attitudes surveys, media content analyses (both quantitative and qualitative), and tracking the amount of contact with target groups. In Europe the most effective long-term campaigns are illustrated by two cases: those of Spain and Ireland to rebrand after joining the EU.

The campaigns might, according to Leonard et al. (2002), build on competition or cooperation. Competition occurs when one government sends messages to the same key audiences abroad as another government or governments, all aiming to win the audience over to achieve their goals, and the countries' policy goals are seen as contradictory. A cooperative public diplomacy suggests working together in fields and regions where competition might be abandoned, especially in those such as democracy promotion, human rights, and good governance.

Public diplomacy is still perceived as a bilateral action, but nowadays we are also confronted with a multilateral form of it.

SEE ALSO: ▶ Advertising   ▶ Branding   ▶ Foreign Correspondents   ▶ Framing of the News   ▶ Globalization of the Media   ▶ Globalization Theories   ▶ Image   ▶ Media Diplomacy   ▶ Propaganda   ▶ Public Opinion   ▶ Public Relations   ▶ Spin Doctor

References and Suggested Readings

Anholt, S., & Hildreth, J. (2004). *Brand America: The mother of all brands.* London: Cyan Communications.

Gilboa, E. (2001). Diplomacy in the media age: Three models of uses and effects. *Diplomacy and Statecraft*, 12(2), 1–28.

van Ham, P. (2001). The rise of brand state: The postmodern politics of image and reputation. *Foreign Affairs*, 80(5), 3–6.

Hiebert, R. E. (2003). Public relations and propaganda in framing the Iraq War: A preliminary review. *Public Relations Review*, 29(3), 243–255.

Leonard, M., Stead, C., & Smewing, C. (2002). *Public diplomacy.* London: Foreign Policy Centre.

Melissen, J. (ed.) (2005). *The new public diplomacy: Soft power in international relations.* London: Palgrave Macmillan.

Nye, J. (2004). *Soft power: The means to success in world politics.* New York: Public Affairs.

Ociepka, B., & Ryniejska-Kiełdanowicz, M. (2005). Public diplomacy and EU enlargement: The case of Poland. *Discussion Papers in Diplomacy*, 99, 1–19.

Signitzer, B. H., & Coombs, T. (1992). Public relations and public diplomacy: Conceptual convergence. *Public Relations Review*, 18(2), 137–147.

Public Goods

Peter A. Thompson

Unitec New Zealand

The idea of public goods has been subject to considerable debate and contestation. The term is generally used to classify products or services that are not diminished through usage and for which charges cannot be levied on individual consumption (e.g., street lighting). The concept of public goods is significant for media and communication scholars because it potentially applies to some forms of broadcasting and informational or audiovisual products and services. Such classifications also have implications for contemporary media policy debates concerning the regulation of communication technologies and the legitimate role of state intervention in market activities (→ Communication and Law; Media Policy).

THEORETICAL CONSIDERATIONS

In contemporary economic theory, the notion of public goods refers to products or services that exhibit the two key characteristics of *nonrivalry* and *nonexcludability* (Ver Eecke 1999; Shankar & Pavitt 2002). Nonrivalry means that the consumption of the goods by one person does not preclude consumption by another. When, say, a loaf of bread is eaten, it ceases to be available to anyone else. In contrast, the reception of a television program can be extended to extra viewers at no additional cost without diminishing its availability (i.e., Pareto efficiency; see Samuelson 1964; Minasian 1964). Nonexcludability, meanwhile, means that there is no technically practical or cost-effective way of preventing additional consumption without payment (free riding). For example, if a community organized a neighborhood patrol to deter crime, any increase in security would extend to all residents in the area irrespective of whether they personally contributed to the initiative. Likewise, an unencrypted broadcast or Internet website can potentially be used by an unlimited number of nonpaying users. If consumers of the product or service cannot be required to pay, the private sector is likely to underprovide them in a purely commercial market (Ver Eecke 1999).

Goods that are excludable and rivalrous are more likely to be provided by the private sector. However, market inefficiencies in pricing and information mechanisms mean that goods that are socially beneficial may also be undersupplied or underconsumed. Products and services that confer benefits external to individual private consumption are known as *merit goods* (Fiorito & Kollintzas 2002). For example, commercial broadcasters often prioritize populist genres that maximize ratings and revenue rather than educational programs that may enhance informed citizenship.

The underprovision of public/merit goods is an important consideration in explaining the role of the state or public sector in economic theory. Some scholars categorize particular products or services as intrinsic public/merit goods that require state provision or subsidy (e.g., national defense, public parks, or public service broadcasting). However, there is both theoretical and political disputation about *which* goods and services – if any – require state intervention and the extent to which this should complement or substitute for their provision by the private sector (Ver Eecke 1999; Fursich & Roushanzamir 2001). Although distinct, public, private, and merit goods are therefore better understood as *ideal types* that are not necessarily mutually exclusive in their application to empirical examples (Ver Eecke 1999). For example, a public broadcaster might include light entertainment in the schedule that a subscription broadcaster provides as a private good, while a commercial free-to-air broadcaster's schedule could include news and documentaries with merit-good value (see Anderson & Coate 2000; Samuelson 1964; Minasian 1964).

REGULATORY AND TECHNOLOGICAL ISSUES

The trend toward international free trade regimes has increased pressure on governments to restrict their provision of public/merit goods to cases of demonstrable market failure. In the EU, for instance, public broadcasting interventions must be clearly delineated and proportionally funded to avoid market distortion ($\rightarrow$ Public Service Broadcasting: Law and Policy; European Union: Communication Law). However, the assumption that efficient commercial markets are a natural state of affairs overlooks the point that economic activity is embedded in social, political, and legal institutional arrangements (e.g., enforcement of property laws). Whether or not a product or service can be categorized as public or private depends on these underlying structures. Consequently, reconfigurations of regulatory and technological arrangements alter the base conditions upon which the classification and legitimization of public goods are premised.

Informational or audiovisual goods are particularly contentious because different institutional arrangements potentially alter their nonrivalrous or nonexcludable character.

This is reflected in recent tensions between commercial and open-source software providers (→ Open Source) and controversies over Internet-based media file-sharing services such as Napster (see Becker & Clement 2006; also Stewart et al. 2004). The combination of market liberalization, digitalization, and media convergence is especially significant here: Digital media facilitate the potentially unlimited replication (nonrivalry) and distribution (nonexcludability) of informational or audiovisual goods (→ Digitization and Media Convergence). However, artificial scarcity (i.e., the elimination of non-excludability) can be imposed through conditional access or encryption technology and intellectual property regulations (→ Intellectual Property Law). The potential to transform public goods into private goods (→ Commodification of the Media) and vice versa explains why these concepts are subject to ideological, legal, and technical contestation.

SEE ALSO: ▶ Commodification of the Media ▶ Communication and Law ▶ Copyright ▶ Digitization and Media Convergence ▶ European Union: Communication Law ▶ Intellectual Property Law ▶ Media Policy ▶ Open Source ▶ Public Service Broadcasting: Law and Policy

References and Suggested Readings

Anderson, S., & Coate, S. (2000). *Market provision of public goods: The case of broadcasting*. NBER Working Paper No. 7513, January. Cambridge, MA: National Bureau of Economic Research.

Becker, J. U., & Clement, M. (2006). Dynamics of illegal participation in peer-to-peer networks: Why do people illegally share media files? *Journal of Media Economics*, 19(1), 7–32.

Fiorito, R., & Kollintzas, T. (2002). *Public goods, merit goods, and the relation between private and government consumption*. CEPR discussion paper No. 3617. Athens: Athens University of Economics and Business.

Fursich, E., & Roushanzamir, E. P. L. (2001). Corporate expansion, textual expansion: Commodification model of communication. *Journal of Communication Inquiry*, 25(4), 375–395.

Minasian, J. R. (1964). Television pricing and the theory of public goods. *Journal of Law and Economics*, 7, 71–80.

Samuelson, P. A. (1964). Public goods and subscription TV: Correction of the record. *Journal of Law and Economics*, 7, 81–83.

Shankar, A., & Pavitt, C. (2002). Resource and public goods dilemmas: A new issue for communication research. *Review of Communication*, 2(3), 251–272.

Stewart, C. M., Gil-Egui, G., & Pileggi, M. S. (2004). The city park as a public good reference for Internet policy making. *Information, Communication and Society*, 7(3), 337–363.

Ver Eecke, W. (1999). Public goods: An ideal concept. *Journal of Socio-Economics*, 28(2), 139–156.

Public Interest

Stylianos Papathanassopoulos

National and Kapodistrian University of Athens

As mass media play an increasing role in our societies by providing an arena of public debate and making politicians, policies, and relevant facts widely known, they are expected to follow certain rules of conduct. These rules and the normative media theories they draw upon typically imply presumptions as to the public interest the media should serve (McQuail 1992; 2005; → Journalism: Normative Theories). Presumptions about what is the public interest, directly or indirectly, determine the institutional set-up of media systems, legal regulations, and media policy measures as well as journalistic codes of ethic and performance standards (→ Communication and Law; Ethics in Journalism; Ethics of Media Content; Media Performance; Media Policy).

Not surprisingly, there is no agreed definition of the public interest, although its history goes back to classical times. The modern understanding of the concept can be traced back to the Enlightenment era when political philosophers who discussed the notion of interests in general, especially partisan interests and the aggregation of private interests, developed the idea of a public interest as a normative objective of political action. The various meanings of the concept we can find today may be subdivided into *substantive* and *procedural* interpretations. While the former are concerned with the content of political actions and their consequences, the latter focus on the quality of decision-making processes (Alexander 2002). For example, procedural interpretations of the public interest are implied in the concept of deliberative democracy and in → Habermas's idea of procedural rationality created in → political discourse (→ Deliberativeness in Political Communication). Instances of substantive interpretations are the three main views distinguished by McQuail (2005): utilitarianism, unitary, and common interest approaches.

Utilitarianism, or the majoritarian view, equates the public interest with aggregated individual values and preferences. The public interest is merely the sum of individuals' wealth, happiness, and avoidance of pain. Therefore, the state's role must be limited to maximizing individuals' benefit according to the overall popular vote. In the case of the media the public interest will be best achieved by free market forces and by giving the public what it says it wants (Veljanovski 1990). A common assumption is that audience ratings and public opinion polls indicate the preferences of the citizens (→ Audience Research; Nielsen Ratings; Readership Research; Public Opinion; Public Opinion Polling; Survey). On the other hand, this involves the risk of a "tyranny of the majority." Also, pleasing the majority in the media market may lead to a mainstreaming of media content and an erosion of quality standards (→ Commercialization: Impact on Media Content; Political Media Content, Quality Criteria in; Quality of the News).

By contrast, the *unitary* approach derives the public interest from a collective moral imperative that transcends particular or private interests. In other words, the public interest necessarily takes precedence over the interests of individuals, in order to pursue a vision of an ideal society (Berki 1979). The public interest is decided by reference to some single dominant value or ideology. However, this would work only in a paternalist (or even nondemocratic) system in which decisions about what is good are made by guardians or experts. As to political communication, the unitarian approach may lead to a "manufacture of consent" since the media will tend to confirm the political status quo (or the "official" ideology as defined by the ruling elite or party).

A third approach conceptualizes the public interest as *common interest* (Held 1970; McQuail 1992; 2003). In this view the public interest is not an aggregation of individual interests, but rather a shared interest. In other words, the public interest is equated with the interests all citizens have in common. Based on this idea modern states provide public services of transport, power, water, and even broadcasting. Basic features of national broadcasting systems and the services they provide (for example, frequency allocations, access to political parties, rules for advertising) are thus justified on grounds of a wider "common good," transcending individual choices and preferences ($\rightarrow$ Public Service Broadcasting: Law and Policy). The principle of media freedom may itself be supported on grounds of long-term benefits to society that are not immediately apparent to many individual citizens. A key element of the common interest approach is the notion of accountability which stresses that media freedom has to be balanced by responsibility (McQuail 2003; $\rightarrow$ Accountability of the Media; Accountability of the News).

In one way or another, the public interest has been the subject of three different sorts of skepticism. First, it has a rather vague and confusing meaning that seems to include the public welfare, the common good, and the national interest (Dennis 2002). Second, it is hardly possible to identify empirically where the public interest lies. And third, there is some doubt whether the practices and institutions of modern politics and the media are such that the public interest is pursued, even if there is agreement on how it should be defined. By and large, the conventional wisdom even among political and social theorists is that vested and concentrated interests often are more able to promote their interests at the expense of the public interest.

SEE ALSO: ▶ Accountability of the Media ▶ Accountability of the News ▶ Audience Research ▶ Commercialization: Impact on Media Content ▶ Communication and Law ▶ Deliberativeness in Political Communication ▶ Ethics in Journalism ▶ Ethics of Media Content ▶ Habermas, Jürgen ▶ Journalism: Normative Theories ▶ Media Performance ▶ Media Policy ▶ Nielsen Ratings ▶ Political Discourse ▶ Political Media Content, Quality Criteria in ▶ Public Opinion ▶ Public Opinion Polling ▶ Public Service Broadcasting: Law and Policy ▶ Quality of the News ▶ Readership Research ▶ Survey

References and Suggested Readings

Alexander, E. R. (2002). The public interest in planning: From legitimation to substantive plan evaluation. *Planning Theory*, 1, 226–249.

Berki, R. N. (1979). State and society: An antithesis of modern political thought. In J. E. S. Hayward & R. N. Berki (eds.), *State and society in contemporary Europe*. Oxford: Robertson, pp. 1–20.

Dennis, E. E. (2002). The press and the public interest: A definitional dilemma. In D. McQuail (ed.), *McQuail's reader in mass communication theory*. London: Sage, pp. 161–170.

Held, V. (1970). *The public interest and individual interests*. New York: Basic Books.

McQuail, D. (1992). *Media performance: Mass communication and the public interest*. London: Sage.

McQuail. D. (2003). *Media accountability and freedom of publication*. London: Sage.

McQuail, D. (2005). *McQuail's mass communication theory*, 5th edn. London: Sage.

Veljanovski, C. (1990). Market driven broadcasting: Not myth but reality. *Intermedia*, 18(6), 17–21.

Public Journalism

David D. Kurpius

Louisiana State University

Public journalism is a movement that arose principally among journalists in the United States during the late twentieth century, as an effort to draw the people to the media at a time of declining readership and viewership by showing the value of the media in civic life. Public journalism is also known as "civic," or less often "community," journalism. The movement developed in part as an answer to the decline of civic participation that scholars noted (Yankelovich 1991; Merritt 1998; Rosen 1999; Putnam 2000) at a time of renewal in many cities (Sirianni & Friedland 2001). Public journalism refocused news on issues and engagement using a community approach. Its founders believed that journalism could improve public dialogue by developing content that citizens engaged in the deliberative process could use in their communities to develop solutions to common problems.

Public journalism inspired discussion among professionals and scholars about the craft of journalism. The debate between → Walter Lippmann and John Dewey in the 1920s marked a seminal time in determining the role of professional journalists in the United States. Lippmann focused on informing elites and using the media to monitor those in power. Dewey believed citizens were capable of a greater participatory role beyond simply voting. In his view, everyday citizens would deliberate on issues if given the information and the opportunity. Lippmann's view prevailed, and American journalism spent the better part of a century pursuing greater professionalism and more scientific reporting methods. Public journalism marks a return to Dewey's view of journalism in democratic life (→ Journalists' Role Perception; Professionalization of Journalism).

Some critics argue that public journalism is just good "shoe-leather journalism," implying a tradition of close-to-the-ground reporting and editing, but traditional journalists spend more time in places of power (such as city hall) than in ordinary life (→ News Sources). By rooting stories in communities, journalists capture the richness of civic conversations. Public journalism encourages journalists to probe systematically from the bottom up, starting with citizens. The top-down model of traditional journalism typically starts with officials and their issue frames (→ Framing of the News). Public journalism starts with those living in communities – their concerns, issues, aspirations, and problems – and builds meaningful comparisons, illuminates trends, and seeks out solutions for citizens to consider. Instead of leaving out officials and experts, the process may prevent elites from framing issues without considering alternative community frames.

The techniques public journalists employ encourage contextual reporting. Reporters develop sources after considering a range of potential stakeholders. "Real people" sources are not simply the opening storyline but the main threads that hold the story together throughout the coverage. Public journalists seek to portray the similarities and differences among stakeholders and look for common ground. The journalists do not select the solutions, but leave the people to decide. By reporting on potential outcomes, journalists help the process go well among citizens.

Professionals and scholars developed public journalism through experimentation and observation. What public journalism seeks to accomplish has come to define the movement.

Other characteristics include cultivating diverse sources from all strata of civic life, finding high-quality information for citizens to use, and providing feedback from citizens as well as the information needed for mobilization.

FOUNDATIONS IN THE UNITED STATES

Public journalism took shape in the late 1980s and early 1990s. Experiments began in Georgia, but the *Wichita Eagle* of Kansas conducted the first major newspaper project in 1990, when editor Davis "Buzz" Merritt wanted to give the people a voice in election coverage. In another early project, the *Charlotte Observer* ran a series called Taking Back Our Neighborhoods. The paper partnered with broadcast stations to cover housing and crime, leading to changes in policing housing and in housing code enforcement.

On television ($\rightarrow$ Television News), public journalism developed in parallel. It began with public stations that developed local public affairs coverage. For example, the Wisconsin Collaborative Project connected stations in small and medium markets to develop cooperative coverage of regional issues. Television eventually connected with print ($\rightarrow$ Newspaper Journalism), when commercial broadcasters created project partnerships with newspapers. Such collaboration became a core element of public journalism.

The longest running collaboration is "We the People Wisconsin," involving Wisconsin Public Broadcasting (the eleven stations of Wisconsin Public Radio and seven stations of Wisconsin Public Television), the commercial CBS affiliate for Madison (WISC-TV on VHF broadcast and cable), the *Wisconsin State Journal* (the main outlet of the Capital Newspapers chain of southern Wisconsin), and Wood Communications, a public relations firm in the region. The partnership continually redefined ways to bring citizens into the deliberative process, developing town hall meetings, mock courtroom hearings, and conferences on issues such as health-care.

Foundation funding promoted public journalism. The Knight Foundation funded the Project on Public Life and the Press, led by Jay Rosen at New York University. The Pew Charitable Trusts created the Pew Center for Civic Journalism, under the direction of Ed Fouhy and Jan Schaffer. During its decade-long run, the Pew Center held workshops, created opportunities for journalists to share experiences, and funded grants. The grants were small compared to the budgets of news businesses but were large enough, usually up to $20,000, to seed experiments. The US Corporation for Public Broadcasting (CPB) and Public Broadcasting System (PBS) ($\rightarrow$ Public Broadcasting Systems) joint Challenge Fund, with support from the Pew Charitable Trusts, supported Best Practices in Journalism, an effort to improve broadcast coverage of local politics by running campaign coverage workshops from 2000 to 2004. Another offshoot of the Pew Center, the J-Lab Institute for Interactive Journalism, received support from the Knight Foundation and from the Ethics and Excellence in Journalism Foundation of Oklahoma. J-Lab continues to focus on interactive journalism and incorporates ideas from public journalism.

Many public journalism grants favored *partnerships*, which combine the capacity of broadcasting to reach a wide audience and raise awareness of a problem with the resources of newspapers capable of reporting stories more deeply. Early grants supported the hiring of people for community liaison; they set up listening posts, organized town hall meetings, and connected to communities. These strategies shortened the start-up time journalists needed for gathering information about community concerns and aspirations. Large public journalism projects would likely have been too costly for media outlets without these partnerships.

BENEFITS AND CRITICISMS

Public journalism alters long-entrenched patterns of journalistic practice. Newspapers engaged in public journalism use more graphics to present issues and solutions (Coleman 2000). On television, public journalism coverage uses more diverse sources, including women, minorities, and non-elites (Kurpius 2002). Partnerships accompanied increased volunteerism, better political processes, and improved citizenship; the problem-solving frames worked better than traditional human-interest or historical frames; and the opportunities for feedback encouraged citizens to get involved (Nichols et al. 2006).

Early *critics* objected that public journalism pandered to the public as a marketing ploy to sell news or advertising. Others said either that it was no different from good journalism (→ Standards of News), or that it gave too much power over the focus of coverage to citizens, who are not well enough informed to understand complex and difficult aspects of public life (→ Public Sphere). Still other critics said that public journalism imposes the editor's view of political processes on citizens and presumes that editors know the public interest best. The town hall meetings drew fire for failing to produce thoughtful debate. These criticisms diminished in the latter part of the 1990s.

One main criticism has persisted: that public journalism undermines journalistic detachment and the *quest for objectivity*, a core professional norm for journalism (→ Objectivity in Reporting). Public journalism projects challenge the idea of detachment by encouraging journalists to spend time in communities, getting to know their ideas and their issues. Objectivity may be unachievable, a fact professional journalists can skirt by seeking truth and accuracy through lesser, more-realistic goals, such as fairness, balance, depth, and context. Innovative television news managers found ways to alter journalistic routines at the station when implementing public journalism, without raising objections, but not every newsroom had such leadership.

A recent criticism is that public journalism is *too expensive for daily practice*. Deep, contextual news coverage of issues may require resources that news organizations lack (Hamilton 2006). Other ways to fund hard news might relieve the pressures to make a profit, as did the Pew Center grants, which moved news businesses not only to try public journalism but also to delve into reporting on trends facing their communities.

Although newspapers and broadcast stations across the United States practiced public journalism, the experimentation was difficult to sustain. Foundation funding created only enclaves of innovation within newsrooms. A partnership among media organizations often depended on core individuals to keep it going and would falter and die once the key actors left. News outlets would let community liaisons go once foundation money ran out, and the ties they built to the community would wither. Or when the reporters practicing public journalism left for other jobs, the trust they had developed within the community would not transfer to the reporters replacing them. The amount of time journalists spent getting to know the community well instead of turning out daily stories caused economic stress in the system. The commercial media struggled to justify the costs of conducting such an intensive form of reporting.

Public journalism emerged in response to the primarily commercial US media system and did not spread intact to other countries (→ Commercialization of the Media; United States of America: Media System). Although scholars around the world study the phenomenon, they treat public journalism as a phase in US journalism practice.

Foundations that supported public journalism have turned to other issues, but its influence endures. "We the People Wisconsin" is still an active media partnership that reinvents itself, but at a slower pace. Individual public journalists continue to practice their craft at television stations and newspapers, but, in the absence of the labels and the debate, they weave the elements of public journalism into daily routines. The experiments bearing the label and the resulting discussion of the craft aimed at altering coverage routines (→ News Routines). The introspection, research, and development arguably made journalism better.

SEE ALSO: ► Commercialization of the Media ► Framing of the News ► Journalists' Role Perception ► Lippmann, Walter ► News Routines ► News Sources ► Newspaper Journalism ► Objectivity in Reporting ► Professionalization of Journalism ► Public Broadcasting Systems ► Public Sphere ► Standards of News ► Television News ► United States of America: Media System

References and Suggested Readings

Coleman, R. (2000). Use of visual communication in public journalism. *Newspaper Research Journal*, 21(4), 17–37.

Coleman, R., & Wasike, B. (2004). Visual elements in public journalism newspapers in an election: A content analysis of the photographs and graphics in campaign 2000. *Journal of Communication*, 54, 456–473.

Eksterowicz, A. J., & Roberts, R. N. (2000). *Public journalism and political knowledge*. Lanham, MD: Rowman and Littlefield.

Friedland, L. (1995). Public television as public sphere: The case of the Wisconsin Collaborative Project. *Journal of Broadcasting and Electronic Media*, 39, 147–176.

Hamilton, J. (2006). *All the news that's fit to sell: How the market transforms information into news*. Princeton, NJ: Princeton University Press.

Kurpius, D. D. (2002). Sources and civic journalism: Changing patterns of reporting? *Journalism and Mass Communication Quarterly*, 79, 853–866.

Merritt, D. (1998). *Public journalism and public life: Why telling the news is not enough*, 2nd edn. Mahwah, NJ: Lawrence Erlbaum.

Nichols, S. L., Friedland, L. A., Rojos, H., Cho, J., & Shaw, D. V. (2006). Examining the effects of public journalism on civil society from 1994 to 2002: Organizational factors, project features, story frames, and citizen engagement. *Journalism and Mass Communication Quarterly*, 83, 77–100.

Poindexter, P. M., Heider, D., & McCombs, M. (2006). Watchdog or good neighbor? The public's expectations of local news. *Harvard International Journal of Press/Politics*, 11, 77–88.

Putnam, R. D. (2000). *Bowling alone: The collapse and revival of American community*. New York: Simon and Schuster.

Rosen, J. (1999). *What are journalists for?* New Haven, CT: Yale University Press.

Sirianni, C., & Friedland, L. (2001). *Civic innovation in America: Community empowerment, public policy, and the movement for civic renewal*. Berkeley, CA: University of California Press.

Yankelovich, D. (1991). *Coming to public judgment: Making democracy work in a complex world*. Syracuse, NY: Syracuse University Press.

Public Meetings

Theresa Castor

University of Wisconsin-Parkside

A public meeting is a gathering in which there are limited, if any, restrictions on who may participate. Public meetings, as an ideal, are a form of democracy (→ Public Sphere), but in fact are often viewed as frustrating and futile. Researchers have studied issues and topics related to public meetings (e.g., leadership, public participation); there is now increased attention on studying public meetings themselves as structured communication events. Labeling an event as a meeting calls attention to the communicative dimensions of this activity. Communication scholars have examined public meetings as situations in which identity, social action, and culture, among other practices, are enacted.

Scholars have specified two or, more commonly, three participants as a minimum for constituting a meeting. While people may gather in a variety of situations, not all gatherings are labeled as meetings; e.g., it would be unusual to call a gathering of friends a meeting. A meeting is explicitly framed as such by participants, but not all meetings are public. For those that are, the public may be involved as observers or participants. Public meetings usually have a *specific structure* and *rules for participation* (e.g., parliamentary procedures or *Robert's Rules of Order*). One characteristic of public meetings that distinguishes them from organizational meetings is that the latter form is more open in terms of participation. Also, the latter will have several audiences, some of which may not even be physically present at the time of a meeting but may know of the discussion through mediated forms of communication, such as print or television broadcast. Several types of meetings fall within the domain of public meetings, including public hearings, public inquiries, town meetings, and some board meetings (this last area intersects the domains of the public and organizational study).

Tracy and Dimock (2004) outline two major *research traditions* that provide an understanding of public meetings: public deliberation and public participation. The former area focuses on a normative ideal for the type of communication that should occur during public meetings: talk is rational and assumes equality among participants. Public participation research examines views of participants regarding public meetings. Tracy and Dimock fault both areas for failing to pay attention to the actual communication practices associated with public meetings.

Language and social interaction scholars have used various *perspectives* to study the actual communication practices associated with public meetings; these perspectives include → ethnography of communication, → discourse analysis, → ethnomethodology, → conversation analysis, speech act theory, and critical/narrative approaches. While meetings have been a part of the background context for many studies, Schwartzman (1989) was among the first to call attention to the need to study meetings in and of themselves as communication events. Applying an ethnography of communication framework, Schwartzman identified the varying structures, purposes, participants, settings, and norms for meetings. Several studies have highlighted the role of culture in meeting discourse (e.g., Brison 1992). Because talk and culture are interconnected, participants may have varying assumptions regarding the purpose of talk during a meeting (e.g., to convey information, to express emotions, to present arguments, etc.). Discourse analysts have shown how differences in participant background can contribute to different meanings for words that are used during meetings, possibly leading to sustained disagreement (e.g., Gephart 1992). More recently, the action-implicative discourse analytic approach (→ Action-Implicative Discourse Analysis) has been applied specifically to examining school board meetings and how participants, through their language use, construct identity and negotiate their interactional dilemmas (e.g., Tracy & Ashcraft 2001).

One *challenge* in the study of public meetings deals with definition. As described earlier, public meetings have been included in many studies as part of a context, but not necessarily as the main focus per se. One reason for this relates to how the unit of analysis is defined for a given study. For example, the topic of focus may be the group (e.g., a governing board) or the purpose (e.g., decision-making, problem-solving, deliberation). Focusing on the group as the unit of study, however, highlights participants rather than communication. Orientation to purpose brings the focus back to communication, but identifying type of talk ahead of time forecloses consideration of the multiple forms of talk that may occur during a public meeting and what those forms may contribute to the various outcomes of a meeting. The most promising future direction for research on public meetings is the development of a practical theory approach (Craig 1989). Practical theory examines communication as naturally occurring practices and seeks to understand the situated ideals of participants for their communication practices. Within the frame of public meetings, a key issue is how participants manage multiple, and possibly competing, goals such as how to develop a consensus or community while voicing individual preferences.

SEE ALSO: ▶ Action-Implicative Discourse Analysis ▶ Conversation Analysis ▶ Deliberativeness in Political Communication ▶ Discourse Analysis ▶ Ethnography of Communication ▶ Ethnomethodology ▶ Language and Social Interaction ▶ Public Sphere

References and Suggested Readings

Boden, D. (1994). *The business of talk: Organizations in action*. Cambridge: Polity.

Brison, K. J. (1992). *Just talk: Gossip, meetings, and power in a Papua New Guinea village*. Berkeley, CA: University of California Press.

Craig, R. T. (1989). Communication as a practical discipline. In B. Dervin, L. Grossberg, B. J. O'Keefe, & E. Wartella (eds.), *Rethinking communication*, vol. 1. Newbury Park, CA: Sage, pp. 97–122.

Gephart, R. P. (1992). Sensemaking, communicative distortion and the logic of public inquiry legitimation. *Industrial Crisis Quarterly*, 6, 115–135.

McComas, K. A. (2001). Theory and practice of public meetings. *Communication Theory*, 11, 36–55.

Schwartzman, H. B. (1989). *The meeting: Gatherings in organizations and communities*. New York: Plenum.

Tracy, K. (2005). Reconstructing communicative practices: Action-implicative discourse analysis. In K. L. Fitch & R. E. Sanders (eds.), *Handbook of language and social interaction*. Mahwah, NJ: Lawrence Erlbaum, pp. 301–319.

Tracy, K., & Ashcraft, C. (2001). Crafting policies about controversial values: How wording disputes manage a group dilemma. *Journal of Applied Communication Research*, 29, 294–316.

Tracy, K., & Dimock, A. (2004). Meetings: Discursive sites for building and fragmenting community. In P. J. Kabfleisch (ed.), *Communication yearbook*, vol. 28. Mahwah, NJ: Lawrence Erlbaum, pp. 127–165.

Van Vree, W. (1999). *Meetings, manners and civilization: The development of modern meeting behavior*. London: Leicester University Press.

Public Opinion

Carroll J. Glynn
Ohio State University

Michael E. Huge
Ohio State University

Bearing the dubious distinction of being one of the oldest, yet least understood, concepts in social science, *public opinion* continues to inspire and perplex scholars from communication and other fields. The term can be adequately defined as a general measure of the directionality and strength of issue-specific views and sentiments held by a relevant group. Public opinion bears a sort of syntactical internal contradiction: While "public" denotes the group and the universal, "opinion" on its own is typically associated with the individual and considered a somewhat internal, subjective formulation. The rise of survey research during the early twentieth century further complicated matters with a trend toward quantifying public opinion as a simple aggregation of individual survey responses (→ Survey; Public Opinion Polling). The rejection of such mathematical reductions – along with the suggestion that public opinion was in fact a group-level social force iteratively constructed through interpersonal interaction and media use (→ Interpersonal Communication; Political Media Use; Media Use by Social Variable) – set the stage for a social science debate that has continued for well over 50 years.

HISTORICAL APPROACHES

The French term "l'opinion publique," originally attributed to sixteenth-century French Renaissance writer Montaigne, was adopted in European thinking as political power and decision-making shifted away from the monarchy and toward the citizenry during the Enlightenment. With the advent of the printing press (→ Printing, History of), knowledge became more distributed within societies, and this led to a realization that it might be possible to arrive at better decisional outcomes if more affected parties (i.e., the citizenry) were consulted. Until recent times, however, the citizenry considered to have a voice consisted primarily of land-owning, wealthy white males. One of the earliest problems to arise in conceptualizing what constituted public opinion was the difficulty of coming to some type of decisional outcome at the end of a public opinion process in which many different viewpoints were voiced. When parties disagreed, it was difficult to discern (1) whose views should be most prominently considered and (2) how other ideas could be eliminated. Additional debate centered on how "rational" a group could be considered in arriving at a public viewpoint. While some argued for an ideal speech situation, in which all points of view could be heard and equally considered, concern remained that public debate would be sullied by an emotional mob mentality in which rash decisions would be reached through manipulative means.

With these challenges in mind, Enlightenment-era thinkers set out to incorporate the views of the public into governmental decisions, while at the same time balancing this democratic input with the presumed knowledge and experience of government officials. In this way, a democratic government could consider the will of the people while maintaining stability against abrupt shifts in sentiment that could overrun the long-term authority of the state. This potential for mob-like behavior is often referred to as the "tyranny of the majority." Divergent views of the role of public opinion in a democracy (i.e., a mandate from the people or merely the views of those affected by decisions) were typified by the 1920s debate between → Walter Lippmann and John Dewey (Splichal 1999). Dewey believed that the more people included in arriving at a public opinion outcome, the better off the entire society would be. From Lippmann's point of view, governmental decisions were best left to elected and appointed officials who were free to use public opinion as a guide to varying degrees.

This debate and other public opinion conceptualizations generated in the early twentieth century marked a shift from approaching public opinion as a philosophical subject to a perspective more rooted in the increasingly systematic approaches of social science (Binkley 1928). Yet this trend toward more scientifically rigorous methods created another debate, with one side seeing public opinion as an aggregation of survey responses, while others were more interested in public opinion as a socially constructed force that developed through media use and interpersonal conversation. For the survey-oriented group, George Gallup's 1936 prediction of the United States presidential race was a watershed moment. With careful sampling techniques created to replicate the basic demography of the electorate, Gallup's poll was able to correctly predict Franklin D. Roosevelt as the winner of the election with far fewer respondents than the *Literary Digest* poll, which had incorrectly predicted that Alfred Landon would win. Gallup's reputation was further improved when he correctly predicted the Labour Party's surprise 1945 victory in the United Kingdom's general election (→ Election Polls and Forecasts; Election Surveys). This led some to argue that public opinion was quite simply a collection of individual responses tightly linked to electoral outcomes.

For those more interested in social aspects of public opinion (Cooley 1962 [1st pub. 1909]; Tarde 1969 [1st pub. 1901]), public opinion was conceptualized as a type of normative force, which had the ability to influence media presentations and conversations about public issues (→ Public Opinion, Media Effects on). Public opinion was seen as a force opposed to tradition and reason. Long before the conceptualization of a two-step flow involving the media and subsequent interpersonal discussion, Tarde saw the important role that media played in disseminating new ideas, noting that the press had the ability to superimpose a kind of "public mind" upon citizens, who were more likely to talk about the ideas set forth in the media (→ Two-Step Flow of Communication). Blumer (1948) rejected polling as a means of measuring public opinion. He asserted that the real value of public opinion was its ability to represent the views of many as a single force capable of influencing those in positions of power, governmental or otherwise.

PUBLIC OPINION PROCESSES: INFORMATION OR SOCIAL CONTROL?

From a societal perspective, public opinion can function in a number of different ways. Some scholars (Habermas 1989 [1st pub. 1962]; → Habermas, Jürgen) argue for the merits of thinking about public opinion as a rational, information-based phenomenon in which the best ideas will percolate to the top of the public agenda. Within the confines of the "public sphere," citizens are exposed to a number of different ideas and opinions that they can hold or improve upon (→ Public Sphere). In a manner akin to free market systems, the ideas that hold the most value are in the highest demand, while less popular ideas are pushed aside.

Others (Noelle-Neumann 1993; → Noelle-Neumann, Elisabeth) counter that public opinion is in fact a method of social control. Acknowledging that societies must be held together by some level of group-wide cohesion, this view posits a heavy influence of the mass media upon the general public. Instead of debating within a rational and unbiased opinion climate, most citizens are instead limited to considering the views put forth in newspapers or on television. Furthermore, these debates tend to mimic news coverage, allowing the views of the news media to become the dominant views within the public. The social control aspect is also involved within interpersonal opinion exchanges. Noelle-Neumann's "spiral of silence" theory predicts that those who believe that their viewpoint is in the minority will be less likely to express that viewpoint (→ Spiral of Silence; Climate of Opinion). Majority opinions are more likely to be expressed, leading to a spiraling effect in which majority opinions are overrepresented, whereas minority ones are underrepresented. This collective phenomenon is said to be rooted in individuals' fear of becoming socially isolated from a group as a result of expressing an unpopular opinion.

The validity of both views (i.e., public opinion as rational information exchange versus public opinion as social control) can be seen in different opinion contexts, and it must be acknowledged that both play an important role in opinion exchange. The notion of individuals fearing social ostracism as a result of expressing an unpopular view highlights the often-neglected role that emotions and affective considerations play in public opinion processes. Scholars have long noted that relatively new or underdeveloped opinions tend to be based less on reason and more on "gut reactions" to ideas or individuals (Zajonc 1980). While such opinions might be considered low in opinion quality, they are nonetheless interesting from a research perspective because they are often the basis for opinions that could become more developed, better reasoned, and higher in opinion quality.

LEVELS OF ANALYSIS

Perhaps the most difficult component of studying public opinion lies in conceptualizing public opinion processes with respect to different levels of analysis. As Pan and McLeod (1991) noted, the spiral of silence theory captures the inherent multilevel nature of public opinion as a social force. At the individual level, people connect with their social environment by talking to others and through exposure to media outlets. From this information-gathering process, they form perceptions of the "climate of opinion" surrounding a given topic. In this way, perceiving opinions can be seen as analogous to perceiving social norms in terms of looking to others for guidance as to what is and what is not acceptable in a given situation (→ Social Perception). In other words, the opinion climate at the macro-level impacts individual perceptions of opinion at the micro-level. Internalizing the opinion climate impacts individual expressions of opinion, and this further impacts the macro-level opinion climate. With the increasing popularity of multilevel modeling approaches in the social sciences, public opinion scholars may be on the brink of a better-specified model of this dynamic and iterative process.

PUBLIC OPINION AND THE MEDIA

Given the importance of the contextual effects in understanding public opinion, researchers interested in media effects, information processing, and political psychology have all contributed to public opinion knowledge. Over the past few decades, media effects research has shifted from investigating the direct effects (i.e., strong or limited effects) of messages to a more information-based cognitive approach (→ Media Effects; Media Effects, History of). The information-processing approach seeks to identify how new, outside information – most of which is received by individuals via media outlets – is integrated with already-existing information. For those who see opinion formation as a continual, iterative process influenced by both pre-existing views and new contextual information, it is important to consider the characteristics of the mechanisms though which this new information is delivered.

A good example of this shift can be seen in agenda-setting research (McCombs & Shaw 1972), which initially focused on matching prominent news stories with lists of what the public perceived to be important issues (→ Agenda-Setting Effects). More recently, agenda-setting research has explored possible mechanisms (e.g., priming) through which this media effect might take place. Other research has focused on how the agenda-setting function can cause shifts in public opinion that go beyond a simple listing of what is important (→ Priming Theory). In other words, agenda-setting research could be a much stronger theoretical framework if differently "set" agendas were shown to impact individual opinions as well as perceptions of macro-level opinion in a significantly different manner. Zaller (1992) presented another view of the impact of media and other messages on public opinion. In his Receive-Accept-Sample (RAS) model, people receive information, accept it or reject it on the basis of whether it fits with prior beliefs, and then sample from recent considerations when asked to offer their own opinion. Zaller also posited the existence of two-sided message flows, in which differing views on an issue are offered for individuals to consider (→ Political Cognitions; Political Knowledge). Political awareness is a key mediating variable in Zaller's model, and those of moderate political awareness are seen as the most vulnerable to the dueling messages offered in two-sided flows.

TECHNOLOGY AND DEMOCRATIC OUTCOMES

In western societies, advances in information technology have historically led to increases in citizen access to political information and political power. Since the introduction of movable type, continually improving information technology has led to an overall trend of increased accessibility for citizens in terms of communicating their views to elected and appointed public officials. In other words, it has become easier for individuals to impact public opinion by contributing to the overall context or opinion climate in which issues are considered (→ Communication Technology and Democracy). Within that overall trend, though, there have been and will continue to be anti-democratic perturbations, whether in the form of → censorship, surveillance, or elite control of opinion debates through technological means.

But exactly how will this new technology be harnessed for democratic outcomes? The barriers to news creation and dissemination are no longer as high as they once were. The recent explosion in popularity of web logs (i.e., blogs; → Blogger) indicates that many individuals are willing and able to put forth their own views and content for mass consumption. Indeed, through web links, e-newsletters, a plethora of cable and satellite television channels, and the increasing portability of wireless and hand-held communication technology, it seems that the potential for broadcasting information – political or otherwise – is almost limitless. Yet it remains to be seen whether the increasing availability of political information will have a marked impact on public opinion processes. It is possible that the people who were interested in politics before the Internet revolution will be the same people who make use of new technology. Problems with access, such as the → digital divide, remain an issue for many, especially in developing nations around the world.

The key to unleashing the potential of technology's role in facilitating the exchange of public opinion rests with government's willingness to allocate more explicit decision-making authority – whether in the form of online deliberations or otherwise – to the general public. This has been and will continue to be a key hurdle for effectively employing information technology as a public opinion tool. Representative democracy is a compromise between the idea that all should have some form of access to decision-making authority and the notion that raw public opinion is too fickle to serve as a basis for a functioning democracy. Newspapers, radio, and television have certainly – each in its own way – improved the transparency of the operations of government while also allowing for the views of common citizens to be broadcast on a wide scale (e.g., letters to the editor, radio call-in shows). Fishkin (1991) and other deliberative scholars (→ Deliberative Polls) argue that this potential exists for online deliberative forums because the Internet ameliorates the effects of many key barriers to a more inclusive, deliberative democratic system (i.e., by bringing people together, controlling conversation, providing uniform access to relevant information).

FUTURE DIRECTIONS

To truly understand public opinion as it relates to society at large, however, social science first needs to address more basic questions regarding the exchange of political information, in terms of both interpersonal interaction and media exposure. Fundamental public opinion issues still need further consideration and explication: How do political ideas from the outside world enter the consciousness of individuals and become integrated with already-held → attitudes, beliefs, and opinions? What role does → emotion play in opinion formation?

With roots in political science and social psychology, mass communication research and public opinion studies are of a similar scientific pedigree. Recent attempts to realign these two formerly diverging fields of research signal an encouraging move toward recognizing public opinion as an inherently communication-centered phenomenon. Encompassing message production, media sociology, content analysis, media exposure effects, individual processing and other cognitive approaches, and interpersonal interaction, as well as a host of perception-based interpretations of social reality, public opinion can be seen as a chance to embark on truly interdisciplinary research (→ Media and Perceptions of Reality; Media Production and Content; Content Analysis, Quantitative; Content Analysis, Qualitative; Exposure to Communication Content). With the increasing speed of technological advancement, the channels by which information passes between sender and receiver are part of an increasingly complex and multifaceted process. Though polling information is available for almost any topic or political candidate, scholars and citizens alike recognize that there is more to the process than simply adding up the number of people who say they are for or against an issue.

Perhaps the tallest hurdle remaining for public opinion scholars is specifying and modeling key contextual factors of public opinion climates. Spiral of silence research gained much attention by noting that the perception of majority pressure can impact the likelihood of individual opinion expression. However, scholars have more recently recognized that perceptions of majority and minority pressures can vary according to the perceived strength of opinions as well as perceptions of how much agreement there is among a group or community.

SEE ALSO: ▶ Agenda-Setting Effects ▶ Attitudes ▶ Behavioral Norms: Perception through the Media ▶ Blogger ▶ Censorship ▶ Climate of Opinion ▶ Communication Technology and Democracy ▶ Content Analysis, Qualitative ▶ Content Analysis, Quantitative ▶ Deliberative Polls ▶ Digital Divide ▶ Election Polls and Forecasts ▶ Election Surveys ▶ Emotion ▶ Exposure to Communication Content ▶ Habermas, Jürgen ▶ Interpersonal Communication ▶ Lippmann, Walter ▶ Media Effects ▶ Media Effects, History of ▶ Media and Perceptions of Reality ▶ Media Production and Content ▶ Media Use by Social Variable ▶ Noelle-Neumann, Elisabeth ▶ Political Cognitions ▶ Political Knowledge ▶ Political Media Use ▶ Priming Theory ▶ Printing, History of ▶ Public Opinion, Media Effects on ▶ Public Opinion Polling ▶ Public Sphere ▶ Rhetoric, Vernacular ▶ Social Perception ▶ Spiral of Silence ▶ Survey ▶ Two-Step Flow of Communication

References and Suggested Readings

Binkley, R. C. (1928). The concept of public opinion in the social sciences. *Social Forces*, 6, 389–396.
Blumer, H. (1948). Public opinion and public opinion polling. *American Sociological Review*, 13, 542–549.
Cooley, C. H. (1962). *Social organization*. Brunswick, NJ: Transaction Books.
Fishkin, J. S. (1991). *Democracy and deliberation*. New Haven, CT: Yale University Press.

Habermas, J. (1989). *The structural transformation of the public sphere: An inquiry into a category of bourgeois society.* Cambridge, MA: MIT Press.

McCombs, M. E., & Shaw, D. L. (1972). The agenda-setting function of mass media. *Public Opinion Quarterly*, 36, 176–187.

Noelle-Neumann, E. (1993). *The spiral of silence: Public opinion – our social skin.* Chicago: University of Chicago Press.

Pan, Z., & McLeod, J. M. (1991). Multilevel analysis in mass communication research. *Communication Research*, 18(2), 140–173.

Splichal, S. (1999). *Public opinion: Developments and controversies in the twentieth century.* New York: Rowan and Littlefield.

Tarde, G. (1969). The public and the crowd. In Terry N. Clark (ed.), *Gabriel Tarde on communication and social influence: Selected papers.* Chicago: University of Chicago Press, pp. 277–294.

Zajonc, R. B. (1980). Feeling and thinking: Preferences need no inferences. *American Psychologist*, 35(2), 151–175.

Zaller, J. R. (1992). *The nature and origins of mass opinion.* New York: Cambridge University Press.

Public Opinion, Media Effects on

Erich Lamp

Johannes Gutenberg University of Mainz

Hans Mathias Kepplinger

Johannes Gutenberg University of Mainz

Because there are various concepts of → public opinion there are no general statements about the effects of mass media on it. Instead, the effects of mass media have to be related to specific concepts. Moreover, different study designs and methods have to be taken into consideration. According to the *quantitative concept*, public opinion is regarded as the distribution of individual opinions within a population and measured by representative opinion polls (→ Survey). According to this approach, the intensity and tone of media coverage directly influence public opinion. Most studies are based on a linear-effect model (→ Linear and Nonlinear Models of Causal Analysis): the more often the media cover an issue, the more people believe it to be important (→ Agenda-Setting Effects); and the more often the media present certain opinions, the more people adopt these opinions. The intensity and tone of media coverage are measured by quantitative content analysis (→ Content Analysis, Quantitative). In some studies, they are not measured but estimated; possible effects are concluded from media use (Robinson 1976). As well as the intensity and tone of media coverage, the framing of news stories can influence public opinion. Framing refers to the media's reporting of issues or events structured along certain perspectives, and to the audience's processing of that content according to predetermined schemas (→ Schemas; Schemas and Media Effects). As demonstrated in several studies, people's interpretations and conclusions are mostly in line with media frames (→ Framing Effects).

MEDIA EFFECTS IN THE QUANTITATIVE CONCEPT OF PUBLIC OPINION

Methodological Designs

The assumed influence of media coverage on public opinion can be analyzed using cross-sectional or longitudinal designs (→ Longitudinal Analysis). In *cross-sectional designs*, the distribution of media coverage on several issues, or the distribution of various opinions on one issue, is compared over a short period of time (several days or weeks) to the distribution of corresponding opinions within the population.

In *longitudinal designs*, the development of intensity and/or tone of media coverage on individual issues (or persons, institutions, etc.) during a rather long period of time (several months or years) is compared to the development of corresponding opinions (Ader 1995). In most studies, general trends in media coverage are compared with general trends in public opinion (aggregate data analysis). Here, the intensity of media use and the type of coverage presented by different mass media is neglected (MacKuen 1981; Page & Shapiro 1992, pp. 341–347). In a few studies, based on the intensity of individual media use and the type of coverage presented by the relevant media, an index of media input is calculated and related to opinions held by individuals (individual data analysis; Kepplinger et al. 1991; → Scales and Indices). If media coverage has an effect on public opinion, trends in public opinion should be predictable from data about trends of media coverage. This has been done using advanced mathematical models of the relationship between causes and effects (Fan 1988; Zaller 1992; → Time-Series Analysis).

As the term implies, media coverage is related to something which gets covered – events, opinions, etc. Media coverage might or might not present an adequate picture of the distribution of opinions or the changing number of certain events in the course of time (→ Reality and Media Reality; Social Perception). Some people might have first-hand information about the reality covered by the media, others might not. Opinions can be influenced by either individual experience or media coverage, or by both sources of information. In these cases information based on personal experience can contradict or support information provided by the mass media. Depending on the mixture of information, personal experience can minimize or maximize media effects (→ Perceived Reality as a Social Process). Therefore, several authors have tried to separate the relative influence of real-world indicators and media coverage on public opinion (Combs & Slovic 1979; Erbring et al. 1980; Behr & Iyengar 1985).

Influence on Behaviors

Media-induced public opinion may *influence behavior*. For example, in the early seventies the coverage of German news media painted a picture showing that a breakdown of the oil supply in the country was ahead – although there was enough crude oil in stock. Because people became concerned they took precautions and bought unusual quantities of gasoline and diesel, which in turn led to scattered bottlenecks in delivery and sharp price increases. Six years later, when the quantity of imported oil really had dropped considerably, the media rarely covered this development and, in consequence, the population did not become concerned and did not change their habits (Kepplinger 1983).

Media-induced images of reality are also relevant for voting decisions. For example, although in 1992 there was an economic upturn in the US, the television networks presented the situation of the economy as twice as bad as in the previous year. Thus most Americans thought of the economic situation as bad (Ladd 1993). Since the assessment of the economic situation has a strong impact on the image of leading politicians, George Bush's popularity went into freefall and challenger Bill Clinton won the election (Katz & Baldassare 1994).

Influence on Social Perception

According to the *functional concept* of public opinion, societies need a consensus on some basic issues. A consensus can only be achieved if at least a significant minority accepts which issue should be discussed, and if the formation of opinions is based on individual insight (see below) or on social forces. The functional concept stresses the importance of the latter. In this case, media coverage can be regarded as an intervening variable which modifies the psychological dynamic of opinion formation. As → Walter Lippmann (Lippmann 1922) and others have stressed, the pictures in our heads about groups, events, and the like are often attended with representations of how other people think about these objects. Likewise one's own opinions, attitudes, and intended behavior are seen in the light of the positions held by others. The formation of public opinion thus emerges from the individual's actual interaction with other people together with the symbolic interaction with generalized others; both influence one's own opinions and behavior.

Perceptions of how most other people think stem from the individual's direct experience, mainly through conversation, as well as indirectly from the media. Media coverage therefore influences not only how people imagine politicians, whom they have rarely met personally, for example, but also how they imagine the → climate of opinion (Fields & Schuman 1976; Gunther 1998). The perception of the climate of opinion can affect whether people are willing to speak out in public or whether they keep silent (→ Spiral of Silence). For example, in the eighties the German news media covered nuclear energy unfavorably. In consequence, an increasing part of the population thought the majority would oppose nuclear power plants. Supporters of nuclear energy were decreasingly willing to voice their position in public. In the course of ten years the relative majority of supporters became a minority while the initial minority of opponents became the relative majority (Noelle-Neumann 1991).

If the mass media present an inadequate picture of the distribution of opinion in society, they may convince members of the minority that they represent the majority opinion (→ False Consensus) and make members of the majority believe they belong to a minority (→ Pluralistic Ignorance). These conclusions might be suggested by most people's conviction that the media have a stronger impact on other people than on themselves (→ Third-Person Effects). This in turn can influence individuals' willingness to express their opinions in public (Mutz 1989), and thus explain the emergence of a silent majority: through the agency of the mass media the views of elites and avant-gardes may incorrectly appear as being widely held. The minority position can thus appear as a majority opinion, which causes the actual majority to keep silent or reduces their willingness to speak out.

MEDIA ROLE IN THE QUALITATIVE CONCEPT OF PUBLIC OPINION

According to the *qualitative concept* public opinion is the consequence of intellectual insights. In this approach the media serve as a forum for discourse, and media coverage is not primarily seen as the cause of opinions but as the prerequisite of reasonable conclusions (Habermas 1989). Because only a small portion of the population is interested in such discourse and has enough knowledge to take part (Neuman 1986), the qualitative concept is also referred to as the "elite concept of public opinion."

According to the qualitative concept, media coverage and public opinion are more or less identical. This is especially true for the coverage of high-quality media such as the leading newspapers (→ Quality Press). Therefore, public opinion can be deduced from media coverage. This is an idea held by many politicians, who often distrust opinion polls (Herbst 1998; → Public Opinion Polling). As far as media coverage shapes the opinions of the majority, there are similarities between the qualitative and quantitative concept that have largely been neglected: present trends in media coverage can be interpreted as future trends in mass opinions. For instance, the spread of minority positions in society can be analyzed by multi-step models which include direct and indirect media effects (→ Media Effects: Direct and Indirect Effects) on various types of individuals and groups (Hilgartner & Bosk 1988).

SEE ALSO: ▶ Agenda-Setting Effects ▶ Climate of Opinion ▶ Content Analysis, Quantitative ▶ False Consensus ▶ Framing Effects ▶ Linear and Nonlinear Models of Causal Analysis ▶ Lippmann, Walter ▶ Longitudinal Analysis ▶ Media Effects: Direct and Indirect Effects ▶ Perceived Reality as a Social Process ▶ Pluralistic Ignorance ▶ Public Opinion ▶ Public Opinion Polling ▶ Quality Press ▶ Reality and Media Reality ▶ Scales and Indices ▶ Schemas ▶ Schemas and Media Effects ▶ Social Perception ▶ Spiral of Silence ▶ Survey ▶ Third-Person Effects ▶ Time-Series Analysis

References and Suggested Readings

Ader, C. R. (1995). A longitudinal study of agenda setting for the issue of environmental pollution. *Journalism and Mass Communication Quarterly*, 72, 300–311.

Behr, R. L., & Iyengar, S. (1985). Television news, real-world cues, and changes in the public agenda. *Public Opinion Quarterly*, 49, 38–57.

Combs, B., & Slovic, P. (1979). Newspaper coverage of causes of death. *Journalism Quarterly*, 56, 837–843.

Erbring, L., Goldenberg, E. N., & Miller, A. H. (1980). Front-page news and real-world cues: A new look at agenda-setting by the media. *American Journal of Political Science*, 24, 16–49.

Fan, D. P. (1988). *Predictions of public opinion from the mass media: Computer content analysis and mathematical modeling*. New York: Greenwood.

Fields, J. M., & Schuman, H. (1976). Public beliefs about the beliefs of the public. *Public Opinion Quarterly*, 40, 427–448.

Gunther, A. C. (1998). The persuasive press inference: Effects of mass media on perceived public opinion. *Communication Research*, 25, 486–504.

Habermas, J. (1989). *The structural transformation of the public sphere: An inquiry into a category of bourgeois society*. Cambridge, MA: MIT, Press.

Herbst, S. (1998). *Reading public opinion: How political actors view the democratic process*. Chicago, IL: University of Chicago Press.

Hilgartner, S., & Bosk, C. L. (1988). The rise and fall of social problems: A public arenas model. *American Journal of Sociology*, 94, 53–78.

Katz, C., & Baldassare, M. (1994). Popularity in a freefall: Measuring a spiral of silence at the end of the Bush presidency. *International Journal of Public Opinion Research*, 6, 1–12.

Kepplinger, H. M. (1983). German media and oil supply in 1978 and 1979. In N. Smith & L. J. Theberge (eds.), *Energy coverage – media panic: An international perspective*. New York: Longman, pp. 22–49.

Kepplinger, H. M., Brosius, H.-B., & Staab, J. F. (1991). Opinion formation in mediated conflicts and crises: A theory of cognitive-affective media effects. *International Journal of Public Opinion Research*, 3, 132–156.

Ladd, E. C. (1993). The 1992 US National Election. *International Journal of Public Opinion Research*, 5, 1–21.

Lippmann, W. (1922). *Public opinion*. New York: Macmillan.

MacKuen, M. B. (1981). Social communication and the mass policy agenda. In M. B. MacKuen & S. L. Coombs (eds.), *More than news: Media power in public affairs*. London: Sage, pp. 19–144.

Mutz, D. C. (1989). The influence of perceptions of media influence: Third person effects and the public expression of opinions. *International Journal of Public Opinion Research*, 1, 3–23.

Neuman, R. W. (1986). *The paradox of mass politics: Knowledge and opinion in the American electorate*. Cambridge, MA: Harvard University Press.

Noelle-Neumann, E. (1991). The theory of public opinion: The concept of the spiral of silence. In J. A. Anderson (ed.), *Communication yearbook*, 14. Newbury Park, CA: Sage, pp. 256–287.

Page, B. J., & Shapiro, R. I. (1992). *The rational public: Fifty years of trends in Americans' policy preferences*. Chicago, IL: University of Chicago Press.

Robinson, M. J. (1976). Public affairs in television and the growth of political malaise: The case of "The selling of the Pentagon." *American Political Science Review*, 70, 409–432.

Zaller, J. (1992). *The nature and origins of mass opinion*. Cambridge, MA: Cambridge University Press.

Public Opinion Polling

Thomas Petersen

Allensbach Institute

The term "public opinion polling" generally refers collectively to both the representative → survey method and to the institutes that specialize in employing this method, particularly to commercial survey institutes. Other terms commonly employed in this context are: "public opinion research," "survey research", or simply, if somewhat confusingly, → "public opinion." The term "demoscopy" (Greek: "observation of the public"), originally suggested by American scientist Stuart Dodd (Dodd 1946), is also commonly used in some European countries, particularly in connection with political debate, although it has not gained a foothold in English-speaking countries.

Along with media content analysis (→ Content Analysis, Quantitative), the laboratory experiment (→ Experiment, Laboratory), and participant → observation, public opinion polling is one of the most important tools in empirical communication research. Survey research serves as a vital source of information in the social sciences, as well as in the areas of market research, media research, and the political sphere.

HISTORY

The three cornerstones of survey research are: the standardization of the investigative technique, i.e., completing → interviews using a firmly worded questionnaire; analyzing the findings in aggregate, in other words, observing respondents as a group, not as individuals; and the random selection of respondents to form a group representative of the total population in question (→ Sampling, Random). These three core elements of opinion research were first combined systematically in the early twentieth century, although they had already been employed previously in a number of statistical surveys and research projects.

Starting in the early Middle Ages at the latest, there were a number of attempts to investigate the population's opinions on current issues by conducting standardized surveys of a great number of people. The first document that can be viewed, at least in terms of its approach, as a *standardized questionnaire* designed to ascertain opinion, stems from the year 811. It is a list of questions compiled by Emperor Charlemagne to be answered by local dignitaries in the provinces of his realm. The questions were designed to investigate the reasons for symptoms of unrest in the empire at that time, for instance, the growing number of men deserting from the army (Petersen et al. 2004). Beginning in the late eighteenth century, we find a steady series of developments in survey method, culminating during the nineteenth and early twentieth centuries in a rich tradition of empirical social research based on surveys. A number of remarkable studies were completed from the mid-nineteenth century onwards, especially in Germany (cf. Oberschall 1965).

Attempts to apply *statistical principles* (→ Statistics, Descriptive) to people date back even further. The Old Testament describes a census conducted by King David (2 Samuel 24); and statistical data on the population was collected regularly in the Roman empire, for example by the census documented in the nativity story in the Gospel according to Luke (Luke 2:1–3). During the eighteenth century, the so-called "moral statisticians" addressed the question of why the number of suicides, crimes, births, and other seemingly arbitrary acts remained constant from year to year. Gradually, they realized that even acts resulting from highly individual motives adhere to calculable statistical laws when viewed in terms of society as a whole.

The development that ultimately revolutionized survey research and, consequently, broad swaths of the social sciences was the concept of selecting respondents according to the *principle of random statistics*. The first survey of this kind was completed by British economist Arthur Bowley in 1912 (Bowley 1915). The breakthrough of the modern method of social research based on representative samples, however, came when American researchers George Gallup, Elmo Roper, and Archibald Crossley employed this technique for their forecasts of the 1936 US presidential elections.

Aside from choosing respondents using a technique that was essentially based on the principle of random selection, another novel aspect of their investigation was the *use of interviewers* to question respondents face-to-face. Prior to this study, questionnaires were commonly sent out by mail. By using the face-to-face technique, Gallup, Roper, and Crossley insured that the sample was representative, and, moreover, they also found that when contacted personally by interviewers, a substantial share of the randomly selected respondents were actually willing to participate in the survey. Of course, the methods employed then have been refined in many ways in the meantime, but the fundamental methodological principles used are still applied in all reputable representative surveys today.

FUNDAMENTAL METHODOLOGICAL PRINCIPLES

Although representative survey findings are now a standard feature in newspaper and television reporting (→ Precision Journalism; Polls and the Media), the survey method still seems somewhat puzzling to many, who wonder how it is possible to draw firm conclusions about the opinions of a population of millions based on interviews with just one or two thousand people. These doubts would be justified if the goal of survey research were to ascertain the opinions and modes of behavior of each single person in all their complexity, but surveys are not intended for that kind of individual → case study. When it comes to opinion polling, individual members of society are not the object of investigation, but rather society as a whole.

In completing surveys, strict *rules regarding standardization and structuring* must be adhered to: as far as possible, all respondents are to be treated in the same way, regardless of whether they are university professors or unskilled workers. All respondents are posed the same questions, using identical question wordings and response alternatives. This technique provides no information about the special characteristics and motives of individual respondents. Rather, it enables researchers to determine what respondents think about a certain issue on average (cf. Noelle-Neumann & Petersen 2005, 65–79).

In public opinion polls the respondents are not selected arbitrarily, but in accordance with strict rules that insure that the group of people interviewed is *representative of the total population*, thus enabling researchers to generalize the responses obtained during the interview (→ Generalizability). Representative samples can be drawn using two different techniques. The "random method" adheres to the lottery principle, with samples being selected at random from the total universe. The fundamental principle is that every member of the population or group of people under investigation must have an equal chance of being included in the sample. The second technique for drawing representative samples is the "quota method." Using this method, interviewers select respondents who display certain predetermined attributes, such as sex, age group, occupational group, size of place of residence, etc. Taken as a whole, the attributes stipulated in the interviewers' quota instructions represent a scaled-down model of the total population (Taylor 1995; → Sampling, Nonrandom).

METHODOLOGICAL ASPECTS

Over the course of the last few decades, research on survey methodology has resulted in a highly diverse body of literature. Numerous basic research studies have been conducted on various aspects of the survey procedure, although the bulk of such research generally focuses on sampling and data analysis. In recent years, research on the first of these two thematic areas, sampling techniques, has mainly concentrated on the fact that *response rates* – i.e., the share of persons selected for a sample who can actually be contacted and who are willing to complete the interview – are steadily declining in many countries around the world. Research on analytical techniques has been boosted by the greatly increased computing capacity of modern computers, which allows even extremely complex multi-variate analysis methods to be employed with relative ease. In contrast, research on how interviewers affect respondent behavior has become somewhat less important in recent years, as telephone and online surveys have largely replaced face-to-face surveys.

So far, remarkably little basic research has been completed on the subject of *questionnaire methods*. At first glance, this seems surprising, since the questionnaire is the survey method's most important tool. Without a good questionnaire, even the most complex analytical methods are of no use at all. Unlike research on sampling and analytical methods, there is no solid mathematical foundation for research on questionnaire techniques. Although survey research pioneers such as Hadley Cantril (1944) and Stanley Payne (1951) investigated the effects of various question wordings via a series of split-ballot experiments in the 1940s and 1950s, it was not until the 1980s that this area began to attract more attention again. In this respect, findings and methods from the field of cognitive psychology played an important role, as reflected in the work of researchers such as George Bishop, Norman Bradburn, Seymour Sudman, and Norbert Schwarz (cf. Sudman et al. 1996). In contrast, only a few isolated studies have dealt with the issue of how various wordings affect respondents emotionally or how the questionnaire orchestration affects response behavior. Another aspect of questionnaire methodology that has been neglected thus far is the effect of illustrations, lists, cards, or other items presented to respondents during the interview. The lack of basic research on this aspect is largely attributable to the current predominance of the telephone survey method, which has depleted the array of methods that can be employed in surveys. Now, however, the emergence of online surveys has begun to revive the relevance of some of these aspects (cf. Couper et al. 2001). From another aspect, little progress has been made in adapting measurement techniques from the field of individual psychology to the requirements of survey research, despite some very promising approaches (Ring 1992).

Since the early days of survey research, numerous variations on the public opinion polling method have been developed, to suit the specific investigative task at hand. One example in this context is the *controlled field experiment* ("split-ballot experiment"; → Experiment, Field), which can play a major role not only in investigating media or advertising effects but also in basic methodological research, since it enables researchers to combine the evidentiary logic of the experiment with the generalizable findings of representative surveys (Petersen 2002).

Another example is the *panel technique*, whereby the same group of respondents is interviewed on several separate occasions. This method is particularly important when analyzing effects that cannot be investigated experimentally, thus playing a significant role in both social research and market research (Hansen 1982). In recent years, there has also been a surge in various technically supported measurement techniques and in "access panels," whereby respondents are selected from a previously recruited pool of people who are willing to participate, although such techniques play only a minor role in academic research.

SOCIAL SIGNIFICANCE OF OPINION POLLS

In the meantime, survey research has become an integral part of many areas of life. It is probably the most important research tool in the empirical social sciences, for example in communication research, political science and sociology. It plays a central role in the business world. Today, representative surveys are naturally conducted in conjunction with product launches, advertising campaigns and new design concepts of all kinds. Survey research plays a particularly vital role in the political process and the mass media, especially during election campaigns.

Right from the start, *election forecasts* (→ Election Polls and Forecasts) have been particularly important for survey institutes since they allow researchers to compare the data on party strength ascertained before an election with the actual election outcome, thus providing a rare opportunity to test the reliability of the survey method against external criteria. For decades, election surveys have also been the target of critical remarks from politicians and journalists, due to the alleged influence of published election forecasts on voting behavior. Contrary to common assumptions, however, research to date indicates that the effect of such forecasts on voting behavior is actually only slight. At any rate, the influence exerted by polls on voting behavior is certainly far less significant than the effect of other forms of media reporting. Yet even if election forecasts did exert a major influence on voting behavior, it is fair to ask whether this would necessarily have a negative influence on the democratic process, as many people assume. Representative surveys are not the only source of information on the relative strength of the political parties prior to an election, but they are certainly the most reliable source. Particularly for politically astute, tactically minded voters, this information can be important, contributing to well-informed voting decisions. Without the publication of election polls, the void would simply be filled by less well-founded speculation.

SEE ALSO: ▶ Case Studies ▶ Content Analysis, Quantitative ▶ Election Polls and Forecasts ▶ Experiment, Field ▶ Experiment, Laboratory ▶ Generalizability ▶ Interview ▶ Observation ▶ Polls and the Media ▶ Precision Journalism ▶ Public Opinion ▶ Sampling, Nonrandom ▶ Sampling, Random ▶ Statistics, Descriptive ▶ Survey

References and Suggested Readings

Bowley, A. (1915). *Livelihood and poverty*. London: Bell.

Cantril, H. (1944). *Gauging public opinion*. Princeton, NJ: Princeton University Press.

Couper, M. P., Traugott, M. W., & Lamias, M. J. (2001). Web survey design and administration. *Public Opinion Quarterly*, 65, 230–253.

Dodd, S. (1946). Toward world surveying. *Public Opinion Quarterly*, 10, 470–483.

Hansen, J. (1982). *Das Panel: Zur Analyse von Verhaltens- und Einstellungswandel* [The use of panel surveys to analyze change in behavior and attitude]. Opladen: Westdeutscher.

Noelle-Neumann, E., & Petersen, T. (2005). *Alle, nicht jeder: Einführung in die Methoden der Demoskopie* [All but not each: Introduction to the methods of survey research], 4th edn. Berlin: Springer.

Oberschall, A. (1965). *Empirical social research in Germany 1848–1914*. Paris: Mouton.

Payne, S. (1951). *The art of asking questions*. Princeton, NJ: Princeton University Press.

Petersen, T. (2002). *Das Feldexperiment in der Umfrageforschung* [The field experiment in survey research]. Frankfurt am Main: Campus.

Petersen, T., Sabel, P., Grube, N., & Voß, P. (2004). Der Fragebogen Karls des Großen. Ein Dokument aus der Vorgeschichte der Umfrageforschung [Charlemagne's questionnaire: A document from the very beginnings of survey research]. *Kölner Zeitschrift für Soziologie und Sozialpsychologie* 56, 736–745.

Ring, E. (1992). *Signale der Gesellschaft: Psychologische Diagnostik in der Umfrageforschung* [Societal signals: Psychological diagnostics in survey research]. Göttingen: Verlag für angewandte Psychologie.

Sudman, S., Bradburn, N., & Schwarz, N. (1996). *Thinking about answers: The application of cognitive processes to survey methodology.* San Francisco, CA: Jossey-Bass.

Taylor, H. (1995). Horses for courses: How different countries measure public opinion in very different ways. *The Public Perspective* (February/March), 3–7.

Public Relations

A. A. Betteke van Ruler

University of Amsterdam

Robert L. Heath

University of Houston

However old the practice of public relations is (Heath 2005a), in the identity we know today it became a serious professional practice in the latter part of the nineteenth century in the USA and in other democratized parts of the world, especially in Europe. Its emergence paralleled the development of mass production society, as a means both for promoting goods and services and for engaging in public policy debates and issues management. The twentieth century witnessed the profession's development as a selected set of strategic best practices, an academic discipline to prepare future practitioners, and a subject for refinements through sophisticated scholarly investigation and discussion. Public relations is on its way to becoming a matured practice all over the world, not least because academic and professional development research continues to mature by generating a wide variety of perspectives and theoretical approaches.

NATURE AND IMAGE OF PUBLIC RELATIONS

In the opinion of some, public relations can be defined as the art of stealthy manipulation of → public opinion, of the opinions of consumers and of politicians. As viewed by some, it consists of spinning the truth to the selfish interest of some organization or interest, issue advocate, person, or viewpoint – usually to the disadvantage of others (→ Spin Doctor).

In contrast, public relations has equally been seen as a *professional practice and academic discipline* dedicated to spreading rational and trustworthy information from and about an organization in order to open up the organization and its practices for those who are interested (→ Professionalization of Public Relations). At the same time, public relations is also seen as a professional practice and academic discipline dedicated to fostering effective two-way communication between some organization or entity, such as an industry, and persons whose opinions can make or break the future success of the sponsor. Some discussants of the nature of public relations, for example in South Africa,

New Zealand, and the USA, have advocated that instead of focusing on fostering sham relationships, senior practitioners are first of all the consciences of their employers. They know better than other disciplines the moral standards by which their employers are judged. They advocate that first the organization must be good before it can be effective in its communication efforts. The core goal of public relations is then not so much to open the organization or produce good relationships as to help the organization to produce quality and acceptable strategic decisions.

Practitioners recognize both that the *challenge of ethics* is broad and that the devil is in the detail. Each strategic decision as well as each word that is spread can pose ethical challenges and, consequently, needs to be discussed in terms of its consequences for the well-being of the organization, of its publics, and of society at large. The first step in public relations is to create sound management policy that deserves the fruits of good will, as John W. Hill, the co-founding principal of Hill & Knowlton, argued in the mid-1900s. At the time of his retirement in the late 1960s, his firm was the largest in the world. "Public confidence in the corporation as an institution must be earned and deserved. 'Smart publicity' will never replace sound management policies and acts in building a solid foundation of good will," he rightly claimed (Hill 1958, 163).

HISTORY OF PUBLIC RELATIONS

Europe

To many, modern public relations was born in the USA at the end of the nineteenth century. That may be so for the naming of this phenomenon but not for the practice itself. World history in general and European history in particular offer many instances of what can be termed evidence of public relations practice, if not by that name. In Europe, public relations as practice has a long history (see for an overview, van Ruler & Verčič 2004). The period of the Enlightenment, as developed in the eighteenth century in France and Germany, strongly influenced the evaluation and practice of public relations in many European countries. In the eighteenth century, science and knowledge were no longer seen as being relevant only for the elite, but had to be diffused. One of the countries that were the first to institutionalize this concept as a practice was the Netherlands. The means for the diffusion of knowledge became known as "voorlichting," which is a literal Dutch translation of "enlightenment."

In the Netherlands the concept of "voorlichting" soon developed into institutionalized "giving full information to all people to enable them to mature and emancipate." Already in the mid-nineteenth century, the administration as well as civil society organizations started to introduce "voorlichters," specialists who traveled around to give information about health, good farming, housekeeping, sexuality, politics, etc. At the same time, the elite remained skeptical about this full enlightenment of ordinary people. That is why most of the time "voorlichting" was also used to show people how to conduct themselves as good citizens/subordinates and to control their behavior. When industrialization became a fact (late 1800s), industries started to provide information about themselves to the press as well as to the general public. The first official press departments originated in the early 1900s. The government soon followed. Dutch journalists, however, preferred to keep direct access to administrators and politicians. Thanks to the strong "pillarization" (denominational *segregation*) of the society, with each pillar using its own media and therefore its own political contacts, their lobby was successful for a long time and the governmental public relations departments were forced to aim their press releases at foreign journalists only.

Directly after World War II public relations became an established part of company life. The Dutch claim to have established the first national public relations association, in early 1946. There was an enormous growth in the area during the 1980s, when US management approaches became the vogue.

In *Germany* also, public relations has a long history, based on the concept of "Öffentlichkeit-sarbeit," which can be translated as "work for the public sphere." According to Bentele (1997), the first press offices engaged in politics and economics as well as in communities, associations, and organizations originated in the early 1900s. Alfred Krupp, founder of the steel company Krupp, established the first press department in a private company in 1870. The duty of this department was to read all newspapers that were considered important to the firm and at the same time to write articles, brochures, and "correspondences" in order to advertise products and the firm as a whole. As in the Netherlands, a characteristic feature of this first period is that public relations was used both to inform and to manipulate.

During the Weimar Republic (1918–1933), new social conditions arose such as the parliamentary, democratic state and an economically independent and active press; the media, no longer directed or controlled by the state, gave a boost to the growth of public relations. After the National Socialists came to power, the conditions of public relations changed abruptly. In sharp contrast with the Weimar period, the media were now controlled and manipulated by the party. After the end of World War II in 1945, not only did public relations have to redefine itself under the new conditions of a parliamentary democracy, it also had to dissociate itself from (Nazi) propaganda. The US influence on West German society was widely felt in the development of postwar public relations: besides new German advertising and public relations agencies, branches of US agencies started to settle in Germany (and in many other European countries), and today research in public relations has been established in several German-speaking universities in Germany, Switzerland, and Austria. Similar distancing occurred among US practitioners, who rejected the connection between propaganda and public relations even though they had initially embraced the connection and cut their professional teeth on propaganda efforts in support of both world wars.

Another country with early maturation of public relations is the *United Kingdom*. L'Etang (2004) placed the beginning of public relations in Britain in the 1920s. Emphasis focused especially on the role of local government, which contributed to public relations ideology and key concepts of professionalism. These articulated a strong public service ethos, laying the foundation of the (now Chartered) Institute of Public Relations, which was established in 1948. It all started with an emphasis on public service rather than on business activities being the roots of public relations in the UK (as well as in most of the Scandinavian countries and in Northern Ireland). Today, public relations seems more oriented toward propaganda and control, even within governmental departments.

Public relations is big business *all over Europe*, in the western as well as the eastern European countries. In most countries US agencies as well as US scholars have dominated the development, except for the German-speaking countries, Scandinavia, and France. In most of the eastern Europe countries public relations could only begin to flourish after the fall of the Soviet Regime in 1989. In all these countries public relations is growing rapidly and many universities provide bachelor's as well as master's degrees in public relations (often, however, named communication management or corporate communication). There is yet hardly any theory building in these countries and the practice has to lean on German, French, and Anglo-American approaches. Despite the US influence, robust innovations and new directions are being explored that may add important refinements to the understanding and practice of public relations internationally.

United States of America

Modern public relations in the United States started in the mid-nineteenth century. Its rise paralleled the mass media's growth, which allowed mass-produced publicity and promotion, as well as the sort of issues management that resulted from the efforts of the robber barons to craft the public policy that was needed to support a mass production society. The practice in the USA has been dominated by public relations agencies, such as Hill & Knowlton, Burson-Marsteller, and Porter Novelli, as well as the public relations departments of major corporations. It has also been a valued tool of activism and the management of government agencies. Scott Cutlip (1994) has written in depth on the history of public relations agencies in the United States. In Cutlip's opinion, the beginnings of modern public relations are found in the *American Revolution*, which brought the struggle for power between the patrician-led patriots and the commercial-propertied Tories – as well as indicting the British monarch for conditions that had become insufferable in the minds of leading colonial radicals. The twentieth-century developments in this field are directly tied to the power struggles evoked by the political reform movements led by master politicians from Theodore Roosevelt to Bill Clinton. These movements reflected strong tides of protest against entrenched power groups.

As a profession, the public relations vocation began with the establishment of the Publicity Bureau in Boston on the eve of the twentieth century and grew into large organizations. Starting with the rise of powerful monopolies, the concentration of wealth and power, and the rough-shod tactics of the robber barons in exploiting human labor and the nation's resources, contemporary public relations emerged out of the melee of the opposing forces in this period of the nation's rapid growth and emergence from isolationism into an imperial power, most of all for promotional and propagandistic reasons, Cutlip (1994) said. Efforts to refine the practice produced an interest in reshaping the profession as public affairs and issues management.

Although not the first pioneer in public relations, Ivy Lee remains today one of the most influential who helped define and build public relations. As a former journalist, he issued his *Declaration of principles* of public relations, which were, over time, to have a profound influence on the evolution of press agentry into publicity and of publicity into public relations. In an era of "the public be damned," his declaration accentuated the positive right of the public to know:

> This is not a secret press bureau. All our work is done in the open. We aim to supply news. This is not an advertising agency; if you think any of our matter ought properly to go to your

business office, do not use it. Our matter is accurate. Further details on any subject treated will be supplied promptly, and any editor will be assisted most cheerfully in verifying directly any statement of fact … In brief, our plan is frankly, and openly, on behalf of business concerns and public institutions, to supply the press and public of the United States prompt and accurate information concerning subjects which it is of value and interest to the public to know about. (Cutlip 1994, 45)

Also famous worldwide is Edward Bernays, who defined public relations as propaganda and the engineering of consent in the early 1900s.

Other Parts of the World

In other parts of the world public relations has been a timeless craft and now is a growing field. As on other continents, the practice of public relations in Asia can be traced back for over a thousand years, ever since emperors realized the importance of public opinion and building harmonious relationships with people.

The use of modern public relations started in the 1970s. In China, for example, public relations became popular after President Deng Xiaoping's decision to open China to the west. The popularity of the TV series *Miss Public Relations* in the late 1980s and early 1990s colored the perception of public relations among the Chinese, as the Chinese public relations scholars Flora Hung and Regina Chen detailed in Sriramesh (2004), where the development of public relations in Asia is described. The TV show, which showed young women hosting guests at expensive hotels, led most Chinese to think that public relations professionals were only involved in guest relations. In recent years, as multinational companies established a foothold in the country, Chinese practitioners and scholars wanted to incorporate western perspectives of public relations practice. The fundamental question was how to apply the western concept of public relations – brought in by young scholars who had studied in the United States – in a Chinese context. With the unique characteristic in Chinese culture of maintaining harmonious relationships with people, relationships are more critical and require more distinct obligations in China than in the west, Hung and Chen claim. That is why public relations in Asian countries can best be seen as a combination of western (USA-oriented) approaches and the so-called personal influence approach.

Due to the constraints of an encyclopedia entry, we cannot give here a full picture of the development of public relations in the world. We encourage our readers to familiarize themselves with overviews of public relations on the different continents, as well as *The global public relations handbook* (Sriramesh & Verčič 2003), the *Encyclopedia of public relations* (Heath 2005b), and articles in *Public Relations Review* on the development of public relations in specific countries, for example in Latin America and Africa.

PUBLIC RELATIONS RESEARCH

The scholarly literature on public relations features one *generic principle* of public relations: It is the function that communicates for each organization and helps its management to favorably position the organization to earn the favor of targeted markets, audiences, publics, and society at large. This, however, is accomplished in different ways and guided by different theories. These theories define the different approaches to public relations, as can be found in the literature of the discipline. Some scholars seek one general theory of public relations. Perhaps it is to be seen as a proof of the effort to achieve the maturity of the discipline that so many perspectives exist and are challenged by so many researchers. Each perspective offers a unique and important contribution to theory building and valuable strategies to guide and foster ethical practice. For more details than can be provided here on theories and perspectives, see Bentele et al. (2005) (only in German), Botan and Hazleton (2006), Hansen-Horn and Neff (2007), Heath (2001b), and many other handbooks, as well as the *Encyclopedia of public relations* (Heath 2005b).

The Information Model

The information model of public relations focuses on the dissemination of information, which targets groups to inform (enlighten) them about the plans of the organization and the decisions made. In the former Soviet countries in Europe, one of the major topics is the education of the organization as well as the public to practice this information model, instead of the propagandistic persuasion model of the Soviet regime (Tampere 2003).

The information model is rooted in classical mass communication theories, such as the two-step flow of information (and the multi-step flow), the diffusion of innovations theory, the knowledge gap theory, the → uses-and-gratifications approach, and → information processing theories (→ Two-Step Flow of Communication; Diffusion of Information and Innovation; Knowledge Gap Effects). Successful public relations in this approach engages in informing the right people at the right time about the plans and decisions of the organization, but most people are not easy to reach directly, and the most widely used channels to inform key, targeted members of the public and society at large are consequently the mass media. Thus, informational communication management is primarily broadcasting management.

The Persuasion Model

The persuasion model of public relations focuses on the → persuasion of target groups to accept the organization's view on relevant issues, and is also known as the → corporate communication approach (van Riel & Fombrun 2007). The basis for this approach stems from Bernays's theory of public relations as propaganda (for an overview of his ideas, see Cutlip 1994), and the expanded introduction of a psychological approach to mass communication instead of a sociological one in the study of public relations, which give this model wings. The key aspect of these theories is the seeking of control through the assumptions of asymmetrical propaganda.

John Hill (1963, 6) offered tried and true advice for practitioners to be cautious about how they seek to persuade: "It functions in the dissemination of information and facts when non-controversial matters are involved. But when controversy exists, public relations may become the advocate before the bar of public opinion, seeking to win support through interpretation of facts and the power of persuasion." Whether such communication options on matters of controversy are → propaganda or rhetoric (→ Rhetorical Studies) can be examined by the extent to which the message is manipulated to obscure enlightened choice or framed to maximize it. Hill realized that propaganda could not be the rationale for public relations, but knew that organizations could not and should not avoid engaging in controversy, which starts with information and includes the interpretation of that information and the application of it to make informed and enlightened decisions.

Receiving and processing the message (which is key in the information model) is not enough here; the targeted public must also be convinced there is a predefined meaning for the situation rather than one that emerges through dialogue. Successful public relations, by this logic, means "*convinced publics*," or ensuring a positive image is held by important target groups. Since it is difficult to convince people, research is thought to be important for discovering what the publics will accept. Persuasive public relations is therefore primarily → *impression management*. Defined by both means and ends, persuasion can corrupt public relations if it presumes only to advantage the source and to control the judgments and actions of a targeted public.

The Critical Model

Habermas (1962; → Habermas, Jürgen) claimed that the development of public relations and advertising changed open democratic → discourse into a non-critical force of acclamation of the powerful elite. In light of this view, critical models of public relations have been developed, with a main tradition in the United Kingdom. Cottle (2003) edited a volume with different critical approaches (see also Davis 2002). Critical approaches to public relations are rooted in symbolic interactionism, the cultural approach of Stuart Hall, the sociology of news production, and social drama theory.

As in the persuasion model, public relations is seen as a persuasive power, tough not from the angle of the benefit of the organization, but from the angle of the benefit to (or deficit from) society as a whole. What may be successful public relations for the organization is not necessarily successful (or even detrimental) for society, these scholars argue. Critical perspectives will call public relations impression management or spinning.

The Two-Way-Symmetry Model

Grunig et al. (2002) offered a critical view, but not so much from a societal perspective as from a strategic management perspective based on the logics of → systems theory. They call the scientific persuasion model an asymmetrical approach to public relations that presumes that to solve a relationship problem a key public has only to alter its view to conform to that preferred by the organization. Grunig et al. prefer a two-way-symmetrical model, in which relationships are built and maintained through → interaction. The essence of the interaction is to understand the concerns of a public through research, make those concerns known to management, and seek appropriate changes in management policy. The aim of the relationship is the creation of consensus on important issues to avoid conflict and assure cooperation, for the sake of the publics as well as of the organization itself.

To accomplish this outcome, it is important to focus on communication processes not toward publics or target groups, but between interdependent parties. The premise is that communication between parties will lead to a *balance of interests*. Another premise is that parties are willing to act as involved and rational citizens instead of selfish consumers and producers. Theoretically this approach is rooted in balance theories of communication, e.g., co-orientation models (→ Co-Orientation Model of Public Relations; Intereffication Approach in Public Relations). In this approach, successful communication management is seen as negotiating with the publics for an acceptable meaning of issues, which is a matter of balancing the give and take. By this logic, two-way-symmetrical public relations is primarily negotiation management.

The Interpersonal Model

Most public relations theories are closely associated with mass communication. As early as 1984, Ferguson promoted the use of interorganizational and interpersonal relationship as the focus in public relations theory. Yet, in most public relations literature, relationships are conceptualized for the most part as interactions between groups ("publics") rather than individuals, Toth (2007) claimed.

Sallot was one of the first scholars to explore the rich interconnectedness of public relations practice and theory and interpersonal communication (IPC) theory in several presentations (see for an overview Sallot, 2005). Only recently (see, e.g., Botan & Hazleton 2006) have researchers started to apply IPC theory in a comprehensive manner to public relations and practice. The central logic of public relations theory derived from IPC theory is that relationship quality counts and that the quality of what is done by relational partners can increase or decrease the harmony between the partners. *Harmonious relationships* lead from and to an incentive to cooperate and support, to distribute resources that are available in the relationship. Disharmony results from qualitatively inferior relationships that give participants a motive to sanction relational partners.

Another typical interpersonal approach to public relations is the *interpersonal influence model*, developed in Asia (Sriramesh 2004) in order to feature the importance of interorganizational and interpersonal relationships in Asian countries. It is critical in this approach to make efforts to cultivate interorganizational and interpersonal relationships by exchanging gifts, favors, and hospitality and do this in an ethical manner. In this approach, successful public relations is most of all people management.

The Reflective Model

The reflective model of public relations (called communication management) is trying to integrate many of the leading perspectives on public relations. Dialogue is an important strategy to develop trust, but it is rather naïve to believe that it is an answer to all mistrust (van Ruler & Verčič 2005). First of all, it is impossible to engage all publics, let alone public opinion, in this dialogue; second, in most cases interests are fuzzy or conflicting. That is why managers use all kinds of strategies, including manipulation of frames (persuasion), in order to earn the favor of publics and get things done. The constraint on this manipulation is public legitimacy, which, because of increased public counteraction, has become increasingly necessary for business to survive.

The reflective model differentiates between the societal/institutional and the economic/administrative roles each organization plays in its public relations. The *economic role* is concerned with the meso- (group) and micro- (interpersonal) level of communication among members of the organization, and between the organization and its publics in order to become legitimate in the eyes of specific publics. The *societal role* is concerned with the macro-level of societal legitimization. Public relations is concerned with the reproduction of the underlying principles that enable organizations to emerge, develop, and prosper. Living in an organizational society, these organizational challenges are communicatively enacted.

This model also differentiates between the organization as organization and as institution. The reflective model looks at the organization as an empirical realization of an institution in society, and the organizational dimension is subordinate to the institutional dimension when it comes to survival. That is why public relations is empirically working in and through the social construction of public identity. In this approach, public relations is primarily concerned with public legitimatization, and in order to get public license to operate, it focuses on public opinion (the public sphere) as a quantity as well as a quality. The institutional dimension of an organization triggers the reflective model of public relations, while the organizational dimension triggers the existing models, now seen as strategies of the reflective model (van Ruler & Verčič 2005).

The primary concerns of public relations from a reflective approach are an organization's inclusiveness and preservation of the "license to operate." As marketing is viewing organization from a market view, reflective communication management is viewing organization from a societal or public view. The basic question in this approach to communication management lies in the empirical definition of what is seen as legitimate.

The Rhetorical Model

The rhetorical model builds on what has been called the rhetorical heritage reaching back to treatises central to the humanities, crafted by Plato, Aristotle, Isocrates, Quintilian, and many others, including more recently the work of Kenneth Burke and Chaim Perelman. This body of literature continues to be a robust part of the standard curriculum of well-educated persons and vital to the democratic spirit of countries around the world (Heath 2001a, 2007; → Rhetorical Theory of Public Relations).

The essence of the rhetorical model at its best is to know the strategies and forces that lead to co-created meaning, collaborative decision-making, and identification. It can also be applied to evil ends using offensive means. Enriched by reflective management and guided by the commitment to demonstrate cases through fact, weigh the values central to each case, and seek to recommend the wisest policy, public relations can apply the rhetorical heritage to increase the likelihood that interested markets, audiences, and publics can make enlightened choices as stakeholders and stakeseekers.

The essence of rhetoric is *statement and counter-statement*. It is advisory, invitational, and propositional, with as its basic paradigm a thoughtful contest between choices. At its best, it can lead to enlightenment and wise choice. At its worse, it obscures, obfuscates, and centers on ad hominem dispute that ultimately may be damaging (Ihlen 2002).

Thus, the theory and practice of public relations as relying on the rhetorical heritage arm it better to engage in discourse as the rationale for individual and collective decision-making in society. This approach allows insights into how meaning is crafted, how ideas are enlivened and framed, and the rich connections between the meanings of the actions of companies and those of other organizations, which are also part of the meaning they create, as well as yield to, in the fostering of harmonious and mutually beneficial relationships. In these endeavors, character counts, a theme that continues to be central to the rhetorical heritage. Not only does the character of the organization speaking add to or detract from the impact its opinions and information have, but the kinds of statements made, the care for the interests of others, and the efforts to achieve enlightenment and reveal good character add to the reputation of the organization.

In more current terms, the rhetorical model presumes that society is created for the collective management of risks. Each individual and organization is conjoined in this arrangement. Dialogue is the rationale for bringing information to bear on risks, but the evaluation of such information is not centered in one body, but institutionalized for the collective good of all members of the society.

THE FUTURE OF PUBLIC RELATIONS

The major work of Sriramesh and Verčič (2003), *The global public relations handbook*, shows that the democratization of the world, especially in the latter half of the twentieth century, goes hand in hand with an enormous growth of public relations all over the world, as well as the necessity of viewing public relations on a global scale. The rapid expansion of new communication technologies such as → satellite television and the → Internet has increased the dissemination of information about products, services, and lifestyles around much of the world, Sriramesh and Verčič claim. Coupled with the freedom that accompanies democratization, the result has been a significant increase in the global demand for products and services, as well as of global suppliers who can meet this demand.

As a result, countries in Africa, Asia, the Middle-East, eastern Europe, and Latin America have already become, or will soon become, major centers of manufacturing as well as consumption, requiring the organizations of these countries to trade and communicate with a global audience. The *formation of multinational trading blocks* has also contributed to shrinking the global market, thereby increasing organizational activities among and between trading blocks. These factors, Sriramesh and Verčič claim, have contributed to a significant spurt in global communication, placing public relations practitioners at the forefront of managing the relationships among people of varied nations and cultures on behalf of organizations of all types. For professionals to engage in strategic public relations management in a global setting, it is essential that they have knowledge of globalization and competencies in multicultural communication (→ Globalization Theories).

The major works of Heath (2001b) and Botan and Hazleton (2006) show how robust the discourse on public relations theory and practice has become. From the 1970s, when much of the discourse on the topic existed in a few textbooks, professional trade publications, and the emerging *Public Relations Review*, the discipline has grown steadily. The breadth and depth of analysis have increased. The discipline is slowly becoming less derivative and more original in its theory building. It continues to seek to make critical and practical advances that have pedagogical and real-world application.

Last but certainly not least, globalization and the necessity of corporate social responsibility will urge public relations to rethink its ethical devices and its position in the organization as well as in society (→ Public Relations Ethics). The question is how public relations, with such a tarnished image, can grow steadily into a professional and academic discipline by realizing its potential for making society more fully functional.

SEE ALSO: ► Change Management and Communication ► Consensus-Oriented Public Relations ► Contingency Model of Conflict ► Co-Orientation Model of Public Relations ► Corporate Communication ► Corporate Social Responsibility ► Crisis Communication ► Cultural Topoi in Public Relations ► Diffusion of Information and Innovation ► Discourse ► Excellence Theory in Public Relations ► Globalization Theories ► Habermas, Jürgen ► Impression Management ► Information Processing ► Interaction ► Intereffication Approach in Public Relations ► Internet ► Issue Management ► Knowledge Gap Effects ► Legitimacy Gap Theory ► Persuasion ► Professionalization of Public Relations ► Propaganda ► Public Affairs ► Public Diplomacy ► Public Opinion ► Public Relations Ethics ► Public Relations, Inter-cultural ► Rhetorical Studies ► Rhetorical Theory of Public Relations ► Satellite Television ► Spin Doctor ► Systems Theory ► Two-Step Flow of Communication ► Uses and Gratifications

References and Suggested Readings

Bentele, G. (1997). PR-Historiographie und funktional-integrative Schichtung: Ein neuer Ansatz zur PR-Geschichtsschreibung [PR historiography and functional-integral stratification: A new approach to PR historiography]. In P. Szyska (ed.), *Auf der Suche nach Identität: PR-Geschichte als Theoriebaustein* [The quest for identity: PR history as theoretical constituent]. Berlin: Vistas, pp. 137–169.

Bentele, G., Fröhlich, R., & Szyska, P. (eds.) (2005). *Handbuch der Public Relations: Wissenschaftliche Grundlagen und berufliches Handeln* [Handbook of public relations: Scientific perspectives and professional action]. Wiesbaden: VS Verlag für Sozialwissenschaften.

Botan, C. H., & Hazleton, V. (eds.) (2006). *Public relations theory II*. Mahwah, NJ: Lawrence Erlbaum.

Cottle, S. (ed.) (2003). *News, public relations and power*. Thousand Oaks, CA: Sage.

Cutlip, S. C. (1994). *The unseen power: Public relations – a history*. Hillsdale, NJ: Lawrence Erlbaum.

Cutlip, S. C., Center, A. H., & Broom, G. M. (2000). *Effective public relations*. Upper Saddle River, NJ: Prentice Hall.

Davis, A. (2002). *Public relations democracy: Public relations, politics, and the mass media in Britain*. Manchester and New York: Manchester University Press.

Ferguson, M. A. (1984). Building theory in public relations: Interorganizational relationships as a public relations paradigm. Paper presented to the Public Relations Division at the annual meeting of the Association for Education in Journalism and Mass Communications, Gainesville, FL.

Grunig, L. A., Grunig, J. E., & Dozier, D. M. (2002). *Excellent public relations and effective organizations: A study of communication management in three countries*. Mahwah, NJ: Lawrence Erlbaum.

Habermas, J. (1962). *Strukturwandel der Öffentlichkeit: Untersuchungen zu einer Kategorie der bürgerlichen Gesellschaft* [Change of the structure of the public sphere: Investigation into a category of citizen's society]. Darmstadt: Luchterhand.

Hansen-Horn, T. L., & Neff, B. D. (eds.) (2007). *Public relations: From theory to practice*. Boston: Pearson.

Heath, R. L. (2001a). A rhetorical enactment rationale for public relations: The good organization communicating well. In R. L. Heath (ed.), *Handbook of public relations*. Thousand Oaks, CA: Sage, pp. 31–50.

Heath, R. L. (ed.) (2001b). *Handbook of public relations*. Thousand Oaks, CA: Sage.

Heath, R. L. (2005a). Antecedents of modern public relations. In R. L. Heath (ed.), *Encyclopedia of public relations*. Thousand Oaks, CA: Sage, pp. 32–37.

Heath, R.L. (ed.) (2005b). *Encyclopedia of public relations*. Thousand Oaks, CA: Sage.

Heath, R. L. (2007). Rhetorical theory, public relations, and meaning: Giving voice to ideas. In T. L. Hansen-Horn & B. D. Neff (eds.), *Public relations: From theory to practice*. Boston: Pearson, pp. 208–226.

Hill, J. W. (1958). *Corporate public relations: Arm of modern management*. New York: Harper.

Hill, J. W. (1963). *The making of a public relations man*. New York: David McKay.

Ihlen, Ø. (2002). Rhetoric and resources: Notes for a new approach to public relations and issues management. *Journal of Public Affairs*, 2(4), 259–269.

L'Etang, J. (2004). *Public relations in Britain: A history of professional practice in the 20th century*. Mahwah, NJ: Lawrence Erlbaum.

Riel, C. B. M. van, & Fombrun, C. J. (2007). *Essentials of corporate communication*. London and New York: Routledge.

Ruler, B. van, & Verčič, D. (eds.) (2004). *Public relations and communication management in Europe*. Berlin and New York: Mouton de Gruyter.

Ruler, B. van, & Verčič, D. (2005). Reflective communication management: Future ways for public relations research. In P. J. Kalbfleisch (ed.), *Communication yearbook 29*. Mahwah, NJ: Lawrence Erlbaum, pp. 239–274.

Sallot, L. M. (2005). Interpersonal communication theory. In R. L. Heath (ed.), *Encyclopedia of public relations*. Thousand Oaks, CA: Sage, pp. 442–444.

Sriramesh, K. (ed.) (2004). *Public relations in Asia: An anthology*. Singapore: Thompson Learning.

Sriramesh, K., & Verčič, D. (eds.) (2003). *The global public relations handbook: Theory, research, and practice*. Mahwah, NJ: Lawrence Erlbaum.

Tampere, K. (2003). *Public relations in a transition society 1989–2002: Using a stakeholder approach in organizational communications and relations analyses*. Jyväskylä: University of Jyväskylä.

Toth, E. L. (2007). Creating public relations through interpersonal communication: A review essay. Paper presented to the Public Relations Division at the annual convention of the International Communication Association, San Francisco, May.

Public Relations Ethics

Shannon A. Bowen

University of Maryland

A core responsibility of communicators in public relations is to manage issues (→ Issue Management; Communication Management). Public relations holds the substantial moral responsibility of defining issues, communicating about those issues with publics and the media, and working to prevent and resolve problems between organizations and publics. This weighty responsibility includes deciding what concepts are related or unrelated to an issue, what facts are relevant or irrelevant, and what potential solutions exist. A moral responsibility to conduct these activities in an ethical manner is inherent in pursuits of such significance, and public relations professionals worldwide are therefore obligated to act with ethical rectitude by the very nature of their responsibilities (→ Corporate Social Responsibility).

Critics argue that public relations has no ethical compass, engages in unrestrained advocacy, or even that it is among the most immoral of fields (→ Advertising Ethics; Ethics in Journalism). Proponents argue that public relations professionals should (and do) act as "ethical consciences" within their organizations, or for clients. Both points of view are able to offer examples and cases in which their beliefs are illustrated. Ethical public relations is one of the foundations of the research supporting excellent public relations management (Verčič et al. 1996; Grunig 2001; Bowen 2007), making management more reflective and responsible to external publics. Others (van Ruler & Verčič 2005) expound on the societal role of the legitimation of organizations in society and the role that public relations plays in enabling communication that contributes to social discourse. Although debate continues, the majority of scholars and authorities on public relations argue that the field has a basis in ethics stemming from the moral nature of informed free choice, education and rational debate on issues, and the duty of dialogue.

Consideration of the power held by public relations to communicate and define issues necessitates analysis of public relations activities through the lens of moral philosophy. Both utilitarian and deontological (Kantian) approaches support the view of public relations as an ethical pursuit. A utilitarian analysis concludes that public relations serves the interest of the greater good by providing a free and open flow of information and discourse for the greatest number of people, thereby benefiting society as a moral good.

Philosopher Immanuel Kant's deontological approach provides arguably the most rigorous and analytical moral analysis yet developed. Autonomy is central to Kant's deontological approach because he argued that *only* the rational will, free of subjectivity, can conduct an ethical analysis. Rational autonomy, or free moral choice, implies the knowledge, access to information, and debate of competing interests necessary to make an analytically sound judgment of right versus wrong. Therefore, the public relations function bears a moral responsibility because it facilitates communication between organizations and publics, supporting the ethical standards of autonomy and dialogue.

Ethical issues are also examined in terms of asking whether they maintain the dignity and respect of the involved publics and organization(s), as well as whether the moral test of a good will can be met. If it can, the intention behind the decision is one to uphold a moral choice rather than serve selfish ends. In this sense, public relations is responsible for consistent organizational decision-making that helps build long-term relationships with publics. Research shows that these relationships are based on trust, among other variables. Ethical decisions work to enhance trust, and trust enhances the reputation of the organization as a credible and morally responsible entity (→ Trust of Publics).

Analysis of ethical issues is complex and time-consuming for public relations professionals, particularly in industries with an inherent level of danger, risk, or proneness to crises. The extent to which ethical analyses take place in public relations practice varies widely. The degree to which the public relations executive acts as an ethics counselor to management depends not only on the type of industry involved, but also upon the expertise, age, ethics background or training, credibility, and persistence of the public relations professional.

As the builders of relationships and stewards of organizational reputation, public relations professionals are also obligated *to act as ethics counsel*. Research in public relations has shown that the public relations executive acting as an ethics counselor to the CEOs and top decision-makers is a common role in many organizations. These senior-level public relations executives are charged with examining issues from multiple perspectives, including those of publics external to the organization, to determine ethical organizational actions and policy. Because of the extensive research conducted by public relations, as well as the relationships public relations professionals maintain with publics, the function is ideally situated to consider the views and needs of publics who would not, otherwise, have a voice in management decision-making.

Public relations professionals often ascribe to codes of ethics held by *professional associations*, such as the International Public Relations Association (IPRA) across many countries, the European Public Relations Education and Research Association (Euprera) with membership in Europe, the Public Relations Society of America (PRSA) in the US, or the International Association of Business Communicators (IABC) with members in most countries. Each of these organizations holds a code of ethics applying to its membership, encouraging responsible, professional, credible, and well-intentioned public relations activities. The content of these codes of ethics varies not by country but by organization; for instance, the PRSA code attempts to offer practical professional guidance geared toward consultants and agency practitioners, while the IPRA code specifies certain moral duties that much be upheld, involving dignity and respect, human rights, and so on. The first code of ethics specific to modern public relations was codified by Ivy Lee in 1906, and the Arthur W. Page Society, based in the US, works to advance the ethical principles Page used in his distinguished public relations career at AT&T.

Although codes of ethics evidence good intent, they often provide conduct guidelines rather than the framework for a comprehensive moral analysis. Therefore, public relations scholars have worked to create formalized means of analyzing ethical dilemmas: Bowen (2004, 2005) created a deontological analysis; Bivins (1992) a systems-theory based analysis; Tilley (2005) a management approach; and, Pearson (1989) a dialogue-based approach. Both academically and professionally, public relations ethics is growing in demand, in responsibility, and in importance. Though no single person or function can be the entire "conscience" of an organization, public relations is ideally situated to know and counsel top management on the values of publics when resolving ethical issues. Public relations managers conduct moral analyses to guide the activities of their organizations, their clients, and their communications with publics and the media. Attention to ethical decision-making facilitates the building and maintenance of relationships, which is the overall goal of the public relations function.

SEE ALSO: ▶ Advertising Ethics ▶ Communication Management ▶ Corporate Social Responsibility ▶ Ethics in Journalism ▶ Ethics of Media Content ▶ Issue Management ▶ Organization–Public Relationships ▶ Professionalization of Public Relations ▶ Public Relations ▶ Trust of Publics

References and Suggested Readings

Bivins, T. H. (1992). A systems model for ethical decision making in public relations. *Public Relations Review*, 18(4), 365–383.

Bowen, S. A. (2004). Expansion of ethics as the tenth generic principle of public relations excellence: A Kantian theory and model for managing ethical issues. *Journal of Public Relations Research*, 16(1), 65–92.

Bowen, S. A. (2005). A practical model for ethical decision making in issues management and public relations. *Journal of Public Relations Research*, 17(3), 191–216.

Bowen, S. A. (2007). The extent of ethics. In E. L. Toth (ed.), *The future of excellence in public relations and communication management: Challenges for the next generation*. Mahwah, NJ: Lawrence Erlbaum, pp. 275–297.

Grunig, J. E. (2001). Two-way symmetrical public relations: Past, present, and future. In R. L. Heath (ed.), *Handbook of public relations*. Thousand Oaks, CA: Sage, pp. 11–30.

Koten, J. A. (ed.) (2004). *Building trust: Leading CEOs speak out – How they create it, strengthen it, sustain it*. New York: Arthur W. Page Society.

Pearson, R. (1989). Business ethics as communication ethics: Public relations practice and the idea of dialogue. In C. H. Botan & V. Hazleton, Jr. (eds.), *Public relations theory*. Hillsdale, NJ: Lawrence Erlbaum, pp. 111–131.

Seeger, M. W. (1997). *Ethics and organizational communication*. Cresskill, NJ: Hampton Press.

Tilley, E. (2005). The ethics pyramid: Making ethics unavoidable in the public relations process. *Journal of Mass Media Ethics*, 20(4), 305–320.

van Ruler, B., & Verčič, D. (2005). Reflective communication management: Future ways for public relations research. *Communication Yearbook*, 29, 239–273.

Verčič, D., Grunig, L. A., & Grunig, J. E. (1996). Global and specific principles of public relations: Evidence from Slovenia. In H. M. Culbertson & N. Chen (eds.), *International public relations: A comparative analysis*. Mahwah, NJ: Lawrence Erlbaum, pp. 31–65.

Public Relations Evaluation

Don W. Stacks

University of Miami

Evaluation is a management tool that allows the user to establish whether a project or campaign has had its intended effect. Effective evaluation is at the center of any public relations effort and should be a basic element of any planned public relations action. In reality, however, evaluation is often overlooked or not undertaken for a variety of reasons, including costs, lack of resources, or simply a failure to understand how to conduct basic evaluation. Basic evaluation provides the user not only with information on how well the project worked, but also with an indication during the project as to whether it is "on target," or "on phase" (→ Public Relations).

Further, effective evaluations are based on *four assumptions*, that are tied to project outcomes and/or business or client needs. First, public relations evaluation assumes that the decision-making process is basically the same across all entities or businesses. This assumption establishes that evaluation is both systematic and applicable to a variety of situations. Second, all evaluation is based on realistic goals with measurable outcomes based on a set strategy and tactics that are implemented to bring the strategies to life. That is, all evaluation has expectations that are rooted in daily practice, associated with specific strategies (that, in turn, employ specific tactics), aimed at meeting measurable objectives (that, in turn, are tuned to "reachable" goals tied to client or business goals). Third, evaluation is divided into three general stages: development, refinement, and evaluation. This assumption suggests that evaluation is a continual process, which begins with project evaluation, is refined as it is implemented, and has a final evaluation against its objectives and ultimately against the client or business goals. Finally, evaluation is knowledge-based and behavior-driven. This assumption underlies the fact that evaluation decisions are made with forethought and that there are measurable criteria against which project outcomes can be tested.

PUBLIC RELATIONS GOALS AND OBJECTIVES

As noted above, all public relations projects must start with realistic goals and measurable objectives. These goals and objectives derive from the problem statement – a statement that succinctly states what the project is seeking to do, what ends it is trying to achieve. The problem statement will in turn focus on the public relations goal, that will be tied to both tactical (output) and strategic (outtake and outcome) decision-making. An output is a tactic, e.g., a media release, video news release (VNR), or speech. It is the technical element and comprises what is to be done to meet the objectives. The outtake is the initial evaluation of the output: has it accomplished its intended purpose? The outcome is whether or not the strategy that employed the tactics actually "moved the needle," met or surpassed its objectives to reach both public relations and client/business goals.

A goal is simply something that is desired. In a political campaign, it is to win the election (→ Election Campaign Communication). In a → branding project it is to establish, maintain, or expand the → brand. In a corporate project it may be to have employees sign up for certain benefits. The goal should be reasonable; the desire to corner 100 percent of a market with a new brand may be achievable, but improbable. Objectives come from goals. They are the things we seek to assess during and at the end of the project. *Public relations objectives* fall into three areas: informational (was the message sent out, received, and understood?), motivational (did it change or reinforce attitudes and behavioral intentions?), and behavioral (did the targeted audience do what the message asked?). Informational and behavioral objectives are fairly easy to set and evaluate; motivational objectives, however, are harder and require that the evaluation assess cognitive, affective, and intended behavioral aspirations. Good evaluation will employ a *triangulated research approach* – it will use multiple research methods to evaluate each of the three objectives during and after the project (→ Triangulation).

EVALUATION PHASES

All evaluation is phase-oriented. The first phase *develops the project* and its evaluation. This pre-project phase sets or establishes the benchmarks against which the project will be evaluated at selected times. Benchmarking is a form of evaluation in and of itself; it provides the project with a current knowledge base against which to plan and helps to establish realistic objectives. The benchmark phase also provides information about competition, identifies potential problems, and may help to preplan strategy in cases where objectives are not being met.

The second phase occurs once the project has begun and, based on periodic evaluation, *refines the strategy and tactics employed* to meet specified objectives (or may result in the altering of the objectives themselves).

The third phase occurs post-project as a *final evaluation* and establishes whether the objectives have been met and the goal achieved. Final evaluation reviews the entire project, from benchmarking to final outcome and provides evaluation of strategy and tactics, as well as a cost–benefit analysis.

EVALUATION METHODS

Evaluation methods employed in a public relations project run the gamut of possible → research methods. Some evaluation simply requires counting whether a target audience – possibly an intervening audience, such as editors or reporters – receives, evaluates, and then forwards the outputs to the intended → public. Other evaluation may require outtake analyses: were the messages transmitted to targeted publics with the intended results, that is, was the tone of the actual article or broadcast what was intended? This goes beyond a count of simple pick-up, it looks at how the message was evaluated by a third party whose endorsement may add to or detract from its intended effect.

Similar research methods are employed across the three phases of evaluation. They are generally classified as being either formal (scientific and quantitative; → Quantitative Methodology) or informal (humanistic or qualitative; → Qualitative Methodology). During the developmental phase, however, a third methodology is typically added – historical or secondary research. Throughout the public relations project different methods are employed and compared one against the other to insure that the evaluation is providing decision-makers with reliable and valid information.

Reliability and Validity

Evaluation methods differ in terms of both → reliability and → validity of the "data" collected and analyzed. The terms "qualitative" and "humanistic" are applied to data gathered with the intent of a deep understanding of specific individuals or cases but not meant to be extended to a larger population or public. The difference is to be found in use. Quantitative data establish norms (or parameters) against which groups can be compared, but in establishing a norm any individual differences are lost.

Quantitative methods have established ways of testing for reliability of response or observation. As such, they can tell the evaluator within a certain degree of confidence that the responses will be similar among other members of the public from which they were taken. Once reliability has been established, validity of response can be established – both in terms of logical and of statistical analyses. Hence, an advantage of the quantitative method is that reliability and validity can be judged and extrapolation to larger groups possibly inferred.

Qualitative data, on the other hand, comes from a much smaller sample and often from the interview of selected individuals. Qualitative data has a deeper meaning, is valid only for those persons being interviewed, and has real reliability problems – that is, it is valid for that group or individual, but may not reliably represent others from the public from which they come.

Evaluation Methodologies

Evaluation methods can be divided into *four general classes* – historical/secondary, qualitative, quantitative, and content analysis. Historical/secondary methods evaluate extant data. Qualitative methods collect data from individuals or small groups of individuals whose → generalizability is limited but which is valid for those individuals; the data obtained is typically based on what was said or interpreted. Quantitative methods generally seek to gather information that can be reduced to numeric evaluation and in the case of survey or poll methods may be generalized to larger groups. Content analysis is a combination of qualitative and quantitative methods and examines the actual messages that are employed in public relations projects or campaigns (→ Content Analysis, Quantitative; Content Analysis, Qualitative).

Historical/Secondary Methods

Almost all projects will have some historical context from which to obtain the data required to establish where the project is before it actually begins. This information may come from association sources, previous research, annual reports, and news reporting of similar industries or products or persons. In many cases other departments may have the data required to establish a starting point. The Internet has made the gathering of historical and secondary data, as well as access to documentation, much easier than before. The gathering and evaluation of extant information often points to gaps in the project knowledge base, places where additional data is required to gain the "big picture" of the project and its project environment. In the rare case where data are missing, contemporary information must be obtained – primarily through qualitative and quantitative methods.

Qualitative Methods

Three qualitative methods found in public relations evaluation are in-depth interviews, focus groups, systematic observation/participant observation, and the → case study. *In-depth interviews* are the most controlled of the qualitative methods and are often used when trying to obtain data from opinion leaders, innovators, or people who are held in high esteem through their contact with target audiences (→ Interview, Qualitative). *Focus groups*, or what have been called "controlled group discussions," allow for a degree of control over questions, but allow participants to qualify their ideas, agree or disagree with others, and "tag on" to current threads of conversation; they provide the researcher with invaluable insight as to why something may or may not work. *Observation* – whether simple systematic "environmental scanning" or a planned participant observation study –

provides information about the real-world activities of people (→ Observation). Observation is something that is often overlooked in planned evaluation, but is a method that provides additional insight into project management.

The *case study* is an in-depth look at previous projects or campaigns from a historical perspective and is found in three different forms. The linear approach examines the case from beginning to end, with a focus on the particular elements employed in the project – basic research undertaken, project objectives, project programming, and project evaluation – as a static analysis of the case under study. Process-oriented case studies take into consideration the feedback process associated with the case, with evaluation first appearing at the second of four phases (fact-finding/problem analysis, strategic planning, action, and assessment). The grounded case study takes a management-by-objective (MBO) approach and includes analysis of the project's financial impact and its impact on the business bottom line. Traditionally, linear and process-oriented case studies have focused on the communication process while the grounded case study has looked more at business strategy. All provide essential information for the planning of a public relations project or campaign.

Quantitative Methods

Quantitative methods can be further divided into scientific and social scientific camps. Most public relations evaluation takes a social science approach and focuses on survey and poll methodology in gathering data on small samples of larger populations or publics.

Survey or poll methodology seeks to understand the attitudes or behavioral intentions (norms) of target audiences (→ Survey; Public Opinion Polling). Polls are shorter, more behavior-oriented collections of questions that seek to take snapshots of the target. Surveys are much longer and take an in-depth look at the target audience or public. Both collect samples (representative or nonrepresentative members of the population or universe being studied), most commonly face to face, by telephone, by mail, or on the → Internet. Sample selection can conducted as a "probability" or convenience ("nonprobability") sampling. Probability sampling occurs when all members of the population have equal chances of being selected; convenience sampling occurs when only those present in a given environment are selected to participate in data gathering (e.g., random intercept or mall survey; → Sampling, Random; Sampling, Nonrandom).

Scientific approaches are more *experimental*, where variables of interest ("independent variables," such as messages or channels) are varied and their impact on desired outcome variables ("dependent variables," such as purchase intent, relationship, reputation). Very sophisticated projects may even simulate under differing conditions the projected impact of the project on the outcome(s) of interest (→ Experimental Design).

Content analysis spans the qualitative–quantitative gulf. Since the method examines messages, it may be considered qualitative and as such may evaluate message content via rhetorical analysis thematic structure, purpose, and so forth. However, content analysis also allows a quantitative evaluation of the message such as number of words, basic tone of message, number of times a certain word or phrase is found, readability indices (e.g., Flesch Reading Ease or Flesch–Kincaid Grade Level indices), or type–token ratio. Content analysis has been computerized for faster analysis with the Internet allowing for almost real-time message acquisition and analysis.

Establishing Metrics

Prior to actually beginning data acquisition, evaluation metrics need to be established. A metric is a way to provide both focused and continuous project evaluation. Metrics run the gamut from dashboards to scorecards. Metrics are management tools that take the results of data gathered through qualitative and quantitative methods and relate them to project objectives, specific outtakes or outcomes, or other indicators that are monitored and evaluated on a regular basis.

Some metrics, such as *balanced scorecards*, are evaluated on a regular basis, but not continuously. Dashboards, on the other hand, are set up to monitor data as it comes in and provide day-by-day, minute-by-minute evaluations. What is common to each, however, is the data gathered, some of which may be compared to pre-project benchmarks or to established benchmarks throughout the project. Scorecards typically examine specific indicators against other indicators – either competitor-based or project-based – and are presented typically as numeric data. Dashboards are often more graphical and present data in terms of analogical measures, such as clocks, fever graphs, or other chart-like presentations. Evaluation metrics should be established during the pre-project, development phase.

Developmental Phase Methodology

Developmental phase evaluation focuses primarily on gathering data against which to compare project results over the life of the project. As such, it often begins with a set of methods that are neither qualitative nor quantitative. Development phase research is often rooted in historical or secondary research. It may, of course collect new data to update what has been obtained from historical and secondary sources or, because of a lack of historical or secondary research, require that benchmark data be gathered as a pre-project requirement through qualitative or quantitative methods.

In preparing for a project or campaign certain information should be readily available. This information may be collected, culled, and interpreted to establish an initial baseline or benchmark against which periodic checks can be conducted at later phases. An all too common characteristic of previous public relations evaluation has been a failure to establish a baseline – often based on the assumption that data at this stage is too expensive to gather.

During the developmental phase in-depth interviews, focus groups, observation, and previous case studies provide the background against which to compare the public relations activities during the campaign. Selected interviews and focus groups may be employed to gather an in-depth understanding of what strategies and tactics will produce the desired results and when and where secondary benchmarks (employed during the refinement phase) should be gathered. The developmental phase will set the actionable and measurable objectives to be met during the campaign.

Quantitative methods seek to establish the expected attitudinal and behavioral norms as target audience/public benchmarks. Survey methodology is often applied where historical/secondary analysis fails to produce expected attitudinal or behavioral norms. In some cases the projected campaign will be submitted to experimental method and a simulated campaign run against differing conditions (market or competition, for instance).

Content analyses are often undertaken to better understand how similar messaging has been interpreted by opinion leaders or reactions of focus groups to messages. This may take the form of pre-project message testing, concept testing, and so forth.

Refinement Phase Methodology

During the refinement phase evaluations are undertaken to see if the project is on target and schedule. This phase employs survey or poll, in-depth interview, focus group, and content analyses methods, often triangulated to provide the normative data required for larger population against the deeper and "richer" data from interviews and focus groups. Content analyses provide indicators that key messaging is getting out and that opinion leaders, editors, or reporters are on message. Observation continues to be an important informal methodology, such as observing during the day how many times and how people communicate on message ("word of mouth").

Data gathered during the refinement phase is evaluated against set objectives. This evaluation allows for alterations in strategy and tactics once the project has begun. As with most planned events, once the project is kicked off many things may alter the way intended messages are interpreted: the competition may engage in counter-messaging, or the target audience simply is not getting the information or, once received, is not being motivated to act. Finally, refinement phase evaluation seeks to make better predictions about actual behavior – that which drives the return on investment and project goals in most cases.

Final Phase Methodology

Final phase methodology is typically divided into three areas. First, was the goal met? Did the project move the needle? Did it meet or surpass expectations and how did it contribute to the client or company bottom line? Second, each objective is examined to evaluate both the strategy and tactics employed. Were objectives met? Were they on target? Were they on schedule? All the data gathered during the development and refinement stages are evaluated against final outcome(s). In some ways this is a meta-evaluation of the campaign and may yield an internal case study that can be used for future projects as baseline or benchmark data. Finally, a cost–product evaluation is undertaken. Here the evaluation focuses on whether the project was cost-effective, that the goal(s) and objective(s) were on target. Was the project cost-effective or were developmental estimates off so that the project could have come in for less? These are the hard questions that are always asked at the final evaluation phase.

Evaluation is an important factor in any public relations project. It should be planned across three phases and take into account both the project goal(s) and the objective(s). Objectives must be actionable and measurable and the methods selected to gather data should be triangulated to gain the best insight into project effectiveness.

SEE ALSO: ▶ Branding ▶ Brands ▶ Case Studies ▶ Content Analysis, Qualitative ▶ Content Analysis, Quantitative ▶ Election Campaign Communication ▶ Experimental Design ▶ Generalizability ▶ Internet ▶ Interview, Qualitative ▶ Measurement Theory ▶ Observation ▶ Public ▶ Public Opinion Polling ▶ Public Relations ▶ Qualitative

Methodology ▶ Quantitative Methodology ▶ Reliability ▶ Research Methods ▶ Sampling, Nonrandom ▶ Sampling, Random ▶ Survey ▶ Triangulation ▶ Validity

References and Suggested Readings

Brody, E. W., & Stone, G. C. (1989). *Public relations research*. New York: Praeger.

Broom, G. M., & Dozier, D. M. (1990). *Using research in public relations: Applications to program management*. Englewood Cliffs, NJ: Prentice Hall.

Carroll, T., & Stacks, D. W. (2004). *Bibliography of public relations measurement*. Gainesville, FL: Institute for Public Relations.

Hocking, J. E., Stacks, D. W., & McDermott, S. T. (2003). *Communication research*, 3rd edn. Boston: Allyn and Bacon.

Stacks, D. W. (2002). *Primer of public relations research*. New York: Guilford.

Stacks, D. W. (2006). *Dictionary of public relations measurement and research*. Gainesville, FL: Institute for Public Relations.

Public Relations Field Dynamics

Peter Szyszka

Zurich University of Applied Sciences

Systems theory reveals that organizations are integrated into their social environment by means of a network of relationships (→ Systems Theory). In part, this rationale of organizational success motivated Harlow, who used the term → "public relations" (PR) to describe the field of "all types of relations an organization has with its publics" (1957, xi; → Organization–Public Relationships). Systems theory and relationship analysis help explain why PR can be reciprocally activated: an organization and its reference groups observe, analyze, and rate each other regularly, particularly when it seems to be relevant because of expected risks and chances. On the organizational side, it is the task of PR activities to arrange these processes as communication management and to intervene communicatively if it seems to be necessary or expedient.

How each organization understands and appreciates its reference groups' opinions, acceptance, and/or behavior will affect how the organization responds to these groups. For effective PR interventions to be made, the relevant reference groups must be identified and their positions on various issues evaluated, along with their attitudes toward the organization. This, in turn, requires appropriate methods. The concept of public relations field dynamics – presented to a professional audience for the first time in 1992 – is one such method. It can be used to identify central qualities of PR, to demonstrate them in context, and to track them over time (→ Organizational Image; Corporate Reputation).

THEORETICAL CONCEPT

The model of public relations field dynamics (PRFD) offers a simple but effective instrument for the observation and description of changes in the relationships between several organizations and publics in any network. For instance, the *situational theory of publics* (→ Publics: Situational Theory) makes it possible to define – on the basis of three indicators (awareness of problems, awareness of consternation, and disposition of engagement) – the attitude of each single reference group toward an organization, and allows practitioners to predict behavior by analyzing the situation (Grunig & Hunt 1984). Alternatively, the *system of markets of opinion* can be applied to differentiate several basic frames of public communication (Szyszka 2005). The PRFD method provides a combined observation and graphical presentation of different reference groups in a group field, and clarifies changes in the network of relationships by comparing the results over time and by various positions on a specific issue.

The PRFD model also works with *three indicators*: valuation of relationship, valuation of → attitude, and degree of influence. Initially, the current status of the relationships between an organization and its reference groups is identified and graphically presented. The synopsis of the findings also makes clear and measurable the relationships between the different reference groups. If the status is defined periodically or if it changes under the influence of incidents (e.g., disputes), the dynamic in the field of PR can be demonstrated and strategically evaluated. In order to make prognoses it is not sufficient to evaluate the actual situation (i.e., take a snapshot). As this situation is the result of a process whose further development should be predicted, the earlier development of the group field has also to be included in the analysis.

Issue management tracks the development of issue careers in public communication in order to draw conclusions with regard to risks, chances, or the possible need for action (→ Issue Management). PRFD focuses – under the influence of the development of public communication – on the reference groups. The two methods complement each other. Methodologically, the PRFD system is adapted from the system for the multiple-level observation of groups (SYMLOG) theory proposed by Bales and Cohen (1979), which is a social psychological method for the analysis of the development of relationships in small groups. In its graphic representation, SYMLOG takes the form of a three-dimensional field diagram. The two orthogonal dimensions – "task orientation" (controlled versus emotionally expressive behavior on the vertical axis) and "social emotional orientation" (friendliness versus unfriendliness on the horizontal axis) – build a field in which a third, also bipolar dimension called "degree of influence" (dominance versus submissiveness) is positioned as a target circle. Springston adapted the SYMLOG model to describe PR in an appropriate way (Springston et al. 1992; Springston & Keyton 2001). While the dimensions of "social emotional orientation" and "degree of influence" have been retained, he changed the dimension of "task orientation" to one of "community orientation versus self-orientation."

These dimensions can be described as follows. By measuring respondents' perceptions, the dimension of "friendly versus unfriendly relationship" *(valuation of relationship)* expresses the basic orientation of a reference group as an attitude toward the organization and other relevant groups. It thereby reflects social trust or distrust, acceptance or insecurity. The decisive factors at this point are reciprocal interests and their orientation, combined with consternation and existential orientation as social emotional influencing factors. The overall evaluation of the relationship of one or several reference groups to an organization as friendly versus unfriendly (friend or foe) at first sight appears stereotypical

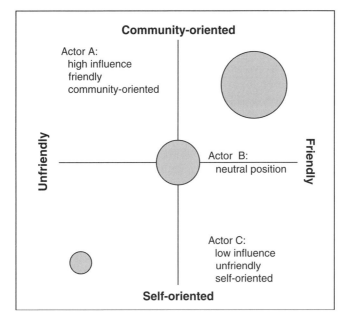

Figure 1   Field diagram of the perceived relational landscape

in that it differentiates groups that are expected to be supporters and groups with opposing interests and therefore with a potential for conflict. But between these two polarities, all levels of interaction – including the neutral position – can be scaled.

The dimension of "community orientation versus self-orientation" *(valuation of attitude)* shows how far a reference group evaluates another of the organization's reference groups or the organization itself as community-oriented or self-oriented. This judgment is important for understanding the decisions and the behavior of an organization. For example, willingness to examine the interests of social groups and their concerns can be considered as a recognizable intention to seek social integration (community orientation) and will therefore receive a positive valuation. The consequent focusing of an organization on the question of cost-efficiency (expense) and economic benefit (self-orientation) will be followed by a critical or negative valuation from the reference groups.

The dimension of "low influence versus high influence capability" *(degree of influence)* shows the potential degree of influence a reference group ascribes to another relevant group or to the organization. In situations without conflicts only a part of this potential is used, because further exertion of influence is not necessary. Only in conflict situations (e.g., concerning sensitive subjects or problematic constellations of interests) will the full potential of influence be tapped, in order for the group to accomplish its own interests –. Knowledge about these potentials belongs to individual PR experts and cannot be shown with PRFD.

Figure 1 illustrates the field diagram of PRFD methodology, placing the friendly–unfriendly dimension on the horizontal axis and the community-orientation–self-orientation dimension on the vertical axis. The influence dimension is demonstrated by circle size within the field. The selection of these three dimensions offers five essential advantages. (1) Each dimension makes an independent statement; the bipolarity of the scale positions them unambiguously. (2) The dimensions are orthogonal, i.e,. they are independent of each other, so alterations to one dimension will not automatically affect the others. (3) Any positioning in the field diagram entails an evaluation of quality or importance; value can be deduced only in the entire context of PR. (4) The field diagram allows issue analysts to reproduce comparative alterations of opinions and attitudes over time. (5) As all actors in any field are in relationships with each other, developments and alterations in the field can be observed and presented (Springston et al. 1992; Springston & Keyton 2001).

FINDINGS AND PERSPECTIVES

PR activities are ideally a process in which target-oriented action requires a strategic activity intent and the decision to follow a procedure is based on systematic analysis. Issue analysis enables PR professionals to appraise communicative trends and potential consequences of public communications in the context of organization-political decisions in order to consult managers, to take precautions against or to prepare for expected controversies and conflicts, and to initiate specific communicative measures. PRFD as an analysis tool gives PR professionals the possibility of considering the relevant publics of an organization as a system of mutual influences. Springston et al. (1992) implied that the use of this tool not only makes clear who are allies or antagonists but also shows who – due to their own neutral position – can be considered as a potential mediator in conflict situations. Considering the development of the field diagrams in time lapse, it is possible to observe changes in positions and parameters and to estimate the degree of the polarization or unification of publics. This analysis allows practitioners to make inferences about the organization, about how it reflects the preferred issue position of others, and about how that can affect social trust. Thus, it is possible to make predictions about the risks faced by an organization that follows its organization-political interests and aims as well as the opportunities for strategic and communication-strategic actions.

Finally, by means of PRFD, it is possible to *answer three central questions* about the analysis of the public relations of an organization. (1) Which basic attitude do publics have toward an organization? (2) How will the basic organization-political orientation of an organization be evaluated? (3) What kind of influence can different publics exert by implicit and explicit actions? Questions, for example, about the different roles and the different organizational relevance of several reference groups, about situational influencing factors, or about the differentiation of various publics can be formulated in relation to the comparative issue context and lead to models, methods, and procedures for communicating about differences. PRFD does not, therefore, recommend a specific stance on various issues but serves as an instrument for analysis.

The PRFD methodology can aid practitioners in their efforts to develop statements about the current condition of several publics. In the context of issues and problems, the reactions and attitudes of key publics can be predicted. Here public communication can be understood as a system of markets of opinion (SMO). This offers the possibility of differentiating publics in different markets of opinion geared to a specific focus on topics and specific key values. Such a model clarifies the fact that assessments of an issue can differ. For example, the issue of personnel reductions may be differently assessed in the personnel and financial markets, because they offer different conditions (social versus economic acceptance) for accepting key policies. However, the way the competing interests of different publics have to be handled depends, for example, on dominance, majority, and dependency within a certain market field. PRFD connects reference groups to a collective field diagram, as SMO positions opinion markets with partial interests in the common public opinion market.

PRFD provides a social psychological model capable of providing adaptable approaches and models for the description of central issues of PR. In this sense, PRFD is a component of awareness in PR research. The fact that the method has not been widely accepted some 15 years after its first publication (e.g., in the USA: Grunig & Hunt 1984; Botan & Hazleton 2006; in Germany: Röttger 2004, Bentele et al. 2005) does not argue against the method.

SEE ALSO: ▶ Attitudes ▶ Consensus-Oriented Public Relations ▶ Corporate Reputation ▶ Cultural Topoi in Public Relations ▶ Excellence Theory in Public Relations ▶ Issue Management ▶ Legitimacy Gap Theory ▶ Organization–Public Relationships ▶ Organizational Image ▶ Public Affairs ▶ Public Relations ▶ Publics: Situational Theory ▶ Stakeholder Theory ▶ Systems Theory

References and Suggested Readings

Bales, R. F., & Cohen, S. P. (1979). *SYMLOG: System for the multiple-level observation of groups*. New York: Free Press.
Bentele, G., Fröhlich, R., & Szyszka, P. (eds.) (2005). *Handbuch der Public Relations*. Wiesbaden: Verlag für Sozialwissenschaften.
Botan, C. H., & Hazleton, V. (eds.) (2006). *Public relations theory II*. Mahwah, NJ, and London: Lawrence Erlbaum.
Grunig, J. E., & Hunt, T. (1984). *Managing public relations*. New York: Thomson Learning.
Harlow, R. F. (1957). *Social science in public relations*. New York. Harper.
Röttger, U. (ed.) (2004). *Theorien der Public Relations*. Wiesbaden: Verlag für Sozialwissenschaften.
Springston, J. K., & Keyton, J. (2001). Public relations field dynamics. In R. L. Heath (ed.), *Handbook of public relations*. Thousand Oaks, CA: Sage, pp. 115–126.
Springston, J. K., Keyton, J., Leichty, G. B., & Metzger, J. (1992). Field dynamics and public relations theory: Toward the management of multiple publics. *Journal of Public Relations Research*, 4(2), 81–100.
Szyszka, P. (2005). Understanding public relations functions as an opportunity for organizational development. Paper presented at the 7th Annual EUPRERA Conference, Lisbon, November 11.

Public Relations: Global Firms

Nilanjana Bardhan

Southern Illinois University Carbondale

After World War II, a spurt in the growth of multinational companies and worldwide trade led to the concomitant growth of global advertising and marketing agencies and networks around the world. Such growth was the inevitable outcome of the need to coordinate the → advertising and → marketing of goods and services in the various markets that were joining the global trade flow and becoming part of the multinational market domain (→ Globalization Theories). In the marketing mix, the global expansion of public relations firms got a late start. However, in the 1950s, the growing realization of the cost-effectiveness of public relations in relation to advertising and marketing, along with an increased understanding that → public relations can effectively support advertising and marketing efforts through reputation management, media relations, and relationship building with diverse publics around the world led to the start of the expansion of international/global public relations firms and activities (→ Professionalization of Public Relations; Corporate Reputation; Organizational Image).

The rate of expansion increased especially from the late 1980s onwards with the demise of the former Soviet Union, the spread of market globalization in more countries, the spatial compression enabled by communication technologies and travel, increasing global competition, and financial deregulations worldwide. The demand for global public relations services were coming from a growing number of companies doing more business in unfamiliar markets, companies that were faced with the need to culturally understand and build mutually beneficial relations with a complex array of publics, government, and the media of various countries, a service that is beyond the scope of just advertising and marketing. Global public relations firms and networks have positioned themselves as entities that possess the knowledge, expertise, and resources to provide these services in an increasingly interconnected world with complex business communication needs.

BRIEF HISTORY

As a communications profession, public relations, as it is understood today, was born in the United States and also had an early start in Britain. Two US firms with early international vision and aspirations were Hill and Knowlton and Burson-Marsteller. Lured by the business potential of the formation of the European Economic Community, the former entered Europe in the 1960s and soon after the Asia Pacific region. Burson-Marsteller, Hill and Knowlton's main international competitor, closely followed suit. Edelman PR (the only independently owned global public relations firm today) was also an early player in joining the expansion of global firms (Morley 1998). In Britain, in the 1980s, Shandwick (now Weber-Shandwick) provided major competition to the US-based firms as it entered the race to provide global public relations services to multinational clients. It established a strong presence in the Asia Pacific region in addition to Europe, after acquiring International Public Relations Group (IPRG), a strong network of public relations firms spanning Japan to Australia, brought together by the enterprising Taiji Kohara of Japan who entered the public relations business in the 1960s (Morley 1998).

The reach of public relations firms today is indeed global. Most of the global firms have a presence in the major metropolitan cities of the world. They provide a full range of public relations services such as strategy and program development, creativity, tools and materials development, implementation, and evaluation and measurement (Rudgard 2003). Some of the global firms (and now networks) have built a reputation for being specialists at providing certain types of public relations services, such as public affairs, financial affairs, travel, health-care, technology, or sports marketing. Today, there are close to two dozen global public relations firms that provide worldwide services, mainly based in the US or in Europe. While they also provide services to domestic clients, their international accounts generate between 40 and 70 percent of their revenues (Wilcox & Cameron 2006).

THE NEED FOR PR FIRMS IN TODAY'S GLOBAL MARKETPLACE

According to Amy Rudgard (2003), head of public relations for Lego in Europe, clients hire global firms or networks for a number of reasons, among them control and consistency over global campaigns, lack of in-house resources, personnel, and expertise, lack of the international experience or resources at the current client, rapid business growth, and entry into new and unfamiliar markets, or the sudden occurrence of a crisis with international repercussions that demands quick action. Further reasons are that the management of some clients with global needs does not perceive the financial value of maintaining a full-fledged in-house international PR team at all times, or that global firms with local affiliates are better rooted in the local culture of various markets.

All of these reasons suggest that an increasing number of businesses, in addition to multinational companies, are in need of coordinated public relations services that transcend national cultures and customs (→ Globalization of Organizations). Along with business, several organizations that span national borders, such as nongovernmental agencies and international agencies, also utilize the services of global public relations firms.

OWNERSHIP PATTERNS AND TRENDS

Until the 1970s, most public relations firms were independently held or publicly owned. However, they were gradually bought over by large advertising firms as they were turning out to be lucrative investments. Another advantage for the advertising firms was that they could provide seamless services to clients with international advertising as well as public relations needs. That trend further shifted as global media and communication operations began to converge rapidly after the late 1980s, leading to the growth of large → media conglomerates with diversified holdings (→ Globalization of the Media). While they maintain their names, most global advertising and public relations firms today are owned by such large conglomerates. For example, the Interpublic Group owns Foote, Cone and Belding along with other advertising agencies and some of the largest global public relations firms such as Weber-Shandwick and Golin/Harris International. The largest conglomerate, however, is Omnicom (roughly US$8.6 billion in revenues), which owns global public relations firms such as Fleishman-Hillard, Porter Novelli, and Ketchum (Wilcox & Cameron 2006).

There are two main reasons for this ownership trend. The first is that large multi-national companies with communication needs in various markets of the world can shop under one roof and expect seamless integrated marketing communication services, i.e., the melding of public relations, advertising, and marketing, in the various countries in which they do business. The other reason is purely financial. Global public relations firms are increasingly proving to be worthwhile investments for large media conglomerates (Wilcox & Cameron 2006).

It needs to be pointed out, however, that not all clients with international public relations needs may desire the one-size-fits-all approach, especially if they feel the need to conduct more locally tailored public relations programs in disparate market cultures. These clients feel the need for less standardized and more personal and culturally focused services. Having to hire one global firm with international offices is not the only option. Such clients can pick and choose from other available options when constructing their global public relations account.

OPTIONS AVAILABLE TO CLIENTS FOR STRUCTURING GLOBAL PR ACCOUNTS

The trend of building networks (e.g., WorldCom, IPREX, Pinnacle), whether comprised of partially owned affiliates or independently owned smaller firms worldwide, is on the rise in global public relations. As a result, clients with global public relations needs have at least *four main options available* to them for structuring their global accounts. First, as mentioned already, there is the option of going with a wholly owned firm that has its own offices in different cities created by the parent firm and bearing the same name. Second, a client can go with the wholly owned network approach. Such a network is composed of local firms that have been acquired by the lead firm, but the local firms retain their local staff, management, and identities. A third option is to go with a main firm that is also part of a network because of equity participation with firms in other countries. The fourth option is to go with a looser (in terms of ownership) network that is a consortium of independently owned firms located in different countries that work together to support the needs of each other's international clients (Heylin et al. 1991).

Each arrangement has its *strengths and weaknesses*. Wholly owned firms with their own offices may have some offices that are weaker than others. In this case, the quality of service would not be uniform in all markets, but central coordination would be a plus. The second option has the advantage of offering services that are rooted in the local culture and knowledge of public relations of the various markets where the affiliates exist (Heylin et al. 1991). A disadvantage for clients with global priorities could be lack of coordination between various markets. However, such an option would be ideal for a client that prioritizes the local over global centralization. The same advantages and dis-advantages would apply to the third and fourth options, except that a further disadvantage in the case of the fourth option would be a lack of leadership and centralization in a network of independently owned firms with their own cultures, loyalties, and client priorities.

The choice comes down to the client's needs. A multinational client shopping for international public relations services would have to consider whether its needs are more global, local, or glocal; the infrastructure of its multinational operations; and whether there is greater need for centralization or for decentralization in the management of the account (Rudgard 2003).

FUTURE DEVELOPMENTS

The landscape of world business has changed dramatically in the last couple of decades. Business activities and communication are criss-crossing national and cultural borders at a rate not known before. However, greater fluidity also means greater intercultural contact, and this reality carries with it the high potential of intercultural communication conflict between clients and the publics in new contact zones. As global public relations firms and networks work to connect disparate market cultures, and establish a presence in recently marketized cultures (parts of South America, Africa, and Asia; eastern Europe; and Russia) where market-capitalist PR is a new concept, their primary challenges become obvious.

In addition to providing the more standard services that these firms and networks provide to their clients, they also have to effectively play the role of intercultural boundary spanners at various levels in the global business communication matrix (→ Public Relations, Intercultural). They also have to effectively address the challenge of anti-globalization sentiments, especially those directed against their multinational clients, and counsel their clients to be far-sighted and socially responsible members of the globalization process (Vogl 2001; → Issue Management; Corporate Social Responsibility).

SEE ALSO: ▶ Advertising ▶ Corporate Reputation ▶ Corporate Social Responsibility ▶ Globalization of the Media ▶ Globalization of Organizations ▶ Globalization Theories ▶ Issue Management ▶ Marketing ▶ Media Conglomerates ▶ Organizational Image ▶ Professionalization of Public Relations ▶ Public Relations ▶ Public Relations, Intercultural

References and Suggested Readings

Capozzi, L. (2001). Parlez-vous relations publiques? The human resources challenges of international public relations. *Strategist*, 7, 16–18.

Edson, A. (1997). Taking your place on the global stage. *Strategist*, 3, 31–33.

Heylin, A., Haywood, R., & Trevitt, G. (1991). Organizing the international operation. In M. Nally (ed.), *International public relations in practice*. London: Kogan Page, pp. 15–27.

Morley, M. (1998). *How to manage your global reputation*. New York: New York University Press.

Rudgard, A. (2003). Serving public relations globally: The agency perspective. In K. Sriramesh & D. Verčič (eds.), *The global public relations handbook*. Mahwah, NJ: Lawrence Erlbaum, pp. 459–477.

Taaffe, P. (2004). The future of global public relations: An agency perspective. *Strategist*, 10, 22–23.

Vogl, F. (2001). International corporate ethics and the challenges to public relations. *Strategist*, 7, 19–22.

Wilcox, D., & Cameron, G. (2006). *Public relations strategies and tactics*, 8th edn. Boston: Pearson Education.

Public Relations, Intercultural

Krishnamurthy Sriramesh

Nanyang Technological University

Although public relations practice is slightly ahead of the public relations body of knowledge, both have developed ethnocentrically in the twentieth century, based predominantly on experience and research from the United States and to a lesser extent from some countries in Europe (Sriramesh & Vercic 2003; Van Ruler & Vercic 2004). However, public relations practice, or many of the publicity activities that we have come to characterize as → public relations today, took place in pre-biblical times in many ancient cultures. There is evidence of such communication practices in ancient civilizations in Egypt, Saudi Arabia, India, and China, among others (Sriramesh & Vercic 2003; Sriramesh 2004). However, in its "modern" avatar (incarnation), public relations practice is perceived around the world to be a western (predominantly American) phenomenon (→ Communication Modes, Western).

INTERCULTURAL ASPECTS IN PUBLIC RELATIONS RESEARCH

The body of knowledge of public relations is relatively young and ethnocentric. Grunig and Hickson (1979) concluded that of the 4,141 books and articles on the subject of public relations prior to 1976, only 63 had some research component, a clear sign of the lack of development of the "science" of public relations by that time. Although there has been a noticeable spurt in public relations scholarship in the last 30 years (→ Communication as a Field and Discipline), it is only in the last five to ten years that the body of knowledge has diversified to some extent, based on descriptions of experiences from other regions of the world. Even so, most of the studies in this genre have focused on public relations as a phenomenon in a single country, and to a lesser extent one region, and there is very little literature that compares public relations practices across countries or cultures. So it is reasonable to conclude that theorizing about intercultural public relations is in its infancy (→ Intercultural and Intergroup Communication). It is important to recognize that whereas international public relations is almost always also intercultural, intercultural public relations need not always be international.

The three-nation research project funded by the International Association of Business Communicators (IABC) that has come to be recognized as the *Excellence Project* (Grunig et al. 2002) was arguably the first research attempt to compare public relations across cultures (albeit in three Anglo-Saxon countries: the US, Canada, and the UK) by using the same research design and survey questionnaire to gather data in all countries. When it began in 1987, this project was also the first effort to study the linkage between culture (both societal and corporate; → Culture: Definitions and Concepts; Cultural Patterns and Communication) and public relations, as evidenced by the first *Body of knowledge report* published by the Public Relations Society of America (PRSA) in 1988, which did not make any reference to culture as a variable in public relations practice.

Beginning in 1990, several graduate students studying in the United States began conducting studies of public relations in a few countries in Asia, principally in India,

China, Taiwan, South Korea, Singapore, Japan, and Thailand. Although their efforts have been helpful in extending the pedagogy beyond a few western countries, thereby reducing to some extent the ethnocentricity of the body of knowledge, there is clearly a paucity in the depth of information from these countries; while many other Asian nations, as well as those from Africa, the Caribbean, and Latin America, have received even less representation in the literature in English for many reasons, including language.

Globalization has made it imperative to address these hitherto neglected areas, which is why there is increased attention to international and intercultural public relations now. In fact, one can reasonably argue that there is no such thing as "domestic" public relations any longer because of the rapid globalization of even small organizations as a result of better communication infrastructure, lower trade barriers, etc. This makes it essential for organizations to consider environmental variables in designing public relations strategies and tactics. Public relations practitioners have traditionally relied on anecdotal evidence to guide their forays into new markets, and in many respects they continue to do so even now because of the scarcity of "intercultural" public relations knowledge. Practitioners have found out, sometimes the hard way, that anecdotal evidence is not always a good method for learning. Three key variables (among others) make organizational environments challenging for intercultural public relations practitioners: the culture, the political and economic system, and the media system. Of these, culture is the only variable to have been empirically linked with public relations so far, albeit by few studies. Unfortunately, culture continues to be treated as an afterthought in the public relations body of knowledge (Sriramesh 2006), which is why one can make a reasonable argument that the current body of knowledge of public relations is ethnocentric (Sriramesh 2002).

CULTURE AND PUBLIC RELATIONS: THE MISSING LINK

The link between organizations and culture has been made in a variety of disciplines, such as organizational behavior (→ Organizational Communication). Similarly, culture and communication are two sides of the same coin. Because communication is the primary underpinning of public relations, the logical connection between culture and public relations is easy to discern. Both *societal* culture (Sriramesh & White 1992) and *corporate* culture (Sriramesh et al. 1992) influence public relations practice. This distinction is important because public relations people communicate with → audiences external and internal to the organization and should have familiarity with the cultural idiosyncrasies of these key stakeholders (→ Stakeholder Theory) in order to communicate effectively with them. Yet less than a handful of empirical studies have assessed how culture affects public relations (see a review of these studies in Sriramesh 2006). It is even more interesting that of the three environmental variables mentioned above, culture has the greatest number of studies linking it with public relations. That is as good an indicator as any of the extent to which intercultural issues have been ignored in public relations pedagogy. Further, beginning with the IABC project, most of the studies linking public relations with culture have relied almost exclusively on Hofstede's dimensions of culture, although even Hofstede noted that culture is much more than the dimensions he was able to measure. The field has barely touched the surface of the many unique cultural idiosyncrasies of individual regions and countries beyond some studies that have discussed *guanxi* ("relations") and *mianzi* ("saving face") in Chinese culture (Sriramesh 2004), and one or two studies that have assessed the influence of *wa* ("harmony"), *amae* ("desire to depend on the goodness of others"), *tatamae* ("public persona and behavior of an individual"), and *honne* ("the private or true self and emotions") in Japanese culture (Sriramesh & Takasaki 2000; → Communication Modes, Asian).

Cultures also differ in the emphasis they place on *interpersonal trust* and the ways in which such trust is established and maintained. In public relations literature this is discussed in terms of the *personal influence model* (Sriramesh & White 1992; Sriramesh 2006). Practitioners from different cultures use different methods of building personal relationships with key stakeholders as a means of increasing the effectiveness of their communication with these stakeholders. This is closely linked to the notion of "relationship building" that seems to have pervaded the body of literature in the past seven years (Hon & Grunig 1999; Ledingham & Bruning 2000). However, interestingly, the core discussion of relationship building in public relations still does not account for culture as the key variable it is. Only when studies have used the core concepts identified in the US or a few western countries in other countries, such as Taiwan and China, has culture been taken into account in applying to other cultures the relationship dimensions identified in the US.

There is plenty of evidence of culture not being given its due in public relations pedagogy, resulting in the ethnocentricity of the body of knowledge. For example, one of the premier research journals of the field, the *Journal of Public Relations Research*, published a special issue titled "Public Relations *Values* [emphasis added] in the New Millennium" as the first issue of the new millennium. Although the thoughtful essays in that special issue discussed activist values, feminist values, rhetorical values, and postmodernist values, not one of them made a single reference to culture, which is the core concept that addresses values in any society. In the entire special issue there was only one reference to culture, when Grunig stated: "[individualistic] Anglo cultures need symmetrical public relations even more than organizations in collective cultures" (Grunig 2000, 39). The same applies to discussions of ethics and public relations (→ Public Relations Ethics) as well, where discussions are silent about ethical values from more ancient cultures such as China or India or cultures in other regions of the world such as Africa or Latin America.

When discussing intercultural public relations, it is important to extend the discussion beyond the traditional (anthropological) notion of culture to include other variables also, such as political economy and media culture. In the rapidly globalizing world of the twenty-first century, such a broader focus is absolutely necessary in order for public relations practice to be more effective.

MEDIA CULTURE

Although almost all textbooks of public relations discuss maintaining relations with the mass media as one of the most important activities of public relations practitioners (→ Media Relations), there has been very little theorizing about the differences in media cultures around the world and their impact on public relations. Global or intercultural public relations ought to study how public relations should be tempered to different media environments. A framework for developing research programs to study the impact of media culture on public relations was presented in Sriramesh and Vercic (2003) and consists of analyzing who owns and controls the media in a country (media control; → Ownership in the Media), who has the ability to penetrate media content (media access; → Access to the Media), and the extent of diffusion of the mass media through the populace (media outreach; → Exposure to Communication Content). Although public relations professionals have been conducting media relations activities cross-nationally and cross-culturally, they are basing them mostly on anecdotal and not empirical evidence. More often than not, such activities have involved imposing western notions of media relations on other parts of the world, with limited effect. So it is imperative for scholars to link media culture with public relations on the basis of empirical evidence.

POLITICAL CULTURE

Western liberal democracy underpins many of the assumptions that pervade the current literature on public relations, because modern public relations has its roots in the west. This is partly why much of the theorizing about public relations is also prescriptive (normative), instructing how it should be practiced in other countries and regions of the world. However, democracy is practiced in myriad forms around the world, because of socio-cultural factors and those relating to level of development. Other forms of political system (e.g., corporatism, communitarianism, or theocracy) exist around the world, and their impact on public relations has not been explored at all. For example, the literature on → issue management assumes a liberal democratic environment where corporations use lobbying to influence legislative decisions and the enactment of public policies. However, in other political systems lobbying may be ill-advised because it is illegal. Also, the term "lobbying" itself may have different connotations in different countries. The body of knowledge has yet to fully explore all these avenues.

The body of knowledge of global, international, and intercultural public relations is very young, with a bright future for development. The rapid pace of globalization requires that scholars pay attention to developing this fledgling field with robust conceptual and empirical studies that can help to increase the efficacy of public relations practitioners globally.

SEE ALSO: ▶ Access to the Media ▶ Audience ▶ Communication as a Field and Discipline ▶ Communication Modes, Asian ▶ Communication Modes, Western ▶ Consensus-Oriented Public Relations ▶ Corporate Social Responsibility ▶ Cultural Patterns and Communication ▶ Culture: Definitions and Concepts ▶ Excellence Theory in Public Relations ▶ Exposure to Communication Content ▶ Intercultural and Intergroup Communication ▶ Intercultural Media Effects ▶ Issue Management ▶ Legitimacy Gap Theory ▶ Media Relations ▶ Organizational Communication ▶ Organization–Public Relationships ▶ Ownership in the Media ▶ Public Relations ▶ Public Relations Ethics ▶ Publics: Situational Theory ▶ Stakeholder Theory

References and Suggested Readings

Grunig, J. E. (2000). Collectivism, collaboration, and societal corporatism as core professional values in public relations. *Journal of Public Relations Research*, 12(1), 23–48.

Grunig, J. E., & Hickson, R. H. (1979). An evaluation of academic research in public relations. *Public Relations Review*, 2(1), 31–43.

Grunig, L. A., Grunig, J. E., & Dozier, D. M. (2002). *Excellent public relations and effective organizations*. Mahwah, NJ: Lawrence Erlbaum.

Hon, L., & Grunig, J. E. (1999). *Guidelines for measuring relationships in public relations*. Gainesville, FL: Institute for Public Relations.

Ledingham, J. A., & Bruning, S. D. (2000). *Public relations as relationship management: A relational approach to the study and practice of public relations*. Mahwah, NJ: Lawrence Erlbaum.

Sriramesh, K. (2002). The dire need for multiculturalism in public relations education: An Asian perspective. *Journal of Communication Management*, 7(1), 54–70.

Sriramesh, K. (2004). *Public relations in Asia: An anthology*. Singapore: Thomson Learning Asia.

Sriramesh, K. (2006). The relationship between culture and public relations. In E. L. Toth (ed.), *The future of excellence in public relations and communication management: Challenges for the next generation*. Mahwah, NJ: Lawrence Erlbaum.

Sriramesh, K., & Takasaki, M. (2000). The impact of culture on Japanese public relations. *Journal of Communication Management*, 3(4), 337–352.

Sriramesh, K., & Vercic, D. (2003). *The global public relations handbook: Theory, research, and practice*. Mahwah, NJ: Lawrence Erlbaum.

Sriramesh, K., & White, J. (1992). Societal culture and public relations. In J. E. Grunig (ed.), *Excellence in public relations and communication management*. Mahwah, NJ: Lawrence Erlbaum.

Sriramesh, K., Grunig, J. E., & Buffington, J. (1992). Corporate culture and public relations. In J. E. Grunig (ed.) *Excellence in public relations and communication management*. Mahwah, NJ: Lawrence Erlbaum.

Van Ruler, B., & Vercic, D. (2004). *Public relations and communication management in Europe*. Berlin: Mouton.

Public Relations: Media Influence

Jan Kleinnijenhuis

Free University Amsterdam

Earning public understanding and acceptance through reports in the press is one of the oldest means–ends schemes in public relations (PR). Firms, governments, NGOs, and interest groups alike use the media to convey their message to their publics. Hence, media influence is a two-step process. Whether PR efforts lead to news items in the media depends on the relations of the company with the media and on the newsworthiness of the publicity efforts (→ Media Relations; News Factors; News Values). Once the media have published the news, PR media influence can be understood through theories about media effects (→ Media Effects; Exposure to Communication Content; Information Processing).

PR media influence is a special field of media effects because of the involvement of stakeholders. Every actor who may affect the company or may be affected by the company is a stakeholder. Typical stakeholders are competitors, investors, financial analysts, interest groups, employees, and consumers. Stakeholders are not simply external publics outside the organization, but active players in the publicity arena themselves, who also invest in media relations. Stakeholders may serve as alternative sources for journalists who want to verify their facts or to present both sides of the argument (Fig. 1, feedback

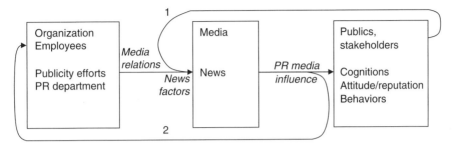

Figure 1   Media relations, news factors, and PR media influence: a reciprocal model

loop 1). Stakeholders may also be located within the organization itself (feedback loop 2). Employees often learn from the press about takeover negotiations, organizational scandals, or the relative performance of their firm as compared to competitors, especially in global firms (→ Public Relations: Global Firms).

From a more abstract point of view, media and journalists, as well as an organization's publics and stakeholders, can be conceived of as actors in an interorganizational communication network (→ Communication Networks; Interorganizational Communication; Social Networks; Network Analysis). A network perspective results in a *reciprocal* model of PR media effects.

INFLUENCE OF THE AMOUNT AND TONE OF THE NEWS

Although it is a basic assumption throughout the PR community that stakeholder perceptions of a firm's reputation rest in part on news coverage (→ Corporate Reputation), only in 1990 was the first large-scale attempt made to test this assumption. Fombrun and Shanley (1990) focused on the amount and tone of the news. The frequency or visibility of the news is often used as a synonym for the amount of news, whereas near-synonyms for the tone of the news are the tenor, direction, valence, or favorability of the news. The authors measured the amount and the tone of the news about firms by means of a content analysis of titles of newspaper articles (→ Content Analysis, Quantitative). With firms as their units of analysis, they regressed the amount and the tone of the news about a firm, together with measures of its financial performance, on its reputation score. Reputations of firms were derived from the Fortune 500 survey among the business elite. They found that the amount of news had a negative effect, i.e., the greater the scrutiny of the firm by the press, the worse its reputation (→ Negativity). On the other hand, the tone of the news had a significant positive effect on corporate reputation, but only for highly diversified firms, especially when the amount of news was large. Stakeholders may have to rely on the news for their information about diversified firms, because it is hard to deduce the reputation of such a firm from elementary knowledge about its core business.

Later studies applied other research designs with mixed results (→ Research Methods). On the basis of a longitudinal research design with yearly data for three firms (→ Longitudinal Analysis), Verčič (2000), for example, found that the yearly change in the amount or tone of the news did not have a significant effect on the yearly change in the perceived trustworthiness of the firm. In addition to different research designs, different → operationalizations of a positive and a negative tone may have been at the heart of these mixed results.

NEWS-TYPE-SPECIFIC INFLUENCES

Recent studies have found that media influence depends in addition on the "news frame," the "news type," or the "attributes" with which an organization is associated in the news (→ Framing Effects; Framing of the News). Among other things, the news may associate organizations with problems or "issues" that arise, with its successes and failures, or with stakeholders who are either supportive or critical of the organization. Each of these three news types (or "frames") has a unique effect on the audience (Meijer 2004).

In *issue news* (e.g., !Philips rolls out sales of energy-efficient light bulbs") an actor (e.g., Philips) promotes or counteracts an issue (e.g., sales of energy-efficient light bulbs). Research on second-level agenda setting and priming shows that the issues with which an organization is associated in the news become salient for evaluation of the organization (Carroll & McCombs 2003; Carroll 2004). On the basis of a correlational second-level agenda-setting study, starting from a 2005 content analysis of press releases and media coverage and aggregated survey data for 28 companies, Kiousis et al. (2007) concluded that a company's attention to issues (or "substantive attributes") in PR messages is transferred to the media agenda, and subsequently to public opinion. Moreover, media adopt the positive or negative issue positions of corporations from the PR news wire. Thus, firms are often quite successful in building the issues that serve to evaluate them.

Priming and *second-level agenda setting* occur also in a business context. Fombrun and Shanley's (1990) early results point to the *special status of issues* related to a company's core business, often labeled as owned issues in the political communication literature. In a study based on a yearly panel survey study and a daily content analysis of the news, 1997–2000, Meijer and Kleinnijenhuis (2006), for example, found that news about a firm's owned issues did indeed increase reputation, even when controlling for former reputation. For example, the reputation of oil company Shell deteriorated in the eyes of audience members who came to associate the company with environmental issues, whereas its reputation improved for audience members who came to associate Shell with its core business. A respondent's issue associations with Shell depended on issue associations with the company in the media from the respondent's personal media palette. Remarkably enough, Shell raised environmental issues itself, because the company wanted to improve its environmental reputation actively after the 1995 Brent Spar affair, in which Greenpeace had successfully accused Shell of using the sea as a trash can to dump the obsolete Brent Spar oil platform.

Corporate reputations depend in a quite different way on news about corporate *success and failure* (e.g., "Upbeat forecast for Philips profits," "Sales dip for Philips"). A defining feature of news about success and failure is that the subject that caused successes and gains or failures and losses remains unspecified. Success breeds success, according to Meijer on the basis of a panel survey study that permitted control for a firm's previous successes (Meijer 2004). For example, most shareholders will follow market hype, whereas only highly aware shareholders will have the self-confidence to act against the hype (e.g., selling shares in a booming market, buying shares in a collapsing market).

EFFECTS OF SUPPORT AND CRITICISM FROM STAKEHOLDERS IN THE NEWS

The literature shows mixed results with regard to effects of news about *support and criticism*. Whether criticisms hit home also depends on stakeholder credibility ($\rightarrow$ Credibility Effects; Consistency Theories). Shah et al. (2002), for example, found that President Clinton was able to restore his reputation after the Monica Lewinsky affair once the moral issue disappeared and press reports came to focus on Republican hardliners who criticized Clinton. Republicans were never deemed credible by Democrats.

The variety of different stakeholders and experts in business news is quite impressive. Business news involves different issue arenas (e.g., corporate finance, mergers and acquisitions, labor relations, consumer affairs), each of them with its own stakeholders and its own experts. In news about mergers and acquisitions, for example, the news may start with rumors, but CEOs usually become the primary definers of the news. Financial analysts and bankers often play the role of experts in this type of news. But if, for example, dismissals are at stake, then employees will easily become the primary definers. Labor unions and a firm's PR spokespersons often will enter the scene also, as will lawyers when the labor dispute is not settled soon. If a firm is prosecuted because of its violations of the law, then CEO and PR spokespersons, as well as lawyers and polling agencies, are likely to become newsworthy. If interest groups, e.g., environmentalists, become the primary definers in the news, then the responsibility for the defense is often with the PR department. In sum, each issue arena raises in the press its own primary definers, adversaries, and experts, whose antagonisms maintain the issue arena to the detriment of other such arenas.

The large number of more or less credible stakeholders in the PR domain makes a precise account of news about their support and criticism difficult, but studies to trace stakeholders are a first step. In their study about the growing prominence of CEOs in corporate news, Park and Berger (2004) found that CEO statements were counterbalanced with stakeholder statements. Stakeholders often cited in CEO press coverage were adversaries (e.g., other executives, board members, union personnel). But experts (e.g., financial analysts, industry analysts, scholars) were cited even more in news items about CEOs.

SEE ALSO: ▶ Agenda-Setting Effects ▶ Communication Management ▶ Communication Networks ▶ Consistency Theories ▶ Content Analysis, Quantitative ▶ Corporate Reputation ▶ Credibility Effects ▶ Crisis Communication ▶ Exposure to Communication Content ▶ Framing Effects ▶ Framing of the News ▶ Information Processing ▶ Intereffication Approach in Public Relations ▶ Interorganizational Communication ▶ Issue Management ▶ Longitudinal Analysis ▶ Media Effects ▶ Media Relations ▶ Negativity ▶ Network Analysis ▶ News Factors ▶ News Values ▶ Operationalization ▶ Positioning Theory ▶ Public Affairs ▶ Public Relations ▶ Public Relations Evaluation ▶ Public Relations Field Dynamics ▶ Public Relations: Global Firms ▶ Public Relations, Intercultural ▶ Research Methods ▶ Social Networks ▶ Stakeholder Theory ▶ Trust of Publics

References and Suggested Readings

Carroll, C. E. (2004). How the mass media influence perceptions of corporate reputation: Exploring agenda-setting effects within business news coverage. Unpublished doctoral dissertation, Austin, University of Texas.

Carroll, C. E., & McCombs, M. (2003). Agenda-setting effects of business news on the public's images and opinions about major corporations. *Corporate Reputation Review*, 16(1), 36–46.

Fombrun, C. J., & Shanley, M. (1990). What's in a name? Reputation building and corporate strategy. *Academy of Management Journal*, 33, 233–258.

Kiousis, S., Popescu, C., & Mitrook, M. (2007). Understanding influence on corporate reputation: An examination of public relations efforts, media coverage, public opinion, and financial performance from an agenda-building and agenda-setting perspective. *Journal of Public Relations Research*, 19, 147–165.

Meijer, M.-M. (2004). *Does success breed success? Effects of news and advertising on corporate reputation*. Amsterdam: Aksant.

Meijer, M.-M., & Kleinnijenhuis, J. (2006). Issue news and corporate reputation: Applying the theories of agenda setting and issue ownership in the field of business communication. *Journal of Communication*, 56(3), 543–559.

Park, D. J., & Berger, B. K. (2004). The presentation of CEOs in the press, 1990–2000: Increasing salience, positive valence, and a focus on competency and personal dimensions of image. *Journal of Public Relations Research*, 16, 93–125.

Shah, D. V., Watts, M. D., Domke, D., & Fan, D. P. (2002). News framing and cueing of issue regimes: Explaining Clinton's public approval in spite of scandal. *Public Opinion Quarterly*, 66, 339–370.

Verčič, D. (2000). Trust in organisations: A study of the relations between media coverage, public perceptions and profitability. Unpublished PhD dissertation, London, London School of Economics and Political Science.

Public Relations Planning

Sherry Devereaux Ferguson

University of Ottawa

The 1952 edition of *Effective Public Relations: Pathway to Public Favor* (Cutlip & Center) set the standard for PR education for decades to come. Chapters 5–7 introduced planning as the second of a three-stage process model. The first step was fact-finding, the second planning, and the third communicating. By 1958, the authors had moved evaluation (originally in step one) to step four. In 1963, Marston created the popular acronym *RACE* (Research, Action, Communication, and Evaluation) to represent the four-stage process conceptualized by Cutlip and Center. As in the earlier model, planning took place at the second stage (→ Public Relations).

THEMES IN PUBLIC RELATIONS (PR) PLANNING

Since 1952, three major themes have emerged in the PR planning literature: a growing emphasis on research as the foundation for planning, increasing stress on linking PR plans to business and corporate plans, and growing emphasis on the need to evaluate communication plans (→ Public Relations Evaluation).

A Growing Emphasis on Research

Funded by the first Arthur W. Page Society research grant, Broom and Dozier researched and wrote *Using Research in Public Relations: Applications to Program Management* (1990). Positioning research as the central element in managing PR programs, this book outlines how research helps to define PR problems and conceptualize the program ("before"), monitor the program's progress and make mid-course corrections ("during"), and assess program impact to learn what did or did not work and why or why not ("after"). In 1992, the International Association of Business Communicators published the results of the Excellence Project, focusing on roles (including research) performed by PR practitioners in countries around the world. Ferguson followed in 1993 with *Mastering the Public Opinion Challenge*, which won the 1994 National Communication Association's Public Relations Innovation, Development, and Educational Achievement (PRIDE) award for best publication in the book category. This book addressed the role of environmental intelligence and strategic planning systems in the tracking and managing of organizational issues (→ Professionalization of Public Relations).

A Growing Focus on Linking to Business and Corporate Plans

By the early 1980s, leading textbooks stressed the need to link PR planning to corporate goals and objectives; and by the end of the decade, these planning models were ensconced in the literature.

Despite a growing recognition of the importance of long-term planning for communication, books and scholarly articles continued to focus, through the 1990s, on contingency planning for crises (with an increasing emphasis, as well, on risk management). Ferguson (1993, 1999, 2000), however, documented a large-scale and unique experiment on the part of the Canadian government to require long-term, research-based communication planning by all departments, agencies, and regions. In 1988, the Privy Council Office (PCO) brought its first government-wide communication policy to life by asking every federal department and agency to submit annual strategic communication plans in October and operational plans in March. The PCO reviewed the plans for conformity to the broad corporate objectives of the government and provided feedback to the strategic planners. Once approved, all subsequent planning efforts (work planning and support planning) were tied to these plans. (See later discussion for definitions of *strategic*, *operational*, and *support* planning.)

By 2000, a spate of articles on → strategic communication planning had appeared, and every professional conference hosted sessions on planning. Led by an editorial board from the Netherlands, Singapore, Slovenia, and the US, *The International Journal of Strategic Communication* published its first issue in January 2006. In Great Britain, the National School of Government established training in strategic communication planning.

A Growing Emphasis on Evaluation

In the late 1980s, a survey of practitioners in Australia, China, Hong Kong, Japan, Malaysia, New Zealand, Papua New Guinea, the Philippines, Singapore, South Africa, South Korea, Taiwan, and Zimbabwe identified the emergence of accountability as a critical concern; and by the 1990s, calls for greater investment in evaluation were coming from professional associations and academics in the US, Britain, Canada, Australia, New Zealand, Germany, and other countries. The Institute for Public Relations Research and Education, the International Public Relations Association, the International Association of Business Communicators, and the Public Relations Society of America (along with chapters in other countries) urged organizations to pay more attention to evaluation.

This new century, which could be dubbed the "*age of accountability*," intensified the challenges to PR planners. With scandals rocking the financial world, organizations grappling with new security issues, and trust in politicians and business leaders at an all-time low, the Internet provided a new means for dissident groups to organize and press their causes. These groups addressed a crazy quilt of political, social, and economic issues. Activist publics employed old strategies such as civil disobedience, teach-ins, and marches, as well as new strategies such as culture jamming. Class action suits gave a voice to the less powerful, and people's tribunals judged people at the highest levels of government. In Seattle, Quebec City, Genoa, Barcelona, and other cities, crowds collected at world summits to protest against globalization. The crowds drew unlikely "march fellows," with organizations as diverse as Greenpeace standing arm in arm with John Birchers and antiabortion activists.

Accountability implies the need to evaluate, and evaluation requires setting goals and objectives – basics in the planning process. In the same way, planning requires research into the opinion environment. So a concomitant stress on research, planning, and evaluation emerged in the PR literature. The increased emphasis on conducting quantitative research (→ Quantitative Methodology) reflected this same shift in focus within both academia and industry.

PLANNING TYPOLOGIES

A major difficulty with talking about communication planning derives from lack of agreement on terminology. PR practitioners use such diverse terms as program plans, action plans, functional plans, project plans, strategic plans, strategies, operational plans, work plans, campaign plans, corporate plans, contingency plans for crises, support plans, communication approaches, communication (or "comm.") plans, and risk management plans to describe the large variety of annual or multi-year communication planning products. Public and non-profit organizations frequently use different terminology to for-profit organizations.

For example, governments use the term "programs" to refer to major ongoing services such as leisure, health, or transportation. Businesses, on the other hand, consider a program to be a large-scale undertaking of limited duration with well-defined deliverables. Similar variations in usage occur at all levels of planning, making it difficult to use consistent terminology across sectors, business units, or industries. For that reason, a careful definition of terms is required to frame any discussion. Moreover, although many more specific forms of planning exist (e.g., market and advertising plans, program plans, management by objectives, etc.), it is beyond the scope of this discussion to identify the full range.

Strategic Planning

Applied in a corporate or communication context, the term *strategic planning* refers to future-oriented, "long-term," and goal-oriented planning. Tied to the mission, mandate, vision, and broad goals or objectives of the organization, strategic planning involves deciding where you want to be at the end of your journey – your ultimate destination. In unstable environments, organizations must revisit their strategic plans on a regular basis to insure goals have not changed since the writing or updating of the last plan. The volatility of planning environments (social, economic, technological, political, cultural, and other) means that definitions of *long-term* have changed from the 1960s (10-year planning cycles) to the 1980s (5-year planning cycles) to the present day (3- to 5-year planning cycles, with annual updates).

Strategic planning can take place at the corporate or highest level of the organization or within the context of programs, branches, or business ventures. Before engaging in high-level planning of any variety (corporate or communication), the organization conducts a situation audit, clarifies its mandate, and writes or updates its mission and vision statements. A *situation audit* looks at the past performance of the organization (its achievements, failures, trends in products and services, and profit performance), forces in the organization's environment (e.g., economic, socio-cultural, technological, political, and demographic), the biases and loyalties of stakeholders (those who have a stake in the success or failure of the organization), and organizational resources. A *mandate* specifies the responsibilities of an organization and assigns authority for pursuing those responsibilities. A mandate generally appears in articles of legislation, incorporation, or charters. A *mission statement* justifies the existence of the organization by defining its purpose or reason for being, values, strategies for achieving its objectives, and behavioral standards. Mission statements guide the *present* actions of the organization. A *vision statement*, on the other hand, says where the organization would like to be at some *future* point – its desired future identity. In that sense, a vision statement is an expansion of the objectives that used to appear in 10- to 20-year strategic plans. In ideal form, vision statements are optimistic, realistic, and eloquent in expression.

After completing these three steps (conducting a situation audit, clarifying its mandate, and rewriting or updating its mission and vision statements), strategic planners move into action – first at the corporate level and subsequently at other levels of the organization. Strategic planners in communication then link their efforts to these different layers of planning (corporate, business, program, or other areas within the organization). Every plan that succeeds the corporate plan links back to these central themes and ideas. In that way, the multi-year corporate plan offers a strategic framework for business units and programs, as well as for communication planners.

The multi-year communication plan typically incorporates the following elements: opinion environment, issues, communication objectives, messages, priorities, strategic considerations (with recommendations as warranted), desired outcomes, and budget. The omission of a heading called *target audiences* derives from the fact that the strategic plan is a broad "motherhood" document. Tied to activities specified at the operational and support planning stages, audiences do not appear in the multi-year or annual strategic plan. Designating audiences at this high level is deemed inappropriate.

Operational Planning

Most commonly used by governments, the term "operational planning" refers to work and project plans. Like the term strategic planning, operational planning originated with the military. Driven by strategic planning and tactical in nature, operational planning involves making choices about how to reach a desired destination. Which vehicles will allow the organization to achieve its strategic goals? Which path will it follow? If strategic planning defines the destination, operational planning sketches a road map for reaching that destination.

Operational planning transforms communication priorities for the immediate planning period (usually one year) into products and services. Such plans also assign priorities to these activities and services, identify key target audiences, designate account-abilities (who will be responsible for carrying out the activities), articulate performance indicators, define evaluation methods and tools, establish milestones and timelines, and identify the resources required to deliver the products and services. Whereas top executives in communication are typically responsible for strategic planning, middle-level managers tend to be responsible for operational planning.

Support Planning

"Support planning" flows from operational planning. Activities identified in the opera-tional planning phase must be brought to life. The organization sets timelines and budgets and assigns responsibilities for accomplishing activities. Planners consider both the strategic responsibilities (e.g., communication objectives and messages) and the tactical (e.g., timing and vehicles for carrying the message). Support planning develops – in a more complete fashion – each of the activities identified in operational plans. Unlike annual or multi-year plans, which cover the full range of an organization's issues and activities, support plans are more limited in scope. The *focus* of the support plan (rather than the longevity, number of activities, or timeline) sets it apart from other types of planning.

Support plans can take the form of "single-use plans" (nonrecurring activities) or "standing plans" (repetitive work and predictable, recurring situations). Redundant once the activity has been carried out and the objective achieved, single-use plans help the organization to manage specific issues, activities, or broad initiatives. Planners write single-use plans for pending policy announcements, upcoming special events, environmental campaigns, press conferences, publications, or capital expenditures. Within the business sector, single-use plans can also apply to programs. Standing plans, by contrast, remain relevant for a lengthier period of time, involve a number of components (e.g., public service announcements, website, and other activities), and have no set length. Com-municators dust off standing plans year after year for events of a recurrent nature (e.g., Secretary Appreciation Day or Recycling Day).

Contingency Planning for Crises

Different from other kinds of planning, crisis communication planning involves anticipation of a situation that could (but not necessarily will) occur. Written in Chinese, the word "crisis" has two characters: one represents danger, the second opportunity. Handled properly, crises can bring increased knowledge of how the organization should function. Common sources of crises are industrial accidents, environmental problems, massive restructuring, union–management conflicts, product recalls, hostile takeovers, acts of terrorism, charges of financial fraud and embezzlement, health threats, major economic and technological changes, and natural disasters. Some result from natural events and others from human actions. Whatever their cause, in the short term, crises can threaten the viability – even the life – of an organization. For that reason, organizations attempt to anticipate and plan for crises. They create categories or typologies to hold various kinds of crises. An airline, for example, might plan for a crash, hostage taking, hijacking, strike, merger, employee layoffs, discovery of a structural fault in aircraft design, air rage, bomb scare, intoxicated pilot, death onboard, food poisoning, weather-related problems, threat of bankruptcy, or service disruption. Planners assess both the probability that the crisis could occur and potential impact in the event of occurrence. They also look for advance indicators of a crisis. Simulations prepare organizations to cope in crisis situations.

Crisis management teams include PR personnel, and crisis management plans have communication components: parties responsible for managing the crisis (team members, chain of command, lead spokespersons, coordinator of operations, alternates, and liaisons to connect with victims' families), required support systems (physical facilities, communication hardware and software, staff requirements, and regulatory requirements), information strategies (key messages, media for carrying messages, target publics for communication, mini-crises that could be activated by the crisis, and sensitivities/cautions in managing the crisis), response and control mechanisms (alert system for activating crisis management network, daily operational guide, system for de-activating crisis management network), evaluation of operations (pre-testing of systems and procedures, post-crisis debriefing, and modifications required), and appendices (principles and regulations governing crisis management). Contingency planning for crises requires the generation of detailed guidelines for dealing with the media. In the situation, publics affected want to be informed and to believe that the organization is taking the necessary actions to better the situation ($\rightarrow$ Crisis Communication).

Planning for Risk Management

Risk management involves assessing and developing strategies to manage potential risks (losses, injuries, or other negative events). Risks may range from threats to the image of the organization to computer viruses or bioterrorism. Many pertain to health or the environment. Strategies for dealing with risk can include avoidance (not purchasing a computer program that carries the risk of being infected with viruses), reduction (installing anti-virus programs), retention (accepting the loss of files when a computer virus strikes), or transfer (suing the company that sold ineffectual virus protection software).

Risk management planners identify the risks, assess the likelihood of occurrence and potential consequences, prioritize the risks based on this assessment, decide on options for managing the risks, develop appropriate responses, and seek approval of their choices. They track the risks to determine whether re-evaluation is necessary at some later point in time. Planners also develop individual plans for high priority risks (→ Risk Communication).

SEE ALSO: ► Crisis Communication ► Health Campaigns, Communication in ► Health Communication ► Organizational Crises, Communication in ► Professionalization of Public Relations ► Public Relations ► Public Relations Evaluation ► Public Relations Roles ► Quantitative Methodology ► Risk Communication ► Strategic Communication

References and Suggested Readings

Broom, G., & Dozier, D. M. (1990). *Using research in public relations: Applications to program management*. Englewood Cliffs, NJ: Prentice Hall.

Cutlip, S. M., & Center, A. H. (1952, 1958). *Effective public relations: Pathway to public favor*. New York: Prentice Hall.

Fearn-Banks, K. (2007). *Crisis communications: A casebook approach*, 2nd edn. Mahwah, NJ: Lawrence Erlbaum.

Ferguson, S. D. (1993). *Mastering the public opinion challenge*. Burr Ridge, IL: Irwin.

Ferguson, S. D. (1998). Constructing a theoretical framework for evaluating public relations programs and activities. In M. Roloff (ed.), *Communication yearbook* 21. Thousand Oaks, CA: Sage, pp. 190–229.

Ferguson, S. D. (1999). *Communication planning: An integrated approach*. Thousand Oaks, CA: Sage.

Ferguson, S. D. (2000). *Researching the public opinion environment: Theories and methods*. Thousand Oaks, CA: Sage.

Grunig, J. E. (ed.) (1992). *Excellence in public relations and communication management*. Hillsdale, NJ: Lawrence Erlbaum.

International Public Relations Association (1994). Public relations evaluation: Professional accountability. Gold Paper 11 (unpublished paper).

Leiss, W. (2004). *Mad cows and mother's milk*, 2nd edn. Montreal: McGill-Queen's University Press.

Marston, J. E. (1963). *The nature of public relations*. New York: McGraw-Hill.

McElreath, M. P. (1989). Priority research questions in the field of public relations for the 1990s: Trends for the past ten years and predictions for the future. Paper presented at the Speech Communication Association, San Francisco, CA.

Raupp, J., & Van Ruler, B. (2006). Trends in public relations and communication management research: A comparison between Germany and the Netherlands, *Journal of Communication Management*, 10, 18–26.

Sandman, P. M. (2006). Fear of fear and panic: Key barriers to effective pandemic pre-crisis communication. Forum on Science and Technology Policy, American Association for the Advancement of Science, Washington, DC.

Smith, R. D. (2005). *Strategic planning for public relations*, 2nd edn. Mahwah, NJ: Lawrence Erlbaum.

Synnott, G., and McKie, D. (1997). International issues in PR: Researching research and prioritizing priorities. *Journal of Public Relations Research*, 9, 259–282.

Ulmer, R. R., Sellnow, T. L., & Seeger, M. W. (2006). *Effective crisis communication: Moving from crisis to opportunity*. Thousand Oaks, CA: Sage.

Public Relations Roles

David M. Dozier

San Diego State University

Organizational roles are abstract maps summarizing the most salient features of the daily activities of organizational members. Katz & Kahn (1978) considered roles central to the structure of organizations; organizations can be regarded as open systems of interrelated roles. Roles are defined as "recurring actions of an individual, appropriately interrelated with the repetitive activities of others so as to yield a predictable outcome" (Katz & Kahn 1978, 189).

In → public relations, practitioners perform a wide range of activities. Despite such diverse activities, researchers have discovered systematic patterns in the roles that practitioners play. Enactment of various roles has important consequences for practitioners and the practice of public relations. Indeed, practitioner roles are among the most studied areas in public relations research.

CONCEPTUAL AND OBSERVED ROLES

Glen Broom began studying roles of practitioners in the 1970s (Broom 1982). Drawing on the relevant literature, Broom conceptualized *four practitioner roles* that he later tested using experimental and survey designs. The "expert prescriber" was conceptualized as the organization's acknowledged expert on public relations. Expert prescribers make recommendations to those who run the organization with the expectation that top managers in organizations will comply. The "communication facilitator" was conceptualized as a "go-between." Practitioners enacting this role are involved in monitoring and enhancing the flow of information between publics and decision-makers inside organizations. The "problem-solving process facilitator" was conceptualized as an assistant to top management, helping senior decision-makers systematically analyze and solve public relations problems for organizations. The "communication technician" was conceptualized as a provider of technical communication services, generating various collateral materials to implement public relations programs. Practitioners enacting this role serve as *journalists-in-residence*, hired for their journalistic skills and expertise.

In a study of US practitioners, Broom found that the roles of expert prescriber, communication facilitator, and problem-solving process facilitator were highly correlated. Although conceptual distinctions could be made between these roles, practitioners enacting one of these roles were very likely to enact the other two roles as well. The communication technician role, however, was not correlated with the other three.

Broom's finding prompted Dozier to conduct exploratory → factor analysis on three practitioner → surveys. Broom's initial findings were replicated. This led to an *inductive reconceptualization* of practitioner roles. The "communication manager" makes communication policies and is held accountable for the success or failure of those decisions. Such practitioners facilitate the flow of information between the public and senior managers and keep top decision-makers in organizations appraised of public reactions to their organizations. The "communication technician" role remains as originally conceptualized by Broom.

Decades later, further research distinguished between the *strategic and administrative manager roles*. The "strategic manager role" consists of conducting evaluation research, using research to segment publics, and performing environmental scanning. The "administrative manager role" involves setting goals and objectives for public relations programs, preparing departmental budgets, and managing organizational responses to public relations problems (Grunig et al. 2002).

All practitioners conduct various role activities to some degree. For some analytic purposes, practitioner roles can be operationalized in terms of predominant role. A practitioner's predominant role is the role set that he or she enacts most frequently. Thus, practitioners who enact manager role activities with greater frequency than technician role activities are enacting the manager role predominantly.

In addition to Broom's 24-item set of practitioner role measures, other scholars have used alternative measurement strategies. Ferguson (1979) developed a 45-item set that measured practitioner perceptions of the appropriateness of various public relations activities (→ Scales and Indices). As such, Ferguson's measures can be viewed as the role received by the practitioner from others in the organization, as well as from other practitioners outside the organization. Berkowitz & Hristodoulakis (1999) developed a 13-item set to measure norms or ideals that apply to the roles of practitioners. Wright (1995) conducted a study of senior-level practitioners and suggested a third major role of communication executive. "Communication executives" hold the rank of corporate senior vice president, reporting directly to the chief executive officer. Toth et al. (1998) identified an "agency profile role," which seemed to fit the duties of practitioners working for public relations firms.

ANTECEDENTS AND CONSEQUENCES OF ROLES

Prior research showed that professional experience in public relations is a positive indicator of manager role enactment (Broom 1982; Dozier & Broom 1995). Women tend to have fewer years of professional experience and fewer years of employment with their current employer. Thus, women are less likely than men to enact the manager role predominantly. Level of formal education has only a weak positive relationship with manager role enactment (Dozier & Broom 1995).

Those enacting the manager role predominantly are more likely to use programmatic research to scan the organization's environment and evaluate the impact of public relations programs, when compared to those enacting the technician role predominantly. Manager role enactment is associated with greater participation in strategic decision-making (Dozier & Broom 1995). Such participation is important to the practice, because proactive "best practices" dictate that practitioners must counsel organizational decision-makers about the public relations implications of various strategic choices before decisions are made. Too often, decision-makers seek public relations help under crisis conditions, after poor choices have been implemented without proper counsel.

Practitioners enacting the manager role predominantly earn higher salaries than practitioners enacting the technician role predominantly. This is true, even after controlling for the professional experience of the practitioner. Job satisfaction, however, is more elusive. Practitioners who participate in strategic decision-making report higher levels of job satisfaction. However, job satisfaction may be affected by the practitioner's desire to pursue the *creative, artistic* aspects of public relations, activities associated with the technician role (Dozier & Gottesman 1982).

CRITICISMS OF ROLES

Creedon (1991) provided the first comprehensive critique of roles research from a feminist perspective. Toth & Grunig (1993), Hon (1995), and Toth et al. (1998) further elaborated this criticism. The feminist critique is important. In the United States, women make up over 61 percent of the public relations labor force (US Department of Labor, 2006). As a female-majority occupation, gender issues in public relations are important.

The critique includes five elements. First, argued the critics, Broom's quantitative measures of roles miss too much texture and nuance of role enactment. Second, the gender of the researcher arguably influences the kind of research questions asked and the methods used to answer those questions. Third, roles research places too much normative value on the manager role while seeming to denigrate the technical aspects of public relations (frequently enacted by women practitioners). Fourth, suggested strategies for overcoming gender discrimination (based on roles) ask women to change their behavior (e.g., enact the manager role more frequently), while leaving the discriminatory ideology of organizations intact. Fifth, the open systems framework for theorizing about practitioner roles provides normative justification for the unequal distribution of power in organizations and society.

ORGANIZATIONAL LEVEL OF ANALYSIS

Most prior research on the roles of practitioners focused on the actual enactment of roles by individual practitioners. Although this research has contributed much to the theory and practice of public relations, the individual level of analysis is problematic for several reasons. First, women enact the technician role predominantly with much greater frequency than men (Dozier & Broom 1995). Relative to women, men tend to enact the manager role predominantly. Second, people attracted to public relations for creative, artistic opportunities may find greater job satisfaction in the production of messages than in strategic planning. Since enactment of the manager role is linked to such desired outcomes as greater participation in strategic planning and higher salaries, enactment of the technician role predominantly seems undesirable. However, the seeming hierarchy of practitioner roles (manager over technician) is an artifact of the level of analysis; the hierarchy disappears when the analysis is shifted to the organizational level.

In the *Excellence Project* (Grunig 1992; Grunig et al. 2002), the most important predictor of excellence in public relations was the knowledge base to enact the strategic manager role and to engage in two-way communication with publics. Moreover, the knowledge base was operationalized as an attribute of the public relations department, not individual practitioners.

Through the multivariate analysis of the factors associated with overall excellence, Grunig et al. (2002) found that the organizations with the excellent public relations also had high expertise in the technical aspects of the practice. This led Dozier & Broom (2006) to theorize that expertise to enact the strategic manager role at the department level led to successful public relations programs over time. This, in turn, empowered the public relations department to capture more resources to enhance the technical expertise of the department.

Excellent public relations departments have a mix of practitioners; some play the manager role predominantly while others play the technician role predominantly. Some seek to participate in the strategic planning of the organization while others use their creative, artistic talents to implement communication programs. Indeed, it is difficult to imagine an excellent public relations department without the full range of expertise. Less-than-excellent public relations departments do not have the requisite strategic management expertise to know what to do with the creative, artistic talent that exists within the department.

Normatively, this shift to the organizational level of analysis suggests dual career tracks for both creative, artistic practitioners and for strategic planners. Both types of roles should be rewarded, because both contribute to the excellence of the public relations department.

SEE ALSO: ▶ Factor Analysis ▶ Professionalization of Public Relations ▶ Public Relations ▶ Public Relations Planning ▶ Scales and Indices ▶ Stakeholder Theory ▶ Strategic Communication ▶ Survey

References and Suggested Readings

Berkowitz, D., & Hristodoulakis, I. (1999). Practitioner roles, public relations education, and professional socialization: An exploratory study. *Journal of Public Relations Research*, 11(1), 91–103.

Broom, G. M. (1982). A comparison of sex roles in public relations. *Public Relations Review*, 8(3), 17–22.

Creedon, P. J. (1991). Public relations and "women's work": Toward a feminist analysis of public relations roles. In J. E. Grunig & L. A. Grunig (eds.), *Public relations research annual* 3. Hillsdale, NJ: Lawrence Erlbaum, pp. 67–84.

Dozier, D. M., & Broom, G. M. (1995). Evolution of the manager role in public relations practice. *Journal of Public Relations Research*, 7(1), 3–26.

Dozier, D. M., & Broom, G. M. (2006). The centrality of practitioner roles in public relations theory. In C. H. Botan & V. Hazleton (eds.), *Public relations theory II*. Mahwah, NJ: Lawrence Erlbaum, pp. 137–170.

Dozier, D. M., & Gottesman, M. (1982). Subjective dimensions of organizational roles among public relations practitioners. Paper presented at the meeting of the Public Relations Division, Association for Education in Journalism, Athens, OH (July).

Ferguson, M. A. (1979). Role norms, implicit relationship attributions and organizational communication: A study of public relations practitioners. Unpublished master's thesis, University of Wisconsin.

Grunig, J. E. (ed.) (1992). *Excellence in public relations and communication management*. Hillsdale, NJ: Lawrence Erlbaum.

Grunig, L. A., Grunig, J. E., & Dozier, D. M. (2002). *Excellent public relations and effective organizations: A study of communication management in three countries*. Mahwah, NJ: Lawrence Erlbaum.

Hon, L. C. (1995). Toward a feminist theory of public relations. *Journal of Public Relations Research*, 7(1), 27–88.

Katz, D., & Kahn, R. L. (1978). *The social psychology of organizations*, rev. edn. New York: John Wiley.

Toth, E. L., & Grunig, L. A. (1993). The missing story of women in public relations. *Journal of Public Relations Research*, 5(3), 153–175.

Toth, E. L., Serini, S. S., Wright, D. K., & Emig, A. G. (1998). Trends in public relations roles: 1990–1995. *Public Relations Review*, 24(2), 145–163.

US Department of Labor, Bureau of Labor Statistics (2006). *Employment and Earnings*. Washington, DC: US Government Printing Office.

Wright, D. K. (1995). The role of corporate public relations executives in the future of employee communications. *Public Relations Review*, 21(3), 181–198.

Public Service Broadcasting: Law and Policy

Damian Tambini

London School of Economics and Political Science

Public service broadcasting (PSB) is funded by the public, and regulated to ensure that it serves the → public interest. Public service broadcasters (PSBs) should be distinguished from state broadcasters, which function mainly to serve the interests of the government, and purely commercial broadcasters, which respond primarily to individual consumer choices rather than to any notion of the broader public interest. PSBs are also distinct from nonprofit local "community broadcasters," which are public-oriented and partly grant-funded, in that PSBs are generally national in scope (→ Community Media).

Almost all countries have some form of national public service as part of their broadcasting ecology, but the size, type, and form of public service broadcasting intervention varies. In Japan and Britain, for example, PSB is funded by a universal license fee and accounts for a significant proportion of all media viewing and listening. In other countries, for example the USA, PSBs rely on less secure forms of funding, such as donations, and only a small fraction of all media use is of PSB content.

THE AIMS AND BASIC STRUCTURES OF PSB

Dimensions in PSB's Societal Functions

The legal basis of the well-established public broadcasting system in Germany can serve as an example for the variety of functions that are expected from the broadcasters. According to German constitutional law scholar Bernd Holznagel, the functional remit of public broadcasters covers eight basic dimensions:

- *Information remit*: the PSB has a duty to convey objective information as a basis for the free forming of opinions. Coverage, therefore, has to be comprehensive, truthful and factual [→ Objectivity in Reporting; Neutrality].

- *Guiding role*: as a source of independent and unbiased information, PSB provides reliable, credible reference points and, consequently, guidance for a free forming of opinion.
- *Role of forum*: PSB has to ensure that all relevant opinions on a particular subject receive a hearing. They have to offer a forum for public discussion in which the relevant social groups can participate [→ Political Discourse].
- *Integration role*: PSB should aim for mutual understanding and, thus, foster social cohesion.
- *Benchmark*: PSB has the obligation to provide guiding, high-quality, and innovative programming. In this way they set standards [→ Quality of the News; Political Media Content, Quality Criteria in].
- *Cultural mission*: PSB programming has to reflect Germany's cultural diversity and the events taking place in all the regions of the country [→ Plurality].
- *Mission to produce*: appropriate fulfilment of the respective obligations cannot be guaranteed by the mere acquisition of foreign productions. Because of that, PSB has a mission to produce independently and creatively.
- *Innovative role*: PSB is encouraged to take an innovative lead in testing and using new technology and new services in the broadcasting sector. [→ Technology and Communication]. (Holznagel 2000, 2)

In order to achieve these goals, PSBs are generally obliged to ensure that their services are universally available, and that they have sufficient independence and funding. Forms of intervention that support public service broadcasting include finance, charters, and governance.

Financing of PSB

NHK in Japan (→ Japan: Media System), the → BBC in the UK, SVT in Sweden (→ Scandinavian States: Media Systems) and ZDF in Germany (→ Germany: Media System) are all examples of public service broadcasters funded by a *universal license fee* on receiver sets. The size of the license fee varies according to local conditions, but in larger markets it can be around $200 per year per television household. In many countries (France, Germany, Italy, Ireland, and Portugal, for example) public broadcasters receive both direct subsidies and advertising revenue.

Public service broadcasters also receive some forms of grant in direct aid from the government (through *taxation, i.e., direct public subsidies*); and smaller countries (such as Portugal and Ireland) are forced to rely more on subsidy through taxation (→ Portugal: Media System). While the US PSB service receives most of its funding from donations, it also receives a significant proportion through government grants.

Indirect public subsidies come mostly in the form of non-market prices for use of the "airwaves" or spectrum frequencies. Most publicly funded broadcasters receive free or cheap spectrum. This means that they do not pay the same charges as a mobile telephony company would pay for the exclusive use of certain frequencies. The value of this indirect subsidy rises rapidly with demand for spectrum, which is in turn driven by innovation, as new services are provided that could use spectrum currently used for television. Some stations receive *voluntary public funding through donations*. For instance, NHK's license fee is technically voluntary, i.e., there is no penalty for non-payment, and people have the right to prevent license collectors entering the home, though there are strong social pressures to pay. The Public Broadcasting Service (PBS) in the US is funded mainly by completely voluntary donations from viewers and listeners.

Some broadcasting systems impose *public service obligations* (such as obligations to provide → news, and educational (→ Instructional Television), cultural, or national programming) on some commercial broadcasters, as a condition of the license to broadcast. In the United Kingdom, the launch of commercial broadcasters alongside the BBC in the 1950s and 1960s was permitted only on the condition that these companies adhered to a strong public service remit. If broadcasters fail to adhere to public service requirements they may lose their licenses. A crucial obligation placed on public service broadcasters is the obligation to present news and current affairs fairly or "impartially."

Founding Statements and Charters

Founding statements and charters state the purposes and aims of the corporation. PSBs' overarching aims and principles tend to be set out either in a license or in a separate founding statement. The BBC, which provides a model for many PSBs around the world, is governed by a *Royal Charter*, which has been renewed and updated every decade or so since the first charter was signed by King George in 1926. The charter sets out the aims of the corporation. For the first years of the corporation they were set out broadly as provision of broadcasting services to "entertain, inform and educate." The Royal Charter approved by the UK government in 2006 changes the general objectives of the corporation and sets out a framework for regulating the provision of nonbroadcasting (such as Internet) services. The public purposes of the BBC for 2007 onwards are as follows: (1) sustaining citizenship and civil society; (2) promoting education and learning; (3) stimulating creativity and cultural excellence; (4) representing the UK, its nations, regions, and communities; (5) bringing the UK to the world and the world to the UK; (6) in promoting its other purposes, helping to deliver to the public the benefit of emerging communications technologies and services and, in addition, taking a leading role in the switchover to digital television (→ Television Broadcasting, Regulation of; Radio Broadcasting, Regulation of).

Accountability and Governance

The regulation, accountability, and governance structures of PSBs attempt to insure that the PSB organization is directly accountable to the public it serves, rather than the government, shareholders, or advertisers. The Netherlands' system of public service broadcasting differs from others, in that public broadcasting channels provide space for programming that is provided by broadcasting associations that represent societal interest groups (→ Netherlands: Media System). Other broadcasters have regional public accountability mechanisms – such as the regional councils in the BBC, or the regulatory authorities in Germany at *Länder* level that exist to monitor and regulate PSB activity.

Some countries, such as Germany, have a separate system for the *financial account-ability* of public service broadcasters. The Commission on Broadcasting Finance (known as the KEF) has since 1975 had responsibility for auditing the accounts of the public broadcasters and insuring that license fees are wisely spent. The BBC has traditionally been a self-regulating organization, with the BBC governors (renamed the BBC Trust in 2006) acting as a body that holds the Corporation to account for content and also financial matters. The BBC reports annually to Parliament, but Parliament has only weak, symbolic sanctions over the BBC. This arrangement has been criticized as providing only weak accountability and an insufficient guarantee of separation of regulatory and management functions, but it has the advantage of underlining the independence of the BBC.

The system of PSB has been explicitly recognized in *international legal instruments* such as the European Convention on Human Rights (ECHR; → European Court of Human Rights). ECHR article 10 explicitly permits states to license broadcasting services. However, the freedom of expression provisions in the ECHR were used in the case of Tele 1 *v.* Austria to establish that national regulators could not restrict terrestrial broadcasters to the national PSBs through refusing to license other broadcasters. There remain some sources of tension between the World Trade Organization attempt to liberalize trade in services (the General Agreement on Trade in Services) and the possible restrictions on free trade between states due to PSBs. Similarly, regional free trade arrangements including the European Union have provided a basis for criticism of PSBs as a form of "state aid" and a barrier to free trade and investment.

PSB IN HISTORICAL PERSPECTIVE

Public service broadcasting has since its inception been based on an attempt to find an alternative to the commercial organization of communications services. The BBC, set up in the 1920s as a consortium of receiver makers, was taken into public ownership in 1926, and a system of noncommercial, publicly funded broadcasting was set up. Within the UK, this was seen by successive UK committees of inquiry as necessary so that the "chaos" of commercial broadcasting in the US was not replicated in the UK. The BBC model has since been widely exported, and hybrid commercial–public service models have evolved in most countries.

For example, in both Japan and Germany in the postwar period a broadcasting system was set up that included a large national public service element. In the case of Germany this broadcaster had many checks and balances to prevent the emergence of a monolithic → propaganda instrument. In the former Soviet bloc, there has been a less successful attempt to develop a mixed ecology of commercial and public service media. The PSBs that have been introduced have struggled to achieve audience share and budget sustainability. In developing countries the principal challenges for PSBs have been financial sustainability and political independence, but there is strong support for PSBs where they are necessary for the protection of minority languages.

Most countries' PSBs operate in a tense relationship with governments. On one hand they must demonstrate that they still merit direct and indirect subsidies, and on the other they can only fulfill their democratic mission by engaging in robust criticism of the government. The use of the BBC model in countries with authoritarian tendencies has been criticized, as it permits too many possibilities for state interference.

ECONOMIC JUSTIFICATIONS OF PSB

Public service broadcasting has been justified with reference to the following main claims about the economic characteristics of broadcasting. First, *broadcasting is a public good.* Public goods, like for example air, or the protection by the military, are goods that are nonrival (my consumption does not diminish yours) and nonexcludable (it is difficult in any case to prevent you consuming them). This has led some to claim that the appropriate level of PSB will not be provided by the market, and that public provision may be the most efficient form of provision.

Second, *broadcasting is a merit good that provides positive externalities.* Education, insurance, and public broadcasting tend to be underprovided by a market because consumers do not choose to consume the amount that serves optimum welfare. In addition, like education, consumption by one individual will have positive benefits in terms of the economic, educational, and democratic health of society as a whole. The BBC argues that broadcasting delivers "public value" that would not be delivered by commercial broadcasting, such as improved democratic, educational, and social cohesion benefits. The contribution of the BBC is measurable through willingness-to-pay → surveys that demonstrate that the average sum that citizens would be willing to pay for a BBC subscription (if this were the only way of getting BBC services) is in excess of the sums currently paid in license fees, thus demonstrating that consumers enjoy a surplus of value. Surveys commissioned by the BBC also show that the amount individuals would be prepared to pay in tax to keep the BBC operating "for the good of society" is also in excess of the current level of the license fee, and in excess of the consumer surplus value.

Third, *spectrum is a scarce resource* and as a result there are a severely limited number of broadcasters. Because choice is limited and broadcasting is a particularly influential and invasive medium, markets will fail and broadcasters must be open and accountable directly to the public and Parliament rather than to shareholders, in order to insure that they provide balanced, plural, and representative forms of content (→ Balance). This rationale is seriously challenged when new platforms such as satellite and broadband show that traditional analog spectrum licenses are no longer a necessary condition of accessing the market.

CHALLENGES TO PUBLIC BROADCASTING

Political pressure on broadcaster independence is the major and permanent pressure on public service broadcasters. The years 2004–5 saw major conflicts regarding the relationship between PSBs and governments in Spain (→ Spain: Media System), Italy (→ Italy: Media System), and the UK. In Spain and the UK the conflicts centered on news coverage of terrorism and security (→ Mediated Terrorism). There are numerous examples in history of disputes between governments and PSBs regarding the appropriate coverage of controversial issues, and governments generally find it hard to resist the temptation to interfere, by attempting to influence high level appointments and editorial policy (→ Media Policy).

The role of governments in relation to broadcasters is a problematic one, and all public broadcasters face a continuing struggle for independence: from societal interests and from governmental influence and control. All of these regulatory arrangements come under pressure from time to time, particularly in relation to sensitive issues such as national security. Key areas of tension between governments and PSBs concern the content of news programming, and the appointment of key figures to management, journalistic, and governance positions within the PSB. In 2004, the Spanish PSB allegedly came under direct pressure from the prime minister to report terrorist bombings. In Italy, PSB independence and impartiality has traditionally been weak. It is generally accepted that there tends to be a division of the main RAI channels between major political parties, and that this informal system has survived successive governments.

Audience decline and fragmentation is a second challenge to PSB. With increasing channel choice and consumer empowerment comes a decline in audience for PSB channels and genres. In the European Broadcasting Union countries, the PSBs' audience shares declined from 39 percent in 1995 to 35.5 percent in 2003 (Ward 2006). For publicly funded broadcasters, declining audiences undermine the legitimacy of charging universal license fees. For advertising funded PBSs, audience loss highlights the increasing costs of providing public service programming. PSBs respond with an attempt to provide popular programming, and leave themselves open to the corresponding criticisms of "dumbing down" or lack of distinctiveness. This could be described as a "downward spiral of PSBs." Fragmentation also leads to pressure for change in the nature of PSB services. For example, some PSBs and their critics argue that the PSB should not have to observe the same high standards – for example of impartiality – if its monopoly position is diminished (→ Audience Segmentation).

Finally, PSBs are increasingly attempting to *launch new services* such as → Internet, satellite, mobile, and high-definition platforms (→ Mobility, Technology for). The extent to which PSBs are able to enter these new markets depends on the detail of their regulatory arrangements. Some (for example in Germany and Japan) are severely curtailed in their ability to launch new services, while others, for example the BBC, have been able to launch a large array of online and other services. New platforms such as reception on PCs and mobile phones undermine the idea of charging a license fee on TV receivers as a way of paying for PSB services. If significant numbers of users access PSB services though platforms other than TV sets, new payment mechanisms may have to be found.

Views on the current and future development of PSBs range from the pessimistic view that it will be impossible to maintain public provision of distinct PSB material to more optimistic views that see the role of PSBs expanding into new on-demand and interactive services. Some have called for a more "decentralized" or "distributed" model of public service broadcasting. This has variously been described as an "arts council of the airwaves," distributing funding for public service content by competitive tender, and as a "public service publisher" (Ofcom 2004) that would commission and distribute content of a public service nature for free.

SEE ALSO: ▶ Audience Segmentation ▶ Balance ▶ BBC ▶ Community Media ▶ European Court of Human Rights ▶ Germany: Media System ▶ Instructional Television ▶ Internet ▶ Italy: Media System ▶ Japan: Media System ▶ Media Policy ▶ Mediated Terrorism ▶ Mobility, Technology for ▶ Netherlands: Media System ▶ Neutrality

▶ News ▶ Objectivity in Reporting ▶ Plurality ▶ Political Discourse ▶ Political Media Content, Quality Criteria in ▶ Portugal: Media System ▶ Propaganda ▶ Public Interest ▶ Quality of the News ▶ Radio Broadcasting, Regulation of ▶ Scandinavian States: Media Systems ▶ Spain: Media System ▶ Survey ▶ Technology and Communication ▶ Television Broadcasting, Regulation of

References and Suggested Readings

Holznagel, B. (2000). The mission of public service broadcasters. *International Journal of Communications Law and Policy*, 13(5), 1–22. (Reprinted in Price & Raboy 2002).

Ofcom (2004). *Ofcom review of public service television broadcasting*, vols. 1, 2, 3. London: Office of Communications.

Price, M., & Raboy, M. (2002). *Public service broadcasting: A documentary reader*. Brussels: European Institute for the Media.

Priebs, N. (2004). Learning from abroad: Regulating public service broadcasting in Germany, Japan and the UK. In D. Tambini & J. Cowling (eds.), *From public service broadcasting to public service communication*. London: Institute for Public Policy Research.

Tambini, D., & Cowling, J. (eds.) (2004). *From public service broadcasting to public service communication*. London: Institute for Public Policy Research.

Ward, D. (2006). Can the market provide? Public service media, market failure and public goods. In C. S. Nissen (ed.), *Making a difference: Public service broadcasting in the European media landscape*. Eastleigh: John Libbey.

Public Sphere

Frank Marcinkowski

University of Münster

The public sphere is an indispensable element of a democratic society and the institutional core of democratic decision-making. Every democratic political order is essentially based on the idea that citizens participate in collectively binding decisions, articulate their interests and opinions openly, listen and evaluate the opinions and arguments of others, and, on that basis, make up their minds. The public sphere establishes an arena of discussion on public affairs and guarantees that all these processes are open to the public.

In everyday usage, the term "public sphere" is associated with "the public", i.e. the people as a whole or a group of people having common interests (e.g., "the reading public"). Scientific definitions of the concept vary across different theoretical schools of thought (→ Public). Mostly the term refers to the institutionalization of a realm of social life for the exchange of information and opinions. The public sphere in the narrower sense is the act of free citizens gathering together for debate in order to achieve a rational regulation of public affairs. Another facet of the concept denotes the structures and contents of the public political debate itself. In a third dimension of the meaning, the term refers to the public spaces in which public communication regularly takes place:

streets and squares, formal and informal gathering places, publicly meeting institutions of the political system, and the arena of the mass media.

HABERMAS AND THE PUBLIC SPHERE

Proponents of *critical theory* working at the Institute for Social Research in Frankfurt had a decisive influence on the development of the concept of the public sphere. The most famous work of the Frankfurt School, *Dialectic of enlightenment* by Max Horkheimer and Theodor W. Adorno (1972), written in the early 1940s while in American exile, focuses on the mass production and consumption of cultural goods as well as their spread via the media. The authors deny any enlightening impact of the predominant media practice in the United States of the 1940s and describe it instead as a form of mass deception. This characteristic of the → "culture industries" necessarily accompanies the development from market capitalism to state and monopoly capitalism. Applied to the concept of the public sphere, the *culture industry thesis* implies three thoughts. The main realm for the exchange of opinions in modern society is the mass media arena. Its commercial basis leads to the standardization and trivialization of all cultural products. Through this, public communication becomes a commodity; its exchange value is more important than its utility value (→ Political Economy of the Media; Commodification of the Media).

Jürgen Habermas, the most prominent representative of the "second generation" of the Frankfurt School, in his seminal work on *The structural transformation of the public sphere* (1989) contrasts the bourgeois public sphere of the liberal democracies of seventeenth- and eighteenth-century Europe with the debased public sphere of late capitalism (→ Habermas, Jürgen). Habermas follows the traditional orientation of critical theory, which is to measure society not according to what it is but according to what it could be. The model of the bourgeois public sphere serves as a normative backdrop against which the transformation and symptoms of decline in the late capitalist welfare state can be shown all the more clearly. Habermas, like Horkheimer and Adorno before him, is less concerned with the sociology of the public sphere than with a comprehensive analysis of society using the public sphere as an analytical "category."

Habermas's understanding of the public sphere takes up Enlightenment philosophy ideas on free deliberation and its inherent potential for rational discussion, debate, and consensus. He points to historical evidence of this in the social developments of Great Britain, France, and Germany after 1680, when the rapidly developing, property-owning, educated bourgeoisie succeeded, for the first time in European history, in openly expressing its demands and developing → *public opinion* as an instrument of critique and of control of state power. The preconditions for this were found in the concrete historical situation at the beginning of the eighteenth century, when the feudal authorities (church, princes, and nobility) disintegrated. As an accompanying development, bourgeois society as well as the new sphere of public authority came into being with national and territorial states. The public sphere as a mediator filled the space between bourgeois society, now a private realm, and the public authority of the state. Places for reasoning and meaningful argument were, in addition to newspapers and journals, a variety of public spaces like pubs, coffee houses, table societies, political clubs, and literary salons, where a self-confident bourgeoisie gathered to contribute everyday knowledge and life-world experience to the discussion of public affairs (→ Coffee Houses as Public Sphere; Public Meetings). Here it was not simply private, partial interests that were moved up against the state, but rather rational critical debate, out of which a discourse-mediated common will emerged.

Precisely because the basis of the public sphere lies in the autonomy of the human life-world from the state, the social structural transformation of the public sphere started, according to Habermas, at the moment when the strict separation between private life and public authority began to erode. With the development of modern welfare states in the late nineteenth century, state authority and civil society became increasingly interwoven. For one, powerful interest groups are increasingly successful in their attempts to influence state decision-making in their favor. For another, the state intervenes ever more deeply in the private realm and in people's economic activities. With the expansion of the social basis of public debates beyond the bounds of the classical educated bourgeoisie, the forms of participation in the public sphere change: the tendency toward active → discourse is eclipsed by passive consumption of public communications. It is no longer general interests and the public good that determine the form and contents of discursive argumentation in the public sphere, but instead unequal partial interests.

The structural transformation brings with it a functional change of the public sphere. With the emergence of the *mediated* public sphere as the central forum of modern societies, the bilateral character and discursiveness that mark the ideal of deliberative assembly lose importance. The public sphere that is now manufactured by the mass media relies on organized contributors. It therefore stands open mainly to powerful and resource-strong actors in the state and economy. The citizens themselves are forced back, as in absolutist states, into the role of spectators ("re-feudalization").

BEYOND HABERMAS

Several authors have taken Habermas's conception as a point of departure for their own theoretical and empirical research on the public sphere. Early on, sociologist Oskar Negt and filmmaker Alexander Kluge (1993) criticized Habermas's concept from a neo-Marxist perspective. They put forward, as opposed to rational discourse, an alternative understanding of the public sphere as a form of organization of collective social experience. In contrast to Habermas's ideal of the bourgeois public sphere, they articulate the notion of an oppositional, proletarian public sphere. In view of the hegemony of the dominant ideology within the bourgeois public sphere, Negt and Kluge seek the conditions of emancipation and self-enlightenment of the proletariat in the counter-public sphere ("counter publicity").

Niklas Luhmann, a longstanding opponent of Habermas within German sociology, thoroughly criticized Habermas's concept of the public sphere, arguing that consensus is not the result but a prerequisite of communication. In order to be able to communicate successfully at all, one must have issues at one's disposal that are accepted by all participants. In the case of political communication, public opinion as "the issues structure of political communication" indicates which issues can be brought forward in the political process with an expectation of being heard. For decision-making, the multitude of opinions is then reduced by means of the decision rules of the political system. Power, and not rationality, is what is decisive here (Luhmann 1970, 1986).

US authors criticizing Habermas's notion of the public sphere refer mainly to the historical inaccuracy and the over-stylized picture of the bourgeois public sphere. It is to that degree questionable whether rational-critical argumentation ever played as powerful a role as Habermas describes. Critics also address the problem of the exclusionary character of the bourgeois public sphere, excluding the working class as well as women. Beyond that, Habermas is found to underestimate the role of science and religion in the bourgeois public sphere in favor of literature. Regarding the media, Habermas is criticized for not recognizing → tabloidization tendencies as early as the seventeenth century and, on the other hand, for drawing an overly one-sided picture of entertainment-oriented television consumers in modern times. Particularly, communication scholars reproach Habermas for having an inadequate understanding of the functions of the modern mass media. With reference to media forms that interlace interpersonal and mass communication, they point out that discourse does not necessarily require direct communication among people who are all present at any one place. They suggest that the public sphere of modern societies should be conceived not as a uniform communication space but instead as a network of more or less closely connected subsidiary public spheres or clusters of denser communication (Calhoun 1992; Roberts & Crossley 2004).

Based on the idea that in modern societies the mass media builds the central arena of public spheres, contemporary empirical work focuses on the deliberative quality of media discourses (→ Deliberativeness in Political Communication). Drawing on normative criteria from the Habermasian model of the public sphere, such as the inclusiveness of discourse, the reciprocity of the participants, the degree of mutual respect, and the level of reflexivity, several studies try to measure the quality of media coverage on controversial policy issues. For example, Gerhards (1997) investigates whether the abortion discourse as reflected in German media meets the demands of Habermas's conception. According to his findings, the media discourse is conducted mainly in the exclusive circle of the political elites, and the participants in the discourse speak more *about* each other than *with* each other. An international comparative study on the same topic shows that public discourse in the United States comes closer to the participatory model of democracy, because here more actors and arguments of civil society are included, while the elite-centered marketplace of ideas and arguments in the German case accords with the model of liberal democracy (Ferree et al. 2002). In both countries the media discourses do not meet the high normative standards of a rational-critical public sphere.

PUBLIC SPHERE REVISITED

Since the 1980s, cognizant of the criticisms and further developing his ideas, Habermas (1985, 1996) has qualified his originally pessimistic view of the potentials of the democratic public sphere. He no longer sees the public sphere as a category typical of an epoch that is tied to historically unique conditions, but rather bases a hope for emancipation and democratization on the universal capacity of human communication for reason and mutual understanding, which can unfold in historically contingent forms of the public sphere. He changes his fictive, ideal-type understanding of the public sphere to a conception of the public sphere "as intermediary system of communication between formally organized and informal face-to-face deliberations in arenas at both the top and the bottom of a political system" (Habermas 2006, 415). The task of the media is to make public and to confront selected issues, arguments, and opinions of the political elites and actors in civil society. Even though mediated communication lacks the defining features of deliberation, it can still function as an arena for perception, identification, and definition of problems related to society as a whole. It thus delivers necessary input for rational decision-making in the institutionalized discourses of the political system (→ Political Discourse). In the working together of everyday talk, mediated public communication, and institutionalized forms of deliberation in the center of the political system, well-grounded opinions on social problems can thus be developed.

SEE ALSO: ► Coffee Houses as Public Sphere ► Commodification of the Media ► Communication Theory and Philosophy ► Culture Industries ► Deliberativeness in Political Communication ► Discourse ► Habermas, Jürgen ► Media History ► Political Discourse ► Political Economy of the Media ► Public ► Public Meetings ► Public Opinion ► Public Sphere, Fragmentation of ► Tabloidization

References and Suggested Readings

Calhoun, C. (ed.) (1992). *Habermas and the public sphere*. Cambridge, MA: MIT Press.

Ferree, M. M., Gamson, W. A., Gerhards, J., & Rucht, D. (2002). *Shaping abortion discourse: Democracy and the public sphere in Germany and the United States*. Cambridge: Cambridge University Press.

Gerhards, J. (1997). Diskursive versus liberale Öffentlichkeit: Eine empirische Auseinandersetzung mit Jürgen Habermas. *Kölner Zeitschrift für Soziologie und Sozialpsychologie*, 49, 1–34.

Habermas, J. (1985). *Theory of communicative action*, vols. 1–2 (trans. T. McCarthy). Boston: Beacon Press. (Original work published 1981).

Habermas, J. (1989). *The structural transformation of the public sphere*. Cambridge, MA: MIT Press. (Original work published 1962).

Habermas, J. (1996). *Between facts and norms: Contributions to a discourse theory of law and democracy* (trans. W. Rehg). Cambridge, MA: MIT Press. (Original work published 1992).

Habermas, J. (2006). Political communication in media society: Does democracy still enjoy an epistemic dimension? The impact of normative theory on empirical research. *Communication Theory*, 16, 411–426.

Horkheimer, M., & Adorno, T. W. (1972). *Dialectic of enlightenment*. New York: Seabury. (Original work published 1944).

Luhmann, N. (1970). Öffentliche Meinung [Public opinion]. *Politische Vierteljahresschrift*, 11, 2–28.

Luhmann, N. (1986). *Ecological communication* (trans. J. Bednarz, Jr.). Cambridge: Polity.

Negt, O., & Kluge, A. (1993). *Public sphere and experience* (trans P. Labanyi, J. O. Daniel, & A. Oksiloff, foreword M. Hansen). Minneapolis, MN: University of Minnesota Press.

Roberts, M., & Crossley, N. (eds.) (2004). *After Habermas: New perspectives on the public sphere*. Oxford: Blackwell.

Public Sphere, Fragmentation of

Frank Marcinkowski

University of Münster

The public sphere is defined as a network of all the communicative spaces within which public affairs are debated and a public opinion is formed (→ Public Sphere; Public Opinion). Such an infrastructure of political communication is crucial for democratic self-government and the social integration of modern society. Both functions seem to be threatened if the public sphere decays into a multitude of arenas that are just loosely connected (if at all) and do not form a coherent space for deliberation (→ Deliberativeness in Political Communication; Political Discourse).

From a sociological point of view the fragmentation (i.e., stratification) of the public sphere seems to be the result either of social inequality (Fraser 1992) or of individualization in the postmodern age (Beck & Beck-Gernsheim 2002). In contrast, communication scholars refer to the media dominance over public communication of current societies. In this view the fragmentation of the mediated public sphere can then be described in at least three distinct dimensions: fragmentation of media channels, fragmentation of content, and fragmentation of audiences (see also Dahlgren 2005).

The enormous growth and the differentiation of the national media systems are focused on in the first dimension. Instead of having only a few radio stations and print media of national importance, there is now a multitude of communication channels, which are all competing with each other. On the one hand, this leads to an extended social range and inclusiveness of the media arena within the public sphere. On the other hand, it also leads to an ongoing decay of this arena into a multitude of media branches and niches that serve a multiplicity of special interests. The → Internet has a special share in the growth of the mediated public sphere. Some authors emphasize that the global infrastructure of the Internet will enable the expansion of the public sphere across national boundaries (Roberts & Crossley 2004). However, the development of a possible global public debate depends on who actually uses the Internet for what reasons and purposes (Sparks 2001). From a democratic point of view the Internet expands the possibilities of political groups and interests that have, up to now, been restrained by the high access barriers of the mainstream media. Thus, the Internet enables the development of new counter-publics and subsidiary publics. However, this could also lead to a locking out of social groups into secluded "cyber ghettos" (Dahlgren 2001).

The vast growth of the media sector, which is formative for the development of the media systems in all western societies, has effectively heightened the media's capacity in addressing and generating media content. In order to fill the multitude of channels with content, more and more areas of human life have to be made a topic of media communication, including areas that are traditionally reserved for personal and private experiences. Fragmentation of media channels thus tends to result in a diversification of content. The competition among more and more media products, combined with limited public attention and the ever-growing market orientation of media products, leads to an overabundance of entertaining media content (→ Competition in Media Systems;

Diversification of Media Markets; Markets of the Media). The majority of information available in today's media does not cater to public affairs deliberation but rather to private interests and the need for amusement. This also applies to the sphere of the Internet, where public debate is a marginalized phenomenon. The playing down of political communication is a quite paradoxical result of the media-driven expansion of the public sphere (McKee 2005).

Developments of media technology and content increasingly allow a more flexible and individualized media usage. This leads to a splitting up of the recipients' attention and a segmentation of media audiences (→ Audience Segmentation). With a growing range of media products and individualized forms of usage, the attention devoted to each single media product inevitably must shrink. Accordingly, political content is perceived in increasingly smaller portions. Moreover, the size of the media audiences that are absorbing identical content is declining, as special interest formats and specialized channels must focus on small target groups in order to be commercially successful. This means that the probability of all members of a society perceiving all relevant topics and problems is diminishing. Hence, if there are no topics of common importance, the probability that a mediated public sphere will resonate in daily interpersonal communication declines.

Most authors, including → Jürgen Habermas, agree that a unitary public sphere is an idealization, for the public discourse has always been divided into a variety of class- and group-specific communication circles. Therefore the seeming fragmentation of the public sphere cannot be blamed on the media development alone. The crucial question, then, is whether or not the segmentation of the public sphere has to be regarded as a challenge to democracy. The optimistic – mostly postmodernist – view argues that special interest media and mainstream media are never hermetically secluded from each other. Exchanges between different media can be found on the level of the producers and on the level of the users. We may therefore expect that people's demands and issue positions diffuse from sub-publics to the national political → public and result in policy outcomes. In this perspective, the fragmentation of channels, contents, and user groups contributes to desirable democratic plurality (Dahlgren 2005). Seen from a pessimistic point of view, the very same fragmentation is worrying, as it is expected to widen gaps of issue knowledge and orientations within the population that cannot be closed with non-medial forms of communication. As a consequence, the mass media would lose its key function of connecting publics, and the public sphere would forfeit its power of social integration (Downey & Fenton 2003). Yet empirical evidence is still lacking for both the optimistic and the pessimistic view. More research is needed, especially on the communicative coupling between mediated and non-mediated arenas of the public sphere.

SEE ALSO: ▶ Audience Segmentation ▶ Competition in Media Systems ▶ Deliberativeness in Political Communication ▶ Diversification of Media Markets ▶ Habermas, Jürgen ▶ Internet ▶ Markets of the Media ▶ Political Discourse ▶ Public ▶ Public Opinion ▶ Public Sphere

References and Suggested Readings

Beck, U., & Beck-Gernsheim, E. (2002). *Individualization: Institutionalized individualism and its social and political consequences*. London: Sage.

Dahlgren, P. (2001). The public sphere and the Net: Structure, space and communication. In L. W. Bennett & R. M. Entman (eds.), *Mediated politics: Communication in the future of democracy*. Cambridge: Cambridge University Press, pp. 33–55.

Dahlgren, P. (2005). The Internet, public spheres, and political communication: Dispersion and deliberation. *Political Communication*, 22, 147–162.

Downey, J., & Fenton, N. (2003). New media, counter publicity and the public sphere. *New Media and Society*, 5, 185–202.

Fraser, N. (1992). Rethinking the public sphere: A contribution to the critique of actually existing democracy. In C. Calhoun (ed.), *Habermas and the public sphere*. Cambridge, MA: MIT Press, pp. 109–142.

McKee, A. (2005). *The public sphere: An introduction*. Cambridge: Cambridge University Press.

Roberts, J. M., & Crossley, N. (2004). Introduction. In N. Crossely & J. M. Roberts (eds.), *After Habermas: New perspectives on the public sphere*. Oxford: Oxford University Press, pp. 1–27.

Sparks, C. (2001). The Internet and the global public sphere. In L. W. Bennett & R. M. Entman (eds.), *Mediated politics: Communication in the future of democracy*. Cambridge: Cambridge University Press, pp. 75–95.

Publics: Situational Theory

Ana Tkalac Verčič

University of Zagreb

During the past 40-odd years, James E. Grunig's situational theory of communication behavior has been developed, changed, empirically tested, and adjusted through new research, with the purpose of defining the communication process and the behavior that results from it. Situational theory seeks to explain why people communicate and when it is most likely that they communicate. The theory also uses communicational behavior to partition the general → public into smaller segments which are most likely to communicate about certain issues. Situational theory also predicts behavioral effects of communication (→ Media Effects), as well as attitudes that are most commonly connected to specific types of communication and types of public for which these consequences are most likely. Finally, the theory describes the process in which a certain, previously unconnected, group of people develops into an activist group that, with its → public opinion, influences the decisions of a certain organization (Grunig 1997).

In the course of its long development, the situational theory of publics has become a significant part of public relations theory and approaches to → communication management (Grunig & Repper 1992), as well as an integral part of the public relations two-way symmetrical model (Grunig 1992).

In its current form, situational theory offers guidelines for segmenting the population into smaller groups (→ Audience Segmentation; Segmentation of the Advertising Audience) relevant for public relations programs. In that sense the theory is comparable with marketing segmentation theories (→ Marketing). Marketing theories offer specific criteria for choosing a segmentation concept; segments have to be mutually exclusive, measurable, reachable, significant for the mission of an organization, and big enough.

Most importantly, though, marketing segments have to show a "differential reaction" to various marketing strategies (Kotler & Andreasen 1987, 124). Situational theory of publics is also used for predicting differential responses, those important for the area of public relations. In addition, it can be used for predicting the effects that communication has on → cognitions, → attitudes, and behavior, as well as forecasting the likelihood of collectively pressurizing an organization (Grunig 1982).

DEVELOPMENT AND BASIC ASSUMPTIONS

The development of the theory began with the assumption of John Dewey and Herbert Blumer (Grunig 1997) that the formation of a public depends mostly on certain problems a group of people share, with the presumption that the consequences of these problems are similar for that group. Blumer (according to Grunig & Hunt 1984) separated the concept of publics from the concept of masses, defining masses as a heterogeneous group of people, unlike the public, which he considered homogeneous. Individuals form a mass not because they share a mutual characteristic but simply because they are all included in the same mass media or live in the same city. On the other hand, members of a public share a common problem and it is this problem that makes them a homogeneous group. A public is formed around issues that influence its members in a similar way. Dewey (according to Grunig 1997) also recognized the key role that publics have in American democracy; once publics recognize a certain problem, stakeholder groups are formed (→ Stakeholder Theory). The main objective of these stakeholder groups is to pressurize the government, thus indirectly controlling organizations.

Members of a public function as a unique system process the same information, and demonstrate similar behavior; that is to say that they represent a structured system in which members discover the same problem and react to it in a similar manner. On the other hand, masses do not behave unanimously (or do not behave at all; they are often inactive). Situational theory builds on the classic concept of publics, formalizing the concept and offering a way of identifying and measuring publics and public opinion (Price 1992).

VARIABLES AND RELATIONSHIPS

In its current form, situational theory comprises two dependent variables (active and passive communication behavior) and three independent variables (problem recognition, constraint recognition, and involvement). Recent research conducted on the model added cognitive and behavioral effects as well as attitudes to the list of dependent variables (Grunig & Childers 1988). The two dependent variables of active and passive communication behavior are also called → information processing and → information seeking.

Grunig based the theory on theories of decision-making in economics and psychology. His first publication of the situational theory was in a monograph on the relationship between communication and economic decision-making, published in 1968 (according to Grunig 1997). The first two variables that the theory is based on were *information seeking* and *problem recognition*; this categorized the theory as a situational theory. Specifically, the independent variable of problem recognition is not a characteristic people transfer from one situation to another, but a person's perception that a certain situation represents or conveys a problem. The next independent variable, *constraint recognition*, was added to the model in research conducted in 1969 and 1971. Grunig discovered that people do not have a need to communicate in situations where certain constraints enable them to make a decision. In 1976, Grunig also added the concept of *involvement* (Grunig 1982), and later that year the concept of a *referent criterion* (a solution transferred from past situations to new ones). The theory was later redefined more than once, but apart from the referent criterion, all dependent and independent variables remained in place.

Independent variables are situational in that they describe perceptions people have about certain situations, especially situations that are problematic or lead to conflict. Situational theory allows a logical connection between these concepts and the classic theorists' idea that problems and situations create publics that change in time. Independent variables can therefore be defined as problem recognition (people realize that something has to be done and stop to think about it); constraint recognition (people perceive that there are limitations that restrain their ability to act); and level of involvement (the level to which people connect to a certain situation; Grunig 1997).

The theory predicts that a high level of problem recognition and a low level of constraint recognition increase both information seeking and information processing (Grunig & Stamm 1979). The level of involvement increases information seeking, but has a lesser influence on information processing. In other words, people rarely seek information on problems that do not concern them, but frequently accidentally process information in low-involvement situations. Since people are more active in their information seeking than in information processing, information seeking and variables that precede it are more likely to produce communication effects than information processing. People who communicate actively develop cognitions that are more organized, have attitudes about the situation more often, and are more frequently involved in behaviors connected to the situation (Grunig 1982; Grunig & Ipes 1983).

Grunig and Disborow (1977) and Grunig (1982, 1983) combined the four variables in order to segment publics in various situations. In the studies mentioned they calculated conditional probabilities in order to predict the possibility of each of the publics being involved in one of two communication behaviors. These probabilities could then be used to plan communication programs for each public. Grunig also estimated probabilities of various communication effects for various combinations of variables. Effects included message retention (→ Memory, Message), cognitions and attitudes (→ Attitudes, Values, and Beliefs, Media Effects on), and certain behaviors. For example, the likelihood that the most active public (high problem recognition and high involvement, low constraint recognition and existence of a referent criterion) will be involved in passive communication behavior was 99 percent, in comparison with the least active public, for whom this likelihood was 63 percent. As for active communication behavior, the likelihood of involvement for the most active public was 77 percent, while for the least active public it was only 20 percent. The most active public had a 99 percent likelihood of having a cognition (for the least active public it was 65 percent), and the possibility of holding an attitude was 74 percent for the most active public and 52 percent for the least active public.

All of the probabilities mentioned help define the implications that situational theory has on forming public relations programs (Grunig & Hunt 1984). If an organization communicates with a public with little chance of information seeking and information processing, it is not necessary to invest time and money in an attempt to send a message. In this type of public, the message will rarely be noticed and, therefore, it will rarely be efficient. The only possibility for communicating with this type of public (if for any reason it is important to the organization) is in communication processing, while communication seeking is very unlikely. If an organization is communicating with a public that is ready to process information, but is not seeking it, the communication strategy must be based on style and creativeness in order to attract the attention of this group. If the communication is aimed at an active public that is likely to actively seek information, it is important to offer them extensive and high-quality arguments in order to discourage them from seeking elsewhere.

EMPIRICAL TESTS OF THE THEORY

In the early days of the theory, the author predicted that each situation will create a unique profile of publics, specific to that situation only. Empirical research of this supposition included, among other things, public affairs, social responsibility, consumer, and employee issues (Grunig 1997; → Public Affairs; Corporate Social Responsibility). However, canonical variants that were the result of the research mentioned earlier pointed to the possibility that in various situations there are four consistent types of public; the *all-issue public* (a public active on all issues); the *apathetic public* (a public not interested in any issue); the *single-issue public* (a public that is active on one issue or a group of connected issues that concern only a very small segment of the population); and the *hot-issue public* (a public active on only one issue that involves almost everyone in a population and is followed with a high media coverage).

Empirical tests of situational theory consistently point to the conclusion that active publics are more likely to show active behavior and are more likely to have cognitions, attitudes, and behavior. However, in its current form, situational theory presupposes the existence of cognitions, attitudes, and behaviors but not their content or valence (Grunig & Childers 1988). People construct their own cognitions, attitudes, and behaviors, in other words, they actively control their own thoughts and behaviors. According to the theory, then, all of the communication efforts aimed at communicating with publics that are not likely to succeed are misguided. Communication campaigns are often based on the idea of changing the level of problem recognition, constraint recognition, and the level of involvement in an audience, the final goal being that of redirecting their behavior in such a way that suits the organization. However, merely exposing an audience to the media cannot lead to the desired effects, since people cannot be influenced by messages they do not seek or process.

Although numerous empirical tests confirmed most of the basic assumptions of the theory, certain elements are still not completely without question. Situational theory of publics in its current form says nothing about the valence of attitudes. Research shows that cognitions and attitudes rarely precede communication behavior; and that people do not seek and process information in order to confirm their existing attitudes but instead they seek information that is of relevance to them (Grunig 1997). Even though attitudes, cognitions, and behavior (according to the situational theory) are a result of communication behavior and not its source, even the author of the theory agrees that including these variables in the theory is necessary.

The question that still remains unanswered by the theory is: can messages create publics? The question of creating publics through the media and media messages is based on another question, namely: how are behavior and communication messages linked? According to situational theory the answer is in creating publics in various ways (for example through → interpersonal communication), but not in using mass media. Only in situations in which individuals form publics will those publics seek and process information on a certain issue.

SEE ALSO: ▶ Attitudes   ▶ Attitudes, Values, and Beliefs, Media Effects on   ▶ Audience Segmentation   ▶ Cognition   ▶ Communication Management   ▶ Corporate Social Responsibility   ▶ Excellence Theory in Public Relations   ▶ Information Processing   ▶ Information Seeking   ▶ Interpersonal Communication   ▶ Marketing   ▶ Media Effects   ▶ Memory, Message   ▶ Public   ▶ Public Affairs   ▶ Public Opinion   ▶ Public Relations   ▶ Segmentation of the Advertising Audience   ▶ Stakeholder Theory

References and Suggested Readings

Grunig J. E. (1982). The message–attitude–behavior relationship: Communication behaviors of organizations. *Communication Research*, 9, 163–200.

Grunig, J. E. (1983). Communication behaviors and attitudes of environmental publics: Two studies. *Journalism Monographs*, 81.

Grunig, J. E. (1992). Systems of internal communication. In J. Grunig (ed.), *Excellence in public relations and communications management*. Hillsdale, NJ: Lawrence Erlbaum, pp. 531–575.

Grunig J. E. (1997). A situational theory of publics: Conceptual history, recent challenges and new research. In D. Moss, T. MacManus, & D. Vercic (eds.), *Public relations research: An international perspective*. London: International Thomson Business Press.

Grunig, J. E., & Childers, L. (1988). Reconstruction of a situational theory of communication: Internal and external concepts as identifiers of publics for AIDS. Paper presented at the Association for Education in Journalism and Mass Communication, Portland, OR (August).

Grunig, J., & Disborow, J. B. (1977). Developing a probabilistic model for communication decision making. *Communication Research*, 4, 145–168.

Grunig, J. E., & Hunt, T. (1984). *Managing public relations*. New York: Holt, Rinehart and Winston.

Grunig, J. E., & Ipes, D. A. (1983). The anatomy of a campaign against drunk driving. *Public Relations Review*, 9(2), 36–53.

Grunig, J. E., & Repper, F. C. (1992). Strategic management, publics, and issues. In J. Grunig (ed.), *Excellence in public relations and communications management*. Hillsdale, NJ: Lawrence Erlbaum.

Grunig, J. E., & Stamm, K. R. (1979). Cognitive strategies and the resolution of environmental issues: A second study. *Journalism Quarterly*, 56, 715–726.

Kotler, P., & Andreasen, A. R. (1987). *Strategic marketing for nonprofit organizations*, 3rd edn. Englewood Cliffs, NJ: Prentice Hall.

Price, V. (1992). *Public opinion*. Newbury Park, CA: Sage.

Qualitative Methodology

Armin Scholl

University of Münster

Qualitative methodology includes a variety and diversity of methods, procedures, and research designs. All kinds of qualitative methods have in common that their main research aim is a deeper understanding of the research object. Therefore, they are nonstandardized tools that can be adapted flexibly to every kind of research object, which can better be called research subjects because qualitative methods do not measure them objectively but interact with them, insofar as method is not a neutral tool in order to gain knowledge about researched subjects but is part of the social reality investigated.

AIMS OF QUALITATIVE METHODOLOGY

Qualitative methods try to discover new hypotheses rather than testing hypotheses deductively derived from known theories; they explore new phenomena and describe them intensively ("thick description") and from different perspectives (→ Triangulation). This is essential for the most prominent approaches in qualitative methodology, such as → grounded theory, ethnography (→ Ethnography of Communication), → case studies, social → hermeneutics or → phenomenology, feminist methodology (→ Feminist and Gender Studies), or action research (→ Participatory Action Research). They all have several research aims in common.

First and basically, qualitative methodology is *directed at the understanding of the social world* that qualitative researchers explore and investigate (→ Verstehen vs Erklären). Social research, therefore, tries to reconstruct the social constructions of people's cognitions, emotions, communications, or actions. Understanding and meaning cannot be taken for granted but need a great effort to recover within the research process by way of intensive interaction between researcher and the people researched (or the texts researched; → Text and Intertextuality). Epistemologically, meaning is itself not a given object but must be "negotiated" in social interaction (→ Language and Social Interaction). Understanding can be characterized as the process of exploring and (re)constructing meaning.

Second, every piece of scientific knowledge and the process of gaining it are necessarily *context-bound* and in consequence strictly relative to this context. Context originates both from within the social reality and social interactions investigated and from the interaction between the researcher and the researched subject (people, actions, etc.) or object (texts, visual material, etc.). The researcher's methods and tools for gaining knowledge are not considered neutral or technical instruments but establish, develop, and affect the research context. Even basic key terms and concepts used in research projects are not only defined by the researcher but elaborated within the data collection process through communication and "negotiation" with the informant or research subject being investigated.

Third, research outcomes are not only achieved results within a research process, but can be characterized as being *dynamic knowledge* in an epistemological sense. This is the reason why research instruments have to be open, flexible, and adaptive to the research subject or object. Research instruments are not the fixed tools of operationalized theories that have to be completely and finally developed before fieldwork begins (→ Operationalization). Instead, they have to be changed (and changeable) within research interaction according to the requirements of the individual and case-specific research situation.

Fourth, the procedure of qualitative research is *primarily inductive* insofar as it starts with research questions and temporarily "ends" with → hypotheses. The research process is spiral instead of linear because there is a permanent dynamic inherent, which includes developing, testing, and changing research questions, premises, hypotheses, instruments, and tools. At the end of the study there should be a better and deeper understanding of the research subject investigated. Consequently, research methods need to be reflected at each stage of the research process with respect to their contribution to the research results.

DIFFERENT QUALITATIVE APPROACHES

The different approaches mentioned above emphasize different aspects of qualitative research, although there are many commonalities in fundamental research aims and in epistemology.

Phenomenology is the study of human phenomena and experiences in everyday life. As social phenomena are not entirely conscious for the people experiencing them, the researcher has to explore different perspectives to gain a full picture of the phenomena being investigated. The foreground of the participants' life-world can be researched by asking the participants about their subjective perceptions. The background of the participants' experiences can be explored by asking other participants about their understanding of the researched person's actions or by observing the participants' actions within their social context. The main aim of phenomenological research strategy is to gain a holistic impression and a deeper understanding of the phenomenon researched and its nature by changing the perspectives of research.

A very similar approach, although less philosophical and more practical, is *ethnographical research*, which emphasizes → field research in natural settings and the investigation of people's everyday lives. The researcher adopts an insider's perspective, trying to understand how people understand and construct the world they are involved in. Thus, ethnographical investigators primarily rely on participant → observation, in-depth interviews. and analysis of (private) documents; data collection is eclectic (→ Document Analysis; Interview, Qualitative). Ethnographic researchers do not confine themselves to a single and short-term research contact but establish a longer contact and intensive relationship with the field under study (community, group, organization, etc.). Another characteristic of ethnographic research is reflexivity, which is particularly relevant for the researcher's ambivalent role and status within the field as both (distant) observer and (close) participant.

Grounded theory emphasizes the spiral and strictly inductive research process: Instead of establishing hypotheses at the beginning of a study, researchers start their investigations only with open research questions. The research process is considered a permanent alternation of data collection and data analysis. Thus, sampling procedures are not planned systematically in advance, but the researcher enters the field with a convenient sample of first interviews, observations, or gathered document materials (→ Sampling, Nonrandom). Provisional theoretical concepts are identified from the first distinct events or incidents in the data. Then further data are gathered by either the same method or different methods and are analyzed in detail. New questions arise from the data, which need to be answered with the help of further data, and so on. The process of data collection and data analysis comes to an end when no further concepts or dimensions emerge from the data and theoretical saturation is reached. Of course the researcher still may discover a "negative case" that does not fit the concepts elaborated. Then the theory must be modified or extended.

Case studies privilege in-depth inquiry over coverage when trying to understand the case and its complexity rather than to generalize from the case to a certain population of individuals or organizations. As is true for the approaches previously described, the participants' interpretation of their actions or of their worldview is at the center of the investigation; case studies are rather long-term investigations than one-shot studies; and they follow an inductive logic. The case study approach slightly differs from the other approaches, insofar as its explorative character is less demanding. The results of case studies are considered descriptive (rather than leading to hypotheses or theories), heuristic and provisional (rather than saturated), and particular (rather than generalized).

Another claim for qualitative methodology is made by feminist methodologies and by action research. Although *feminist methodologies* are not methodologies in a strict sense but can be understood as a (meta-)theoretical approach or perspective, they suggest a preference for qualitative methodology and its practical or political consequences. They sensitize the researcher to the politics and power influences underlying each methodology and each method. As research and methodological rules are mostly masculine – most researchers have been male – the dominating role of objectivity in research and methodology is itself masculinist. Instead, feminist methodology insists on the positionality ("standpoint epistemology") and reflexivity ("logic of self-reference") of social research and the researcher. It is a critical methodology and has normative implications for social practice, claiming justice and equality between sexes. Implications for research designs include the empowerment of the people researched and the cooperative production of knowledge.

This is also and particularly true for *action research*, which aims to change practice with the help of and for the participants researched. Social scientific research causes political consequences in two different ways: with respect to the relationship between researcher and researched and with regard to the change or improvement of social practice outside the research process. Action research helps the participants researched to reflect their own practice and to change a criticized situation. In this perspective, all steps in research, from the early stage of defining the research problem to the final data analysis, result from the processes of negotiation and cooperation between researcher and participant.

METHODS IN QUALITATIVE RESEARCH PRACTICE

Prominent methods in qualitative methodology are participant observation, in-depth interviews, narrative interviews, qualitative content analysis (→ Content Analysis, Qualitative), → discourse analysis, → conversation analysis, social scientific hermeneutics, etc. They will be described shortly.

With the help of *observation*, events and actions can be investigated. Observation can either be direct (nonparticipant) or participant. There is a preference for participant observation in qualitative research, particularly when an ethnographical approach is chosen, because in direct observation the observer is cut off from the people he or she observes and therefore cannot ask the meanings of or reasons for their actions and behaviors. Practically, researchers or observers first have to gain access to the field, which implies defining their role as more or less active participants in the field or situation observed. Then observers make a record of their impressions of the situation. As human behavior is complex, observers permanently select particular elements of the situation to be observed. Furthermore, observing includes interpreting the meaning of the impressions made, insofar as observation is an observer's subjective, selective, and sense-making activity. In qualitative observation there is no standardized schedule with predetermined categories; instead observers record relevant impressions with detailed but unstructured field notes and sometimes with the help of video equipment. Although qualitative observation is unstructured in terms of measurement, it must be well prepared according to the research aim, to the role the observers take within the field they observe, and to the technology the observers use to record their observation.

In *in-depth-interviews* the researcher or interviewer uses an interview guide consisting of open-ended key questions and of probing follow-ups. The guide has a flexible order and structure so that the interview can be conducted as a dialogue with the respondent. It enables the respondents to express their point of view, to emphasize the aspects relevant for them, to clarify and illustrate the meaning of their responses, etc.

Narrative interviews do not even use interview guides as employed in in-depth interviews, because narrative interviews aim at gaining complete stories told by the respondents. If the respondents talk about their lives, narrative interviews are used for biographical research, life history, or oral history. Storytelling is an open-structured but rule-based dialogue or conversation (→ Storytelling and Narration). It is the aim of biographical research not only to gain true data about the informants' life but also to get an impression of how the story of their life is told, how narratives are constructed.

Unlike individual interviews, *focus groups* consist of moderated discussions among a group of six to ten respondents or discussants. Instead of an interviewer, a moderator manages the conversation by asking questions and developing the discussion. The main aim of a focus group session is to find out how strong arguments are, to test new ideas or products, etc., and this is achieved by discussants' mutual stimulation and controversial debate. As group dynamics emerge spontaneously, the results of the discussion may differ from group to group. Therefore, several groups should be selected to compare the outcomes. Depending on the research question, the samples of focus groups can either be homogeneous or heterogeneous with regard to demographic or other characteristics, real-world groups (families, neighbors, cliques, etc.), or artificial groups (consisting of people who do not know each other). All kinds of qualitative interviews are recorded with the help of an audio tape (sometimes even a video tape), then transcribed and finally analyzed.

Qualitative content analysis is a method to develop categories from texts or visual material including newspaper articles, radio or television programs, and web pages (primary material), but also transcribed interview texts, documents, or video-taped observations (secondary material). Categorization means a step-by-step reduction, abstraction, and generalization of the textual or visual material. This → coding procedure is an inductive and spiral process, because it starts from the material and repeatedly goes back to it in order to check that the categories evolved from the material are correct and do not bias the original, context-bound meaning. Categories summarize, explicate, and structure the original material. They can be sorted on different levels of abstraction. Often categories may be combined in order to develop patterns or typologies of texts or other manifest material (photographs, films, documents, etc.) in further steps of analysis.

A more open and less rule-based kind of interpretation or data analysis is at the center of (social scientific) *hermeneutics*, which is particularly used in analyzing narratives or stories from interviews or texts. Instead of reducing propositional units to more abstract categories, hermeneutic interpretation emphasizes the functional relationship between units and the whole text, narrative, or story. Both formal and content-related characteristics of the language used in interviews, texts, or visual material are brought into play for the interpretation and understanding of meaning and social reality represented in and by the material analyzed.

Conversation analysis can be regarded as a particular kind of hermeneutic analysis that is related to dialogical structure, such as talk, conversations, debates, etc. Language not only represents social reality but is also an expression of human (communicative) action. Participants' utterances and interactional forms are embedded in social rules, structure, and order. With the help of linguistic or semiotic tools these latent structures and patterns can be uncovered (→ Linguistics; Semiotics). Conversation analysis is not only based on communication represented in texts but also takes into consideration nonverbal and extra-verbal overt behaviors.

Discourse analysis combines a text-immanent hermeneutical approach with a context-related interpretation. Similar to conversation analysis, it characterizes discourse not only as a text but as a social practice in everyday life, involving ideology, authority, social rules, power, and even audience. Unlike conversation, discourse represents the struggle for arguments, status, and hierarchy and emphasizes sociological questions rather than linguistic ones. For discourse analysis both naturalistic material (documents, media contents) and interviews may be used. In addition to coding processes employed in qualitative content analysis, discourse analysts combine manifest characteristics of the text with latent power analysis (e.g., in the tradition of Michel Foucault). This is the reason why discourse analysis often follows a critical approach, uncovering the ideology and power relations behind the text.

As texts or other documentary material cannot be separated from their social production, *documentary analysis* also explores the social context of texts for a better understanding of the meaning expressed within them. Therefore, it is necessary to investigate the characteristics of the producers of texts and documents. Documentary analysis is particularly relevant for historical research and for media research in order to evaluate the status, truth, and relevance of documents, media contents, and their production.

Qualitative experiments use a particular stimulus, as do standardized experiments ($\rightarrow$ Experimental Design), but they explore the range of subjects' reactions rather than test hypotheses. Within $\rightarrow$ ethnomethodology Harold Garfinkel has developed so-called breaching experiments to reconstruct everyday rules: By breaching commonsense expectancies, questioning "normal" behaviors, or disrupting ordinary rules, it is possible to make self-evident practices conscious for the practitioner and to demonstrate the effectiveness of invisible rules, structures, and orders. Thus, experimenters use incomplete or inconsistent instructions. Another technique is for researchers to engage in an everyday conversation insisting on the clarification of the other person's position, which obviously disrupts the conversational rule not to question clearly comprehensible statements.

As research instruments are open and flexible, so too are sampling procedures. In qualitative research they are mostly deliberative or purposive. The sample cannot be representative in a quantitative sense but should either be homogeneous, in order to find the small distinction among the sample units, or heterogeneous, in order to cover a maximum of variation and find the commonalities (and differences) among the sample units. A special case of heterogeneous sampling is extreme-case sampling, which is appropriate when the full range of possible answers, positions, and actions needs to be explored. Very often sampling procedures are driven by convenience because or if access to the field or population investigated is hard to gain. However, sampling procedure is far from being arbitrary; instead it is coherent and consistent with the research questions and the theoretical aim of the study.

In sum, qualitative research requires the researcher's fundamental openness within a research process. In a cognitive sense this means that the researcher is open to unexpected aspects and events. In a social sense this means that there are no strict rules either for the researcher (interviewer, observer, coder or interpreter) or for the person interviewed or observed. Critics of qualitative methodology object that the lack of rules may cause arbitrary research results. Furthermore, if these results are strictly context-bound and can only be interpreted within their context, the idea of deciding between true and false results must be abandoned. Finally, the results of qualitative research cannot be generalized, as they are based on only a small number of cases.

EVALUATIVE CRITERIA FOR QUALITATIVE RESEARCH

However, there are evaluative criteria for qualitative research dealing with these problems: First, the most general criterion of qualitative methodology is *clarity of presentation*, which seems trivial as it is an overall criterion for every scientific effort. Process-related reporting of the research process is typical of qualitative methodology, in contrast to a more outcome-related reporting within quantitative methodology. Other researchers can comprehend not only the operationalization of theoretical constructs but each step of the process and can criticize its plausibility.

A second criterion may be called *communicative* → *validity or validation*, which means that the researcher's understanding of an answer, an observation, or a text interpretation will be checked with the research subjects' own interpretation or with other researchers' inferences. On the whole, the qualitative research process includes open and authentic data collection, which inherently promotes validity because it relies not merely on a sketchy research contact but on intensive and extensive interaction.

Third, generalization and *generalizability* can be achieved if the results and conclusions are transferable to other settings and contexts than those under study. Therefore, the sample should be heterogeneous enough with respect to the research question, the context should be elaborated intensively, and the concepts should be abstracted at a high level. Even in case studies results are generalizable, if the case is sufficiently complex to discover general structures rather than single social practices.

Fourth, → reliability of data implies the *stability of the results* within the research process. Also, the systematic use of different methods and research instruments ("triangulation") can provide reliability if the outcomes of different methods are consistent or lead to a coherent holistic impression of cases investigated.

SEE ALSO: ► Case Studies ► Coding ► Content Analysis, Qualitative ► Conversation Analysis ► Discourse Analysis ► Document Analysis ► Ethnography of Communication ► Ethnomethodology ► Experimental Design ► Feminist and Gender Studies ► Field Research ► Generalizability ► Grounded Theory ► Hermeneutics ► Hypothesis ► Interview, Qualitative ► Language and Social Interaction ► Linguistics ► Observation ► Operationalization ► Participatory Action Research ► Phenomenology ► Reliability ► Sampling, Nonrandom ► Semiotics ► Storytelling and Narration ► Text and Intertextuality ► Triangulation ► Validity ► Verstehen vs Erklären

References and Suggested Readings

Creswell, J. W. (1994). *Research design: Qualitative and quantitative approaches.* Thousand Oaks, CA, London, and New Delhi: Sage.

Denzin, N. K., & Lincoln, Y. S. (eds.) (2000). *Handbook of qualitative research,* 2nd edn. Thousand Oaks, CA: Sage.

Punch, K. F. (2005). *Introduction to social research: Quantitative and qualitative approaches,* 2nd edn. London, Thousand Oaks, CA, and New Delhi: Sage.

Ragin, C. C. (1994). *Constructing social research: The unity and diversity of method.* Thousand Oaks, CA: Pine Forge Press.

Seale, C., Gobo, G., Gubrium, J. F., & Silverman, D. (eds.) (2004). *Qualitative research practice.* London, Thousand Oaks, CA, and New Delhi: Sage.

Somekh, B., & Lewin, C. (eds.) (2005). *Research methods in the social sciences.* London, Thousand Oaks, CA, and New Delhi: Sage.

Quality of the News

Adam Jacobsson

Stockholm University

Eva-Maria Jacobsson

Royal Institute of Technology

Quality of the news is a difficult and complex concept to define. Who determines what is good quality and what is not? Quality depends in part on what → uses and gratifications are demanded from the media. Taking a liberal standpoint one could say that quality is what the audience wants. Another view would be to let media professionals, such as journalists and editors, act as moral agents and establish a set of criteria that defines good quality. The literature has, in sum, taken the view of professionals as the starting point.

A high-quality news service isexpected to help citizens make informed decisions that in turn will help develop society. This view has support from disciplines other than journalism and mass communication studies, such as economics. Here, a high-quality news service is perceived to help economic development, as it reduces uncertainty by providing accurate and reliable information. In political science the media is seen as the → fourth estate, informing citizens, maintaining checks and balances on the political process, and thereby increasing the efficiency of government and helping to resolve social conflict by giving a multifaceted description of events, among other things. The above functions are largely supported by what the journalism and mass communication literature describes as commonly shared professional standards of → journalism (→ Standards of News; Journalism: Normative Theories). Sometimes, however, there is tension between these standards and a demand for a lighter kind of news reporting, geared toward entertaining sensationalism, that pits professionalism against commercialism (→ Commercialization of the Media). In fact, Downs (1957) showed that it is theoretically irrational for citizens to vote, since it is highly unlikely that any individual citizen's vote would be crucial. Therefore, the audience should have a preference for entertainment rather than hard-to-digest quality news about political affairs. Hence, the personal rewards gained by attaining and digesting quality news may be lower than the personal cost of obtaining them. Also, the individual news consumer may not internalize the benefits to society of having well-informed citizens. However, a US study by Gladney (1996) polled editors and readers of 251 newspapers, grouped by size of circulation, asking them to rank 18 measures of news quality, and found that there was less divergence between readers and editors than the logic based on Downs would predict.

MEASURES OF NEWS QUALITY

Generally, research divides the definitions of news media quality into three sub-categories: content, organizational, and financial commitment (Hollifield 2006).

Content is a matter of several aspects, but some measures are: → balance and fairness – lack of → sensationalism; → accuracy – lack of bias (→ Bias in the News); news interpretation (→ Interpretive Journalism); relevance of the news presented and reliance on authoritative sources (→ News Sources); comprehensive coverage and presentation of multiple points of view; favorable coverage of different groups in society; strong local coverage (→ Local News); the community press standard – emphasis on community values and institutions; a strong editorial page; visual appeal; and good writing.

Organizational aspects of quality can be divided into two major categories. Editorial quality includes: editorial independence and courage – freedom from outside pressure by political interest groups and economic forces (→ Freedom of the Press, Concept of); impartiality – fairness in gathering and reporting news (→ Fairness Doctrine); influence with opinion leaders; and community leadership – willingness to take an active role in the betterment and welfare of the community. Journalistic staff features include: professionalism – e.g., the level of education, experience, and willingness to fight against wrong; staff enterprise – aggressive and original reporting; decency; and integrity – a keen sense of professional ethics (→ Ethics in Journalism).

The content and organizational measures of news quality have a long tradition in the literature but have suffered critique for being too subjective and difficult to replicate. These measures are usually judgments by panels of professional experts and are by definition difficult to duplicate. As a response to this critique, measures of financial commitment emerged (Litman & Bridges 1986; Bogart 1981, 2004; → Qualitative Methodology).

Financial commitment can be divided into four sub-categories. *Copy* includes the advertising–editorial copy ratio, the amounts of locally produced copy and nonadvertising copy, the length of stories in terms of offering readers depth, and the number of in-depth, investigative, or interpretive stories. *Graphics* includes the amount of visual and graphic material. *Journalistic* includes the size of the news staff, reporter workloads, and the number of stories or amount of time devoted to news programming. *Technical* includes the number of → news agencies subscribed to and investment in news-gathering technologies such as satellite trucks. These criteria are not measurements of news quality per se, but are considered to be a measure of the amount of resources that are needed to produce such quality (Litman & Bridges 1986). The quantitative measures of financial commitment require little, if any, subjective judgments and are thus better suited to duplication (→ Quantitative Methodology).

THE USE OF QUALITY MEASURES

The above measures of quality have been devised for the purpose of measuring not so much quality per se as how other institutional factors and the degree of competition affect news quality. Increased news media competition has in a number of studies been shown to be linked to higher measures of news quality. News media (print and broadcast) have been found to increase their financial commitment in news production as the intensity of competition over market shares increases. Studies have also shown that high-quality newspapers and broadcasters do better in terms of → circulation/ratings than do low-quality ones. In fact, increased measures of quality not only affect relative market shares, but also increase total news demand in a given market. However, these findings originate in research undertaken in either the US or other developed markets that feature a very low degree of competition after a century of news media consolidation (→ Consolidation of Media Markets). More recent international research indicates, however, that in conditions of hyper-competition, more competition may in fact yield lower-quality news products (Hollifield 2006; van der Wurff & van Cuilenburg 2001; Becker et al. 2006).

Concerning the effects of public ownership of news media (→ Ownership in the Media), research has shown that profit margins are higher in publicly owned news media companies due to pressures from investors. News organizations often respond to these pressures by cutting the largest cost item, i.e., personnel, thereby reducing financial commitment and leading to lower scores in other measures of news quality.

IMPLICATIONS OF MEDIA QUALITY

Different groups value news quality differently. From a professional viewpoint, high scores in the above quality measures or awards such as Pulitzer prizes constitute success. Taking the view of readers, circulation is a proper measure, while investors would value profitability. Research has established a positive link between quality and circulation/ratings, while high circulation/ratings do not necessarily imply high profitability.

A problem in this research is how to establish causality between different measures of quality and factors that affect and are affected by news quality. Quality has been found to positively affect circulation/ratings, but a strong case is made for the reverse causality. Given the logic that in order to achieve a high measure of quality a news organization needs financial commitment, which in turn comes from high circulation/ratings, then small newspapers/broadcasters do not have the same resources as big ones to produce quality news. This effect is amplified by the fact that advertisers tend to converge on high-circulation/ratings news organizations (→ Advertising, Economics of). Gladney (1990) found that smaller newspapers can't really compete with big ones in staff enterprise, staff professionalism, news interpretation, and comprehensive news coverage, as these demand greater resources. Logan and Sutter (2004) found that 91 percent of all Pulitzer prizes in 1997 went to newspapers in the top quintile in terms of circulation the same year. This is not surprising, as the news industry exhibits increasing returns to scale. That is, producing a news item is costly while distribution to the audience is very cheap. It therefore makes economic sense to have few producers investing in news production.

The literature is not clear on whether the measurements of news quality are valid for all socio-economic groups in society. Concerns have been voiced that the measures used are elitist in character, mainly appealing to the well-educated urban classes. In studies by Gladney (1990, 1996) editors at larger, often metropolitan, newspapers emphasized staff enterprise, staff professionalism, and comprehensive news coverage. Their counterparts at smaller newspapers placed greater value on community leadership, strong local news coverage, decency, and the community press standard, which is an "emphasis on news coverage that focuses on common community values and helps give readers a sense of individual existence and worth." (Gladney 1990, 62). Readers were found to largely hold these same values, especially concerning strong local press coverage and the community press standard, confirming earlier research. Hence, large (metropolitan) and small (local) news media can fulfill different functions, with the latter complementing the former in terms of more locally focused news. This illuminates the difficulty of applying one standard of excellence to all news markets.

Another channel through which the size of circulation/ratings can affect measures of quality is the risk of media capture, which describes a situation where the content of a news organization is controlled by some external political or economic organization (Besley & Prat 2006). If this influence is attained by economic means such as bribes or ownership, smaller, poorer news organizations are likely to be more susceptible than wealthier ones. As the economic performance of news organizations declines with increased competition, high degrees of competition may then increase the risk of media capture, which is relevant for the organizational quality measures of editorial courage, decency, accuracy, etc. Apart from leading to media capture, extreme competition is also likely to reduce measures of financial commitment as revenues drop. The research on the negative effects of competition is small and recent (Hollifield 2006; Becker et al. 2006; van der Wurff & van Cuilenburg 2001), which to a large extent is a result of the fact most research is focused on the consolidated US media market. However, more international research is needed on this issue, as many emerging economies exhibit extreme levels of media competition.

SEE ALSO: ▶ Accuracy ▶ Advertising, Economics of ▶ Balance ▶ Bias in the News ▶ Circulation ▶ Commercialization of the Media ▶ Consolidation of Media Markets ▶ Ethics in Journalism ▶ Fairness Doctrine ▶ Fourth Estate ▶ Freedom of the Press, Concept of ▶ Interpretive Journalism ▶ Journalism ▶ Journalism: Normative Theories ▶ Local News ▶ News Agencies ▶ News Sources ▶ Ownership in the Media ▶ Political Media Content, Quality Criteria in ▶ Qualitative Methodology ▶ Quantitative Methodology ▶ Sensationalism ▶ Standards of News ▶ Uses and Gratifications

References and Suggested Readings

Becker, L. B., Hollifield, C. A., Jacobsson, A., Jacobsson, E-M., & Vlad, T. (2006). Examining the suspected adverse effects of competition on media performance. Paper presented at the Journalism Studies Interest Group at the International Communication Association conference in Dresden, Germany, June 19–23.

Besley, T., & Prat, A. (2006). Handcuffs for the grabbing hand? Media capture and government accountability. *American Economic Review*, 96(3), 720–736.

Bogart, L. (1981). *Press and public: Who reads what, when , where and why in American newspapers.* Hillsdale, NJ: Lawrence Erlbaum.

Bogart, L. (2004). Reflections on content quality in newspapers. *Newspaper Research Journal*, 25(1), 40–53.

Downs, A. (1957). *An economic theory of democracy.* New York: Harper and Row.

Gladney, G. (1990). Newspaper excellence: How editors of small and large papers judge quality. *Newspaper Research Journal*, 11(2), 58–72.

Gladney, G. (1996). How editors and readers rank and rate the importance of eighteen traditional standards of newspaper excellence. *Journalism and Mass Communication Quarterly*, 73(2), 319–331.

Hollifield, C. A. (2006). News media performance in hypercompetitive markets: An extended model. *International Journal on Media Management*, 8(2), 60–69.

Kim, K-H., & Meyer, P. (2005). Survey yields five factors of newspaper quality. *Newspaper Research Journal*, 26(1), 6–15.

Lacy, S., & Blanchard, A. (2003). The impact of public ownership, profits, and competition on number of newsroom employees and starting salaries in mid-sized daily newspapers. *Journalism and Mass Communication Quarterly*, 80(1), 949–968.

Litman, B., & Bridges, J. (1986). An economic analysis of daily newspaper performance. *Newspaper Research Journal*, 7(3), 9–26.

Logan, B., & Sutter, D. (2004). Newspaper quality, Pulitzer prizes, and newspaper circulation. *Atlantic Economic Journal*, 32(2), 100–112.

van der Wurff, R., & van Cuilenburg, J. (2001). Impact of moderate and ruinous competition on diversity: The Dutch television market. *Journal of Media Economics*, 14(4), 213–229.

Quality Press

Stephan Russ-Mohl
University of Lugano

Although communication researchers talk and write eloquently about the quality press and seem to have a clear concept what the term means, hardly anyone has made an effort to define it. A short, impressionistic review of handbooks and lexica as well as of online resources like Wikipedia and Google shows the term "quality" in many media-related contexts. But the "quality press" itself has attracted little attention from researchers (Spassov 2004).

Nevertheless, there seems to be an unwritten consensus that those newspapers and newsmagazines are considered quality press that (1) address the "intelligentsia" (Sparks & Campbell 1987, 456), i.e., the elites and decision-makers of a country; (2) are distributed nationally rather than regionally; and (3) provide a broad and in-depth coverage of news and background information. A recent German definition (Raabe 2006) emphasizes additionally that quality papers frequently cooperate internationally with other quality print media; that they often have local or regional editions for several big cities, including the capital of the country; and that they offer a journalistically rich "menu" to readers as well as an attractive readership to advertisers – including sporadic supplements.

The term "quality press" implicitly contains a clear value judgment. Labeling some newspapers "quality press" implies inevitably that all the other press products are *not* "quality press." This can be unfair, as regional newspapers or even the boulevard press differ in terms of their quality, too. Besides that, even the quality newspapers and magazines differ among themselves and from country to country.

PRECONDITIONS OF A QUALITY PRESS

A non-negotiable precondition of quality press is press freedom and democracy – though even dictatorships may try to create the impression that quality papers continue to exist, as Hitler's propaganda minister Joseph Goebbels did: in Nazi Germany for many years the *Frankfurter Zeitung* benefited from this policy. It was the newspaper that had more leeway to place messages "between the lines" than the others (Gillessen 1986). Otherwise, the quality press depends on the existence of the following conditions:

- *Degree of education and "demand" of publics*: an educated and literate readership has to exist, and it has to be willing to pay for news and information.

- *Cultural tradition*: in "northern" countries a "habit" of reading newspapers seems to have grown, whereas in "southern" countries such a tradition is limited to very small elites.
- *Sales system*: where newspapers have to compete at the newsstand daily, it is less likely that quality press will develop.
- *Degree of centralization*: in countries like France, Great Britain, and Austria the so-called quality press is concentrated in the capital. In more decentralized countries like the US, Germany, and Switzerland quality papers are more "equally" distributed among different cities and regions, and thus have a broader base from which to be nourished.
- *Size of countries*: in smaller countries, it is more difficult to develop quality press – but countries like Denmark, the Netherlands, and Switzerland prove that there are exceptions to this rule.

IDENTIFYING THE QUALITY PRESS

No single researcher can give a solid overview of the quality press throughout the world. The earliest and still most prominent attempt to identify the "club" of quality newspapers worldwide dates back to the late 1960s: Merrill (1968, 32–44) cited different rankings made until then in the Merrill Elite Press Pyramid. Among the world's top 10 papers were the *New York Times, Neue Zürcher Zeitung, Le Monde*, the *Guardian, The Times, Pravda, Jen-min Jih-pao* (Peking), *Borba* (Belgrade), *Osservatore Romano* (Vatican City), and *ABC* (Madrid). While the idea of identifying elite newspapers certainly makes sense, Merrill's ranking itself seems dubious. Though based on experts' judgments from various continents, his list of 10 newspapers contains four from countries where press freedom as the basic requirement for developing a quality press was nonexistent at that time. *Pravda, Jen-min Jih-pao*, and *Borba* were organs controlled by communist or socialist governments, and *ABC* was censored by the fascist Franco regime. Further, the *Osservatore Romano* is controlled more by the Catholic church than by a politically "independent" publisher.

More recent rankings include a look ahead in the *Columbia Journalism Review* (1999) into the twenty-first century, in which only American newspapers were ranked by top editors, and a study by the German media watchdog organization Internationale Medienhilfe based on the judgments of 1,000 media experts in 50 countries. According to the latter, the top five newspapers in the world in the year 2005 were (1) the *Financial Times* (UK), (2) the *Wall Street Journal* (USA), (3) *Frankfurter Allgemeine Zeitung* (Germany), (4) *Le Monde* (France), and (5) *Neue Zuercher Zeitung* (Switzerland). Due to the scandals in which the *New York Times* was involved, it ranked only sixth in this review (*Neue Zürcher Zeitung* 2005).

Reviewing the literature and picking out just a few countries, some "obvious" examples of the quality press are: in France, *Le Monde, Le Figaro*, and the *Herald Tribune* (an American newspaper published in Paris); in Germany, *Frankfurter Allgemeine Zeitung, Süddeutsche Zeitung, Die Welt*, the business newspapers *Handelsblatt* and *Financial Times Deutschland*, and as weeklies *Der Spiegel* and *Die Zeit*; in Great Britain, the *Independent*, the *Guardian*, the business newspaper the *Financial Times*, and the newsmagazine *The Economist*; in Italy, *Corriere della Sera* and the business newspaper *Il Sole-24 Ore*; in Japan, *Asahi Shimbun*; in Spain, *El Pais*; in Switzerland, *Neue Zürcher Zeitung, Tagesanzeiger* (internationally much less "visible"), and the weeklies *Facts* and *Weltwoche*; in the US, the *New York Times*, the *Washington Post*, the *Los Angeles Times*, the *Wall Street Journal* (the world's leading business paper), the weekly newsmagazines *Time* and *Newsweek*, and the *New Yorker* as a cultural highlight.

The difficulty in defining its characteristics apart, the quality press in many western countries has become an endangered species. Book titles like *The vanishing newspaper* (Meyer 2004), and magazine stories addressing "journalism without journalists" (Lemann 2006) or analyzing the sharp decrease in foreign correspondence (Arnett 1998), can be seen as alarming. As classified → advertising is shifting to the Internet, the web is eating up newspapers' revenue sources. And many users, particularly younger ones, have become accustomed to receiving information for free online, which poses a threat to the survival of the quality press. While the public debate concentrates on bloggers and "citizen journalists" endangering professional journalism, the other real threat for quality journalism may be the rise and the professionalization of public relations (PR). If a scenario developed by Ries and Ries (2002) should come true, PR will expand at the expense of advertising – and thus the resource basis for quality journalism will erode further.

SEE ALSO: ▶ Advertising ▶ Comparative Research ▶ Quality of the News ▶ Rating Methods

References and Suggested Readings

Arnett, P. (1998). Goodbye, world! *American Journalism Review*, Nov./Dec. At www.ajr.org/Article.asp?id=3288.
Columbia Journalism Review (1999). America's best newspapers. Nov./Dec. At www.archives.cjr.org/year/99/6/best.asp, accessed April 5, 2007.
Gillessen, G. (1986). *Auf verlorenem Posten: Die Frankfurter Zeitung im Dritten Reich*. Berlin: Siedler.
Lemann, N. (2006). Amateur hour: Journalism without journalists. *New Yorker*, pp. 44–49 (August 7 and 14).
Merrill, J. (1968). *The elite press: Great newspapers of the world*. New York: Pitman.
Meyer, P. (2004). *The vanishing newspaper*. Columbia: University of Missouri Press.
Neue Zürcher Zeitung (2005). Die renommiertesten Blätter: Weltweite Umfrage unter 1000 Personen. July 8.
Raabe, J. (2006). Qualitätszeitungen. In G. Bentele, H-B. Brosius, & O. Jarren (eds.), *Lexikon Kommunikations- und Medienwissenschaft*. Wiesbaden: VS Verlag für Sozialwissenschaften, p. 236.
Ries, A., & Ries, L. (2002). *The fall of advertising and the rise of PR*. New York: HarperCollins.
Sparks, C., & Campbell, M. (1987). The "inscribed reader" of the British quality press. *European Journal of Communication*, 2, 455–472.
Spassov, O. (2004). The quality of the press in southeast Europe: To be or not to be. In O. Spassov (ed.), *The quality of the press in southeast Europe*. Sofia: Southeast European Media Center, pp. 7–35.

Quantitative Methodology

Armin Scholl

University of Münster

The results of polls tell us how many people intend to vote for a certain political party, watch TV more than four hours a day, or favor a certain TV program. We call methods of collecting and analyzing such data "quantitative methodology" because individuals' attributes are counted in large numbers. One can count not only single persons (→ Survey), but also propositions within texts, visual elements within pictures or sequences of film material (→ Content Analysis, Quantitative), or observed actions and overt behaviors (→ Observation). Counting people, words, the duration of a TV program, and so on is deeply rooted in our everyday lives and nothing artificial. Quantitative methodology joins these basic social phenomena but works out systematic (methodological) rules to a complex pattern of standards.

AIMS OF QUANTITATIVE METHODOLOGY

The main aim of quantitative methodology is comparison and measurement (→ Measurement Theory). To compare individuals, text units, or behaviors it is necessary to have a common basis as a starting point for comparison. Without commonalities or standards no comparisons can be made. The logic of quantitative methodology is basically the *logic of standardization*, which implies reducing context complexity around the research object in question. With the help of standardization it is possible to measure the attributes of research units. Measurement is related to the attributes of research units; research units, however, are not viewed in their (complex) entirety but reduced to variables that can be analyzed separately.

One can standardize either different features of the research process or the research process as a whole. Standardizing the entire research process means proceeding systematically and in a certain order of procedures. We start with research questions or with → hypotheses referring to a specific research object. Research questions without hypotheses, which are potential answers to these questions, imply an explorative research strategy. If hypotheses, which can be deduced from abstract theories, are available, a confirmative research strategy will be preferred to test whether the hypotheses are right or false. Regardless of the research strategy being explorative or confirmative, a second step requires research method(s) that are adequate to answer the research questions or to test the hypotheses. Theoretical concepts must be translated into empirical indicators – a process we call → operationalization. Furthermore, a sample of research units needs to be selected. The following process of data collection demands a direct contact and interaction between researcher and the research field explored. After collection, the data will be analyzed with quantitative (statistical) tools and interpreted in the context of the research questions or hypotheses. Each step of the research process is checked according to scientific rules to which a given scientific community agrees within a certain scientific context.

METHODS AND INSTRUMENTS

We can now take a closer look at several steps of the research process and their particular standardization. The most relevant objects of standardization are the research instrument and the research situation. In *polls and surveys* people are questioned about their opinion toward certain social phenomena. The respondent's opinion is treated as a variable that can be separated from other (measurable) attributes. The wording and the order of the questions are laid down in a questionnaire. The interviewer is admonished to follow the interviewing rules strictly and not to use his/her own words. The respondent has to fit his/her answers to preformed categories of answers, such as "strongly agree," "somewhat agree," "don't know," "somewhat disagree," and "strongly disagree." It is the respondent's task to translate the mental representation of his/her opinion into the given (i.e., communicated) categories and to select the category that best fits his/her opinion. This procedure ignores the respondent's own semantic representation of his/her opinion and the context of the cognitive process that forms this opinion, as well as other cognitive and communicative aspects related to the opinion in question, such as prototypical examples, narratives, etc. (→ Cognition; Attitudes). For the purpose of comparison the respondent's answer is only of interest as the standardized semantic result of the preceded complex and context-related or context-bound cognitive processes of opinion formatting. Typical variables collected in surveys may be attributes (gender, age, income, etc.), opinions or attitudes (toward social phenomena, such as norms), knowledge (of persons, structures, processes, etc.), or behaviors (hours of TV watched, voting, etc.).

The research instrument of *content analysis* is called "code-book." It includes a set of standardized semantic categories of attributes that are relevant with regard to the research questions, and which the coder searches within the documents (text, proposition, photograph, film, etc.; → Photography). Coding categories can be formal elements (such as the length of an article, the position of an article within a → newspaper, etc.), semantic variables (such as the theme of an article, actor-related categories, etc.), or pragmatic variables (such as the assessments of actors, organizations, arguments, etc.). Although → coding is not an automatic process (with the exception of computer-aided content analysis; → Text Analysis, Computer-Aided), a deeper or hermeneutical understanding of the text or propositions within the text is not necessary for coding. The coder's task is to assign textual or visual elements to the given categories. A coding manual or commentary contains the coding rules the coder has to apply to the document that has to be coded.

With regard to *observational methods*, the observer pays attention to overt behaviors or apparent attributes of observed people, which s/he records in a code sheet or a list with given categories. Other concomitants spontaneously observed are not of interest in the context of the standardized schedule. The coding process works analogously to the coding process of content analysis.

RESEARCH DESIGNS

As well as the research instrument and the research situation, the complete research design and the process of data collection can also be standardized. Within *experimental research* designs (→ Experimental Design) independent variables are controlled with the help of manipulated stimulus material or the treatment of experimental subjects. In order to test causal effects, subjects are randomly allocated to experimental groups and/or a control group. The experimental group, for instance, is exposed to a horror movie to find out whether this stimulus causes anxiety reactions (→ Fear Induction through Media Content). The proof for the causal effect of the movie content on the media user's emotional state either requires the comparison between a pre-test and a post-test measurement, or a comparison between the measurement of the experimental group after presenting the stimulus material and that of the control group, which is exposed to no stimulus material at all or to a neutral stimulus material.

In the first experimental design comparing *two measurements of the same subjects*, the experimental subjects should show more feelings or reactions of anxiety after viewing the horror movie than before viewing it to put the anxious response exclusively down to the movie and not to any other circumstances. This experimental design only proves the causal effect hypothesized if repeated measurement of the same subjects does not sensitize the subjects toward the measurement instrument, and consequently does not bias the measurement results. In the second experimental design *comparing different subjects* those subjects of the experimental group should show more feelings or reactions of anxiety than the subjects of the control group who viewed a neutral movie to put anxiety exclusively down to the reception of the horror movie and not to other attributes of the subjects or the research situation. This experimental design only proves the causal effect hypothesized if the stimulus materials of the experimental group and the control group clearly differ and if both groups are comparable (identical) with regard to other relevant subjects' attributes.

There are further research designs in quantitative and standardized methodology, such as trend or panel designs, which are often applied in polls on voting behavior or on political attitude change. In *trend studies* the same research instrument is used for different samples at different points of time. Points of time can be chosen very closely (e.g., daily) and data can be analyzed with the help of time-series statistics (→ Longitudinal Analysis). As the samples differ at each point of time, only aggregated differences can be measured. To measure individual differences, panel designs should be applied. In panel designs, standardized measurements can be repeated several times for the same sample, but not as often as in trend designs because subjects become sensitized to the research instrument and bias their responses. Furthermore, sample size in panel designs con-tinuously diminishes because of "panel mortality," i.e., respondents' decreasing coopera-tion in participating in the survey. As a result, the sample may be biased or become too small for complex statistical analysis.

LOGIC OF SAMPLING PROCEDURE AND SAMPLING TECHNIQUE

Quantification of data also has consequences for sampling procedures because quantitat-ive methodology requires sufficiently large samples (of respondents or text units) for data analysis. The general aim of sampling is the generalization of the results (→ Generalizability). The most far-reaching kind of generalization is a representative sample, which means that the distribution of relevant variables in the sample corresponds to the distribution of these variables in the total population. A *random sampling* technique tries to maintain the chance of getting into the sample (approximately) equal for every unit (respondent, text, observed person, etc.). Although the probability of getting into the sample is low if the total population is large, it will never be zero. The procedure of random sampling needs practical conditions that make sure the distributions within the sample are representative of the distributions within the total population (→ Sampling, Random). If some relevant parameters of the total population are known, a *quota-sampling* is also possible. The distributions of these variables in the total population serve as quota instructions for the sampling procedure, which makes sure that the distributions in the sample represent the distributions in the total population. Other sampling procedures and techniques vary according to the research question or the data-collection method applied. In experiments, for instance, samples need not be representative, but should be selected at random; this is important for the statistical testing of the hypotheses (→ Sampling, Nonrandom).

DATA ANALYSIS

All steps taken to standardize the process of data collection reduce the complex information about individuals or text units to separate variables and categories, abstracted from their context. With the help of statistical data analysis we can now count the number of individuals or units with regard to the collected variables (univariate statistics) and we can correlate the variables (bivariate statistics; → Correlation Analysis). Information about the sample distribution is expressed as means and standard deviation of variables; information about the correlation of variables can be documented in cross-tabulations or mean comparisons between group variables (such as gender, categories of age, education, etc.).

It is also possible to test *complex theoretical models* with many variables (multivariate statistics). Several statistical tools discover structures within the data (e.g., → Factor Analysis; Cluster Analysis; Discriminant Analysis); others use a confirmative logic to test models (e.g., variance of analysis; → Regression Analysis; Structural Equation). The complexity lost or reduced within the process of data collection by standardizing the variables and neglecting the context of variables can partly be re-established by analyzing the correlation between the separately collected abstract variables. The analytical outcome may be a complex relationship between variables, which enables the researcher to reconstruct context (→ Statistics, Descriptive; Statistics, Explanatory).

EVALUATIVE CRITERIA FOR QUANTITATIVE RESEARCH

Quantitative methodology is based on certain criteria to assess its quality. These criteria are objectivity (→ Objectivity in Science), → validity, and → reliability. The notion of "objectivity" is somewhat misleading because it does not imply truth in an epistemological sense. Instead, objectivity is related to the research process and procedures. Research procedures have to be systematically planned and carried out. Researchers have to bear in mind the scientific rules that the scientific community agrees on. In that sense, objectivity has a normative aspect and is therefore replaced by the notion of "*intersubjectivity*" (→ Critical Rationalism).

The same is true for *validity*: a research instrument is valid if it measures what it claims to measure. Validity is a criterion to assess the relationship between theoretical concept and empirical indicator. To measure the relevance of media coverage on a certain theme with the help of the position of articles in a newspaper makes sense because front-page news is considered more relevant than articles placed at the back of the newspaper. Although this example seems obvious, the rule to assess validity follows a circular logic, as validity can only be ascertained within scientific discourse and not with the help of a formal procedure.

In contrast to validity, *reliability* is a formal criterion, which can be mathematically calculated as a coefficient of agreement. Reliability is related to the stability of the research instrument. A research instrument is reliable if its repeated use does not change the outcome. In content analysis the coding scheme is reliable if different coders use it in the same way with the same coding results (inter-coder-reliability) or if the same coder uses it the same way at the beginning of the coding procedure as at its end (intra-coder-reliability). The same is true for observation with the exception that an observed situation cannot be reobserved (if it is not recorded). Therefore, intra-coder-reliability can only be simulated by observing similar situations. In surveys reliability is related to similar instruments (questions in the questionnaire). If different questions that are supposed to measure the same construct lead to similar or equal answers, these questions are considered reliable.

In sum, quantitative methodology is characterized by a relationship between *standardization* of research instruments, research situations, and research designs, *quantification* of analysis, *generalization* of results gained from samples, and *systematizing* research procedures. Research is a technical and rule-based process. The underlying premise says that standardizing method and research procedure creates a common basis of preconditions, which allows for comparison across different research objects. As a consequence, the research object is measured in a standardized way and can only be explored in terms of standardized and quantified variables. It is cut off from its individual context but it can be analyzed systematically. Furthermore, standardization is the only way to analyze data quantitatively. To collect a sizeable amount of data is of immense value for the generalization of empirical results because the probability of variety within data increases – even if not necessarily in a linear fashion – with the number of objects researched.

CRITIQUE AND DEFENSE

For the reasons mentioned above researchers who prefer → qualitative methodology object to quantitative methodology, and claim that the complexity lost within the process of data collection neglects the problem of understanding and interpretation (→ Verstehen vs Erklären). A respondent's selection of a certain category from a given set of categories would not imply that she or he understands the category in the same way as the researcher does or other respondents do. Selecting a certain category by interpreting it as the best fit for one's own opinion would be only a vague indicator for the "true" value of the opinion in question. Using standardized data-collection methods would only catch the researcher's presumption of what a question or a category means. Whether the meaning insinuated by the researcher fits the authentic meaning of the "research object" or not could not be technically assessed.

From a *meta-theoretical perspective* it is possible to reconstruct the communication model that underlies quantitative or standardized methodology: it is a stimulus–response model because quantitative methodology supposes that standardizing the meaning of the research stimulus (questions in surveys, categories in content analysis and in observation) causes the standardized understanding of the research object (respondents in surveys), of the coder (in content analysis), or of the observer (in observation).

Advocates of quantitative methodology, however, use the premise of nonsystematic or random error that accompanies the process of measurement. Although a standardized instrument (questionnaire, code-book, observation schedule) is not able to represent the "true" value itself, it is a statistically probable estimation of it. Every bias (deviation from the "true" value) is less probable than the collected value, unless the measurement has been carried out correctly. Systematic errors only occur if and when attributes of the data-collection process itself interfere with attributes of the object (respondent, text, observed person).

Critics may again object that interferences between the measurement process and the measured attribute cannot be avoided and are typical of social phenomena, as the process of data collection is a social process itself. From a constructivist epistemological viewpoint (→ Constructivism) it is indeed not possible to separate both kinds of "realities" (data collection and data itself). Constructivists claim that we should not even speak of (measured) data but of (constructed) facts, as measurement can be considered a social process following and violating the methodological rules developed and declared valid by the scientific community.

We need not solve this problem of epistemological argumentation here because it is more fundamental than the alternative between a quantitative and qualitative methodology. As a consequence of constructivist objections we should not interpret validity in an ontological but in a pragmatic sense. The "correct" use of data-collection and data-analysis tools is not an indicator of truth or approximation to reality but a pragmatic consensus within a scientific community in a given social and historical context. Again, the argumentation is based on standardization: if all researchers use the tools of data collection in the same way, the results can be compared and discussed. If the rules change and other research instruments are developed, they should be compared with the old ones either to find a new agreement among the scientific community or to compete for the better way.

SEE ALSO: ▶ Attitudes ▶ Coding ▶ Cognition ▶ Constructivism ▶ Content Analysis, Quantitative ▶ Cluster Analysis ▶ Correlation Analysis ▶ Critical Rationalism ▶ Discriminant Analysis ▶ Experimental Design ▶ Factor Analysis ▶ Fear Induction through Media Content ▶ Generalizability ▶ Hypothesis ▶ Longitudinal Analysis ▶ Measurement Theory ▶ Newspaper ▶ Objectivity in Science ▶ Observation ▶ Operationalization ▶ Photography ▶ Qualitative Methodology ▶ Regression Analysis ▶ Reliability ▶ Sampling, Nonrandom ▶ Sampling, Random ▶ Statistics, Descriptive ▶ Statistics, Explanatory ▶ Structural Equation ▶ Survey ▶ Text Analysis, Computer-Aided ▶ Validity ▶ Verstehen vs Erklären

References and Suggested Readings

Adèr, H. J. (ed.) (1999). *Research methodology in the life, behavioural and social sciences.* London, Thousand Oaks, CA, and New Delhi: Sage.

Creswell, J. W. (1994). *Research design: Qualitative and quantitative approaches.* London, Thousand Oaks, CA, and New Delhi: Sage.

Kaplan, D. (ed.) (2004). *Handbook of quantitative methodology for the social sciences.* London, Thousand Oaks, CA, and New Delhi: Sage.

Punch, K. F. (2005). *Introduction to social research: Quantitative and qualitative approaches,* 2nd edn. London, Thousand Oaks, CA, and New Delhi: Sage.

Ragin, C. C. (1994). *Constructing social research: The unity and diversity of method.* Thousand Oaks, CA: Pine Forge.

Somekh, B., & Lewin, C. (eds.) (2005). *Research methods in the social sciences.* London, Thousand Oaks, CA, and New Delhi: Sage.

Questions and Questioning

Irene Koshik

University of Illinois at Urbana-Champaign

Any discussion of questions and questioning needs to distinguish between questions as a linguistic form and the various social actions that are accomplished through this form. Questions, or "interrogatives," can be formed in a variety of ways. One type of question uses a specific question word: "which," "when," "why," "where," "who," "whose," "whom," or "how," forming what is called a *wh-question*, e.g., "Who was that lady?," "Where did you play basketball?," "Met whom?" Another question type is the *yes/no question*, i.e., a question to which a "yes" or "no" answer is generally expected. These questions are usually formed in English by inversion of subject and auxiliary, e.g., "Is Al here today?" If there is no auxiliary, the "do auxiliary" is added. Increasingly in informal oral English, the auxiliary is left out, e.g., "You home?" Other languages use phrases or particles, rather than inversion, to indicate that a preceding or following utterance is a yes/no question. Yes/no questions can also be formed syntactically in the same way that declarative statements are formed, using upward instead of downward intonation, e.g., "You're home?" Quirk et al. (1985) call these *declarative questions*. Other types of questions are *tag questions*, which are a type of yes/no question, e.g., "They're a lovely family now aren't they?" and *alternative questions*, e.g., "Didju say *wide*spread or *white*spread?"

RELATIONSHIPS BETWEEN FORM, FUNCTION, AND RESPONSE

According to conversation analysts, questions are *first pair parts* ($\rightarrow$ Conversation Analysis). This means that they initiate courses of action and make certain kinds of responses to these actions relevant and expectable. To some extent, the grammatical form of the question puts constraints on the form of answer that is relevant and expectable. Wh-questions make relevant answers that replace the question word; i.e., *who* questions elicit person references, *where*, place references. Yes/no questions make relevant *yes* or *no* answers. Alternative questions make relevant answers that choose one of the alternatives. However, participants can choose to design responses to questions in ways that do not conform to the grammatical form of the question. For example, when participants disagree with a presupposition embedded in a yes/no question, and providing either a *yes* or *no* answer would imply agreement with this presupposition, participants can choose to give a *non-type-conforming* answer that displays that the question is in some way problematic (Raymond 2003).

Questions are not only used to ask for new information. They are used to initiate repair on someone else's prior talk, e.g., "Huh?" or "Met whom?" and they also perform a variety of social actions such as invitations ("Wanna come down and have a bite of lunch with me?"), offers ("Would you like a cup of coffee?"), complaints ("Why is it that *we* have to go *there*?"), and requests ("Can I have your light?"). At the beginning of a phone conversation, a question such as "Is Judy there?" is also a request, i.e., to speak to Judy. When questions are used to perform actions such as invitations, offers, and requests, recipients often respond by first answering the question, and then dealing with the action performed by the question (Schegloff forthcoming). For example, in response to the phone request, "Is Judy there?" the response "Yeah, just a second." first answers the question: "Yeah," and then responds to the request, indicating that it is being complied with: "just a second."

Like other kinds of initiating actions and their responses, the ways that particular questions are used in particular contexts to perform particular actions are often culture specific. The English telephone request "Is Judy there?" may be heard as an information-seeking question in other cultures. And in some cultures, it is perfectly acceptable on a first encounter to ask adults questions such as "How old are you?" or "How much money do you make at your job?" In North America, it is not.

There are two different types of responses to the actions that questions initiate. With some exceptions, those that forward the action initiated by the question and, in the process, promote social solidarity are called *preferred responses*, and those that block the action initiated by the question are *dispreferred responses* (Schegloff forthcoming). For example, accepting an invitation is *preferred* and rejecting it is *dispreferred*. However, not all responses that forward the action initiated by the question are preferred. Exceptions include self-deprecations, e.g. "I look fat in this dress, don't I?" and some offers, e.g., "Would you like the last piece of cake?" Of course, people can and do give dispreferred responses, but they generally do these in ways that mark them as dispreferred, e.g., by delaying them with silence and discourse markers such as "well," mitigating them, and providing accounts. These response preferences are not personal, psychological preferences, but structural and social preferences. Even if someone invites a person they dislike to a party, and that person does not want to come, their refusal is still a dispreferred response. In fact, they may even end up coming if they can't think of an acceptable account for refusing.

Aside from this action preference, the design of the question itself can convey a preference for a certain type of answer. Linguistics uses the term *conducive* to describe this preference (Quirk et al. 1985). For example, the questions "Didn't he arrive yet?" and "Do you really want to leave now?" seem to expect negative answers because of the *negative polarity item* "yet" and the *intensifier* "really." The questions "Did someone call?" and "Hasn't the boat left already?" seem to expect affirmative answers because of the positive polarity items "someone" and "already." These questions are conducive because they display the questioner's epistemic stance (Koshik 2005). Because of the preference for agreement, the answers prefer agreement with this stance.

Some questions, commonly known as *rhetorical questions*, are so strongly conducive that they are not heard as questions but as making a claim, or assertion, of the opposite polarity to that of the question. Because of this polarity reversal, Koshik (2005) calls these questions "reversed polarity questions." They are often used as accusations, challenges, or complaints, e.g., "when have I." (i.e., I never have), said in response to a friend's accusation that Shelley was blowing off her girlfriends for guys, and "oh who cares!" (i.e., no one [except you] cares), said by a teenage boy in response to his parents' attempts to correct his grammar.

QUESTIONS IN INSTITUTIONAL TALK

Questions play an important role in institutional talk. According to Drew and Heritage (1992), question–answer sequences are the dominant form of interaction in many types of institutional talk, e.g. counseling interviews, medical interactions, broadcast news interviews (→ Broadcast Talk), survey interviews (→ Survey; Interview, Standardized), employment interviews, emergency calls, courtroom interactions, and pedagogical interactions (→ Educational Communication). Questions are used to enact institutional roles, with the professional often leading the lay person through a series of question-initiated sequences, creating interactional asymmetry.

Questions reflect institutional norms, are central to accomplishing institutional goals, and are designed in special ways to meet these goals. Broadcast news interviewers design questions to strike a balance between the "journalistic norms of impartiality and adversarialness" (Clayman & Heritage 2002). For example, interviewers use reversed polarity questions to challenge interviewees, without directly giving their opinions, e.g., "Doesn't that suggest that your party is still immature/irresponsible/undisciplined/unserious?" Teachers in one-on-one writing conferences use similar questions as hints to enable students to perform error correction successfully (Koshik 2005). For example, after a student explains how a portion of his text is relevant to his thesis, the teacher says, "Good. Did you tell me that?" conveying, "You didn't write in your essay what you just told me orally, but you should have." Attorneys in the courtroom can design yes/no questions to challenge the truth or adequacy of a witness's evidence. These questions often contain presuppositions which support their views. Lawyers can then require witnesses to answer with type-conforming questions, asking that answers beyond simple "yes" and "no" be stricken from the record (Atkinson & Drew 1979; → Discourse in the Law). In contrast, survey interview questions are designed to avoid presuppositions (Raymond 2003). Doctors use questions to elicit the patient's history in medical examinations, and to maintain control over what is talked about (Drew & Heritage 1992; → Doctor–Patient Talk).

Many of the questions asked by the professional in institutional talk are *known-information* questions, i.e., questions to which the questioner knows the answer. Lawyers and broadcast news interviewers are expected to know answers to the questions they ask of witnesses and interviewees; they are asking these questions for an overhearing audience (Drew & Heritage 1992). Known-information questions are so common in North American and British pedagogy that they are identified with doing teaching, even when done outside institutional settings, e.g. when parents help children with homework. They engender a special three-part sequence, which Mehan (1979) calls "initiation, response, evaluation." In the third turn after the student's correct answer, the teacher typically evaluates the answer as correct, e.g., "good!" This evaluation does not treat the answer as new information. It would be odd for a teacher, or even a lawyer or news interviewer, to follow an answer to a known-information question with an information receipt such as "oh," displaying that the answer was news to them (Drew & Heritage 1992).

SEE ALSO: ▶ Broadcast Talk ▶ Conversation Analysis ▶ Directives ▶ Discourse in the Law ▶ Doctor–Patient Talk ▶ Educational Communication ▶ Interview, Standardized ▶ Linguistic Pragmatics ▶ Survey

References and Suggested Readings

Atkinson, J. M., & Drew, P. (1979). *Order in court: The organization of verbal interaction in juridical settings*. London: Macmillan.

Clayman, S. E., & Heritage, J. (2002). Questioning presidents: Journalistic deference and adversarialness in the press conferences of U.S. presidents Eisenhower and Reagan. *Journal of Communication*, 2, 749–775.

Drew, P., & Heritage, J. (1992). Analyzing talk at work: An introduction. In P. Drew & J. Heritage (eds.), *Talk at work*. Cambridge: Cambridge University Press, pp. 3–65.

Koshik, I. (2005). *Beyond rhetorical questions: Assertive questions in everyday interaction*. Amsterdam: John Benjamins.

Mehan, H. (1979). *Learning lessons: Social organization in the classroom*. Cambridge, MA: Harvard University Press.

Quirk, R., Greenbaum, S., Leech, G., & Svartvik, J. (1985). *A comprehensive grammar of the English language*. New York: Longman.

Raymond, G. (2003). Grammar and social organization: Yes/no interrogatives and the structure of responding. *American Sociological Review*, 68, 939–967.

Schegloff, E. A. (1984). On some questions and ambiguities in conversation. In J. M. Atkinson & J. Heritage (eds.), *Structures of social action*. Cambridge: Cambridge University Press, pp. 28–52.

Schegloff, E. A. (forthcoming). *A primer of conversation analysis: Sequence organization*. Cambridge: Cambridge University Press.

Weber, E. G. (1993). *Varieties of questions in English conversation*, vol. III. Amsterdam: John Benjamins.

R

Radical Media

Clemencia Rodríguez

University of Oklahoma

"Radical media" is a term used by communication scholars to refer to information and communication technologies used by radical media activists to bring about social change (→ Activist Media; Social Movements and Communication). In this sense, the word "radical" means the expression of ideas, opinions, and options to reorganize society that are not sanctioned by the established social order. British communication scholar John Downing coined the term in his volume *Radical media*, where he critiques the term "alternative media" as oxymoronic because "[e]verything, at some point, is alternative to something else" (1984, ix). For Downing, the designation radical media needs to be based on a careful historical examination of the medium's context, content, and consequences. Under certain cultural and political conditions, content that in other contexts would be deemed apolitical and inoffensive can yield tremendous social change when transmitted by radical media; thus, context determines the "radicalness" of the content in each case. Also, the medium's organization does not necessarily mean that the content is radical; each case has to be examined in order to establish if and to what extent the medium's content is in fact radical, depending on its potential to strengthen resistance politics and bring about social change.

Radical media serve both progressive and authoritarian social movements. In the first case, radical media are used by radical media activists including environmentalists, women, ethnic minorities, and human rights groups among others. In the latter case, radical media express the views of fundamentalist, racist, or fascist movements that revolve around "radically negative forces" (Downing 2001, ix), such as white supremacy, and religious fundamentalist organizations (→ Civil Rights Movement and the Media).

The *goal of radical media* is twofold. First, radical media express someone's intent to critique, resist, and transform the establishment. Second, radical media are used by activists to build solidarity and support around their agendas. In this sense, radical media develop a series of vertical and lateral communication and information actions and messages.

Radical media come in "a colossal variety of formats" (Downing 2001, x) that range through print media (→ Newspaper), → radio, → television, → video, film, puppets, woodcuts, → dance, → posters, → cartoons, → graffiti, murals, → theatre, performance art, and culture jamming.

With several co-authors, Downing has studied the role(s) of radical media in different geographical, cultural, and political contexts that include radical radio and print media and the fall of the dictatorship in Portugal in the 1970s; the free radio movement in Italy from 1970 to 2000; the case of access television in the United States during the 1980s and 1990s; the case of samizdat in the former Soviet bloc; and the case of Free Radio Berkeley in the United States.

SEE ALSO: ▶ Activist Media ▶ Cartoons ▶ Civil Rights Movement and the Media ▶ Community Media ▶ Dance ▶ Graffiti ▶ Newspaper ▶ Poster ▶ Radio ▶ Social Movements and Communication ▶ Television ▶ Theatre ▶ Video

References and Suggested Readings

Atton, C. (2002). *Alternative media*. London: Sage.
Downing, J. (1984). *Radical media: The political organization of alternative communication*. Boston, MA: South End Press.
Downing, J. (2001). *Radical media: Rebellious communication and social movements*. London: Sage.
Rodríguez, C. (2001). *Fissures in the mediascape: An international study of citizens' media*. Cresskill, NJ: Hampton Press.

Radio

Douglas Ferguson
College of Charleston

Radio is a media technology that permits one person or organization to communicate with many receivers over large distances via the electromagnetic spectrum and radiated electrons. Listening to radio is possible by modulating voice (→ Broadcast Talk) or music (→ Popular Music) onto a radio wave that transmits at a predetermined signal. A radio receiver is tuned to the modulated carrier wave broadcasting at that frequency and the radio circuitry amplifies the voice or music, after discarding the carrier frequency wave (→ Radio Technology; Information and Communication Technology, Development of).

Radio is a ubiquitous and inexpensive means of mass communication. Audiences need not be literate, making radio accessible to everyone with the most basic language skills, or in the case of music, no language at all (→ Exposure to Radio). Depending on the characteristics of the radio frequency, programs can be heard around the world (→ International Radio), but are typically limited to a small geographic area. The device that became known as the radio took its name from radio waves, the band of frequencies that made the technology possible. Before that, it was more commonly known as "the wireless" because it operated without a physical connection.

Radio was demonstrated by Guglielmo Marconi in 1895, in work based on the earlier theory of Heinrich Hertz and ideas by Nikola Tesla. Marconi's transmitter and receiver used Morse code to communicate radiotelegraphy. The unmodulated carrier frequency was turned off and on, signaling a short or long (dot–dash) signal that could be interpreted by a trained receiver, making radio an effective means of point-to-point communication, especially from ship to shore.

Radio transformed into the first medium of live mass (point-to-many) communication when Reginald Fessenden and Lee de Forest demonstrated voice and music broadcasts in 1906 and 1907. David Sarnoff of the American Marconi Company first proposed a commercial enterprise in his "radio box" memo of 1916, although Charles Herrold had earlier begun regularly scheduled broadcasts in San Jose, California. The United States began licensing frequencies in 1920, when the necessary radio patents had been pooled by the Radio Corporation of America (RCA). By 1922, radio was a national craze in the US, with more broadcasters than available frequencies (→ Attending to the Mass Media). The Federal Radio Commission (FRC, later the FCC) was the government agency in the US that brought some order to the chaos by 1927 (→ Radio Broadcasting, Regulation of). The radio medium became advertiser-supported when one of the original RCA partners and patent-holders, AT&T, successfully experimented with "toll broadcasting" on its New York station WEAF in 1922 (→ Radio Networks).

Until the popularity of television grew after World War II, radio was the most widely used mass medium, from the 1920s through the late 1940s. Many of the program → genres that exist on television today (e.g., game shows, sitcoms, serialized dramas) were first conceived for radio. After television, radio stations switched to specialized music formats to attract a new audience that often stays loyal because of the unique content or the compelling on-air personality of the announcer (→ Audience Segmentation). In the US, public radio is a designated band of frequencies for noncommercial content.

Radio operates in different ways. AM (amplitude modulation) radio modulates the desired content onto the carrier wave using the vertical strength of the frequency. To combat audio interference from other sources of electromagnetic frequencies (e.g., thunderstorms), Edwin Armstrong developed FM (frequency modulation) radio, which modulated the frequency itself horizontally. Satellite radio (XM and Sirius) are federally licensed digital audio radio service (DARS) frequencies in the US that transmit signals from a high-power geostationary satellite to subscription-only receivers. Finally, HD radio is a method for allowing terrestrial (AM and FM) radio broadcasters to modulate digital (CD-quality) signals onto the same carrier wave used for analog signals, allowing radio content to be received by old and new radios alike on the same band and frequency. Signal compression will eventually allow more content per individual frequencies (called a channel).

Radio stations are *licensed* by individual countries, and radio frequencies are controlled by international treaties and agencies. In the United States, nearly 14,000 radio stations broadcast to over 300 million potential listeners. Radio audiences age 12 and above are measured by Arbitron to assist in the determination of advertising rates. The Radio Advertising Bureau and the National Association of Broadcasters are two important trade organizations. Ownership of radio stations was deregulated in the US by the Telecommunications Act of 1996, which allows a single company to own a limitless number of commercial stations as long as no market area designated by Arbitron has more than eight stations per owner. Clear Channel owns over 1,400 stations, making it the largest owner (→ Ownership in the Media).

Media effects research grew out of early studies of radio in → Paul Lazarsfeld's Office of Radio Research, with seminal studies of, for example, voting behavior as influenced by radio (→ Media Effects, History of). On the other hand, some researchers studied radio from a → uses-and-gratifications perspective. Among these, Herta Herzog examined why people listened to daytime dramas (i.e., soap operas). Hadley Cantril studied, for example, the panic that followed the 1938 Halloween broadcast (by Orson Welles and the Mercury Theatre) of H. G. Wells's epic *War of the Worlds*. Interviews with listeners were used to explain why one million of the six million listeners believed the fictional broadcast to be real.

After the introduction of television, many mass communication researchers and theorists turned their attention to the world of video, which exerts a potentially more powerful influence and consumes many more hours per day of public attention. Still, radio functions as the ultimate portable medium and continues to reach nearly everyone, especially in commuting automobiles. In publications such as the *Journal of Radio Studies*, some studies now focus on how broadcast radio competes with satellite radio and other forms of portable audio media.

SEE ALSO: ▶ Attending to the Mass Media ▶ Audience Research ▶ Audience Segmentation ▶ Broadcast Talk ▶ Exposure to Radio ▶ Genre ▶ Information and Communication Technology, Development of ▶ International Radio ▶ Lazarsfeld, Paul F. ▶ Media Effects, History of ▶ Ownership in the Media ▶ Popular Music ▶ Radio Broadcasting, Regulation of ▶ Radio for Development ▶ Radio Networks ▶ Radio Technology ▶ Uses and Gratifications

References and Suggested Readings

Dunning, J. (1998). *On the air: The encyclopedia of old-time radio*. New York: Oxford University Press.
Lackmann, R. W. (2000). *The encyclopedia of American radio*. New York: Checkmark Books.
Warren, J. (2005). *Radio: The book*. Boston: Focal Press.

Radio Broadcasting, Regulation of

William R. Davie
University of Louisiana

The radio spectrum is viewed as a natural and scarce resource available to all nations. Even though the rules establishing the allocation of bandwidth and assignment of frequencies vary, common principles apply to all countries. The *legal rationale for controls* over licensing is generally based on four principles: (1) recognition of spectrum as a valuable resource; (2) conservation of bandwidth due to spectrum scarcity; (3) prevention of technical interference between channels; and (4) radio broadcasting's potential to influence society. These general principles serve as the starting point for regulating ownership, technology, and programming content (→ Radio; Radio: Social History).

GLOBAL HISTORY AND INTERNATIONAL ACTION

Before radio's ship-to-shore communication evolved into broadcasting early in the twentieth century, nations recognized the imperative of using wireless telegraphy at sea to save lives and cargo. The International Radiotelegraph Convention of 1906 established policies that held radio frequencies should be registered, signal interference prevented, and proprietary restraints against sending and receiving signals lifted.

Nations began drawing up rules beyond maritime services in the 1920s, and eventually formed an international body to oversee radio regulations. The agreement of 1927 allocated the middle frequency band (MF = 10 kHz to 30 MHz) for broadcasting, maritime communications, land mobile radio, and amateur services. In 1932, the Madrid General Radio Regulations Conference established the *International Telecommunication Union (ITU)*. From its base in Geneva, Switzerland, the ITU today is an arm of the United Nations and effectively manages radio traffic across borders while settling international disputes. A select comparison of countries will show how legal systems contrast both in terms of radio ownership and content restrictions.

NATIONAL REGULATIONS

US and Europe

The origin of radio-broadcast regulation in the *US* was prompted by a treaty dispute with Canada, which US Secretary of Commerce Herbert Hoover was powerless to resolve under existing law. Congress consequently moved to grant his office more power under the Radio Control Bill of 1927, and in 1934 it established the → Federal Communications Commission (FCC) in order to protect the "public interest, convenience and necessity" of broadcasting. Those terms continue to guide American radio regulations, and in the decades since it was created, the FCC has enforced a wide variety of rules from restricting indecent content to limiting the numbers of stations one group can own. In 1996, the Telecommunications Act was passed to allow more competition in radio and to deregulate other elements of the law (see http://wireless.fcc.gov/rules.html; → United States of America: Media System; Communication Law and Policy: North America).

In *Britain*, the British Broadcasting Corporation (→ BBC) is an independent public organization, which for 80 years was run by a board of governors, who were replaced in 2007 by a trust of 11 members. Britons support the BBC through license fees, and in return the "Beeb" has supplied domestic and global audiences with a wealth of radio programs, but private stations now compete with the BBC under the Independent Broadcasting Authority (IBA). The 1990 Broadcasting Act created licenses rather than franchises for British broadcasters, yet, unlike the US model, private radio stations had to gain approval for programming formats. When radio groups began taking over multiple stations, the UK devised a system of ownership points to prevent any one group from reaching too wide an audience. Britain also adopted a new technical standard for radio digital broadcasting, Eureka 147 (→ United Kingdom: Media System; Public Service Broadcasting: Law and Policy).

The Association of German Broadcasters (ARD) became the organizing agency for radio in West *Germany* following the fall of the Third Reich. The ARD was modeled after the British public service system, which afforded independence from the government without reliance on advertising revenue. It was originally comprised of nine independent broadcasting corporations covering various regions of the country. After the fall of the Berlin wall the newly founded public broadcasting stations in East Germany were incorporated into the system. Boards of representatives from political parties, industrial unions, religious groups, and other associations monitor the independent public channels. German households support public radio with a fee, but advertising also generates revenue. One of the key principles of broadcasting in Germany is the freedom from governmental interference in terms of program content. No public official can control or censor German programming, but the Federal Constitutional Court has ruled that public radio must give voice to a variety of opinions. That protection corresponds with the European Convention on Human Rights, which has influenced radio broadcasting in other countries as well.

France moved from a public monopoly operated under the Office de Radiodiffusion Télévision Française (ORTF) to both a public and a private system of licensing in the early 1980s. In 1984, France adopted its first commercial radio law allowing private stations to seek advertising for support. Today, private-sector radio attracts more than two thirds of the listening audience in France, but Radio France continues to operate seven public channels as well (→ Communication Law and Policy: Europe).

African Nations

Radio is the dominant medium for *African countries*, and the majority of systems reflect their colonial fathers. France used radio as a means for disseminating its language and culture among Africans. Britain encouraged natives to preserve their culture and language by radio after years of using the medium exclusively for its colonists rather than natives. The Ghana Broadcasting Corporation (GBC) stands as an example of the British model since it became the first country to gain independence in 1957. Ghana's state-run radio system fell victim to political patronage, however, and failed to realize the BBC ideal of broadcast independence. Following deregulation in the 1990s, private stations replaced the GBC as the most popular channels for Ghanans.

African countries tend to rely primarily on national broadcasting systems with studios located in the capital or the nation's largest city. Nigeria and South Africa's broadcast systems stand apart among those on the continent for their development of regional systems of radio. Following widespread deregulation, hundreds of independent or community radio stations sprung up across Africa. Legal structures vary, but governments generally apply stricter controls over broadcasters than western powers. Zambia, for example, licenses private radio stations, but forbids news bulletins on them. Clandestine radio channels assumed an important role in African broadcasting during the 1990s. The infamous *Radio des Mille Collines* (Radio of a Thousand Hills) in Rwanda enflamed genocidal hatred contributing to the mass murder of millions in 1994. As a result, humanitarian stations were established by the United Nations to broadcast messages of peace to Africa's war-torn regions (→ Africa: Media Systems; Communication Law and Policy: Africa).

Asia

Two key distinctions in radio regulation are the extent to which the government applies legal controls over content, and the measure to which privatization of radio ownership has occurred. Radio Singapura of Singapore for example was originally government operated but became privatized in 1994. Radio Singapura is still subject to government censorship ostensibly to protect the multicultural population from offensive and violent content. Singapore law forbids the denigration of races or religions in addition to banning pornography or violence "contrary to the public interest." The Media Development Authority of Singapore exercises censorship whenever it detects programming that might put the public at risk. In *Japan*, Nippon Hoso Kyokai (NHK) operates three radio services required by law to elevate cultural values for both national and community interests. Article 44 of the Broadcast Law of Japan requires NHK to conduct research and development in radio, and serve foreign countries with Japanese programming that will contribute to international understanding (→ Japan: Media System).

At the other end of the spectrum, the Democratic People's Republic of *North Korea* operates a government-run system of radio connecting Pyongyang by radio wire to more than 4,000 "broadcasting booths" located in farms, factories, and other public places. The government forbids reception of foreign channels on any North Korean radio receiver. *South Korea*'s National Security Law prevents its citizens from listening to Pyongyang's radio propaganda if the government in Seoul determines that they are doing so to help North Korean efforts. In addition to South Korea's 100-plus radio stations operated by two networks, American Armed Forces radio is popular, and internet-based radio stations are cropping up on broadband websites. One independent Internet radio station operated by North Korean defectors was forced to vacate its offices following a protest from the Pyongyang government, but continued webcasting from private offices (→ South Korea: Media System; Communication Law and Policy: Asia).

Shanghai signed on to the first American radio station in *China*, but the Minister of Communications established the first Chinese public radio channel in 1927. The Chinese Communist Party established its first radio station, New China, in 1945, in the southern province of Yunin, and took over nationalist transmitters in 1949. At the beginning of the twenty-first century, China used a three-tiered broadcasting system based on geography – municipal, regional, and national networks – funded by governments at each level. Radio in China remains a state-run system with no private ownership but with some competition among individual stations and networks (→ China: Media System).

Latin America

The rule of law in Latin America is by no means airtight and the politicization of radio airwaves is a defining factor. In *Mexico*, a privatization bill was enacted in 2000 over the loud protests of government-run radio stations, which charged that political patronage was involved in the new law. In *Venezuela*, the 1999 constitution introduced by President Hugo Chavez promised freedom of expression for broadcasters, but human-rights groups observed prior restraint was ordered by judicial fiat, and more recently a widespread suspension of radio and television stations critical of the Chavez administration was ordered.

In *Brazil*, privately owned radio stations are required to carry government-sponsored programs including a one-hour evening newscast produced by the government, *Hora do Brazil*. Community radio stations have reached listeners in rural areas of the country, but not always legally. ANATEL, Brazil's telecommunications regulatory agency, has shut down renegade community stations broadcasting without a license.

Radio stations in *Chile* were nationalized under Salvador Allende's regime in the early 1970s, but eventually were sold to political groups representing the Socialists, Communists, and Christian Democrats. Today, the Roman Catholic Church also broadcasts over a radio network in Chile.

In *Colombia*, the National Institute of Radio and Television offers program content for both private and government-owned stations. The two largest networks are required by law to broadcast shortwave for Colombian interests outside the country.

The international scope of foreign investments in radio systems and the extent to which countries legally restrict foreign ownership for reasons of national security, culture, or economy has changed in recent years. Brazil opened its cable television industry to foreign ownership, but not its radio stations. Chile, on the other hand, applies no restrictions to foreign investments in radio, and India recently raised its limit to over 70 percent to attract foreign investment.

Only American and Puerto Rican citizens were allowed to hold US radio licenses until 1996 when a cap was placed on direct foreign investments of 20 percent for private firms, and 25 percent for holding companies. Following September 11, 2001, a select committee of government agents was authorized to approve foreign ownership in US radio licenses on a case-by-case basis (→ Communication Law and Policy: South America).

SEE ALSO: ▶ Africa: Media Systems ▶ BBC ▶ China: Media System ▶ Communication Law and Policy: Africa ▶ Communication Law and Policy: Asia ▶ Communication Law and Policy: Europe ▶ Communication Law and Policy: Middle East ▶ Communication Law and Policy: North America ▶ Communication Law and Policy: South America ▶ European Union: Communication Law ▶ Federal Communications Commission (FCC) ▶ Foreign Policy and the Media ▶ International Radio ▶ Japan: Media System ▶ South Korea: Media System ▶ Public Service Broadcasting: Law and Policy ▶ Radio ▶ Radio: Social History ▶ Telecommunications: Law and Policy ▶ United Kingdom: Media System ▶ United Nations, Communication Policies of ▶ United States of America: Media System

References and Suggested Readings

Bourgault, L. M. (1995). *Mass media in Sub-Saharan Africa*. Bloomington, IN: Indiana University Press.

Boyd, D. A. (1999). *Broadcasting in the Arab World: A survey of the electronic media in the Middle East*, 3rd edn. Ames, IA: Iowa State University Press.

Fardon, R., & Furniss, G. (2000). *African broadcast cultures: Radio in transition.* Westport, CT: Praeger.

Mytton, G. (2004). Africa. In C. H. Sterling (ed.), *Encyclopedia of radio vol. 1: The museum of broadcast communications.* New York: Taylor and Francis Books.

Walker, A. (1992). *A skyful of freedom: Sixty years of the BBC World Service.* London: Brookside Books.

Ziegler, D., & Asante, M. (1992). *Thunder and silence: The mass media in Africa.* Trenton, NJ: Africa World Press.

Radio for Development

Robert Huesca

Trinity University

Radio for development is the strategic use of this medium to effect social changes beneficial to a community, nation, or region. Within the study and practice of communication for national development and social change, → radio has claimed a prominent place for a variety of reasons. As an aural medium, radio obviates the need for a literate audience, making it an attractive medium for states and agencies working with impoverished populations that lack access to schools or other forms of literacy training. In addition, radio is an inexpensive medium for its audience, and therefore enjoys a wide range of diffusion even among rural people with scant resources for material not directly related to their basic needs. Finally, radio is relatively inexpensive to produce and distribute, making it an attractive medium for donor agencies concerned with per capita costs for reaching underdeveloped audiences with pro-social messages. Indeed, among all communication media (print, film, telephone, television, and new media), radio consistently enjoys the highest rates of diffusion and use in the developing world (→ Exposure to Radio).

EARLY THEORIES AND METHODS

Along with the broad use of radio for development, a wide range of approaches and methods has emerged with its evolution and deployment. In the early years of development communication (the 1950s through the 1960s), which were dominated by modernization theories, the focus of scholars and practitioners was both on the mere exposure to radio and on the diffusion of "good information" (→ Diffusion of Information and Innovation; Modernization). For *modernization theorists*, radio, along with other mass media, was considered an "index of development." Indeed, in the early 1960s, the United Nations Educational, Scientific, and Cultural Organization (→ UNESCO) issued standards for media sufficiency that identified the per capita requirement of five radios per 100 inhabitants as a measure of minimal development. As the primary, transnational organization conducting research into communication and development at the time, UNESCO reflected the assumptions of scholars that radio and other media functioned as "magic multipliers" of development and as the gateways to "empathy" and social mobility needed in the transition away from traditional values and beliefs (→ Empathy Theory). Many social surveys at the time demonstrated correlations between media exposure and wider economic and political participation.

During this period, however, neither radio nor other mass media generally were seen as a simple panacea for underdevelopment, as is sometimes erroneously asserted by some scholars. Rather, radio was to be combined with information relevant to development objectives in a process of diffusion aimed at attitude and behavior change. Early development efforts were often guided and assessed by the theoretical propositions delineated in Rogers's *Diffusion of innovations* (1962), which prescribed messages aimed at achieving attitude changes among individuals considered to be early adopters of new technologies and practices (→ Opinion Leader; Rogers, Everett). By the time his book was first published, Rogers had documented some 5,000 diffusion projects, many of them using radio in the development process. These early approaches to radio for development are often represented in the shorthand phrase "the dominant paradigm of communication," which generally conceptualizes media use as a one-way, top-down spread of information from experts to beneficiaries.

CONCEPTUAL CHALLENGES

The dominant paradigm of radio for development was challenged in both theory and practice in the 1970s when there was a confluence of intellectual and social factors. Many of the leading theories and practices emerged from Latin America, including: (1) Paolo Freire's work on dialogic pedagogy; (2) dependency theory's critique of capitalism; and (3) liberation theology's option for the poor (→ Dependency Theories). All of these movements reacted against the top-down model of development and called for communication practices that relied on the *participation of grassroots communities*, which were viewed as crucial partners in efforts to design and implement particular projects (→ Participatory Communication).

The social and political context of this movement reinforced its direction. Within Latin America, a turn toward authoritarian government spurred a strong call to return to civilian rule, which accompanied democratic models of communication. On the global stage, former colonies from Africa and Asia took their place within international organizations, such as UNESCO, and pushed agendas such as the call for a → New World Information and Communication Order (NWICO). Indeed, in 1977 UNESCO published what has become known as the "Belgrade Document," which had a strong impact on radio for development. In it, UNESCO identified the goals of access, participation, and self-management for radio development projects.

Actually, the practice of grassroots radio in Latin America preceded the theory. As far back as 1947, Radio Sutatenza, established by a Roman Catholic priest in Colombia, began using a *community model of radio for development*. The station's success at promoting community participation in radio for development stimulated numerous other broadcast projects that ultimately led to the formation of the Latin American Association of Radio Education (ALER). Since then, hundreds, if not thousands, of small community radio stations have taken root around the world. They tend to define development broadly and rely on various means of support including educational institutions, international aid organizations, churches, listener contributions, and even advertising. Successful models of participatory radio for development include: listening clubs, where people meet to discuss programs and then ask questions and offer responses to broadcasters either in writing or on tape; cassette forums, where local populations submit opinions, suggestions, and questions to broadcasters serving rural populations; "people's reporters," who are representatives elected by communities to act as local journalists and submit news to radio stations; and community centers that broadcast cultural events and public affairs programs. Regardless of their particular practices, most participatory uses of radio tend to work with existing nongovernmental organizations and other civil society groups to increase their impact in achieving development objectives and goals.

Participatory approaches have been so successful that virtually all radio for development projects today make blanket claims to incorporate access and dialogue into their activities. This has led to vigorous *theoretical debates* attempting to refine this robust concept. At one end of the theoretical debates, scholars have identified approaches that conceptualize participation merely as a means to an end, or as the practical necessity of identifying salient topics, concepts, language, and actors to most effectively deliver media products such as radio dramas, public service announcements, or songs with pro-social messages. At the other end of the debates is a school that posits participation as an end in and of itself. This approach understands participation as practically a moral mandate wherein the beneficiaries of any program should be directly involved at every stage of production. Deep participation in the communication process is thought to contribute to multiple outcomes ranging from material gains to psychological empowerment.

REFORMING EARLY APPROACHES

In a move stemming from these theoretical debates, some clear descendents of the dominant paradigm approach to radio for development have undergone rigorous reformulation since the 1990s. Two complementary approaches in particular stand out as robust methods of implementing radio for development projects: → social marketing and → entertainment education. *Social marketing* traces its roots to the advertising industry and adopts the industry's primary objective of persuading individuals to change their attitudes and behaviors. Drawing on research and methods from consumer behavior, social marketing attaches pro-social messages to industry techniques of influencing market segments through radio advertising, announcements, and programs.

Similarly, *entertainment education* borrows techniques prevalent within various media industries and aimed at mass audiences. As indicated in its name, this approach designs projects that use media strategically both to entertain and to educate audiences about development issues, with the aim of changing attitudes and behavior (Singhal 2004). Entertainment education programs are founded on Albert Bandura's social learning theory and create programming with characters that model pro-social beliefs, attitudes, and behaviors (→ Observational Learning).

A recent review of 14 cases of radio dramas from Latin America, Africa, and south Asia demonstrated the contemporary strength and influence of Bandura's social learning theory and the entertainment education approaches to radio for development (Myers 2002;

→ Development Communication: Africa; Development Communication: Asia; Development Communication: Latin America). Like social marketing projects, entertainment education radio programs rely on formative research of audience segments, consisting largely of focus groups and surveys. This formative research is vital to shaping pro-social messages that are largely determined in advance by donor agencies. At this time, the most commonly funded programs focus on family planning and AIDS prevention (→ Health Communication). They are sometimes evaluated through survey techniques that measure message retention, attitudes, and reported behavior changes. Social marketing and entertainment education share a clear lineage from dominant paradigm approaches in their top-down transmission orientation to communication that focuses on individual attitudes and behaviors.

FUTURE DIRECTIONS FOR RADIO

As with all development communication projects, the future of radio for development will be shaped by a combination of technological advances and the agendas of donor agencies, international organizations, and communication scholars. In the mid-1990s, radio for development was given renewed life by the advent of *wind-up or "clockwork" radios* that operated without the need for electricity or batteries. Despite their sustainable qualities and relative affordability, the wind-up sets have generally been beyond the means of many of the world's poorest people. New developments in solar-powered sets, however, are once again trying to place radios in the hands of individuals who do not have access to electricity or batteries.

Aside from technological challenges, the agendas of *donor agencies* vary by region, which will shape future uses of radio for development. US programs, such as the Agency for International Development and the Centers for Disease Control and Prevention, prefer programs that reflect the dominant paradigm tradition. These sorts of programs reach mass audiences and generate quantitative data, such as ratings points and attitude measures, that are demanded by donor agencies in their evaluation requirements. European foundations and religious organizations, however, have been more supportive traditionally of community radio approaches that strive for local participation and control of communication. This approach to radio for development is also supported by international organizations such as the United Nations Development Program and UNESCO, which currently are focused on promoting democracy locally, nationally, and internationally. These institutions have identified corporate media as an impediment to democratic communication practices, while noting the rise of civil society groups and nongovernmental organizations in the regulation of societies. This emphasis on democratizing communication will provide support and encouragement for more participatory and community radio for development projects.

Finally, scholars continue to debate *theoretical questions* in development communication and will influence radio for development practices in the future. The notion of participation has been the most robust concept in the field of development communication over the past quarter century, but scholars have adopted it in complex and nuanced ways. Many scholars continue to devote energy to democratic theories of radio as well as social marketing and entertainment education approaches to the medium. Both approaches to radio for development will continue to have adherents, proponents, and defenders in the long term.

SEE ALSO: ▶ Dependency Theories ▶ Development Communication: Africa ▶ Development Communication: Asia ▶ Development Communication: Latin America ▶ Diffusion of Information and Innovation ▶ Empathy Theory ▶ Entertainment Education ▶ Exposure to Radio ▶ Health Communication ▶ Modernization ▶ New World Information and Communication Order (NWICO) ▶ Observational Learning ▶ Opinion Leader ▶ Participatory Communication ▶ Planned Social Change through Communication ▶ Radio ▶ Rogers, Everett ▶ Social Marketing ▶ UNESCO

References and Suggested Readings

Adam, G., & Harford, N. (1998). *Health on air: A guide to creative radio for development*. London: Health Unlimited.

Fisher, H. A. (1990). Community radio as a tool for development. *Media Development*, 4, 19–24.

Gumucio Dagron, A. (2001). *Making waves: Stories of participatory communication for social change: A report to the Rockefeller Foundation*. New York: Rockefeller Foundation.

Katz, E., & Wedell, G. (1977). *Broadcasting in the third world: Promise and performance*. Cambridge, MA: Harvard University Press.

Mody, B. (1991). *Designing messages for development communication: An audience participatory-based approach*. Thousand Oaks: Sage.

Myers, M. (2002). *Institutional review of educational radio dramas*. Atlanta: Centers for Disease Control and Prevention.

O'Sullivan-Ryan, J., & Kaplún, M. (1978). *Communication methods to promote grass-roots participation: A summary of research findings from Latin America, and an annotated bibliography*. Paris: UNESCO.

Rogers, E. (1962). *Diffusion of innovations*. New York: Free Press.

Singhal, A. (2004). *Entertainment-education and social change: History, research, and practice*. Mahwah, NJ: Lawrence Erlbaum.

Vargas, L. (1995). *Social uses and radio practices: The use of participatory radio by ethnic minorities in Mexico*. Boulder, CO: Westview Press.

Radio France Internationale

Olivier J. Tchouaffe

University of Texas at Austin

Radio France Internationale began in 1929 with the creation of the French national office of radio broadcasting. Two years later, in 1931, Radio France began broadcasting to French colonies in 20 languages under the name *Poste Colonial*. Its target audience was French expatriate colonizers and a few natives, termed *évolués*, who had been trained to speak French and engage in low-status labor, such as nursing, postal clerking, and the infantry, which whites were not allowed to perform in the colonies. In 1938, Poste

Colonial was renamed Paris Mondial, and was then jettisoned during the pro-Nazi Vichy regime (1940–1944), resuming after liberation. In 1964 the French government created the ORTF (French Radio and Television Broadcasting). In 1974 Radio France became a separate entity from the ORTF. The following year, on January 6, 1975, Radio France Internationale (RFI) was created as a subsidiary of Radio France (→ International Radio; France: Media System).

From 1987 RFI was independent from Radio France and broadcast news and public affairs programs around the world in 19 languages on shortwave frequencies 24 hours a day. In Paris, RFI could be heard on the FM band; the station could also be accessed in France via satellites and the Internet. From 1991 RFI could be heard on FM in 27 African countries. It was estimated that RFI had a global audience of 44 million listeners, roughly three-fifths of them in Africa. This number surpassed many African domestic radio services, including Africa No 1, a Panafricanist radio station broadcasting from Libreville, Gabon. The rest of RFI's audience was spread out worldwide, with 24 percent in the Middle East, 9 percent in Latin America, 5.3 percent in Asia, 5 percent in the Pacific, 4.7 percent in Europe and 0.8 percent in Northern America (Vittin 1997). During the → Francophonies, an annual worldwide event in which all the former French colonies celebrate their cultures, RFI usually worked in tandem with other powerful francophone radio services such as Radio Canada and Radio Suisse Romande in order to extend Francophonie worldwide.

In the middle of the first decade of the twenty-first century, RFI had a workforce of 850, including 350 correspondents worldwide. RFI's influence also extended beyond radio to other media such as newspapers. Journalists such as Philippe Leymarie and Stephen Smith, who wrote regularly for → *Le Monde Diplomatique*, frequently broadcast on RFI. RFI also worked in tandem with the Francophone TV channel TV5 to expand French audiovisual presence globally, in order to compete with major players such as the → BBC World Service, CNN International (→ CNN), and Qatar's Al Jazeera (→ Arab Satellite TV News). As of June 2005, roughly two million people were visiting RFI's website each month.

In *Africa*, the popularity of international radio services such as RFI, the BBC World Service, → Voice of America, and → Deutsche Welle was entirely due to the media monopoly in many African states, which turned local and national radio into a government mouthpiece. Within this context, African audiences saw international radio as providing "objective" news that seemed less biased and more complex than state → propaganda (→ Africa: Media Systems). These international radio services managed to retain their influence even after the wind of democratization swept Africa in the early 1990s. According to Vittin (2002), RFI serves as the official voice of France because the service is entirely funded by the French government. This includes the French Foreign Ministry (€71 million in 2004) as well as the French Ministry of Communication (€53 million in 2004) (Roy 2004).

However, this funding raised controversies regarding agenda setting, French national interests, and the desire for objective news. Vittin (2002) argues that there are dangers when important → news regarding the continent is framed by journalists in Paris or New York (→ Framing of the News). News within that context becomes a tool to inter-nationalize French or US perspectives about a particular African situation. As a result, descriptions may be packaged with national self-interest or lack analytical nuances. This *management of information* may also legitimate and validate some points of views at the expense of others, creating a disequilibrium in a particular public sphere. Within this context, Zanasoumo Roger Nouma claims that RFI's implicit mission is cheerleading for French corporations and helping to implement their strategies on a global basis, and quotes RFI's former chairman, Fouad Benhalla, as openly claiming that RFI's mission is to offer an official French vision of world events (Nouma 1990, 65, 106).

SEE ALSO: ► Africa: Media Systems ► Americanization of the Media ► Arab Satellite TV News ► BBC World Service ► CNN ► Deutsche Welle ► Framing of the News ► France: Media System ► Francophonie ► International Radio ► Le Monde Diplomatique ► News ► Propaganda ► Radio Free Europe/Radio Liberty ► Vatican Radio ► Voice of America

References and Suggested Readings

Nouma, Z. R. (1990). Radio France Internationale: Instrument de la présence française dans le monde, doctoral thesis, Lille University II.
Roy, A. (2004). La Voix de la France. *L'Humanité* (August 21). At humanite.fr/journal, accessed September 26, 2007.
Vittin, T. (1997). Les Radios internationales, acteurs de la vie politique en Afrique noire. In A.-J. Tudesq (ed.), *Les médias, acteurs de la vie internationale*. Paris: Éditions Apogée.
Vittin, T. (2002). In T. Mattelart (ed.), *La Mondialisation des médias contre la censure*. Brussels: De Boeck, pp. 82–102.

Radio Free Europe/Radio Liberty

John D. H. Downing

Southern Illinois University

Radio Free Europe and Radio Liberty were among the half dozen major broadcast information sources for the Soviet bloc from soon after World War II until the final collapse of the Soviet system in 1991. The two shortwave stations were covertly founded in 1950 (Radio Free Europe) and 1953 (Radio Liberation from Bolshevism, its initial title) by the US Central Intelligence Agency. Radio Liberty broadcast to the citizens of the Soviet Union, and Radio Free Europe to most of the sovietized eastern and central Europe, including the Balkan states. Radio Liberty's signal began to reach the USSR with any strength only in 1960 (→ International Radio).

THE STATIONS' HISTORY AND GOALS

There were exceptions to the coverage. One was the German Democratic Republic, which was covered by RIAS (Radio in the American Sector) broadcasting out of West Berlin, and another was Albania, where the absence of shortwave sets in the country and the scarcity of Albanian speakers in the USA rendered the project impracticable. Yugoslavia was defined, after the 1948 Stalin–Tito break, as a halfway house of sorts between the Soviet bloc and the west, and began to receive a multilingual "South Slav" broadcast service only in 1993 as the federal Yugoslav republic disintegrated into its constituent elements. The three Baltic republics, for a complex variety of reasons, were not fully covered until the 1980s, while the USSR's non-Russophones received very little attention.

Officially, both stations' funding was provided at the outset by an ongoing nationwide campaign within the USA to protect citizens in both zones from the effects of monopoly Communist Party control over the flow of information (→ Propaganda). Ostensibly, the Crusade for Freedom (the campaign's title), inaugurated by President Eisenhower, collected annually a host of small contributions from around the USA, referred to as "truth dollars," which provided the stations with their financial base. In reality, at most only around 20 percent of RFE's funding was procured from the Crusade, and none for RL.

This reality was unknown to a large proportion of the stations' staff, and came as a bitter shock to some who, when the truth finally emerged in 1967, felt they had been lied to. Their sentiments were shared by a number of public figures, who were less disturbed at the truth itself than that the Crusade's everyday barrage of appeals and advertising had misled the public into subsidizing a government spying agency. Other longstanding critics of the stations – some of whom objected to their trenchantly anti-Soviet tone, others who wanted them to instigate armed revolt in Soviet bloc countries – found in the revelation supporting evidence for their views.

TURBULENCES AND CHANGES OF SITE

This episode led to a period of some turbulence in the stations' life which eventually, after a series of congressional and presidential inquiries and reports, led to the *removal of the CIA's control over the stations*. The Agency was replaced in 1974 by the Board for International Broadcasting, whose initial two top figures were a former assistant secretary of state and a former director of news at CBS. In 1976 the two stations were administratively merged as RFE/RL, Inc., and in 1978 almost all operations shifted to Munich in Germany. Paradoxically, many of the staff found the new management considerably more intrusive and heavy-handed than the CIA, which had largely followed the pattern of the British Foreign Office's fairly light touch in managing the → BBC's overseas service.

In 1981 the headquarters in Munich were bombed, causing four people to be injured and US$2 million worth of damage. Stasi files secured from the GDR after 1989 indicate that the money and equipment were supplied by Romania's Ceaucescu regime, but that the wreckers were from a variety of nations, led by Ilyich Ramírez Sánchez, better known to the → tabloid press as the professional terrorist "Carlos the Jackal."

In 1993, following the final collapse of the Soviet bloc, the Clinton administration moved the operation to Prague, where President Havel offered a site rent-free in the city center. The services were considerably reduced, with the Hungarian service being cut out altogether. In 1998, the US Congress placed the new Radio Free Iran and Radio Free Iraq under RFE/RL control, and in 2002 Radio Free Afghanistan.

As of 2007, RFE/RL was broadcasting nearly 1,000 hours a week to its traditional target zones and to southwestern Asia, and had bureaus in 19 countries. Since 1996 RFE/

RL has built over 500 transmitter sites to enable AM and FM broadcasts as well as its traditional shortwave service. The languages in which it broadcast were Albanian, Arabic, Armenian, Avar, Azerbaijani, Bashkir, Belarusian, Bosnian, Chechen, Circassian, Crimean Tatar, Croatian, Dari, Georgian, Kazakh, Kyrgyz, Macedonian, Montenegrin, Pashto, Persian, Romanian, Russian, Serbian, Tajik, Tatar, Turkmen, Ukrainian, and Uzbek. RFE/RL has also built up an electronic information service more recently, which according to its website has been receiving over 20 million hits a day.

DISTINCTIVE CHARACTER

The main difference between the RFE/RL stations and the → BBC World Service, → Deutsche Welle, → Voice of America, or → Radio France Internationale was that while the latter aimed to provide an international news service, RFE/RL endeavored to be the honest domestic news service – not without international coverage, to be sure – that the nations and republics in the Soviet zone were lacking. They were staffed to a great extent by refugees and expatriates from the various Soviet bloc nations, who set themselves the task very often of diffusing samizdat publications that would otherwise have reached rather few people in major cities. In this way, they could amplify muzzled public opinion and maintain some semblance of internal debate within each of the nations independent of the regimes. However, especially in the early years, their form of address was sometimes very local and specific, for example naming a factory manager who was a sexual predator and warning him that justice would await him once the regime collapsed.

Reactions to these stations varied sharply across the political spectrum, as well as within the Soviet zone itself (aside from the political leadership, whose views may easily be deduced). For VoA and BBC adherents, the two stations were often seen as very aggressive in style to the point of being counter-productive. For the West German government, where the Munich office was located, this sharp style ran counter to their drive to develop an effective working relationship with the Eastern bloc (*Ostpolitik*), in the interests both of keeping the two parts of Germany in communication, and in terms of national economic opportunities for business and trade with Moscow. For others on the political right, the stations repeatedly failed to deliver the real goods, in other words. stimulating uprising against the Soviet yoke.

Within the stations themselves, there was an almost equally *wide spectrum of political opinions*, some of which surfaced directly in broadcasts and some of which did not. In Radio Liberty, for example, the sudden new rush of Jewish Russian émigré professionals beginning in the late 1970s led to frequent tension between the newer arrivals and the older generation of gentile Russians, some of them racist nationalists, intuitively skeptical that a Jewish person could be a true Russian. It was also widely recognized both that the Soviet regimes infiltrated their own people into RFE/RL, and that some station staff had a pro-fascist background and present.

THE POLITICS OF BROADCAST JAMMING

The Soviet bloc regimes routinely sought to jam RFE/RL broadcasting. Estimates and reports vary, but as of 1961 there were approximately 1,400 local and long-distance jamming stations altogether. Different regimes operated jamming at different times, with Poland largely ceasing from 1956 onwards, though the Russians continued to jam broadcasts in Polish. According to one Polish spokesperson at the time, the energy needed would have supplied electric power to a medium-sized town. In 1981 the BBC World Service estimated that four days of jamming cost Soviet Russia as much as the BBC's Russian Service for a whole year. On the other hand, especially in large cities, it was generally all too effective, though the determined could sometimes still hear the broadcasts by listening at twilight or in the evening, when the signal was at its clearest, or in the countryside.

However, jamming also interfered with some local broadcasting. Counter-jamming measures were undertaken at different times by the western stations. From time to time, in response to negotiations between the Soviet bloc and the west, the Soviets would reduce or pause their jamming, but these windows rarely lasted very long. In late November 1988, however, the Soviet Union suddenly and without fanfare stopped jamming. This proved to be of particular importance during the attempted coup against President Gorbachev in August 1991 by those determined to reinstate the old Soviet system. Because jamming was not in place, western news services, in particular CNN, were able both to broadcast what was happening and to be seen in the major Soviet cities. This most likely had a powerful impact on consolidating the opposition to the coup, which rapidly and boldly expressed itself across the USSR, and thus led to the coup's failure, almost without bloodshed.

ROLE OF THE STATIONS IN POLITICAL UPHEAVALS

Hungary, 1956

As the determined Hungarian revolution against Soviet colonization developed in late 1956, RFE was caught in an extreme dilemma. Should it simply report events as they transpired, or encourage people to take their rebellion to new heights? The situation was further complicated by the fact that some informed global opinion judged that the Soviets, having withdrawn militarily, would not return, while others suspected the worst. Some RFE staff, with the interim premier Imre Nagy's past in mind, were skeptical that he had become a nationalist leader, while others were prepared to give him the benefit of the doubt. In the event, some very ugly street murders of unarmed party officials in Budapest gave the Soviet Politburo members in favor of military action the rationale they needed to press for intervention. The situation was uncertain from day to day.

Nonetheless, a review of broadcasting output subsequently determined that a considerable amount of the tone of broadcasts had been highly emotional in a way that would easily encourage Hungarian listeners to think the west would intervene to protect the revolutionaries. Thus, while no evidence was available that any direct message had been broadcast urging listeners to expect western action, the impression lingered for many decades that RFE in particular had whipped up expectations in Hungary to the point of getting people killed, or later executed, in the name of help that was never going to be forthcoming. Domestic criticism of the station within the USA repeatedly harked back to this episode.

The Prague Spring, 1968

With this in mind, the Czech and Slovak broadcasters in the station found themselves in a paradoxical position during the Prague Spring. When the gradual cultural thaw in intellectual and literary circles – symbolized by the first republishing of Kafka since the 1948 communist coup – came very rapidly to galvanize the entire Czech and Slovak publics, the RFE Czechoslovakia service found itself compelled by management, as well as its own political inhibitions, to tread with the greatest caution. No one wanted to be accused a second time of stimulating a revolt whose consequences would be borne exclusively on the spot. Nor did the staff want to propose or even endorse any actions that could be used by Soviet hardliners as a rationale for armed intervention.

Thus with the temporary explosion of freedom in media within Czechoslovakia itself, RFE found itself constantly behind the times, since it would have been direct anti-Soviet provocation to install any of its own reporters in the country. Indeed, at one point the station found itself urging moderation and caution on the reformers, who seemed to be overly insouciant of the temptation they were presenting to Soviet hawks. When the Soviet invasion came, they were assiduous in urging Czechs and Slovaks to stay calm and not to engage in any pointless heroics.

Polish Solidarity, Perestroika, and the Soviet System's Collapse

The emergence of Poland's huge Solidarity labor movement in 1979–1980, the 1981 imposition of martial law in Poland to avoid Soviet intervention, the collapse from within of the Polish regime, and the emergence of Gorbachev as reformist Soviet leader bent on the reconstruction (*perestroika*) of Soviet life, all presented RFE/RL with unparalleled new opportunities. It was unexpected that RFE would add to its critiques of the regimes' failures critical commentary on the timidity of the Polish Catholic hierarchy, which until then had constituted something of a sacred cow, but it was a sign both of the times and of RFE's maturity that this was possible. RFE also expanded its pop music programs, highly popular with Soviet bloc youth. RL's new Russian director concluded that Gorbachev's policies were more of a threat to the old Soviet system than to the west, and so steered away from the knee-jerk suspicion of many of the old guard staff regarding the changes underway.

In the few days following the nuclear power plant disaster in Chernobyl in 1986 the Soviet response – or rather nonresponse – confirmed the old guard in their skepticism, until the Kremlin's sudden switch to acknowledging the disaster some 72 hours after the event. In contrast, President Gorbachev's frankness in publicly recognizing the mess the USSR had gotten itself into by invading Afghanistan (our "bleeding wound") was a sign of change. Not only however did RL involve itself constructively with the new direction the USSR was taking, but for the first time it also began seriously to engage with broadcasting to the non-Russophone republics of the Soviet Union.

The trajectory of these two stations is an absorbing one. Inevitably, after 1991, voices called for their closure, since their ultimate mission had been achieved. The counterargument was that their service was still needed as nations long deprived of a vigorous news market struggled to develop democratic broadcasting. In some ways slimmed down, but also with some new projects, RFE/RL has continued up to the present to be actively engaged in producing quality international news (see website at www.rferl.org).

SEE ALSO: ▶ BBC ▶ BBC World Service ▶ Deutsche Welle ▶ International Radio ▶ Propaganda ▶ Radio France Internationale ▶ Tabloid Press ▶ Voice of America

References and Suggested Readings

Nelson, M. (1997). *War of the black heavens: The battles of western broadcasting in the Cold War.* Syracuse, NY: Syracuse University Press.

Puddington, A. (2000). *Broadcasting freedom: The Cold War triumph of Radio Free Europe and Radio Liberty.* Lexington: University Press of Kentucky.

Semelin, J. (1997). *La liberté aux bouts des ondes: Du coup de Prague à la chute du Mur de Berlin.* Paris: Belfond.

Radio Networks

Daniel G. McDonald

Ohio State University

A traditional → radio network consists of a series of radio broadcasting stations connected in some way (typically by broadcast, landline, microwave, or satellite; → Radio Technology) so that each of the stations can carry the same programs or advertisements (→ Advertising). Often, the stations will carry the programs simultaneously, but under some circumstances (e.g., stations in differing time zones), a program or set of programs may be delayed for a given length of time. In both cases, the network serves to extend the audience beyond that which would have been available without the network. The linkage between stations may take the form of very different stations linked for the convenience of sharing particular content, or may take the form of one primary station linked to multiple "repeater" stations in which the repeater simply rebroadcasts whatever it receives from the primary station. More recently, with the advent of satellite channels and the → Internet, the radio network label has been applied to describe any audio service involving a large number of receivers, rather than stations, although it is questionable whether a system involving only one transmission device should be considered a network.

NETWORK PREDECESSORS

The idea of program origination in one location and an audience for the program in other locations is somewhat older than radio itself, having been demonstrated with the telephone during the 1880s and 1890s. In Budapest, brothers Antoine and Francois Puskas linked telephone subscribers to a commercial service offering news and entertainment for about 40 years, beginning in 1893 (Sterling & Kittross 1978, 39). While the Puskas's service might be more similar to radio broadcasting than radio network broadcasting, experiments in the US in 1885 engaged audiences for music programs in two different locations (New York Times 1885), and by 1890 several cities were connected for telephone transmissions of musical and comedy entertainment. By this time, college boat races had already been "transmitted" to two different audiences 400 miles apart, and predictions were being made that all major cities east of the Mississippi river would soon be joined by telephone entertainment, with various channels available at "the push of a button" (New York Times 1890). In 1909, Lee DeForest included a simultaneous radio/telephone broadcast experiment in which 21 mayors in their own cities talked into the telephones in their offices, engaging in a discussion that was broadcast via radiowaves to all the cities, so that each mayor could hear all the others (Chicago Daily Tribune 1909).

DEVELOPMENT OF RADIO NETWORKS

Experiments with radio networking began during the early 1920s. By the mid-1920s, permanent radio networks had been established in the United Kingdom, the US, and a number of other countries. One of the earliest radio networks was the *British Broadcasting Company*, later the British Broadcasting Corporation (→ BBC; United Kingdom: Media System). In 1922, the Post Office was charged with organizing broadcasting in such a way as to avoid the chaos that had ensued in the US, where inventors, manufacturers, and audiences were all dealing with a "frontier" situation in which, with radio's rapid development, no one was certain how it could be used to make money, or how it should be regulated (→ Radio Broadcasting, Regulation of). F. J. Brown of the Post Office visited the US prior to beginning work on British broadcasting policy in order to learn from what had happened there (Briggs 1995). British manufacturers and the public were eager for regular radio broadcasting. Marconi had moved to England soon after his demonstration of wireless telegraphy (→ Telegraph, History of), where his presence helped to spur on other inventors and entrepreneurs. By 1922, the Post Office had licensed some experimental stations (2LO and 2MT), and later the same year the BBC.

Formed in October 1922 by a group of wireless manufacturers (including Marconi), the BBC began broadcasting from Marconi's London studio on November 14. Broadcasts from Birmingham and Manchester soon followed. Within three years, the BBC could be heard nearly everywhere in the UK. The group of manufacturers who began the BBC saw broadcasting as a commercial enterprise, a stimulus for the sale of radio receivers. A major influence on the growth of the philosophy of regulation of the BBC, and of radio networks in the country, was John Reith, who envisaged the BBC as an independent broadcasting system broadcasting information and entertainment for the public good, free from political or commercial pressure (→ Public Broadcasting Systems; Public Broadcasting, History of). This tension between the use of the spectrum for the public good and for commercial enterprise became one of the major points of debate in most countries, and has been resolved in many different ways.

In the *United States*, where privately owned experimental stations had been broadcasting, sporadic hook-ups between stations occurred occasionally during the early 1920s, much like the telephone experiments of the 1890s (→ United States of America: Media System). For security reasons, amateur stations had been shut down during World War I, and the

US Navy had requisitioned Marconi's and other foreign radio investments in the US. As a result, the US Navy developed the world's most powerful transmitter and created a patents pool of radio technology from which its suppliers could freely draw for the duration of the war.

General Electric (GE) and American Telephone & Telegraph (AT&T) were heavily involved in radio from an early period, and during the war served as suppliers for the Navy. This appropriation of patents and technologies allowed a number of technological advances and standardization to occur. After the war, GE was able to use its influence to help control which patents were being released by the Navy so that a certain level of standardization could be achieved. Along with these developments, British Marconi was able to join with other companies in the formation of Radio Corporation of America (RCA; Balk 2006).

In 1920, the US Navy had transferred the Marconi stations it had confiscated to RCA. With RCA's collection of stations, a radio network was probably inevitable. There was no generally accepted means of radio support – toll stations, taxes on receivers, or simple funding through set sales were all considered. Additionally, producing programs for many stations proved to be a monumental and costly task. In 1925, plans began for a "broadcasting service association" for stations, and by 1926 the National Broadcasting Company was formed, advertised as "Radio for 26,000,000 homes" (Balk 2006). The first broadcast in late November linked 25 stations. Within two months, a second NBC network, the "Blue" network debuted. In 1927, the Columbia Broadcasting Company (later Columbia Broadcasting System) began operations as a third major network in the US. Although a series of stations formed an educational radio network in the 1930s, it was not until the late 1960s that a truly public (noncommercial) radio network, National Public Radio (NPR), was formed in the US.

Development of radio networks around the world tended to follow a pattern similar to that in the UK (broadcasting as a government-sanctioned public good) or in the US (broadcasting as a commercial enterprise), although elements of both traditions appear in all countries. Egypt, for example, included early experimentation similar to that in the US, but opted for a system heavily influenced by the BBC. In 1932, the Egyptian government employed the British Marconi Company to provide a noncommercial radio service for Egypt (Boyd 1999; → Egypt: Media System). In smaller countries, an international audience is often obtained with a powerful radio station rather than through a network. Czech Radio began broadcasting in 1923, and continues today in multiple regional stations as well as Internet locations. Radio Prague, the international component of Czech Radio, began as a station in 1936, and is considered more like a network today because of the array of content it produces in association with stations in other countries (e.g., Croatia, Romania, Australia, and the US), and the extent of offerings in multiple languages via broadcast and over the Internet (→ Czech Republic: Media System; International Radio).

GOLDEN AGE OF RADIO NETWORKS AND AFTER

The motivation behind radio networks is to bring content to audiences that are separated by distance. For most large countries, network radio broadcasting is needed for full geographic coverage, so network broadcasting of some sort became important in providing news, education, and entertainment for the country (→ Radio News). In hindsight, network radio broadcasting before the diffusion of television forms a kind of golden age for network broadcasting. In a pre-television era, network news, drama, comedy, and music provide access to information and talent undreamed of before radio's diffusion (→ Radio: Social History). Typically, → television takes over many of the news and entertainment functions for most people and provides the added visual dimension, that forces changes in network radio content, whether the network is commercial or noncommercial (→ Television, Visual Characteristics of).

In the television era, radio networks must adapt by finding which particular niches it fills better than television. This may be in terms of geography or content. For example, radio networks may have access to audiences in places where it is difficult to receive television signals, such as remote villages or islands or in places where terrain blocks television signals. In the South Pacific, Radio Polynesia links a number of radio stations through FM and shortwave broadcasting to pool resources to provide a radio network in which the stations are separated by hundreds of miles and different forms of government.

In regard to content niches, radio networks provide all-news programming, religious programming, or other specialized programming geared for particular uses, such as background music in stores or other businesses. In addition, because the bulk of the audience has shifted to television in many countries, highly specialized programming (right or left of the political spectrum, for example) can be successful for certain radio networks. In the US, certain ad hoc networks sometimes form around groups of stations reaching particular audiences, providing advertisers with access to those people in a way that could not be easily achieved through advertising on hundreds of local stations around the country.

RECENT DEVELOPMENTS

Satellite radio broadcasting also provides a challenge to network broadcasting. Satellite broadcasting may not be a true network, but it offers the listener the same kind of experience: the same content wherever he or she may go within the country. Geographically large countries, such as the US and Canada, offer opportunities for satellite radio to have many of the same functions as network radio in the golden age. At the turn of the twenty-first century Sirius and XM satellite radio competed in the US and Canada, although a merger of the two was announced in early 2007. The difference between satellite radio and network radio broadcasting is that network broadcasting is typically thought of as involving a number of local stations, each broadcasting within its own area, and in that way much of the country is covered, while with satellite radio, a few satellites (two or more, depending on the size of the country) cover a huge geographic area, so that the entire country is covered, also offering many different channels. A satellite radio service may be thought of as providing the content of 100 (or more) content-specialized radio networks. In an interesting turn of events, satellite radio in the US, where commercial broadcasting is perhaps at its most commercial, satellite radio is primarily financed by subscription.

In the UK and countries where the population tends to be more densely packed, there is less need for satellite radio networks. Instead, much of the current focus in radio is on achieving higher quality through digital broadcasting or high definition radio. Digital

Audio Broadcasting (DAB) has also taken hold in southern parts of Canada, where the population is also relatively dense. With traditional radio broadcasting, reflections occur from buildings or natural terrain which tend to interfere with clear reception of signals. With digital audio broadcasting, the reflections are used in selection of the strongest signal at any given time, and competing signals are rejected.

The introduction of digital programming (as opposed to digital broadcasting) has signaled the arrival of a different kind of network as well, with some local stations serving almost as repeater transmitters from a centralized programmer, yet each projecting a unique identity within its base community.

The Internet has seen the arrival of still more types of audio providers who classify themselves as radio networks, although they are more like a station with multiple types of content at the same time. The "network" designation undoubtedly comes from the practice of → satellite television services that began referring to themselves as networks in the 1980s, because they covered large geographic areas either through direct broadcasting from satellite or through distribution over → cable television.

What began as experimental services designed to provide the same content to audiences separated over distances has evolved during the last century, and continues to evolve today. In current terminology, a radio network refers as easily to an audio service with wide geographic coverage as much as it does to interconnected stations sharing content. Although radio networks in many parts of the world continue their traditional structure and role in disseminating → information, educational materials, and entertainment, recent developments in the area of digital broadcasting and multiple audio formats delivered via the Internet insure that radio networks will continue to evolve (→ Educational Communication; Educational Media; Educational Media Content).

SEE ALSO: ▶ Advertising   ▶ Advertising, History of   ▶ Audience Segmentation   ▶ BBC ▶ Cable Television   ▶ Convergence of Media Systems   ▶ Czech Republic: Media System ▶ Educational Communication   ▶ Educational Media   ▶ Educational Media Content   ▶ Egypt: Media System   ▶ Exposure to Radio   ▶ Information   ▶ International Radio   ▶ Internet   ▶ Public Broadcasting, History of   ▶ Public Broadcasting Systems ▶ Radio   ▶ Radio Broadcasting, Regulation of   ▶ Radio News   ▶ Radio: Social History ▶ Radio Technology   ▶ Satellite Television   ▶ Telegraph, History of   ▶ Television   ▶ Television, Visual Characteristics of   ▶ United Kingdom: Media System   ▶ United States of America: Media System

References and Suggested Readings

Balk, A. (2006). *The rise of radio*. Jefferson, NC: McFarland.

Boyd, D. A. (1999). *Broadcasting in the Arab world*. Ames: Iowa State University Press.

Briggs, A. (1995). *The birth of broadcasting*. New York: Oxford University Press.

Chicago Daily Tribune (1909). Unique talkfest of the mayors of twenty-one cities through the new wireless telephone. *Chicago Daily Tribune*, January 3, p. D1.

New York Times (1885). A telephone concert. *New York Times*, January 30, p. 2.

New York Times (1890). Music over the wires. *New York Times*, October 9, p. 3.

Sterling, C. H., & Kittross, J. M. (1978). *Stay tuned: A concise history of American broadcasting*. Belmont, CA: Wadsworth.

Radio News

Douglas Ferguson

College of Charleston

Timely information delivered over radio waves dates back to the earliest stations and before (→ Radio; Radio: Social History; News). Lee de Forest reported the election night results via radio in 1916 and the first licensed US station to report election returns was KDKA in 1920. By 1924, radio broadcasts became a major influence on → public opinion because they could report live events. Radio news in the UK first gained attention during the General Strike of 1926, which briefly halted newspaper publication.

Radio → newscasts, however, did not appear in the US until the 1930s, relegating emergency and event coverage to the wireless medium. By 1933, the wire services that supplied news to most newspapers decided to withhold news wire stories from radio, until radio newscasters agreed to limit their reporting to twice per day, at times (9.30 a.m. and 9 p.m., for just five minutes) that protected the newspapers (→ News Agencies, History of). By 1935 competing wire services began to supply US radio stations and the newspaper–radio war was over by 1939 (Culbert 1976).

Unlike the US and the UK, radio in many other countries was controlled by the government. In Germany, for example, Hans Fritzsche began offering news broadcasts on behalf of the von Papen regime's Wireless News Service in 1932, which fell under the control of Joseph Goebbels's Propaganda Ministry in 1933. During the Nuremberg tribunal at the close of World War II, Fritzsche was prosecuted for distorting the news in the 1930s and 1940s (→ Propaganda in World War II).

Research interest in US radio news began in 1940 during the campaign between Franklin Roosevelt and Wendell Willkie. Surveys conducted by → Paul Lazarsfeld suggested that most voters considered radio superior to newspapers for political news. His studies also noted that reinforcement was the main effect of radio coverage, with listeners' predispositions supported by their choice of candidate speaking on the radio. Radio began a long broadcast tradition of reporting the horse race aspects of political contests (→ Elections and Media, History of).

World War II greatly expanded the importance of radio news, making reputations for future television commentators Edward R. Murrow, Walter Cronkite, and others. In the UK people began to equate hearing something on the BBC as knowing the truth, according to an observation by George Orwell in 1944. After the arrival of television in the late 1940s, radio news became a supplementary service, still focusing on live events and breaking news. Until the → Internet era began, newspapers and television enjoyed a long era of news dominance (→ Newspaper Journalism; Broadcast Journalism).

Academic journals that regularly report on radio news are *Journalism and Mass Communication Quarterly* (originally *JQ*), *Journal of Broadcasting and Electronic Media* (*JOBEM*), and *Journal of Radio Studies* (*JRS*). The latter journal has focused more on history and international studies than on US radio news, with only seven articles on radio news in its first 14 years of publication. *JQ* has emphasized newspaper journalism and television news, with 15 articles with the words "radio" and "news" in the title since the 1970s.

JOBEM focuses almost entirely on television news, with only three articles specifically on radio news in the past two decades.

The three dominant *areas of radio news research* are ownership/competition, listenership, and news director perceptions. Research on ownership starts with the notion that large corporations are inherently inferior when it comes to serving local audiences (→ Ownership in the Media). In the US, the → Federal Communications Commission (FCC) dictates that stations operate in the public interest, serving local audiences (→ Radio Broadcasting, Regulation of). Radio news is generally considered a linchpin of local service. Most recent studies about the demise of localism focus on Clear Channel and its dominant position in the United States (over 1,200 stations). *Listenership studies* typically provide a descriptive profile of the audiences for radio news (→ Audience Research). Most provide a snapshot of a particular point in time, while the rest attempt to study trends. Often such research emulates newspaper readership studies. Surveys of radio news directors have assessed trends and the present status of radio news, including newsroom profitability, salaries, staff diversity, careers, and internships.

Some observers take a dim view of the *future of radio news*, as television and online sources have overshadowed radio (→ Television News; Online Media). Radio talk shows have supplanted regular newscasts, particularly on the AM stations in the US. Radio stations facing economic difficulties found it easier to fill time with local and syndicated talk shows rather than maintain full-fledged news departments. The blurring of lines between radio news reporting and talk radio commentary has been a concern for many years. National Public Radio is apparently the only US source of radio news with a long-term prospect, although it has endured periodic threats from legislators who object to its political leanings. The → BBC World Service, → Deutsche Welle, → Voice of America, Radio Netherlands, and Radio Australia are also options for those who want news from the radio.

SEE ALSO: ▶ Audience Research ▶ BBC World Service ▶ Broadcast Journalism ▶ Deutsche Welle ▶ Elections and Media, History of ▶ Federal Communications Commission (FCC) ▶ Internet ▶ Lazarsfeld, Paul F. ▶ News ▶ News Agencies, History of ▶ Newscast ▶ Newspaper Journalism ▶ Online Media ▶ Ownership in the Media ▶ Propaganda in World War II ▶ Public Opinion ▶ Radio ▶ Radio Broadcasting, Regulation of ▶ Radio: Social History ▶ Television News ▶ Voice of America

References and Suggested Readings

Bromley, M. (2001). *No news is bad news*. New York: Longman.
Crook, T. (1998). *International radio journalism*. London: Routledge.
Culbert, D. H. (1976). *News for everyman: Radio and foreign affairs in thirties America*. Westport, CT: Greenwood.
Jackaway, G. (1995). *Media at war: Radio's challenge to the newspapers, 1924–1939*. Westport, CT: Greenwood.

Radio: Social History

Chris Priestman

Staffordshire University

The introduction of → radio broadcasting during the 1920s released a tide of social changes, which have profoundly affected every society in the world, changes that have subsequently been amplified by → television and information and communication technology (→ Television: Social History; Information and Communication Technology, Development of). By the end of the twentieth century these electronic media had become so embedded in social, political, and economic processes that it is hard today to conceive of a world without their influence. Their defining characteristic as public media is that they provide systems for communicating simultaneously with large, geographically dispersed → audiences via pathways that are immediate and capable of delivering messages live: they abolish the delay between production and reception inherent in all earlier public media. Their combined effect has been greatly to accelerate the formation and shaping of cultural consciousness within societies (Hilmes 1997). They provide mechanisms of continuous reference and comparison by which individuals perceive their relationships beyond their immediate private sphere. The few social groups yet to be reached by radio have nevertheless felt the effects of communications-driven political and economic change indirectly.

THEORETICAL FRAMING

The social history of radio occupies a small proportion of the literature in comparison with film, print, television, or the → Internet (→ Printing, History of). The systematic study of the mass media gained momentum in the 1960s and 1970s, by which time, despite the far greater worldwide ownership of radio receivers, the social impacts of television were preoccupying the industrialized nations. Subsequently the theorization of the → public sphere has been influential in attempts to discern (1) how each component of the mass media influences social change, and (2) which forces are dominant in shaping each medium: economic, political, or technological (→ Habermas, Jürgen).

Radio's social history can be traced through a number of marked stages, arising from changes that are either *endogenous* (i.e., internal to the radio industry and typically driven by advances in technology) or *exogenous* (i.e., due to alterations in external conditions of culture, economy, or politics that force change on the radio world). The manner and pace of these developments has varied from continent to continent according to relative wealth and stage of industrialization (→ Communication Inequality).

INHERENT ADAPTABILITY

The facilities and institutions for systematic public broadcasting began to emerge in Europe and North America from 1922. The history of radio since then has been remarkable for the variety of uses and listening locations to which the radio *receiver* has been successfully adapted. Many authors have observed that the source of the medium's adaptability and enduring social role lies in its paradoxical offer to the listener of both a highly personal choice of aural accompaniment to private life and, simultaneously, a means of participation in the shared experience of a tangible public community of concurrent listeners (e.g., Douglas 1999). Key illustrations of the significance of this personal/public engagement can be found in the field of health information: messages about personal health matters have been embedded in a variety of programming, their potency being attributed to the combined effect of preserving the anonymity of the listener, while normalizing their isolated experience (→ Health Communication and Journalism).

EARLY POLITICAL AND ECONOMIC SHAPING

In its initial development radio was a point-to-point system, transmitting in Morse code and then, following the first demonstration in 1906, via the human voice (→ Telegraph, History of). It was rapidly adopted as a means of sending messages, "one to few," by the military and civilian emergency and other services. Although outside radio's mass communications role, the numerous social impacts these nonpublic applications cannot be overlooked, be these via extensions to military capability or to the effectiveness of civilian rescue and policing.

   The social significance of the pre-1920s era of radio lay less with either its content or the numbers of listeners, but in the sense of expectation it created in the popular imagination at the *idea* of what might be achievable in a world where voices could be transmitted through the ether; early electronics manufactures envisaged new business opportunities; owners of newspapers and organizers of live entertainments saw a threat to their livelihoods and responded defensively; governments realized the need for new systems of regulation to decide who would be allowed to communicate what and to whom (→ Radio Broadcasting, Regulation of). The first decision to fundamentally shape radio for the twentieth century was that, for the general public, it would be a one-way medium with government agencies licensing companies or consortia to transmit on given frequencies. The manufacturers built receivers accordingly. The second pivotal decision, which has shaped the subsequent development of all broadcasting, was to determine how to fund radio services. European nations favored a public service model in which a national broadcast network would be funded from the public purse or, as in the case of the → BBC in the UK, from an annual license fee attached to the ownership of a radio receiver; while America opted for a commercial model in which privately owned broadcasters fund their competing services through on-air advertising (→ Public Broadcasting Systems; Public Broadcasting, History of).

POTENCY OF RADIO MESSAGES

In these parallel models, from the late 1920s and into the 1930s, the mains-powered "wireless" found its place at the heart of the domestic living space of an increasing proportion of households across North America, Europe, New Zealand, and Australia. In the period leading up to 1939 further aspects of radio's position in the public sphere were established: the different funding models placed different emphasis on the proportions of information, entertainment, and education they broadcast, with the imperatives of winning advertising inclining the commercial model toward entertainment while the underpinning ideology of the public service model attached higher importance to radio's educational role; transmission was often confined to a particular limited number of hours in the day; radio's close relationship with the commercial recording industry was established as playing their recorded products on air began to drive sales – of gramophone discs and players as well as radios.

During the lead-up to World War II, as radio ownership continued to increase, its importance as a potent propaganda tool became sharply evident. The imperial nations of the day invested in increasingly powerful transmission technologies in order to reach their colonies and allies overseas (→ BBC World Service). Significantly, radio was then the only mass medium able to reach pre-literate audiences, a fact that clearly framed the spread of state-sponsored "external" radio services from the 1930s onwards and, more recently, → UNESCO's many local radio development projects (→ Radio for Development).

Radio broadcasting proved to be of critical importance to both sides during World War II and of greater pervasive and persuasive influence on public opinion than the press. Among the complex of factors involved were: the rapid provision of → news perceived as authoritative and up to date, including occasional "as live" reports from the front line using early mobile recording equipment; recognition by political leaders that talking "direct to the nation" had real impact on morale; and recognition also of the power of musical, comic, and dramatic entertainment to foster a sense of belonging and unity among a national audience. While radio has not occupied quite such a singular role in subsequent national crises in western nations, its power to influence the collective actions of listeners continues to be evident, for example through the catalytic role attributed to particular radio broadcasters in fomenting the Rwandan genocide of 1994 (Kellow & Steeves 1998) or the overthrow of the Milosevic dictatorship in Yugoslavia in 2000 (Collin 2004).

SHIFTING LISTENING PATTERNS POST-WORLD WAR II

During the 1950s endogenous and exogenous factors forced a radical shift in radio's position in listeners' lives, which enabled it to become a major facilitator of the processes of post-World War II political democratization and social change in the west. The key technological innovation was the mass manufacture of transistors, which made the new receivers both portable and cheap to buy (→ Radio Technology). For rural and less developed societies with little or no access to mains electricity the availability of afford-able battery-powered radios created a surge in radio listening and in many such parts of the world it remains the dominant mass medium. With portability the choice of station became a personal matter: radio could now go with the individual listener, including – importantly – in the car; as a direct consequence the demand for ever more culturally and demographically differentiated stations grew. The major exogenous co-factors were closely associated: first, the postwar economic boom brought with it the rapid rise in disposable income in the industrialized nations, which in its turn transformed the economic and cultural environment into which radio stations broadcast; second, television began rapidly to supplant the wireless as the centerpiece of the domestic living space (→ Television: History of). A significant outcome of this shift was that the fortunes of the radio industry become ever more closely entwined with those of the record industry such that today the overwhelming majority of total radio output around the world is of recorded popular music, catering to individuated tastes ($\rightarrow$ Music Industry). Radio's ability to reach across cultural boundaries ($\rightarrow$ International Radio) has been largely responsible for the mixing of musical traditions that have given rise to the proliferation of popular music genres and cultures, from the evolution of rock 'n' roll in the southern USA onwards.

The closeness of the radio station's relationship to its listeners, however, has been built through talk (Scannell 1996). The words and voices of presenters and contributors define the appeal to audiences both according to social grouping (by class, age, language, etc.) and identification with the locality ($\rightarrow$ Broadcast Talk).

The arrival of truly portable tape recorders in the 1940s enabled the voices of "ordinary people" to be heard on the radio, expressing opinion and giving glimpses directly into their ways of life: they could be recorded at their places of work, on the streets, and in their homes as components of news reports or as the subjects of documentary exploration. From the late 1960s the radio phone-in emerged as a yet more immediate means of putting listeners on air, paving the way for the "talk radio" genre. Talk radio stations themselves typically describe the verbal sparring between hosts and contributors as entertainment, while critics tend to regard their output as disproportionately influential on public opinion, especially during election campaigns (Hendy 2000).

Toward the end of the twentieth century claims of both music and speech-oriented stations to significant interactivity between presenter and listener became key markers in their social raison d'être: for stations funded by government or license fee, interactivity has become emblematic of their public service; for commercial stations it is key to nurturing the listener identification and loyalty that they sell to advertisers; for "third sector" stations it is central to their representative appeal to supporters and potential donors. It remains to be seen how the twentieth-century constructs of collective identification and station loyalty will fare in the face of the post-1990s proliferation of digital platforms through which radio can now be heard and the accompanying processes of deregulation ($\rightarrow$ Convergence of Media Systems; Public Sphere, Fragmentation of).

SEE ALSO: ▶ Audience ▶ BBC ▶ BBC World Service ▶ Broadcast Talk ▶ Communication Inequality ▶ Convergence of Media Systems ▶ Habermas, Jürgen ▶ Health Communication and Journalism ▶ Information and Communication Technology, Development of ▶ International Radio ▶ Internet ▶ Media History ▶ Music Industry ▶ News ▶ Online Media ▶ Printing, History of ▶ Public Broadcasting, History of ▶ Public Broadcasting Systems ▶ Public Sphere ▶ Public Sphere, Fragmentation of ▶ Radio ▶ Radio Broadcasting, Regulation of ▶ Radio for Development ▶ Radio Technology ▶ Telegraph, History of ▶ Television ▶ Television, History of ▶ Television: Social History ▶ UNESCO

References and Suggested Readings

Briggs, A., & Burke, P. (2002). *A social history of the media: From Gutenberg to the Internet.* Cambridge: Polity, pp. 152–163, 216–233.

Collin, M. (2004). *This is Serbia calling: Rock 'n' roll radio and Belgrade's underground resistance.* London: Serpent's Tail.

Douglas, S. J. (1999). The zen of listening. In *Listening in: Radio and the American imagination.* New York: Times Books.

Habermas, J. (1989). *The structural transformation of the public sphere.* Cambridge: Polity.

Hendy, D. (2000). Culture. In *Radio in the global age.* Cambridge: Polity.

Hilmes, M. (1997). The nation's voice. In *Radio voices: American broadcasting 1922–1952.* Minneapolis: University of Minnesota Press.

Kellow, C. L., & Steeves, H. L. (1998). The role of Radio in the Rwandan genocide. *Journal of Communication,* 48(3), 107–128.

Scannell, P. (1996). *Radio, television and modern life.* Oxford: Blackwell, pp. 22–25.

Scannell, P., & Cardiff, D. (1991). *A social history of British broadcasting: Serving the nation.* Oxford: Blackwell.

Winston, B. (1998). Wireless and radio. *Media technology and society: A history: From the printing press to the superhighway.* London: Routledge.

Radio Technology

David Hendy

University of Westminster

The history of radio technology can be divided *chronologically* into four main eras: experimentation with basic equipment between the 1890s and 1920s; broadcasting to mass audiences using established processes between the 1930s and 1950s; adjustment to the arrival of television from the 1950s; and, finally, the emergence of digital radio technology from the late 1980s.

This history can also be viewed *thematically*, by distinguishing between developments in the capture and manipulation of sound by program-makers, the transmission of those sounds across the ether, and the ways they have been heard by listeners. What unites each era and each theme is a recurring tension between the push for technological improvement – such as a desire to attain higher fidelity sound – and an equally powerful determination among producers *and* listeners to maintain radio's status as cheap, easy to operate, and instantly accessible. Another perennial tension is between the centripetal *and* centrifugal forces that technology unleashed on the medium (→ Information and Communication Technology, Development of).

EXPERIMENTAL PERIOD

The origins of "wireless" are complex. Though Gugliemo Marconi (1871–1937) is popularly credited with being its founding father, most academic authors stress the medium's emergence through a broad front of inventive acts in electrical science during the second half of the nineteenth century. The British scientist James Clerk Maxwell and the German scientist Heinrich Hertz, for instance, had first theorized, and then verified, the existence of electromagnetic waves by the 1880s. It was another British scientist, Oliver Lodge, who had developed a "coherer" able to "syntonize" sending and receiving equipment to the same electromagnetic frequency – and demonstrated a Morse code signal being transmitted by precisely this means across a distance of some 55 meters by 1894. Alexander Popov in Russia, Augusto Righi in Italy, Edouard Branley in France, and Roberto Landell de Moura in Brazil, all worked along much the same lines at the time.

Marconi's achievement was thus not to have "invented" radio but to have seen its commercial potential as a signaling system – for merchant shipping, say, or the armed forces – and then to have shown, by sending the letter *S* across the Atlantic in 1901, just how far a signal could travel when transmitted from tall masts and refracted from the ionosphere to a point over the horizon. It was also Marconi who seized the initiative internationally by claiming general-purpose patent rights in 1896 (→ Technology, Social Construction of).

This was wireless telegraphy, however, not wireless telephony (→ Telegraph, History of). Conveying more than a series of dots and dashes required the electromagnetic signal to be *"modulated" as a continuous wave* – something achieved by the Danish scientist Valdemar Poulsen in 1902, and then demonstrated more sensationally in 1906 by the Canadian Reginald Fessenden when he transmitted voices and music across a wide stretch of the Massachusetts coastline. It was this event that effectively marked the beginnings of radio as a means of mass communication, since it broke with Marconi's limited conception of the technology as a means of private, one-to-one contact, and hinted at David Sarnoff's later, and much quoted, vision of a "music box" available in every home providing entertainment and information to the public: a vision that turned the perceived fault in wireless transmission – that it traveled in all directions so that anybody with receiving equipment could listen – into its prime virtue (→ Public Broadcasting, History of).

What made this feasible technically – and created the potential for a general audience – was a second wave of invention that radically *amplified* the rather weak signals hitherto achieved: Ambrose Fleming's adaptation of Edison's light-bulb into a "diode" valve in 1904; Lee De Forest's addition of a third valve, the "audion," in 1906; the creation of simple receiving sets that drew on the electrical properties of crystals – as tested by the German scientist Karl Braun – to "tune" into signals of differing wavelengths; and, by the mid-1920s, the manufacture of "dynamic" loudspeakers that allowed headphones to be discarded in favor of communal listening.

THE DOMESTICATION OF RADIO

Radio's experimental period therefore ended with its domestication. Simple crystal kits, or unwieldy receivers lashed to a spaghetti of unsightly batteries and aerials, steadily evolved into more aesthetically pleasing – and more effective – valve sets, tastefully wrapped in wood or Bakelite, relatively easy to tune and to run off a mains electricity supply, each occupying pride of place in the living rooms of suburban Europe and America. The period also ended with enforced reductions in the number of those actually broadcasting. As more and more private operators had appeared – there were some 150 in Britain and at least 500 in the United States by 1921 – national regulators and commercial interests asserted the *need for interference* to be minimized. The drive to create centralized monopolies such as the → BBC, commercial cartels such as the Radio Corporation of America, and a panoply of national and international regulatory bodies: all this had many underlying social and political causes (→ Media Conglomerates; Radio Broadcasting, Regulation of). But, at another level, it was a response to the perceived dangers of chaos in the ether, at a time when transmitters were crude and scientific understanding of the effect of atmospheric conditions on electromagnetic waves was barely developed (→ Radio: Social History; Radio Networks; Communication Technology Standards).

The underlying technology of radio was firmly established by the beginning of the 1930s. Yet the fact that regular broadcasting emerged only two decades after the start of wireless communication meant techniques of program-making were still evolving. Mixers, for example, appeared only in the late 1920s. The number of microphones in each studio increased thereafter, creating more "perspective" in dramatic or musical performances. By the 1930s, the BBC was using the *dramatic control panel*, a kind of mixing desk linking several studios at once and allowing producers to assemble baroque, multilayered programs encompassing recitals, orchestral music, and narration in complex forms – to the evident bafflement of many listeners. Other technology pointed radio in the direction of greater intimacy. More sensitive microphones, for instance, allowed for a less declamatory style of speech – and, as Chanan (1995) has shown, played a part in encouraging a sensual, "crooning" style of singing, as heard on American radio in the songs of Rudy Vallee and Bing Crosby.

EARLY RECORDING TECHNIQUES

The biggest challenge was in finding a convenient means of recording. Within the BBC, three very different types of machine were employed in the 1930s: the Blattnerphone, and its successor the Marconi–Stille system, which impressed signals in magnetic form on steel wire or steel tape; the Philips–Miller system, which used film track; and a machine that recorded directly onto wax discs. None was ideal: material was bulky or expensive, and processing was slow. Steel tape, for instance, could be edited only by the laborious welding of joints.

Nevertheless, by 1940 the Corporation was using some 40 *static disc recorders*. And for those wishing to record on location, machines were by now regularly carried on large vans. War acted as a major spur to miniaturization, since there was huge demand for reports from the front line. The BBC developed a "Type-C" recorder mounted on ambulances and, from 1943, the "midget," equipped with double-sided discs allowing nearly three minutes' recording each side and weighing only 16 kilograms. German engineers, however, had already succeeded in producing an even lighter *magnetic tape recorder*, which made recordings infinitely easier to edit. When the Allies overwhelmed Nazi forces in 1945, some of these portable *Tonschreibers* were seized, and subsequently remodelled by British and American firms. Within a decade, most recording was done on magnetic tape. The medium was becoming ever more mobile and fleet of foot in its production capacity.

RESPONSES TO TELEVISION

By now, of course, there was → television, and radio had to carve out a new role for itself (→ Television: Social History). Miniaturization and portability was one means of insuring its continued pre-eminence, since television struggled to report distant events smoothly and cheaply without a great deal of advanced planning: radio was still the more instant of the two media. It also had a reservoir of experience built up over decades. The BBC's first outside broadcast for radio had been in 1923; in 1939 it was doing some 5,000 a year. By World War II, the ad hoc use of telephone lines for "hook-ups" had been replaced by the permanent leasing of higher-specification cables, so that program material could be distributed easily and quickly from one part of a country to another; mobile transmitters had also been deployed.

Two other technical responses to television came in the form of VHF – which used *frequency modulation (FM)*, as opposed to the amplitude modulation (AM) of medium wave and long wave – and *stereophony*. Together, they offered vastly improved sound quality. Both technologies were prewar in origin, but took root from the late 1950s. VHF/FM was largely static-free; stereo allowed producers to create a "sound stage," overlap dialogue, create movement. The combined effect was to offer listeners a greater degree of clarity and naturalism, in much the same way that color made television images more vivid. Studios, equipped with multi-track recorders and effects units, became the site of experimentation in the new art of "radiophonics." Among European public service broadcasters, there was even talk in the 1970s of radio creating a form of "sound cinema."

In the US, stereo and FM had more influence in music radio, where it offered an alternative to an increasingly over-formatted AM sector. It was on FM that aficionados appreciated the complex, layered, rock albums of the period, and where a counterculture seeking heightened sensory experiences briefly thrived. For the radio establishment, however, FM's overriding advantage was more prosaic: because its signals were highly localized, it multiplied dramatically the number of stations that could be squeezed onto the air. In the US, especially, radio now became more localized than it had been since the early 1920s. The number of formats and markets proliferated, and, as they did so, radio shifted from being a mass, "national" medium to one predominantly serving a range of niche audiences, defined by locality, age, or musical taste. An important dimension to this fragmentation in listening was the widespread adoption of battery-powered, portable *transistor radios*. The technology, unveiled in 1947, drew on a science of semiconductors more than half a century old, and subsequently took another decade to become commercially viable. By the 1960s, however, its impact appeared irreversible. Though radio was displaced from the living room, it had found a multitude of new homes: the kitchen, the bedroom, cars, and even, by the 1980s, in one's pocket as a kind of "personal hi-fi." Television captured the family audience, but portability and cheapness made radio far more ubiquitous, especially in the developing world. In the west, the transistor also helped radio to forge a close association with teenage culture and all its musical sub-genres. Technology was applied to the cause of "consumer choice," and *narrow*casting took over from *broad*casting.

DIGITIZATION

In one sense, digitization simply accelerates these trends. Digital recording and transmission, first employed systematically by European broadcasters in the mid-1990s, provides even higher fidelity sound than anything captured on tape and aired on FM.

Since binary code also allows more data to be compressed into the broadcasting spectrum, it multiplies again the number of stations that can take to the air. On the → Internet, meanwhile, *streaming* enables new operators to reach small but global audiences, and *podcasting* pushes radio further in the direction of personalized listening (→ Digital Media, History of).

As in the past, however, new technology has a paradoxical influence. Authors such as Douglas (1999) rightly acknowledge radio's continued "technical insurgency": its protean ability – via the "radio hams" of the 1920s, the pirates of the 1980s, and the bedroom deejays of the Internet age – to be an alternative medium, to evade full rationalization by corporate interests (→ Alternative Journalism). Others suggest that ever since stations first hooked up to each other via phone lines in the 1920s, "networking" – whether analogue or digital – has created an increasingly professionalized, *standardized industry*. The current pervasiveness of technology capable of delivering centrally produced programs to every station owned by a single chain, and of "automated" play-out systems that replace human beings in each studio, hints at a rather more mechanized, *impersonal* future, where the "infinite" choice offered by "unique" formats is largely illusory.

SEE ALSO: ▶ Alternative Journalism ▶ BBC ▶ Communication Technology Standards ▶ Digital Media, History of ▶ Information and Communication Technology, Development of ▶ Internet ▶ Media Conglomerates ▶ Public Broadcasting, History of ▶ Radio Broadcasting, Regulation of ▶ Radio Networks ▶ Radio: Social History ▶ Technology, Social Construction of ▶ Telegraph, History of ▶ Television ▶ Television: Social History

References and Suggested Readings

Chanan, M. (1995). *Repeated takes*. London: Verso.
Douglas, S. (1999). *Listening in: Radio and the American imagination*. New York: Times Books.
Hendy, D. (2000). *Radio in the global age*. Cambridge: Polity.
Pawley, E. (1972). *BBC engineering 1922–1972*. London: BBC.
Winston, B. (1998). *Media technology and society: A history*. London: Routledge.

Rating Methods

James G. Webster

Northwestern University

A rating, as the term is most often used in media industries, is an estimate of the size and demographic composition of a radio, television, or Internet audience. Such metrics are of enormous importance to advertiser-supported media because they set the value of the time used to run commercial messages. The larger and more desirable the audience, the more the media can charge advertisers. Ratings are typically measures of exposure to media based on surveys of various target populations conducted by "third-party" firms independent of the sales transaction. The practice of ratings research emerged in the United States in the 1930s, and has since been refined and adopted worldwide (→ Nielsen Ratings). However, new technologies that allow people to consume a wide range of media anywhere, at any time, coupled with the desire of advertisers to reach ever-more narrowly drawn markets, have strained current systems of audience measurement. Ratings companies have responded by developing new methods to keep pace with the demands of their client industries (→ People-Meter).

Audience ratings are most often based on some form of probability sampling, and as such are subject to the same kinds of non-response and sampling error that occur in any survey research (→ Survey; Sampling, Random). In dozens of countries, ratings companies provide commercial and government clients with estimates of national audiences. In a subset of those countries, including the US and China, firms provide more localized measurement of cities and regions. Two factors are pressing sample sizes to their limit. The increasing abundance of new media delivery systems, including broadband delivery systems and video-on-demand, has fragmented audiences, reducing the size of any one outlet's audience. Concurrently, advertisers are more apt to be concerned with tightly defined target audiences. Under such circumstances, even large national samples are quickly whittled down to a very small number of respondents in the audience of interest, producing unacceptably high levels of sampling error. To address this problem, ratings firms are devising strategies to increase sample sizes, or basing their estimates on technologies that afford census-like numbers of respondents.

MEASURES OF EXPOSURE

The methods used to measure media exposure are, in large part, what set ratings apart from other forms of survey research. As US radio grew into an advertiser-supported medium in the late 1920s, it became essential to quantify its audience. The first such effort, launched in 1930, used telephone recall techniques to ascertain listening in the previous 24 hours. A few years later, "telephone coincidental" techniques, which asked respondents what they were listening to at the time of the call, were introduced in an effort to reduce response errors attributable to faulty memories. Telephones are still used in ratings research today, though usually in support of other methods that provide more copious data on exposure.

Diaries are inexpensive paper booklets that require a respondent to make a written log of their radio listening or television viewing, usually for one week. Diary formats vary by medium, but all offer some sort of grid that divides each day into quarter hours or broader "dayparts." In television measurement, a diary is assigned to each set in the sample household. In radio, each individual in the sample carries a diary. At the end of the survey week, the diaries are mailed to a processing center where they are coded, checked for logical errors and omissions, and ultimately turned into ratings reports.

If they are properly filled out, diaries provide a wealth of information, including audience demographics, at relatively low cost. Nonetheless, although they are, at this writing, in widespread use, they suffer from a number of problems that make them increasingly problematic for audience measurement. Diaries necessarily require some literacy. They suffer from relatively low response rates that, even with financial incentives, sometimes dip below 30 percent. Data collection is slow, and prone to a variety of processing and response errors. Most importantly, the new media environment, with remote controls, hundreds of channels, and various recording and delivery devices, simply overwhelms the ability of even conscientious diary-keepers to produce an accurate, contemporaneous record of their media use.

Meters, devices attached to receivers and producing a continuous paper record of tuning behavior, were introduced in radio measurement in the early 1940s by Arthur C. Nielsen. These were "household" meters that could record when sets were on, and the station to which they were tuned, but were incapable of identifying who within the household was listening. In the 1950s, household meters were adapted to television measurement. Such meters eventually made an electronic record of set use that could be retrieved over telephone lines to produce "overnight" ratings. They were the principal method of national television measurement in the US until the late 1980s, and continue to be used in some local markets.

Household meters have a number of advantages. They are fast, relatively unobtrusive, require no literacy, and produce vast amounts of accurate set-tuning data over long periods of time. Compared with diaries, however, they are expensive. Their cost is justified only in larger markets (e.g., nations and major cities). Moreover, household meters produce no demographic information, so they must typically be used in conjunction with diaries.

A new generation of meters called *people-meters*, introduced in the late 1980s, provided a means to quickly gather demographic information. They work much like household meters, but feature a set-top box and/or hand-held devices that allow respondents to press a button signaling their presence in front of the set. People-meters are currently the preferred way to measure television audiences around the world. They do require some effort on the part of respondents, however, and so are more obtrusive and prone to respondent fatigue and error than is ideal. Newer generations of more passive, portable devices are being introduced.

All the aforementioned techniques gather data from samples. Even large national panels, which might exceed 10,000 households, can be insufficient to estimate the audience for a very small network, or to assess the behaviors of a narrowly defined market segment. Media industries are now studying the possibility of harnessing the data created by *digital set-top boxes*. These are analogous to household meters operating in millions of homes, and might provide a way to study highly fragmented digital media consumption. There are, however, at least three problems with this approach. First, it presents obvious concerns about privacy. Second, not all homes subscribe to digital cable or satellites, and even those that do won't necessarily have all their sets attached to the service. Hence, it is impossible to determine the total audience for all channels. Third, like all household meters, the technology provides no "people data," though mathematical models can approximate demographic composition.

Internet audience measurement has also presented some relatively new opportunities to measure user behaviors. One approach, sometimes labeled "user-centric," mirrors conventional ratings research. Here a probability sample of users is recruited to provide information. However, since Internet access is gained via a computer, it is a relatively simple and inexpensive proposition to install a piece of software on the user's machine that records and reports the URLs the user visits. This, in effect, turns each computer into a metering device, and allows research firms to create much larger panels than would be economically viable with conventional metering. Alternatively, a "server-centric" approach takes advantage of the fact that all Internet traffic is managed by computers called servers. They can record the total number of times information is requested and fed to users. This goes beyond sampling and represents a census of use. Unfortunately, server "hits" can be difficult to decipher. While there are techniques to differentiate returning versus new visitors, or identify their place of origin, this approach cannot provide reliable demographic information about Internet audiences. It can, however, be combined with user-centric data to provide highly detailed estimates of exposure, including the use of media streamed over the Internet.

MEASURES OF ENGAGEMENT

Another consequence of newer media that allow people to see what they want when they want it is some erosion in the value of simple exposure as the metric upon which media time is bought and sold. DVRs and other on-demand technologies make it relatively simple for audiences to avoid commercials. Increasingly, advertisers are demanding some measure of the extent to which audiences are involved or engaged with the media they consume. The general theory is that engaged audience members will be less inclined to look away, more receptive to advertising, and better able to recall brand messages.

"Qualitative" ratings are nothing new. In some countries with strong traditions of public service broadcasting, finding out how much people like or learn from programming is an ongoing practice. Historically, in the more commercially oriented US, qualitative ratings have foundered. Current definitions of engagement include various affects, attentiveness, recall, intentions, and behaviors. For these factors to constitute an ongoing system of ratings, the industry must reach some consensus on the definition of engagement, valid measures of the construct, and whether the value of such supplemental ratings ultimately justifies the cost.

RATINGS QUALITY

Ratings are subject to various sources of error, including sampling, response, non-response, and processing error. The first three are familiar to survey researchers. The last speaks to the fact that ratings are a complex product manufactured from various inputs, including different measures of behavior as well as program and advertising information. All such forms of error have relatively objective meanings and can generally be ameliorated with the application of sufficient resources.

However, there are more subjective criteria that affect the quality of ratings data. Take, for example, something as fundamental as the definition of exposure to television. Should the audience for a program include those who watched the show in real time as well as those who recorded it? If the latter, does their inclusion depend upon how quickly they replayed the program? Is a delay of a few minutes, or hours, or days acceptable? There are no objectively right answers, but the resolution can have profound consequences for different ratings consumers. As a consequence, ratings are inevitably the product of an ongoing process of negotiation among different industry and government players, often with competing interests. That very tension is probably the best guarantee that ratings maintain a reasonable degree of quality.

SEE ALSO: ▶ Advertising ▶ Audience Research ▶ Audience Segmentation ▶ Exposure to Television ▶ Media Marketing ▶ Nielsen Ratings ▶ People-Meter ▶ Sampling, Random ▶ Survey

References and Suggested Readings

Ang, I. (1991). *Desperately seeking the audience*. London: Routledge.

Beville, H. (1988). *Audience ratings: Radio, television, and cable*, rev. edn. Hillsdale, NJ: Lawrence Erlbaum.

Ettema, J. S., & Whitney, D. C. (1994). *Audiencemaking: How the media create the audience*. Thousand Oaks, CA: Sage.

Napoli, P. M. (2003). *Audience economics: Media institutions and the audience marketplace*. New York: Columbia University Press.

Webster, J. G., & Phalen, P. F. (1997). *The mass audience: Rediscovering the dominant model*. Mahwah, NJ: Lawrence Erlbaum.

Webster, J. G., Phalen, P. F., & Lichty, L. W. (2006). *Ratings analysis: The theory and practice of audience research*, 3rd edn. Mahwah, NJ: Lawrence Erlbaum.

Readership Research

Rüdiger Schulz

Allensbach Institute

Readership research employs empirical methods to investigate print media usage, focusing mainly on → magazines and → newspapers that appear periodically. Of primary importance in this context are readership analyses that ascertain findings on print-media coverage (reach or cumulative audience) and readership structure (composition of readership to describe print-media target groups). These methods are supplemented by reception analyses, which investigate reading habits in a more general sense.

A distinction can be drawn here between readership research as *media advertising research*, which deals with the performance of a print medium as an advertising medium, and as *editorial readership research*, which is aimed at optimizing newspaper and magazine content and/or layout. The lion's share of applied readership research focuses on optimizing media planning for advertising purposes (→ Advertisement Campaign Management; Advertising Effectiveness, Measurement of) as well as optimizing the content and layout of print products. In comparison, academic reception research, which is designed to ascertain more fundamental insights into readership, plays a relatively minor role. The dominance of media advertising research in practice can be explained by its far-reaching economic significance (→ Advertising, Economics of; Cost and Revenue Structures in the Media).

HISTORICAL DEVELOPMENT

The origins of systematic readership research based on empirical methods go back a very long way. In the US, for example, standardized questionnaires (→ Interview, Standardized) were already being used in the early 1920s to conduct commercially motivated mass surveys among newspaper readers (to help publications respond to readers' interests and thus increase circulation, to provide evidence of readers' interest levels and purchasing power, and thus increase advertising revenues). In 1921 George Hotchkiss conducted a written survey among wealthy and well-educated New York residents to investigate their newspaper-reading habits. His self-administered survey method was further developed by Ralph O. Nafziger and his students at the University of Wisconsin. During the same period, George Gallup was working on a different approach at the University of Iowa. Gallup developed the face-to-face survey method based on interviews with a representative cross-section of readers, a method he first employed in 1927 to conduct copy tests to establish whether particular articles were read in full, merely glanced through or paid no attention at all (→ Survey).

The *widening spectrum of print media* available, for example the ever-increasing number of new general-interest and special-interest magazine titles, has brought with it an increasing necessity for comparative readership coverage and readership-structure findings upon which commercial advertisers and advertising agencies can base their media-planning decisions. Investigations funded jointly by several publishers have in the meantime been superseded by syndicated national readership surveys in many countries. If readership surveys are to obtain accurate findings, above all for titles with a small circulation and low coverage, they require very large samples, which also means very large research budgets. The need to raise substantial funding led to *joint industry surveys* commissioned by a great number of publishing houses and conducted by large market-research companies. These surveys are often overseen by technical advisory commissions that serve to lend the findings a legitimate, "quasi-official" status, thus raising general acceptance levels. Typical examples of such joint industry readership surveys include: the MRI in the US, the NRS survey in the UK, the media analyses (MA) in Germany, or the AMPS in South Africa.

In his "Summary of current readership research" for the Worldwide Readership Symposium 2005 in Prague, Erhard Meier reported on 91 readership surveys from 71 countries, a fact that reflects both the centralization and the globalization of research companies today. Multinational organizations such as Ipsos, AC Nielsen, Milward Brown, or TNS each presently conduct national readership surveys in 10 or more different countries. Sample sizes range from 1000 (Bahrain and Zambia) to about 250,000 respondents (India).

BASIC DEFINITIONS AND METHODS

Newspaper or magazine circulation says little in itself about the number of people a print medium actually reaches. The reality of the situation is far more complex: many copies are printed but distributed free of charge rather than sold or are not distributed at all, other copies are sold but are not read and, above all, a great number of copies are used by more than just one person, e.g., at home, at work, or in a doctor's waiting room. Despite the fact that data supplied by publishing houses is verified by so-called *Audit Bureaus of Circulation* in many countries to prevent manipulation, the question of how many readers a print medium actually reaches remains unanswered.

What is a "Reader"?

Because circulation data fails to paint the complete picture, it is necessary to conduct readership surveys based on broad samples. In order to do this, it is necessary to *define exactly who qualifies as a reader*. Should only people who read a publication from cover to cover very carefully be counted or do people who just flick through a publication, stopping only to read a few headlines or glance at a few pictures also qualify as readers? What if a publication is read more than once: do all reading events count? Does it only count if a publication is read on one specific day or does it count if it was read at any time within the issue period or even well beyond the issue period, e.g., at some time in the last three months? Clear definitions of who counts as a reader are essential as they provide the buyers (advertisers and advertising agencies) as well as the sellers (publishing houses) of advertising space with what equates to a mutually acceptable currency.

The most common of such currencies is *Average Issue Readership (AIR)*, i.e., the number of people who have read or looked at some or all of the average issue of a publication. Just flicking through is enough: it is not necessary to have read a publication through carefully to have come into contact with an advertisement placed there. *Average Readers per Copy (ARPC)* can be calculated by dividing average-issue readership by average circulation. There are many different ways of measuring average-issue readership. The four main techniques are described here, namely: "Through-the-Book," "Recent Reading," "First Reading Yesterday," and "Readership Diaries."

Through-the-Book Technique

The oldest of these methods is the *Through-the-Book (TTB)* technique, which was first used in 1936 to estimate the readership of Life Magazine. It is the only one of the four approaches described here to employ recognition of a specific issue to estimate readership. Respondents are shown actual full issues of publications; stripped or skeletonized issues are often used to reduce the burden on both respondents and interviewers when a great number of publications are presented in one interview. Bill Simmons and Alfred Politz are pioneers of the TTB approach. Empirical tests have shown that TTB estimates are prone to both overclaims (e.g., caused by perceived social desirability or prestige effects) and underclaims (e.g., caused by forgetfulness), as well as to frequent confusion of similar print titles with the same kind of content. To prevent confusion, similar titles are often presented together in a group. The age of the issues presented also has a major influence on findings. If the issue is too old, there is a danger that respondents will have forgotten about having read it, whereas if the issue is very recent it may not yet have accumulated its full audience.

The most common method for measuring readership today is the *Recent Reading (RR)* technique, which was brought into use by the Institute of Practitioners in Advertising in 1952. In Europe, it is also known as the IPA technique. There are two fundamental differences between RR and TTB. First, respondents are not asked whether they came into contact with one specific issue of a newspaper or magazine, but about contact with any issue. "The readership estimate depends not on the respondent's ability to *recognize* a specific issue as one they have previously read, but on their accurate *recall* of when it was that they last came into contact with the publication in question" (Brown 1999, 65). Second, the question mainly used to estimate readership in this technique is: "When did you last read or look at any copy of . . . (title)," and it is posed either as an open question or with response categories, e.g., "yesterday"/"within the last seven days"/"between one week and one month ago," and so on. Even in this case, where the information requested seems to be so simple, there is still a danger that respondents may not provide reliable answers from memory. In particular, if the most recent reading event is already quite some time ago, a telescoping effect is often observed, i.e., respondents believe something happened more recently than it actually did.

Intensive methodology research has uncovered two further phenomena limiting the accuracy of the RR technique. The first is *replicated readership*, which comes about when people spread their readership of a given issue over more than one issue period, leading to overestimation. The second is *parallel readership*, which occurs when two or more issues of the same publication are read in the same period, leading to an underestimation of average-issue readership. Although these two sources of error cancel each other out to a certain extent, empirical tests indicate that the net effect tends to be understatement.

Many readership surveys supplement the main recent-reading question by asking about *frequency of reading*. A distinction can be drawn here between questions using verbal scales (e.g., "almost always," "quite often," or "only occasionally"), questions using numerical scales (e.g., "How many out of twelve issues of magazine XYZ have you read in the past 12 months?"), and questions that employ a combination of verbal and numerical scales. However, these frequency questions also depend on an ability to remember events to such a degree of accuracy that many respondents are likely to struggle to respond reliably. In order to increase recall accuracy in particular, and to eliminate biases caused by replicated reading, readership researchers have experimented with ways to reduce the recall period, e.g., by including questions about First Reading Yesterday (FRY).

A further method referred to earlier for estimating readership data is *Readership Diaries*. Households selected at random are asked to regularly record all the newspapers and magazines they read during a specified period of time (e.g., 1 month) in a diary, including additional details on which issue was read, how much was read, whether the issue in question was being read for the first time, etc. Researchers face serious methodological problems when using the readership diaries method; recruiting a representative cross-section of panel members, for instance, and ensuring they continue to participate reliably over time can prove extremely difficult. A further drawback of diaries is the tendency of respondents to behave unnaturally (conditioning effect).

Methodological Problems

All of the methods employed to estimate print-media readership described so far suffer from *one common weakness*, in that they all rely exclusively on statements provided by respondents, who may fail to recall past events correctly or filter responses according to social norms, e.g., social desirability. The accuracy of readership estimates ascertained using these methods therefore depends on the number and type of visual aids employed or the length of time that has elapsed since the reading event took place. Alternative approaches to ascertaining readership data involve *technical measurement techniques* designed to gather data independently of replies provided by respondents ("measurements not responses"). Examples of this type of approach are: the use of *eye cameras* to track reading, electromagnetic sensors fitted to wristwatches to register page contacts, portable bar-code scanners to register publication details, or hidden cameras to validate page-contact findings. However, these methods have so far not progressed beyond laboratory tests conducted under unrealistic conditions.

Erhard Meier's review of methodological observations referred to above shows that most national readership surveys continue to be based on face-to-face interviews with broad samples of the population. Of the 91 national readership studies conducted around the world during the review period, 71 used face-to-face interviews, of which the majority (63) were conducted with pen and paper, 5 as computer-assisted personal interviews (CAPI), and 3 as double screen CAPI interviews. A total of 10 national studies used self-completion questionnaires and 7 used computer-assisted telephone interviews (CATI). There are a few countries where a mix of methods is used, e.g., telephone interviews combined with self-completion (Norway), face-to-face interviews with pen and paper supplemented by subsamples conducted using CATI, or (in the Netherlands and Germany) subsamples using computer-assisted self-interviews (CASI).

Because large national readership surveys often include several hundred different newspaper and magazine titles, it is common practice to pose *screening questions* at the beginning of interviews to reduce the title load per respondent by excluding those titles respondents "only know by name," or titles that are completely "unknown" to them. Subsequent questions, usually beginning with the frequency question followed by the recency question, are only posed on the remaining publications. *Logo cards*, either in black and white or in color, are the main form of visual aid employed in face-to-face readership interviews to assist respondents' recall, as well as to help avoid title confusion. Print titles and categories (dailies, weeklies, fortnightlies, monthlies, etc.) are often rotated to counterbalance possible order effects. In many readership surveys, respondents are then posed a number of supplementary questions to establish, for example, how long, where, and on how many days reading took place, or to ascertain their "relationship" with the publication read, e.g., by asking about the amount read ("all/nearly all," "over half," "about half," "less than half," etc.). In order to establish reader "involvement," respondents are also often asked to gauge how much they would "miss" a publication if it were no longer published.

Another way of reducing load per respondent employed in certain large national readership surveys is to *split the titles* included, e.g., to create two groups of 150 publications and conduct a survey for each. The findings from the two representative surveys are fused to create one combined dataset. This so-called "marriage of data" via common connecting links (e.g., socio-demographic or attitude variables) is, however, wide open to methodological criticism.

Rudimentary contact data (having "read or flicked through" a newspaper or magazine) tells advertisers little about the potential effectiveness of their adverts. In contrast, *data on the quality of reading*, allows conclusions to be drawn about the chances readers have of coming into contact with advertisements, which is a prerequisite for advertising effectiveness. Respondents who have read a publication carefully from cover to cover, for example, are more likely to come into contact with a particular advertisement than those who have only taken a look inside, flicked through briefly (→ Copy Test and Starch Test).

In summing up his comprehensive review of methods developed in the field of readership research, Michael Brown states that there is no "gold standard," no single, inalienable currency that provides an equally valid measure of readership across the entire spectrum of print titles and categories: "All methods have differing advantages and limitations. Arguments as to methods' 'validity,' in any absolute sense, are arid; they should be judged by their ability to deliver readership estimates which allow comparisons between different newspapers and magazines which are minimally biased" (Brown 1999, 83). For as long as there are no universally accepted methods, it will continue to prove difficult to further harmonize the many different techniques being employed to estimate readership around the world today, as well as to establish common methodological standards. This is essential, however, for international advertising planning in an increasingly globalized world economy.

EDITORIAL READERSHIP RESEARCH

While newspaper and magazine readership in newly developed countries is rising in line with alphabetization, it is in decline in many developed industrial countries. In the US, the *fall in newspaper readership* in recent decades is so dramatic that it represents a cultural shift away from newspaper reading. Fewer and fewer young people are becoming regular newspaper readers and many magazines are, to an increasing degree, only being read sporadically. Young people in particular read print media more impatiently and selectively, tending to scan rather than read thoroughly (→ Exposure to Print Media).

Empirical readership research has an important role to play in optimizing print media, providing vital insights for decision-makers. Surveys among readers based on the *copy test* technique, for example, can be used to establish which of the items in an issue read yesterday or the day before yesterday were "read in full," "only scanned," or "not looked at at all." Here too, attempts have been made recently to introduce *technical measurement* to avoid relying on readers' questionable ability to respond reliably from memory. One example is the "*Reader Scan*" method, whereby a small panel of readers electronically mark the point up to which an article has been read during the act of reading. However, along with the apparent gains in accuracy, this method also brings with it a number of problems. For example, there are difficulties with gathering representative samples for such studies as it is normally only possible to attract participants with above-average motivation as readers. It is also impossible to completely counter conditioning effects in such tests ("unnatural behavior").

The increasing intermedia competition has breathed new life into readership research in recent years and new perspectives are opening up, for example research into the networking of cross-media usage between print and online media ("print in a multimedia world," "integrated communication").

SEE ALSO: ▶Advertisement Campaign Management ▶Advertising, Economics of ▶Advertising Effectiveness, Measurement of ▶Copy Test and Starch Test ▶Cost and Revenue Structures in the Media ▶Exposure to Print Media ▶Interview, Standardized ▶Magazine ▶Media Performance ▶Newspaper ▶Survey

References and Suggested Readings

Belson, W. (1962). *Studies in readership*. London: Business publications on behalf of the Institute of Practitioners in Advertising.

Brown, M. (1999). *Effective print media measurement: Audiences . . . and more*. Harrow: Ipsos-RSL.

Joyce, T. (1987). A comparison of recent reading and full through-the-book. In H. Henry (ed.), *Readership research: Theory and practice: Proceedings of the third international symposium, Salzburg*. Amsterdam: Elsevier, pp. 116–122.

List, D. (2006). Measuring audiences to printed publications. At www.audiencedialogue.org, accessed December 2006.

Lysaker, R. (1989). Towards a gold standard. In H. Henry (ed.), *Readership research: Theory and practice: Proceedings of the fourth international symposium, Barcelona*. London: Research Services and British Market Research Bureau, pp. 172–179.

Meier, E. (2005). Looking for best practice. *Session papers from the Worldwide Readership Research Symposium (Prague)*. Harrow: Ipsos, pp. 1–9.

Politz, A. (1967). *Media studies: An experimental study comparing magazine audiences by two questioning procedures*. New York: Alfred Politz.

Schreiber, R., & Schiller, C. (1984). Electro-mechanical devices for recording readership: A report of a development project. In H. Henry (ed.), *Readership research: Proceedings of the second international symposium, Montreal*. Amsterdam: Elsevier, pp. 198–199.

Tennstädt, F., & Hansen, J. (1982). Validating the recency and through-the-book techniques. In H. Henry (ed.), *Readership research: Theory and practice: Proceedings of the first international symposium, New Orleans*. London: Sigmatext, pp. 229–241.

Real-Time Ratings (RTR)

Andreas Fahr

Ludwig Maximilian University of Mainz

Real-time rating (RTR) methods – also called "real-time response" or "continuous response measurement" (CRM) – collect judgments or evaluation data from a subject during media exposure (→ Exposure to Communication Content; Audience Research). While questionnaires provide data about the outcome of a perception (e.g., television viewing), RTR focuses on the process of viewing. Besides the application to academic questions of reception research, it is widely used within the media industry for testing → television programs or movies before they are aired or released. Applications range from commercial television or radio programs, → advertising research, to measuring judgment processes in presidential debates (→ Televised Debates). It can also be used for content analysis of television programs or speeches (e.g., measuring perceived degree of violence, dimensions of characters' behavior, interaction, etc.; → Content Analysis, Quantitative).

DEVELOPMENT: "LITTLE ANNIE"

The idea of real-time response measurement dates back to the late 1930s and early 1940s when → Paul F. Lazarsfeld and Frank Stanton introduced their "program analyzer," which was later adopted by CBS and major advertising companies. Their first system, affectionately named "Little Annie," consisted of two cylinders, about five inches long with a diameter of an inch. One cylinder had a red push-button at the end and the other a green button. The members of the audience held one in each hand with the thumb positioned to press on the button. Viewers were instructed to press the green button to indicate their liking of a radio program, and the red button if they were to feel uncomfortable about the program. Pushing neither button indicated indifference. Audience response charts on paper showed patterns of likers and dislikers for up to 10 persons at a time.

In the later years a set of 100 stations called "Big Annie" was developed. The first generations of these kinds of program analyzers were used for program and film testing, for example, at Columbia University's Bureau of Applied Social Research, McCann Erickson, or CBS. In the years following the introduction of the program analyzer, the idea was adopted for a number of similar devices. The main differences were in the way participants' judgments were collected: five- to ten-point scale push-button systems were developed as well as seven-point scale dialers, and ones with ten or more points (→ Scales; Scales and Indices). But basically the idea itself remained the same (Millard 1992).

The boom of microcomputers in the 1980s led to refinement in data collection, display, and analysis. Today participants in RTR studies signal their reactions to exposure mostly by means of a dialer, joystick, or slider using a predetermined scale (mood, judgment, → attitudes, etc.). More or less any scale suitable for real-time reactions can be used. Hence, RTR can be considered as a continuous report on one repeated question (e.g., How much do I like what I see?), producing panel data that are dynamically sensitive to the subtle effects of the stimulus. Since results are nothing more than highly autocorrelated time-series data (→ Time-Series Analysis), a wide range of data analysis techniques can be employed.

APPLICATIONS TODAY

Compared to traditional → surveys, the results of RTR are far more precise, letting the researcher pinpoint which parts of audiovisual stimuli are responsible for the so-called peaks or spikes during exposure. For example, one can describe how the appearance of a certain character influences judgments, how music can contribute to changes in evaluations, how humor moderates perception, how dynamic a plot is perceived to be, and more. Moreover the technique is also described as a measure of audience → "attention" (Millard 1992), semantic processing, attitudes, or other psychological states or mental processes (Biocca et al. 1994). In general, Biocca et al. (1994) define the measure as subjects' self-reports of changes in psychological state or judgment.

Furthermore RTR can also be used as a continuous *measure of changing message content* or a way to code communication behaviors. Measures of hedonic response (like/dislike) are found in a majority of the measures. Concerning validity, subjects report that the measure reflects their feelings about a program accurately. Moreover, RTR proves to be a sensitive indicator for attitudes toward a fictional or real character (often measured in the context of political or presidential debates). Finally, the measure allows for the investigation of whether our overall evaluation of a media stimulus is triggered largely by an overall judgment of that stimulus (mean-driven judgment), rather than by individual events or scenes of a program – whether it be cumulative, multiplicative, linear or nonlinear (e.g., peaks, spikes, punch-lines, appearance of important actors, peripeteia).

High *attention to a program* can be indicated by high frequency of use and wide range of movement of the dialer. Studies show a positive correlation between this kind of activity and memory recall of these parts of the program. However, critics point to the fact that high involvement in the program may lead to the subject forgetting to use the dialer, giving rise to a false interpretation of psychological deafness or boredom. The nonuse of the handheld device can therefore mean opposite things: being completely absorbed or completely bored. Implementing a secondary task reaction-time design into the research setting could address the problem, but would at the same time make the viewing situation more artificial and the task more complicated.

The participants could also be asked how involved they felt during a decisive part of the program and relate this answer to the individual real-time response data. If high reported involvement is accompanied by no scale movement, these subjects should be analyzed carefully, separately, or even eliminated from analysis. Another important issue in this context is that subjects utilize the given scale to a different degree. If the sample size is low, this scaling problem is often not leveled out sufficiently. Again, cross-checks with questionnaires – asking subjects about their highest and lowest scores in relation to their personal range – could help adjust RTR data. In some cases, it might even be helpful to standardize the mean series.

VALIDITY OF THE METHOD

One other major constraint of RTR measurement is that it is only one-dimensional. As the online evaluation task requires some cognitive effort, valid results can be expected only if subjects concentrate on one dimension only for evaluation. For example, it is relatively easy for subjects to indicate whether they like what they see or not. More difficult and less valid would be the question of whether a magazine, show, film, etc. is entertaining or informative. Moreover, reactivity of RTR measurements is often criticized, meaning that the task itself modifies the perception process or does not indicate what should be measured – hence, → validity is violated. As stated above, if participants are asked to indicate their involvement in a movie by means of RTR, very high involvement might make viewers forget to use the dialer because they are too engaged in the program (→ Involvement with Media Content). Similarly, if viewers are continuously evaluating their state, they might not be able to become engaged with the media content. Hence, the task should be easy and participants be given time to get used to the method.

Compared to RTR measures a questionnaire can ask for retrospective judgment on a greater variety of criteria. However, a retrospective judgment may be quite different from an online judgment. After watching a movie, quite a lot is already forgotten; messages have already been processed on a higher level, rationalized, adjusted to one's reference system, and often altered because of → social desirability. If one wants to collect data on spontaneous, immediate impressions, RTR is the ideal measurement technique. Continuous audience response research is of high value when applied to pilot programs, TV commercials, movies, or political advertising at a point in production where they can still be changed. Taken together, the most effective means of audience research is a combination of several techniques. For audience profiling and ex post facto judgment, a questionnaire is employed. For continuous judgments RTR is needed, and for validation purposes and enrichment of RTR data, focus groups can be very useful (→ Qualitative Methodology).

SEE ALSO: ▶ Advertising ▶ Attention ▶ Attitudes ▶ Attitudes, Values, and Beliefs, Media Effects on ▶ Audience Research ▶ Content Analysis, Quantitative ▶ Exposure to Communication Content ▶ Involvement with Media Content ▶ Lazarsfeld, Paul F. ▶ Qualitative Methodology ▶ Scales ▶ Scales and Indices ▶ Social Desirability ▶ Survey ▶ Televised Debates ▶ Television ▶ Time-Series Analysis ▶ Validity

References and Suggested Readings

Biocca, F., David, P., & West, M. (1994). Continuous response measurement (CRM): A computerized tool for research on the cognitive processing of communication messages. In A. Lang (ed.), *Measuring psychological responses to media messages*. Hillsdale, NJ: Lawrence Erlbaum, pp. 15–64.

Maier, J., Maurer, M., Reinemann, C., & Faas, T. (2006). Reliability and validity of real-time response measurement: A comparison of two studies of a televised debate in Germany. *International Journal of Public Opinion Research*, 19(1), 53–73.

Millard, W. J. (1992). A history of handsets for direct measurement of audience response. *International Journal of Public Opinion Research*, 4(1), 1–17.

Realism

Klaus Bruhn Jensen

University of Copenhagen

A classic position in the history of ideas and theory of science, realism assumes that the world exists independently of human minds, and that it lends itself to intersubjective inquiry, even if humans – individually, collectively, and as a species – may be unable to understand reality in all its aspects (Nagel 1986). In recent theory of science, realism has regained influence in comparison with other major positions such as → critical rationalism and → constructivism. Pavitt (1999) suggested that realism is currently the dominant position in theory of science, and that it informs the practice of much current media and communication research. (In literary and other aesthetic theory, realism denotes fictional

Table 1   Three domains of reality, incorporating three types of phenomena

	The real	The actual	The empirical
Experiences	x	x	x
Events	x	x	
Mechanisms	x		

forms that represent reality in the categories of everyday experience [→ Fiction; Realism in Film and Photography; Reality and Media Reality].)

The general tenets of realism can be laid out with reference to three components of Roy Bhaskar's (1979) influential *critical realism*.

Ontological realism: rejecting skepticist and idealist premises – that no knowledge of the empirical world is possible, or that reality equals the sum of our conceptions of it – realism questions such "anthropocentrism": "Copernicus argued that the universe does not revolve around man. And yet in philosophy we still represent things as if it did" (Bhaskar cited in Archer et al. 1998, 45).

Epistemological relativism: from a moderately constructivist position, realism assumes that human knowledge of both nature and other minds depends on an iterative sequence of perceptions, cognitions, and inferences, all of which are open to question, rejection, and revision in a community of researchers. In the process, reality serves as a limit condition or regulatory ideal, without which the range of natural and cultural phenomena that one encounters in science as well as in daily life would be inexplicable.

Judgmental rationality: science depend on the exercise of rationality, which, at some point, must end in (fallible) judgments about what to do next – as an individual scholar, a scientific field, or a society. The business of science is to continuously compare and contrast alternative accounts, considering the widest possible range of criteria and means for examining reality.

Critical realism further emphasizes the *transfactuality* or *stratification* of reality. Several kinds of facts are real, including aesthetic experience and its biological foundations, micro-social order as well as macro-social infrastructure. Such facts are not reducible to each other, but enter into relationships of emergence, and they call for complementary forms of inquiry (Jensen 2002). One methodological implication is that research must consider three domains or levels of reality (Table 1). The *empirical* domain is the source of concrete evidence – *experience* of the world. By experiencing and documenting, for example, how journalists collect information, and how readers respond to it as news, researchers procure a necessary though not sufficient condition of empirical studies. The *actual* status of this documentation is a matter of inference. It is by characterizing and conceptualizing empirical materials as evidence of *events* (e.g., reporter–source interactions or decodings) that one may infer their place in mediated communication. The domain of the *real* is the most inclusive. Research ultimately seeks to establish the *mechanisms* that may account for events (e.g., a system of political communication that operates according to economic prerogatives and professional routines, as well as ideals of citizenship).

In sum, experiences, events, and mechanisms are all real. Experiences are available to be selected and analyzed by researchers as evidence of events. However, the distinctive task of research is to interpret or explain the underlying mechanisms with reference to theoretical concepts and frameworks.

SEE ALSO: ► Constructivism   ► Critical Rationalism   ► Fiction   ► Realism in Film and Photography   ► Reality and Media Reality

References and Suggested Readings

Archer, M., Bhaskar, R., Collier, A., Lawson, T., & Norrie, A. (eds.) (1998). *Critical realism: Essential readings*. London: Routledge.

Bhaskar, R. (1979). *The possibility of naturalism*. Brighton: Harvester Press.

Jensen, K. B. (2002). The complementarity of qualitative and quantitative methodologies in media and communication research. In K. B. Jensen (ed.), *A handbook of media and communication research: Qualitative and quantitative methodologies*. London: Routledge, pp. 254–272.

Nagel, T. (1986). *The view from nowhere*. Oxford: Oxford University Press.

Pavitt, C. (1999). The third way: Scientific realism and communication theory. *Communication Theory*, 9(2), 162–188.

Realism in Film and Photography

Theo van Leeuwen

University of Technology, Sydney

From its very beginnings, photography was understood and experienced in terms of its capacity for realism. "It is not merely the likeness which is precious . . . but the sense of nearness involved in the thing . . . the fact of the very shadow of the person lying there fixed forever," wrote Elizabeth Barret in 1843 (quoted in Sontag 1977, 183). Soon it would be used to record events and document many aspects of the world, not just in people's family albums, but also in science, medical training, police work, military reconnaissance, and many other spheres of activity. Yet photography also developed into an art form, with highly allegorical *tableaux vivants* that "combined the sensuous beauty of the fine print with the moral beauty of the fine image" (Mike Weaver, quoted in Wells 2000, 262). In the twentieth century both these aspects of photography would continue to develop: documentary photography and → photojournalism with masters such as Erich Salomon, Cartier-Bresson, and Robert Frank; and photography as a form of modern art with, for instance, the formal, quasi-abstract landscapes of Edward Weston and the nudes of Bill Brandt.

In a similar way film started both as a medium for capturing reality and as a new form of theatre (→ Film as Popular Culture). As the Lumière brothers sent cameramen across the world to record sites of interest including *The Grand Canal of Venice*, shot from a gondola, Georges Méliès, who had been a magician, built the world's first film studio in Montreuil and used the medium for trick films such as *The Man with the Rubber Head* and *Disappearance of a Lady*, and for science fiction fantasies such as *Trip to the Moon* and *Voyage across the Impossible* (→ Animation). The two kinds of films looked very different. In Lumière's *Arrival of a Train at the Station of La Ciotat* (1896), one of the earliest films ever to be screened, a train enters a station and moves toward the camera, and the people on the platform too move toward or away from the camera. In Méliès's films the camera was static, positioned in front of a stage, observing the spectacle, rather than in the middle of the action.

REALISM IN THE HISTORY OF FILM THEORY

These two sides of photography and film have also dominated theory and criticism. In the 1950s, André Bazin (1971) called film "the deathmask of reality" and advocated the use of long takes that show events unfolding in real time and renege on the medium's capacity to condense or, occasionally, expand time through editing. In the same period, Siegfried Kracauer wrote that photography and film should aim for an "impersonal, completely artless camera record" (1960, 12) and "represent significant aspects of physical reality without trying to overwhelm that reality – so that the raw material focused upon is both left intact and made transparent" (1960, 23). Almost all significant new developments in the cinema of the time claimed to advance the cause of realism – postwar neorealism in Italy, the early *nouvelle vague* films in France, the British kitchen sink dramas of the late 1950s and early 1960s, and the *cinema vérité* style of US documentary filmmakers such as Pennebaker, the Maysles brothers, Leacock, and Wiseman.

For others film could only be an art insofar as it went *beyond* the "simple" reproduction of reality. The constructivist Soviet filmmakers and theorists of the 1920s, for instance, experimented with "creative geography," constructing a nonexistent location by combining shots taken in different locations and using editing to make them seem adjacent. In the 1930s Rudolf Arnheim (1967) argued that only the medium's shortcomings, the way in which it *reduces* what it records, could allow it to develop into a new art form. The absence of the third dimension, the absence of colour (in the black-and-white era), and the absence of the nonvisual world of the senses should not be seen as a loss, he said, but as a gain: "Only gradually . . . the possibility of utilising the difference between film and real life for the purpose of making formally significant images was realised" (Arnheim 1967, 42).

In the 1960s the dominant realist aesthetic was challenged by a combination of → semiotics and Marxism. In *Mythologies* (1977), → Roland Barthes attacked *The Family of Man*, a key 1950s exhibition of documentary photographs that featured Dorothy Lange's iconic 1930s portrait of a poverty-stricken mother and child on the cover of its catalogue. Barthes denounced as a bourgeois "myth" the exhibition's aim to show the universality of human actions across the world: "The failure of photography seems to me flagrant in this connection: to reproduce death or birth tells us, literally, nothing . . . Yes, these are facts of nature, universal facts. But if one removes History from them, there is nothing more to be said" (Barthes 1977, 101). As in the Soviet Union of the 1920s, realism was now seen as a bourgeois art form that naturalizes the status quo of bourgeois society.

Bertolt Brecht became an important reference point for both filmmakers and theorists. "Less than at any time does a simple reproduction of reality tell us anything about reality," Brecht had said in the 1930s, "Therefore something has to actually be constructed, something artificial, something set up" (quoted in Wells 2000, 108).

In the late 1960s, filmmakers like Godard would heed this call and use Brecht's "alienation effect" to insure audiences would realize they were looking at a film, at something constructed, rather than at a "mechanical" record of reality. Film theorist Colin MacCabe (1974), in the pages of the then very prominent UK film journal *Screen* denounced the "classic realist text," which, he argued, presents the dominant discourse, not as a → discourse, but as objective fact. Although other discourses can get a hearing in "classic realist texts," they are "between quotation marks," while the dominant discourse functions like the voice of the omniscient narrator in realist novels and always has the last word. Only films that do not privilege one discourse and leave the inevitable contradictions unresolved could be truly "revolutionary" and allow viewers to examine the issues for themselves.

INFLUENCE OF NEW TECHNOLOGIES ON THEORY

As theorists argued against the idea that photography and film can record reality "as it is", and as this anti-realist view was taught to generations of media students, photography and film themselves began to be overtaken, first by video, and then by the new digital media with their much greater potential for image manipulation (→ Digital Imagery). The strongest reaction against this development came from photojournalists. In a celebrated article titled "The end of photography as we have known it", Fred Ritchen argued that photography's "fact-based, mechanistic qualities, which have been able to change world opinion even against the most powerful governments, have been devalued to a point where photography is much less a threat to the established points of view. The debate encouraged by the photographs of the Vietnam War will probably not occur again. Photography becomes poetry, and those whose position is less than lyrical suffer the most" (Ritchen 1991, 14).

In the second half of the twentieth century, the market for photojournalism would contract and → magazines would increasingly rely on *stock imagery* for their illustrations (→ Stock Photography). Image banks now allow magazine publishers to cheaply and quickly download photographs to illustrate almost any kind of article. The photographs they distribute have lost their function of recording specific people, places, and events, as they must be reusable, and focus on connoting the kinds of themes publishers might wish to illustrate. Press photographs are increasingly posed and "set up," rather than "captured." Ambitious young photographers no longer follow the call of Cartier-Bresson to record the "decisive moment," but focus on studio work and on photography as an art form. In → Hollywood film, the disaster movies of the early 1970s inaugurated a return to the studios and to the construction of often dystopic future worlds. "Dramatized documentaries" became increasingly indistinguishable from → fiction films and today's "reality television" differs from the *cinema vérité* of the 1960s and early 1970s in that it no longer pretends that what the viewer sees would have occurred in the same view if no cameras had been present (→ Reality TV).

Yet at the level of technology the issue of realism still dominates. Computer games for instance are constantly praised for their level of realism (→ Video Games). The more they approach the look and the level of resolution of photography and film, the better. This development is also reflected in a new theory of visual realism that takes its clues from the linguistic theory of modality (Kress & Van Leeuwen 2006, 154ff.; → Linguistics). The question they ask is not "How real is this image?" but "*As* how real does it represent what it represents?" They list the indicators of this kind of "surface" realism (level of detail, use of color, rendering of lighting, and so on) and describe how these indicators are used in different types of images. In their theory, images that are in fact records of reality can therefore have "low modality" and images that are entirely constructed "high modality," just as → paintings may also be "photorealistic." In the heyday of photographic and filmic realism, the crucial questions were: Has the reality in front of the camera been tampered with or rearranged? Has anything been "set up" for the camera, or re-enacted? In the age of digital technology, the questions are: *As* how real is this represented? How real does it *look*?

TRUTH AND REALITY

As Hodge & Kress have said, "appeals to something like truth and reality are fundamental in the social construction of meaning" (1988, 121). People will always need clues as to whether they can use the information in images as a reliable guide for judgment and action. The "guarantee" that was formerly provided by the ability of film and photography (and video) to provide a "mechanical duplicate" of reality is of course still used in some areas, for instance in surveillance. But in other areas, for instance in the media, it is retreating, and new "guarantees" have perhaps not yet developed to the point that we can again judge the reliability of images with confidence. The idea that we can know reality through visual examination, which has been so fundamental in the age of empirical science, is increasing undermined, both by theorizing it out of existence and by the malleability of the new media and the new modes of image-making (→ Objectivity in Science; Objectivity in Reporting).

Raymond Williams is right of course: "There are many real forces – from inner feelings to underlying social and historical movements – which are either not accessible to ordinary observation or not at all represented in how things appear, so that a realism 'of the surface' can miss important realities" (1983, 260). But in representing such realities it is harder to exclude the subjectivities and interpretations that empirical observation and the "mechanical duplication of reality" claimed to exclude, and therefore harder to agree on what the facts are. For the time being, the Mathematician from Brecht's *Life of Galileo* appears to have, again, gained the upper hand – Galilei: "Perhaps Your Excellency would like to observe these impossible and unnecessary stars through this telescope?" Mathematician: "One might be inclined to answer that your instrument, showing something that logically cannot exist, can hardly be a very reliable instrument."

SEE ALSO: ▶ Animation ▶ Barthes, Roland ▶ Digital Imagery ▶ Discourse ▶ Fiction ▶ Film as Popular Culture ▶ Film Theory ▶ Hollywood ▶ Linguistics ▶ Magazine ▶ Objectivity in Reporting ▶ Objectivity in Science ▶ Painting ▶ Photojournalism ▶ Reality TV ▶ Semiotics ▶ Stock Photography ▶ Video Games

References and Suggested Readings

Arnheim, R. (1967). *Film as art*. Berkeley and Los Angeles: University of California Press. (Original work published 1933.)

Barthes, R. (1970). *Mythologies*. London: Paladin. (Original work published 1957).

Barthes, R (1984). *Camera Lucida*. London: Paladin. (Original work published 1980).

Bazin, A. (1971). *What is cinema?*, vol. II. Berkeley and Los Angeles: University of California Press. (Original work published 1958).

Hodge, R., & Kress, G. (1988). *Social semiotics*. Cambridge: Polity.

Kracauer, S. (1960). *Theory of film: The redemption of physical reality*. New York: Oxford University Press.

Kress, G., & Van Leeuwen, T. (2006). *Reading images: The grammar of visual design*, 2nd edn. London: Routledge.

MacCabe, C. (1974). Realism and the cinema: Notes on some Brechtian theses. *Screen*, 15(2), 7–27.

Ritchen, F. (1991). The end of photography as we have known it. In P. Wombell (ed.), *Photovideo: Photography in the age of the computer*. London: Rovers Oram.

Sontag, S. (1977). *On photography*. Harmondsworth: Penguin.

Wells, L. (ed.) (2000). *Photography: A critical introduction*. London: Routledge.

Williams, R. (1983). *Keywords: A vocabulary of culture and society*. London: Flamingo.

Reality and Media Reality

Michael Morgan

University of Massachusetts Amherst

Since the earliest days of mass media, researchers, social critics, politicians, and the general public have been concerned about the extent to which media representations reflect or deviate from "reality." Over the years, a great deal of research and public debate have revolved around the kinds of images of the world that are created and disseminated by media, and how they compare to the "real world" as revealed by official statistics or other objective indicators (→ Media and Perceptions of Reality).

REALITY AS SOCIAL REALITY

The first problem research in this tradition must confront is the question of what constitutes "reality," which is a topic of longstanding philosophical deliberation. Similarly complex is the question of how – and even whether – we can comprehend reality. Many theorists argue that humans construct what is perceived (and treated) as reality through social, cultural, and psychological mechanisms and structures. In a sense, this reflects Shakespeare's notion in *Hamlet* that "There is nothing either good or bad, but thinking makes it so" (act II, scene ii). Berger & Luckman (1966) argued that reality is knowable only as a mediated phenomenon, and that this is always ultimately a social process. Through intersubjectivity, we share a sense of "everyday reality" with others, but this is socially and culturally constructed (→ Constructivism).

There is thus a fundamental debate over whether media and reality can be meaningfully compared; if reality is unknowable, then attempting to compare it to media is a futile enterprise (Schulz 1976). Given that, some researchers, rather than comparing news media to some standard of "reality," have examined social, institutional, and psychological explanations for how journalists make decisions about what to cover (or not cover), and how (Donsbach 2004).

On the other hand, even if reality does not exist outside of human (cultural) construction and interpretation, and is constructed (rather than discovered) through human investigation and manipulation of symbol systems, many researchers still believe that the world represented in media can be compared to certain facts about life and society. From that perspective, the task is to determine the most useful and reliable indicators of how the media world deviates from observable structural parameters, or to compare mediated representations and unmediated experiences of the "same" event or phenomenon (Donsbach 2003).

For example, in a series of studies, Kepplinger compared the coverage of the oil supply in Germany with data on actual reserves (1979); media coverage of air and water quality with real-world biological measurements (1992); and the political activities of the German parliament with the coverage of politics by the emerging media in the postwar period (2002). Studies in this vein often show sharp disjunctures between "reality" and media coverage.

Media can also construct multiple (and often conflicting) realities. For example, comparative international analyses have shown how the US and "others" are presented by the press in different countries in the context of the "war on terror" and the war in Iraq (Nohrstedt & Ottosen 2005), or how media in Israel and Jordan each portrayed the peace process (Wolfsfeld et al. 2002).

On the other hand, the very "unreality" of media can also have a powerful impact on our sense of reality. As Fiske (1987, 21) argues, television is "an essentially realistic medium because of its ability to carry a socially convincing sense of the real." In Brazil, a telenovela can provide interpretive frames that shape how viewers perceive contemporary political events (Porto 2005). As Pearson (2005, 406) notes, Mexicans are fond of saying "Life is like a telenovela," to the point that "the line between *the* world and *a* world is often difficult to distinguish."

Although many scholars concerned with the correspondence of media to reality tend to focus on news, for purposes of this discussion, the distinctions among news, scripted programs, and "reality television" are not especially relevant (→ Reality TV). At a more general level, media themselves can constitute a way of knowing (Chesebro 1984). Media representations are "real" in the sense that dreams, stories, legends, and → rumors are real – they exist as phenomenological narratives and representations (→ Narrative News Story; Storytelling and Narration). That is, a statement about an event is not *the* event itself, but it *is* nonetheless itself *an* event.

Comparative measures of media and reality allow researchers to see how closely media stories reflect the facts of society and provide a basis for follow-up studies in different media, and/or in other societies, and/or over time. There is no expectation of any particular correspondence between reality and media reality; the key theoretical and empirical task is to illuminate specific and systematic discrepancies in order to better understand media institutions and to provide a basis for further inquiry into how media images inform our constructions of social reality.

Large portions of what we know (or think we know) are based not on first-hand experience, but on media representations of life, society, groups, and institutions. Researchers in the *cultivation analysis tradition*, for example, point out that most people have limited, if any, experience of places such as courtrooms, police stations, prisons, or hospitals, but that we have extensive and vivid images about what transpires in such locations, as well as about the sorts of people who work in them (→ Cultivation Theory; Cultivation Effects). Media provide us with a vast range of representations of things about which we have no direct knowledge, and these account for many of our "intersubjective" beliefs.

ANALYSES OF MEDIA CONTENT

Systematically coded, quantitative content analysis has been frequently employed to illuminate how media construct different aspects of reality (→ Content Analysis, Quantitative). An online bibliography of content analyses listed in *Communication Abstracts* between 1990 and 1997 features 428 separate entries (Neuendorf 2000).

These studies cover an immense range of topics. Studies comparing reality and media reality have examined issues as diverse as the portrayal of persons over 50 in television commercials; alcohol and tobacco use in daytime → soap operas; → news coverage of infectious diseases; women scientists in popular → magazines; sex and contraception in prime-time programs; art and artists on network television news; television's messages about the environment; the image of journalists on prime-time television; and hundreds more (→ Media Production and Content).

The number of areas in which the "real world" and the media world can be compared is virtually boundless. Entering the phrase "media portrayals of" into the Google → search engine will produce tens of thousands of hits, with links to a broad range of articles and sites that examine media representations. Researchers have explored the correspondence between reality and media reality in relation to dozens of wide-ranging topics, including girls and women (→ Women in the Media, Images of; Sex Role Stereotypes in the Media), ethnic minorities, weight loss surgery, bipolar disorder, terrorism, hate crimes, sex in the workplace, sports, suicide, poverty, aging, and many more.

Early Studies

In the 1930s and 1940s, many content analyses were conducted on then burgeoning forms of popular culture, including movies, radio, song lyrics, and magazines. The technique was applied to television almost immediately after it emerged. Early studies by Smythe (1954) and Head (1954) established basic parameters for examining television's representations of demography (gender, age, class, race, occupations) and violence that other studies would emulate for decades to come. Smythe (1954) analyzed a week of New York television programs in 1951, 1952, and 1953 and Head (1954) studied a 13-week sample of 1952 network programs. It is noteworthy that Smythe began his report with the caveat that "Reality is too elusive a concept to be pinned down definitively" (p. 143).

Both of these seminal studies found that the *demography of the television world* diverged sharply from the real world. On television, there were twice as many male characters as female characters, and males tended to be older than females. Adults were vastly over-represented in the television world; at that time, over half of the US population, but only a quarter of the TV population, was younger than 20 or older than 50.

Most TV characters were white Americans. "American Negroes" accounted for 2 percent of the TV world. Non-Americans were mostly English, Italian, and French; there were no Jews, Africans, Indians, or Asians other than Chinese, who represented 0.2 percent of the TV population (compared to 22 percent of the world's population at that time).

Violence on television occurred at a rate of 6.2 acts per hour (Smythe 1954), and was far more frequent on children's programs (22.4 acts per hour for "children's drama" and 36.6 per hour for "children's comedy drama"). Both studies found that the most common program type was crime drama (→ Violence as Media Content).

These early studies found that upper- and upper-middle-class *occupations* were greatly over-represented, as were certain occupations at the lower and higher ends of the employment scale. Over half of television characters, compared to about 10 percent of the US population, were professionals, managers, service workers, and private household workers. The latter reflect the dominance of upper-class characters, who typically (in the media reality of the times) had servants at home. Occupations such as operatives, craftsmen, and farmers were virtually invisible in the TV world, but they accounted for nearly 50 percent of the actual workforce. In terms of specific occupations, teachers were the "cleanest, kindest, and fairest," while scientists were "the least honest, least kind, and most unfair." Lawyers were the "dirtiest" of all occupational types (Smythe 1954, 155).

Dozens of studies conducted in the intervening decades have confirmed and replicated the portraits of the TV world drawn by Smythe and Head, especially with regard to gender, class, and violence. One notable exception is that the number of African-American characters has increased over time.

Cultural Indicators

Other studies have continued to focus on television, given the medium's dominant role as the most widely shared storyteller of contemporary culture. One of the most sustained investigations of media reality was → George Gerbner's Cultural Indicators Project. Starting in 1967 and continuing into the late 1990s and beyond, an annual week-long sample of prime-time and weekend daytime US network broadcast programming was systematically coded for hundreds of aspects of the world as portrayed on television and the people who live in that world. The project accumulated data on thousands of programs and tens of thousands of characters over more than 30 years.

Many of the project's findings echo those of Smythe and Head despite the passage of time. Although the percentage of women in the TV world did increase somewhat over the years (from 27 percent of the TV world in the 1970s to 35 percent in the 1990s), males continued to outnumber females. Daytime serials and game shows are more balanced, but females are especially under-represented in children's and news programs. Women are twice as likely to play the role of wife as men are to play the role of husband. Women age faster than do men, and are more likely to be shown as "evil" as they age. Older people appear far less on television than an accurate representation of reality would require. People over 65 account for over 12 percent of the actual US population but less than 3 percent in the television world, and older women are especially scarce on television.

Poor and working-class people continue to be nearly invisible on television, appearing in less than one-tenth of their actual population share, while middle-class characters are over-represented, as are professionals (doctors, lawyers, judges, business moguls, among others). White males are consistently over-represented. Villains and "bad guys" are disproportionately from the lower classes and more likely to be represented as people of color or mentally ill. The percentage of African-Americans in network prime-time programs has increased (but only among males), roughly matching their corresponding percentage in the US population (about 12 percent). Asian/Pacific characters account for less than half, and Latino characters are less than one-third, of their real proportion of the US population, while Native Americans are nearly invisible.

Media reality is violent. Between 60 and 70 percent of the network programs in each weekly sample contained *violence*, with 4 to 6 acts of violence per hour. The small year-to-year fluctuations in these data show no clear pattern or tendency, and taken as a whole the patterns seem highly consistent over the decades. Among major characters, 40 percent commit violence and 43 percent are victims. On children's programs, over 80 percent of males and two-thirds of females are involved in violence. Fewer than 2 percent of characters are shown as having any physical disability, and just over 1 percent are portrayed as mentally ill, but over 70 percent characters who are portrayed as mentally ill commit violence. (In reality, mental illness does not predict violence.)

Another large-scale study of television content in the US, the National Television Violence Study, examined 10,000 hours of programming between 1994 and 1997, and found many parallel patterns, with about 60 percent of prime-time programs featuring violence, with no major differences between broadcast and cable fare. Children's shows were even more likely to contain violence, with an average of 14 episodes of violence per hour, compared to six in other programs. Beyond the sheer frequency with which violence is encountered in the media world, the reality of media violence bears little resemblance to the reality of violence. Nearly six out of ten violent incidents do not depict any pain, and about half depict no harm; close to 90 percent show no blood or gore.

Other Patterns

Stories of *crime and violence* dominate news coverage as well as fictional programs, and the coverage does not match real-world crime patterns. Murder accounts for a disproportionate amount of both local and national news; murder suspects represent 0.13 percent of all those arrested, but 25 percent of all suspects in the news. From 1970 to 2000, almost a quarter of all stories were crime-related, although corporate crime typically receives relatively little attention.

The amount of crime coverage in television news does not reflect actual crime rates; editorial decisions and judgments of news value determine coverage, locally and nationally. Also, television network news over-represents white victims and under-represents African-American victims. African-Americans are more likely to be shown as perpetrators of crime and less likely than whites to be portrayed as police officers.

Researchers have pointed out many other significant discrepancies between the reality of crime statistics and television's depictions of crime and violence. Perpetrators of crime are apprehended and convicted far more often on television than in reality. Women on television are more likely than men to be victims of homicide (the reverse is true in reality), and women on television are three times as likely to commit crime as are women in reality. Homicides account for 79 percent of the crimes in the television world, compared to only 0.01 percent of actual crimes (Brown 2001). Conversely, nearly 70 percent of actual crimes are theft or robbery, but these are only 5 percent of the crimes portrayed on television.

ACCOUNTING FOR MEDIA REALITY

Many varied factors account for these patterns, but the central explanations are commercial and cultural. Even the earliest content analysts of television pointed to the *commercial context of programming* as the major explanation for the media reality they found ($\rightarrow$ Commercialization: Impact on Media Content). Commercial media content is designed to feel familiar, to reproduce formulas, and to gratify common audience expectations; a program that strays too far from the mold would be jarring to the audience. Commercial media have always thrived on imitating the successful; fear of losing the audience drives programming decisions. The patterns described here also have deep cultural and historical roots that predate modern media; current media are not the source of these images, but television in particular has mass-produced and mass-distributed them to an unprecedented degree ($\rightarrow$ Television: Social History). All eras and cultures have relied on stories to express and represent both reality and ideology, but never before has any society produced and consumed as many stories as we do now.

The stories and images of the media reflect popular ideological and commercial values, including the glorification of youth culture, particular intersections of race, class, and gender, the valorization of certain occupations, ritualistic struggles between good and evil, and so on. As with any cultural or industrial product, television stories reflect the values, priorities, and needs of those who produce them. This explains why so many aspects of media reality appear to have changed little in more than half a century of research. Slow, gradual changes in cultural reality do come to be reflected in media reality (and vice versa), but without meaningful change in the dominant institutional commercial structures, significant changes in media reality are unlikely to be seen.

SEE ALSO: ► Balance ► Bias in the News ► Commercialization: Impact on Media Content ► Construction of Reality through the News ► Constructivism ► Content Analysis, Quantitative ► Cultivation Effects ► Cultivation Theory ► Entertainment Content and Reality Perception ► Fantasy–Reality Distinction ► Gerbner, George ► Magazine ► Media and Perceptions of Reality ► Media Production and Content ► Narrative News Story ► News ► Realism ► Reality TV ► Rumor ► Search Engines ► Sex Role Stereotypes in the Media ► Soap Operas ► Storytelling and Narration ► Television: Social History ► Truth and Media Content ► Violence as Media Content ► Women in the Media, Images of

References and Suggested Readings

Berger, P. L., & Luckmann, T. (1966). *The social construction of reality: A treatise in the sociology of knowledge*. Garden City, NY: Doubleday.

Brown, N. J. (2001). A comparison of fictional television crime and crime index statistics. *Communication Research Reports*, 18(2), 192–199.

Center for Communication and Social Policy (1998). *National television violence study*, vol. III. Thousand Oaks, CA: Sage.

Chesebro, J. W. (1984). The media reality: Epistemological functions of media in cultural systems. *Critical Studies in Mass Communication*, 1, 111–130.

Donsbach, W. (2003). Objectivity in reporting. In D. H. Johnston (ed.), *Encyclopedia of international media and communication*. San Diego, CA: Academic Press, pp. 383–391.

Donsbach, W. (2004). Psychology of news decisions: Factors behind journalists' professional behavior. *Journalism*, 5(2), 131–157.

Fiske, J. (1987). *Television culture*. London: Routledge.

Gerbner, G. (1972). Violence and television drama: Trends and symbolic functions. In G. A. Comstock & E. Rubinstein (eds.), *Television and social behavior*, vol. 1, *Content and control*. Washington, DC: US Government Printing Office, pp. 28–187.

Gerbner, G. (1994). Women and minorities on TV: A study in casting and fate. *Media Development*, 41(2), 38–44.

Gerbner, G., Gross, L., Jackson-Beeck, M., Jeffries-Fox, S., & Signorielli, N. (1978). Cultural indicators: Violence profile no. 9. *Journal of Communication*, 28(3), 176–207.

Head, S. W. (1954). Content analysis of television drama programs. *Quarterly of Film, Radio, and Television*, 9(2), 175–194.

Kepplinger, H. M. (1979). Creating a crisis: German mass media and oil supply in 1973/74. *Public Opinion Quarterly*, 43, 285–296.

Kepplinger, H. M. (1992). Artificial horizons: How the press presented and how the population received technology in Germany from 1965–1986. In S. Rothman (ed.), *The mass media in liberal democratic society*. New York: Paragon House, pp. 147–176.

Kepplinger, H. M. (2002). Mediatization of politics: Theory and data. *Journal of Communication*, 52(4), 972–986.

Neuendorf, K. (2000). *The content analysis guidebook online*. At academic.csuohio.edu/kneuendorf/content/bibs/comabsbib.htm, accessed August 8, 2006.

Nohrstedt, S. A., & Ottosen, R. (eds.) (2005). *Global war: Local views: Media images of the Iraq war*. Gothenburg: Nordicom.

Pearson, R. C. (2005). Fact or fiction? Narrative and reality in the Mexican telenovela. *Television and New Media*, 6(4), 400–406.

Porto, M. P. (2005). Political controversies in Brazilian TV fiction: Viewers' interpretations of the telenovela *Terra Nostra*. *Television and New Media*, 6(4), 342–359.

Schulz, W. (1976). *Die Konstruktion von Realität in den Nachrichtenmedien: Analyse der aktuellen Berichterstattung*. Freiburg and Munich: Alber.

Signorielli, N. (1984). The demography of the television world. In G. Melischek, K. E. Rosengren, & J. Stappers (eds.), *Cultural indicators: An international symposium*. Vienna: Austrian Academy of Sciences Press, pp. 137–157.

Smythe, D. W. (1954). Reality as presented by television. *Public Opinion Quarterly*, 18, 143–156.

Wolfsfeld, G., Khouri, R., & Peri, Y. (2002). News about the other in Jordan and Israel: Does peace make a difference? *Political Communication*, 19, 189–210.

Reality TV

Mark Andrejevic
University of Iowa

Reality TV became an increasingly prevalent global entertainment → genre in the 1990s and early 2000s. The popularity of reality shows with producers is due in large part to the fact that they represent a cheap, flexible form of programming that is easily customizable to different audiences and lends itself to forms of interaction and participation associated with new communication technologies (→ Interactivity, Concept of; Digitization and Media Convergence). As an entertainment genre that relies on the unscripted interactions of people who are not professional actors, reality TV develops and discards formats at a rapid rate, parasitizing the permutations available in everyday life – including everything from romance to warfare – for raw material. Reality-based formats can be differentiated from → news and other informational or documentary programming insofar as their focus is not on bringing the public realm of politics into the private sphere, but on publicizing the private and intimate (→ Television News; Tabloidization). The emphasis is not on matters of public interest for the purpose of democratic participation, but on therapy and social experimentation for the purpose of diversion (→ Enjoyment/Entertainment Seeking; Media Democracy). Reality formats make their claim to reality on the basis of their lack of scriptwriters and professional actors, but they are, for the most part, highly edited portrayals of patently contrived situations.

The global success of the genre is based in part on the fact that since reality TV formats rely not on contrived scenarios and contests rather than on the talent of individual actors or scriptwriters, they are easily exportable. Successful formats rapidly replicate themselves from region to region, drawing cast members from local populations. Thus, for example, the *Big Brother* format, which isolates a group of strangers in a house where they compete to be the last one voted out by viewers, was pioneered in the Netherlands but became successful in local versions across Europe and in the Americas, Australia, and Asia, as well as in regional versions in Africa and the Middle East (→ Globalization of the Media; International Television).

The reality TV boom in the early twenty-first century was built around successful blockbuster formats like *Survivor* and *Big Brother*, but reality TV, broadly construed, has been around since the dawn of television. For example, *Candid Camera*, a prank format that films unsuspecting people placed in humorous situations, was a format that migrated from radio (where it was called *Candid Microphone*) to TV in 1948 (→ Television). Game shows and talk shows, both perennial entertainment formats, share with reality TV a reliance on at least partially unscripted interactions featuring non-actors. The development of lightweight cameras and recording equipment facilitated the migration of reality-based formats from the soundstage to the home, the street, the school, the workplace, and beyond (→ Documentary Film, History of). As this happened, the scope and reach of reality-based programming grew to encompass a broader range of human experience, some contrived, some based in the events of daily life, many a combination of both. At the same time, the expansion of cable TV increased the demand for cheap, quickly produced content – a demand that reality TV was uniquely positioned to fill thanks to its reliance on the inexpensive or free labor of non-professional actors and, in many cases, on found scenarios, sets, and even video (as in the case of shows like *America's Funniest Home Videos* – a format made possible by the advent of cheap, portable video cameras) (→ Cable Television).

As the number of channels and the amount of programming time devoted to reality formats have expanded, so too has the range of the formats that can be described as reality-based entertainment. Susan Murray and Laurie Ouellette (2004), for example, list *sub-genres* including, the "gamedoc" (in which cast members compete for prizes as their daily lives are recorded), the dating show, the makeover show, the "docusoap" (a reality TV version of the → soap opera in which the focus is on open-ended dramatic narratives), the talent contest, court and police shows, and celebrity formats that feature behind-the-scenes glimpses of the real lives of the rich and famous – or the formerly rich and famous. The proliferation of formats has led to two new TV award categories in the United States and a cable channel devoted entirely to reality programming.

Reality fare ranges from expensive and highly produced blockbusters like, in the United States, *Survivor* and *American Idol* to cheap, quick-hit dating formats and even compilations of video images captured by security cameras. All of these formats rely on the interactive promise that characterizes the era of media convergence: that non-professionals can contribute to the creation of media content. This participation comes either in the form of selected members of the viewing population crossing over to the other side of the TV screen, or in forms of direct participation fostered by interactive formats that invite people either to send in their own videos or to shape the outcome of the show by "voting," usually by phone, Internet, or text message (→ Convergence of Media Systems). Viewers tend to describe the appeal of reality TV in terms of the ease with which they can identify with the non-professional cast members and the suspense provided by the fact that outcomes are not scripted in advance.

The booming popularity of reality formats represents not just the rise of a genre, but also a shift in industry practice (→ Media Economics). Even the most successful formats are expected to make most of their money during their first run rather than in rerun syndication. The flexibility of the genre has disrupted the rhythm of the typical television season in the United States, allowing producers to switch shows mid-season and to debut new shows during summer prime-time slots, typically devoted to reruns. Moreover, reality formats lend themselves to the integration of content and advertising, as illustrated by successful formats like *American Idol* in the United States, which features prominent product placement deals, and doubles as a promotional vehicle for the singers, whose albums and concert tours generate additional revenues for producers.

SEE ALSO: ▶ Cable Television   ▶ Convergence of Media Systems   ▶ Digitization and Media Convergence   ▶ Documentary Film, History of   ▶ Enjoyment/Entertainment Seeking   ▶ Genre   ▶ Globalization of the Media   ▶ Interactivity, Concept of   ▶ International Television   ▶ Media Democracy   ▶ Media Economics   ▶ News   ▶ Soap Operas ▶ Tabloidization   ▶ Television   ▶ Television News

References and Suggested Readings

Andersen, R. (1995). *Consumer culture and TV programming*. Boulder, CO: Westview Press.

Andrejevic, M. (2001). The kinder, gentler gaze of Big Brother: Reality TV in the era of digital capitalism. *New Media and Society*, 4(2), 251–270.

Andrejevic, M. (2004). *Reality TV: The work of being watched*. Lanham, MD: Rowman and Littlefield.

Brenton, S., & Cohen, R. (2003). *Shooting people: Adventures in reality TV*. London: Verso.

Corner, J. (2002). Performing the real. *Television and New Media*, 3(3), 255–270.

Dovey, J. (2000). *Freakshow: First person media and factual television*. London: Pluto Press.

Fetveit, A. (1994). Reality TV in the digital era. *Media, Culture, and Society*, 21, 787–804.

Hill, A. (2005). *Reality TV: Audiences and popular factual television*. London and New York: Routledge.

Hill, A., & Palmer, G. (2002). Big Brother. *Television and New Media*, special issue, 3(3).

Holmes, S., & Jermyn, D. (eds.) (2004). *Understanding reality television*. London and New York: Routledge.

Kilborn, R. (1994). "How real can you get?" Recent developments in "reality" television. *European Journal of Communication*, 9, 421–439.

Kilborn, R. (2003). *Staging the real: Factual TV programming in the age of Big Brother*. Manchester: Manchester University Press.

Murray, S., & Ouellette, L. (eds.) (2004). *Reality TV: Remaking television culture*. New York: New York University Press.

Smith, M. J., & Wood, A. F. (eds.) (2003). *Survivor lessons: Essays on communication and reality television*. Jefferson, NC: McFarland.

Reasoned Action, Theory of

Martin Fishbein

University of Pennsylvania

The theory of reasoned action (TRA) is a general theory of behavior that was first introduced in 1967 by Martin Fishbein, and was extended by Fishbein and Icek Ajzen (e.g., Fishbein & Ajzen 1975; Ajzen & Fishbein 1980). Developed largely in response to the repeated failure of traditional → attitude measures to predict specific behaviors, the theory began with the premise that the simplest and most efficient way to predict a given behavior was to ask a person whether he or she was or was not going to perform that behavior. Thus, according to the theory, performance or non-performance of a given behavior is primarily determined by the strength of a person's intention to perform (or to not perform) that behavior, where intention is defined as the subjective likelihood that one will perform (or try to perform) the behavior in question (→ Attitude-Behavior Consistency; Planned Behavior, Theory of).

THEORY

Although the theory focuses upon behavioral intentions (e.g., to jog 20 minutes every day), it can also *predict and explain intentions to engage in categories of behavior* (e.g., to exercise) or to reach certain goals (e.g., to lose weight). According to the theory, however, unlike the strong relation between intentions to engage in a given behavior and behavioral performance, there is no necessary relation between intentions to engage in a behavioral category and whether one does (or does not) perform any single behavior in that category or between intentions to reach a specific goal and goal attainment. Thus, although the theory can predict and explain any intention, the TRA recognizes that only intentions to engage in volitionally controlled behaviors will consistently lead to accurate behavioral predictions.

The intention (I) to perform a given behavior (B) is, in turn, viewed as a *function of two basic factors*: the person's attitude toward performing the behavior (i.e., one's overall positive or negative feeling about personally performing the behavior – Ab) and/or the person's subjective norm concerning his or her performance of the behavior (i.e., the person's perception that his or her important others think that he or she should [or should not] perform the behavior in question – SN). Algebraically, this can be expressed as: $B \sim I = w_1Ab + w_2SN$, where w_1 and w_2 are weights indicating the relative importance of attitudes and subjective norms as determinants of intention. It is important to recognize that the relative importance of these two psychosocial variables as determinants of intention will depend upon both the behavior and the population being considered. Thus, for example, one behavior may be primarily determined by attitudinal considerations while another may be primarily influenced by perceived norms. Similarly, a behavior that is attitudinally driven in one population or culture may be normatively driven in another. While some behaviors may be entirely under attitudinal control (i.e., w_2 may be zero) others may be entirely under normative control (i.e., w_1 may be zero).

The theory also considers the *determinants of attitudes and subjective norms*. On the basis of Fishbein's earlier (1963) → expectancy value model, attitudes are viewed as a function of behavioral beliefs and their evaluative aspects. Algebraically: $Ab = f(\Sigma b_i e_i)$, where Ab = the attitude toward performing the behavior, b_i = belief that performing the behavior will lead to outcome "i" and e_i = the evaluation of outcome "i." Somewhat similarly, subjective norms are viewed as a function of normative beliefs and motivations to comply. Algebraically: $SN = f(\Sigma Nb_i Mc_i)$, where SN = the subjective norm, Nb_i = the normative belief that referent "i" thinks one should (or should not) perform the behavior and Mc_i = the motivation to comply, in general, with referent "i".

Generally speaking, the more one believes that performing a given behavior will lead to positive outcomes and/or will prevent negative outcomes, the more favorable will be one's attitude toward performing that behavior. Similarly, the more one believes that specific referents (i.e., individuals or groups) think that one should (or should not) perform the behavior, and the more one is motivated to comply with those referents, the stronger will be the perceived pressure (i.e., the subjective norm) to perform (or to not perform) that behavior.

It is at the level of behavioral and normative beliefs that the *substantive uniqueness of each behavior* comes into play. Even if two behaviors appear quite similar, the outcomes (or consequences) of, for example, buying a Ford may be very different from those associated with buying a Toyota. Similarly, a specific referent's support or opposition to my always using a condom for vaginal sex with my main partner may be very different from his or her support or opposition to my always using a condom for vaginal sex with an occasional partner. According to the theory, these specific behavioral and normative beliefs about the behavior in question must be identified in order to fully understand the determinants of that behavior. Although an investigator can sit in her or his office and develop measures of attitudes and subjective norms, she or he cannot tell you what a given population (or a given person) believes about performing a given behavior. Thus one must go to members of that population to identify salient behavioral and normative beliefs. To put this somewhat differently, according to the theory, one must understand the behavior from the perspective of the population one is considering.

Finally, the TRA also considers the role played by more traditional demographic, economic, personality, attitudinal, and other individual difference variables, such as perceived risk (→ Risk Perceptions) or → sensation seeking. According to the model, these types of variables primarily play an indirect role in influencing behavior. That is, these "distal" or "background" factors may or may not influence the behavioral or normative beliefs underlying attitudes and norms. Thus, for example, while men and women may hold different beliefs about performing some behaviors, they may hold very similar beliefs with respect to others. Similarly rich and poor, old and young, those from developing and developed countries, those with favorable and unfavorable attitudes toward religion, and those who have or who have not used drugs may hold different attitudinal and normative beliefs with respect to one behavior but may hold similar beliefs with respect to another. Thus, according to the theory, there is no necessary relation between these "distal" or "background" variables and any given behavior. Nevertheless, distal variables such as cultural and personality differences and differences in a wide range of values may influence underlying beliefs, and when they do so, they are likely to also be associated with the behavior in question.

APPLICATION OF THE THEORY

In order to apply the TRA, one must first *identify the behavior* (or behaviors) that one wishes to understand, predict, change, or reinforce. Unfortunately, this is not as simple or straightforward as is often assumed. As indicated above, it is important to distinguish between behaviors, behavioral categories, and goals. Moreover, from the perspective of the TRA, the definition of a behavior involves several elements: an action (joining, using, buying, selling), the target (the navy, condoms, a Ford), and the context (after graduating high school, for vaginal sex with an occasional partner).

Clearly, a change in any one of the elements changes the behavior under consideration. Thus, for example, as indicated above, joining the navy is a different behavior than is joining the Army (a change in target). Similarly, using a condom for vaginal sex with an occasional partner is a different behavior than is using a condom for vaginal sex with one's spouse (a change in context). Moreover, in predicting and assessing behavior, it is also important to include an additional element – time. For example, an assessment of whether one bought a car in the past three months is different from an assessment of whether one bought a car in the past two years. Consistent with this, the intention to buy a car in the next three months is very different from the intention to buy a car in the next two years.

The second step in applying the TRA is to *identify the specific population* to be considered. As indicated above, for any given behavior, both the relative importance of attitudes and norms as determinants of intention (and/or behavior) and the substantive content of the behavioral and normative beliefs underlying these determinants may also vary as a function of the population under consideration. Thus, it is imperative to define the population (or populations) to be considered.

Once one or more behaviors and target populations have been identified, the TRA can be used to understand why some members of a target population are performing the behavior and others are not. That is, by obtaining measures of each of the central variables in the theory (i.e., beliefs, attitudes, norms, intentions, and behavior), one can determine whether a given behavior (e.g., getting a mammogram) is not being performed because people have not formed intentions to get a mammogram or because they are unable to act on their intentions. Similarly, one can determine, for the population under consideration, whether intention is influenced primarily by attitudes or norms. Finally, one can identify the specific behavioral or normative beliefs that discriminate between those who do or do not (intend to) perform the behavior.

For accurate prediction and full understanding of a given behavior, measures of beliefs, attitudes, norms, and intention must all correspond exactly to the behavior to be predicted. That is, each of the measures should contain the same four elements as the behavior. This is known as the *principle of correspondence or compatibility*, and is central to the TRA. This does not mean, however, that one must always measure behaviors and intentions at a specific level of all four behavioral elements. If one is interested in predicting whether one will or will not get a mammogram in the next six months, beliefs, attitudes, norms, and intentions must all be assessed with respect to "my getting a mammogram in the next six months." However, if one is interested in predicting whether one will or will not get a mammogram at Women's Hospital in the next six months, beliefs, attitudes, norms, and intentions must all be assessed with respect to "my getting a mammogram at Women's Hospital the next six months."

In 1991, Ajzen introduced the theory of planned behavior, which extended the TRA by adding the concept of perceived behavioral control as a predictor of both intention and behavior. And in 2000, Fishbein introduced the *integrative model*, which extended the theory of planned behavior by expanding the normative component to include descriptive as well as injunctive norms, and by explicitly acknowledging the role of skills and abilities and facilitating factors as moderators of the intention–behavior relationship. The reasoned action approach has been used successfully to predict and/or explain a wide variety of behaviors, including such things as wearing safety helmets, smoking marijuana, voting, eating at fast food restaurants, smoking cigarettes, drinking alcohol, entering an alcohol treatment program, using birth control pills, breast feeding, donating blood, wearing seat belts, condom use, church attendance, and engaging in premarital sexual behavior (see, e.g., Ajzen et al. 2007; Van den Putte 1993).

SEE ALSO: ▶ Attitude-Behavior Consistency ▶ Attitudes ▶ Expectancy Value Model ▶ Planned Behavior, Theory of ▶ Risk Perceptions ▶ Sensation Seeking ▶ Social Norms

References and Suggested Readings

Ajzen, I. (1991). The theory of planned behavior. *Organizational Behavior and Human Decision Processes*, 50(2), 179–211.

Ajzen, I., & Fishbein, M. (1980). *Understanding attitudes and predicting social behavior*. Englewood Cliffs, NJ: Prentice Hall.

Ajzen, I., Albarracin, D., & Hornik, R. (eds.) (2007). *Prediction and change of health behavior: Applying the reasoned action approach*. Mahwah, NJ: Lawrence Erlbaum.

Fishbein, M. (1963). An investigation of the relationships between beliefs about an object and the attitude toward that object. *Human Relations*, 16, 233–240.

Fishbein, M. (1967). Attitude and the prediction of behavior. In M. Fishbein (ed.), *Readings in attitude theory and measurement*. New York: John Wiley, pp. 477–492.

Fishbein, M. (2000). The role of theory in HIV prevention. *AIDS Care*, 12(3), 273–278.

Fishbein, M., & Ajzen, I. (1975). *Belief, attitude, intention and behavior: An introduction to theory and research*. Boston: Addison-Wesley.

Van den Putte, B. (1993). On the theory of reasoned action. Unpublished doctoral dissertation. University of Amsterdam.

Reciprocal Effects

Hans Mathias Kepplinger
Johannes Gutenberg University of Mainz

Originally, the term "reciprocal effects" was used by Kurt Lang and Gladys Engel Lang (1953) to describe the behavior of people in front of TV cameras. Here it is used in a broader sense. It denotes all the effects of the mass media on actual and potential subjects of media coverage (→ Media Effects; Media Effects: Direct and Indirect Effects). Included are the effects of media coverage that mentions subjects personally or explicitly deals with individuals and topics closely related to them. Subjects are distinguished from bystanders who are not directly or indirectly addressed by media coverage. With respect to the time when reciprocal effects occur, anticipatory, immediate, and corrective reactions are distinguished. *Anticipatory reactions* intend to avoid or seek to bring about media coverage. *Immediate reactions* are instantaneous consequences of interactions between media people (reporters, camera men, etc.) and the protagonists of media reports. *Corrective reactions* are produced by existing news coverage. When we look at reciprocal effects, there is no given distinction between cause and effect, because every element can be seen as both cause and effect. For example, a report might be seen as an effect of a subject's prior behavior while also being the cause of his subsequent emotions. Thus, the traditionally linear model of media effects becomes a *feedback* model of media relations: the personality or behavior of subjects stimulates media reports that, in turn, directly influence the cognitions, appraisals, emotions, and behavior of subjects (→ Linear and Nonlinear Models of Causal Analysis).

CAUSES AND TYPES OF EFFECTS

We can distinguish seven different causes and types of reciprocal effects.

(1) *Awareness of reports:* because the subjects of news reports are highly involved in the issue at hand, they are motivated to hear and see considerably more reports than

are bystanders (→ Exposure to Communication Content; Involvement with Media Content). As a result, subjects are subjected to an unusually strong dose of media information.

(2) *Appraisals of reports:* according to attribution theory (→ Attribution Processes), actors tend to attribute their misbehavior to circumstances whereas observers tend to attribute it to the actors' personality (Jones & Nisbett 1972). Journalists are professional observers; therefore they tend to attribute behavior to the actors' personality and describe it correspondingly. As a consequence, the subjects of negative news reports (→ Negativity) often see themselves as victims of circumstances and believe they would be mis-represented if reported as independent actors who are fully responsible for their mistakes. Because most subjects are not aware of perception differences between actors and observers, they tend to blame reporters for unfair coverage, which in turn might be perceived by reporters and editors as unfair criticism.

(3) *Assumptions about effect upon others:* most people attribute stronger negative effects of media messages to others than to themselves (→ Third-Person Effects). People who are highly involved in an issue tend to estimate the effect of news reports as stronger than neutral people do. Because the subjects of news reports are more involved in the issues reported, are more aware of the coverage, and have more background information than bystanders, they overestimate the effect of media on others even more.

(4) *Estimating public opinion:* the subjects of media reports can use four types of data to estimate the reports' effect on the population in general – opinion polls, media reports, expert analysis, and their own impressions drawn from discussions with people (→ Public Opinion, Media Effects on; Media Campaigns and Perceptions of Reality). Opinion polls are not always at hand, for example, in the immediate outbreak of a crisis (→ Crisis Communication; Public Opinion Polling). Therefore, subjects might draw their own conclusions about public opinion from media reports, partly by assuming certain effects of the mass media on the general population, partly by assuming that media coverage represents or reflects public opinion. Subjects who generally mistrust the validity of opinion polls, those without regular access to opinion polls, and those facing the beginning of a crisis rely first and foremost on media coverage to estimate public opinion (Herbst 1998).

(5) *Observing behavioral changes:* people who are associated with the subjects of media reports are generally more acutely aware of these reports than are average bystanders, in part because these people know the individuals depicted but also because usually they react on a personal level to the reports. Therefore, media reports have a remarkable influence upon the cognitions, appraisals, and behavior of those associated with the subjects. In the case of negative reports, these people may question the accuracy of coverage or turn away from the subjects. In the case of positive reporting, these people may applaud it and turn their attention more closely to the subjects. The subjects of reports will observe these behavioral changes. In addition, they will attribute such changes to themselves by misinterpreting them. For example, subjects will interpret an unusually short greeting, actually caused by time pressure, as an attempt to avoid them.

(6) *Emotions evoked by reports:* emotions are reactions to psychological arousal (→ Excitation and Arousal) and → cognition. Cognitions include the perceived causes of

positive and negative events. Negative events that are perceived as being caused by given circumstances stimulate sadness, while the same events perceived as being caused by individual behavior stimulate anger (Nerb & Spada 2001). Because the subjects of negative reports attribute their depiction to the personal motives and agendas of journalists and editors, the subjects develop feelings of anger or similar emotions, such as annoyance. Because the subjects know that they cannot rectify every reader's, listener's, or viewer's image of them, they develop feelings of powerlessness. In contrast, positive reports will stimulate strong positive emotions such as happiness, hope, and pride.

(7) *Interactions of emotions and observations:* generally, people develop consistent emotions and observations (→ Appraisal Theory). For example, if the subjects of media reports believe others are avoiding them, they will feel abandoned. Subjects' observations might very well reflect real changes in the behavior of people around them. It might also be that the subjects are imagining behavioral changes. Emotions and perceived behavioral changes (real or attributed) reinforce each other, which, in turn, leads to the creation of an insular emotional state where subjects stay stuck in emotional patterns and thereby modify their own behavior (Kepplinger & Glaab 2005).

TIME OF REACTIONS

Concerning the time and pattern of reaction to media reports, we can distinguish between four types.

Anticipatory reactions are due to the fact that the increasing availability of media information to the general public has changed the balance of power between politicians and political institutions on the one hand, and journalists on the other (→ Media Logic; Mediatization of Politics). Because of the increasing dependency of politicians, business people, artists, etc. on media coverage, they adapt their public behavior to the needs of the media, even when this is counter-productive to their original mission. Here, two strategies have to be distinguished – agenda building to establish favorable coverage and policy cutting to avoid unfavorable coverage (→ Agenda Building). Expecting favorable coverage, these people frame information given to the media according to their policy (Linsky 1986; Hutcheson et al. 2004), they shape events to fit media coverage, and they stage events that would not occur if it wasn't for the expectation of media coverage (→ Media Events and Pseudo-Events). Fearing unfavorable media coverage, politicians, business people, and other public actors avoid making unpopular decisions (→ Symbolic Politics).

Immediate reactions occur when decision-makers and journalists interact and exert a mutual influence. Professionals are aware of this influence and behave accordingly. Decision-makers and journalists play roles according to social expectations. Furthermore, the personal and ideological distance between journalists and subjects also has an impact on their verbal and nonverbal behavior (→ Nonverbal Signals, Effects of). It is relatively strong in more polarized societies and in contexts where the media is more partisan. The subjects of TV coverage are also influenced by the presence of cameras, lights, and staff. Some are stimulated by these circumstances; others feel insecure or even frightened. The ability to handle this medium effectively has an impact on career prospects (→ Public Relations Roles).

Corrective reactions are behavioral changes due to the anticipation of the positive or negative effects of media coverage on others. There are two major reasons why subjects respond to media reports. Because subjects are so aware of positive reports and sensitive to issues related to themselves, they are strongly influenced by those reports. They therefore also tend to overestimate the impact of reports upon the wider public more than bystanders do. In the aftermath of positive reports, their subjects will seek to take action to capitalize on their popularity and, for example, will make certain decisions that they know will benefit from added media coverage. These decisions might have consequences that otherwise would not have occurred. In the aftermath of negative reports, the situation is more complex ($\rightarrow$ Scandalization in the News). Because subjects are convinced that their actions have been misrepresented, they are confronted with a critical choice. They can do nothing, hoping the coverage will end quickly; or they can react in order to minimize the anticipated effects on the general public and their customers and/ or clients. Both choices are risky because both can ultimately stimulate more negative coverage than otherwise.

Finally, *feedback loops* can occur. Thus far, journalists' behavior and news reports have been interpreted as causes, and the behavior of politicians and other decision-makers as effects. This is insufficient for three reasons. First, the behavior of subjects can also be regarded as the cause of journalists' behavior and of news reports. Second, subjects' expectations of the motives, goals, and behavior of journalists, as well as journalists' expectations of the motives, goals, and behavior of subjects, can influence the subjects' own behavior, which in turn can influence the journalists' behavior. For example, preparing for an interview, politicians as well as journalists may expect a sharp controversy, which from the outset will influence their behavior toward each other. To put this more formally: the expectations and behavior of each actor influence the other and immediately interact with the expectations and behavior of the interlocutor. Third, the direct and indirect effects of news reports can themselves cause new news reports. Again, to put this more formally: the effects of former media coverage on subjects' behavior can cause subsequent media coverage dealing with the behavior stimulated (Fishman 1980) or with the former media coverage.

SEE ALSO: ▶ Agenda Building ▶ Appraisal Theory ▶ Attribution Processes ▶ Cognition ▶ Crisis Communication ▶ Excitation and Arousal ▶ Exposure to Communication Content ▶ Involvement with Media Content ▶ Linear and Nonlinear Models of Causal Analysis ▶ Media Campaigns and Perceptions of Reality ▶ Media Effects ▶ Media Effects: Direct and Indirect Effects ▶ Media Events and Pseudo-Events ▶ Media Logic ▶ Media as Political Actors ▶ Mediatization of Politics ▶ Negativity ▶ Nonverbal Signals, Effects of ▶ Public Opinion, Media Effects on ▶ Public Opinion Polling ▶ Public Relations Roles ▶ Scandalization in the News ▶ Social Capital, Media Effects on ▶ Symbolic Politics ▶ Third-Person Effects

References and Suggested Readings

Bruschke, J., & Loges, W. E. (1999). Relationship between pretrial publicity and trial outcomes. *Journal of Communication*, 49, 104–120.

Fishman, M. (1980). *Manufacturing the news*. Austin, TX: University of Texas.

Herbst, S. (1998). *Reading public opinion: How political actors view the democratic process*. Chicago: University of Chicago Press.

Hutcheson, J., Domke, D., Billeaudeaux, A., & Garland, P. (2004). U.S. national identity, political elites, and patriotic press following September 11. *Political Communication*, 21, 27–50.

Jones, E. E., & Nisbett, R. E. (1972). The actor and the observer: Divergent perceptions of causes of behavior. In E. E. Jones , D. E. Kanouse, H. H. Kelley, R. E. Nisbett, S. Valins, & B. Weiner (eds.), *Attribution: Perceiving the causes of behaviour*. Morristown, NJ: General Learning Press, pp. 79–94.

Kepplinger, H. M. (2007). Reciprocal effects. Toward a theory of mass media effects on decision makers. *Harvard International Journal of Press Politics*, 12, 3–23.

Kepplinger, H. M., & Glaab, S. (2005). Reziproke Effekte: Folgen ungewollter Öffentlichkeit [Reciprocal effects: Consequences of undesired publicity]. In A. Beater & S. Habermeier (eds.), *Verletzungen von Persönlichkeitsrechten durch die Medien* [Violations of privacy by the mass media]. Tübingen: Mohr Siebeck, pp. 117–137.

Lang, K., & Lang, G. (1953). The unique perspective of television and its effect: A pilot study. *American Sociological Review*, 18, 3–12.

Linsky, M. (1986). *Impact: How the press affects federal policymaking*. New York: W. W. Norton.

Nerb, J., & Spada, H. (2001). Evaluation of environmental problems: A coherence model of cognition and emotion. *Cognition and Emotion*, 15, 521–555.

Reciprocity and Compensation in Interaction

Miles L. Patterson

University of Missouri-St. Louis

Social interaction is a complex, yet often subtle, process through which humans transmit information, pursue social goals, and initiate and sustain relationships. Even in the current digital age with its various forms of remote communication, face-to-face interaction is still critical for our social and emotional well-being. One way of characterizing the give-and-take between people in interactions is in terms of the relative changes partners make in their behavior over time; specifically, compensation and reciprocation. Compensation refers to a pattern of balancing or controlling the partner's behavioral intimacy by moving in the opposite direction. Thus, too much intimacy by one person precipitates avoidance and too little intimacy precipitates approach. In contrast, when a partner's behavioral intimacy is matched or intensified, the resulting pattern is described as reciprocation. On the verbal side of interactions, reciprocation or matching of self-disclosure seems to be the dominant pattern. Although verbal communication is obviously important, nonverbal communication typically has a greater impact than the verbal on social judgments, interpersonal attitudes, and influence (Patterson 2002). In fact, most of the research and theory on compensation and reciprocation has focused on nonverbal communication. Consequently, this discussion examines the evolution of our understanding of compensation and reciprocation in nonverbal communication (→ Nonverbal Signals, Effects of).

REACTIVE ADJUSTMENTS IN INTERACTION

How and why do people make behavioral adjustments relative to their partners in the course of interaction? The systematic pursuit of this question can be traced back to Argyle and Dean's (1965) *equilibrium theory*. Argyle and Dean (1965) proposed that a small set of behaviors, including distance, gaze, smiling, and verbal intimacy, was critical in reflecting the behavioral intimacy or involvement in an interaction. Thus, as the underlying intimacy in a relationship increased, e.g., from initial strangers to acquaintances to good friends or lovers, the comfortable level of involvement also increased. Furthermore, equilibrium theory posited that interaction partners were motivated to maintain a comfortable or appropriate level of involvement over the course of an interaction. When there was a deviation from the appropriate level of involvement, reactive adjustments were predicted that would help to restore equilibrium to a comfortable level.

For example, if Bill approached a little too close to Mary and exceeded her comfort level, she might reduce the overall level of involvement by decreasing her gaze and reducing her smiling. Thus, her reactive adjustment might help to restore equilibrium in their behavioral involvement. In other words, the reduction in gaze and smiling compensated for the too close approach. Compensation might also occur when there was too little involvement for one or both partners. For example, if the seating arrangement required two good friends to sit too far apart, they might compensate for this increased distance by substantially increasing gaze toward one another. Early research on equilibrium theory not only provided strong support for the predicted compensatory adjustments of equilibrium theory, but also expanded the set of relevant behaviors to include touch, body orientation, posture, and body lean (Patterson 1973). That is, compensation might occur in any combination of one or more of these behaviors.

The results of a few studies, however, directly contradicted the predictions of equilibrium theory. Instead of compensating for increased involvement, individuals increased, or reciprocated, the higher involvement of a partner. In hindsight, it is likely that the dominant pattern of compensation found in the research was a product of the relationships (i.e., the lack of them) between the interactants and the types of experimental settings sampled. Typically this research employed confederates initiating a spatial intrusion, high level of gaze, or a touch on their unsuspecting partners in settings where their partners had little control over their immediate environments. Given these circumstances, it is not surprising that most people compensated by leaving the setting, turning away, or avoiding gaze in response to the confederate's increased involvement. This kind of pattern might not be expected between good friends interacting at home or at work. In fact, reciprocation might be more common in interactions between friends, family members, or lovers. Consequently, explaining both compensation and reciprocation required something more than equilibrium theory.

AROUSAL THEORIES

Early research demonstrated that recipients of high levels of nonverbal involvement, such as a close approach and touch, often experienced increased arousal (e.g., McBride et al.

1965; → Proxemics). Thus, arousal seemed a likely mediator directing nonverbal adjustments. For example, the *arousal-labeling theory* proposed that when the partner's change of nonverbal behavior was sufficient to produce arousal, an emotion-labeling or self-attribution process was initiated (Patterson 1976). Next, if the resulting emotional state was positive (e.g., liking, love, comfort), then the individual would reciprocate the partner's increased involvement. For example, a close approach, smile, and touch from a good friend would increase arousal, be labeled as liking, and lead to reciprocating the friend's high involvement. This might take the form of smiling back at the friend and increasing gaze. If similar behavior was initiated unexpectedly by a stranger, arousal would also be increased, but be labeled as discomfort and lead to compensation. Thus, the recipient might turn away and avoid gaze in attempting to re-establish some degree of comfort and control in the setting.

From the mid-1970s to the mid-1980s, several other theories also enlisted arousal as a central process directing both compensation and reciprocation across a wide range of relationships (see Burgoon et al. 1995 for a review). In spite of important differences among the theories, common to all of them was the determining role of affective state in directing reactive adjustments, i.e., negative states precipitated compensation and positive states precipitated reciprocation.

Arousal theories improved on equilibrium theory by offering explanations of both compensation and reciprocation. Nevertheless, in terms of explaining the dynamic give-and-take of interactions, they also shared two basic *limitations*. First, the theories were all reactive in nature. That is, they were limited in explaining B's reaction to A's change in behavior and could not address the reasons behind A's behavior in the first place. Furthermore, some interactions are more or less scripted and do not proceed in a simple, reactive fashion. For example, in initiating a greeting, interactants are not simply reacting to one another, but are following a common script for greetings. A second limitation was that the arousal theories were all affect driven. That is, according to the arousal theories, a person's affective reaction to a partner's behavior necessarily determined the behavioral adjustment. Specifically, positive emotional reactions (liking, love, comfort) precipitated reciprocation, whereas negative emotional reactions (anxiety, fear, discomfort) precipitated compensation. Although this certainly happens at times, there are many occasions when we cannot let our immediate emotional reactions determine our behavior. For example, if the boss approaches closely and puts a hand on your shoulder as she asks you to take on another responsibility, you are not likely to pull away (compensation), even though your affective response may be negative.

FUNCTIONAL APPROACH

The important limitations of arousal-based theories suggested that a different approach was needed to explain behavioral adjustments and, more generally, the initiation and development of interactions. The functional model provided such a perspective by focusing on the functions of interactions (Patterson 1983). Specifically, the functional model posited that individuals are not only reactive in relating to their partners, but also proactive in initiating goal-oriented behavior. Thus, patterns of compensation or reciprocation may be initiated independent of a person's underlying affective reaction to a partner. Nevertheless, affect in the functional model still provides a critical role in the initiation of, and reaction to, patterns of nonverbal behavior as a kind of "default" setting in interactions.

The presence of particular goals, however, such as gaining compliance from another person or deceiving someone, can override the role of affect in determining nonverbal behavior. The proactive manifestation of compensation and reciprocation may be seen in interaction strategies precipitated by interpersonal expectancies (Ickes et al. 1982). For example, in the case of a self-fulfilling prophecy, specific expectancies about a partner may result in reciprocating the behavior *anticipated* from the partner. Thus, a positive expectancy about a partner increases the likelihood that an actor will initiate the open and friendly behavior expected of the partner. In other words, the actor's expectation precipitates a behavioral strategy of reciprocation and facilitates the expected behavior from the partner; i.e., a self-fulfilling prophecy. Sometimes, interpersonal expectancies can precipitate a contrasting strategy of compensation. That is, the actor tries to overcome the partner's anticipated behavior by initiating an opposing (or compensatory) strategy. Thus, if it is important and if the partner's reactions seem malleable, an actor might be more open and friendly to a presumably cold, unfriendly person. That is, the actor compensates for the unfriendly expectancy by behaving in warmer and friendlier fashion in attempting to alter the expected outcome.

CURRENT TRENDS

Although the study of interactive behavior is still a major focus of research, in recent years there has been less attention paid to the specific contrast between compensation and reciprocation. Instead, there is greater interest in the *social utility of behavioral adjustments*, consistent with both the functional approach and an evolutionary perspective on interactive behavior. For example, research indicates that interpersonal rapport is reflected in partners mutually displaying positive expressions, visual attention, and behavioral coordination with one another (Tickle-Degnen 2006). Related research on behavioral mimicry also shows that the automatic copying of a partner's movements and expressions increases liking and social bonds (Lakin et al. 2003). In fact, both rapport and mimicry are special cases of reciprocation.

The current emphasis on reciprocation in the form of behavioral rapport and mimicry provides additional evidence for the pragmatic value of behavioral adjustments. In interactions with friends, matching and mimicry serve to increase liking and foster stronger relationships. In turn, the increased attachment is adaptive because it facilitates subsequent cooperation and interdependence. Although this form of reciprocation typically happens automatically and outside of awareness, strategically mimicking a partner's behavior can also facilitate increased liking and influence. For example, individuals who are ostracized or otherwise in need of social support are also more likely to initiate mimicry with their more secure partners (Lakin et al. 2003). Compensation is, however, also adaptive in managing the discomfort of a partner's inappropriate involvement and in trying to modify a partner's attitudes and behavior. Thus, these complementary patterns of behavioral adjustment are important, but often subtle, elements in navigating our social environments and managing our relationships with others.

SEE ALSO: ▶ Disclosure in Interpersonal Communication   ▶ Eye Behavior   ▶ Facial Expressions   ▶ Gaze in Interaction   ▶ Gestures and Kinesics   ▶ Initial Interaction   ▶ Interaction Adaptation Theory   ▶ Interpersonal Communication   ▶ Nonverbal Signals, Effects of ▶ Proxemics

References and Suggested Readings

Argyle, M., & Dean, J. (1965). Eye-contact, distance, and affiliation. *Sociometry*, 28, 289–304.

Burgoon, J. K., Stern, L. A., & Dillman, L. (1995). *Interpersonal adaptation: Dyadic adaptation patterns*. Cambridge: Cambridge University Press.

Ickes, W., Patterson, M. L., Rajecki, D. W., & Tanford, S. (1982). Behavioral and cognitive consequences to reciprocal versus compensatory responses to preinteraction expectancies. *Social Cognition*, 1, 160–190.

Lakin, J. L., Jeffris, V. E., Cheng, C. M., & Chartrand, T. L. (2003). The chameleon effect as social glue: Evidence for the evolutionary significance of nonconscious mimicry. *Journal of Nonverbal Behavior*, 27, 145–162.

McBride, G., King, M. C., & James, J. W. (1965). Social proximity effects of galvanic skin responses in adult humans. *Journal of Psychology*, 61, 153–157.

Patterson, M. L. (1973). Compensation in nonverbal immediacy behaviors: A review. *Sociometry*, 36, 237–252.

Patterson, M. L. (1976). An arousal model of interpersonal intimacy. *Psychological Review*, 83, 235–245.

Patterson, M. L. (1983). *Nonverbal behavior: A functional perspective*. New York: Springer.

Patterson, M. L. (2002). Psychology of nonverbal communication and interpersonal interaction. In *Encyclopedia of life support systems (EOLSS)*. Oxford: Developed under the Auspices of the UNESCO, Eolss Publishers. At www.eolss.net.

Tickle-Degnen, L. (2006). Nonverbal behavior and its function in the ecosystem of rapport. In V. Manusov & M. L. Patterson (eds.), *The Sage handbook of nonverbal communication*. Thousand Oaks, CA: Sage:, pp. 381–399.

Regression Analysis

Alan M. Rubin

Kent State University

The essence of scientific research is explaining and predicting relationships among variables. Two or more variables co-vary and are related if their values systematically correspond to each other. In other words, as one value increases or decreases, the other value consistently or systematically increases or decreases (→ Correlation Analysis). For example, researchers might observe the amount of Internet use increases from younger to older adolescence, leading them to expect a relationship between Internet use and age of adolescents.

As scientists seek to explain phenomena, they employ various empirical measures to express relationships among two or more variables. *Correlation* is a measure of such relationships. The Pearson product–moment correlation coefficient assesses the magnitude and direction of a relationship between two linear variables, and describes how proportional the values of the variables are to each other (StatSoft 2006). A multiple correlation coefficient does this for three or more variables, such as age, education level, and amount of Internet use. There are similar tests, such as gamma and phi, for relationships among nonlinear, categorical, or rank-order variables (→ Measurement Theory).

From a correlation coefficient we might conclude there is a positive and significant relationship between amount of Internet use and age of adolescents. A correlation coefficient ranges from 0.0 (no relationship) to 1.0 (a perfect relationship between the variables' values). The coefficients can be positive (the variables increase or decrease in unison) or negative (as one variable increases, the other decreases, or vice versa).

REGRESSION AND PREDICTION

Regression is typically used for research designs having one or more continuous independent or predictor variables. Based on correlation, regression moves beyond examining whether a relationship exists between variables to assessing the nature of the relationship (Kerlinger & Pedhazur 1973). Regression analyzes the variability of the criterion or dependent variable based on the information from one or more predictor or independent variables (Pedhazur & Schmelkin 1991), seeking to explain which independent variables best predict the dependent variable. For example, we might try to predict income level from people's age, experience, and amount of education. Or we might try to predict level of fear from the amount of time people spend watching television and how realistic they feel television content is.

Prediction is the essence of science. Regression analysis seeks to uncover how much one or more independent variables predict the dependent variable. It seeks to explain the dependent variable's sources of variance, and to answer, "What values in the dependent variable can we expect given certain values of the independent variable(s)?" (Vogt 1993, 192). Good regression models can predict one's income or one's level of fear from the predictor variables.

Simple and Multiple Regression

The regression equation involves one or more independent variables. Regression analysis estimates the coefficients of that equation, involving the independent variables, which best predict the value of the dependent variable. The regression equation indicates the nature and proximity of the variables, specifically how well we can predict values of the dependent variable by knowing the values of the independent variable(s) (Vogt 1993). The equation is represented by the regression line, which depicts the relationship between the variables. The sum of squares refers to the deviation or variance of a score from the average score of a distribution; it is fundamental to regression analysis (StatSoft 2006). The regression line or least-squares line is a line on the graph or scatterplot that depicts the lowest sum of squared distances of all data points. We fit our data to the best-fitting straight line based on this least-squares criterion (Blalock 1979).

Simple regression analysis contains one continuous predictor variable. The equation for simple linear regression refers to the regression of *Y* scores on *X* scores, or how the dependent variable scores depend on the independent variable scores. The simple regression equation seeking for a design with one predictor variable, X, and one dependent variable, Y, is.

$$Y = a + bX$$

where X is the independent variable score, Y is the predicted dependent variable score, a is the intercept constant (i.e., where the regression line intercepts the Y axis), and b is the regression coefficient (i.e., the change in Y with the change in one unit of X). The simple linear regression equation seeks to uncover how much an independent variable explains or predicts the dependent variable.

Multiple regression analysis contains the simple regression designs for two or more continuous independent variables. The regression equation for a multiple regression design with three predictor variables, X_1, X_2, and X_3, and one dependent variable, Y, is.

$$Y = a + bX_1 + bX_2 + bX_3$$

where X_1, X_2, and X_3 are the scores on three independent variables, Y is the predicted dependent variable score, a is the intercept constant, and b is the unstandardized regression coefficient (used with raw scores). The multiple linear regression equation seeks to uncover how two or more independent variables explain or predict the dependent variable. If the regression coefficient b were to be standardized in these equations, it would be represented by β (beta), whereby all variables are standardized to a mean of 0.0 and a standard deviation of 1.0.

Based on the size of each regression coefficient, researchers can compare the contribution of each independent variable for predicting the dependent variable. Multiple R indicates the strength of the relationship. The proportion of explained variance for the predictor or set of predictors is depicted by R^2 and F is the test of significance of the relationship. If the predictor variables are intercorrelated, such multicolinearity makes it difficult to assess individual predictor contributions to the regression equation.

Multiple regression, then, estimates the separate and collective contributions of two or more independent variables to explaining the dependent variable (Kerlinger & Pedhazur 1973). Multiple regression analysis assesses the relationship between a dependent variable and a set of independent variables, seeking to learn how the continuous independent variables, such as age, level of education, academic performance, and amount of television viewing, explain or predict the dependent variable, such as the amount of Internet use. Or communication researchers might want to learn how, collectively, knowledge, skill, *and* motivation enhance communication competence, and whether knowledge, skill, *or* motivation is more instrumental to enhancing communication competence. Once the researchers measure the three predictor variables – knowledge, skill, and motivation – they can assess how the variables, collectively, explain a communicator's level of competence, and which one, if any, better explains a communicator's competence. Or, in a typical transaction, a salesperson might want to learn which attribute – price, gas mileage, or reliability – predicts a consumer's decision to buy an automobile. Once the salesperson gathers the information across many transactions, he or she can learn which attribute is, or which attributes are, better predictors of car purchases.

Additional Considerations

Statistical programs allow researchers to enter the predictors into the regression equation using forward, backward, stepwise, or hierarchical techniques. Depending on the objective, a researcher might choose to enter all predictors simultaneously. Forward entry sequentially adds predictors having the highest correlations with the criterion variable. Backward entry enters all predictors and then removes one at a time based on the weakest significance. Using stepwise regression, the computer selects predictors that add incrementally and significantly to the equation, based on the set tolerance criterion. If the researcher's goal was to test a communication model, he or she would enter the predictor variables in blocks, hierarchically, according to the sequential steps in the model.

We also can expand the relationships examined by regression analysis to include two or more criterion variables. For example, we might examine how knowledge, skill, and motivation predict communication competence *and* satisfaction. Or we might analyze how amount and type of television viewing predict distrust *and* fear. Monge (1980) explains the application of multivariate multiple regression to communication research. In addition, such techniques as binary and logistic regression can be used to expand the manner of how we can examine relationships via regression analysis to include discrete, categorical, and other nonlinear variables (Norusis 1999).

BRIEF EXAMPLES

A few brief examples help illustrate the application of regression analysis in communication research. Sypher and Zorn (1986), for example, used stepwise multiple regression in their organizational study, and found, of four communication-related abilities, cognitive differentiation accounted for the most variance when predicting job level and upward mobility. Those with more developed cognitive abilities tended to be promoted to higher levels in organizations than did those with lesser cognitive abilities.

Ohr and Schrott (2001) used regression analysis to examine determinants of political → information seeking in a local German election: social expectations to be politically informed; a personal duty to stay politically informed; a desire to express political orientations by voting; and the entertainment aspect of politics. They found that campaign information seeking can be explained reasonably well by these determinants, especially social expectations to be politically informed (→ Election Campaign Communication).

In the media context, Rubin et al. (1985) used hierarchical multiple regression and found news affinity, perceived news realism, and news-viewing motives predicted parasocial interaction with favorite television news personalities (→ Parasocial Interactions and Relationships). Those who sought information when viewing the news, and felt news content was realistic and important, developed a greater sense of parasocial interaction with newscasters than their counterparts.

Loges (1994) also used hierarchical multiple regression, and found support for the hypothesis that media dependency relations (→ Media System Dependency Theory) with → newspapers, → magazines, → radio, and → television are more intense the more threatening one perceives the social and natural environment to be. Controlling for demographics, Loges found that threat significantly added to the explained variance in dependency.

Using hierarchical regression, Slater (2003) found that gender, → sensation seeking, aggression, and frequency of → Internet use contributed to explaining the use of violent media content and violent website content. Alienation from school and family partially mediated the effects of sensation seeking and aggression on using violent Internet content.

Path analysis uses several regression analyses to test the path model, seeking to explain complex directional relationships between independent and dependent variables. Rubin and McHugh (1987), for example, examined an explanatory model of perceived importance of parasocial relationships, moving from television exposure through interpersonal attraction and parasocial interaction to perceived relationship importance. They found that social attraction and parasocial interaction significantly predicted perceived relationship importance.

SEE ALSO: ▶ Correlation Analysis ▶ Election Campaign Communication ▶ Factor Analysis ▶ Information Seeking ▶ Internet ▶ Magazine ▶ Measurement Theory ▶ Media System Dependency Theory ▶ Newspaper ▶ Parasocial Interactions and Relationships ▶ Radio ▶ Sensation Seeking ▶ Statistics, Descriptive ▶ Statistics, Explanatory ▶ Television

References and Suggested Readings

Blalock, H. M., Jr. (1979). *Social statistics*, 2nd edn. New York: McGraw-Hill.

Kerlinger, F. N., & Pedhazur, E. J. (1973). *Multiple regression in behavioral research*. New York: Holt, Rinehart and Winston.

Loges, W. E. (1994). Canaries in the coal mine: Perceptions of threat and media dependency system relations. *Communication Research*, 21, 5–23.

Monge, P. R. (1980). Multivariate multiple regression. In P. R. Monge & J. N. Capella (eds.), *Multivariate techniques in human communication research*. New York: Academic Press, pp. 13–56.

Norusis, M. J. (1999). *SPSS regression models 10.0*. Chicago: SPSS.

Ohr, D., & Schrott, P. R. (2001). Campaigns and information seeking: Evidence from a German state election. *European Journal of Communication*, 16, 419–449.

Pedhazur, E. J., & Schmelkin, L. P. (1991). *Measurement, design, and analysis: An integrated approach*. Hillsdale, NJ: Lawrence Erlbaum.

Rubin, A. M., Perse, E. M., & Powell, R. A. (1985). Loneliness, parasocial interaction, and local television news viewing. *Human Communication Research*, 12, 155–180.

Rubin, R. B., & McHugh, M. P. (1987). Development of parasocial interaction relationships. *Journal of Broadcasting and Electronic Media*, 31, 279–292.

Slater, M. D. (2003). Alienation, aggression, and sensation seeking as predictors of adolescent use of violent film, computer, and website content. *Journal of Communication*, 53(1), 105–121.

StatSoft, Inc. (2006). *Electronic statistics textbook*. Tulsa, OK: StatSoft. Also at www.statsoft.com/textbook/stathome.html, accessed August 30, 2007.

Sypher, B. D., & Zorn, T. E., Jr. (1986). Communication-related abilities and upward mobility: A longitudinal investigation. *Human Communication Research*, 12, 420–431.

Vogt, W. P. (1993). *Dictionary of statistics and methodology*. Newbury Park, CA: Sage.

Reification

Kim D. Hester-Williams

Sonoma State University

"Popular communication" can be characterized by the various ways in which the general public engages popular forms of communication including radio, → television, film, → popular music, and print media such as magazines, newspapers, and popular literature, as well as new technologies such as the Internet, email, and mobile phones (→ Communication: Definitions and Concepts). In addition to their general utility, these cultural objects inform and entertain the general public and are directed toward mass audience reception. The conspicuous consumption of popular forms of communication reveals a complex set of interactions with these modes of communication (→ Popular Communication).

Popular communication in the twenty-first century has transformed human → interaction by providing for seemingly limitless possibilities. In so doing, contemporary popular communication has subverted traditional forms of communication such as letters and the telephone. As more personalized and private communication is increasingly no longer the dominant form of communication, the reification of human communication has become pervasive. In the context of popular communication, "reification" can be described as the process by which popular communicative interactions between persons and the personal relationships indicative of those interactions are converted into objects that are thereby depersonalized and often function as a commodity.

This concept of reification is derived from Marxist studies and includes the theory that, as human beings become considered as physical objects they are deprived of subjectivity, that is, a consciousness of individual agency. Reification, according to this Marxist view, subsequently produces the effect of alienation. Within the parameters of popular communication, reification and alienation can be identified through such examples as television talk shows and reality shows which often feature intimate discussions and interactions between persons and groups of persons that are directed and mass-marketed to television viewers who consume such discussions and interactions as commodities. Through this process of reification viewers become part of a communicative exchange, which, ultimately, results in the commodification of human relations (→ Commodification of the Media).

The → Internet provides another such example of popular communication and reification. Many websites such as MySpace, which is marketed to users as "a space for friends," as well as Internet chatrooms and email represent modes of popular communication that have also become a significant vehicle for marketing goods and products to consumers. In addition, mobile phones can be used to connect to the Internet, check email, and download and access popular music, all of which is mediated by the marketing strategies of mobile phone and other corporate companies (→ Electronic Mail; Commercialization of the Media; Commercialization: Impact on Media Content). Consequently, the mobile phone has evolved into more than simply a way for people to communicate. Rather, mobile phones provide yet another example of the reification of human contact through popular communication as they have become another means for transforming the communicative process into a commodity. However, these modes of popular communication alone do not produce reification. Instead, these cultural artifacts are part of a larger complex interplay between → popular culture, commercial culture, market forces, and the need for human beings to communicate and interact socially.

In addressing the *intersections between commodity culture and popular communication*, current popular communication scholarship has continued to provide a historical and comparative view of these popular communicative processes while also examining the areas of race, ethnicity, gender, sexuality, social class, globalization, audience reception, and information technologies as they relate and contribute to an understanding of the social and cultural consequences of such processes (→ Cultural Studies; Social Movements and Communication). Scholars have continued to develop interdisciplinary theories and methodologies to trace the effects of reification through popular communication on human beings and the society at large. Scholars of popular communication, for instance, generally agree that attention to national as well as global market forces on information technology and culture is one of many significant factors in identifying the potential social and cultural consequences of popular communication and reification. Audience reception is yet another popular field of inquiry within popular communication studies (→ Audience). Many scholars in these emergent fields posit that it remains to be seen how popular communication artifacts and technologies will ultimately be used – as a tool for creating community beyond cultural and social divides such as race, gender, sexuality, and class, or will they persist as a way of continuing to create markets and consumers?

SEE ALSO: ▶ Audience ▶ Commercialization of the Media ▶ Commercialization: Impact on Media Content ▶ Commodification of the Media ▶ Communication: Definitions and Concepts ▶ Cultural Studies ▶ Electronic Mail ▶ Interaction ▶ Internet ▶ Interpersonal Communication ▶ Language and Social Interaction ▶ Media Effects ▶ Popular Communication ▶ Popular Culture ▶ Popular Music ▶ Media and Perceptions of Reality ▶ Social Movements and Communication ▶ Technology and Communication ▶ Television

References and Suggested Readings

Burris, V. (1988). Reification: A Marxist perspective. *California Sociologist*, 10, 22–43.
Butsch, R. (2003). Popular communication audiences: A historical research agenda. *Popular Communication*, 1(1), 15–21.
Carey, J. (1989). *Communication as culture: Essays on media and society*. Boston: Unwin Hyman.
Harris, L., Kiernan, V. G., & Miliband, R. (1983). *A dictionary of Marxist thought*. Cambridge, MA: Harvard University Press.
Mazzarella, S. R., & Pecora, N. (2003). Editors' introduction: Mapping the field of popular communication. *Popular Communication*, 1(1), 1–4.
Stevenson, N. (1995). *Understanding media cultures: Social theory and mass communication*. London: Sage.
Valdivia, A. N. (2003). *A companion to media studies*. London: Blackwell.

Relational Control

Frank E. Millar

University of Wyoming

Relational control is the most dynamic of the three dimensions of social relationships proposed by Millar and Rogers (1987) – the other two are trust and intimacy. Control represents the vertical "distance" between the persons in an ongoing interaction; it refers to the pattern of rights and obligations to define or direct and to defer or accept the other's assertions while constructing the continually re-produced form of any interpersonal relationship. The temporal relevance of control is the present, since the right to direct and the obligation to accept the dyad's form varies by topics, social roles, and social settings. Functionally, control structures serve to regulate how each person acts toward and with the other and the dyad's ability to accomplish interdependent and individual goals (→ Social Interaction Structure). Subjective judgments about the vertical distance between persons are encapsulated in the notions of freedom and equity. Freedom concerns the possibility of one's own actions affecting the forms and outcomes of the relationship, while equity judgments concern the fairness of one's own rewards in comparison to the other's, considering the amount and type of one's contributions to the relationship (→ Social Exchange).

Relational control has been most frequently measured with the Relational Communication Control Coding System (RCCCS) or some modification of it. A comprehensive report of the development, application, and modifications of RCCCS is provided in Rogers and Escudero (2004). Briefly, the RCCCS uses a three-digit code to categorize any speech turn; the first digit codes the *speaker*, the second codes the verbalization's *format*, and the third classifies the turn's *response mode* relative to the prior statement from the previous speaker. The three-digit code is then assigned a control code; an attempt to define the relationship is called a one-up movement ($\uparrow$); a request or acceptance of the other's definition is called a one-down movement ($\downarrow$), and a non-demanding, non-accepting, leveling utterance is called a one-across movement ($\rightarrow$). Combining contiguous control codes creates three types of transacts termed *complementary* ($\uparrow\downarrow$ or $\downarrow\uparrow$), *symmetrical* ($\uparrow\uparrow$, $\downarrow\downarrow$, or $\rightarrow\rightarrow$) and *transitory* ($\rightarrow\uparrow$, $\uparrow\rightarrow$, $\rightarrow\downarrow$, or $\downarrow\rightarrow$), thereby measuring the two primary theoretical constructs (i.e., complementarity and symmetry) that prompted the coding scheme's creation (Rogers 1982). Although seemingly complex, the reliability and validity estimates of RCCCS are good to excellent by conventional social science standards. The RCCCS has been used to describe the relational control dimension of verbal utterances in a variety of interpersonal settings such as husband–wife conversations, superior–subordinate interactions, and three-or-more-person family therapy sessions, and recent modifications include the coding of nonverbal behaviors in interpersonal interactions (Rogers & Escudero 2004).

A variety of measures of the relational control dimension is possible with RCCCS. Two that have received a fair amount of empirical attention are dominance and redundancy. *Dominance* is operationally defined as the number of one-up moves responded to with a one-down maneuver (dominance = given $\uparrow$, %$\downarrow$). Dominance is a momentary outcome in an ongoing conversation where one person asserts a definition of the relationship and the other accepts that assertion (e.g., the wife says "Let's go out to dinner" and the husband replies "OK. Good idea."). In husband–wife relationships, the more the husband is in a dominant position relative to his wife, the more marital satisfaction he reports, but the same correlation is not observed with wife dominance scores. Further, the greater the couple's dominance ratio indicating that the husband is in a dominant position considerably more than his wife, (1) the less he understands his wife and (2) the more redundant and rigid or less flexible the couple's control structure. (*Redundancy* is operationally defined as the sum of the absolute deviation from random use of the nine transactional configurations indexed by the RCCCS. Either highly redundant or highly chaotic patterns are problematic for the relationship.)

Dominance, a momentary relational structure, is not to be confused with *domineering-ness*, which is a measure of an individual's use of one-up moves (domineeringness = $\uparrow$/ total number of maneuvers uttered by the speaker). Dominance and domineeringness are independent measures; that is, the frequency of dominance cannot be predicted by the frequency of one-up moves even though the more domineering one person is the lower the other's dominance score. This statistical independence is an important, consistent finding; it empirically supports the conceptual distinction between individual and relational measures, and reminds scholars that communication processes cannot be additively reconstructed from or reduced to measures of individual actions and perceptions. Research consistently shows that, in husband–wife conversations, the more domineering statements issued by the wife, (1) the less marital satisfaction she reports and (2) the less communication satisfaction both she and her husband report. Husband domineeringness is not consistently related with either spouse's reported levels of marital satisfaction, although it is slightly correlated with the frequency of conflicts observed in marital conversations. (A verbal conflict is depicted by at least three consecutive one-up moves by the two speakers with RCCCS codes.)

Just as biological systems continually reproduce their structure by and through their own processes, so communication systems reproduce their relational form by and through their message performances. Describing this self-regulating feature of interpersonal relationships is the concern of the relational control construct and the focus of RCCCS coding procedures.

SEE ALSO: ▶ Social Exchange   ▶ Social Interaction Structure

References and Suggested Readings

Millar, F. E. (1994). The structure of interpersonal structuring processes: A relational view. In R. L. Conville (ed.), *Uses of "structure" in communication studies*. Westport, CT: Praeger, pp. 39–60.
Millar, F. E., & Rogers, L. E. (1987). Relational dimensions of interpersonal dynamics. In M. E. Roloff & G. R. Miller (eds.), *Interpersonal processes: New directions in communication research*. Newbury Park, CA: Sage, pp. 117–139.
Rogers, L. E. (1982). Symmetry and complementarity: Evolution and evaluation of an idea. In C. Wilder-Mott & J. H. Weakland (eds.), *Rigor and imagination: Essays from the legacy of Gregory Bateson*. New York: Praeger, pp. 231–251.
Rogers, L. E., & Escudero, V. (eds.) (2004). *Relational communication: An interactional perspective to the study of process and form*. Mahwah, NJ: Lawrence Erlbaum.

Relational Dialectics

Leslie A. Baxter
University of Iowa

Relational dialectics is an interpretive theory of meaning-making in familial and non-kin relationships (→ Meaning). Formally articulated in 1996 by Leslie Baxter and Barbara Montgomery, the theory is grounded in the philosophy of dialogism articulated by Russian language philosopher → Mikhail Bakhtin (→ Dialogic Perspectives). It relies primarily on qualitative methods with a goal of rendering a rich understanding of the meaning-making process (→ Qualitative Methodology). Unlike many interpretive theories, however, relational dialectics theory (RDT) challenges interpretivism's focus on consensual, unified meanings, emphasizing instead the fragmented and contested nature of meaning-making. Further, RDT moves from subjective sense-making of individuals to focus on → discourse. The theory can be summarized in *three core propositions*.

The *first proposition* is that meanings emerge from the struggle of different, often *opposing, discourses* (→ Text and Intertextuality). Following Bakhtin, all of meaning-making can be understood metaphorically and literally as a dialogue. Everyday dialogue presupposes difference in the unique perspectives of the interlocutors. To Bakhtin, all meaning-making can be understood as a dialogue – the interplay of different, ideologically freighted discourses. Bakhtin's lifelong intellectual project was critical of monologues of all kinds – authoritative discourses that foreclose the struggle of competing discourses by centering a single discursive point of view. Meaning-making becomes calcified when only one discourse occupies the centripetal center and all other systems of meaning have been rendered mute. RDT seeks to reclaim discursive conflict in relating, adopting a radical skepticism of relational monologues.

To date, RDT-informed researchers have identified a variety of competing discourses in romantic, marital, and familial relationships. Three dialogues appear common across a wide range of relationship experiences. First, relationship parties give voice to a discourse of individualism that interpenetrates with a discourse of connection. Second, relationship parties navigate the discursive struggle between a discourse of openness, candor, and honesty on the one hand, and a discourse of discretion and privacy on the other hand. Third, the communication activity of relationship parties is rendered intelligible by a discourse of certainty and predictability in play with a discourse of uncertainty, novelty, and spontaneity. Other discursive struggles are specific to particular relationship types. For example, stepfamily communication is often characterized by the discursive struggle of stepparent-as-parent with and against stepparent-as-outsider. Existing research has, for the most part, been centered in the first proposition, to the relative neglect of the other two propositions.

The *second proposition* is that the interpenetration of discourses is *both synchronic and diachronic* (→ Linguistics; Semiotics). Meanings emerge in any given interaction moment, and in this sense, they are, at least momentarily, synchronically fixed. But meanings are also fluid; in subsequent interactions, relational parties might jointly construct meanings that reproduce the old meanings, or they could jointly produce new meanings. In either case

– reproduction or production – meaning-making is envisioned as ongoing communicative work that results from discursive struggle.

Some constructed meanings function to elide, or skirt, the struggle of discourses to the extent possible. For example, parties can privilege one discourse at a given moment and thereby mute all discursive rivals. If, over time, one discourse is reproduced again and again, it becomes authoritative. RDT argues, however, that it is effortful for parties to sustain authoritative discourses. Communication holds the potential for rupture, and centrifugal discourses, while removed from the centripetal center, can never be completely silenced. The struggle of competing discourses is also elided when relationship parties jointly construct meanings that involve an inversion across time with respect to which discourses are centered and which are marginalized. This diachronic ebb and flow moves back and forth, with centered and marginalized discourses changing places in the meaning-making process. This pattern of meaning-making appears quite common among relationship parties. Discursive struggles are also elided when relationship parties construct ambiguous or equivocal meanings. Ambiguity is a discursive lubricant, allowing meaning to slide between discourses, appearing to embrace them all.

Other meaning-making emerges from the interplay of discourses. Hybrid constructions combine or mix competing discourses. A new meaning emerges from the struggle, one that draws upon elements of multiple discourses. Another kind of discursive mixture is what Bakhtin refers to as an aesthetic moment; that is, meaning-making in which discourses are no longer framed as oppositional but instead merge in a way that profoundly alters each meaning system. These aesthetic meanings are crafted along new discursive lines, akin to chemical reactions.

The *third proposition* is that the interpenetration of competing discourses *constitutes social reality* (→ Constructivism). In this third proposition, RDT joins a growing number of theories committed to a constitutive view in which communication is positioned to construct the social world, not merely to represent an objective world that precedes communication. What is unique about RDT is its articulation of the mechanism by which such construction takes place: the tensionality of difference. The constitutive process includes a decentering of the sovereign self in which the individual's dispositions, attitudes, beliefs, and social positions are thought to precede communication. Communication is deployed by the sovereign self to serve his or her preformed goals. By contrast, according to RDT, consciousness and identity are continually formed through communication with different others. In decentering the sovereign self, interpersonal conflict and power are shifted from the individual unit of analysis to focus instead on discourse.

SEE ALSO: ▶ Bakhtin, Mikhail ▶ Constructivism ▶ Dialogic Perspectives ▶ Discourse ▶ Linguistics ▶ Meaning ▶ Qualitative Methodology ▶ Semiotics ▶ Text and Intertextuality

References and Suggested Readings

Baxter, L. A. (2004). Distinguished scholar article: Relationships as dialogues. *Personal Relationships*, 11, 1–23.

Baxter, L. A. (2006). Relational dialectics theory: Multivocal dialogues of family communication. In D. O. Braithwaite & L. A. Baxter (eds.), *Engaging theories in family communication: Multiple perspectives*. Thousand Oaks, CA: Sage, pp. 130–145.

Baxter, L. A. (2007). Mikhail Bakhtin and the philosophy of dialogism. In P. Arneson (ed.), *Perspectives on philosophy of communication*. West Lafayette, IN: Purdue University Press, pp. 247–268.

Baxter, L. A., & Braithwaite, D. O. (in press). Relational dialectics theory: Crafting meaning from competing discourses. In L. A. Baxter & D. O. Braithwaite (eds.), *Engaging theories in interpersonal communication*. Thousand Oaks, CA: Sage.

Baxter, L. A., & Montgomery, B. M. (1996). *Relating: Dialogues and dialectics*. New York: Guilford.

Relational Maintenance

Marianne Dainton

La Salle University

Relational maintenance refers to activities that occur in interpersonal relationships after the relationship is developed and before the relationship is terminated (Stafford 1994). Although the term implies a temporal stage of relationship life, communication scholars have more frequently focused on the processes that sustain a relationship. For example, Dindia & Canary (1993) identified four common *definitions of relational maintenance*: (1) the process of keeping a relationship in existence; (2) the process of keeping a relationship in a specified state or condition; (3) the process of keeping a relationship in satisfactory condition; and (4) the process of keeping a relationship in repair (→ Relationship Development).

There are several controversies within relational maintenance scholarship, including theoretical commitment and views of intentionality. For example, three major theories have emerged. The first is *equity theory* (→ Social Exchange). Associated with the work of Canary, Stafford, and colleagues, equity theory posits that maintenance behaviors are both rewards and costs. These authors identified seven maintenance strategies: "positivity" (being cheerful and optimistic), "openness" (self-disclosure and direct discussion of the relationship), "assurances" (messages stressing commitment), "network" (relying on common friends and affiliations), "sharing tasks" (accomplishing instrumental responsibilities), "advice" (expressing opinions and support), and "integrative conflict management" (e.g., cooperating, apologizing). Research indicates that these strategies are consistent and strong predictors of relational characteristics such as satisfaction, commitment, and love.

The second theoretical approach is a *dialectical perspective* (→ Relational Dialectics). Championed by scholars such as Baxter and Montgomery (1996), the dialectical approach focuses on the ways that contradictory tensions are managed in order to sustain the relationship. For example, a dialectical tension might involve the desire for both predictability and novelty in the relationship. Eight management strategies have been identified. These include "denial" (rejecting the existence of a tension), "disorientation" (ignoring the ability to actively manage tensions), "spiraling inversion" (responding to first one, then the other pole), "segmentation" (partitioning the relationship by topic/ activity), "balance" (partially fulfilling the demands of each pole), "integration" (responding to both poles simultaneously), "recalibration" (temporarily synthesizing the contra-diction so opposing forces are no longer viewed as opposite), and "reaffirmation" (celebrating the stimulation that contradictory tensions provides).

Finally, *systems approaches* have been touted as the ideal theory for understanding maintenance processes (Stafford 1994; → Systems Theory). Systems approaches allow for an understanding of how mutual and reciprocal influences affect the balance of the relationship. In his seminal study of maintenance processes, Ayres (1983) found that three strategies – "avoidance", "balance," and "directness" – functioned to sustain a relationship's equilibrium.

Although these theories have provided insights into maintenance processes, they have not provided a full picture. Equity theory, for example, is biased toward western notions of relationships. The dialectical perspective provides an intuitive means for understanding relationships, but does not provide a mechanism for predicting which relationships will be maintained and which will not. And, despite the potential usefulness of the systems perspective, relatively little maintenance research has adopted this view. A significant area for future scholarship is the development of a theory or theories that more fully explain the maintenance process.

A second ongoing controversy is the extent to which maintenance is achieved intentionally. At issue is whether maintenance is effortful and planned (i.e., it is *strategic*), or whether it also occurs as a by-product of everyday interaction (i.e., it is *routine maintenance*). Dindia (2000) identified three possible relationships between strategic and routine maintenance. First, she argued that some behaviors might start off as strategies for relational partners, but become routinized over time. Second, some behaviors might be performed primarily strategically by some partners and primarily routinely by others. Finally, Dindia proposed that the same behavior might on some occasions be used strategically, and on other occasions be used routinely. Tentative support has been found for all three possibilities, and for the proposal that routine maintenance may be a stronger predictor of relationship satisfaction than strategic maintenance (Dainton & Aylor 2002). However, the larger question of when and why maintenance is performed strategically vs routinely has not yet been answered.

Regardless of theoretical perspective or stance on intentionality, much of the published research has used *self-report data* (→ Research Methods). Although communication is presumed to be the central mechanism for relational maintenance, the sheer difficulty of capturing real-life interactions in real-life settings makes research focused on actual communication problematic. Whether strategic or routine, relational maintenance is embedded in the rocky terrain of daily life, and is rarely on public view. Future research will need to devise creative methods to fully investigate maintenance communication.

Moreover, although scholars have learned a great deal about the cognitions and behaviors that relational partners use for maintenance, network and cultural influences have largely been ignored. Future research needs to put maintenance in context, investigat-ing the extent to which cultural norms, as well as family members, other relationships, and social structures, affect the maintenance process.

Finally, nearly all of the research has focused on dating and marital relationships, but clearly *other types of relationships* are maintained (→ Dating Relationships; Marital Communication). Scholars are just beginning to investigate the maintenance of friendships, family relationships, co-worker relationships, and the like. An intriguing but as yet unanswered question is the extent to which the same maintenance processes operate across contexts. Early results indicate that there are some maintenance activities that occur in numerous relationship forms, including providing support and talking about the relationship. The relative importance of these more generic strategies vs the contextually determined and/or relationally idiosyncratic behaviors is an area for future research.

SEE ALSO: ► Dating Relationships   ► Marital Communication   ► Relational Dialectics
► Relationship Development   ► Research Methods   ► Social Exchange   ► Systems Theory

References and Suggested Readings

Ayres, J. (1983). Strategies to maintain relationships: Their identification and perceived usage. *Communication Quarterly*, 31, 62–67.

Baxter, L. A., & Montgomery, B. M. (1996). *Relating: Dialogues and dialectics*. New York: Guilford.

Canary, D. J., & Dainton, M. (eds.) (2003). *Maintaining relationships through communication: Relational, contextual, and cultural variations*. Hillsdale, NJ: Lawrence Erlbaum.

Canary, D. J., & Stafford, L. (eds.) (1994). *Communication and relational maintenance*. New York: Academic Press.

Dainton, M., & Aylor, B. A. (2002). Routine and strategic maintenance efforts: Behavioral patterns, variations associated with relational length, and the prediction of relational characteristics. *Communication Monographs*, 69, 52–66.

Dindia, K. (2000). Relational maintenance. In C. Hendrick & S. S. Hendrick (eds.), *Close relationships: A sourcebook*. Thousand Oaks, CA: Sage, pp. 287–300.

Dindia, K., & Canary, D. J. (1993). Definitions and theoretical perspectives on maintaining relationships. *Journal of Social and Personal Relationships*, 10, 163–173.

Harvey, J. H., & Wenzel, A. (eds.) (2001). *Close romantic relationships: Maintenance and enhancement*. Mahwah, NJ: Lawrence Erlbaum.

Stafford, L. (1994). Tracing the threads of spider webs. In D. J. Canary & L. Stafford (eds.), *Communication and relational maintenance*. New York: Academic Press, pp. 297–306.

Relational Schemas

Ascan F. Koerner

University of Minnesota

Schemas are defined as large-scale cognitive structures representing general knowledge, often also described as subjective theories, about some object or concept (Smith 1998). Their main functions include aiding in the interpretation of external stimuli, directing attention to specific types of external information, and guiding the retrieval and judgment of information from memory. That is, schemas play a central role in information processing and how persons understand and act in their social worlds. It follows that relational schemas organize knowledge of relationships in long-term memory and play an important role in the cognitive processes that precede, accompany, and follow interpersonal communication (→ Schemas, Knowledge Structures, and Social Interaction).

Specifically, *relational* schemas can be defined as interrelated pieces of declarative and procedural knowledge about relationships that resides in long-term memory (Baldwin 1992). In this context, declarative knowledge is defined as descriptive knowledge of the attributes and features of things, whereas procedural knowledge refers to a person's knowledge of if-then contingencies. The declarative and procedural knowledge contained in relational schemas overlaps with three subsets of knowledge that are often considered to be independent and to constitute their own schemas: self-, other-, and relationship-schemas. *Self-schemas* organize knowledge about the self, including knowledge of thoughts and emotions, goals and plans for the future, and memory of past experiences. *Other-schemas* represent knowledge about others with whom one has relationships. Knowledge of others mirrors knowledge of self in that it includes representations of others' thoughts and emotions, goals and plans for the future, and past experiences. The main difference is that, depending on how well one knows the other, these representations are much more limited than those of self.

Finally, *relationship-schemas* contain memories of past and expectations of future interactions with others. They include knowledge of experienced and expected behavioral sequences between self and other that is used to interpret and to plan behavior. These interaction sequences can be very specific and rigid interpersonal scripts (Abelson 1981) for routine behaviors, such as greeting someone, or more abstract and flexible memory organization packets (MOP) (Kellermann 1995) and plans (Berger 2002) for reaching goals in novel interactions. Although these three sub-schemas are often conceptualized as being isolated from each other, Baldwin (1992) demonstrated that these three subsets of knowledge are so highly interdependent on one another (i.e., any change in one will effect changes in the others) that they actually all belong to the same, highly abstract cognitive schema.

Like other schemas, relational schemas are hierarchically organized and exist at least at three levels of generality (Koerner & Fitzpatrick 2002). At the most general level is knowledge that applies to all social relationships, the general social schema. Such general social knowledge includes beliefs and pragmatic rules that apply to all interactions, like the norm of reciprocity (→ Reciprocity and Compensation in Interaction) or the need to be truthful and relevant when communicating (→ Deception Detection Accuracy). On the second level are relationship-type schemas that include knowledge specific to the different types of relationships one has, such as romantic partner, co-worker, sibling, and best friend. The knowledge stored in schemas at this level is different from the knowledge in the general social schema and applies to all relationships of that type (Fletcher 1993). On the most specific level are relationship-specific schemas that contain knowledge that applies to only one particular relationship a person has with one specific other person. These schemas contain memories, attributions, and experiences made within the context of that particular relationship and allow individuals to adapt their thoughts, behaviors, and interpretations to that particular relationship. These particular relationship beliefs are what make each relationship unique and distinguishable from other relationships.

The knowledge contained at the level of more specific schemas is different from the knowledge that exists at more general levels, and a person's complete mental representation of a relationship combines knowledge from all three levels. Thus, similarities of mental representations of relationships with different persons are the result of shared knowledge drawn from either the general social schema or the relationship-type schema. By contrast, differences in mental representations of relationships with different persons are due to unique information contained either in relationship-type or in relationship-specific schemas. Consequently, there must be a process that determines which information is retrieved and used in relational information processing. Originally, Koerner and Fitzpatrick (2002) proposed a sequential process in which relationship-specific knowledge is accessed first and general social knowledge last, which would explain why more specific knowledge has supremacy over more general knowledge in information processing. An equally plausible alternative that is more consistent with parallel processing is a recursive or iterative process that accesses knowledge at all levels of specificity simultaneously and that assigns more specific knowledge primacy over more general knowledge if there is a conflict between knowledge at the different levels of abstraction. A similar process should be involved when storing relationship experiences in memory. Truly unique experiences are stored in relationship-specific schemas, whereas experiences that are made with several others are stored in relationship-type schemas or the general social schema.

SEE ALSO: ▶ Cognition   ▶ Communication: Definitions and Concepts   ▶ Communication: Relationship Rules   ▶ Deception Detection Accuracy   ▶ Information Processing: ▶ Self-Concept   ▶ Memory, Person   ▶ Reciprocity and Compensation in Interaction ▶ Schemas, Knowledge Structures, and Social Interaction

References and Suggested Readings

Abelson, R. P. (1981). The psychological status of the script concept. *American Psychologist*, 36, 715–729.

Baldwin, M. W. (1992). Relational schemas and the processing of social information. *Psychological Bulletin*, 112, 461–484.

Berger, C. R. (2002). Goals and knowledge structures in social interactions. In M. L. Knapp & J. A. Daly (eds.), *Handbook of interpersonal communication*, 3rd edn. Thousand Oaks, CA: Sage, pp. 181–212.

Fletcher, G. J. O. (1993). Cognition in close relationships. *New Zealand Journal of Psychology*, 22, 69–81.

Kellermann, K. (1995). The conversation MOP: A model of patterned and pliable behavior. In D. E. Hewes (ed.), *The cognitive bases of interpersonal communication*. Hillsdale, NJ: Lawrence Erlbaum, pp. 181–221.

Koerner, A. F., & Fitzpatrick, M. A. (2002). Toward a theory of family communication. *Communication Theory*, 12, 70–91.

Smith, E. R. (1998). Mental representation and memory. In D. T. Gilbert, S. T. Fiske, & G. Lindzey (eds.), *The handbook of social psychology*, 4th edn. Boston: McGraw-Hill, pp. 391–445.

Relational Termination

Anita L. Vangelisti
University of Texas at Austin

Approximately 50 percent of first-time marriages, and an even higher percentage of remarriages, end in separation or divorce. Because researchers and theorists are concerned with the prevalence of relational termination, they have devoted a great deal of effort to understanding the antecedents, processes, and consequences associated with divorce and the dissolution of romantic relationships.

A number of the *characteristics that people bring to marriage* are associated with the likelihood that they will divorce. For instance, socio-demographic variables such as age and income predict the early termination of marriages. The divorce rate is particularly high for those who marry in their teens as it is for people in lower income groups, those with low-status occupations, and those with less education (Kitson et al. 1985). Relatively stable personality variables, such as neuroticism, also have been linked to the dissolution of marriage (Kelly & Conley 1987).

In addition to the characteristics that people bring to their romantic relationships, the *way partners interact* with each other predicts relational dissolution (Vangelisti 2002; → Marital Communication). Individuals who are dissatisfied with their relationship display more negative affect and less positive affect when communicating with their partner than do those who are satisfied, and the expression of negative affect predicts declines in marital satisfaction over time. Further, there are two sequences of behavior that distinguish happy from unhappy couples. The first involves the reciprocation of negative affect. People who tend to respond to their partner's negative behavior with negative behavior are less satisfied than those who do not. The second involves one partner communicating in "demanding" ways (e.g., trying to engage the other) while the other withdraws (e.g., tries to avoid the issue at hand). Labeled the demand–withdraw pattern, this behavioral sequence has been consistently associated with marital dissatisfaction and divorce (→ Interpersonal Conflict).

Because marital and other romantic relationships take place in the context of social networks, *family and friends* also influence relational stability. Generally, perceptions of approval from a partner's network and network support are positively linked to relational stability, as is the amount of overlap between partners' social networks (Sprecher et al. 2006).

The termination of marital and other romantic relationships occurs over time and involves interaction between relational partners. In other words, it is a *process rather than an event*. A number of researchers have put forth models describing the stages that couples go through when their relationships come apart (e.g., Knapp 1978). The models are similar in several ways. For instance, most note that the dissolution of romantic relationships starts when one or both partners recognize there is a problem and begin to evaluate the relationship. Next, the models suggest that partners discuss their relational problems. These discussions may be direct or indirect and may involve efforts to repair the relationship. The models also indicate that people go to their social network to talk about their relationship, seek advice, or provide an account of why their relationship is ending. Finally, most of the models suggest that after the relationship ends, partners engage in behaviors that help them recover from the dissolution. While some of the models describe the termination process as a series of steps, all of them acknowledge that relational partners may progress through the steps at different rates and in different sequences and that partners may even skip some steps (→ Relationship Development).

Rather than describe the dissolution process itself, some researchers have focused specifically on the *tactics that people use to end their relationships*. For instance, Cody (1982) found that people who initiated a breakup with a romantic partner tended to use one of several strategies including: (1) positive tone (apologizing, trying not to hurt the partner); (2) negative identity management (noting the importance of dating other people); (3) justification (explaining the reason for the breakup); (4) behavioral de-escalation (avoiding contact); and (5) de-escalation (saying that partners should "cool off" for a period of time).

Relationship dissolution is *stressful* for most people. Individuals who are divorced report lower levels of well-being, more health problems, more loneliness and social isolation, and more economic difficulties than do those who are married. Longitudinal studies indicate that divorce causes psychological distress; however, there also is evidence suggesting that people have certain individual differences that make them vulnerable to divorce (Mastekaasa 1994). Moreover, a small number of studies show that divorce can be linked to positive outcomes such as personal growth and autonomy (Marks 1996).

Like adults, children typically find divorce stressful: Children whose parents have divorced tend to have poorer psychological adjustment, lower academic achievement, and more behavioral problems than do those whose parents have not divorced (Hetherington et al. 1985). It is worth noting, though, that the differences between children with divorced parents and those with continually married parents are relatively small. In addition, children's adjustment to divorce is influenced by social and economic resources (Amato 1993). There is strong evidence that the conflict associated with divorce, rather than the divorce itself, accounts for the lower well-being of children from divorced families. Further, children whose parents have economic difficulties after divorce appear to be more negatively influenced than those whose parents do not experience such difficulties.

Although the prevalence of relational termination has stimulated a great deal of study, researchers' understanding of divorce and relational dissolution is still fragmented. Most studies focus on direct associations between predictors and outcomes when, in reality, many of these associations may be mediated by other factors. Also, much of the literature is based on the assumption that characteristics that occur early in relationships determine relationship outcomes. Because the process of relational termination likely is non-linear and is influenced at different points in time by different variables, understanding the process will require longitudinal studies that examine relationship variables at multiple points in time.

SEE ALSO: ► Dating Relationships ► Interpersonal Communication ► Interpersonal Conflict ► Marital Communication ► Relationship Development

References and Suggested Readings

Amato, P. R. (1993). Children's adjustment to divorce: Theories, hypotheses, and empirical support. *Journal of Marriage and the Family*, 55, 23–38.

Cody, M. J. (1982). A typology of disengagement strategies and an examination of the role intimacy, reactions to inequity, and relational problems play in strategy selection. *Communication Monographs*, 49, 148–170.

Hetherington, E. M., Cox, M., & Cox, R. (1985). Long-term effects of divorce and remarriage on the adjustment of children. *Journal of the American Academy of Psychiatry*, 24, 518–530.

Kelly, E. L., & Conley, J. J. (1987). Personality and compatibility: A prospective analysis of marital stability and marital satisfaction. *Journal of Personality and Social Psychology*, 52, 27–40.

Kitson, G. C., Barbi, K. B., & Roach, M. J. (1985). Who divorces and why? A review. *Journal of Family Issues*, 6, 255–293.

Knapp, M. L. (1978). *Social intercourse: From greeting to goodbye*. Boston: Allyn and Bacon.

Marks, N. F. (1996). Flying solo at midlife: Gender, marital status, and psychological well-being. *Journal of Marriage and the Family*, 58, 917–932.

Mastekaasa, A. (1994). Psychological well-being and marital dissolution. *Journal of Family Issues*, 15, 208–228.

Sprecher, S., Felmlee, D., Schmeeckle, M., & Shu, X. (2006). No breakup occurs on an island: Social networks and relationship dissolution. In M. A. Fine & J. H. Harvey (eds.), *Handbook of divorce and relationship dissolution*. Mahwah, NJ: Lawrence Erlbaum, pp. 457–478.

Vangelisti, A. L. (2002). Interpersonal processes in romantic relationships. In M. L. Knapp & J. A. Daly (eds.), *Handbook of interpersonal communication*. Thousand Oaks, CA: Sage, pp. 643–679.

Relational Uncertainty

Leanne K. Knobloch

University of Illinois

Relational uncertainty is the degree of confidence people have in their perceptions of involvement within interpersonal relationships. The construct has its roots in → Uncertainty Reduction Theory (URT; Berger & Calabrese 1975), which emphasized the relevance of uncertainty to interactions between strangers (→ Initial Interaction). As scholars began to examine URT in the domain of close relationships, they recognized the need to reconceptualize uncertainty in ways that attended to features of intimate associations (Knobloch & Solomon 2002a). The relational uncertainty construct was developed to fill this void.

Relational uncertainty is an umbrella term that refers to ambiguity arising from self, partner, and relationship sources (Berger & Bradac 1982). *Self uncertainty* indexes the questions people have about their own participation in the relationship ("How certain am I about my goals for this relationship?"). *Partner uncertainty* involves the doubts individuals experience about their partner's participation in the relationship ("How certain am I about my partner's goals for this relationship?"). *Relationship uncertainty* is the ambiguity people feel about the state of the relationship itself ("How certain am I about the future of this relationship?"). Whereas self and partner uncertainty encompass questions about individuals, relationship uncertainty exists at a higher level of abstraction because it focuses on the dyad as a unit. The three sources of relational uncertainty are both conceptually and empirically distinct.

The *sources* of relational uncertainty can be further distinguished by content areas (Knobloch & Solomon 1999). In the context of courtship, self and partner uncertainty involve the questions people have about their desire for the relationship, their evaluation of its value, and their goals for its progression. Relationship uncertainty includes the ambiguity individuals experience about the norms for appropriate behavior, the mutuality of feelings between partners, the definition of the association, and the future of the relationship (→ Expectancy Violation).

Scholars have conceptualized relational uncertainty at two *levels of abstraction*. It exists on a global level as people's overall ambiguity about a relationship ("How certain are you about the status of this relationship?"). It also occurs on an episodic level as the doubts generated by discrete events ("How much uncertainty did you experience because of this episode?"). Scholars have collected data on both people's retrospective accounts of unexpected events (Planalp et al. 1988) and their appraisals of hypothetical episodes (Knobloch & Solomon 2002b).

Relational uncertainty can have several *consequences*. It may provoke face threats because individuals lack information about how their partner will respond to messages. Consequently, people tend to avoid open communication under conditions of ambiguity (Knobloch 2006). Individuals experiencing relational uncertainty engage in more topic avoidance, are less likely to express jealousy to their partner, and are more apt to refrain from discussing unexpected events. Moreover, people grappling with relational uncertainty produce date request messages that are less affiliative, less relationally focused, and less explicit. Relational uncertainty may also make it harder for individuals to glean information from conversation. Under conditions of relational uncertainty, dating partners have trouble recognizing relationship-focused messages, experience problems deriving inferences from utterances, and report that conversation is difficult (Knobloch & Solomon 2005). Thus, relational uncertainty may impede people's ability to process messages (→ Relationship Development).

At the episodic level, scholars have investigated how individuals manage uncertainty increasing events (→ Information Seeking). Both distal and proximal features of the situation govern people's responses to unexpected episodes. Three predictors have garnered the most research attention (Knobloch 2005). Intimacy is a distal parameter that is positively associated with direct information seeking strategies. Cognitions and emotions are proximal parameters that also predict information seeking strategies.

Questions remain about the *advantages and disadvantages* of relational uncertainty (Knobloch 2007). On the one hand, research suggests that relational uncertainty may be dissatisfying. People experiencing ambiguity appraise irritating partner behavior to be more severe, feel more negative emotion, and perceive network members to be less supportive of their courtship. Further, individuals typically view unexpected events to be negatively valenced. On the other hand, scholars have theorized that relational uncertainty may be beneficial by providing romance, excitement, and opportunities to affirm commitment (Knobloch & Solomon 2002a; Livingston 1980). More research is needed to determine the boundary conditions that make relational uncertainty helpful or harmful to intimate associations ($\rightarrow$ Uncertainty Management).

Two other directions for future research involve the link between relational uncertainty and communication. First, most studies have examined people's global communication strategies rather than features of their utterances, so work is necessary to shed light on characteristics of messages. Second, scholars have focused on understanding how relational uncertainty predicts message production, so research is required to illuminate the connection between relational uncertainty and message processing.

SEE ALSO: ► Expectancy Violation ► Information Seeking ► Initial Interaction ► Relationship Development ► Uncertainty Management ► Uncertainty Reduction Theory

References and Suggested Readings

Berger, C. R., & Bradac, J. J. (1982). *Language and social knowledge: Uncertainty in interpersonal relationships*. London: Edward Arnold.

Berger, C. R., & Calabrese, R. J. (1975). Some explorations in initial interaction and beyond: Toward a developmental theory of interpersonal communication. *Human Communication Research*, 1, 99–112.

Knobloch, L. K. (2005). Evaluating a contextual model of responses to relational uncertainty increasing events: The role of intimacy, appraisals, and emotions. *Human Communication Research*, 31(1), 60–101.

Knobloch, L. K. (2006). Relational uncertainty and message production within courtship: Features of date request messages. *Human Communication Research*, 32(3), 244–273.

Knobloch, L. K. (2007). The dark side of relational uncertainty: Obstacle or opportunity? In B. Spitzberg & W. Cupach (eds.), *The dark side of interpersonal communication*, 2nd edn. Mahwah, NJ: Lawrence Erlbaum, pp. 31–59.

Knobloch, L. K., & Carpenter-Theune, K. E. (2004). Topic avoidance in developing romantic relationships: Associations with intimacy and relational uncertainty. *Communication Research*, 31(2), 173–205.

Knobloch, L. K., & Solomon, D. H. (1999). Measuring the sources and content of relational uncertainty. *Communication Studies*, 50(4), 261–278.

Knobloch, L. K., & Solomon, D. H. (2002a). Information seeking beyond initial interaction: Negotiating relational uncertainty within close relationships. *Human Communication Research*, 28(2), 243–257.

Knobloch, L. K., & Solomon, D. H. (2002b). Intimacy and the magnitude and experience of episodic relational uncertainty within romantic relationships. *Personal Relationships*, 9, 457–478.

Knobloch, L. K., & Solomon, D. H. (2005). Relational uncertainty and relational information processing: Questions without answers? *Communication Research*, 32(3), 349–388.

Livingston, K. R. (1980). Love as a process of reducing uncertainty: Cognitive theory. In K. S. Pope (ed.), *On love and loving*. San Francisco, CA: Jossey-Bass, pp. 133–151.

Planalp, S., Rutherford, D. K., & Honeycutt, J. M. (1988). Events that increase uncertainty in personal relationships II: Replication and extension. *Human Communication Research*, 14(4), 516–547.

Relationship Development

Rebecca B. Rubin

Kent State University

Since the dawn of interpersonal communication research in the early 1970s, communication researchers have been interested in relationship development processes. Theories focused on how strangers develop more personal and intimate alliances with others over time, couples work to maintain relationships, and partners cope when they fall apart or disintegrate. Extensions and applications of these basic theories into work, family, cross-cultural, and mediated arenas followed.

Several important *relationship development theories*, advanced in the 1970s, laid the foundation for the next 30 years. Altman and Taylor's (1973) Social Penetration Theory claimed that relationships develop because people expect the amount and nature of rewards accrued by continuing will exceed the potential costs. Communicators exchange an increasingly broad number of topics, going into more depth on some and staying superficial on others. But as the topics and depth progress from non-intimate areas to more intimate ones, the layers are peeled, like an onion, and the relationship develops. Relational dissolution (i.e., depenetration) follows the same process, but in reverse.

Duck's (1973) description of the phases of breaking up was consistent with this approach, but examined satisfaction with the relationship, possible confrontation about complaints, means of dealing with one's social network, and retrospection on the breakup (→ Relational Termination). Rogers (Rogers & Farace 1975) described another relational approach to development based on analysis of conversations; symmetrical or complementary transactions connote similar types of relationships (→ Transactional Models).

Charles Berger's → Uncertainty Reduction Theory (URT) has generated the most research in the communication field (Berger & Calabrese 1975). On the basis of attraction theories developed by Newcomb, Asch, Miller, and Heider (Knapp et al. 2002; Rubin & Rubin 2001), Berger identified three main stages of development: entry, person, and exit. Berger and associates developed and tested 21 theorems centered on seven essential communication concepts: amount of communication, nonverbal affiliative expressiveness, information-seeking behavior, intimacy level, reciprocity, similarity, and liking. Research also examined five main strategies for reducing uncertainty: interrogation, self-disclosure, detecting deception, environmental structuring, and deviation testing (→ Disclosure in Interpersonal Communication; Deception Detection Accuracy; Information Seeking). The process of development was conceived as a series of proactive (predictions) and retroactive (explanations) attributions about the other person before, during, and after interaction (→ Attribution Processes).

Miller & Steinberg's (1975) Goal-Plan-Action model proposed that relationships move from non-interpersonal (where demographic/stereotypic attributions are based on cultural/sociological information) to interpersonal (in which psychological information is used to create personal/private attributions). Central concepts of this model are control (people intentionally try to affect others) and exchange of rewards (with reduction of costs). Three main skills necessary for development are empathy, self-disclosure, and small talk (→ Empathy Theory; Interpersonal Communication Competence and Social Skills).

Knapp's (1978) Staircase Model was based on Murray Davis's 1973 book *Intimate relations* and Social Penetration Theory. Knapp identified five stages of coming together – initiating, experimenting, intensifying, integrating, bonding – and five stages of coming apart – differentiating, circumscribing, stagnating, avoiding, and terminating. Progression through the stages depends on interactions that take place and amount of information exchanged.

The 1980s produced extensions of these theories and some new directions (Berger & Gudykunst 1991). Judee Burgoon and Jerold Hale (1984) extracted fundamental topics in the relational area. Gudykunst extended URT to the intercultural communication arena, and Leslie Baxter, following Duck's work, continued to examine elements such as disengagement, turning points, and other stages (→ Relational Maintenance). This latter approach was continued into the 1990s and until today by those following more of a dialectical approach.

Researchers have investigated development in several *types of relationships*. Most research has focused on romantic or potentially romantic interactions (Vangelisti 2002; → Dating Relationships). These works identified attraction and attribution as key elements in moving from one stage to another (→ Interpersonal Attraction). Studies of friendship among acquaintances and roommates, dissolution, and conflict among family members or spouses abound. Best known in this area is the work of Baxter and Bullis on turning points, Bochner on families, and Fitzpatrick on marital couple types.

Additional research has looked at interpersonal relationships across cultures, identifying mainly the uncertainty that is inherent in cultural differences. URT in work relationships has taken the form of socialization and assimilation; later work has looked at uncertain situations such as job transfers, stress, and burnout. A similar applied area is the health field, with URT applied to provider–patient and caregiver–patient relationships.

Extensions to mediated relationships began with examination of URT to explain parasocial relationship development with television characters and online relationships (Walther & Parks 2002; → Mediated Social Interaction). In effect, with so many relationships today initiated online and with the help of mobile phones, email, and instant messaging (IM) programs, long-distance relationship development (see Stafford 2005) becomes more than interpersonal – almost hyperpersonal (→ Long-Distance Relationships; Online Relationships). Thus focus on the medium has replaced prior investigations into the process.

SEE ALSO: ► Attribution Processes ► Dating Relationships ► Deception Detection Accuracy ► Disclosure in Interpersonal Communication ► Empathy Theory ► Friendship and Communication ► Information Seeking ► Interpersonal Attraction ► Interpersonal Communication Competence and Social Skills ► Long-Distance Relationships ► Mediated Social Interaction ► Online Relationships ► Relational Maintenance ► Relational Termination ► Transactional Models ► Uncertainty Reduction Theory

References and Suggested Readings

Altman, I., & Taylor, D. (1973). *Social penetration: The development of interpersonal relationships.* New York: Holt, Rinehart and Winston.

Berger, C. R., & Calabrese, R. J. (1975). Some explorations in initial interaction and beyond: Toward a developmental theory of interpersonal communication. *Human Communication Research*, 1, 99–112.

Berger, C. R., & Gudykunst, W. B. (1991). Uncertainty and communication. In B. Dervin & M. Voight (eds.), *Progress in communication sciences*. Norwood, NJ: Ablex, pp. 21–66.

Burgoon, J. K., & Hale, J. L. (1984). The fundamental topoi of relational communication. *Communication Monographs*, 51, 193–214.

Davis, Murray, S. (1973). *Intimate relations*. New York: Free Press.

Duck, S. W. (1973). *Personal relationships and personal constructs*. London: John Wiley.

Knapp, M. L. (1978). *Social intercourse: From greetings to goodbye*. Boston: Allyn and Bacon.

Knapp, M. L., Daly, J. A., Albada, K. F., & Miller, G. R. (2002). Background and current trends in the study of interpersonal communication. In M. L. Knapp & J. A. Daly (eds.), *Handbook of interpersonal communication*, 2nd edn. Thousand Oaks, CA: Sage, pp. 3–20.

Miller, G. R., & Steinberg, M. (1975). *Between people: A new analysis of interpersonal communication*. Chicago: Science Research Associates.

Rogers, L. E., & Farace, V. (1975). Analysis of relational communication in dyads. *Human Communication Research*, 1, 229–239.

Rubin, R. B., & Rubin, A. M. (2001). Attribution in social and parasocial relationships. In V. Manusov & J. H. Harvey (eds.), *Attribution, communication behavior, and close relationships*. Cambridge: Cambridge University Press, pp. 320–337.

Stafford, L. (2005). *Maintaining long-distance and cross-residential relationships*. Mahwah, NJ: Lawrence Erlbaum.

Vangelisti, A. L. (2002). Interpersonal processes in romantic relationships. In J. A. Daly & M. L. Knapp (eds.), *Handbook of interpersonal communication*, 3rd edn. Thousand Oaks, CA: Sage, pp. 643–679.

Walther, J. B., & Parks, M. R. (2002). Cues filtered out, cues filtered in: Computer-mediated communication and relationships. In M. L. Knapp & J. A. Daly (eds.), *Handbook of interpersonal communication*, 3rd edn. Thousand Oaks, CA: Sage, pp. 529–563.

Reliability

Klaus Krippendorff

University of Pennsylvania

Linguistically, the word "reliability" occurs in contexts of relying on something, for example, on one's tools, someone else's service, given measuring instruments, or data. In the conduct of science, the reliability of data is an important bottleneck for the construction of theories or scientific conjectures, and for giving reasonable advice.

Data usually are the primary and therefore the most direct representations of typically transient phenomena that researchers are interested in theorizing, conceptualizing, or explaining. Interviews, public happenings, historical events, natural catastrophes, even scientific experiments do not last long enough for important details to be inspected (→ Research Methods; Experimental Design). Moreover, phenomena cannot be compared unless they co-occur. Analysis, comparison, and research of diverse transient and non-synchronous phenomena cannot proceed without relying on sufficiently durable representations of them: data for short. Even archaeological artifacts that have endured natural decay, often thought to be direct and unmistakably obvious data, are not data unless they can be seen as the products of a distant culture that archaeologists seek to understand. Observations, when committed to memory, may seem individually more real than phenomena talked about by others, but they have no intersubjective status until they are recorded, described, or transcribed, until they have become data for more than one person. Thus, one speaks of data when a community can handle them in the absence of phenomena of interest to that community.

EPISTEMOLOGY OF RELIABILITY

Reliability is a measure of the extent to which a community can trust data as stand-ins for unavailable phenomena. *Sources of unreliability* are many. Measuring instruments may malfunction, be influenced by variables that are irrelevant to what is to be measured, or be misread. When asked for their opinions, interviewees may answer to please the interviewer. Witnesses may testify from recollections that are distorted by self-interests, enriched by recent insights, or informed by explanations heard from third parties. Medical doctors may disagree on the diagnosis of a patient. Content analysts may have conflicting assessments of what a text means. Demonstrating the reliability of data means ruling out all conceivable sources of uncertainty that could have contributed to the data's present form.

Assessing the reliability of data entails two *epistemological difficulties*. Not only are many phenomena that data aim to represent transitory, but, even when they are not so, it is the act of generating data that makes them into known phenomena. For example, one does not know the time of the day unless there is a clock to observe. One does not know the meaning of a text unless one reads it. One does not know the category of an event unless someone categorizes it. Data are relatively durable descriptions that create what they describe. This fact is the most important reason why researchers need to assure themselves and each other that the data they have generated or obtained from other sources are reliable in the sense of representing something real and are, hence, worthy of attention. Obtaining such assurances presents two problems: how to assess the reliability of data, and once measured, whether their unreliability is tolerable or not.

TWO COMPATIBLE CONCEPTS OF RELIABILITY

There are two concepts of reliability in use. (1) From the perspective of → *measurement theory*, reliability amounts to an assurance that a method of generating data is free of influence from circumstances that are extraneous to the processes of observation, description, or measurement. Establishing this kind of reliability means measuring the extent to which the variation in data is free of variation from spurious causes. Such tests require duplicating the data-making effort under a variety of circumstances that could affect the data. These duplications must be independent of each other and obtained under the very conditions under which one would like the data to be stable. For example, if human coders are involved, one wants to use coders whose kind can be found elsewhere (→ Content Analysis, Quantitative). For interview data, one wants to be sure that the personality of the interviewer does not affect what interviewees say (→ Interview; Survey).

If the temperature of medical patients is measured, one may want to be sure that room temperature does not influence the outcome. The extent of agreement among these duplications is interpreted as the degree to which data can be considered reliable and, hence, trusted.

(2) From the perspective of *interpretation theory*, reliability amounts to an assurance that researchers interpret their data consensually. Establishing this kind of reliability means demonstrating that the members of a scientific community agree on the meaning of the data they analyze. Unlike measurement theory, interpretation theory recognizes that researchers may have different backgrounds, interests, and theoretical orientations that lead them to different interpretations of the same data. Seeing the same phenomenon from different perspectives is typical, often considered instructive, and not counted as evidence of unreliability. It is when data are taken as evidence about phenomena not under researchers' control, say, about historical events, witness accounts, or statistical facts, that unreliability can become an issue. A method for establishing this kind of reliability is triangulation. Data are reliable when, after accounting for explainable differences in approaches and perspectives, three or more sets of data imply the same thing. Unreliability becomes evident, however, when one researcher's claim of what the data represent contradicts the claims made by others. When one researcher considers his or her data as evidence for "A" while others consider their data as evidence for "not A," the two claims cannot both be true. Data that cannot be triangulated erode an interpretive community's trust in them. From the perspective of interpretation theory, therefore, reliability assures a community that its members are talking about the same phenomena – without availability of these phenomena independent of talking about them.

Whereas measurement theory focuses on the process of generating data and attempts to assure researchers that their data are representative of real as opposed to spurious phenomena, interpretation theory concerns itself with what measurement theory tries to accomplish, namely that researchers agree regarding whether they are investigating the same phenomena. Both concepts of reliability rely on achieving substantial agreement.

RELIABILITY AND AGREEMENT

The reliability of a particular technological device often is an either/or proposition; for example, does the engine of a car start or not? The reliability of a class of devices usually is the failure rate of its members, indicated by a statistic; for example, the repair record of a particular model of car. However, when humans are involved in generating data, especially by recording observations or reading texts – from recording the numerical values read from a measuring instrument to judging whether published statements are favorable or unfavorable to a candidate for political office – their reliability depends on agreement among independently obtained records of observations, readings, or judgments.

Agreement is not truth, and reliability, therefore, must not be confused with → validity. Validity is the quality of research results, statistical findings, measurements, or propositions being true in the sense that they do represent the phenomena they claim to represent. To establish validity requires validating evidence. Predictions, for example, are not valid until they come true. By contrast, from the measurement theory perspective, reliability assures that data are generated with all conceivable precautions against

Table 1   Kinds of reliability and validity for comparison

	What is measured?	Errors registered by the measure
Stability	Agreement between the results of repeated applications of the same process to the same set of phenomena	Intra-observer inconsistencies
Reproducibility	Agreement between the results of applying several supposedly identical processes to the same set of phenomena	Intra-observer inconsistencies + Inter-observer disagreement
Accuracy	Agreement between an accepted standard and the results of applying one or more supposedly identical processes to the same set of phenomena	Intra-observer inconsistencies + Inter-observer disagreement + Disagreement with a standard
Validity	Agreement between research results and what they claim to represent	Intra-observer inconsistencies + Inter-observer disagreement + Disagreement with a standard + Disagreement with evidence

extraneous influence from the data-making process; from the perspective of interpretation theory, reliability insures that all available data triangulate and their interpretations are consistent with each other – in the absence of evidence of what these data actually represent. Since validating evidence is rarely available while data are being analyzed, reliability often is the only criterion available to empirical researchers.

KINDS OF RELIABILITY

There are three kinds of reliability: stability, reproducibility, and accuracy, which may be contrasted with validity. They are distinguished by registering different kinds of errors and having unequal strengths (Table 1).

Stability is also called test–retest reliability, reproducibility test–test reliability, and accuracy test–standard reliability. While all three reliabilities (and incidentally validity as well) are determined by measuring agreement, the data for stability, reproducibility, and accuracy (and validity) differ. As the table suggests, stability reacts to just one kind of error, replicability to two, and accuracy to three. It follows that accuracy is the strongest and stability the weakest form of reliability. In most practical situations, however, replicability is preferred.

MEASURING RELIABILITY

From the measurement theory perspective, reliability is the degree to which a data-making process is reproducible in a variety of situations, by different but identically instructed observers or interpreters, or by different measuring devices that are designed to respond to the same phenomena in identical ways. From the interpretation theory perspective, reliability is rarely actually measured, but assessed in terms of the degree to which separate researchers concur in the use of data claimed to be about the same phenomena.

Where humans are involved as observers, researchers, coders, translators, or inter-preters, *appropriate measures of reliability* – reproducibility in particular – must do the following:

1 Treat the observers involved as interchangeable (the point of replicability being that any qualified observer should be able to comprehend the given instructions for what is to be done, observe, read, or interpret the phenomena in question, and record them accordingly).
2 Measure the extent of the (dis)agreement or (in)compatibilities among many (at least two) independently working observers or researchers regarding the descriptions or categorizations of a given set of phenomena (recording units).
3 Compare the observed (dis)agreements or (in)compatibilities with what would be expected when the accounts of these phenomena were chance events. In order to be interpretable as the absence of reliability, chance must be defined as the condition of no correlation between the descriptions collectively used to account for the phenomena in question and the phenomena to which they were meant to apply. For example, chance would be observed when observers assigned their descriptions to the phenomena by throwing dice.
4 Be independent of the number and kind of descriptions available to each phenomenon (so as to yield reliability measures that are comparable across variables with different numbers of values or scales of measurement).
5 Define a scale that is anchored in at least two points with meaningful reliability inter-pretations: perfect reliability (typically 1.000) and the absence of any reliability or chance agreement (typically 0.000).
6   Yield values that are comparable across levels of measurements, where different levels – nominal, ordinal, interval, and ratio metrics – are involved.

There are only a few statistics that satisfy these criteria, and researchers should examine them in the above terms before settling on one.

CRITICAL VALUES

The second question concerns the conditions under which somewhat unreliable data may still be trusted for use in subsequent analyses or rejected as too misleading. Some researchers look for a fixed numerical cut-off point in the scale that an agreement coefficient defines. Save for perfect agreement, there are no magical numbers, however. Cut-off points depend on the costs of losing one's reputation, resources, or affecting others' well-being by drawing false conclusions from unreliable data. When someone's life is at stake, for example in criminal proceedings or in medical diagnoses, or when decisions between war and peace are made dependent on imperfect data, the costs of wrong conclusions are high and that cut-off point must be high as well. In academic research, where the consequences of wrong conclusions may be less drastic, reliability standards may be more relaxed but should never be ignored.

While reliable data cannot guarantee valid conclusions – researchers can make mistakes in analyzing perfectly reliable data – unreliable data always reduce the probability of drawing valid conclusions from them. This relationship between reliability and validity renders reliability assessments an important safeguard against potentially invalid research results.

SEE ALSO: ▶ Content Analysis, Quantitative ▶ Experimental Design ▶ Interview ▶ Measurement Theory ▶ Research Methods ▶ Survey ▶ Validity

References and Suggested Readings

Krippendorff, K. (2004). *Content analysis: An introduction to its methodology.* Thousand Oaks, CA: Sage.

Religion and Popular Communication

Jon Radwan

Seton Hall University

"Communication" derives from the Latin term *communicare* meaning to share or impart and to make common (→ Communication: Definitions and Concepts). "Popular communication" refers to those efforts of, by, and for the people that establish and maintain this sharing and commonality (→ Popular Communication). In this sense, communication is the basic requirement for sustaining any social group. "The people" are generally understood as the average or common members of a society, the masses, and are contrasted with elite sub-groups that possess an unusual degree of power, wealth, or information. "The people" are also distinguished from "others," who are nonmembers of any particular group at issue but are members of their own social groups (→ Popular Culture).

"Religion" has a more obscure etymology, with Latin and Old French derivations pointing to binding and reconnection, reverence, rereading, gathering, and care. From a philosophical perspective, religions are belief systems or worldviews that posit a divine order for both human life and the universe as a whole. There is significant diversity of belief among world religions regarding the structure of this divine order, but human recognition of a spiritual "depth dimension" is universal. From a communication perspective, a religion is a more or less organized social movement working to unify a people by advocating and passing on ways of life that are in accord with its vision of divine order.

EARLY HISTORY

Historically, universality of religion suggests that sharing spiritual experience was one of the first goals of human communication. Early human culture is characterized by oral, gestural, and graphic media. Early *graphic evidence* of religious communication is recognized in Upper Paleolithic cave art (40,000 to 10,000 BCE); the scale (murals up to 20 feet in length, 20 feet above floor level), location (some nearly inaccessible, others in cave galleries for popular viewing), permanence (a consistent message across hundreds of generations), and expense (requiring extensive scaffolding, assistants, tools and pigment, lighting) all demonstrate how cave art expresses awe and reverence. Paleolithic oral (myths, legends, dramas) and gestural or performative (songs, dances, rituals, etc.) communication traditions are more difficult to trace, but archaeological evidence of interment and other ritual practices is clear as early as 160,000 years ago (→ Storytelling and Narration). Each subsequent media revolution enables new forms of expression, but orality, visual symbolism, and ritual performance are the fundamental modes of popular religious communication (→ Rituals in Popular Communication).

Architecture presents another early avenue of popular religious expression, serving to mark sacred spaces or times and create appropriate ritual environments. Numerous megalithic calendars and tombs dating from 5000 BCE show both precise astronomical knowledge and considerable labor invested in transporting and positioning massive stones. As agriculture developed, temples and shrines became important structures within the new and growing cities.

Many religions vector toward sacred locations and architecture – ritualized travel to a distant site represents both the first mass form of international communication and a fundamental pattern for socio-religious movements (→ Social Movements and Communication). Pilgrimage sites are still vital centers for disseminating religious knowledge, styles, and imagery. The holy city of Mecca in Saudi Arabia is a prime example, today it is estimated that over 2.5 million Muslim pilgrims visit and worship in the month of Zil al-Hijjah.

WRITING

With the development of alphabetic writing circa 2000 BCE, the myths and meta-narratives of oral religious traditions could be recorded and distributed with a broader reach and a new degree of uniformity and precision. The sacred texts and commentary of manuscript culture became important to many religions, forging a close relationship between religion and literacy. With Islam, reading the Koran in Arabic is considered a spiritual obligation for everyone. Judaism and Christianity also advanced literacy, but for most people religious communication remained oral and performative. Hinduism is an exemplar – it is the oldest active world religion, developing out of the already ancient Vedic oral tradition between 3000 and 1000 BCE. The Hindu Vedas are revealed sacred texts, but they are experienced orally and referred to as *Shruti*, "that which has been heard."

Manuscript culture remains active, as with Judaism and the Torah, but religious communication changed radically as printing technologies developed worldwide. Buddhist scriptures and artwork were printed with woodblocks as early as the sixth century CE, and in Europe Gutenberg's *Bible* (1455) represents a landmark event; the movable-type press inaugurated mass production of books, a much more portable and durable medium than manuscripts. Martin Luther's publication of *Ninety-five theses* in 1517 sparked the Protestant Reformation and ultimately pushed the spread of literacy by encouraging vernacular translation and personal interpretation of the Bible. Later, when paper became less expensive and presses more common, religious newspapers and periodicals flourished. This was especially true in the "new world" of North America, where religious books and tracts were used extensively to spread both literacy and morality from the educated east to the wilds of the expanding western frontier.

MODERN MEDIA

The end of the nineteenth century saw the development of electronic media in the west. Telegraph and telephone are primarily interpersonal media and had minimal impact on popular religious communication, but the development of → radio at the turn of the century introduced a revolutionary pattern of dissemination, broadcasting (→ Telegraph, History of; Radio: Social History). Prior to broadcast media, religious communication was relatively local. Pilgrimage site art and architecture could share a uniform message with millions, but it took hundreds of years; print media introduced portability and faster distribution on a larger scale, but were limited to literate receivers. With broadcasting, a uniform oral message is shared nearly instantaneously on a mass scale. By the 1930s radio was firmly established as the mass medium for both Europe and North America, with television following a similar growth pattern in the 1960s. Religious programming in the United States was among the earliest genres because commercial broadcasters interpreted their legal obligation to operate in the → public interest as a call to provide major religions with weekly airtime and programming support. Today religion remains the third most widely syndicated radio format in the United States. In the 1980s, cable and satellite networks extended the broadcast pattern to a national and international scale, and numerous churches and faith-based organizations have embraced this expanded opportunity for mass ministry by founding their own studios and channels, many operating 24 hours a day, seven days a week (→ Cable Television; Satellite Television; International Television; Morality and Taste in Media Content).

With the turn of the twenty-first century, *computer media* are rapidly developing alongside both the fundamental oral, graphic, and performative media and the now firmly established print and broadcast media. The → Internet enables nearly all users to communicate on a global scale in both text and audio-visual formats, and religious content and interaction abound. In contrast to the unilateral quality of broadcast and print media, computers enable both dissemination and bilateral interaction – sender and receiver can converse and discuss all issues, including religion, with greater speed and reach than ever before. However, just as literacy rates limit the reach and efficacy of print, economic conditions limit the scale of broadcast and computer media. In developed countries where technology is common and networks are established, mass-mediated and web-based religious communication can be enormously influential, but in developing countries the impact is much less apparent.

In the future, as computer media undoubtedly spread, religious content and interaction will grow along with global networks. Extensive use of electronic media for religious purposes makes it clear that communication *about* religion is well served by all media, but religious communication itself, the rites that express reverence, awe, devotion, and belonging, tend to be more interpersonal than mediated. With radio and television some rituals are broadcast, yet presence at and participation in a physical communal event is usually considered necessary for sacred purposes. Popular religious communication remains fundamentally oral and visual, especially within ritual performance contexts.

SEE ALSO: ▶ Cable Television ▶ Communication: Definitions and Concepts ▶ International Television ▶ Internet ▶ Morality and Taste in Media Content ▶ Popular Communication ▶ Popular Culture ▶ Public Interest ▶ Radio ▶ Radio: Social History ▶ Rhetoric and Religion ▶ Rituals in Popular Communication ▶ Satellite Television ▶ Social Movements and Communication ▶ Storytelling and Narration ▶ Telegraph, History of

References and Suggested Readings

James, W. (1958). *The varieties of religious experience*. New York: Mentor.
Malinowski, B. (1948). *Magic, science and religion*. Boston: Beacon Press.
Maslow, A. H. (1970). *Religions, values, and peak-experiences*. New York: Penguin.
McDannell, C. (1998). *Material Christianity: Religion and popular culture in America*. New Haven, CT: Yale University Press.
Nord, D. P. (2004). *Faith in reading: Religious publishing and the birth of mass media in America*. New York: Oxford University Press.
Ostling, R. N. (1984). Evangelical publishing and broadcasting. In G. Marsden (ed.), *Evangelicalism and modern America*. Grand Rapids, MI: W. B. Eerdmans.
Weber, M. (1922). *The sociology of religion*. Boston: Beacon Press.

Remediation

Jay David Bolter

Georgia Institute of Technology

Remediation (Bolter & Grusin 1999) refers to a historical process through which newer media forms interact with earlier ones. On the very first page of *Understanding media* (1964), → Marshall McLuhan noted that the "'content' of any medium is always another medium: the content of writing is speech, just as the written word is the content of print." Remediation proceeds from this insight, but understands the process as more complex and historically nuanced.

The relationship between media is not a linear process of replacement or incorporation, as McLuhan suggested; instead, the media of a given culture enter into a configuration of relationships involving cooperation as well as competition among numerous media. When a new medium is introduced (e.g., film at the beginning of the twentieth century, television in the middle, or the computer at the end), the whole configuration may shift. Designers and producers working in the new medium may seek to take over the roles previously played by the established media, and their counterparts in the established media may respond either by yielding easily or by reasserting their own roles (→ Design

Theory). This dual *process of appropriation and reappropriation* will remain ongoing as long as the various media remain vigorous. Today, printed materials (books, magazines, newspapers), film, television, and radio remain important, although practitioners in these media have had to adjust their roles because of the introduction of digital forms.

One might generalize and claim that Hollywood film remediates the novel, or that computer games remediate film. Used more precisely, however, the term "remediation" describes specific creative acts: the computer game *The Lord of the Rings: The Two Towers* remediates the Peter Jackson films, which in turn remediate the novels by J. R. R. Tolkien. Remediation is not a mere transfer of content. In the quotation from *Understanding media* above, McLuhan himself put the word "content" in quotation marks, indicating that the distinction of form and content was problematic for him. By the same token, new media producers do not remediate content per se, but rather the representational practices of a previous media form.

For example, some *video and computer games* borrow and refashion camera techniques and narrative elements from film (→ Video Games). Such games have radically extended the first-person (or subjective) camera. In film, the subjective camera locates the viewer in the persona of one or a few main characters (→ Cinematography). Early generations of action and role-playing games put the player almost exclusively into the viewing position of the main figure. This practice (which may in fact have been adopted to make the rendering of computer graphics more efficient) was promoted as a defining advantage of games over film. Games were and are still claimed to be interactive (→ Interactivity, Concept of): not only can the player see through the eyes of the main character, but he or she can act as the main character, usually by fighting opponents and gaining various forms of treasure. Later games have become more sophisticated in their camerawork, refashioning many Hollywood techniques quite explicitly in so-called cut scenes over which the player has no control. Game producers, however, continue to insist on the advantage of games as a representational practice: they are interactive, not fully determined by the game designer.

This claim to greater authenticity (or sometimes even "reality") is a defining aspect of remediation in general. For this reason, acts of remediation establish an ambivalent relationship between the remediating and remediated forms. The producers of the new form borrow representational elements from the older one, but, in refashioning those elements, they further make an implicit or explicit claim that their new form is in some way better, i.e., more authentic or more realistic.

Bolter and Grusin (1999) identified two main *representational strategies* of remediation: transparency and hypermediacy. *Transparency* is a strategy that dates back at least to Renaissance painting, in which the artist or producer tries to erase the evidence of the medium: to make the medium disappear so that viewers may feel as if they were in the presence of the object or scene represented. Examples include linear-perspective painting, so-called "straight photography," Hollywood narrative cinema, and digital interactive narratives. *Hypermediacy* is the opposite strategy, in which the producer acknowledges and even celebrates the process of mediation. Examples include avant-garde cinema, postmodern architecture, and many forms of digital installation and performance art (→ Art as Communication). As approaches to remediation, a focus on either transparency or hypermediacy indicates whether the producer is inclined to cover up or to acknowledge a dependence on earlier media forms. The strategy of transparency often makes a direct appeal to nature, denying its dependence on these earlier forms.

Remediation is one theoretical approach to comparative media studies. Intermediality is another term that covers, for instance, an approach currently pursued by a variety of scholars in Europe and Canada (→ Intermediality). While intermediality often implies synchronic studies of media forms, remediation entails a historical approach (→ Media History). This historical perspective is grounded in a conviction that there is a relationship between formal strategies of representation and the ideologies of particular times and cultural groups. Strategies of remediation are also strategies for affirming cultural identities. Thus, the so-called music-video and remix generation may favor a strategy of hybridity and hypermediacy, while older viewers may prefer the transparency that still characterizes Hollywood films.

SEE ALSO: ▶ Art as Communication ▶ Cinematography ▶ Design Theory ▶ Interactivity, Concept of ▶ Intermediality ▶ McLuhan, Marshall ▶ Media History ▶ Video Games

References and Suggested Readings

Bolter, J. D., & Grusin, R. (1999). *Remediation: Understanding new media.* Cambridge, MA: MIT Press.
Fetveit, A., & Stald, G. S. (eds.) (in preparation). *Digital aesthetics and communication: Conceptual and theoretical reassessments.*
Manovich, L. (2001). *The language of new media.* Cambridge, MA: MIT Press.
McLuhan, M. (1964). *Understanding media.* New York: McGraw-Hill.
Müller, J. E. (1996). *Intermedialität, Formen moderner kultureller Kommunikation.* Münster: Nordus Publikationen.
Qvortrup, L., & Philipsen, H. (eds.) (in preparation). *Moving media studies: Remediation revisited.*
Spielmann, Y. (1998). *Intermedialität: Das System Peter Greenaway.* Munich: Wilhelm Fink.

Research Dissemination

Jon F. Kerner

US National Cancer Institute

When considering how the lessons learned from science can be used by those audiences who might benefit from them, the term "research dissemination" (Lomas 1993) has been coined to focus on the active process by which information gleaned from science is actively communicated to those audiences who are thought to be most likely to benefit from this information. However, there is considerable confusion in terminology among those who focus on this important issue. Thus, "communication," "diffusion," and "dissemination" are often used interchangeably to describe the processes by which information from science is moved into the public or practice domains (→ Diffusion of

Information and Innovation). Similarly when focused on the benefits of research dissemination processes, knowledge transfer, translational research, research translation, knowledge integration, and knowledge implementation are often presented as comparable outcomes from research dissemination.

With respect to research dissemination processes, the terms "communication," "diffusion," and "dissemination" have overlapping but different meanings. As such, they are often confused with one another. In simplest terms, *communication* is the provision of information through sounds and signs (sight) that can be transmitted to single individuals, small and large groups, organizations, communities, and mass populations. Communication can also be transmitted through other senses (e.g., touch, smell), but this is usually restricted to transmissions to a single individual or between individuals, and rarely extends to larger groups or populations (→ Communication: Definitions and Concepts). *Dissemination* simply means to scatter widely, and the term "diffusion" is often used as a synonym for dissemination. *Diffusion*, in the context of chemistry, is the spontaneous migration of substances from regions where their concentration is high to regions where their concentration is low.

Thus, in the context of information and knowledge, prior to the availability of mass communication technologies (e.g., the printing press; → Media History) information and knowledge were largely concentrated within religious and private libraries, universities, and academies, and communication was limited to correspondence and the distribution of a limited number of handwritten texts (Eisenstein 1979; Chartier 1987). Diffusion of information, where it did occur, was also limited to storytellers (e.g., religious) and oral reporters of official information (e.g., town criers). With the advent of mass communication technologies, diffusion of information became more rapid, the ability to actively disseminate information to larger audiences became possible, and the ability to tailor the information for particular audiences became a reality.

PASSIVE VERSUS ACTIVE COMMUNICATION

In the modern context of communication, diffusion and dissemination reflect a different level of action or effort to perhaps achieve the same outcome (i.e., widespread exposure to information). Thus, diffusion is often conceived as a relatively passive process, whereby "natural" channels of communication (e.g., word of mouth, reading) allow information to diffuse through individuals and social networks into larger populations, albeit slowly over time. With respect to information related to new ideas or technologies, this process has been labeled the diffusion of innovation (Rogers 2003) whereby creators of new information or innovators pass information on to early adopters and information continues to be communicated and used over time following an S-shaped curve (from mid to late adopters) until all the population of potential information users have been exposed to the innovation and most if not all are able to use it (→ Rogers, Everett).

Dissemination, on the other hand, is associated with more active efforts to accelerate the transmission of information beyond passive individual communication channels to reach a wider audience and larger populations more quickly than passive diffusion (Lomas 1993). Effective dissemination involves several steps: (1) identifying audience characteristics that may make them more or less receptive to, or interested in, the information being disseminated (→ Audience Research); (2) understanding the context in which the information is likely to be used; (3) framing the information to maximize audience receptivity and contextual relevance (→ Framing Effects); and (4) creating feedback mechanisms that allow monitoring of information exposure and use, enabling modification of dissemination strategies as receptivity and context change over time.

UNDERSTANDING DIFFERENT AUDIENCES

The → audiences in communication are many and varied, and are often recognized by the channels through which communication takes place to them. Thus, for example, the media, both entertainment and → news, are seen as a communication channel to reach the general public. While media do segment the general public (e.g., demographically, psychographically, and geographically; → Audience Segmentation) to address the different appetites for information, media communication is designed to reach masses of individuals in a wide variety of personal settings (e.g., home, work, recreation). With respect to research dissemination, the news media in particular are regularly contacted by research agencies to alert them to new findings. As such both the news media and the research community may usually be focused on novelty rather than the significance of new scientific knowledge.

Commercial communication also reaches out to market segments of the general public, and has a broader set of communication channels including point of sale, personal sales representatives, as well as traditional media outlets. With the advent of the → Internet, and computerized tracking of purchasing behavior, commercial communication has the led the way in developing and implementing individually tailored communications that frames the information in the context of past purchasing behavior patterns based on market research data collection. Thus, for example, discount coupons provided at supermarket checkout counters are tailored to past purchases, increasing the probability that similar or related products will obtained. Similarly, Internet sales websites provide their customers with email reminders and other forms of electronic communications about new opportunities to purchase goods or services that reflect their interests and past purchasing behavior.

Political communication, to promote candidates for office or political ideologies, has also adopted many of the commercial communication strategies of market research, market segmentation, and message framing to shape the information to fit the values or beliefs of target constituencies (→ Political Communication; Strategic Framing). While not nearly as sophisticated as either commercial or political communication, government and nongovernment organization communication efforts to reach the general public (e.g., to promote health, social well-being, and national security) have also attempted to take advantage of new communication technologies to improve the receptivity of information being communicated (→ Health Communication). While communication interventions vary widely in the extent to which information about the audience shapes the messages being communicated, they all share one thing in common: broad reach is more important than the magnitude of the response to the information communicated. Thus, for example, a small percentage increase in sales or change in voting behavior across a large population is considered more significant than a large impact in a relatively small proportion of the general population.

Dissemination on the other hand, while sharing many of the same concerns about audience characteristics as communication, is much more focused on the *context in which information is used*, and as such seeks to achieve a larger impact on a relatively limited population of information users who share the same practice context. For example, in the health arena, there are three very different practice contexts in which information may be used: public health, primary care, and disease specialty care practice. Disseminating research information about new approaches to promote health and prevent disease to public health practitioners, needs to recognize: (1) the level of training of most public health practitioners (e.g., masters or bachelors trained) to translate information into practical knowledge that can be applied in public health practice context; (2) the variation in resources in international, national, state, and local public health practice contexts that make possible or make difficult the implementation of public health interventions based on new health promotion information; and (3) the extent to which public health practitioners working for long periods of time in resource-limited practice contexts may or may not be amenable to change.

Similarly in *clinical practice settings*, dissemination of research information to improve quality of care must be designed with three factors in mind: the rate of the dissemination for new clinically relevant information, the time constraints of clinical practice, and the variation in clinical infrastructure resources. With the explosion of access to research information and other information sources (e.g., patient blogs, professional associations) available to patients and providers from the Internet, a key challenge for both patients and providers is to sort through the enormous amount of information to separate the wheat from the chaff ($\rightarrow$ Health Communication and the Internet). For example, if the words "heart disease" are inserted into a Google search, 87,300,000 hits are returned. Similarly, if a search is made for "cancer control," one gets 116,000,000 hits. Thus, for two of the leading causes of death in the developed world, there are over 200,000,000 links to information on the web from which to choose. In any service delivery context, but particularly in the clinical care context, this is a great deal of information to sort through and integrate into practice.

In the primary *care practice context*, the communication and dissemination challenges are even greater because patients may be coming in with any number of signs or symptoms of a health-related problem, in contrast to the disease specialty context where the focus of both patients and providers is on one group of diseases or disorders ($\rightarrow$ Patient–Provider Communication). In primary care practice, patients may or may not be as motivated to search the web to find out more about their potential problem, compared to patients with a pre-existing condition seeking a specialist. For primary care practitioners, the challenge is not only to have the latest information on the signs or symptoms of the problems being presented at the point of patient contact, but also to have the time to review with the patient their broader personal and family health history information and a set of preventive medicine strategies designed to also promote health (e.g., smoking cessation, improved diet, increased physical activity).

New information management and communication technologies like the electronic medical record (EMR; with information from the practice) and the electronic health record (EHR; with information from the patient) hold the promise of providing *real-time communication* between practitioners and their patients, as well as providing the opportunity to disseminate to practitioners, at the point of patient contact, key decision aids based on patient-specific information such as test results or patient self-reported health status. It remains unclear to what extent current practitioners and patients will be willing to adopt these new forms of electronic communication and dissemination. To date the adoption of both EMRs and EHRs has been slow, particularly among smaller freestanding practices unaffiliated with large health-care systems.

In more specialized care contexts, the knowledge gap between the practitioner "expert" and the patient continues to narrow, as many patients take advantage of *open access to health and illness research information* available through the world wide web. Highly motivated patients will seek out and attempt to digest large amounts of treatment and follow-up information, frequently sharing this research information in their communications with their practitioners. This, in turn, can put a special burden on the practitioners who must not only become familiar with this research information but must also integrate it with their own tacit knowledge from practice experience as well their own efforts to keep up with the new information emerging from research.

As such, the process of shared decision-making and knowledge integration may become more the norm in the future, which in turn may help speed the process of research dissemination and use of new knowledge as it emerges from research innovations. As new generations enter the health service delivery workforce and become adult patients, the familiarity and comfort with electronic forms of communication, information seeking, and the electronic tools for increasing channels for communication and dissemination may lead to expanded shared decision-making between practice experts and knowledgeable patients. New approaches for integrating explicit knowledge from science with tacit knowledge from practice and patient experience will be needed (Kerner 2006).

RESEARCH INFORMATION AND PRACTICE KNOWLEDGE

As noted above in the context of health-care, the communication and dissemination of research information can lead to new knowledge, when the information is either put to immediate use or is understood in the context of a practice framework. Thus, information may or may not lead to new knowledge depending on how it is presented and how it is understood. Prior to the twentieth century, communication and diffusion of information were relatively slow processes that depended on the spoken or written word. This permitted time to deliberate about new research information and put it into context, and may have provided more time for information to be transformed into knowledge. Since the advent of modern communication technologies (radio, television, the Internet), more and more information from research and other sources is being transmitted with less and less time to digest the information. As such, one unintended consequence of the explosion of information available seven days a week, 24 hours a day, is that there is a signal-to-noise ratio problem with too much information being processed and too little time to contextualize the information into knowledge.

Instant messaging, instantly reviewing and replying to emails from PDAs (personal digital assistants), and the many and varied means by which people can now communicate with each other around the world, have provided multiple avenues for quickly sharing new information, reacting to changing situations in real time, and potentially speeding up the rate at which new information can be transformed into new knowledge by those with the time to deliberate about what the information may mean in their context (→ Technology and Communication). However, the shift from slow and deliberative communication and research dissemination technologies to instantaneous technologies may inadvertently contribute to the creation of a growing class of individuals who turn away from much of this new information and focus only on the things they can learn from their personal experience (→ Digital Divide). The impact of such a disparity may be the creation of large "knowledge gaps" that could impact many aspects of society (Viswanath & Finnegan 1996; → Knowledge Gap Effects).

KNOWLEDGE TRANSFER VERSUS KNOWLEDGE INTEGRATION

As more and more communication channels are opened, the temptation to push large amounts of research information out to as broad an audience as possible is great. The explosion of web links on the Internet with respect to virtually any topic imaginable is but one example of this high information push priority. All sectors of society are flooding the communication channels with new information resources, be they government, commercial, or NGOs (→ Knowledge Management). While facilitating communication and diffusion of information, these expanded communication channels also provide new challenges for disseminating information to those audiences who are most interested in the particular information being disseminated (i.e., pull), and have the resources (e.g., time, infrastructure) to transform this new information into knowledge that can be used.

In the field of research dissemination and implementation, the terms "knowledge transfer" and "knowledge integration" have been used to differentiate the push-only approach from the research dissemination approach which recognizes the importance of push, pull, and infrastructure to take advantage of new information and translate it into usable knowledge (Lomas 1993; Orleans 2002; Kerner 2006). A key to knowledge integration is to recognize the importance placed on information and knowledge gained from tacit experience in a practice context as well as explicit information and knowledge gained from research. In most *knowledge transfer dissemination approaches*, the assumption is often that the only information and knowledge worth disseminating is explicit. This may help to explain why the diffusion and dissemination of explicit new information from research falls on deaf ears when it contradicts or undermines long-held beliefs and assumptions based on experience within the context in which the information would be used.

Knowledge integration, on the other hand, recognizes that explicit information gained from research may or may not fit the context in which the information could be used and transformed into practice knowledge. As such, knowledge integration models for research dissemination require that an exchange of information take place between the advocates of explicit research information and those who value tacit knowledge from context-specific experience. When such an information exchange is valued by both parties, an informed decision can be made within a particular knowledge use context that weighs the benefits and costs of using the information from both research and experience.

OUTLOOK

The explosion of new communication channels in the twentieth and twenty-first centuries have provided both great opportunities and great challenges in transforming research information into knowledge that can be applied to improve the human condition. Research dissemination, when focused on knowledge integration and communication exchange, can help the process of transforming large amounts of new information based on research and practice into knowledge that can be useful and applied.

However, with rapid innovation in communication technologies comes the real concern that disparities will be exacerbated between those ready, willing, and able to take advantage of the information revolution, and those who are left behind because of limited access to, and limited understanding of, the new communication technologies. Research dissemination strategies must be developed to sort out how best to integrate the information-disadvantaged. Thus, all can benefit from the opportunities provided by these new mechanisms for communication, diffusion, and dissemination of research and the integration of research with practice, particularly when focused on the underserved.

SEE ALSO: ▶ Audience ▶ Audience Research ▶ Audience Segmentation ▶ Communication: Definitions and Concepts ▶ Diffusion of Information and Innovation ▶ Digital Divide ▶ Framing Effects ▶ Health Communication ▶ Health Communication and the Internet ▶ Internet ▶ Knowledge Gap Effects ▶ Knowledge Management ▶ Media History ▶ News ▶ Patient–Provider Communication ▶ Political Communication ▶ Rogers, Everett ▶ Strategic Framing ▶ Technology and Communication

References and Suggested Readings

Chartier, R. (1987). *The cultural uses of print in early modern France* (trans. L. G. Cochrane). Princeton: Princeton University Press.

Eisenstein, E. L. (1979). *The printing press as an agent of change: Communications and cultural transformations in early modern Europe*, 2 vols. Cambridge and New York: Cambridge University Press.

Kerner, J. (2006). Knowledge translation versus knowledge integration: A "funder's" perspective. *Journal of Continuing Education in the Health Professions*, 26(1), 72–80.

Lomas, J. (1993). Diffusion, dissemination, and implementation: Who should do what? *Annals of the New York Academy of Sciences*, 703, 226–237.

Orleans, C. T. (2002). Designing for dissemination. Conference presentation, Washington, DC, Sept. 19, 2002. Available at http://dccps.nci.nih.gov/d4d/pdfs/challenge_translation.pdf, accessed June 15, 2007.

Rogers, E. (2003). *Diffusion of innovation*, 5th edn. New York: Free Press.

Viswanath, K., & Finnegan, J. R. (1996). The knowledge gap hypothesis: Twenty-five years later. In B. Burleson (ed.), *Communication yearbook*, vol. 19. Thousand Oaks, CA: Sage, pp. 187–227.

Research Ethics

Patrick Lee Plaisance
Colorado State University

As the field of ethics addresses the philosophical foundations for standards of behavior and treatment of others when personal, social, and professional values conflict, social science researchers in general and communication researchers in particular are required to consider ethical implications of their work. Ethics is a process of deliberation that helps illuminate the dimensions and implications of our moral agency. It enables us to draw upon broad moral values to help question or justify a decision that will affect others. As professionals whose work both depends upon the willingness of others to cooperate and whose work can have direct or indirect bearing on the welfare of others, researchers are obligated to ensure their activities reflect commonly accepted ethical standards. Potential risks to subjects of research vary depending upon the nature of the questions explored and the methodologies used, but researchers are obligated as professionals to uphold fundamental values involving reduction of potential harm and respect due to all research participants as autonomous agents (→ Research Methods).

These and other fundamental values are rooted in the moral philosophy of Aristotle, Kant, Hegel, and others. These theorists proposed frameworks to assess the "good" or what constitutes "goodness." Kant, for example, proposed a system of moral law that places a premium on our "absolute" duties to respect and promote the exercise of free will and the capacity for reason that separates humans from the animal kingdom. This capacity is what enables us to pursue "moral" lives as well as physical, emotional and intellectual ones. Failure to carry out this duty to respect others as autonomous, rational beings constitutes a failure of moral agency. Such precepts of moral philosophy provide the foundation for the subfield of the philosophy of ethics, which is concerned with how we might deliberate among conflicting options in a dilemma by applying moral principles.

Thus, the distinction between the related topics of moral philosophy and ethics is subtle but significant. While morality refers to a set of beliefs about what constitutes right and wrong, ethics, Frankena said, is the intellectual work that addresses "moral problems and moral judgment" (1963, 3). Ethical deliberation does not merely assert the "truth" of moral claims; it enables us to argue for the legitimate, reason-based application of moral claims in a given case. Ethics is the study of questions regarding what individuals might be obliged to do in certain situations, and how one might construct a compelling argument to place a premium on one value over another in a given situation when legitimate values, such as the pursuit of truth and the concern to minimize harm, come into conflict.

ETHICS IN RESEARCH

Numerous governmental and scientific organizations around the world have formally adopted ethical codes or guidelines to ensure researchers uphold key, broadly accepted ethical principles. Many calls for research ethics guidelines were responses to examples of research conduct that was perceived to be abusive, destructive, or unethical in some way. Charles Babbage (1970) wrote about the lack of ethics and honesty in British science in the nineteenth century.

The global scientific community was shocked by the horrors of Nazi research on human beings during the Nuremburg trials after World War II. In the US, from 1932 to 1972, medical treatment for syphilis was withheld from 600 poor African-American men in rural Alabama during the infamous Tuskegee syphilis study. The ensuing outcry resulted in the establishment of the National Commission for the Protection of Human Subjects of Biomedical and Behavioral Research in the 1970s. In 1979, the commission released the widely known Belmont Report, "Ethical principles and guidelines for the protection of human subjects of research."

The Belmont Report

The Belmont Report (National Commission for the Protection of Human Subjects of Biomedical and Behavioral Research 1979) put forward three basic principles that have become widely embraced as fundamental considerations that determine the ethical validity of any research effort: respect for persons, beneficence, and justice.

Respect for persons: "[I]ndividuals should be treated as autonomous agents, and ... persons with diminished autonomy are entitled to protection." The report states: "To show lack of respect for an autonomous agent is to repudiate that person's considered judgments, to deny an individual the freedom to act on those considered judgments, or to withhold information necessary to make a considered judgment, when there are no compelling reasons to do so."

Beneficence: "Persons are treated in an ethical manner not only by respecting their decisions and protecting them from harm, but also by making efforts to secure their well-being. ... In this document, beneficence is understood ... as an obligation." The report continues: "[I]nvestigators and members of their institutions are obliged to give forethought to the maximization of benefits and the reduction of risk that might occur from the research investigation."

Justice: "An injustice occurs when some benefit to which a person is entitled is denied without good reason or when some burden is imposed unduly." The report refers to the Tuskegee study specifically, stating, "These subjects were deprived of demonstrably effective treatment in order not to interrupt the project, long after such treatment became generally available."

Many ethical codes and guidelines are explicit in the need for such standards to protect the credibility and public support of the research enterprise. Concern about and attention to research ethics has spawned a body of literature explicating how ethics should inform particular types of research as well as calling more generally for heightened ethical sensitivity on the part of scientists (see Kitchener 2000; Shamoo & Resnik 2003; Rollin 2006).

Research ethics and oversight boards have been formalized around the globe. In the US, the National Institutes of Health's Office of Human Subjects Research is associated with institutional review boards, or IRBs, that are located within the administrations of universities and other research centers. IRBs are charged with approving research protocols for any projects involving federal funding, but most universities require IRB approval for all projects, funded or not. Other countries, most notably in eastern Europe, have national research ethics committees (RECs). Most European Union members have established a network of federal, state, and local research ethics review committees (Institute of Science and Ethics 2005), many similar to the IRB system. Several studies have found that emphasis on research ethics in Africa, Southeast Asia, and Latin America is minimal, inconsistent or under development (Ezcurra 2001; World Health Organization 2002; Kirigia et al. 2005). China's Ministry of Science and Technology has responded to a recent pattern of apparent scientific misconduct by pledging more aggressive enforcement of ethical standards (Yidong & Xin 2006).

ETHICAL STANDARDS FOR SOCIAL SCIENCE

As social-science research and communications studies have expanded and matured, institutions and researcher networks have reconsidered the efficacy of research-ethics oversight systems that were originally established for work in medicine, bio-engineering, and other more clinical settings. European and North American organizations, such as the UK Economic and Social Research Council, the European Commission's Information Society Technologies Programme, the Social Sciences and Humanities Research Ethics Special Working Committee in Canada, and the Association for the Accreditation of Human Research Protection Programs in the US, have promoted standards intended to address the range of social-science methodologies and field-specific risk assessment.

At the same time, social scientists have been urged to consider the idea of "risk," not just in a personal or health-related sense, but as a concept that had interpersonal and social dimensions as well. According to the "Research Ethics Framework" adopted for UK researchers in 2006 by the Economic and Social Research Council, "The form of vigilance required for the management of physical risk used in medical research is inappropriate for the management of social risks that may be present in social science research" (Economic and Social Research Council 2006, 22). Social-science researchers have argued that strict application of clinical standards to survey, ethnographic, and other methodologies have stifled research, threatened academic freedom, and constitute an unpardonable paternalistic approach (American Association of University Professors 2006).

Most notably, this has concerned qualitative researchers (→ Qualitative Methodology) and those involved in environmental- and social-justice projects. "[D]esigning culturally valid ethical procedures for research involves adopting a new perspective, one that derives from the ethnic groups themselves rather than one that starts from prior assumptions of what constitutes human values of respect, care and justice.... With rare exceptions, current professional standards and federal regulations for the protection of research participants fail to provide the guidance needed to achieve the responsible conduct of ethnocultural research" (Trimble & Fisher 2006, xii, xv). The American Association of University Professors adopted a resolution urging that "research whose methodology consists entirely of collecting data by surveys, conducting interviews, or observing behavior in public places be exempt from the requirement of IRB review" (2006, 3–4) and that institutions "formulate a separate set of procedures for research that is not federally funded" (p. 6).

Field-specific research and academic associations have also adopted ethics guidelines that are often tailored for dominant methodological practices. The code of the American Sociological Association provides guidelines on research conducted in public settings and the use of publicly available information. The code applies eight key values – integrity, fairness, professional and social responsibility, equality of opportunity, confidentiality, honesty and openness, respect for self and others, and freedom and safety – to the areas of teaching, research, publications, and relationships. The → International Communication Association (ICA) has not adopted a code of professional ethics but instead offers members a general policy statement that embraces broad standards similar to those of AEJMC and NCA (International Communication Association 2006).

Research on → Internet use and online communication has also raised questions about the need for more specific ethics guidelines (→ Research Ethics: Internet Research). The European Commission's ethics code for socio-economic research emphasizes that such research must acknowledge that what users consider "private" is shifting in response to new technologies, yet researchers risk breaching the trust of subjects by unintended disclosure of material such as drafts attached to emails. Research quality can also be threatened by problems of authenticity, originality, and reliability of Internet data (Dench et al. 2004). Stern also cautioned that, "Given [the nature of both] online communication and research, those who study Internet users and communities may find themselves particularly likely to come across distressing information in their research" (2003, 249). This is because the anonymity and public reach of the Internet appears to promote self-disclosure (Reid 1996; Miller & Gergen 1998; Thompson 1999), which increases the likelihood that researchers will come across expressions that otherwise may have gone unnoticed.

Many Internet researchers dispute whether much of their work in collecting and assessing online communication is research that involves actual human subjects. In response, the US Department of Health and Human Services has stated that online research does involve human subjects if: (1) there is some element of "interaction or intervention with a living person that would not be occurring except for the research project at hand," or (2) "identifiable private data/information will be obtained for this research in a form associable with the individual" (Stern 2003, 255).

SEE ALSO: ▶ Applied Communication Research ▶ Ethics of Media Content ▶ International Communication Association (ICA) ▶ Internet ▶ Online Research ▶ Qualitative Methodology ▶ Research Ethics: Internet Research ▶ Research Methods

References and Suggested Readings

American Association of University Professors (2006). Academic freedom and the Institutional Review Board. At www.aaup.org/AAUP/About/committees/committee+repts/CommA/ResearchonHumanSubjects.htm, accessed May 22, 2007.

Babbage, C. (1970; 1st pub. 1830). *Reflections on the decline of science in England.* New York: Augustus Kelley.

Dench, S., Iphofen, R., & Huws, U. (2004). *RESPECT Project: A European Union code of ethics for socio-economic research.* Brighton: Institute for Employment Studies. Also at www.respectproject.org/pubs/ethics.php, accessed May 22, 2007.

Economic and Social Research Council (2006). *Research ethics framework*. At www.esrc.ac.uk/ESRCInfoCentre/Images/ESRC_Re_Ethics_Frame_tcm6-11291.pdf, accessed June 5, 2007.

Ezcurra, R. R. (2001). Composition and operation of selected research ethics review committees in Latin America. IRB 23, 9–12.

Frankena, W. K. (1963). *Ethics*. Englewood Cliffs, NJ: Prentice Hall.

Institute of Science and Ethics (2005). Provision of support for producing a European directory of local ethics committees (LECs). At http://ec.europa.eu/research/conferences/2005/recs/pdf/lec_finalreport.pdf, accessed June 8, 2007.

International Communication Association (2006). ICA general statement on standards. At www.icahdq.org/aboutica/ethics.asp, accessed June 12, 2007.

Kirigia, J. M., Wambebe, C., & Baba-Mousa, A. (2005). Status of national bioethics committees in the WHO African region. *BMC Medical Ethics*, 6, E10.

Kitchener, K. S. (2000). *Foundations of ethical practice, research and teaching in psychology*. Mahwah, NJ: Lawrence Erlbaum.

Miller, J., & Gergen, K. (1998). Life on the line: The therapeutic potentials of computer-mediated communication. *Journal of Marital and Family Therapy*, 24(2), 189–202.

National Commission for the Protection of Human Subjects of Biomedical and Behavioral Research (1979). The Belmont report: Ethical principles and guidelines for the protection of human subjects of research. At http://ohsr.od.nih.gov/guidelines/belmont.html, accessed June 5, 2007.

Reid, E. (1996). Informed consent in the study of on-line communities: A reflection on the effects of computer-mediated social research. *The Information Society*, 12(2), 169–174.

Rollin, B. E. (2006). *Science and ethics*. New York: Cambridge University Press.

Shamoo, A. E., & Resnik, D. B. (2003). *Responsible conduct of research*. New York: Oxford University Press.

Stern, S. R. (2003). Encountering distressing information in online research: A consideration of legal and ethical responsibilities. *New Media and Society*, 5(2), 249–266.

Thompson, S. (1999). The Internet and its potential influence on suicide. *Psychiatric Bulletin*, 23(8), 449–451.

Trimble, J. E., & Fisher, C. B. (eds.) (2006). *The handbook of ethical research with ethnocultural populations and communities*. Thousand Oaks, CA: Sage.

World Health Organization (2002). Ethics in health research. New Delhi: WHO Southeast Asian Regional Office.

Yidong, G., & Xin, H. (2006). Research ethics: China's science ministry fires a barrage of measures at misconduct. *Science*, 312(5781), 1728–1729.

Research Ethics: Internet Research

Charles Ess

Drury University

Internet research ethics (IRE) attempts to clarify and resolve ethical dilemmas encountered by researchers who use the → Internet as a medium for their research – for example, doing online surveys – and/or focus on the various forms of interactions observable online, such as virtual communities, social networks like MySpace, web pages, instant messaging, and other forms of computer-mediated communication (→ Online Research; Research Ethics).

IRE is further complicated as researchers may draw on *humanities* ethical guidelines, which usually treat someone posting material online as an *author* (White 2002), and/or *social science* guidelines, which treat posters as *subjects* who thus require traditional human subjects protections (Bruckman 2002). Because the Internet connects researchers and those they study across national boundaries, additional complications arise as researchers are constrained by diverse national laws, such as those regarding privacy and data privacy protection, and contrasting research ethics, as countries vary considerably with regard to how human subjects are to be treated.

IRE has been systematically addressed in Germany with regard to the ethics of online surveys (Arbeitskreis Deutscher Markt- und Sozialforschungsinstitute et al. 2001; → Survey); in Norway as part of a larger research ethics framework (NESH 2003); by the American Psychological Association (Kraut et al. 2004); and, with greater emphasis on the interdisciplinary and international issues of IRE, in the ethical guidelines developed by the Association of Internet Researchers (AoIR 2002).

In the Anglo-American world, much of the interest in IRE is driven by *research oversight committees*, such as the institutional review boards (IRBs) responsible for protecting human subjects in the United States (Buchanan 2002). Such protections minimally include guarantees of subject anonymity, confidentiality of personal information and research data, and a right to informed consent (see Lawson 2004). In addition, subjects are to be exposed to *minimal* risks and *only* as these are justified by the research's benefits. This *consequentialist* approach in the Anglo-American world contrasts with a more absolute approach elsewhere to protection of these and other basic rights such as privacy (European Commission 1995; NESH 2003). Moreover, different research *methodologies* require distinctive ethical approaches (Markham 2004). Participant-observation approaches have received the widest attention (Sveningsson 2004; Bromseth 2006; → Research Methods). Other methodologies, ranging from discourse analysis to online surveys, will often present different sorts of ethical problems and resolutions (Ess forthcoming).

While especially the AoIR guidelines find extensive use in a variety of disciplines and countries, as our uses of the Internet develop, new ethical concerns continue to arise. For example, how should researchers respond to sensitive and disturbing information online, such as apparently serious considerations of suicide in a blog or home page – especially as posted by minors (Stern 2004)? Blogging opens up new ethical questions regarding citation practices, plagiarism, and libel. Similarly, the explosive popularity, particularly among young people, of social networking venues such as Facebook, MySpace, and others raises important issues beyond those of potential sexual predation. These include the restrictions, if any, that might be justified regarding the content a user is allowed to post. As the Internet continues its explosive diffusion throughout the world – over 1 billion people on the planet have regular access to the Internet – an IRE is needed that is recognized as legitimate for all participants while at the same time respecting the diverse ethical traditions defining distinctive national and cultural identities.

SEE ALSO: ▶ Copyright ▶ Internet ▶ Internet: International Regulation ▶ Internet Law and Regulation ▶ Online Research ▶ Qualitative Methodology ▶ Quantitative Methodology ▶ Research Ethics ▶ Research Methods ▶ Survey

References and Suggested Readings

AoIR (2002). Ethical guidelines for internet research. At www.aoir.org/reports/ethics.pdf, accessed August 19, 2006.

Arbeitskreis Deutscher Markt- und Sozialforschungsinstitute, Arbeitsgemeinschaft Sozialwissenschaftlicher Institute, Berufsverband Deutscher Markt- und Sozialforscher, und Deutsche Gesellschaft für Online-Forschung. (2001). *Standards zur Qualitätssicherung für Online-Befragungen* [Quality assurance standards for online questionnaires]. At www.adm-ev.de/quali_online.html, accessed August 19, 2006.

Bromseth, J. (2006). Genre trouble and the body that mattered: Negotiations of gender, sexuality and identity in a Scandinavian mailing list community for lesbian and bisexual women. PhD dissertation. Norwegian University of Science and Technology, Trondheim.

Bruckman, A. (2002). Studying the amateur artist: A perspective on disguising data collected in human subjects research on the Internet. *Ethics and Information Technology*, 4(3), 217–231. At www.nyu.edu/projects/nissenbaum/ethics_bru_full.html, accessed August 19, 2006.

Buchanan, E. (2002). Internet research ethics and institutional review board policy: New challenges, new opportunities. *Advances in Library Organization and Management*, 19, 85–100.

Buchanan, E. (ed.) (2004). *Readings in virtual research ethics: Issues and controversies*. Hershey, PA: Information Science.

Ess, C. (forthcoming). Internet research ethics. In A. Joinson, K. McKenna, T. Postmes, and U.-D. Reips (eds.), *Oxford handbook of Internet psychology*. Oxford: Oxford University Press.

European Commission (1995). Directive 95/46/EC of the European Parliament and of the Council of 24 October 1995 on the Protection of Individuals with Regard to the Processing of Personal Data and on the Free Movement of Such Data. At http://ec.europa.eu/justice_home/fsj/privacy/law/index_en.htm, accessed August 19, 2006.

Johns, M. D., Chen, S. S., & Hall, G. J. (eds.) (2004). *Online social research: Methods, issues, and ethics*. New York: Peter Lang.

Kraut, R., Olson, J., Banaji, M., Bruckman, A., Cohen, J., & Couper, M. (2004). Psychological research online: Report of the scientific affairs' advisory group on the conduct of research on the Internet. *American Psychologist*, 59(2), 105–117.

Lawson, D. (2004). Blurring the boundaries: Ethical considerations for online research using synchronous CMC forums. In E. Buchanan (ed.), *Readings in virtual research ethics: Issues and controversies*. Hershey, PA: Information Science, pp. 80–100.

Markham, A. (2004). Representation in online ethnographies: A matter of context sensitivity. In M. D. Johns, S. S. Chen, & G. J. Hall (eds.), *Online social research: Methods, issues, and ethics*. New York: Peter Lang, pp. 141–155.

NESH (National Committee for Research Ethics in the Social Sciences and the Humanities) (2003). Research ethics guidelines for Internet research. At www.etikkom.no/Engelsk/Publications/internet03, accessed August 19, 2006.

Reips, U.-D. (2002). Internet-based psychological experimenting: Five dos and five don'ts. *Social Science Computer Review*, 20(3), 241–249. At www.psychologie.unizh.ch/sowi/team/reips/papers/Reips2002.pdf, accessed August 19, 2006.

Stern, S. R. (2004). Studying adolescents online: A consideration of ethical issues. In E. Buchanan (ed.), *Readings in virtual research ethics: Issues and controversies*. Hershey, PA: Information Science, pp. 274–287.

Sveningsson, M. (2004). Ethics in Internet ethnography. In E. Buchanan (ed.), *Readings in virtual research ethics: Issues and controversies*. Hershey, PA: Information Science, pp. 45–61.

Walther, J. (2002). Research ethics in Internet-enabled research: Human subjects issues and methodological myopia. *Ethics and Information Technology*, 4(3), 205–216. At www.nyu.edu/projects/nissenbaum/ethics_walther.html, accessed August 19, 2006.

White, M. (2002). Representations or people? *Ethics and Information Technology*, 4(3), 249–266. At www.nyu.edu/projects/nissenbaum/ethics_white.html, accessed August 19, 2006.

Research Methods

Hans-Bernd Brosius

Ludwig Maximilian University of Munich

Alongside theories, research methods shape academic disciplines such as communication. Whereas theories determine the subject matter (i.e., the part of reality a discipline is looking at), methods determine how a discipline gathers information about its subject matter. Which methods are acceptable and how methods are applied is subject to an ongoing debate and communication process within a scientific community. The correct application of research methods ensures that scientific results (1) are collected systematically; (2) are independent of the scholar who collected them; and (3) can be replicated by other scholars. In other words, research methods increase the credibility of results, and hence improve their quality.

This entry provides an overview of the methods being used in communication research. Scattered around the encyclopedia are some 80 entries on research methods. This overview entry will try to refer to most of them so that the reader can easily find more information on a given keyword. Besides the specific methods a vast body of literature provides interested readers with information on the theory of science and research focusing on the question of how we find evidence for our theories, whether we can eventually prove or falsify theories with the data collected, as well as how research depends on our conceptualization of science in general. Some of the most well-known authors in the field of general methodology are Karl Popper (1935) and Thomas Kuhn (1962). Popper's basic argument is that theories in general cannot be verified, because we cannot know – neither in the present, nor in the past and future – about all events and facts relevant to the theory. Consequently, theories can only be falsified; good theories are those that survive plenty of falsification attempts (→ Critical Rationalism). Kuhn argues that science does not develop in a linear fashion. Instead, scientific revolutions change the → paradigm according to which research is conducted, thereby establishing a new view on the types of problems a discipline should address and the way of building theories about them.

Research methods can be grouped in three sub-fields: (1) data collection; (2) data analysis; and (3) study design. The kind of method through which a researcher collects data depends on whether he or she uses → quantitative methodology or → qualitative methodology. *Quantitative approaches* collect data from a large number of subjects, and are usually aimed at describing characteristics of, and trends in, the general population (e.g., a country) or at identifying differences between sub-groups (e.g., men vs women). Most of the time, only few attributes of subjects are measured. Typical studies with quantitative methodology are representative → surveys among the general public. *Qualitative approaches* collect data from only a small number of subjects, and are usually aimed at describing individuals or small groups according to their behavior in an area relevant to communication, for example how politicians use the Internet. Most of the time, many attributes of subjects are collected in order to describe the complex nature of that subject's behavior or attitudes. Studies with qualitative methodology are often in-depth → interviews with individuals who are typical of the study's subject.

DATA COLLECTION

Data collection can be conducted with (1) self-characterization of respondents; (2) observation of respondents' behavior (→ Observation; Case Studies); (3) analysis of media or communication content (→ Content Analysis, Qualitative; Discourse Analysis; Historiography; Document Analysis); and (4) measurement of physiological parameters.

Respondents in *interviews* characterize themselves either in front of an interviewer who is asking questions (→ Interview, Qualitative; Interview, Standardized) or in written questionnaires (mail survey, online survey). The interviewer will ask questions either via the telephone or face to face. Telephone surveys have become extremely popular because they are fast, inexpensive, and easy to control (all interviewers are located in one spot). Computer-assisted telephone interviewing (CATI) makes it convenient to design, conduct, and analyze telephone interviews. Face-to-face interviews have the advantage of a higher response rate and better illustration. Visual materials can be used to illustrate → scales, ranges, and so on. However, face-to-face interviews are more expensive, and the effects of the interviewer on the quality of the interviews pose a potential problem. Mail surveys usually suffer from a very low response rate, unless the researcher notifies respondents in advance and highlights the importance of the study. The term survey is used to describe mainly face-to-face interviews or telephone interviews with samples of the general population of a country. Professional survey-research institutes (e.g., Gallup or Roper in the US; Allensbach in Germany) offer representative results for those who are interested in → public opinion.

Other than surveys, *qualitative interviews* are less standardized. The order and the wording of questions are to some degree dependent on the course of the interview. Instead of collecting a limited series of individual attributes (e.g., which party do you vote for, how many hours of television do you watch on a normal weekday), qualitative interviewers try to dig deeper and collect information about an individual as a whole. At the same time, there are neither a fixed number of people under investigation, nor a precise sampling procedure. Researchers often use theoretical saturation as a criterion to stop doing further interviewing. This means that interviews are conducted as long as the researcher has the impression that he/she still gets valuable information about the research topic.

Observation of subjects' behavior is a multifaceted method. In general, researchers develop a coding scheme that counts the occurrence, frequency, and/or duration of certain behavioral instances. One of the most frequent observation methods is telemetry: devices built into the television set of a sample of television viewers (→ People-Meter) enable researchers to identify the channel any subject is watching at a given point in time. As a result, ratings for a given television show can be computed (→ Nielsen Ratings). Other types of observations are conducted while people are engaged in group discussions. Their points of view, their nonverbal behavior, their arguments, and so on can be observed and counted.

Analysis of *communication content* can be conducted in several ways, depending on the type of study. Qualitative content analysis is used when data has already been collected from expert – ethnographic or historiographic – interviews. Quantitative content analysis is used to analyze larger amounts of mostly mass media messages like newspaper articles or television news (→ Content Analysis, Quantitative). The results of content analyses may be used to make three types of inferences: (1) to the context in which a message was created; (2) to the motives and intentions of the communicator (journalists, public relations people); and (3) to possible effects of media messages. All three inferences are only valid if additional data, such as survey results, interviews with journalists, etc. is incorporated into the study. *Physiological measurement* (still) plays a minor role in communication research (→ Physiological Measurement). Examples of fields in which this methodology is used are media use and reception (→ Exposure to Communication Content) as well as the effects of media violence (→ Violence as Media Content, Effects of). Recipients' heart rates, electrodermal activity, or blood pressure are used to identify physiological arousal, which in turn can help to predict phenomena such as involvement with a media message, activation, and/or processing quality.

DATA ANALYSIS

Whether data was collected using qualitative or quantitative methods, it needs interpretation and analysis. There is a whole spectrum of methods to do this. In the qualitative realm, the collected texts are reordered, interpreted, and reconstructed in order to find general ideas behind the text surface. The qualitative analysis is a combination of inductive and deductive processes. Theories and hypotheses are developed, compared against the textual material, rephrased, and compared again.

Quantitative data is mostly analyzed using a wide spectrum of statistical procedures and tests. These can be divided into descriptive and explanatory statistics (→ Statistics, Descriptive; Statistics, Explanatory). *Descriptive statistics* include the central tendencies of variables in a sample, such as arithmetic means, median, or standard deviation, as well as the distribution of frequencies for a given variable, such as the percentage of voters voting for each of a country's parties. *Explanatory statistics* are designed to test the relationship between two or more variables (→ Correlation Analysis; Factor Analysis; Cluster Analysis) and try to identify causal orders. They include group comparisons (t-test, analysis of variance) and predictions of a dependent variable by one or more independent variables (→ Regression Analysis; Discriminant Analysis; Structural Equation). Most of these analyses are parametric – they are based on statistical distributions, mainly the so-called normal distribution. Less frequently used are different types of → nonparametric analysis.

The adequate application of statistical procedures requires knowledge about the *measurement level* on which data was collected (→ Measurement Theory). Variables on the nominal level have a limited number of values that are mutually exclusive. A typical variable on the nominal level is gender. It has two values: "male" and "female." Each observation in a data set has a value for gender, either one or the other. Nominal variables with two values are called dichotomous; when they have more than two values they are called polytomous. Variables on the ordinal level of measurement have a limited number of values that can be arranged in a rank order (the best, the second best, the third best, etc.). Grades in school are an example of rank-order data. Subjects in a sample can either have a unique rank each or can be tied, i.e., they share a rank. Variables on the interval level have values with equal distances. The interval level is most often found with Likert scales.

STUDY DESIGN

One of the most important issues in social sciences is the question of *causality*: in a complex social environment, how can we be sure that a given phenomenon A is the cause for another phenomenon B? Can it not be the other way round, i.e., B causes A, or even more likely that A and B are caused by a third phenomenon, C? The only study design that yields true causal relationships is the → experimental design (→ Experiment, Laboratory). Experiments are built upon two groups of subjects: the experimental group and the control group. These groups are created by dividing a set of subjects into two halfs, using either randomizing or matching procedures. As a result, the groups do not differ systematically in any variable. Ideally, all attributes of the subjects are distributed equally. Given this, the two groups receive a different "treatment."

For example, the experimental group is presented a violent media stimulus, the control group a non-violent. The different treatments form the independent variable. After presentation, subjects' reactions are measured, e.g., their aggressive tendencies. These reactions form the dependent variable. If the two groups differ in their reactions, the cause must be the different treatments, as we assume that the two groups are identical in any other regard. This can only be stated if there are no other differences between the two groups; statistically speaking, there are no error variables. Many error variables can occur during the presentation. Consequently, researchers try to standardize the exposure to the stimulus material as much as they can. This leads to high degree of internal → *validity*. On the other hand, this procedure also creates rather artificial situations in which subjects are likely to behave differently from natural situations. Thus, the degree of external validity is low. The interpretation of the results of this experiment would claim that violent media content leads to aggressive tendencies among its viewers.

The experimental design can also be used outside the "laboratory." Field experiments and natural experiments are conducted in the social environment of the subjects (→ Experiment, Field; Experiment, Natural; Comparative Research). It is more difficult to find two parallel groups of individuals, and it is even more difficult to control for error variables that occur during presentation. These types of experiments have a higher degree of external validity at the cost of lower internal validity. Any other non-experimental design does not allow for a causal interpretation of the relationship between two or more variables.

Communication processes occur over time. As a consequence, it is often not appropriate to investigate subjects' communication behavior only once at a given point in time (cross-sectional analysis). A repetition of investigations over time is called → *longitudinal analysis*. This kind of analysis can either be conducted as trend study or as panel study. Trend studies are often found during election campaigns. Surveys among samples of the electorate are conducted on a regular basis, using a "fresh" random sample every time. The results can be used to show developments in party or candidate preferences over time. However, trend analyses do not show whether individuals have changed their opinions and/or preferences. This can be shown by using panel studies. In these studies, the same subjects are surveyed at different points in time. Panel surveys, therefore, do not only show the gross development of public opinion, they also show how individuals have changed their views and what might have caused the changes. Problems arise regarding so-called "panel mortality," i.e., respondents refusing to participate in the study any longer and dropping out of the panel. Increasing the time period of investigation increases panel mortality as well. In addition, panel studies are more expensive because panels need a lot more administration.

Another type of design is called → *Delphi Studies*. In order to get assessment about future developments, researchers conduct mail or telephone surveys with experts in a certain field. Their responses are aggregated and sent out to the experts once more. Experts can then revoke their original responses in light of the results, i.e., the responses of the other experts. It is assumed that the results converge after the second survey, which in turn leads to more valid predictions.

Surveys and questionnaires often include standardized measures, mostly scales that explore a certain construct such as personality traits, → attitudes, or person → perceptions. Standardized measures are pre-tested and validated. Researchers therefore know about the distribution of the measures in a given population. A good overview of such measures is given by Rubin et al. (1994).

QUALITY MEASURES OF RESEARCH

The quality of research methods is also an issue of methodological consideration. Systematization and objectivity (→ Objectivity in Science) have already been named as prerequisites of good research. They make given results independent of the particular researcher's views or expectations, and enable other researchers to repeat the study, as long as all steps of a study are laid open in the publication. Particularly in the area of quantitative methodology, two further measures of quality are applicable: → reliability and validity. *Reliability* indicates whether categories in a code-book (content analysis), questions in a survey, or categories in observation sheets measure a stable construct or not. The most common form of reliability is test-retest-reliability. After a certain interval, the same subjects are being measured again. If the first and the second measurement lead to the same results, the corresponding instrument (code-book, questionnaire) is reliable. Other forms of reliability include parallel-test or split-half-reliability. The degree of reliability varies between 0 (not reliable at all) and 1 (completely reliable). Without reliable measures, any conclusion or interpretation might be misleading or at least dependent on the situation in which the data was collected.

Validity refers to the question of whether a measured construct really measures what it intends to measure. In other words, the → operationalization, i.e., the translation of theoretical concepts into measurement operations, should be valid. A good example for missing validity is the attempt to measure the construct "intelligence" by the perimeter of people's heads. It is obvious that head perimeter has nothing to do with intelligence. The validity of a measure is very difficult to obtain and determine. Mostly, researchers rely on face validity using prior knowledge or common sense to estimate validity. Criterion validity uses an existing measure to validate a new one. Intelligence tests are often validated by using teachers' judgments of their students' intellectual capability. The question arises, then, of whether such judgments are valid themselves.

Another quality measure is the → *generalizability* of results. As most research is conducted using random samples or nonrandom samples, results can only be generalized to a population if – and only if – a sample is representative of a certain population (→ Sampling, Random; Sampling, Nonrandom). Representativeness means that the distribution of attributes and variables in a sample is equivalent to the distribution in the given population.

Most of these quality criteria refer to quantitative methodology. It is much harder to establish such criteria for qualitative research. In particular, researchers have to prove that their results and interpretations are independent of their personality, or have to lay open how their own views and attitudes are related to their subjects. Triangulation is one way of increasing the quality of research (→ Triangulation). It includes employment of different methods, theories, or data sources on the same research topic in order to capture the phenomena in a broader way.

SEE ALSO: ▶ Attitudes ▶ Case Studies ▶ Cluster Analysis ▶ Comparative Research ▶ Content Analysis, Qualitative ▶ Content Analysis, Quantitative ▶ Correlation Analysis ▶ Critical Rationalism ▶ Delphi Studies ▶ Discourse Analysis ▶ Discriminant Analysis ▶ Document Analysis ▶ Experiment, Field ▶ Experiment, Laboratory ▶ Experiment, Natural ▶ Experimental Design ▶ Exposure to Communication Content ▶ Factor Analysis ▶ Generalizability ▶ Historiography ▶ Interview ▶ Interview, Qualitative ▶ Interview, Standardized ▶ Longitudinal Analysis ▶ Measurement Theory ▶ Nielsen Ratings ▶ Non-parametric Analysis ▶ Objectivity in Science ▶ Observation ▶ Operationalization ▶ Paradigm ▶ People-Meter ▶ Perception ▶ Physiological Measurement ▶ Public Opinion ▶ Qualitative Methodology ▶ Quantitative Methodology ▶ Regression Analysis ▶ Reliability ▶ Sampling, Nonrandom ▶ Sampling, Random ▶ Scales ▶ Statistics, Descriptive ▶ Statistics, Explanatory ▶ Structural Equation ▶ Survey ▶ Triangulation ▶ Validity ▶ Violence as Media Content, Effects of

References and Suggested Readings

Aneshensel, C. S. (2002). *Theory-based data analysis for the social sciences.* Thousand Oaks, CA: Pine Forge.

Babbie, E. (1990). *Survey research methods,* 2nd edn. Belmont, CA: Wadsworth/Thomson Learning.

Babbie, E. (2001). *The practice of social research,* 9th edn. Belmont, CA: Wadsworth/Thomson Learning.

Denzin, N. K., & Lincoln, Y. S. (eds.) (2000). *Handbook of qualitative research,* 2nd edn. Thousand Oaks, CA: Sage.

Flick, U. (2006). *An introduction to qualitative research,* 3rd edn. Thousand Oaks, CA: Sage.

Frey, L. R., Botan, C. H., & Kreps, G. L. (2000). *Investigating communication: An introduction to research methods,* 2nd edn. Needham Heights, MA: Allyn and Bacon.

Hinkle, D. E., Wiersma, W., & Jurs, S. G. (1994). *Applied statistics for the behavioral sciences,* 3rd edn. Boston: Houghton Mifflin.

Katzer, J., Cook, K. H., & Crouch, W. W. (1998). *Evaluating information: A guide for users of social science research,* 4th edn. Boston: McGraw-Hill.

Krippendorf, K. (2004). *Content analysis: An introduction to its methodology,* 2nd edn. Thousand Oaks, CA: Sage.

Kuhn, T. S. (1962). *The structure of scientific revolutions.* Chicago: University of Chicago Press.

Myers, A., & Hansen, C. (1997). *Experimental psychology,* 4th edn. Pacific Grove, CA: Brooks/Cole.

Popper, K. R. (1935). *Logik der Forschung: Zur Erkenntnistheorie der modernen Naturwissenschaft.* Vienna: Julius Springer. English version pub. 1959 as *The logic of scientific discovery.* New York: Basic Books.

Rubin, R. B., Palmgreen, P., & Sypher, H. E. (1994). *Communication research measures: A sourcebook*. New York: Guilford.

Shadish, W. R., Cook, T. D., & Campbell, D. T. (2002). *Experimental and quasi-experimental designs for generalized causal inference*. Boston: Houghton Mifflin.

Tabachnick, B., & Fidell, L. (2007). *Using multivariate statistics*. Boston: Pearson Education.

Watts, J. H., & Van den Berg, S. A. (1995). *Research methods for communication science*. Needham Heights, MA: Allyn and Bacon.

Wimmer, R. D., & Dominick, J. R. (2003). *Mass media research: An introduction*, 7th edn. Belmont, CA: Wadsworth/Thomson Learning.

Response Sets

Roland Mangold

Stuttgart Media University

In many social empirical studies subjects are provoked by situational conditions to exhibit reactive behavior patterns. From these reactions (e.g., marking point 5 on a seven-point rating scale), the kind and the strength of the subjects' behavioral dispositions (e.g., beliefs, personality traits or states, emotional feelings) may be inferred. For reliable and valid conclusions to be drawn from collected data (→ Test Theory), the subjects' reactions should only depend on these inner states under study, and not be influenced by other factors that are irrelevant to the research topic. In other words, the methods chosen for the measurement of values in a study (→ Scales) should provide data that resembles the "real values" of these inner states as close as possible.

The error part of measured values should also be minimized. An error occurs during measurement because values obtained are superimposed by a random distortion. In addition, values may be biased by systematic influences. For example, subjects participating in a social study tend to develop hypotheses concerning the goal of that study. As a consequence, they might react in accordance with their assumptions, and this response tendency causes a systematic error. A systematic bias also occurs if a subject in an interview gives answers that are formulated with respect to → social desirability. As a rule, data-collection methods that are based on processes of verbal communication (i.e., → interviews, questionnaires, and psychometric tests) are all more or less subjected to the influence of response sets. It should be the researcher's intention to keep their negative biasing effects on collected data as small as possible.

DEFINITION AND TYPES OF RESPONSE SETS

A response set is defined as a subject's tendency to react to the stimuli presented to him or her in an interview, a questionnaire, or a psychometric test (questions, test items) in a way that reveals a certain pattern. This pattern interferes with the values indicating the intensity or strength of the internal state or trait to be measured. As a consequence, it is made difficult to assess the 'true' values of the variables in the focus of research. Response sets *reflect general human reaction tendencies*, e.g., to answer questions in such a way that the partner will consider the person's verbal utterance to be relevant to the ongoing communication (Grice 1975). Response sets may also be related to a person's specific characteristics (e.g., not being able to say "no" to a communication partner).

Response sets that become obvious in characteristic answering patterns in social research are the acquiescence response set, the nay-saying response set, the central tendency, the tendency toward the extreme, and a random answering tendency. Two more response sets – faking and the tendency toward social desirability – are related to the content of the questions or test items. The *acquiescence response set* is based on a subject's tendency to predominantly answer questions in an affirmative way. A nay-saying response set, by contrast, is effective if a subject tends to give mostly negative answers to questions. A central tendency describes an answering pattern that consists of subjects frequently selecting the middle points of a rating scale ($\rightarrow$ Scales and Indices).

In contrast, a *tendency toward the extreme* will be observed if mainly extreme (i.e., the highest or the lowest) numbers on a rating scale are checked as answers. Guessing or answering at random occurs if a subject does not know the correct answer or does not want to deal with the question's content. By faking, a person is intentionally giving answers that do not express what he or she really thinks or feels, but what he or she wants the experimenter to hear or read (e.g., when a person applies for a job and does not want the HR manager to know about their real opinion). The tendency toward social desirability is effective when a person is giving answers that are strongly oriented toward general norms and values as seen by the person.

DETERMINANTS OF RESPONSE SETS

As indicated, it has been argued whether response sets reflect a general tendency of subjects to react or whether they should be attributed to specific personal characteristics. For example, if test items for the measurement of a personal trait or state (e.g., anxiety) are constructed in such a way that affirmative answers are indicating stronger intensity of this trait or state, a higher test score might really indicate a higher intensity of that state or trait. However, a high test score may also simply be the consequence of an acquiescence tendency. As a third possibility, this acquiescence tendency could be related to the personal state or trait; as a consequence a high test score would reflect both strong intensity (i.e., anxiety) and an effective acquiescence tendency.

In empirical investigations, the acquiescence tendency has been found to be *related to specific behavioral dispositions*: subjects exhibiting a strong acquiescence tendency tend to act in a reserved and docile way toward other persons. In addition, persons with this tendency have been found to be less competent in social interaction ($\rightarrow$ Interpersonal Communication Competence and Social Skills). Contradictory results, however, have been provided by the observation that the acquiescence tendency varies considerably between tests and that only weak correlations between this tendency and behavior outside test situations have been found. Furthermore, a tendency toward faking as well as a social desirability tendency have been found especially for those questionnaire items that are related to norms and the value systems of the social environment the subject is living in ($\rightarrow$ Interview, Standardized; Public Opinion Polling).

IMPLICATIONS FOR RESEARCH PRACTICES

Avoiding Response Sets

Response sets affecting measurements in social studies can be minimized in their effects by carefully constructing the methods used for data collection. In order to reduce the acquiescence and nay-saying tendency, the alternatives provided for the subject's answers (e.g., in multiple-choice items) should be balanced out with respect to "yes" and "no" answers. For example, if the intensity of a person's anxiety is to be measured, approximately half the "yes" and half the "no" answers should indicate a higher intensity of this state. Effects of central tendency can be limited by avoiding middle points on rating scales, and choosing an even number of points when constructing the scales ($\rightarrow$ Rating Methods). However, if people perceive the intensity or strength of the personal state or trait they are asked about as best represented by a value right in the middle, between the two extremes, they might be irritated by the omission of a central answering point. To avoid response sets in general the subjects' cooperation should be asked for by *providing comprehensible instructions* for the test or questionnaire, as well as unambiguous formulations of test or questionnaire items. In that way subjects establishing unfounded assumptions concerning the intentions of the study can be avoided. As subjects tend to react in correspondence with their prevailing hypotheses about the study, obscure and incomprehensible texts in data-collection methods can intensify biasing tendencies and by that increase the error proportion of obtained data.

Controlling Response Sets

In addition to a careful design of instructions and questions or test items, the strength of some of the content-oriented response sets (i.e., social desirability, faking) can be estimated by the inclusion of scales specifically constructed for that purpose. These scales will make biasing tendencies obvious during data analysis and thus might indicate that the subject's test results should be interpreted with great care. Moreover, if the correlations between these scales indicate that response sets and the variable(s) to be measured are known, a mathematical correction procedure can be applied to exclude biasing tendencies from received data ($\rightarrow$ Statistics, Descriptive).

For example, some personality tests contain so-called frankness or faking scales. The construction of items for these scales is based on the assumption that for some questions the correct answers be will known beforehand. If, for example, a subject says "no" to a question like "Have you ever been dishonest?" or "Have you ever lied?", such an answer indicates a tendency of the subject to fake test results, assuming that everybody has lied at least once in their life. As soon as the frequency of positive answers to items of this faking scale exceeds a certain threshold, an interpretation of test results should be performed with care.

Social Processes Underlying Response Sets

Response sets should be appraised with respect to the fact that empirical studies in social sciences are conducted within social situations. A context is established, in which data based on the subject's reaction is of importance for the experimenter as well as for the subject. An experimenter is interested in acquiring unbiased data, which does not restrict → reliability too much and which allows for valid interpretations (→ Validity). For the subject the score achieved in a test or a questionnaire can have *severe consequences* if, for example, the chance to get a job depends on the results, and "wrong" answers (at least in the subject's perception) are perceived as dramatically reducing the likelihood of success.

If a person is anxious to influence test or questionnaire results in a certain direction, that does not necessarily mean they intend to present themselves in a better light. In some cases subjects dissimulate, e.g., if a person is undergoing a testing procedure for the army and wants to avoid being selected. On the basis of a single answering sheet it is mostly impossible to decide whether a response set was active or not, and which response set has to be taken into account. Furthermore, a biasing tendency does not necessarily have to be a consequence of deliberate faking. *Unconscious biases in answering* can occur, e.g., if a subject is not experienced in filling out tests or answering questions in questionnaires and if they have difficulties in understanding the formulation of instructions, questions, or answering alternatives.

Given the likelihood of incompatible interests between the experimenter and the subject participating in a test, there is only a small chance that response sets will be avoided. Subjects tend to cooperate when they realize that the data collected in the study will be used to compute aggregated parameters like means and frequency tables, and that no values specific to individuals are made public. It is a further advantage if the goals of the study and the procedure are explained to the subjects at length and if they are explicitly asked for their cooperation. In general, it is important to make the relationship between the subjects' cooperation, the goal of the study, and the quality of acquired data obvious to the subjects.

Response sets should be understood in the light of a general *tendency of subjects to influence the results* of studies they are involved in. Some subjects have been observed to compliantly follow experimenters' instructions and to be surprisingly willing to oblige the experimenter and the study in general. Cooperation can also be based on a tendency to relent to social pressure in the testing situation or on the desire for social appreciation when the subjects are anxious to exhibit only behavior perceived to be acceptable to the peer group or the experimenter.

Subjects, however, have also been observed to demonstrate *destructive or negativistic behavior* that might result in abandoning their participation in the study. Such destructive behavior is intensified if the subjects consider the questions, answering alternatives, or scales as not being clear or useful to them. Negative behavior is also increased if subjects recognize a social pressure to react in a specific way, or if they feel misled in some way.

SEE ALSO: ▶ Election Surveys ▶ Interpersonal Communication Competence and Social Skills ▶ Interview ▶ Interview, Standardized ▶ Measurement Theory ▶ Public Opinion Polling ▶ Rating Methods ▶ Reliability ▶ Scales ▶ Scales and Indices ▶ Social Desirability ▶ Statistics, Descriptive ▶ Survey ▶ Test Theory ▶ Validity

References and Suggested Readings

Bachman, J. G., & O'Malley, P. M. (1984). Yea-saying, nay-saying, and going to extremes: Black–white differences in response styles. *Public Opinion Quarterly*, 48, 491–509.

Cronbach, L. J. (1950). Further evidence on response sets and test design. *Educational and Psychological Measurement*, 6, 474–494.

Grice, H. P. (1975). Logic and conversation. In P. Cole & J. L. Morgan (eds.), *Speech acts*. New York: Academic Press, pp. 41–58.

Hamilton, D. L. (1968). Personality attributes associated with extreme response style. *Psychological Bulletin*, 69, 192–203.

Hui, C. H., & Triandis, H. C. (1985). The instability of response sets. *Public Opinion Quarterly*, 49, 253–260.

Meisels, M., & Ford, L. H. (1990). Social desirability, response set, and semantic differential evaluative judgments. *Journal of Social Psychology*, 78, 45–54.

Schinka, J. A., Velicer, W. F., & Weiner, I. B. (eds.) (2003). *Handbook of psychology: Research methods in psychology*, vol. 2. Hoboken, NJ: John Wiley.

Shaugnessy, J. J., Zechmeister, E. B., & Zechmeister, J. S. (2006). *Research methods in psychology*, 7th edn. Boston, NJ: McGraw-Hill.

Wilcox, C., Siegelman, L., & Cook, E. (1989). Some like it hot: Individual differences in response to group feeling thermometers. *Public Opinion Quarterly*, 53, 246–257.

Reticence

Lynne Kelly

University of Hartford

Reticence is a communication problem with cognitive, affective, and behavioral dimensions and is due to the belief that one is better off remaining silent than risking appearing foolish (Keaten & Kelly 2000). Reticent individuals tend to avoid communication in social and public contexts, particularly novel situations that have the potential for negative evaluation. The publication of Gerald M. Phillips's first article on reticence in 1965 was groundbreaking in that it expanded scholarly interest in communication anxiety and avoidance problems beyond fear of public speaking (→ Speech Anxiety), spawning cognate constructs such as communication apprehension (McCroskey 1970) and launching a major new line of research (→ Communication Apprehension and Social Anxiety).

Reticent individuals view themselves as incompetent communicators, and measured against norms about appropriate levels of talkativeness in social situations (→ Social Norms), they tend to fall short. Reticence is typified by a set of faulty beliefs about communication, such as that good communicators speak spontaneously and one must be born with good communication skills. The adoption of this set of beliefs creates anxiety and feelings of helplessness. Reticent individuals fear negative evaluation and appearing foolish, and they have learned to associate anxiety with communication, which contributes to their avoidance and withdrawal pattern.

Although there is debate about how much overlap exists between reticence and cognate constructs, there are theoretical distinctions. Stage fright and speech anxiety refer to fear of public speaking; reticent individuals often fear giving speeches, but their anxiety about communication extends to social situations. Communication apprehension involves fear or anxiety across contexts, similarly to reticence, but does not include faulty beliefs or skill deficits (→ Communication Apprehension).

HISTORY OF THE RETICENCE CONSTRUCT

Although Phillips developed the reticence construct, he credited F. Laura Muir with introducing it to him. First defined as a personality-based, anxiety disorder (Phillips 1965), by 1977 reticence was reconceptualized as a problem of inadequate communication skills (Phillips 1977) and remained as such throughout Phillips's work. Drawing on his 1968 definition, Phillips (1984, 52) defined reticence as: "when people *avoid communication because they believe they will lose more by talking than by remaining silent.*" This served as the definition of reticence from 1977 until 1997, when Phillips published his final article on reticence. He posited that the major characteristic of reticent persons is avoidance of social situations in which they feel inept. Reticent persons may or may not have deficient social skills, but they think they do, and most do. Thus, the conceptualization of reticence for two decades was clearly about reticent *behavior*. Phillips felt that whether or not reticent people experience anxiety is not important.

In a refinement of the construct in which he adopted the term *communication incompetence* as a replacement for reticence, Phillips (1991) (1) identified the classical canons of rhetoric – invention, disposition, style, delivery, and memory – as the major sub-processes that are involved in a competent act of communication, and (2) argued that the reticent communicator may be incompetent in one or more of these rhetorical sub-processes.

Another aspect of reticence, introduced in the 1970s and remaining as a central component, is reticent individuals' adherence to a faulty set of cognitions or beliefs (Kelly et al. 1995). These beliefs contribute to the reticent person's avoidance of communication and ineptitude as a speaker, and include, among others, (1) an exaggerated sense of self-importance; (2) a conviction that speaking is not that important; and (3) a belief that it is better to be quiet and let people think you are a fool than prove it by talking.

Thus, the conceptualization of reticence throughout the decades of the 1980s and 1990s included cognitive and behavioral dimensions and recognition of an anxiety (i.e., affective) component that was considered irrelevant to treatment of the problem. The behavioral dimension was central, involving avoidance and ineptitude brought on by skills deficits in the rhetorical sub-processes. The cognitive component was the faulty belief system that justifies the reticent person's avoidance of communication.

The most recent reconceptualization, offered by Keaten and Kelly (2000), modified some aspects of the construct while retaining most of its essential features. To the cognitive and behavioral dimensions, Keaten and Kelly added the affective component, arguing that reticent individuals' anxiety about communication is relevant. Their definition, derived from the belief that "it is better to remain silent than risk appearing foolish" (2000, 168), represented a departure from Phillips's (1984) definition, and was supported by research findings (Keaten et al. 2000). Their conceptualization was further elaborated as a model of reticence in which reticence is viewed as part of a cycle of social interaction constituted by six components: need, perceived incompetence, perceived helplessness, anxiety, devaluation, and withdrawal.

MEASUREMENT OF RETICENCE

Until 1997, the procedure used to assess reticence for both treatment and research purposes, developed by Phillips, was an individual screening interview. Interviewers were instructors in a special course for reticent college students. The brief interview followed a protocol in which students were asked questions about the communication difficulties they experienced. On the basis of student responses and observation of their verbal and nonverbal behaviors, the interviewers determined which students were appropriate candidates for the treatment. The final decision to enroll a student in the program was made jointly by the interviewer and the student. Thus, individuals were deemed to be reticent through the screening process, which continues to be the method used to assess reticence for treatment purposes. The concurrent validity of the method was established by Sours (1979).

Keaten et al. (1997) published a 24-item standardized measure called the Reticence Scale (RS), which has been used to assess reticence for research. The RS measures six dimensions of reticence experienced in social situations: (1) feelings of anxiety; (2) knowledge of conversational topics; (3) timing skills; (4) organization of thoughts; (5) delivery skills; and (6) memory. The scale has obtained good reliabilities and there is support for its construct and concurrent validity. More recently, a 12-item version of the scale has been tested which also has good reliability (Kelly & Keaten in press).

TREATMENT OF RETICENCE

Launched in spring of 1965 by Phillips, the Reticence Program at the Pennsylvania State University was designed as a treatment for reticence (→ Communication Apprehension: Intervention Techniques). In the early 1970s the program was modified to incorporate the educational philosophy of Robert Mager, an approach that better fit the changed definition of reticence as deficient communication skills. The program was offered through an introductory college speech course and has been implemented at other universities.

"Rhetoritherapy" was the term Phillips coined to designate the skills training approach used in the Reticence Program. As Phillips & Sokoloff (1979, 389) defined it, rhetoritherapy is "a form of systematic, individualized instruction directed at improving speech performance in mundane, task, and social situations." The cognitive restructuring component of the training aims to change reticent students' faulty beliefs about communication. They are encouraged to set realistic goals and to perceive situations as rhetorical, i.e., as opportunities for achieving social goals.

Given the emphasis of rhetoritherapy on speech as a means to accomplish goals, Mager's (1972) concept of goal analysis became the centerpiece of the program. The goal analysis method helps students pinpoint realistic goals, identify behavioral criteria indicating goal achievement, and develop specific plans of action. Students set goals for communication contexts (e.g., social conversation, public speaking), prepare goal analyses, implement actions, and evaluate their performance. They begin with easier goals and work on achieving progressively more difficult ones, practicing the communication techniques they are taught. A study by Keaten et al. (2003) provides support for the effectiveness of the goal analysis approach.

Phillips was adamant later in his career that his method was behavior modification, aimed at improving skills in the rhetorical sub-processes representing the five canons of Aristotelean rhetoric (Phillips 1991). The five canons as applied to rhetoritherapy are: (1) *invention*, the process of sizing up a social situation to determine topics for communication; (2) *disposition*, the process of arranging ideas in a sequence; (3) *style*, the word choices for expressing the ideas; (4) *delivery*, the actual presentation of the ideas; and (5) *memory*, the process of drawing upon resources such as what has been successful in similar situations in the past (→ Arrangement and Rhetoric; Invention and Rhetoric; Style and Rhetoric; Delivery and Rhetoric; Memory and Rhetoric).

Since the 1970s, studies of the Reticence Program have employed self-evaluation papers, standardized scales, and observer ratings and have consistently found the program to help reticent students. The earliest study – by Metzger in 1974 – compared assessments of improvement by the instructor, the students, and observers, and found that students showed noticeable or at least adequate improvement, although a few showed only minimal improvement. McKinney's (1980) results indicated that students in the Reticence Program reported significant decreases in anxiety and avoidance behavior on all items concerned with social interaction, class participation, group discussion, and interviewing, and on most public speaking items. Kelly and Keaten's (1992) study found a greater reduction in self-reported shyness and communication apprehension for those in the Reticence Program than for those in either a speech course or a control group.

Because of limited research, there is less evidence for the long-term effectiveness of rhetoritherapy. Oerkvitz (1975) assessed participants' perceptions of their improvement one year or more after completion of the program and found that 75 percent of respondents said that they had improved, 17 percent had not, and some gave mixed responses. Similarly, Kelly (1992) mailed a questionnaire to former Reticence Program participants, with 91 percent of respondents reporting that they had improved their communication skills upon completion of the program and 87 percent reporting continuing positive benefits. They indicated greater confidence, less fear, communication skill improvement, and more control over their behavior as results of the program.

Research on the impact of the program on reticent beliefs (Keaten et al. 2000) revealed a moderate treatment effect for three of seven beliefs: "The most significant changes in beliefs center around the relationship between communicative ability and skill development … reticent individuals begin to realize that communication skills can be learned … they learn that preparation is a vital component of effective speaking" (2000, 144). Another study – of the perceived effectiveness of the components of rhetoritherapy (Keaten et al. 2003) – found that respondents viewed the rehearsal and performance of a speech and an oral interpretation of literature as most helpful. Additionally, they reported that goal analysis was helpful, practice was more helpful than instruction, and the supportive classroom environment was instrumental in the development of their communication skills.

Together, these studies demonstrated the effectiveness of the rhetoritherapy approach as a treatment for reticence. The treatment has been found to reduce anxiety about communicating, to change faulty beliefs, and to a lesser degree to improve behavior.

SEE ALSO: ▶ Arrangement and Rhetoric ▶ Communication Apprehension ▶ Communication Apprehension: Intervention Techniques ▶ Communication Apprehension and Social Anxiety ▶ Delivery and Rhetoric ▶ Invention and Rhetoric ▶ Memory and Rhetoric ▶ Social Norms ▶ Speech Anxiety ▶ Stage Fright ▶ Style and Rhetoric

References and Suggested Readings

Keaten, J. A., & Kelly, L. (2000). Reticence: An affirmation and revision. *Communication Education*, 49, 165–177.

Keaten, J. A., Kelly, L., & Finch, C. (1997). Development of an instrument to measure reticence. *Communication Quarterly*, 45, 37–54.

Keaten, J. A., Kelly, L., & Finch, C. (2000). Effectiveness of the Penn State Program in changing beliefs associated with reticence. *Communication Education*, 49, 134–145.

Keaten, J. A., Kelly, L., & Finch, C. (2003). Student perceptions of the helpfulness of the Pennsylvania State University Reticence Program components. *Communication Research Reports*, 20, 151–160.

Kelly, L. (1992). The long-term effects of rhetoritherapy. Unpublished manuscript, University of Hartford, West Hartford, CT.

Kelly, L., & Keaten, J. A. (1992). A test of the effectiveness of the Reticence Program at the Pennsylvania State University. *Communication Education*, 41, 361–374.

Kelly, L., & Keaten, J. A. (in press). Development of the Affect for Communication Channels Scale. *Journal of Communication*.

Kelly, L., Phillips, G. M., & Keaten, J. A. (1995). *Teaching people to speak well: Training and remediation of communication reticence*. Cresskill, NJ: Hampton Press.

Mager, R. F. (1972). *Goal analysis*. Belmont, CA: Fearon.

McCroskey, J. C. (1970). Measures of communication-bound anxiety. *Speech Monographs*, 37, 269–277.

McKinney, B. C. (1980). Comparison of students in self-selected speech options on four measures of reticence and cognate problems. Unpublished Master's thesis, Pennsylvania State University, University Park, PA.

Metzger, N. J. (1974). The effects of a rhetorical method of instruction on a selected population of reticent students. Unpublished doctoral dissertation, Pennsylvania State University, University Park, PA.

Oerkvitz, S. K. (1975). Reports of continuing effects of instruction in a specially designed speech course for reticent students. Unpublished Master's thesis, Pennsylvania State University, University Park, PA.

Phillips, G. M. (1965). The problem of reticence. *Pennsylvania Speech Annual*, 22, 22–38.

Phillips, G. M. (1968). Reticence: Pathology of the normal speaker. *Speech Monographs*, 35, 39–49.

Phillips, G. M. (1977). Rhetoritherapy versus the medical model: Dealing with reticence. *Communication Education*, 26, 34–43.

Phillips, G. M. (1984). Reticence: A perspective on social withdrawal. In J. A. Daly & J. C. McCroskey (eds.), *Avoiding communication: Shyness, reticence and communication apprehension*. Beverly Hills, CA: Sage, pp. 51–66.

Phillips, G. M. (1991). *Communication incompetencies: A theory of training oral performance behavior*. Carbondale, IL: Southern Illinois University Press.

Phillips, G. M. (1997). Reticence: A perspective on social withdrawal. In J. A. Daly, J. C. McCroskey, J. Ayres, T. Hopf, & D. M. Ayres (eds.), *Avoiding communication: Shyness, reticence, and communication apprehension*, 2nd edn. Cresskill, NJ: Hampton Press, pp. 129–150.

Phillips, G. M., & Sokoloff, K. A. (1979). An end to anxiety: Treating speech problems with rhetoritherapy. *Journal of Communication Disorders,* 12, 385–397.

Sours, D. B. (1979). Comparison of judgments by placement interviewers and instructors about the severity of reticence in students enrolled in a special section of a basic speech course. Unpublished Master's thesis, Pennsylvania State University, University Park, PA.

Rhetoric in Africa

Sanya Osha

University of South Africa

This description of rhetoric in Africa will focus on two primary tendencies, namely, the valorization of the virtues of classical antiquity on the one hand, and the highlighting of an ethos of cosmopolitanism and the politics of the private on the other. These two disparate discursive operations are often complementary and give a deeper meaning to the political and cultural formations of the contemporary age.

The academic study of rhetoric studies in Africa is relatively new and South Africa maintains a pivotal position in spreading and entrenching the discipline. In this regard, the efforts and accomplishments of a South African-based French professor of philosophy, Philippe-Joseph Salazar, who founded the Centre for Rhetoric Studies, University of Cape Town, have been seminal. Salazar has not only worked to establish the academic parameters and credentials of the discipline but has also contributed to the creation of the institutions to legitimize the field of study. In particular, he was instrumental in establishing an association for the study of rhetoric and communication in Southern Africa whose reach extends to other parts of Africa and the globe, and which espouses a multidisciplinary ethic (see for instance Salazar et al. 2002).

In addition, one of the ways in which Salazar lays the foundations for the academic viability of the field is by various interrogations of categories such as democracy and race within the context of post-apartheid South Africa (→ Rhetoric and Race). Accordingly, Salazar's important study *An African Athens: Rhetoric and the shaping of democracy in South Africa* (2002) examines the discourses of democracy, multiculturalism, race, cosmopolitanism, public deliberation, and constitutionalism in South Africa (Osha 2005). Within the shores of Africa, Salazar's focus on democracy, multiculturalism, and cosmopolitanism is quite important for moving beyond conventional discourses that fail to address the interconnections between these categories. Along with these general discursive concerns, there have also been elaborate attempts to ground the study of rhetoric beyond Southern Africa, in regions as diverse as West Africa, through the hosting of regular international conferences that attract reputable academics from all over the world. In other words, the institutionalization of the practice has indeed been equally important.

Democracy remains a very topical issue in Africa for many reasons. The problems of governance have been the bane of postcolonial development. Ethnic conflicts, wars, and genocide continue to plague the African continent, as events and developments in Rwanda, Liberia, Sierra Leone, Ivory Coast, the Democratic Republic of Congo, Somalia, and so many other countries demonstrate. The global community wishes to see Africa democratize and develop, and in this connection external theories of democracy and development are frequently advanced. A dominant *rhetoric of democracy* offered by the Bretton Woods institutional order for postcolonial African nations includes the following conditionalities: good governance, public accountability, fiscal discipline, and economic liberalization. This dominant rhetoric of democracy is often proffered without an elaborate historical context. Salazar and other scholars (for example, Cassin 1998) re-establish the rhetorical and historical connections between Athenian conceptions of democracy and modern modes of governmentality. By making this connection, scholars of rhetoric in Africa historicize, and grant depth to, the problem of governance in contemporary times.

The historicization of the rhetoric of democracy in contemporary times is not a merely anachronistic maneuver. Scholars of rhetoric also investigate categories such as race, multiculturalism, cosmopolitanism, and sexuality, as we have noted in the case of Salazar. These various preoccupations give the study of rhetoric a contemporary flavor and relevance. In his reflections on these issues, Salazar advances a notion of multiculturalism (rainbowism), tolerance, and a new understanding of the semiotics of the body within a globalizing, cosmopolitan South African context (→ Rhetoric, Vernacular). The investigation of cosmopolitan sensibilities, the ethics of good living, and the technologies of the self in the neo-liberal age is usually conducted within the context of broader historical dimensions. In this way, we come to understand that the competitive spirit of sport and its modern sublimation owe much to the medieval thrust to domesticate human activities that were usually bloody or unduly harmful. The contemporary cult of the body and the cult of personality regarding the ruler (caesarism) can be traced to distinct historical formations, and part of the success of rhetoric studies has been to unravel the antecedents of these traces.

As mentioned, the study of rhetoric in Africa has moved in *two central directions*. First, there has been a powerful tendency to foreground the importance of classical studies and knowledges. Second, the gains made from the initial maneuver are then transferred to explorations of contemporary phenomena and problems. Scholars of rhetoric studies have also situated the contemporary political instrumentalization of the concept of democracy within a much broader conceptual canvas than is usually attempted by scholars in other disciplines, through a conscious link to Athenian institutional impetuses and forms of life (→ Rhetoric, Greek). The multidisciplinary scope and approach of rhetoric studies in Africa has been considerably assisted by the contributions of scholars such as Charles Calder and Chris Dunton, who employ their backgrounds in literature and literary theory to demonstrate the ways in which contemporary sexualities can be conceptualized. Thus by unearthing the deeper layers of meaning in the concepts that govern contemporary existence, scholars of rhetoric in Africa show that what is assumed to be "new" or "unusual" has wider and perhaps more illustrious historical origins.

SEE ALSO: ▶ Rhetoric, Greek   ▶ Rhetoric and Race   ▶ Rhetoric, Vernacular

References and Suggested Readings

Cassin, B. (1998). Speak, if you are a man, or the transcendental exclusion. In J.-J. Goux & P. R. Wood (eds.), *Terror and consensus: Vicissitudes of French thought*. Stanford, CA: Stanford University Press, pp. 13–24.

Osha, S. (2005). Race, rhetoric and a postmodern world. *Quest: An African Journal of Philosophy/ Revue Africaine de Philosophie*, 19, 77–89.

Salazar, J.-P. (2002). *An African Athens: Rhetoric and the shaping of democracy in South Africa*. Mahwah, NJ: Lawrence Erlbaum.

Salazar, J.-P., Osha, S., & van Binsbergen, W. (eds.) (2002). *Truth in politics: Rhetorical approaches to democratic deliberation in Africa and beyond*. Special issue of *Quest: An African Journal of Philosophy/Revue Africaine de Philosophie*, 16(1–2).

Rhetoric, Argument, and Persuasion

Frans H. van Eemeren

University of Amsterdam

Rhetoric, argument, and persuasion come together in the study of argumentation. According to a handbook definition, *argumentation* is a verbal, social, and rational activity aimed at convincing a reasonable critic of the acceptability of a standpoint by advancing a constellation of propositions justifying or (in case the standpoint is negative) refuting the proposition expressed in the standpoint (van Eemeren et al. 1996). This definition does justice to the "process–product ambiguity" of the term "argumentation" because it captures not only the activity of advancing reasons but also the discourse or text resulting from it.

THE STUDY OF ARGUMENTATION

Argumentation always pertains to a specific point of view regarding a certain issue. The speaker or writer who advances argumentation defends this *standpoint* to listeners or readers who (are assumed to) doubt the acceptability of the standpoint or have a different standpoint. Argumentation is aimed at convincing them of the acceptability of the standpoint. The person who advances it makes an appeal to their reasonableness by assuming that they will act as reasonable critics when evaluating the argumentation – otherwise advancing argumentation would not make sense (→ Argumentative Discourse; Discourse).

The study of argumentation includes not only philosophical and theoretical investigations of the concepts of rationality and reasonableness inspiring the conceptual frameworks that shape the various models of argumentation, but also empirical and analytic research aimed at explaining argumentative reality and reconstructing it from the perspective of these models, and practical research aimed at a critical appreciation of the various kinds of argumentative practices and systematic improvement when this is due.

In all components of this research program, the effort is concentrated on three problem areas: the analysis, evaluation, and production of argumentative discourse and texts.

So far the study of argumentation has not resulted in a universally accepted theory. The *state of the art* is characterized by the coexistence of a variety of approaches that differ considerably in conceptualization, scope, and theoretical refinement. Some argumentation theorists, especially those having a background in discourse analysis and rhetoric, have a primarily (and sometimes exclusively) descriptive goal. They are interested in finding out how speakers and writers use argumentation to convince or persuade others. Other argumentation theorists, inspired by logic and philosophy, study argumentation for normative purposes. They are interested in developing soundness criteria that must be satisfied for the argumentation to be reasonable. Many argumentation theorists take a middle position and assume that the study of argumentation has a normative as well as a descriptive dimension.

In spite of the differences, argumentation theorists are jointly concerned with *certain research problems*. The first one is the identification of standpoints, argumentation, and other argumentative moves. Another common problem is the identification of elements that remain unexpressed in the discourse, which are often the pivotal points of an argument, in particular *unexpressed premises*. In some cases, the identification of these implicit elements causes considerable problems – usually because there are several possibilities.

Arguers who put forward an argument are not automatically involved in an attempt to logically derive the conclusion from the premises, but they must be aiming for a transfer of acceptance from the explicit premise to the standpoint. In this endeavor they rely on more or less ready-made *argument schemes* – conventionalized ways of relating a premise to a standpoint. Because an argument scheme typifies the justification or refutation the premise provides for the standpoint, examining argument schemes is required for getting to the principles, standards, criteria, and assumptions involved in argument evaluation.

A further problem is the analysis of the *argumentation structure*, which is determined by the way in which the arguments advanced in defense of a standpoint hang together. When it consists of one premise and an unexpressed premise, argumentation is "single," but in practice its structure can be more complex, depending on how the defense has been organized to respond to (anticipated) doubt or criticism. In more complexly structured argumentation the reasons put forward to support a standpoint can be alternative defenses of the standpoint that are unrelated, but they can also be interdependent because the arguments strengthen or complement each other or the one argument supports the other.

Hamblin (1970) demonstrated that a great number of the generally recognized *fallacies* are not covered by the "logical standard definition" of fallacies as arguments that seem valid but are not, because they are not arguments, not invalid, or fallacious for another reason. Most argumentation theorists therefore dropped the standard definition and view fallacies as discussion moves that harm the quality of argumentative discourse. The theorists' problem is to explain when and why this is the case.

These and other problems pertinent to the analysis, evaluation, and production of argumentation are treated differently in the various theoretical approaches to argumentation. Although this is not always acknowledged, most of these approaches are strongly affected by either the dialectical perspective or the rhetorical perspective on argumentation developed in antiquity. *Rhetorically oriented* approaches put an emphasis on factors influencing the effectiveness of argumentation, viewing effectiveness as a matter of "right" rather than fact. If the factual effectiveness of argumentation, in the sense of its actual persuasiveness, is the primary interest, empirical *persuasion research* is required that amounts to empirical testing of attitude change (→ Persuasion). *Dialectically oriented* approaches focus primarily on the quality of argumentation in regulated critical dialogues. They put an emphasis on finding ways of guarding the reasonableness of argumentation. A brief overview of prominent approaches, starting with the "neo-classical" approaches developed by Toulmin and Perelman, will highlight their main points and make clear that they are all indebted to classical rhetoric and dialectic (→ Rhetoric and Dialectic).

OVERVIEW OF PROMINENT APPROACHES

Reacting against the then dominant logical approach to argumentation, Toulmin (1958) presented a model of the "procedural form" of argumentation: the steps that can be distinguished in the defense of a standpoint. It is noteworthy that Toulmin's model is conceptually equivalent to the Roman-Hellenistic *epicheirema* (extended syllogism). According to Toulmin, the soundness of argumentation is primarily determined by the degree to which the *warrant*, which connects the *data* adduced in the argumentation with the *claim* that is defended, is made acceptable by a *backing*. This procedural form of argumentation is "field-independent": the steps that are taken – as represented in the model – are always the same, irrespective of the subject of the argumentation. What kind of backing is required, however, depends on the field to which the standpoint at issue belongs. An ethical justification, for instance, requires a different kind of backing than a legal justification. This means that the evaluation criteria for determining the soundness of argumentation are "field-dependent."

In line with classical rhetoric, Perelman and Olbrechts-Tyteca (1958) regard argumentation as sound if it adduces (more) assent with the standpoint among the audience. Thus the soundness of argumentation is in the *new rhetoric* measured against its effect on the target group, which may be a "particular audience," but can also be the "universal audience" that embodies reasonableness for the speaker or writer. Apart from an overview of elements that can serve as points of departure of argumentation, such as facts and values, Perelman and Olbrechts-Tyteca provide an overview of argument schemes that could convince or persuade the audience. The argument schemes that are distinguished remain for the most part close to the classical topical tradition. There are arguments with a *quasi-logical* argument scheme, but also arguments with a scheme that *structures reality* and arguments with a scheme *based on the structure of reality*.

Out of dissatisfaction with how argumentation was treated in logical textbooks, inspired by Toulmin and to a lesser extent Perelman, since the 1970s an approach to argumentation has been propagated in Canada and the United States that is known as *informal logic*. The label covers a collection of normative approaches to argumentation that remain closer to the practice of argumentation in ordinary language than formal logic. Informal logicians develop norms for interpreting, assessing, and construing argumentation, such as *premise acceptability*, *relevance*, and *sufficiency*. Among informal logicians, Johnson (2000) takes a predominantly logical approach but complements it with a "dialectical tier," whereas Tindale (1999) turns to rhetoric (→ Rhetoric and Logic).

To modern dialecticians argumentation is part of a procedure for resolving differences about the tenability of standpoints by means of a regulated discussion. According to Barth and Krabbe (1982), the dialectical rules that are to be followed must not only be "problem-valid" in the sense of optimally serving the purpose for which they are designed, but also "conventionally valid" in the sense of being intersubjectively acceptable. Building on dialogue logic, they present argumentation in their *formal dialectics* – a term coined by Hamblin – as a regimented dialogue game between a proponent and an opponent of a thesis. Together the parties try to establish whether the thesis can be defended against critical attacks.

Van Eemeren and Grootendorst's (2004) *pragma-dialectical* theory of argumentation connects with formal dialectics. The replacement of "formal" by "pragma" (for "pragmatic") points to the differences, which are inspired by speech act theory, Grice's logic of conversation, and discourse analysis. In the pragma-dialectical model of a *critical discussion* four stages are analytically distinguished, an overview is provided of the speech acts that can play a constructive role in the various stages, and the discussion rules are formulated that must be followed to test the acceptability of a standpoint in a reasonable way. As shown in van Eemeren and Grootendorst (1992), each rule violation, in whatever stage of the discussion, obstructs the resolution and is therefore a fallacy.

In the past decades a powerful *revaluation of rhetoric* has taken place. The irrational image of rhetoric that had come into being has been revised and the sharp division between rhetoric and dialectic appears to require weakening. Several argumentation theorists have become aware that rhetoric as the study of ways of gaining assent is not incompatible with maintaining a critical ideal of reasonableness. Van Eemeren and Houtlosser (2002), for instance, aim to bring about an integration of insight from rhetoric into the pragma-dialectical theory. In their view, there is a rhetorical goal corresponding to each of the dialectical stages of the resolution process. They think that the reconstruction of argumentative discourse and texts can become more precise, and more fully accounted for, if allowance is made for the arguers' *strategic maneuvering* to keep their dialectical and rhetorical pursuits in balance.

In a number of (French) publications, Ducrot and Anscombre have developed a purely *descriptive linguistic approach* to argumentative language use that is in many respects rhetorical. Because they are of the opinion that verbal utterances that – often implicitly – lead the listener or reader to a certain conclusion always involve an argumentative relation, they refer to their theoretical position as *radical argumentativism* (Anscombre & Ducrot 1983). Their approach is characterized by a great interest in words such as "only," "but," "even," and "because" that give the utterances a certain *argumentative force* and *argumentative direction*.

It is remarkable that the rehabilitation of rhetoric in the study of argumentation started at about the same time in various countries. In the 1980s, in the United States several argumentation scholars defended the rational qualities of rhetoric. Wenzel, for one, wanted to give rhetoric full credit, but then emphatically in relation to logic and more in particular dialectics. In Germany, Kopperschmidt claimed that rhetoric is the central concern of argumentation theorists. North American theorists such as Leff, Schiappa, and Zarefsky took up the same position (see van Eemeren et al. 1996). In persuasion research, O'Keefe gave an impetus to the empirical study of argumentation. He tested experimentally the recognition of argumentative moves and, more recently, used "meta-analysis" to check on theoretical claims.

SEE ALSO: ▶ Argumentative Discourse ▶ Discourse ▶ Linguistic Pragmatics ▶ Logos and Rhetoric ▶ Persuasion ▶ Rhetoric and Dialectic ▶ Rhetoric and Logic ▶ Rhetorical Studies ▶ Style and Rhetoric

References and Suggested Readings

Anscombre, J.-C., & Ducrot, O. (1983). *L'argumentation dans la langue*. Liège: Mardaga.

Barth, E. M., & Krabbe, E. C. W. (1982). *From axiom to dialogue: A philosophical study of logics and argumentation*. Berlin: De Gruyter.

Eemeren, F. H. van, & Grootendorst, R. (1992). *Argumentation, communication and fallacies: A pragma-dialectical perspective*. Hillside, NJ: Lawrence Erlbaum.

Eemeren, F. H. van, & Grootendorst, R. (2004). *A systematic theory of argumentation: The pragma-dialectical approach*. Cambridge: Cambridge University Press.

Eemeren, F. H. van, & Houtlosser, P. (2002). Strategic maneuvering: Maintaining a delicate balance. In F. H. van Eemeren & P. Houtlosser (eds.), *Dialectic and rhetoric: The warp and woof of argumentation analysis*. Dordrecht: Kluwer, 131–159.

Eemeren, F. H. van, Grootendorst, R., Snoeck Henkemans, A. F., et al. (1996). *Fundamentals of argumentation theory*. Mahwah, NJ: Lawrence Erlbaum.

Hamblin, C. L. (1970). *Fallacies*. London: Methuen.

Johnson, R. H. (2000). *Manifest rationality: A pragmatic theory of argument*. Mahwah, NJ: Lawrence Erlbaum.

Perelman, C., & Olbrechts-Tyteca, L. (1958). *Traité de l'argumentation: La nouvelle rhétorique*. Paris: Presses Universitaires de France.

Tindale, C. W. (1999). *Acts of arguing: A rhetorical model of argument*. Albany, NY: SUNY Press.

Toulmin, S. E. (1958). *The uses of argument*. Cambridge: Cambridge University Press.

Rhetoric in Central and South America

Esther Paglialunga

University of the Andes

This entry presents an overview of recent rhetorical studies by scholars from universities in Central and South America, where there is a renewed interest in this field. Generally, rhetorical studies in Central and South America are concerned with the main theoretical notions of literary criticism in antiquity; the application of such notions to the analysis of Greek and Roman classical texts (→ Rhetoric, Greek; Rhetoric, Roman); the influence of classical rhetoric on Latin American thought and literature from the discovery of the New World; and → discourse analysis, especially according to modern linguistic theories.

Central American scholars have recently pursued ancient literary theory and documented its influence on historical and contemporary → discourse. For instance, Campuzano (1980) has explored pre-Platonic poetics, and Sparisci Loviselli (2003) has addressed the relation of classical rhetoric to Costa Rican oratory. Critical analysis of contemporary rhetorical discourse is also represented; typical of this scholarship is Alvarez's assessment of the oratory of Jose Marti.

Within *South America*, perhaps the most extensive body of rhetorical studies relates to principles of ancient rhetoric and literary theory ($\rightarrow$ Rhetoric and Poetics). Among these studies, Chichi (2002) has identified and investigated the functions of rhetorical and dialectical resources for refutation in Aristotelian and Platonic texts and their Hellenistic receptions, and Santa Cruz (2003) has examined aspects of rhetoric in Plato. Additionally, a number of scholars have offered surveys of ancient rhetorical theory or literary theory.

Rhetorical studies have also addressed historical and contemporary discourse from the perspective of ancient rhetoric and literary theory. Considerable research has been motivated by the relationship between oratory and other literary genres, especially tragedy (Gastaldi & Gambon 2006). Other studies have interrogated the relationship between rhetoric and political life (Paglialunga 2004), religion (Hansen 2003), education (Pereira 2005), and constructions of the New World (Nava Contreras 2006).

Finally, some studies have applied rhetoric to the problem of discourse composition, particularly in light of contemporary theories of $\rightarrow$ linguistics. For example Narvaja de Arnoux (2001) investigates the role of grammar and style in the writing process, while Dietrich (2003) offers a theoretical-methodological basis for the rhetorical analysis of discourse and the integration of rhetoric, communication, and teaching of languages.

SEE ALSO: ▶ Discourse   ▶ Discourse Analysis   ▶ Linguistics   ▶ Rhetoric, Greek   ▶ Rhetoric and Poetics   ▶ Rhetoric, Roman

References and Suggested Readings

Campuzano, L. (1980). *Breve esbozo de poética preplatónica: Con antología de fragmentos y testimonios*. Havana: Arte y Literatura.

Chichi, G. M. (2002). *Argumentum ad hominem* in Aristotelian rhetoric. *Méthexis*, 15, 29–43.

Dietrich, I. (2003). *Lingüística e jornalismo: Dos sentidos à argumentação*. Cascavel: Edunioeste.

Gastaldi, V., & Gambon, L. (2006). *Sophism and Greek theater*. Baha Blanca: EdiUns.

Hansen, J. A. (2003). Vieira e os estilos cultos: Ut theologia rhetorica. *Rivista di Studi Portoghesi e Brasiliani*, 4, 47–65.

Narvaja de Arnoux, E. (2001). Orden gramatical y estilo en las Artes de Escribir. In G. Parodi (ed.), *Lingüística e interdisciplinariedad: Desafios para el nuevo milenio. Homenaje a Marianne Peronard*. Valparaíso: Editorial Universitaria de Valparaíso.

Nava Contreras, M. (2006). *La curiosidad compartida: Estrategias de la descripción de laNaturaleza en los historiadores antiguos y la crónica de Indias*. Caracas: Academia Nacional de la Historia.

Paglialunga, E. (2004). Lógos poético y lógos político. In A. M. González de Tobia (ed.), *Ética y estética: De Grecia a la modernidad*. La Plata: Centro de Estudios de Lenguas Clásicas, Área Filología Griega, Facultad de Humanidades y Ciencias de la Educación de la Universidad Nacional de la Plata, pp. 269–284.

Pereira, M. A. (2005). *Quintiliano gramático: O papel do mestre de gramática na institutio oratoria*, 2nd edn. São Paulo: Associação Editorial Humanitas.

Santa Cruz, M. I. (2003). Sobre el empleo de pístis y empeiría en Platón. *Apuntes Filosóficos*, 22, 39–47.

Scabuzzo, S., Gastaldi, V., & Gambón, L. (1998). *El discurso judicial en la tragedia de Sofocles*. Bahía Blanca: EDIUNS (Editorial of the Universidad del Sur).

Sparisci Loviselli, L. (2003). Tradición clásica en Costa Rica: La retórica clásica en la oratoria costarricense. In G. Grammatico Amari, A. Arbea Gavilán, & L. M. Edwards (eds.) *América Latina y lo clásico*, 2 vols. Santiago de Chile: Sociedad Chilena de Estudios Clásicos, vol. 1, pp. 275–287.

Rhetoric and Class

Nathaniel I. Córdova

Willamette University

A basic sociological assumption is that human behavior is patterned, not random. Such patterns form social structures or stratifications that reflect the persistent and regularized social relations that the patterns facilitate. The social stratification made possible by these hierarchies affects life chances, resources at our disposal, and relations of inequality in the distribution of social resources and rewards. Hence, at its most basic, research on social class encompasses the study of how societies manifest hierarchies of prestige and power, and how these hierarchies in turn shape a social stratification system and the reception of goods according to the status assigned to positions in the system.

Much difficulty in explicating the concept of social class critically stems from the fact that in complex societies multiple criteria, not just economic factors, are used to identify the set of relations that determine not only what a class is, but the individual's position in the social stratification system. For instance, wealth, prominence, ancestry, prestige, occupation, and level of influence are all possible elements in defining social class. What is more, some of these elements have several valences that might carry difference in the prestige and status granted. For example, although wealth is a primary determinant of social class in the United States, how such wealth is attained is key to locating an individual in the stratification system. The proliferation of class terms (criminal class, jobless class, underclass, working class, professional class, chattering class, and so on), speaks further of how the concept of class, albeit productive, has multiplied to the extent that critical imprecision has become a significant concern. Hence, reliance on class as explanatory concept requires careful attention to matters of definition.

From an early focus on only the persuasive effects of discourse, rhetoric scholars since the 1960s have taken up the call for a more robust critical practice that emphasizes rhetoric as a process and perspective humans undertake. This scholarship has sought to understand rhetoric as epistemic, as mediator of multiple "truths," and as generative grammar for social critique (→ Rhetorical Criticism). The insistence on the sociality and materiality of rhetoric, its implication with ideological discourses, and its formative or constitutive power has continued to facilitate the training of rhetorical lenses onto not just iconic texts but the social construction, negotiation, and performance of symbolic structures. Hence scholars of rhetoric have contributed to our understanding of how social structures are socially constructed phenomena, sustained and reproduced by ideological discursive practices.

Rhetorical scholarship has thus provoked deeper understanding of how social relationships are constructed and sustained by the ongoing discursive activity of people. Therefore, patterns of regularized relationships, concomitant notions of status and roles, and their implications are observable through the way people engage in particular discursive practices. However, simple observation reveals significant contestation over the definition, meaning, and impact of social class as marker of identity. Such indeterminacy is not necessarily a shortcoming from the vantage point of the study of rhetoric, as it effectively demonstrates the constructed, negotiated, and performed nature of our identities as discursive practices.

The central outlook to rhetorical engagement with the subject of social class has been a Marxist critical perspective. Marx's treatment of *class as a dynamic relationship* tied to the overall set of productive processes and relations in society, his notion of class struggle, and the concomitant theory of social progress (especially Marx 1939–1941) have been the central animating impetus for a critical theory that took up the critique of the political economy in which texts, media, mass culture, and other cultural practices served as legitimating discourses for capitalist ideology.

Although Marx's ideas about class conflict and economic determination have been criticized as essentialist, the notion that agon is central to the life of the polis has been given prominence by rhetorical and political theorists. With a critical eye toward such discourses, rhetoric scholars have explored how individuals are integrated into the framework of a social formation and the power of such discourses in shaping attitude, belief, and behavior.

A significant move has been the understanding of how the dominant class must constantly reinvent or rearticulate the set of relationships that assure it of social dominance. An implication of this insight is that the power relation between social classes is inherently unstable and a differential relation. In other words, it is not one element or another that points to class or power, but the relations between the complex of elements that are constitutive of class and social position. This particular struggle for reasserting dominance or hegemony takes place in various contexts, including education, politics, media systems, and others. Hence, the Marxian conflict or "battleground" is not merely about economic, but also cultural, relations. From this vantage point, sustaining a dominant status is a struggle to define and rearticulate the basis for dominance conceived not just economically but also culturally, and thus, symbolically.

Scholars of rhetoric have incorporated these insights into studies about just how such hegemonic struggles take place discursively through privileged representations and articulations that reinforce and reaffirm particular power relations. Highlighting a focus on the power of discourse to reconfigure real economic and material relations, and leveling a critique of idealist (or non-realist) positions that pay attention to the effects of discourse on the consciousness of individuals, some scholars have written on the material instrumentality of discourse to affirm hegemony. Others have commented wisely on the history of this ideological critique as it has emerged within the rhetorical tradition. A productive area continues to be how class permeates media content, and how it frames acceptance or promotes class abjection through popular representations.

Concerned with issues of representation, hegemony, intersectionality of social struggles, pluralism, and poststructural sensibilities against totalizing narratives of social structure, many rhetoricians have been in the vanguard of a critique reflective of widespread disenchantment with the essentialist and homogenizing tendencies of Marxist-inspired critical discourses. Such approaches have been instrumental in rendering a critique of power and the social formations it makes possible, as situated within an economy of discourses that "permeate, characterize and constitute the social body" (Foucault 1980, 93). Scholars in the field of rhetoric have responded fruitfully to these poststructural and postmodern approaches, devoting critical attention to anti-essentialist investigations of social positionality, gender, race, and ethnic identity, and to studies of new social movements as reflective of such concerns. Work on the mystification of power relations, vernacular rhetorics, counter-publics, and outlaw rhetoric has treated the centrality of discursive practices to the reproduction of class consciousness, social positionality, and the possibility of social change.

SEE ALSO: ▶ Critical Theory   ▶ Popular Communication and Social Class   ▶ Post-modernism and Communication   ▶ Rhetoric, Postmodern   ▶ Rhetorical Criticism

References and Suggested Readings

Althusser, L. (1984). Ideology and ideological state apparatuses. In *Essays on ideology* (trans. B. Brewster). London: Verso, pp. 1–60.

Aune, J. A. (1994). *Rhetoric and Marxism*. Boulder, CO: Westview Press.

Charland, M. (1987). Constitutive rhetoric: The case of the *peuple Quebecois*. *Quarterly Journal of Speech*, 73, 133–150.

Cloud, D. L. (1994). The materiality of discourse as oxymoron: A challenge to critical rhetoric. *Western Journal of Communication*, 58, 141–163.

Crowley, S. (1992). Reflections on an argument that won't go away: Or, a turn of the ideological screw. *Quarterly Journal of Speech*, 78, 450–465.

Foucault, M. (1980). *Power/knowledge: Selected interviews and other writings, 1972–1977* (ed. C. Gordon). New York: Pantheon.

Gramsci, A. (1971). *Selections from the prison notebooks* (trans. Q. Hoare & G. N. Smith). Newark, NJ: International.

Greene, R. W. (1998). Another materialism. *Critical Studies in Mass Communication*, 15, 21–41.

Hauser, G. A. (1999). *Vernacular voices: The rhetoric of publics and public spheres*. Columbia, SC: University of South Carolina Press.

Laclau, E., & Mouffe, C. (1985). *Hegemony and socialist strategy* (trans. W. Moore & P. Cammack). London: Verso.

Marx, K. (1939–1941). *Grundrisse der Kritik der politischen Ökonomie. (Rohentwurf) 1857–1858. Anhang, 1850–1859.* 2 vols. Moskow: Verlag für Fremdsprachige Literatur.

McGee, M. C. (1982). A materialist's conception of rhetoric. In R. E. McKerrow (ed.), *Explorations in rhetoric*. Glenview, IL: Scott, Foresman, pp. 23–48.

McKerrow, R. E. (1989). Critical rhetoric: Theory and praxis. *Communication Monographs*, 56, 91–111.

Ono, K., & Sloop, J. (2002). *Shifting borders: Rhetoric, immigration, and California's proposition 187*. Philadelphia: Temple University Press.

Wander, P. (1983). The ideological turn in modern criticism. *Central States Speech Journal*, 34, 1–18.

Wander, P. (ed.) (1993). Introduction, special issue: Ideology and communication. *Western Journal of Communication*, 57, 105–110.

Rhetoric and Dialectic

Peter Mack

University of Warwick

Rhetoric and dialectic are closely related theories of (and trainings in) → persuasion. They have some distinct bodies of doctrine (e.g., the topics of invention and the enthymeme belong to dialectic; the theory of disposition and the figures of speech to rhetoric) but over time they have also overlapped and annexed each other's territory (→ Rhetoric and Philosophy). Theorists today attempt to incorporate the insights and teachings of both subjects into an overarching theory of persuasive communication. These attempts have some instructive historical antecedents which will be the main subject of this article.

DIALECTIC IN GREEK AND ROMAN RHETORIC

To understand the history of the relations between rhetoric and dialectic it is necessary to take account of changes in the definition of dialectic and in the educational context of the two subjects. For Plato dialectic meant the training in philosophy acquired through dialogue and argument. For Aristotle dialectic is the technique of argument used in everyday conversations and in subjects (such as politics or questions of practical behavior) where certain reasoning, which he called analytic, was not possible. Later in antiquity and in the Middle Ages and Renaissance, "dialectic" and "logic" were synonyms, so dialectic included both plausible and certain reason, both the topics and the syllogism. Since the nineteenth century the term "dialectic" has generally been used to refer to the logical method of Hegel and of Marxism. This is connected to the classical Greek idea of dialectic, but is separate from the mainly Latin tradition with which this article is concerned.

Aristotle says that rhetoric and dialectic are counterparts because they are both concerned with questions that cannot be resolved scientifically. Dialectic treats such questions more generally, while rhetoric is concerned with persuasion in the three contexts in which speeches were made in Athens: the law court, the public assembly, and the occasion for celebration or blame. Aristotle was the first to admit the teaching of rhetoric into the school of philosophy and the first to give a systematic account of all the doctrines of rhetoric (→ Rhetoric, Greek). Throughout the Hellenistic world the rhetoric schools were the dominant form of higher education.

When Cicero argued in *De oratore* that orators needed a knowledge of dialectic, for which he wrote his textbook *Topica* and whose doctrines he incorporated in his late synthesis, *Partitiones oratoriae*, he was campaigning for a broadening of rhetorical education. For Quintilian dialectic, including the syllogism, the topics, and the four Stoic forms of inference, were part of the orator's education (→ Rhetoric, Roman). For much of late antiquity and the early Middle Ages it was usual to study rhetoric and dialectic together as constituent parts of the cycle of seven liberal arts. Later in the medieval period the study of logic came to dominate the whole arts course of the universities which were founded then, with rhetoric relegated to the sidelines. In fourteenth-century Italy some teachers of letter-writing, a subject at the margins of the university arts course, revived the imitation of classical Latin and took a more literary approach to the study of Latin rhetoric (→ Rhetoric, Medieval).

DIALECTIC IN EUROPEAN RENAISSANCE

Valla

Lorenzo Valla was appalled by what he saw as the pointless intricacy of late scholastic logic and by logic's domination of the university arts course. His *Repastinatio dialecticae et philosophiae* (1439) is a wide-ranging attack on Aristotelian philosophy. He insists on the wide range of talents and skills required for rhetoric, but argues that this demanding skill need be mastered only by the few people who will become leaders. By contrast dialectic is much simpler, consisting of a small part of one of rhetoric's five skills. For him dialectic is concerned with practical arguing in good Latin. It involves the study of topical invention, careful attention to the implications of words employed, and the presentation of arguments in a small number of forms of argumentation, which need not be stated in full.

Compared with the years required to gain a thorough knowledge of Greek and Latin grammar, dialectic, which everyone needs to study, should take only a few weeks. Valla's polemical work sets out the goal of a simple and accessible dialectic expressed in classical Latin but this goal was most nearly achieved by his enemy, George of Trebizond, whose *Isagoge dialectica* (late 1430s) gives an introduction to Aristotelian logic, including the elements Valla rejected, expressed in classical Latin. Unlike Valla's work, it was a viable teaching book and achieved considerable success with around 60 editions in the fifteenth and sixteenth centuries.

Agricola

Rudolph Agricola's *De inventione dialectica* (1479) treats dialectical invention as the key element in the composition of texts of many different kinds (→ Invention and Rhetoric). Agricola rewrites the topics of invention (for example, definition, genus, cause, and contrary) so as to put more emphasis on the nature of the argumentative relationship defined, on its use in practical arguing, and on the method of producing arguments of each type. Familiarity with the topics of invention enables a writer to find whatever can usefully be said on a topic. The best arguments found must be selected and expressed either as simple expositions or as fully supported and elaborated argumentations. He regards the distinction between exposition and argument as partly a matter of audience (it is exposition when you state something simply to an audience that follows; argumentation when an audience resists and you pile in additional reasons and extort their assent) and texture (exposition is plain; argumentation involves density of reasoning and figures).

Furthermore he argues that emotional persuasion is subject to logical processes (for example, to make someone feel pity for a person you must show them that their fate is both harsh and undeserved). Rather than fitting all works into the traditional rhetorical model of the four-part oration, Agricola argues that many different models are available for the structure of texts and that the writer must think about the appropriate form by reflecting on the arguments he or she has assembled, the nature and attitude of the audience (which will enable him or her to work out the key question to be addressed) and what he or she wants to achieve (→ Arrangement and Rhetoric). One of Agricola's suggestions for practical training in becoming familiar with topics, argumentation, and exposition was the dialectical analysis of a text, for example a speech from Virgil's *Aeneid* or by Cicero. Agricola's dialectical commentary on Cicero's speech *Pro lege Manilia* became the model for the numerous dialectical commentaries written by Latomus, Melanchthon, and Ramus.

In effect Agricola's work proclaimed the new technique of dialectical invention to be the core of the composition of literary, technical, and persuasive works. He presented the moods and figures of the syllogism and the figures of rhetoric, which were easily available in other texts, as necessary add-ons to complete the training in arguing and composition. Although Agricola enjoyed a great reputation in northern Europe, with many publications of his work, his unification of rhetoric and dialectic around dialectical invention ran against the disciplinary boundaries of schools and universities so that teachers took different views on where it should fit within the syllabus. Erasmus combined techniques from both subjects under the umbrella of variation and rhetorical amplification of an existing text in his highly successful *De copia* (1512). The first book, on copia of words, suggests methods of varying or extending the language of a phrase on the basis of figures of grammar and rhetoric, while the second, on copia of things, uses the topics of invention to discover more material within, or to vary the presentation of, something already expressed.

Melanchthon

Philipp Melanchthon was called to Wittenberg at the age of 21 to teach Greek and rhetoric. His *De rhetorica libri tres* (1519) emphasizes the close relationship between rhetoric and dialectic. In his (Aristotelian) view all subjects depend on dialectic, yet dialectic itself became deprived and useless when (presumably in the medieval universities) rhetoric was removed from the schools. He proclaims the common purpose of dialectic and rhetoric, the former restrained and suited to teaching, the latter spreading itself more fully and ready to move an audience.

This book included much of the syllabus of dialectic within the invention section of a rhetoric textbook. But since his audience asked him for even more dialectic, he first produced a short overview of the whole of dialectic, *Compendiaria dialectices ratio* (1520), and then, to complement it, a rhetoric without so much dialectic, *Institutiones rhetoricae* (1521). Melanchthon's first attempt at a comprehensive rhetoric which included the dialectical material that he thought necessary was thus replaced by separate textbooks for the two subjects, including the now traditional areas of overlap, which he later expanded further.

Ramus

Peter Ramus adopted a different approach to the problem of combining rhetoric and dialectic (*Dialecticae libri duo*, 1556). He always expected that rhetoric and dialectic would be taught together and that the theoretical training offered by manuals of the two subjects would be complemented by readings in classical literature and oratory, which would demonstrate the way in which effective persuasive writing combines the skills taught by both. His theory of method obliged him to start at a very general level, proceeding by division to specifics and to avoid all overlaps between subjects.

This encouraged him to declare that dialectic was composed of only two elements, invention and judgment. Invention described the topics, while judgment was sub-divided into the theory of the proposition, the syllogism, and method. By the same simplification, rhetoric comprised only style, that is to say, the tropes and figures, and delivery. Thus while Ramus certainly oversimplified both subjects (partly in the hope that, contrary to frequent practice, the whole of each subject would be covered in class), the claim that he taught a rhetoric without invention needs to be qualified by the observation that he expected his pupils to learn invention within the dialectic studies which they pursued alongside rhetoric. The textbooks of Ramus and Melanchthon enjoyed enormous success throughout northern Europe, without replacing the classical textbooks (for dialectic, Aristotle; for rhetoric, *Rhetorica ad Herennium*, Cicero, and Quintilian) required by the university syllabus (→ Rhetoric, European Renaissance).

SEVENTEENTH CENTURY TO TODAY

In the seventeenth and eighteenth centuries the tendency was for rhetoric and dialectic to be presented separately, with more attention to the emotions in rhetoric manuals as a result of a gradually increasing domestication of Aristotle's *Rhetoric*. George Campbell's *Philosophy of rhetoric* (1776) adapted and absorbed much of the teaching associated with topical invention and syllogistic as part of the foundations of eloquence before going on to discuss purity of language and qualities of style. Where Hugh Blair's *Lectures on rhetoric and belles lettres* (1783) focus on language, taste, style, and criticism, and Alexander Bain's *English composition and rhetoric* (1887) was devoted to the English sentence, paragraphing, figures of speech (organized logically), and intellectual and emotional qualities of style, Richard Whately's *Elements of rhetoric* (1846) included a good deal of dialectic in its discussion of the types of argument and methods of presentation, even though Whately composed a parallel *Elements of logic* (1827), and the two textbooks were often taught together, for example in North American colleges. The nineteenth century saw a gradual decline in the teaching of Aristotelian logic and its replacement with the more mathematical formal logic.

Reactions against the abstractness and lack of application of formal logic have caused some philosophers to attempt to formulate rules for practical arguing (→ Rhetoric, Argument, and Persuasion). Stephen Toulmin's *The uses of argument* (1958), for example, develops a theory that allows people to assess the strength of arguments in practical life, which owes something both to traditional logic and to rhetoric (→ Rhetoric and Logic). Chaim Perelman and Lucie Olbrechts-Tyteca incorporated theories of argumentation, topics of invention, and persuasive principles taken from rhetoric in their *Traité de l'argumentation* (1958), which became known in English as *The new rhetoric* (1969). Since then theorists of communication, working partly from → linguistics, partly from ideas about mass communications and → public relations, and partly from theories of → information connected with computer science (→ Information Processing), have begun to interact with the newly flourishing historians of rhetoric to find new ways of incorporating the insights of the ancient arts of rhetoric and dialectic in a modern and postmodern framework.

SEE ALSO: ▶ Arrangement and Rhetoric ▶ Information ▶ Information Processing ▶ Invention and Rhetoric ▶ Linguistics ▶ Persuasion ▶ Public Relations ▶ Rhetoric, Argument, and Persuasion ▶ Rhetoric, European Renaissance ▶ Rhetoric, Greek ▶ Rhetoric and Logic ▶ Rhetoric, Medieval ▶ Rhetoric and Philosophy ▶ Rhetoric, Roman

References and Suggested Readings

Howell, W. S. (1971). *Eighteenth century British logic and rhetoric*. Princeton: Princeton University Press.

Mack, P. (1993). *Renaissance argument: Valla and Agricola in the traditions of rhetoric and dialectic*. Leiden: Brill.

Monfasani, J. (1976). *George of Trebizond: A biography and a study of his rhetoric and logic*. Leiden: Brill.

Ong, W. J. (1958). *Ramus, method, and the decay of dialogue: From the art of discourse to the art of reason*. Cambridge, MA: Harvard University Press.

Perelman, C., & Olbrechts-Tyteca, L. (1958). *Traité de l'argumentation: La nouvelle rhétorique*. Paris: Presses Universitaires de France. (Published in English as *The new rhetoric: A treatise on argumentation* [trans. J. Wilkinson & P. Weaver]. Notre Dame, IN: University of Notre Dame Press, 1969).

Toulmin, S. E. (1958). *The uses of argument*. Cambridge: Cambridge University Press.

Rhetoric in East Asia: China and Japan

Rudong Chen

Peking University

Chinese rhetorical thought can be traced back to the Spring and Autumn period (770–476 BCE). The word for "rhetoric" in Chinese came from Confucius' (551–479 BCE) speech in *The book of changes*: "The gentleman advances in virtue, and cultivates all the spheres of his duty. His honesty and good faith are the way in which he advances in virtue. His sincere rhetoric (Xiū Cí) is the way in which he fulfills his spheres of duty." In ancient Chinese, "rhetoric" means to decorate oral and written words, to use language appropriately and effectively.

DEVELOPMENT OF RHETORIC IN CHINA

In ancient China, people summed up the functions of rhetoric in four aspects: moral cultivation, life pursuit, interpersonal coordination, and social management. Rhetoric or speech was regarded as one of the abilities and qualities of participating in social management as well as one's pursuit of life, as expressed in Shusun Bao's speech in Xianggong's year 24 of *The Tso Chuen*: "The highest meaning of 'not decaying' is when there is established virtue; the second, when there is established merit; and the third, when there is established speech. They are not forgotten with length of time: this is called three ways of 'not decaying.'" Rhetoric was also regarded as one important means of social management. *The book of songs* said, "If the wording of your decrees is gentle and kind, the people will be of one heart and support you; if the wording of your decrees is pleasing and convincing, the people will feel safe and assured." Ancient Chinese people thought that rhetoric should obey four moral principles: "speak rituals," "speak humanity," "speak loyalty," and "speak truthfulness." They also summarized some rhetorical principles such as the harmony of rhetoric and context, the harmony of "Wén" (refinement) and "Zhì" (simplicity), and the harmony of "Dá" (clear) and "Qiǎo" (literary grace).

Chén Kuí's *Wén Zé* in the Song dynasty is usually regarded as the first systematic rhetoric book of China. Actually, there were many books about rhetoric before the Song dynasty, such as *The book of changes, The analects of Confucius, Lǎo Zi, Hánfēi Zi, Guǐgúzi,* Liú Xiàng's *Shuōyuàn,* Cáo Pī's *Diǎnlùn,* Lù Jī's *Wén Fù,* and Liú Xié's *Wénxīn Diāolóng.* Chén Kuí's *Wén Zé* is a composition book. It put forward some principles of writing, and summed up many rhetorical means, figures of speech and styles (→ Style and Rhetoric).

Modern Chinese rhetoric was established from the beginning of the twentieth century to the 1930s under the influence of western and Japanese rhetoric. The representative books of this period include Lóng Bóchún's *Rhetoric: Introduction to letters,* Tāng Zhèncháng's *Textbook of rhetoric,* Wáng Yì's *Rhetoric,* Táng Yuè's *Figures of speech,* and Chén Wàngdào's *Introduction to rhetoric.* They investigated the objects, scope, and tasks of rhetoric. These studies focused on usage of words and sentences, figures of speech, and style. Until the 1950s, Chinese rhetoric developed independently from modern linguistics. Many new books emerged, such as Lǚ Shūxiāng and Zhū Déxī's *Lectures on grammar and rhetoric,* Zhāng Gōng's *Modern Chinese rhetoric,* Zhāng Zhìgōng's *The outline of rhetoric,* and Ní Bǎoyuán's *Rhetoric.* These studies mainly focused on rhetorical means such as sounds, vocabulary, and grammar, as well as figures of speech, paragraphs, chapters, and style. From the 1980s, the research objects, scope, fields, and tasks of rhetoric changed greatly. Many new books have been published, such as Wáng Déchūn and Chén Chén's *Modern rhetoric,* Zhèng Yuǎnhàn's *Speech stylistics,* Lí Yùnhàn's *Stylistics of Chinese language,* Wáng Xījié's *General rhetoric,* Liú Huànhuī's *Compendium of rhetoric,* Zhāng Liànqiáng's *Studies on the theoretical basis of rhetoric,* and Chén Rùdōng's *Introduction to socio-psychological rhetoric, Cognitive rhetoric,* and *Contemporary rhetoric of Chinese.* In addition, studies on the history of rhetoric phenomena and rhetoric discipline have made great achievements, such as Zhèng Zǐyú's *Rhetoric history of China,* Zhōu Zhènfǔ's *Rhetoric history of China, General history of Chinese rhetoric,* chief-edited by Zhèng Zǐyú and Zōng Tínghǔ, and *Rhetoric phenomena history of China.*

Modern Chinese rhetoric has made great progress. First, understanding of the nature of rhetoric has deepened. The meaning of "rhetoric" has changed gradually from "polishing" and "decorating" to "a purposive, effective and contextual speech communicative act or symbolic act" (→ Rhetoric, Argument, and Persuasion; Rhetorical Studies). Second, the objects and scope of Chinese rhetoric have been extended from rhetorical skills to context, schema of rhetorical communication, laws of rhetorical communication, and discourse comprehension (→ Discourse; Discourse Comprehension). Third, new research methods have been used, such as socio-psychological and cognitive approaches (→ Cognition; Information Processing; Persuasion). Fourth, new rhetorical laws and principles have been revealed, such as "rhetoric fits context, speech purposes, and socio-psychological elements." In a word, Chinese rhetoric has made great achievements from the beginning of the twentieth century to the present day.

RHETORIC IN JAPAN

Rhetoric in East Asia also includes Japanese and Korean rhetoric (→ Rhetoric in East Asia: Korea). Some people believe that *Wénjìng Mìfǔ* was the origin of Japanese rhetoric, but others consider that Japanese rhetoric began from the Meiji era. Meiji rhetoric included five different forms: "rhetoric," "article studies," "Bijigaku" (a free translation of "rhetoric" in Japanese), "Bunshougaku" (eloquence), and "Shujigaku" (the pronunciation of "rhetoric" in Japanese). Modern Japanese rhetoric focuses on methods of writing or composition, especially methods of writing poems (→ Rhetoric and Poetics). Its main content is connotation, structure, form, style of articles, figure of speech, and rhetorical means. The rhetorical studies in Meiji and Taisho can be divided into four types. The first is studies of "Bijigaku," such as Sanae Pakada's *Bijigaku*, Shoyo Tsubouchi's *Bijigaku*, and Hougetu Shimamura's *New Bijigaku*. The second is "rhetoric" studies, such as Shoyo Tsubouchi's *Rhetoric*, Chikarashu Igarashi's *General rhetoric: Composition and application*, Tateki Owada's *Rhetoric*, Hagoromo Takeshima's *Rhetoric*, Seiichi Sasaki's *Rhetorical methods*, Motohiko Hattori's *Rhetoric*, and Yoshiharu Watanabe's *Outline of modern rhetoric*. The third is article or composition studies, such as Chikarashu Igarashi's *New talks on articles* and Totsudo Kato's *Applied rhetoric: Speech and article*. The last one is eloquence or persuasion studies, such as Dai Kuroiwa's *Eloquent rhetoric* and Ryutaro Nagai's *Lectures on elocution*. Modern Japanese rhetoric was influenced by western rhetoric theories from its beginning. Some other western rhetoric books also had a strong influence on Japanese rhetoric, such as Campbell's *Philosophy of rhetoric*, Blair's *Lectures on rhetoric*, and Whately's *Elements of rhetoric*. In addition, modern Japanese rhetoricians absorbed perspectives from ancient rhetorical thought such as Cáo Pī's *Diǎnlùn*, Líu xié's *Wénxīn Diāolóng*, and Chén Kuí's *Wén Zé*.

Japanese rhetoric has developed continuously since the 1930s. Its research fields expanded from forms, structures of articles, writing methods, figure of speech, and style to the cognitive, epistemic, and psychological basis of rhetoric, metaphor, etc., such as Shigehiko Toyama's *Japanese rhetoric*, Akira Nakamura's *Japanese rhetoric*, Ken'ichi Seto's *Epistemic rhetoric*, Tateki Sugeno's *New rhetoric*, and Kanji Hatano's *Modern rhetoric* (→ Rhetoric and Epistemology; Rhetorics: New Rhetorics) In addition, studies on the history of Japanese rhetoric made progress, such as Hiroshi Hayami's *Neoteric Japanese rhetoric* and *The history of Rhetoric: Neoteric Japan*, Shiro Hara's *Studies on the history of Japanese rhetoric*, and Shuntaro Arisawa's *Studies on the evolvement process of Japanese rhetoric in the early and mid Meiji eras*.

Modern Japanese rhetoric flourished in the period from the 1860s to the 1920s while western rhetoric declined. It was more than half a century earlier than the renaissance of western rhetoric. Political reforms in the Meiji era provided a social basis for the rise of modern Japanese rhetoric.

SEE ALSO: ▶ Cognition ▶ Communication Modes, Asian ▶ Discourse ▶ Discourse Comprehension ▶ Information Processing ▶ Persuasion ▶ Rhetoric, Argument, and Persuasion ▶ Rhetoric in East Asia: Korea ▶ Rhetoric and Epistemology ▶ Rhetoric and Poetics ▶ Rhetorical Studies ▶ Rhetorics: New Rhetorics ▶ Style and Rhetoric

References and Suggested Readings

Chen, Ru-dong (2001). Zhongguo Xiucixue: 20 Shijin Huigu Yu 21 Shiji Zhanwang [Chinese rhetoric: Review of the twentieth century and prospect for the twenty-first]. *Pingdingshan Shizhuan Xuebao* [Journal of Pingdingshan Teachers College], no. 3.
Chen, Ru-dong (2005). Xianqin Shiqi de Hanyu Xiucixue Sixiang: Lilun Yu Shijian [Chinese rhetorical thought before the Qin dynasty: Theory and practice]. *Susahak*, no. 3.
Tomasi, M. (2004). *Rhetoric in modern Japan: Western influences on the development of narrative and oratorical style*. Honolulu, HI: University of Hawaii Press.

Rhetoric in East Asia: Korea

WooSoo Park

Hankuk University of Foreign Studies

The history of Korean rhetoric is the history of translation of and communication with its neighboring foreign cultures. From its early period of the Three Kingdoms to the later Yi dynasty, Korea sought its own ways of expression under the influence of Chinese culture. More recently, from the beginning of the twentieth century to its independence from Japanese colonial rule in 1945, the influence of Japanese culture was predominant (→ Rhetoric in East Asia: China and Japan). Since then, Korea has been strongly affected culturally by America (→ Rhetoric in North America: United States).

Before its annexation to Japan in 1910, Korea had maintained a mimetic rivalry with China, especially in terms of *Confucianism*. In traditional Confucian culture, words and expressions are undervalued as mere vehicles for conveying Tao and thoughts. This tendency was enhanced by the introduction of Buddhism and the natural philosophy of Laotzu and Chungtzu, both of which placed emphasis on spiritual identification apart from verbal and literary communication. However, this spiritual and occult tradition was challenged by new ideas: a modern educational system from Japan and democracy from America. While Confucianism is conservative in expression of private emotions and loyal to the established social hierarchy, development of democratic government in Korea went in tandem with the spread of public opinions and public speaking. Rhetoric plays a crucial role in Korea's modernization and development, both politically and economically.

In the Three Kingdoms of Koguryo, Paekche, and Silla, only the ruling classes were literate enough to understand and communicate in Chinese characters, and literacy was equated with political power. However, even in this period, Korean efforts to express their own native thinking found a solution in the inventions of *idu*, *hyangchal*, and *kygyol*, variations of the Chinese language in its syntax and pronunciation. In the later twelfth century, Lee Kyubo (1168–1241) in his essay "A brief commentary on the subtle will in poetry" argues that the subject and content of a poem come before word arrangements. Here he repeats the Confucian doctrine that speech and writing are vehicles to deliver authentic will and virtues of a person. A good style is one that performs this function well. Hence, the study of style in Korean rhetoric is not the end in itself, but the means to manifest the personality of the writer or speaker. The relationship between the will and its expression is also found in the controversy of *li* (the general principle or reason) and *qi* (energy or individuation) among Yi Hwang (1501–1570) and Yi I (1536–1584) and their disciples in the Yi dynasty. *Li* is the equivalent to the invention of a topic; *qi* the arrangement and eloquence of words (→ Invention and Rhetoric; Style and Rhetoric).

While the study of Korean rhetoric and communication foregrounds the literary content, the *proper study of style* is not disregarded. Pak Chiwon (1737–1805) in his introduction to Lee Jaesung's *Sodanjukchi* ("A writer is like a general of soldiers") argues for the importance of style, as Cicero likens the arrangement of words to military strategy. According to Pak, words are like soldiers, the content a general, and historical examples and anecdotes the moats and bulwarks of a castle. Metaphors are similar to the task forces. However, the most important thing is variation of style depending on the given situation. Here Pak emphasizes the efficiency of *sirhak* (practical learning), ignoring the philosophical debate of *li/qi*.

The invention of *Hangul, the Korean alphabet*, in 1443 is the landmark event for self-expression by Koreans. While communication in the Chinese characters was mainly confined to the literati and the yangban (gentlemen) class, hangul made it possible for women and lower people to find ways of self-expression. But the official language of the government was still Chinese, and the practice of direct petition from the people to the king or queen supported the use of the Chinese language, together with the Korean traditional examination for recruiting bureaucrats, which was based on the Chinese classics.

However, hangul became a dominant language, especially with the introduction of Christianity and the translation of the Bible into Korean by early Christian missionaries. The complete Korean Bible was published in 1938. With the introduction and spread of Christianity and the establishment of modernized advanced schools, western rhetoric and pulpit oratory were also introduced into Korean culture. They helped the development of identification of colloquial and literary styles. This development also expedited the increase of literacy. These changes in the ways of expression were accompanied by a desire for democratic society. The publication of the *Independence Newspaper* and "new novels" dealing with love affairs and self-awakening were offshoots of this desire.

The study of rhetoric in Korea before the enlightenment period was mainly focused on the importance of will and content of speech and writing, whereas style and modes of expression were under close attention from the end of the enlightenment throughout the whole of the twentieth century. This study of style is closely related to the scholarship of Japanese rhetoric, which was mainly concerned with stylistics of belles-lettres. The first Korean textbook of rhetoric, *Practically applied composition* (1909) by Choe Jaihak, devotes most of its pages to stylistics and metaphors, with rare attention to invention and arrangement. At the top of the stylistic study in Korea stands Yi Taejun's *Lectures on composition*, which is still published in Korea. Yi's book suggests some examples of composition and then analyzes them in terms of style and diction. Both of these textbooks were written under the strong influence of Japanese rhetorical books.

The independence of Korea from Japan in 1945 opened the floodgates for free speech and self-expression. This time the influence of British and American rhetoric was apparent. Following I. A. Richards, Kim Kirim's *New lectures on composition* focused on remedies for misunderstanding in communication. The need for a remedial rhetoric was evoked by the birth pangs of a new nation, torn asunder by the ideological struggles of communism and democracy. Still, a "reduction" of rhetoric to eloquence and style was perpetuated in the teaching of composition at college and university level.

In the 1990s, Korea experienced a restoration of rhetoric, including invention and logic. This tendency is reinforced by the new university entrance examination, which demands critical inquiry and writing. The introduction of a new law school system is expected to invite further studies of reasoning and logical proof. And feminism is breaking the wall that confined rhetoric to men.

SEE ALSO: ▶ Invention and Rhetoric ▶ Rhetoric in East Asia: China and Japan ▶ Rhetoric and Logic ▶ Rhetoric in North America: United States ▶ Rhetoric, Roman ▶ Rhetoric in South Asia ▶ Rhetorical Studies ▶ Style and Rhetoric

References and Suggested Readings

Choe Jaihak (1909). *Practically applied composition.* Seoul: Huimunkwan.
Kim Kirim (1949). *New lectures on composition.* Seoul: Minjungseokwan.
Yi Taejun (1940). *Lectures on composition.* Seoul: Munjangsa.

Rhetoric in Eastern Europe

Noemi Marin

Florida Atlantic University

Throughout central and eastern Europe (Poland, Czech Republic, Slovakia, Slovenia, Hungary, Romania, and Bulgaria), classical rhetorical studies pertain to a longstanding tradition of research on antiquity, while contemporary rhetoric scholarship focuses on democratic → discourse and the political context in postcommunist times. A major challenge throughout the area is the diffused location of both classical and contemporary (postcommunist) rhetorical research. National academies of sciences along with classical philosophy and philology university programs host most classical and medieval rhetoric research. Scholarship on contemporary rhetorical discourse and political rhetoric can be located under postcommunist studies and philology. Since the fall of communism (1989), rhetorical practices of debate and democratic discourse are also part of postcommunist studies. Rhetoric as a general subject matter is embedded in humanities under programs such as classical studies, philology, linguistics, history, history of literature, ancient history, and classical philosophy. International democratic organizations sponsor new alliances with local, national, or international scope that acknowledge the role of debate and rhetoric for civic engagement, political awareness, and social change.

Important challenges for the study of rhetoric (both classical and contemporary) are shared throughout central and eastern Europe, such as (1) the scarcity of higher education or high school programs that incorporate rhetorical studies (Slovenia, Poland); (2) the diffused location of rhetorical scholarship within national research institutions inherited from the communist past (applicable to all central and eastern European countries listed); (3) problematic access to bibliographical resources or scholarship due to lack of translated materials; (4) terminology inherited from communist times; and (5) difficult international access to information or location of scholarship associated with the history of rhetoric in some countries, due to communist past and regulations (→ Rhetoric and History; Rhetorical Studies). Almost absent as scholarship in the region are deliberative rhetoric and communist rhetoric.

CLASSICAL AND MEDIEVAL RHETORIC IN HIGHER EDUCATION

Most higher education programs in classical studies include classical rhetoric as textual/literary studies within the Greek and Latin programs specific to each university (→ Rhetoric, Greek; Rhetoric, Roman). Natunewicz provides detailed information on the large number of classical scholarship programs for each country of the region in the listings part of the Central and Eastern European Classical Scholarship (CEECS) network (www.ceecs.net).

The three main programs that locate "rhetoric" as a subject matter for study and scholarship are Slovenia (University of Primorska, University of Nova Gorica), Poland (Center for Studies on the Classical Tradition in Poland and East-Central Europe [OBTA]), and Bulgaria (Department of Rhetoric, Faculty of Philosophy, University of Sofia). Based on the profiles of the programs listed above, rhetorical studies signifies rhetoric and pragmatics (Slovenia), classical and medieval rhetoric (Poland), and philosophical or political rhetoric (Bulgaria). The University of Sofia, Bulgaria, lists its Department of Rhetoric as part of the Faculty of Philosophy. The umbrella term "rhetoric" does not explicate methodological or theoretical approaches specific to the mission of the Department. "Faculty" translates for American academic structures as "college" or "school." The Bulgarian example is indicative of the general tendency to utilize such terminology describing academic structures of higher education in the area.

Most national universities in the Czech Republic (Prague, Brno), Romania (Bucharest, Iassi, Cluj-Napoca, Timisoara), Bulgaria (Sofia), Hungary (Budapest), and Slovenia (Ljubljana) have centers or departments dedicated to classical studies, classical philosophy, and classical philology. Such centers and departments feature undergraduate and graduate programs in direct or indirect relation to rhetorical studies, as part of the higher education curricula approved at the level of the national education department or ministry. Depending on the country, the uneven presence of rhetorical research creates difficulty in locating the term and the discipline of "rhetoric" under certain disciplinary studies in multiple departments or university programs.

At the high school level, following an educational tradition of over 50 years, Latin language and literature is part of the humanities high school four-year curriculum in most central and eastern European countries, with requirements set by each national ministry or department of education. For instance, the Romanian high school curriculum (four consecutive years) comprises ancient rhetorical texts to be studied as part of the Latin language and literature requirement. Starting in 2006, the Romanian Ministry of Education and Research introduced Latin language and literature focused on several religious texts from ancient and medieval times. Unique in the region, Slovenia recently included rhetoric as part of the secondary school curriculum (eighth and ninth grades).

CLASSICAL AND MEDIEVAL RHETORIC RESEARCH

In all central and eastern European countries, academies of sciences validate most prestigious scholarship produced at national level. All institutes and centers under the auspices of national academies of sciences share similar formats throughout the region.

Postdoctoral and highly specialized research is organized under different names (institutes, sections, or committees), inheriting the communist format for specialized scholarship. Each national academy of sciences has its own publishing house, thus endorsing the highest levels of research. Accordingly, under the seal of each academy of sciences, numerous publications (in different formats) feature specialized research. Due to coexisting structures from the communist past, knowing the history of publishing houses in the area becomes an imperative for international scholars. Currently, some university press publications in the area announce broader scope for publishing textbooks and graduate work.

In all academies of sciences (Czech Republic, Slovenia, Slovakia, Poland, Hungary, Romania, and Bulgaria) "rhetoric" as a discipline is part of philosophical or philological institutes, depending on the research projects accepted. While the research produced in communist times can add important explorations beneficial to international scholarship, few classical studies produced in communist times have been translated into either English or any other international language. Kumaniecki (1967), in an indicative presentation on classical philology in Poland covering 1945–1965, attests to the wealth of scholarship, while rhetoric remains mostly an embedded focus.

Access to research produced during communism remains more problematic, due to previous political regulations or for translation reasons. Depending on the country, most communist publications require extensive library investigation to find rhetorical scholarship, translations of rhetorical texts, and specific studies on the rhetorical tradition. However, a wealth of both classical and philological research materials has been produced by national academies of sciences and/or university presses in the past 50 years. It is important to note that such materials require both language fluency and understanding of the political and pedagogical past in order to make successful advances in scholarship on specific rhetorical subject matters. National library archives in different countries inherit policies and resources based on the distinct political past of each country. For instance, pre-1989, library access to Byzantine original texts in Romania was under strict censorship laws, hence there is a scarcity of rhetorical research available for continuation of scholarship.

In order to locate *classical rhetorical* scholarship produced in conjunction with national academies of sciences, Natunewicz (2000) provides a detailed description of most classical studies programs in the region. Among them, for the *Czech Republic*, rhetorical scholarship can pertain to the Section of Humanities and Philosophy, Historical Sciences or research produced at the Institute for Classical Studies or the Institute of Philosophy. To name a few Czech Academy of Sciences publications, there are *Philological Letters, Eirene, Folia Philologica*, and *Philosophical Journal*. The *Bulgarian* Academy of Sciences lists institutes focused on studies of classical times and, by extension, on the rhetorical tradition. Among them are the Institute for Literature, the Institute for Philological Studies, and the Institute of History. The *Romanian* Academy (of Sciences) includes large research sections related to classical studies, among which are philology and literature, arts, architecture and audiovisual, historical sciences, and archaeology. The Romanian Academy publication *Classical Studies* is considered the most prestigious national publication on Greek and Roman/Latin studies, in print for the past 50 years. In addition, 40 other serial, periodical, and commemorative publications are listed under classical scholarship. The *Polish* Academy of Sciences (PAN) houses the Committee for Studies on Ancient Culture, along with numerous other committees and institutes related to classical studies. Of international note is the longstanding publication *Journal of Juristic Papyrology*. In 1994, after the fall of communism, the *Slovenian* Academy of Sciences announced its status as the national research entity aligned with the rest of the academies of sciences in the region. Rhetoric as part of classical studies can be found in projects related to philological endeavors. Part of the *Hungarian* Academy of Sciences is the Institute of Philosophy, where there is a Research Group on Communication. The University of Leipzig, once a part of the former East *German* Republic, hosts rhetorical studies focused on style and literary tradition, at the Institute of Classical Philology.

Medieval rhetoric can be studied within the Czech Academy of Sciences, Center for Medieval Studies; or in Poland, at OBTA, among others (→ Rhetoric, Medieval).

CONTEMPORARY RHETORICAL STUDIES

Deeply connected to the development of postcommunist studies in the last decade of the twentieth century, scholarship focusing on rhetoric and democratic discourse has become of academic interest throughout the region. Complex theoretical approaches (rhetoric and culture, critical discourse analysis, political rhetoric, among others) create novel and exciting scholarship on the function of rhetoric in postcommunist times to create civic engagement and social change (→ Rhetoric and Politics).

Since 1989, a plethora of new academic institutions have pursued research on political, historical, philological, and philosophical studies related to communist and postcommunist societies in central and eastern Europe. Hosted by national academic centers as multi-national research projects, rhetorical scholarship brings forth political and civic discourse as part of postcommunist studies in the humanities. Of note are postcommunist academic institutions such as the New Europe College (NEC-Romania) and the Central European University (CEU-Hungary). NGOs, democratic and civil organizations, associations, and alliances at local, national, and international levels feature debate, argumentation, and rhetoric as practical venues to create civic awareness for social change throughout the area.

Extremely important for the development of rhetorical studies in postcommunist times is open access and exchange of scholarship related to classical and current rhetorical studies. After 1990, multiple conferences and symposia have been organized to emphasize contemporary rhetoric and its impact on democracy. In the past decade, several international organizations, associations, and centers have featured rhetoric and democratic discourse as part of research programs and/or projects. Among such multinational alliances are OBTA at Warsaw University, the Center for Rhetorical Studies at the University of Cape Town, the Rhetoric Society of America, and the International Society for the History of Rhetoric. In recent times, *Advances in the History of Rhetoric* has published annually rhetorical scholarship on the region (e.g., Marin 2004, 2006; Ornatowski 2005, 2006).

Research on postcommunist discourse is also part of the International Pragmatics Association conferences, incorporating central and eastern European pragmatics and critical discourse analysis ($\rightarrow$ Discourse Analysis; Linguistic Pragmatics). Similarly, engaging scholarship on argumentation and postcommunist rhetoric is part of international conferences and publications hosted by the International Society for the Study of Argumentation ($\rightarrow$ Argumentative Discourse; Rhetoric, Argumentation, and Persuasion).

Since 1995, most central and eastern European countries joined with the International Debate Education Association (IDEA) to form regional and national organizations that promote democratic education through rhetorical practices of debate and argumentation.

SEE ALSO: ▶ Argumentative Discourse ▶ Communication as a Field and Discipline ▶ Discourse ▶ Discourse Analysis ▶ Linguistic Pragmatics ▶ Rhetoric, Argumentation, and Persuasion ▶ Rhetoric, Greek ▶ Rhetoric and History ▶ Rhetoric, Medieval ▶ Rhetoric and Politics ▶ Rhetoric, Roman ▶ Rhetorical Studies

References and Suggested Readings

Axer, J. (ed.) (2003). *Rhetoric of transformation*. Warsaw: Warsaw University Press.

Kumaniecki, K. (1967). Twenty years of classical philology in Poland (1945–1965). *Greece and Rome*, 14, 61–75.

Marin, N. (2004). Rhetoric at the gates of revolution: Romanian presidential discourse in translation. *Advances in the History of Rhetoric*, 7, 293–312.

Marin, N. (2006). The other side(s) of history: The return of rhetoric. *Advances in the History of Rhetoric*, 9, 209–225.

Marin, N. (2007). *After the fall: Rhetoric in the aftermath of dissent in post-communist times*. New York: Peter Lang.

Natunewicz, C. F. (2000). Classical studies in central and eastern Europe. *Sarmatian Review*, 20(2). At www.ruf.rice.edu/~sarmatia/400/natunewicz.html, accessed September 29, 2007.

Ornatowski, C. M. (2005). "I leapt over the wall, and they made me president": Historical context, rhetorical agency, and the amazing career of Lech Walesa. *Advances in the History of Rhetoric*, 8, 155–192.

Ornatowski, C. M. (2006). Rhetoric and the subject of/in history: Reflections on political transformation. *Advances in the History of Rhetoric*, 9, 187–207.

Riley, K. K. (2007). *Everyday subversion: From joking to revolting in the German Democratic Republic*. East Lansing, MI: Michigan State University Press.

Rhetoric, Epideictic

Ekaterina Haskins

Rensselaer Polytechnic Institute

The term "epideictic" derives from the Greek *epideixis*, translated as "showing forth" or "display." According to Aristotle's classification of rhetorical genres in *The art of rhetoric*, epideictic → discourse is concerned with topics of praise and blame, deals with the present, and is addressed to an audience of spectators, rather than judges (1358a–b). Epideictic relies on verbal amplification (*auxesis*) to portray desirable qualities of the object of praise and to depict the object of blame as base and dishonorable (1368a). Although *The art of rhetoric* identifies epideictic as a distinct form or genre of rhetoric, it also notes that epideictic elements can be used in the other two main genres of oratory, when, for example, a deliberative speaker portrays a particular course of action as more attractive than others and a judicial orator's defense employs amplification to depict the accused in a favorable way (→ Rhetoric, Greek).

Aristotle's classification subsumed under the rubric of epideictic several existing genres, including the speech of praise (*enkomion*), the festival speech (*panêgyrikos logos*), and the Athenian funeral oration (*epitaphios logos*). Aristotle also "disciplined" these genres by collapsing their distinct ideological functions into a neutral category of praise and blame and by turning the → audience into detached observers of the orator's skill (Schiappa 1999, 185–206). In practice, however, each of these genres exceeded the mold into which Aristotle tried to place it: *enkomion* possessed a significant moral and didactic dimension (Poulakos 1987), *panêgyrikos* was often used politically to exhort an audience to follow a course of action (Haskins 2005), and *epitaphios logos* played a major role in constituting Athenian democratic ideology (Loraux 1986).

Aristotle's interpretation of epideictic as display and amplification was tied to his notion of rhetoric as a "useful" art subordinated to substantive knowledge of politics and ethics (*Rhetoric* 1355a, 1356a; → Rhetoric and Ethics; Rhetoric and Politics). An alternative approach to eloquence was championed by Aristotle's older contemporary Isocrates (436–338 BCE), an Athenian educator whose school was a major rival of Plato's Academy. Isocrates posited discourse as an artificer of culture and politics rather than a mere appendage to it (→ Culture: Definitions and Concepts). According to this view, epideictic "appears as that which shapes and cultivates the basic codes of value and belief by which a society or culture lives; it shapes ideologies and imageries with which, and by which, the individual members of a community identify themselves; and, perhaps most significantly, it shapes the fundamental grounds, the 'deep' commitments and presuppositions, that will underlie and ultimately determine decision and debate in particular pragmatic forums" (Walker 2000, 9).

The purview and cultural importance of epideictic expanded during those historical periods when oratory of the type practiced in public arenas of democratic Athens and republican Rome was eclipsed by less explicitly pragmatic types of eloquence. Epideictic discourses occupied a broad range between the extremes of the Isocratean idea of *logos politikos*, "characterized by elevation of subject matter and a certain practical application usually arising from admixture of the deliberative element," and declamatory exercises that treated paradoxical themes (Burgess 1902, 96).

Epideictic rhetoric continued in prominence from late antiquity into the Renaissance (→ Rhetoric, European Renaissance; Rhetoric, Medieval; Rhetoric, Roman; Rhetoric of the Second Sophistic). Its influence on the discursive output of both secular and religious nature owes to its preoccupation with ethical choice and its artful modeling of virtues. The moralizing aspect of epideictic infiltrated many genres, cutting across presumed distinctions between rhetoric and literature, prose and poetry, the private and the public. Its pragmatic-pedagogic aspect cannot be dismissed either, for epideictic declamation formed a cornerstone of humanistic education from Hellenistic times to the nineteenth century, training students in the art of seeing both sides of the same subject (Vickers 1983).

In the twentieth century, several theorists contributed to the perceived primacy of epideictic rhetoric. Richard Weaver argued that all language is "sermonic" insofar as its function of naming is never neutral but shot through with intention and attitude. Chaim Perelman's theorizing of "presence" highlighted display as a key rhetorical strategy in bringing certain elements to "the foreground of the hearer's consciousness" (Perelman & Olbrechts-Tyteca 1969, 142). Kenneth Burke's notion of "terministic screens" similarly insisted that every terminology selects and amplifies some aspects of reality and thereby obscures other aspects (1966). Burke's characterization of rhetoric as a form of communal identification (rather than mere → persuasion) suggested that discourse not only frames reality but also creates grounds for both social → identification and division (1969; → Rhetorics: New Rhetorics).

Together, these insights influenced scholarly inquiry into rhetorical dimensions of a wide spectrum of symbolic action, both verbal and nonverbal (→ Rhetoric, Nonverbal). No longer viewed as a mere supplement to substantive argumentation, "display" is now accorded serious scholarly attention. Contemporary rhetorical studies of display encompass both traditional ceremonial genres of public address as well as a host of primarily visual and spatial forms, from museums and memorials to film and television (→ Rhetoric and Visuality).

SEE ALSO: ▶ Audience ▶ Culture: Definitions and Concepts ▶ Discourse ▶ Identification ▶ Persuasion ▶ Rhetoric and Ethics ▶ Rhetoric, European Renaissance ▶ Rhetoric, Greek ▶ Rhetoric, Medieval ▶ Rhetoric, Nonverbal ▶ Rhetoric and Poetics ▶ Rhetoric and Politics ▶ Rhetoric, Roman ▶ Rhetoric of the Second Sophistic ▶ Rhetorical Studies ▶ Rhetoric and Visuality ▶ Rhetorics: New Rhetorics

References and Suggested Readings

Burgess, T. C. (1902). *Epideictic literature.* Chicago, IL: University of Chicago Press.

Burke, K. (1966). *Language as symbolic action.* Berkeley, CA: University of California Press.

Burke, K. (1969). *A rhetoric of motives.* Berkeley, CA: University of California Press.

Haskins, E. V. (2005). Philosophy, rhetoric, and cultural memory: Rereading Plato's *Menexenus* and Isocrates' *Panegyricus. Rhetoric Society Quarterly,* 35, 25–45.

Loraux, N. (1986). *The invention of Athens: The funeral oration in the classical city* (trans. A. Sheridan). Cambridge, MA: Harvard University Press.

Perelman, C., & Olbrechts-Tyteca, L. (1969). *The new rhetoric: A treatise on argumentation* (trans. J. Wilkinson & P. Weaver). Notre Dame, IN: University of Notre Dame Press.

Poulakos, T. (1987). Isocrates' use of narrative in the *Evagoras*: Epideictic rhetoric and moral action. *Quarterly Journal of Speech*, 73, 317–328.

Schiappa, E. (1999). *The beginnings of rhetorical theory in classical Greece.* New Haven, CT: Yale University Press.

Vickers, B. (1983). Epideictic and epic in the Renaissance. *New Literary History*, 14, 497–537.

Walker, J. (2000). *Rhetoric and poetics in antiquity.* New York: Oxford University Press.

Weaver, R. M. (1970). Language is sermonic. In R. L. Johannesen, R. Strickland, & R. T. Eubanks (eds.), *Language is sermonic: Richard M. Weaver on the nature of rhetoric.* Baton Rouge, LA: Louisiana State University Press, pp. 201–225.

Rhetoric and Epistemology

Robert L. Scott

University of Minnesota, Twin Cities

In 1967 the assertion that rhetoric is epistemic attracted immediate attention from rhetorical scholars. The assertion was taken to imply that rhetoric generated a sort of knowledge. The purpose of the claim was to establish a fresh justification for the study and practice of rhetoric. In short, it was an answer to a line of reason beginning with Plato, who argued that rhetoric was a form of deception, practiced only under questionable circumstances by suspect persons.

The dominant response to the strong tendency to view rhetoric with suspicion was to present the art of → persuasion as vital in making the truth effective. The problem with that position, adherents of the claim that rhetoric is epistemic argued, is that it implies that rhetoric is only necessary under questionable conditions. If truth can be known, but cannot be explained sufficiently by those who know it to gain the assent of others whose assent is somehow necessary, then a sort of lie must be told to the latter by the former. Put differently, those not able to grasp truth must be deceived into thinking that they do. That implies that those who know truth are not in a position simply to demand adherence and perhaps ought to be. Therefore, rhetoric, if justified as making the truth effective, is anti-democratic.

Epistemology, taken as the theory of knowledge, seemed to a number of scholars to be a better platform on which to justify rhetoric; that is, the practice of rhetoric was a way to create a sort of knowledge (→ Communication Theory and Philosophy). The term "epistemology" arose in the sixteenth century. Before then, thinkers simply seemed to assume that we knew what we knew; in short, knowing was not problematic. Philosophers began to take knowing as posing a question: how can we know? Answers to the question varied, but the discussions helped fix "an age of reason." Descartes is often cited as a helpful time-marker in the beginning of the discussion.

Juxtaposing "epistemology" with "rhetoric" as a fresh beginning in justifying rhetoric anew immediately became controversial. In part the controversies arose from the term "knowledge." The question "how can we know?" was treated as if it were "how can we be certain?" Descartes argued for an indisputable starting place for thought. With that foundation, reason must be followed. That entailed setting aside emotion. Emotional responses were, in this realm, improper guides. (Some advocates of the linking of rhetoric and epistemology would argue that this move was the same as setting aside commitment.)

Since rhetoric has always been associated with arguing for probabilities not certainties, the historical thrust of the quest of epistemology is contrary to the claim that rhetoric is epistemic. Quite frequently, however, writers about epistemology have tended to interchange "knowing" and "understanding" in their discussions. For the most part the proponents of rhetoric as epistemic have taken "understanding" as a qualified claim to knowledge rather than taking "knowing" as synonymous with "certainty." These would argue that twentieth century science worked toward probabilities, which can be verified by traditional methods provisionally but are ever open to further research and reinterpretations.

Many rhetoricians hold that science and rhetoric interact in that the gradual establishment of traditions of scientific research has been a result of a constant conversation that is essentially rhetorical, and that the entire enterprise has resulted in an ethical code that scientists must observe in order to assure the integrity of the pursuit of truth, as provisional as that term may be.

In the final section of *The uses of argument*, a book that influenced many rhetorical scholars in the latter twentieth century, Stephen Toulmin writes, "The status of argument has always been somewhat ambiguous." The essential question of "how we think" seems to be a psychological one. "Considered as psychology, the subject is concerned with intellectual, or 'cognitive' processes" (1958, 211, 212).

The claim discussed here may be even more important in the twenty-first century, in which, thus far, cognitive science has flourished. Antonio Damasio firmly sets aside the mind/body problem, arguing in *Descartes' error* (1994) that the question of how we think is material and that we now have the techniques to reveal the activity of the brain. Moreover, we must take the brain as part of the entire nervous system. Damasio argues further that emotion cannot be dismissed as disruptive to reason. Thus commitment is relevant to human action. In a later book, *Looking for Spinoza* (2003), he makes a highly provisional attempt to trace human values as seated in adaptive evolution of brains.

Rhetorical theorists must attend carefully to such developments. Cognitive scientist Walter Freeman has argued that it is not sufficient to study the activity of isolated brains, and that the overriding questions of cognition are how brains interact (1995, 2000); he explicitly says that cognitive scientists must address the phenomenon of communication. These sorts of studies will pose a number of obstacles and challenges for all rhetoricians and surely impact heavily on the claim that rhetoric is epistemic.

SEE ALSO: ► Communication Theory and Philosophy ► Persuasion ► Rhetoric, Argument, and Persuasion ► Rhetoric of Science

References and Suggested Readings

Brookey, R., & Schiappa, E. (eds.) (1998). The epistemological view, thirty years later. *Argumentation and Advocacy*, 35, 1–31.

Cherwitz, R., & Hikins, J. (1986). *Communication and knowledge: An investigation in rhetorical epistemology*. Columbia, SC: University of South Caroline Press.

Damasio, A. R. (1994). *Descartes' error: Emotion, reason, and the human brain*. New York: Putnam.

Damasio, A. R. (2003). *Looking for Spinoza: Joy, sorrow, and the feeling brain*. Orlando, FL: Harcourt.

Freeman, W. J. (1995). *Societies of brains: A study in the neuroscience of love and hate*. Hillsdale, NJ: Lawrence Erlbaum.

Freeman, W. J. (2000). *How brains make up their minds*. New York: Columbia University Press.

Scott, R. (1967). On viewing rhetoric as epistemic. *Central States Speech Journal*, 18, 9–17.

Scott, R. (1976). On viewing rhetoric as epistemic: Ten years later. *Central States Speech Journal*, 27, 258–266.

Scott, R. (1993). Rhetoric is epistemic: What difference does that make? In T. Enos & S. Brown (eds.), *Defining the new rhetorics*. Newbury Park, CA: Sage, pp. 120–136.

Toulmin, S. E. (1958). *The uses of argument*. Cambridge: Cambridge University Press.

Rhetoric and Ethics

Ronald C. Arnett

Duquesne University

The field of communication has historical roots in the interplay of human speech and ethics (→ Communication as a Field and Discipline). Our journals record scholarly investigation of communication ethics beginning in 1934 with Pellegrini's *Quarterly Journal of Speech* essay, "Public speaking and social obligations." The founding scholarly work on speech and ethics is Aristotle's *Nichomachean ethics*. Aristotle's public descriptive account of Homer's narrative responsiveness to Athenian virtues in action establishes the enduring heart of communication ethics – *responsiveness*, commencing with responsiveness to the Athenian polis.

Responsiveness is part of a long heritage begun with *phronesis*, practical wisdom attentive to the interplay of the demands of the situation and a given virtue of the polis, whose application falls to the side of neither excess nor deficiency. Centuries later, this sense of responsiveness continues to propel the communication field's commitment to democracy and the fight against → propaganda spurred by World War II (Wallace 1955). Today, this responsive tradition continues with Michael Hyde's call for communication ethics' response to the emerging era of "post-human" genetic alteration. The communication field's responsiveness to → audience and context acts as a line of demarcation between the rhetoric of communication ethics and the philosophical study of ethics (→ Rhetoric and Philosophy).

FROM VIRTUE ETHICS TO TAINTED GROUND

Contemporary communication ethics theory begins with Aristotle's introduction of responsiveness and "virtue ethics." Variations on virtue ethics exist in differing historical eras, each with a different locus that frames the standard for virtue: (1) the classical world

– virtues and the polis; (2) the medieval world – virtues and the church; (3) the enlightenment – virtues and rationality; and (4) modernity – virtues and the individual. Virtue ethics now competes with other communication ethics theories that refute *one* view of virtues, rejecting the universal claim of "truth," considering bias inevitable, and working hand-in-hand with a postmodern context of narrative and virtue contention (→ Rhetoric and Narrativity; Rhetoric, Postmodern).

Communication ethics in a postmodern context recognizes that differing communication ethics live on biased ground where the rhetoric of competing "goods" shapes our discourse. Bias is unavoidable, as detailed by Hans Georg Gadamer (1986, 238–239). His understanding of philosophical → hermeneutics assumes the ontological reality of bias; recognition of situated, tainted ground links communication ethics to learning about and discovery of different "goods" protected and promoted by those dissimilar to us. *Alterity* is key to Emmanuel Levinas's understanding of ethics as first principle; the initial communicative gesture is recognition of radical alterity, an otherness different from "my kind" or "me." Tainted/biased ground and engagement with alterity/difference requires rhetorical engagement of a communication ethic or "bearing witness," as Amit Pinchevski (2005) suggests.

Tainted ground is the home of radical otherness, represented in a philosophical turn of consequence in the work of Heidegger and Nietzsche; they mark a "disputed" end to the reign of "virtue ethics"; virtue ethics continues without uniform acceptance as we move into an era marked by a "hermeneutic of suspicion." Deconstructive and existential approaches open conversation to theories that openly claim tainted ground in work interestingly akin to that of early sophists, who argued that virtues are polis-dependent (→ Rhetoric, Pre-Socratic). Virtue ethics understood as nurtured by biased ground, whether of a given polis, church, "universal" principle, or individual, rests upon the socially constructed approval of Sandra Harding's (1991) metaphor of *standpoint theory* (→ Rhetoric and Gender; Rhetoric and Race). Standpoint, the admission of tainted ground, rejects conventional thinking, countering individualism, a term coined by Alexis de Tocqueville (2002) in *Democracy in America*. Individualism advocates that one can stand above history, securing a vision of "truth" imposed upon another with universal assurance.

Individualism, according to Tocqueville (2002), is not selfishness, which can unite collective self-interest. Selfishness works with a knowledge of taintedness that individualism rejects. Selfishness permits Franklin to warn us that we must all hang together or hang separately. Individualism proclaims and tells, based upon an assumptive arrogance of untainted perception, missing the pragmatic need for association and the admission of bias.

Concepts such as standpoint, ground, embeddedness, situatedness, social–cultural limits, and the unavoidable bias of tradition place human feet on provincial soil that generates difference. Communication ethics as cosmopolitanism in the twenty-first century must attend to the local and engage learning as the bridge to the other, disclaiming the assumption that we can stand above our own historicity. Communication ethics as responsiveness in this historical moment rests on tainted, biased ground, whether that of speaker, audience, context, and/or content, moving rhetoric to the forefront – a persuasive task responsive to audience and context that provides a public map of the "why" and "how" of a given communication ethics position. Communication ethics, thus, takes a pragmatic rhetorical turn, pivoting on tainted ground, forming a public map of the "for," the "by," and the "about" of communication ethics. Calvin Schrag's (1986) articulation of communication praxis, called in this essay a rhetoric of prepositions ("for," "by," and "about"), frames communication ethics in the interplay of biased/tainted ground and the historical moment, attentive to a rhetorical turn responsive to otherness, context, communicators, and message.

COMMUNICATION ETHICS PRAXIS

Calvin Schrag (1986) defines rhetoric of prepositions, "by," "about," and "for," offering basic coordinates for a rhetoric of public accounting. The key to the use of Schrag's rhetoric of prepositions is that it offers a public accounting of a given communication ethics situated upon tainted/biased ground. Communication ethics praxis unites communication ethics vocabulary with Schrag's communicative praxis, a rhetoric of prepositions: (1) responsiveness – "for"; (2) the human face – "by"; and (3) the good – "about."

Responsiveness: "*For*" assumes that communication ethics engages and influences others. Aristotle's connection of speech and ethics responded to the virtues of the polis, with further responsiveness required by *phronesis*, practical wisdom responsive to unique circumstances/context and ever attentive to dialectical danger of excessive response or deficiency. Aristotle framed "the golden mean" as a moving ethical aim responsive to both excess and deficiency. The golden mean responds to known public virtues and is responsive to the polis and to the "proper" proportion of response. Aristotle's ethics moved phronesis or responsiveness to a recognition of the "proper" sense of "taste" (Gadamer 1986), suspicious of communicative actions of gluttony and/or deprivation.

The communication ethics assumption today is that wariness of communicative acts of excess and deficiency recognizes multiplicity and the rhetorical contention of competing goods. Tainted ground moves us from the "taste" of communication ethics to recognition of "tastes." Communication ethics in a postmodern context meets the historical moment without confidence in universal truth that assures the one "right" response – the "for" of responsiveness lives in the mud of everyday life (Buber 1955), not pristine clarity. This lack of clarity moves from theory and proclamation alone to Levinas's connection of ethics as first principle as responsiveness to the human face.

The human face: "*By*" lives through authors who continue to make a case for communication textured by its ethical implications. Major review essays by Chesebro (1969), Arnett (1987), Johannesen (2001), and Arnett et al. (2006) and journal scholarship continues through human faces situating communication ethics in the forefront. The study and practice of communication ethics rests on biased ground, engaged by a human face embedded in unique historical situations and responsive to others.

The contemporary marker for the study of communication ethics in the US is the theme bestowed upon the annual conference of the Speech Communication Association (now the National Communication Association) in 1983 by vice president Kenneth Anderson. Anderson's proclamation energized James Jaksa's spearheading of a national commission (1984) and later a National Communication Association Division entitled Communication Ethics. Jaksa and Michael Pritchard began the communication ethics summer conference at Northern Michigan University/Gull Lake (1990) with the summer conference moving to Duquesne University (2004). The conferences gave birth to numerous articles, including five edited book projects: (1) Jaksa & Pritchard's (1994) *Communication ethics: Methods of analysis*; (2) Makau and Arnett's (1997) *Communication ethics in an age of diversity*; (3) Bracci & Christians's (2002) *Moral engagement in public life*; and (4) Pat Arneson's (2007) *Exploring communication ethics*. Finally, two of the major Carroll Arnold addresses on communication ethics were delivered at the National Communication Conference by Kenneth Anderson (2003) and Michael Hyde in 2007. Their addresses and ongoing scholarship announce the enduring importance of communication ethics.

The good: The "*about*" of communication ethics, the protection and promotion of a given understanding of the "right" communication act, begins with knowledge of tainted/biased ground. We live in the rhetorical encounter of multiple communication ethics, each protecting and promoting a given good. Recognition of multiplicity necessitates one basic assumption – there is no one agreed-upon entity entitled "the communication ethic." There are multiple communication ethics, each providing rhetorical protection and promoting a given sense of the good. In the field of communication, six major approaches to communication ethics have dominated the scholarship: democratic; universal/humanitarian; codes, procedures, and standards; contextual; narrative; dialogic. Each one protects and promotes a particular good (Arnett et al. 2006).

The "about" of communication ethics in this historical moment assumes that we live and communicate in an era of multiple rhetorical and ethical coordinates: (1) contending understandings of the good; (2) contrasting goods that display themselves in communicative action; and (3) tainted/biased narrative ground(s) upon which communicators, context, and message rest. It is the rhetorical contending of goods and the pragmatic necessity of learning about different goods that shape postmodern engagement with communication ethics (Arnett et al., in press).

The problems that shake local and global communities often rest with contrary commitments to the good, played out in communicative behavior. Differing interest groups work at protecting and promoting different understandings of the good. In an age of diversity and contentiousness "about" what goods should claim our loyalty for protection and promotion, communication ethics begins with learning and asks, "What does the Other seek to protect and promote as a given good?" Additionally, communication ethics in this era abides within an existential reminder, "What one considers a communication ethic will not necessarily meet with the approval of another." The rhetoric of communication ethics in an era of narrative and virtue contention seeks to understand what good is protected and promoted by a given communication ethic.

SEE ALSO: ▶ Audience ▶ Communication as a Field and Discipline ▶ Hermeneutics ▶ Propaganda ▶ Rhetoric and Gender ▶ Rhetoric and Narrativity ▶ Rhetoric and Philosophy ▶ Rhetoric, Postmodern ▶ Rhetoric, Pre-Socratic ▶ Rhetoric and Race

References and Suggested Readings

Andersen, K. E. (2003). *Recovering the civic culture: The imperative of ethical communication.* Boston: Pearson.
Aristotle (1962). *Nicomachean ethics* (trans. M. Ostwald). Indianapolis: Bobbs-Merrill.

Arneson, P. (2007). *Exploring communication ethics: Interviews with influential scholars in the field.* New York: Peter Lang.

Arnett, R. C. (1987). The status of communication ethics scholarship in speech communication journals from 1915–1985. *Central States Journal,* 38, 44–61.

Arnett, R. C., Arneson, P., & Bell, L. M. (2006). Communication ethics: The dialogic turn. *Review of Communication,* 6, 63–93.

Arnett, R. C., Fritz, J. M. H., & Bell, L. M. (in press). *Communication ethics literacy: Dialogue and difference.* Thousand Oaks, CA: Sage.

Bracci, S. L., & Christians, C. G. (eds.) (2002). *Moral engagement in public life: Theorists for contemporary ethics.* New York: Peter Lang.

Buber, M. (1955). *Between man and man* (trans. R. G. Smith). Boston: Beacon.

Chesebro, J. (1969). A construct for assessing ethics in communication. *Central States Speech Journal,* 20, 104–114.

Gadamer, H.-G. (1986). *Truth and method.* New York: Crossroad.

Harding, S. (1991). *Whose science? Whose knowledge? Thinking from women's lives.* Ithaca, NY: Cornell University Press.

Jaksa, J. A., & Pritchard, M. S. (1994). *Communication ethics: Methods of analysis,* 2nd edn. Belmont, CA: Wadsworth.

Johannesen, R. L. (2001). Communication ethics: Centrality, trends, and controversies. *Communication Yearbook,* 25, 201–235.

Makau, J. M., & Arnett, R. C. (eds.) (1997). *Communication ethics in an age of diversity.* Urbana: University of Illinois Press.

Pellegrini, A. M. (1934). Public speaking and social obligations. *Quarterly Journal of Speech,* 20, 345–351.

Pinchevski, A. (2005). *By way of interruption: Levinas and the ethics of communication.* Pittsburgh, PA: Duquesne University Press.

Schrag, C. (1986). *Communicative praxis and the space of subjectivity.* Indianapolis: Indiana University Press.

Tocqueville, Alexis de (2002). *Democracy in America* (trans. H. C. Mansfield & D. Winthrop). Chicago: University of Chicago Press.

Wallace, K. R. (1955). An ethical basis of communication. *Speech Teacher,* 4, 109.

Rhetoric and Ethnography

Elizabeth C. Britt

Northeastern University

"Rhetoric" and "ethnography" are slippery concepts, each describing a practice or methodology as well as a class of textual objects. And while "rhetoric" describes an identifiable field of study more than does "ethnography," which is most often associated with cultural anthropology, each is an inter- and cross-disciplinary enterprise whose character can vary depending on its disciplinary home. Both rhetoric and ethnography – in their multiple meanings – have been individually challenged by postmodernism (→ Postmodernism and Communication), particularly by the loss of faith in grand, totalizing theories and the assumption that language plays a role in the construction of reality. But these challenges have also brought theorists and practitioners of rhetoric and ethnography together to explore how postmodern understandings of each concept can inform the other (→ Ethnography of Communication).

Postmodernism's crisis of representation prompted what has come to be known as the "rhetorical turn" in the humanities and social sciences. Some scholars in disciplines such as history, economics, and anthropology recognized that their knowledge-making practices were thoroughly rhetorical – emerging through argument and contestation and inevitably expressed from some point of view. In cultural anthropology, one outcome of the rhetorical turn has been a reflection on ethnography (literally, "writing culture") as both fieldwork practice and written account. The practices of participant observation (→ Observation) and interviewing (→ Interview, Qualitative), central features of ethnography, are no longer viewed as neutral activities but as interested influences on the objects of study. In addition, the written account of fieldwork (also called an "ethnography") has come to be seen as a kind of fiction, not in the sense of something necessarily untrue, but in the sense of something made (rather than simply reported) by an author (Geertz 1973).

Two publications have had enormous influence over subsequent discussions about the rhetorical nature of ethnography. The central concern of one collection of essays, informed by a postmodern sensibility, is the rhetorical construction of ethnographic authority (Clifford & Marcus 1986). The essays, by anthropologists and a comparative literary theorist, explore the ethical implications of representing cultural "Others" when these representations can never be neutral, as well as the nature of "experimental" writing (writing in forms that challenge the traditional ethnographic genre). Marcus and Fischer (1986) are more explicit about what experimental ethnographies might look like. Marcus and Fischer pay particular attention to the form of ethnography, arguing that any experimentation with form should illustrate the difficulty of representation. As a particularly successful (and early) experiment with form, they cite Bateson (1958), which examines one cultural practice of a tribe of New Guinea headhunters from multiple angles that parallel the author's own emerging understanding of the practice. Marcus and Fischer also survey how experimental ethnographers juxtapose their own voices with the voice of the "Other"; such experiments are designed not only to decenter the authority of the ethnographer but also to illustrate that cultural representations are moments of exchange between differing worldviews.

Largely excluded from these two publications, feminist anthropologists have also contributed to the discussion about the rhetorical nature of ethnography and to experimentation with the genre. In the introduction to Clifford and Marcus (1986), Clifford asserts that feminism has not contributed to ethnographic experimentation; this assertion has been challenged by articles and edited collections, among them Di Leonardo (1991) and Behar and Gordon (1995). Moreover, Mountford (1996) argues that the gender of ethnographers is rhetorical in how ethnographies are written as well as in how the researcher conducts fieldwork. Mountford points to the work of Hurston, historically overlooked in her own discipline, as an example of rhetorical experimentation that highlights gender (as well as race and class); by foregrounding herself as an insider and attending to her own subject position as a researcher, Hurston (especially 1935, 1938) complicates the relationship between observer and observed as well as author and audience.

Ethnographic theorizing within anthropology has prompted contributions by contemporary rhetorical theorists, as well as the "discovery" of canonized thinkers such as Kenneth Burke (see, e.g., Abrahams 2005). But the discipline of rhetoric has also felt the influence of a revitalized ethnography. While compositionists and communication scholars interested in empirically investigating writing and speaking practices have borrowed methods associated with ethnography – particularly participant observation and interviewing – for decades, the rhetorical turn brought newfound interest in ethnography and culture to rhetoric studies. This interest has expanded beyond theorizing about the practice of ethnography; rhetoricians have begun to describe culture itself (e.g., its institutions, objects, practices, and the like) in rhetorical terms. Two such ethnographies are Cintron (1997) and Britt (2001). Questions of the grounding of rhetoric in culture and vice versa have also been taken up more broadly by the interdisciplinary International Rhetoric Culture Project (Strecker et al. 2003).

SEE ALSO: ▶ Culture and Communication, Ethnographic Perspectives on   ▶ Ethnography of Communication   ▶ Ethnomethodology   ▶ Interview, Qualitative   ▶ Microethnography   ▶ Observation   ▶ Postmodernism and Communication

References and Suggested Readings

Abrahams, R. D. (2005). *Everyday life: A poetics of vernacular practices*. Pittsburgh: University of Pennsylvania Press.

Bateson, G. (1958). *Naven: A survey of the problems suggested by a composite picture of the culture of a New Guinea tribe drawn from three points of view*. Stanford, CA: Stanford University Press.

Behar, R., & Gordon, D. A. (eds.) (1995). *Women writing culture*. Berkeley, CA: University of California Press.

Britt, E. C. (2001). *Conceiving normalcy: Rhetoric, law, and the double binds of infertility*. Tuscaloosa, AL: University of Alabama Press.

Cintron, R. (1997). *Angels' town: Chero ways, gang life, and rhetorics of the everyday*. Boston: Beacon Press.

Clifford, J., & Marcus, G. E. (eds.) (1986). *Writing culture: The poetics and politics of ethnography*. Berkeley, CA: University of California Press.

Di Leonardo, M. (1991). *Gender at the crossroads of knowledge: Feminist anthropology in the postmodern era*. Berkeley, CA: University of California Press.

Geertz, C. (1973). *The interpretation of cultures*. New York: Basic Books.

Hurston, Z. N. (1935). *Mules and men*. Philadelphia: Lippincott.

Hurston, Z. N. (1938). *Tell my horse*. Philadelphia: Lippincott.

Marcus, G. E., & Fischer, M. M. J. (1986). *Anthropology as cultural critique: An experimental moment in the human sciences*. Chicago: University of Chicago Press.

Mountford, R. (1996). Engendering ethnography: Insights from the feminist critique of postmodern ethnography. In G. Kirsch & P. Mortensen (eds.), *Ethics and representation in qualitative studies of literacy*. Urbana, IL: National Council of Teachers of English, pp. 205–227.

Strecker, I., Meyer, C., & Tyler, S. (2003). Rhetoric culture: Outline of a project for the study of the interaction of rhetoric and culture. International Rhetoric Culture Project. At http://rhetoric-culture.org/outline.htm, accessed September 8, 2006.

Rhetoric, European Renaissance

Lawrence D. Green

University of Southern California

The goal of rhetoric during the Renaissance was the *mastery* of spoken or written language to affect a *particular* audience in an *intended* and predictable manner. *Mastery* entailed an understanding of language in its relation to human psychology, the use of formal procedures for turning theory into practice, and the education of others in both theory and practice. The focus on *particular* audiences, rather than a universal audience, recognized that listeners or readers could be differentiated and grouped according to their interests in a given topic or problem. Not every *intention* could be realized with every audience, and students were trained to judge whether it was reasonable to expect a particular audience to respond as intended to a particular use of language.

REDISCOVERING THE ANTIQUE TRADITION

Renaissance rhetoric was marked by an enthusiastic return to the major Greek and Roman treatises, combined with efforts to adapt those treatises to the changed circumstances of the early modern period. Cicero (106–43 BCE) had been known during the medieval period for the mechanical prescriptions found in his *De inventione* and the pseudo-Ciceronian *Rhetorica ad Herennium*, and both treatises had been reduced to synopses and epitomes that served immediate needs. Quintilian (c. 35–c. 95 CE) had been known during the medieval period as an imitator of Cicero, based on fragmented and nearly incoherent versions of his *Institutio oratoria* (→ Rhetoric, Roman). Aristotle (384–322 BCE) had been known primarily through his logical and ethical treatises, while the names and works of many other classical writers had simply disappeared (→ Rhetoric, Greek). But in the early fifteenth century, scholars recovered complete copies of Cicero's *De oratore, Orator, Brutus*, many of his personal letters, and most of his speeches, leading to a major re-evaluation of the previously known works and showing the centrality of Roman rhetoric in producing a full civic and private life through → discourse. A complete version of Quintilian's *Institutio oratoria* was discovered in 1416, with its vision of an orator who embodied in himself all the education of his culture, and whose life from cradle to grave was devoted to and governed by rhetoric. As the Byzantine empire crumbled during the fifteenth century, many Greek scholars emigrated, bringing with them works of rhetoric unknown to Latin scholars in the west, along with works previously known only through incomplete or inadequate Latin translations, including Aristotle's *Rhetoric*. Copies of these works circulated throughout western Europe as quickly as they could be transcribed, with eager scholars trading fascicles among themselves as they waited for the next installments to arrive.

These and other classical works all became available as full treatises in a surprisingly short span of time and the effect was electrifying. Where rhetoric had been seen largely as a set of linguistic procedures for intelligent composition and efficient communication, it now was seen as once having been the very heart and soul of a vibrant civilization, fostering civic life and celebrating private life. Renaissance writers, educators, and political and religious figures who wanted to reproduce that vibrancy for their own time embraced classical rhetoric as a major means toward that end. Some of the first books to come from the newly invented printing press were treatises on rhetoric, and the newly recovered classical Latin treatises were edited and published throughout Europe. The Greek treatises were edited, most were translated into Latin (often in competing versions), and some were translated into vernaculars. All of the major Greek and Latin treatises received commentaries that often were much longer than the original treatises themselves. Student textbooks and handbooks soon followed, sometimes building upon the prescriptive understandings from the medieval period, but more often ignoring the medieval works to go back directly to the newly recovered classical sources (→ Rhetoric, Medieval). In the first 250 years of print there were over 3,800 books on rhetoric, in over 12,300 printings, by more than 1,700 authors, produced by 3,300 publishers in 310 towns from Finland to Mexico.

THE ANTIQUE TRADITION AND RENAISSANCE SOCIETY AND CULTURE

The Renaissance embrace of classical rhetoric was not without challenges, since many of the institutions of Greek or Roman civic life had little counterpart in the Renaissance, and the regional variations between southern and northern Europe were far more pronounced than those within the small city-state of Athens, or republican Rome, or even imperial Rome. Classical judicial oratory, for example, had almost no practical relation to the processes of legal adjudication in the Renaissance. Classical theory envisaged competing speakers trying to sway juries of hundreds in open gatherings, whereas Renaissance courts often had magistrates in restrictive settings. So also, the institutions that shaped classical political oratory bore no resemblance to the procedures in Renaissance monarchies and principalities, where policies were debated *in camera* and decisions rested with a single person. Commentators were puzzled by classical democracies and republics that seemed to vest political power in uneducated people, and even the small Italian states that offered scope for public oratory restricted the franchise to the elite. A different kind of challenge was presented by the fact that the Renaissance had its own communicative needs that had never been anticipated by classical rhetoric, notably in preaching and official letter writing (*ars praedicandi* and *ars dictaminis*). During the medieval period both of these genres had been addressed in rhetorical terms, and became major concerns in the Renaissance as increasing religious partisanship called for effective sermons (*ars concionandi*) and as letter writing expanded from public officialdom to a wider realm of literate private exchange (*ars epistolographia*).

Renaissance writers responded to these challenges in a variety of ways. Some sought to recast the activities of their own time in terms of classical rhetoric, as with the English definition of a letter as "nothing else but an Oration written, containing the mind of the Orator or writer" (Angel Day, *The English secretorie*, 1586), in which the understandings about a public speech intended for a large audience of strangers are extended to a private meditation intended for a single and familiar reader. Others writers sought to modernize classical rhetoric to embrace Renaissance activities, for example, by adding to the traditional three genres of judicial, political, and ceremonial rhetoric such new genres as explanation (*genus enarrans*), instruction (*genus docens*), and commentary (*ratio commentandi*). To the extent that classical rhetoric was focused on → persuasion and effecting communal action in a civic sphere, Renaissance rhetoric represents a vast expansion to include realms of discourse well beyond persuasion, while at the same time seeking to preserve the underlying structure and understandings that made rhetoric such a force in earlier times. Both of these efforts – extension and modernization – reflected the belief that earlier authors had all been saying versions of the same thing and that their different doctrines were all consonant with one another.

RHETORIC IN THE RENAISSANCE

George of Trebizond (1396–1486), a Greek émigré in Italy, contributed to the syncretic view with his *Rhetoricorum libri V* (1433/4, published c. 1472), which blended the Hellenistic Greek rhetorical theories of Hermogenes (second century BCE) with earlier Latin theories of Cicero, the former from George's old life in the collapsing Byzantine world, the latter from the new western world he hoped to enter. George's syncreticism was more the artifact of a Renaissance writer than of the materials themselves, and what looks like a rehearsal of doctrines from two traditions is actually the *forging of a new rhetoric for the Renaissance*, couched in the language of classical doctrine. Rudolf Agricola (c. 1443–1485) illustrates the same phenomenon in his enormously influential *De inventione dialectica* (1479, published 1515). During the medieval period scholars increasingly assigned to dialectic the argumentative procedures of rhetoric, and then subsumed dialectic into scholastic logic, so that argumentation theory became increasingly remote from the shifting contingencies of everyday life (→ Rhetoric, Argument, and Persuasion). Agricola largely reversed this process by instead using the extraordinarily elaborated dialectical systems to produce vast numbers of inventional strategies for rhetorical argumentation (→ Rhetoric and Dialectic; Logos and Rhetoric).

Rhetoric emerged as the *central educational discipline* in the Renaissance, studied in the simplest provincial classroom and the university lecture hall. At its most basic level, it involved widely available training in practical techniques for manipulating words, while at advanced levels it was a sophisticated exploration of language and psychology. Widespread rhetorical education provided shared understandings of how individuals should communicate, since it trained students both in how to control language and in what to expect of the language of others. Philipp Melanchthon (1497–1560), hailed as the Praeceptor Germaniae, reshaped classical doctrines for Renaissance purposes – and ultimately for Protestant purposes – in his widely circulated textbooks on rhetoric: *De rhetorica libri tres* (1519), *Institutiones rhetoricae* (1521), and *Elementorum rhetorices libri duo* (1529). Melanchthon's school texts were imitated and recast for local purposes throughout Europe by Protestants and Catholics alike. One notable imitation in England was Thomas Wilson's *The arte of rhetorique* (1553), but, unlike Melanchthon's texts intended for the Latin classroom, Wilson advertised that his English text was intended for local preachers, non-Latinate courtiers, and women. In France, Petrus Ramus (1515–1572) proposed a curricular approach to the teaching of dialectic and rhetoric. Those parts of argumentation evidently shared by the two disciplines he assigned to dialectic, so that instruction in rhetoric focused only on those aspects of discourse not shared with dialectic. Pedagogical presentation was made easier by systematic reorganizations of both disciplines – by Ramus himself, starting with *La dialectique* (1555), and with his colleague Audomarus Talaeus (c. 1510–1562) in *Institutiones oratoriae* (1545). This curricular realignment had the effect in much of Europe of encouraging a split between "logic" and rhetoric, between argument and style, when in fact both Ramus and Talaeus insisted that in practice the two disciplines could only function together (→ Rhetoric and Philosophy).

Counterbalancing these uses of formal rhetoric in the classroom were two equally influential but less formal approaches. The Renaissance inherited from late antiquity a program of *exercises in composition* known as the *progymnasmata*, and published in hundreds of editions across Europe. In the form attributed to Aphthonius (fourth century CE), the series began with proverbs and legends suitable for very young boys, and ended with declamations of legal argumentation for grown men. The *progymnasmata* encouraged the invention of dialogues and adoption of unusual *personae* and unfamiliar points of view, with the goal of flexibility and comprehensiveness in speech or writing. The *educational treatises by Desiderius Erasmus* (1466/69–1536) had much the same goal, and were equally widespread and influential. The most famous of these treatises was his *De copia verborum et rerum* (1412), which began as a short exercise for two of his students and gradually grew into a huge treatise that captured the imagination of Renaissance readers. Richness of thought was Erasmus's goal, but the path could only be through richness of language. He provided hundreds of techniques for manipulating words and phrases that would create an unending supply of new combinations of language, thus making possible new combinations of ideas and understandings, and ultimately making mankind better able to appreciate and honor the fullness of God's creation. Most of these techniques derived from his understanding of classical rhetoric, but it put *elocutio* in the service of *inventio*; style was the path to argumentation (→ Invention and Rhetoric; Style and Rhetoric). At its best, Erasmus's *De copia* encouraged the rhetorical ability to perceive and articulate multiple points of view, along with skepticism that any one expression or thought was adequate for the richness of creation. This multiplicity in Erasmus contrasted with the singularity needed by Ramus to systematize his curricular realignments. In subsequent centuries, and in less capable hands, this contrast played itself out as a conflict between skeptical toleration and unrelenting insistence on a single understanding.

SEE ALSO: ▶ Discourse ▶ Invention and Rhetoric ▶ Logos and Rhetoric ▶ Persuasion ▶ Rhetoric, Argument, and Persuasion ▶ Rhetoric and Dialectic ▶ Rhetoric, Greek ▶ Rhetoric, Medieval ▶ Rhetoric and Philosophy ▶ Rhetoric, Roman ▶ Style and Rhetoric

References and Suggested Readings

Fumaroli, M. (1980). *L'Âge de l'éloquence: Rhétorique et "res literaria" de la Renaissance au seuil de l'époque classique.* Geneva: Droz.

Green, L. D., & Murphy, J. J. (2006). *Renaissance rhetoric: Short-title catalogue 1460–1700.* Burlington, VT: Ashgate.

Howell, W. S. (1956). *Logic and rhetoric in England, 1500–1700.* Princeton, NJ: Princeton University Press.

Mack, P. (2002). *Elizabethan rhetoric: Theory and practice.* Cambridge: Cambridge University Press.

Meerhoff, K. (1986). *Rhétorique et poétique au XVIe siècle en France: Du Bellay, Ramus, et les autres.* Leiden: Brill.

Monfasani, J. (1976). *George of Trebizond: A biography and a study of his rhetoric and logic*. Leiden: Brill.

Murphy, J. J. (ed.) (1983). *Renaissance eloquence: Studies in the theory and practice of Renaissance rhetoric*. Berkeley, CA: University of California Press.

Ong, W. J. (1958). *Ramus, method, and the decay of dialogue: From the art of discourse to the art of reason*. Cambridge, MA: Harvard University Press.

Plett, H. F. (2004). *Rhetoric and Renaissance culture*. Berlin: de Gruyter.

Vasoli, C. (1968). *La dialettica e la retorica dell'Umanesimo: "Invenzione" e "metodo" nella cultura del XV e XVI secolo*. Milan: Feltrinelli.

Rhetoric and Gender

Karen A. Foss

University of New Mexico

Rhetoric is the art and study of human symbol use. As a discipline, rhetoric began in ancient Greece as a practical art of persuasion, applied principally to political, legal, and judicial contexts (→ Rhetoric, Greek). Gender refers to the cultural constructs of masculinity and femininity imposed upon biological sex by any particular culture – what it means to be *masculine* or *feminine*. The relationship between rhetoric and gender has played out in four different and progressively complex perspectives in the discipline of rhetorical studies.

GENDER AS EXCLUSION

The starting point of the relationship between rhetoric and gender was one of mutual exclusivity. Gender was not conceptualized as relevant to rhetoric. In fact, however, rhetorical action and standards of eloquence were highly gendered in that rhetoric was synonymous with and considered to be the province of men. The assertion of authority and expertise, the use of logical argument, and the deliberate manipulation of discourse to affect an audience's beliefs and actions were seen as masculine prerogatives (→ Rhetoric and Logic), unsuited to women and even impossible for them to attain given their biological nature (Campbell 1981). Furthermore, women typically were denied the education necessary to learn the art of rhetoric. At every level, then, considerable cultural complicity was required to insure that there was no place for women in rhetoric, a perspective reflected in the formal study of rhetoric. The gendered nature of rhetoric was not a subject for scholarly investigation.

Acknowledgment in the discipline of rhetoric that gender is indeed relevant to rhetoric emerged as part of an interest in gender that accompanied the rebirth of feminism in the 1960s. Betty Friedan's *The feminine mystique* (→ Feminine Mystique), written in 1963, helped launch feminist movements in the United States; in Europe, Simone de Beauvoir's *The second sex* (1953) was a primary inspiration. Feminist social movements challenged contemporary gendered practices and made issues of gender an area of scholarly inquiry across academic disciplines, including the study of rhetoric.

GENDER AS HISTORY

Initial efforts to incorporate gender into rhetoric centered on the recovery of women speakers in history who managed to speak and write despite the cultural proscriptions against such activity. Feminist scholars in rhetoric searched for and found women in every historical time period who achieved renown because of their rhetorical success. Sappho, Aspasia, Cornelia, and Hortensia, for example, were rhetoricians with considerable social and political influence in ancient Greece and Rome. Margery Kempe wrote her autobiography in the Middle Ages, developing a distinctive narrative style, and Anne Askew wrote *Examinations* to document her religious suffering and to argue her case before being burned at the stake in 1546 (Glenn 1997). Most studies, however, focused on those women activists in nineteenth-century Europe and the United States who spoke out on behalf of abolition, temperance, and suffrage (→ Rhetoric and Social Protest). Elizabeth Cady Stanton, Angelina Grimké, Sojourner Truth, Susan B. Anthony, Emma Goldman, and Alice Paul were among those whose rhetorical activism received particular scholarly attention.

Studies of women in history focused principally on *three dimensions*: their significance historically, the obstacles they had to overcome in order to speak, and the degree to which they met traditional rhetorical standards for eloquence. Those selected for study by rhetorical scholars were those whose speeches and writings had been preserved, offering evidence of their noteworthiness and significance. For the most part, these were women speaking on behalf of social and moral causes considered the special province of women.

In addition, the study of important women speakers in history typically was accompanied by a focus on what they had to overcome to succeed rhetorically. Because speaking in public was considered in direct contradiction to the traits of femininity, engaging in rhetorical activity was thought to desex women and to diminish their purity and moral superiority (→ Femininity and Feminine Values). Rhetorical scholars typically explored and addressed the ways women speakers negotiated the obstacle of gender through their choice of arguments, dress, audience adaptation, and other accommodations (Kennedy & O'Shields 1983).

Furthermore, rhetorical scholars measured early women speakers against traditional criteria for eloquence. The discourse of women rhetors was analyzed according to the traditional schemas and expectations for rhetoric in which masculinity was the norm. If they deviated from these criteria, they were found to be at fault; yet meeting them meant they were not entirely feminine. As a result, women were found not to measure up – they were evaluated as unable to perform rhetorically as well as men. A study of Frances Wright offers an example. She was judged a failure as a speaker because, as a woman, she did not meet societal expectations of rhetors – and this in turn lowered her *ethos* (Kendall & Fisher 1974).

GENDER AS STANDPOINT

The realization that the assessment of women rhetors was according to traditional rhetorical – i.e., masculine – standards led to efforts by feminist rhetorical scholars to understand women's rhetorical practices on their own terms. According to *standpoint theory*, women as a group might be expected to favor certain rhetorical processes and practices because of certain cultural conditions and role expectations. Gender as standpoint thus recognizes the distinctive circumstances of a woman's life and the particular interpretations she gives to those circumstances. Rather than assess and evaluate a woman's rhetorical choices according to traditional rhetorical criteria, the particular goals, meanings, and strategies of woman as rhetor began to be considered.

Standpoint theory literally originated in the recognition that the female body will produce a different kind of knowing or ways of making sense of experience. Two French feminists – Hélène Cixous (1976) and Julia Kristeva (1979) – were instrumental in the development of standpoint theory. Cixous coined the phrase *writing the body* to suggest a reconceptualization of women from inferior to powerful, with a linguistic system grounded in an understanding of women's muted subjectivities. Kristeva posited that women have a particular relationship to and conception of time that affects their perspective on and approach to the world. In the United States, Patricia Hill Collins (1990) and Sandra Harding (1991) developed standpoint theory, and Julia Wood (1992) has articulated contemporary meanings of standpoint theory as it relates specifically to the discipline of communication.

When standpoint is the starting point for rhetoric, what counts as significant communication, who is allowed to speak and in what circumstances, and the desired goals and outcomes for a rhetorical transaction are reassessed. For many women, for instance, important communication occurs in the private rather than the public realm, and strategies are directed less at persuading and changing others and more at achieving understanding and community (→ Women's Communication and Language). Furthermore, women need not be important in history for their communication to be considered important, and rhetorical scholars began to examine women's communication across contexts from the private to the public.

Of particular importance has been the enumeration of various *women's rhetorical systems*, some of which contain more expanded options for rhetors than those offered by traditional rhetorical theories. These include Karlyn Kohrs Campbell's discussion of contemporary feminism as oxymoron (1973), Sally Miller Gearhart's articulation of the womanization of rhetoric (1979), and Cheris Kramer's exposition of different linguistic systems for women and men (1974). Karen Foss et al. (1999) summarize the rhetorics of nine contemporary feminist activists and describe rhetorical options such as enactment, violation of expectations, and honoring of multiplicity – strategies not part of the traditional rhetorical canon.

The recognition of multiple identities as standpoint for any rhetorical system was important for initiating a consideration of all kinds of standpoint factors, in addition to gender, that might distinguish the rhetorics of non-dominant group members. Standpoint epistemology opened the way for rhetorical scholars to take into account and begin to examine the rhetorical practices of all kinds of marginalized rhetors (→ Rhetoric and Class; Rhetoric and Race). The result was an increasingly broad understanding of rhetoric. No longer a monolithic ideal from classical Greece, rhetoric is now conceptualized in the plural. A multiplicity of rhetorics exists, many of which simply have not yet been acknowledged or fully explored because they do not meet the traditional expectations and conventions of a rhetorical system.

GENDER AS TRANSFORMATIVE

The acceptance of gender as standpoint – as a variable that cannot help but affect rhetorical sensibilities – led to a debate about the *capacity of gender to transform rhetorical theory* itself. At one end of the debate are those scholars who suggest that rhetoric needs to take gender into account, but that such accounting will not substantially alter what rhetoric is. Celeste Condit, a prime advocate of this position, suggests that diverse genderings should be incorporated into rhetoric, but her version of rhetoric remains synonymous with traditional eloquence (1997). At the other end of the continuum are those scholars, including Sonja Foss, Cindy Griffin, and Karen Foss (1997), who believe that the goal of feminist perspectives generally is to disrupt the ideology of domination wherever it occurs and to facilitate the transformation of knowledge and practices that limit the possibilities of human social life. The incorporation of gender into rhetoric is seen as an intervention that can assist in a reconceptualization of rhetorical theory to help achieve these emancipatory outcomes.

An example of a theory designed to reconceptualize rhetoric is Sonja Foss and Cindy Griffin's *theory of invitational rhetoric* (Foss & Griffin 1995; see also Foss & Foss 2003). These scholars seek to expand rhetorical possibilities by offering a continuum of rhetorical modes ranging from conversion rhetoric to invitational rhetoric. In the process, they develop the invitational possibilities more fully than traditional rhetorical theories have done. Regardless of where scholars fall in terms of their conceptualization of the role of gender in rhetoric, gender is now a fully acknowledged dimension in rhetorical theory, with the capacity to affect if not transform the rhetorical terrain.

SEE ALSO: ▶ Feminine Mystique ▶ Femininity and Feminine Values ▶ Rhetoric and Class ▶ Rhetoric, Greek ▶ Rhetoric and Logic ▶ Rhetoric in North America: United States ▶ Rhetoric and Race ▶ Rhetoric and Social Protest ▶ Rhetoric in Western Europe: Britain ▶ Rhetoric in Western Europe: France ▶ Women's Communication and Language

References and Suggested Readings

Campbell, K. K. (1973). The rhetoric of women's liberation: An oxymoron. *Quarterly Journal of Speech*, 59, 74–86.

Campbell, K. K. (1981). *Man cannot speak for her: A critical study of early feminist rhetoric*, vol. I. Westport, CT: Greenwood Press.

Cixous, H. (1976). Le rire de la Méduse [The laugh of the Medusa] (trans K. Cohen & P. Cohen). *Signs*, 1, 875–93. (Original work published 1975).

Condit, C. M. (1997). In praise of eloquent diversity: Gender and rhetoric as public persuasion. *Women's Studies in Communication*, 20, 91–116.

Foss, S. K., & Foss, K. A. (2003). *Inviting transformation: Presentational speaking for a changing world*, 2nd edn. Prospect Heights, IL: Waveland Press.

Foss, S. K., & Griffin, C. L. (1995). Beyond persuasion: A proposal for an invitational rhetoric. *Communication Monographs*, 62, 2–18.

Foss, S. K., Griffin, C. L., & Foss, K. A. (1997). Transforming rhetoric through feminist reconstruction: A response to the gender diversity perspective. *Women's Studies in Communication*, 20, 117–135.

Foss, K. A., Foss, S. K., & Griffin, C. L. (1999). *Feminist rhetorical theories*. Thousand Oaks, CA: Sage.

Gearhart, S. M. (1979). The womanization of rhetoric. *Women's Studies International Quarterly*, 2, 195–201.

Glenn, C. (1997). *Rhetoric retold: Regendering the tradition from antiquity through the renaissance*. Carbondale, IL: University of Southern Illinois Press.

Harding, S. (1991). *Whose science? Whose knowledge? Thinking from women's lives*. Ithaca, NY: Cornell University Press.

Hill Collins, P. (1990). *Black feminist thought: Knowledge, consciousness, and the politics of empowerment*. Boston: Unwin Hyman.

Kendall, K. E., & Fisher, J. Y. (1974). Frances Wright on women's rights: Eloquence versus ethos. *Quarterly Journal of Speech*, 40, 58–68.

Kennedy, P. S., & O'Shields, G. H. (1983). *We shall be heard: Women speakers in America*. Dubuque, IA: Kendall Hunt.

Kramer [now Kramarae], C. (1974). Women's speech: Separate but unequal? *Quarterly Journal of Speech*, 60, 14–24.

Kristeva, J. (1979). Le temps des femmes [Women's time] (trans. A. Jardine & H. Blake). *Cahiers de recherche de sciences des textes et documents*, 5, 5–19.

Wood, J. T. (1992). Gender and moral voice: Moving from woman's nature to standpoint epistemology. *Women's Studies in Communication*, 15, 1–24.

Rhetoric, Greek

Laurent Pernot
University of Strasbourg

The word "rhetoric" comes from the Greek *rhêtorikê*, which means "the art of speech," "the art of speaking": the etymology shows the role played by the ancient Greeks in the field which constitutes the subject of this article. The art of speaking exists in many civilizations, but Greek antiquity has given it a distinctive, rigorous, and rich theoretical underpinning.

The most common definition in antiquity consists of characterizing rhetoric as the "power of persuasion" or the "art of persuasion." This means that rhetoric aims to win the approval of others by means of speech (→ Rhetorical Studies). The basis of Greek rhetoric is → persuasion: the enigma of persuasion (→ Rhetoric, Argument, and Persuasion). How do we explain the frequent yet mysterious phenomenon that consists of making others freely think something they have not thought before? Rhetoric was invented in order to answer this question. Fundamentally, it aims at understanding, producing, and influencing persuasion. The word "art" (*tekhnê* in Greek) does not limit itself to what modern languages mean by artistic creation, and it also gives the idea of a reasoned approach, of a system of rules for practical usage, and of a technical production.

In its full sense (which was that of the ancients), the word "rhetoric" covers both the theory and the practice of speech; that is to say, treatises, manuals, and abstract discussions, and also presentations and speeches of all kinds.

Rhetoric was developed in Greece during what is known as the "classical" era; that is to say, during the fifth and fourth centuries BCE. It was linked to the regime of the "city" (*polis*), which was a dominating type of political and social organization at that time. A "city" was a small autonomous state of which the inhabitants (or more precisely, some of the inhabitants), called "citizens," managed their affairs by voting and common debates. Such a regime favored public speech and, therefore, rhetoric.

It was at Athens above all, the most important city at the time, that rhetoric was at its height in terms of three aspects: oratorical practice, theory and teaching, and critical and philosophical reflection.

ORATORICAL PRACTICE

The Athenian oratorical practice spread within a legal and political context. By law, parties were obliged to plead their cause personally, without being represented by a lawyer. The public prosecutor's office did not exist, therefore individuals brought the necessary accusations forward. Such a system supposed an effective commitment from the citizens, both as defendants and as prosecutors, within the legal framework. The courts sat all throughout the year and the verdicts were given by the juries, drawn from among citizens of more than 30 years of age, of whom there were several hundreds. In politics, the main organ was the Assembly of people (made up of all the adult citizens with a quorum of 6,000), who exercised the executive power by voting on decrees and by electing magistrates. There was also the Council (composed of 500 citizens aged over 30), who prepared the work of the Assembly. So it was the Athenian institutions themselves that created the rhetoric activity. It was an almost daily activity, considering the frequency with which the courts and assemblies met, and also an activity that took place before a large audience, usually meaning an extremely high number of listeners each time (several hundred or several thousand people). In Athens, during the fifth and fourth centuries BCE, "speaking to the people" constituted a communication situation that is difficult to comprehend today. It was a question of making oneself heard in large crowds, in physically and acoustically uncomfortable conditions, and with a view to real and immediate consequences.

Added to that are the ceremonial speeches made on occasions such as national funerals and religious feast days, as well as ambassadorial speeches given before cities and foreign sovereigns and all sorts of private conferences.

From this assiduous and multiform practice, written traces have been preserved, because during the classical era, the Greek speakers took the habit of publishing their speeches or at least some of them. The three most significant contributions, in both quantity and quality, were those of Demosthenes, Isocrates, and Lysias. They illustrate the Athenian rhetoric practice in all its glory. The published speeches are not necessarily word for word records, but were revised with artistic license and took into account a posteriori the arguments of the other side. Between "oral character" and "literary character," the exchange was constant in Athenian rhetoric.

THEORY AND TEACHING

Oratorical practice relied on a very vigorous teaching. There were many masters of rhetoric in Athens and many different schools. The methods varied but were for the main part oral. They included theoretical lessons, case studies, the learning of exemplar speeches assigned by the master, practical composition exercises on real or fictional subjects, verbal sparring matches between students, as well as gesture and voice training (→ Delivery and Rhetoric; Gestures and Kinesics).

Research into the rhetoric field was conducted in the manuals or treatises that were called *Tekhnai* ("Arts," meaning "of rhetoric"). Two remarkable examples have been preserved and offer complete lessons on rhetoric. One is the *Rhetoric to Alexander*, dated from between 340 and 300 BCE, and which has been wrongly handed down to us under the name of Aristotle (the author could in fact be the orator and historian Anaximenes of Lampsacus). This treatise lists the different types of speeches, then presents the appropriate subjects for each type, then analyses the common means of persuasion in all types of speeches (concerning argumentation as well as style). It finally gives indications regarding which plan to adopt for each type of speech considered (→ Arrangement and Rhetoric). Its aim is to supply as detailed a method as possible, in order to allow speakers to produce the most rich, elegant, and persuasive speeches for each case. Basically, it gives definitions, advice and rules, which stem both from a systematic study of the object and a close examination of usage and norms in place at that time.

The other treatise is the *Rhetoric* by Aristotle, which dates from around 360–325 BCE. For Aristotle, the study of rhetoric took on an intellectual and practical usefulness. It allows truth and justice to triumph within the legal context. It serves to persuade at all times where a didactical presentation is not acceptable and where it must maintain the conviction using common notions (before large audiences); it provides the ability to support opposing arguments and it allows one to defend oneself by speech in case of danger.

Some of the main points covered by Aristotle include the identification of three genres which can be applied to all possible rhetoric speeches (judicial genre, deliberative genre, and epideictic or ceremonial genre; → Rhetoric, Epideictic); the distinction between the two main forms of persuasion: logical persuasion through demonstration (*logos*; → Logos and Rhetoric) and moral persuasion through "character" (*êthos*; → Ethos and Rhetoric) and "passion" (*pathos*; → Pathos and Rhetoric); the psychology used as an agency of proof; the systemization of the "commonplaces" (*topoi*) of argumentation; the distinction between the technical evidence (elaborated by speech) and non-technical evidence (provided by an external source, for example testimonies); and also sentence analysis ("period" notion) and → metaphor (→ Style and Rhetoric).

Aristotle came up with the fundamental idea that, in order to persuade, the existing competencies within the listener must be exploited. A good speaker knows the cognitive competencies and the significant connections of those listening. He builds upon the pre-existing ideas, on accepted values, and in this way can bring about the paradox of persuasion (which was indicated above). Innovation is introduced into the listener's mind from well-known and accepted premises.

CRITICAL AND PHILOSOPHICAL REFLECTION

The Athenians did not only practice and theorize rhetoric; they also analyzed and evaluated it. While the rhetoric phenomenon was developing and becoming more extensive, society at the time had, in fact, reservations and doubts about this new art, which harbored possibilities of excessive subtlety, manipulation, and deception. This mistrust was radically and greatly expressed in Plato's dialogues, which constituted one of the principal chapters in rhetoric history (first half of the fourth century BCE). Plato often dealt with rhetoric; it constituted one of the main themes of his work. Plato ruthlessly criticized what he regarded as the faults of the rhetoric in use in his day: its intellectual and moral weakness as well as its link to democracy (Plato condemned democracy). Against this vulgar rhetoric, he defined the ideal of a "true" rhetoric, which was founded upon truth and justice. The true rhetoric has little in common with what is normally called rhetoric. It is, in reality, science and teaching; it is the speech of philosophy. Ultimately, in its perfection, it is not made for men but for gods.

The Platonic criticism was fruitful, because it sparked off a dialogue between philosophy and rhetoric. It made philosophers understand that rhetoric also concerns them (that is why Aristotle, a philosopher, dealt with rhetoric) and it led orators to take into account the intellectual and moral requirements of philosophy (→ Rhetoric and Philosophy).

When the fourth century BCE came to an end, rhetoric was completely different to what it was at the beginning of the fifth century BCE. Over the period of 150 years, in classical Greece and in particular at Athens, rhetoric became widespread thanks to the constant contact and exchanges between people, institutions, doctrines, and problems.

Subsequently, the elements put in place were never forgotten. They constituted a platform for the later history of rhetoric, not only during antiquity but much later up until the modern era of European and American history.

Even today, Greek rhetoric remains a reference and a source of inspiration for the scholars who are interested in political models, literature, and the philosophical and linguistic aspects of communication.

SEE ALSO: ▶ Arrangement and Rhetoric   ▶ Case Studies   ▶ Delivery and Rhetoric ▶ Ethos and Rhetoric   ▶ Gestures and Kinesics   ▶ Logos and Rhetoric   ▶ Metaphor ▶ Pathos and Rhetoric   ▶ Persuasion   ▶ Rhetoric, Argument, and Persuasion   ▶ Rhetoric, Epideictic   ▶ Rhetoric and Philosophy   ▶ Rhetoric, Pre-Socratic   ▶ Rhetoric of the Second Sophistic   ▶ Rhetorical Studies   ▶ Style and Rhetoric

References and Suggested Readings

Conley, T. M. (1990). *Rhetoric in the European tradition.* Chicago, IL: University of Chicago Press.
Fumaroli, M. (ed.) (1999). *Histoire de la rhétorique dans l'Europe moderne: 1450–1950.* Paris: Presses Universitaires de France.
Gagarin, M. (ed.) (1998). *The oratory of classical Greece.* Austin, TX: University of Texas Press.
Hett, W. S., & Rackham H. (trans.) (1937). *Aristotle, Problems II and Rhetorica ad Alexandrum.* Cambridge, MA: Harvard University Press, pp. 258–449.
Kennedy, G. A. (trans.) (1991). *Aristotle, On rhetoric: A theory of civic discourse.* New York: Oxford: Oxford University Press.
Kennedy, G. A. (1994). *A new history of classical rhetoric.* Princeton, NJ: Princeton University Press.
Pernot, L. (2005). *Rhetoric in antiquity* (trans. W. E. Higgins). Washington, DC: Catholic University of America Press.
Pernot, L. (2006). The rhetoric of religion. *Rhetorica,* 24, 235–254.
Vickers, B. (1988). *In defence of rhetoric.* Oxford: Clarendon Press.

Rhetoric and History

Kathleen J. Turner

Davidson College

The conjoining of the terms "rhetoric" and "history" suggests at least three related but distinct areas of study. One, *the history of rhetoric*, focuses on rhetorical theory and practice during particular periods of time; entries on various aspects of this area abound (e.g., → Rhetoric, Pre-Socratic; Rhetoric, European Renaissance). Two others are the focus here: *rhetorical processes in history* and *the rhetoric of history*.

RHETORICAL PROCESSES IN HISTORY

The study of *rhetorical processes in history* focuses on the ways in which rhetoric functions in historical contexts. As "speech" emerged as a distinct field in the early to mid-1900s, its origins in public address were evidenced in its scholarship (→ Speech Communication, History of). Early inquiries focused on specific speeches and speakers in historical contexts using what came to be known as "historical-critical research," exemplified by the classic three-volume anthology, *A history and criticism of American public address* (Brigance 1943; Hochmuth 1955). In the mid-1960s, publications using this methodological approach came under attack as "cookie cutter" studies that did little to advance either rhetorical theory or the discipline's status in the academy (→ Rhetorical Criticism).

By the 1970s, such challenges met rejoinders from several authors who sought to restore luster to the study of rhetorical processes in history. During a gradual renaissance, many scholars shifted from the assessment of rhetorical texts as distinct products that were historically situated to explorations of historical developments as captured in, and created by, rhetorical processes. Echoing the move in departments of history from "drum and trumpet" topics to social and cultural perspectives, rhetorical scholars increasingly explored historical events as rhetorically constituted.

Two trends characterized this resurgence. A *move toward book-length studies* evolved as scholars found journal articles and book chapters too abbreviated as venues in which to make significant arguments and interpretations. In addition, an emphasis (some scholars would say *re*-emphasis) on the *significance of primary resources* came from the recognition that invaluable insights may be obtained from examining such archival materials as memoranda, correspondence, reports, oral histories, appointment calendars, photographs, and recordings The development of Internet databases and resources has eased access to some archival holdings, and such access is especially valuable given the accelerating graduate study and tenure schedules that encroach on the time required for meticulous historiographical research (→ Historiography).

Studies of rhetorical processes in history still attend to individual rhetors, with particular attention to the speeches of American presidents (e.g., Ritter & Medhurst 2003). Other examinations broaden the scope of "public address" to incorporate differing forms of communication. Ball (1992), for example, uses primary sources from presidential libraries to trace the decision-making processes in the Kennedy and Johnson administrations, connecting the arguments within these small groups to the execution of and justifications for the Vietnam War. In a wide-reaching exploration, Condit & Lucaites (1993) delineate the evolution of the term "equality" from the mid-eighteenth to the end of the twentieth centuries, exploring the crucial role of discourse in developing connotations and applications that shifted across time and subject. "Equality" for white colonists, for example, did not have the same meaning as for black slaves.

Scholars interested in the rhetorical analysis of historical processes agree on its significance, but other aspects are debated. Issues include how rhetorical history should be defined; one characterization is that "rhetorical history," broadly construed, seeks "to understand the context through messages that reflect and construct that context" (Turner 1998, 2), while others suggest that any study of rhetoric that occurred in the past constitutes rhetorical history. Another issue is whether rhetorical history and criticism are so closely related as to be indistinguishable, or constitute distinct perspectives that deserve delineation in order to appreciate their complementary approaches. A third point of difference centers on what the relationship between rhetorical history and rhetorical theory should be: should historical studies be explicitly based on and constructed as contributions to theoretical inquiry, or do they serve other functions? Finally, scholars differ concerning the current status of rhetorical history, with some declaring it to be alive and well while others contend it has been marginalized.

THE RHETORIC OF HISTORY

A more recent area of inquiry, the rhetoric of history, focuses on how the construction of history constitutes an essentially rhetorical process that by its very nature emphasizes certain aspects in certain ways while overlooking others. Paralleling explorations of other specialized discourse communities (e.g., the rhetoric of scientific inquiry and of law), such studies argue that the standard of "objectivity" masks the choices that not only can but must be made in constructing stories of the past (→ Objectivity in Science). These choices include delineating a time frame for the subject, identifying key "characters," developing narrative frameworks, evaluating and using evidence, creating arguments of causality and relationship, employing metaphors, and constructing the historian's own credibility. Central to such analyses is the contention that such choices constitute not mere window dressing but essential epistemological decisions: one's very way of knowing about what and who have gone before is created through the writing of history. The most advanced versions of this argument contend that there *is* no "history" – at least, none that is humanly knowable – beyond what is rhetorically constructed. (→ Constructivism; Rhetoric and Epistemology; Rhetoric of Science)

From this perspective, such cherished criteria as "accuracy" and "facts" depend on not only the individual but also the social and cultural context in which the histories are created and received (→ Memory and Rhetoric). As Carpenter (1995) contends, such historians as Frederick Jackson Turner, Carl Becker, and Barbara Tuchman served as opinion leaders because they created stories that resonated with their audiences and their times. Whether writing for academics, the general public, or both, historians make their arguments within the contexts of the social truths of their times.

Some scholars extend this investigation to explore the rhetorical purposes to which historical arguments are put. Political, social, and economic debates rely on "the lessons of history" to construct cases for both the interpretation of current events and the recommendations for future action. Precisely because historical accounts are rhetorically constructed, the "lessons" drawn from the same events are often diametrically opposed. Arguments over reparations for slavery, for example, pit meta-narratives of white innocence and the individual nature of history against those of white implicature and the institutional nature of history, in contentions that Bacon (2003) asserts reveal the rhetorical nature of historical constructions. Similarly, "the lessons of Vietnam" suggest to some that the United States and its allies should have been more aggressive in their military intervention in Iraq, and to others that they should not have undertaken the venture in the first place.

Gronbeck (1991) suggests *two key forms of argument from the past* to illuminate issues of the present. The "genetic argument" traces the subject of discussion to a particular point of origin, cited as the "beginning" of the story currently being addressed. That originating point may be cast either as an ideal from which the community has gradually but inevitably progressed, or as an ideal to which the community must return in order to realize its potential. The "analogical argument" constructs parallels between historical and current characters, events, or situations to suggest cautionary tales or advisory actions. In both cases, appropriations of the past construct and are constructed by views of the present and the future.

An additional rhetorical use of history celebrates *the past as embodying the essence of the society*. Inspired by Kammen (1991), these studies examine how the commemoration of historical concepts serves to inspire and embody a people. Blair et al. (1991), for example, trace how changing expectations for public monuments reveal the ways in which a society's public memory frames the past, while Biesecker (2002) elucidates how, at the turn of the twenty-first century, such popular "memory texts" as the World War II memorial and the movie *Saving Private Ryan* serve as rhetorical reconstructions of the past to create a sense of national unity and purpose for a fractious American public.

Whether the focus is on rhetorical processes in history or the rhetoric of history, the connection between these two key terms reveals both the interdisciplinary significance of communication as a central liberal art, and the valuable insights to be generated through the interdisciplinary turn in academia.

SEE ALSO: ▶ Constructivism ▶ Historiography ▶ Memory and Rhetoric ▶ Objectivity in Science ▶ Rhetoric and Epistemology ▶ Rhetoric, European Renaissance ▶ Rhetoric, Pre-Socratic ▶ Rhetoric of Science ▶ Rhetorical Criticism ▶ Speech Communication, History of

References and Suggested Readings

Bacon, J. (2003). Reading the reparations debate. *Quarterly Journal of Speech*, 89, 171–185.
Ball, M. A. (1992). *Vietnam-on-the-Potomac*. New York: Praeger.
Biesecker, B. (2002). Remembering World War II: Rhetoric and politics at the turn of the twenty-first century. *Quarterly Journal of Speech*, 88, 393–409.

Blair, C., Jeppeson, M. S., & Pucci, E. (1991). Public memorializing in postmodernity: The Vietnam Veterans Memorial as prototype. *Quarterly Journal of Speech*, 77, 263–288.

Brigance, W. N. (ed.) (1943). *A history and criticism of American public address*, vols. 1 and 2. New York: McGraw-Hill.

Carpenter, R. H. (1995). *History as rhetoric: Style, narrative, and persuasion*. Columbia: University of South Carolina Press.

Condit, C., & Lucaites, J. L. (1993). *Crafting equality: America's Anglo-African word*. Chicago: University of Chicago Press.

Gronbeck, B. E. (1991). Argument from history$_1$ and argument from history$_2$: Uses of the past in public deliberation. In D. Parson (ed.), *Argument in controversy: Proceedings of the seventh SCA/AFA conference on argumentation*. Annandale, VA: Speech Communication Association, 96–99.

Hochmuth, M. (ed.) (1955). *A history and criticism of American public address*, vol. 3. New York: McGraw-Hill.

Kammen, M. (1991). *Mystic chords of memory: The transformation of tradition in American culture*. New York: Vintage Books.

Medhurst, M. (ed.) (1994). *Eisenhower's war of words: Rhetoric and leadership*. East Lansing: Michigan State University Press.

Ritter, K., & Medhurst, M. J. (eds.) (2003). *Presidential speechwriting: From the New Deal to the Reagan revolution and beyond*. College Station: Texas A & M Press.

Turner, K. J. (ed.) (1998). *Doing rhetorical history: Concepts and cases*. Tuscaloosa: University of Alabama Press.

Zarefsky, D. (1990). *Lincoln, Douglas, and slavery: In the crucible of public debate*. Chicago: University of Chicago Press.

Rhetoric and Language

Cornelia Ilie

Örebro University

"Language is itself the collective art of expression, a summary of thousands upon thousands of individual intuitions" (Sapir 1921, 246). When exploring rhetoric in relation to language we usually have in mind the nature and functions of the communication systems used by humans in different times and in different parts of the world. Some of the first important theoreticians of language were in fact rhetoricians, as well as philosophers. A major point of departure in exploring rhetoric is the rhetorical role played by language as a conceptualizing and persuasive tool, as a means of communication and as a bearer of values (Dumarsais 1825; Fontanier 1968; Perelman & Olbrechts-Tyteca 1969; Groupe μ 1976; Barthes 1988).

THE CONCEPT OF RHETORIC

Rhetoric has always been difficult to define, since the term has multiple denotations and connotations. Dictionary definitions most often describe rhetoric as the effective use of language to persuade or as the study of the elements of style and structure in writing or speaking. Typical definitions clearly point to a dualistic nature of rhetoric as understood for much of the past 2,500 years: "rhetoric is the *process* of using language to organize experience and communicate it to others. It is also the *study* of how people use language to organize and communicate experience. The word denotes, as I use it, both a distinctive human activity and the 'science' concerned with understanding that activity. All human beings are 'rhetors' because they naturally conceive as well as share their knowledge of the world by means of discourse" (Knoblauch 1985, 29).

Rhetoric is currently used to mean: (1) a field of study and an academic discipline (→ Rhetorical Studies); (2) social, professional, and/or political skill in language use (→ Rhetoric and Politics); (3) persuasive, stylistic features in language use (→ Style and Rhetoric); and (4) a form of "energy" transfer in language use (following Kennedy 1998). Needless to say, none of these ways of defining rhetoric is exclusive.

In ancient times rhetoric was a vast and influential branch of learning, closely tied to grammar and to logic within the famous medieval trivium (→ Rhetoric, Medieval; Rhetoric and Philosophy). Grammar evolved into a vast field of linguistic studies, which examine and explore the nature, structure, functions, and evolution of language (→ Linguistics). Although linguistics is a much later development than rhetoric, experience and scholarly evidence show that the study of language and rhetoric have been intertwined when required by specific situations and purposes. Important issues of language analysis were addressed by grammarians and philosophers in ancient Greece, Rome, and India (→ Rhetoric, Greek; Rhetoric, Roman; Rhetoric in South Asia). The earliest linguistic debate is found in the pages of Plato (4th century BCE). Further insights were later offered by Aristotle (4th century BCE). When Aristotle first called rhetoric the counterpart to dialectic (*Rhetoric* 1354a), he situated the study of the persuasive functions of language alongside the study of philosophy and science as a vital scholarly endeavor (→ Persuasion).

The term "rhetoric" and its variations in European languages is derived from the Greek *rhêtorikê* (art/technique of a public speaker; from *eirein*, to say, speak), the earliest occurrences of which are in Plato's dialogue *Gorgias* (see Dodds 1959). It is used there, somewhat pejoratively, of the technique of a public speaker or politician. According to Kennedy (1998), almost all cultures have a word for "orator," someone with special skills at public speaking. A common brief definition of "rhetoric" in classical antiquity was "the art of persuasion," or, in Aristotle's formulation (*Rhetoric* 1355b) "an ability, in each [particular] case, to see the available means of persuasion" (Kennedy 1991).

RELATION BETWEEN RHETORIC AND LANGUAGE

In order to understand the dynamic and complex relation between rhetoric and language it is essential to examine the role of natural language use and of human communication mechanisms in shaping and reflecting human thinking processes. This relation can be explored at three levels: (1) semiotic-evolutionary (the role of natural language in enabling distinctively human forms of thinking and communicating effectively); (2) structural-comparative (the role of specific language codes in shaping habitual thought – the "linguistic relativity" of experience); and (3) functional-discursive (the role of linguistic conventions, specialized discursive practices, and particular ideologies in cultivating specialized forms of thought for various situations and purposes).

From a *semiotic-evolutionary perspective*, there is a strong interdependence between language systems and thinking patterns. A central feature of languages is that they are systems of symbols designed for the purpose of communication. It is hardly possible to formulate a meaningful thought without using language. The reason is that, when formulating a thought, we need a particular code to express it with and a corresponding network of meaning relations to enable the transfer of messages (→ Meaning; Semiotics). Since language serves as both an instrument of thought and a means of expression, it reflects and shapes socially and culturally agreed meaning. This explains why one of the most salient characteristics of language by comparison with other communication systems is its flexibility and versatility.

The rhetorical dimension of language use is always present, though in different degrees, since we need to be relevant, both in writing and in speaking, when we communicate a message, so that we may capture and maintain our addressees' attention. We are used to selecting from the wide range of linguistic devices and discursive patterns the register and style that is most appropriate in a specific situation. The much debated distinction made by structuralists between *langue* and *parole* (Saussure 1916), as well as the distinction between the *competence* and *performance* of language users (Chomsky 1965) acquire a new significance in rhetorical theory through a change of focus. Whereas linguistics examines the way in which language is used by human beings, rhetoric examines the active role of human beings when using language. Consequently, the two elements are regarded as complementary in the context-based, goal-oriented, and addressee/audience-targeted process of communication.

From a *structural-comparative perspective*, the situation-adjusted language use involves understanding its persuasive potential as well as the speaker's ability to influence beliefs and behaviors through the power of symbolic action. This viewpoint stood in contrast to the position of many philosophers who treated → discourse as a neutral channel for representing an otherwise objective, independent "truth." Rhetoricians argue instead that the manner and form of discourse is integral to the thing or phenomenon that is described or discussed. Moreover, they emphasized their central role in shaping and motivating collective identity and action. Modern rhetoric follows classical rhetorical theory in treating the relationship between language and meaning as *contextual*, i.e., the meaning of a particular linguistic usage derived from the particular experiences and understanding of a particular audience addressed by a particular speaker at a specific moment in time (→ Linguistic Pragmatics).

From a *functional-discursive perspective*, language acquires meaning and value in actual use depending on socio-cultural contexts and historical conditions. On examining language use, Halliday (1978) proposed three categories of meaning: ideational meaning (relating to overall situation in the world), interpersonal meaning (concerning the relations between communicators), and textual meaning (referring to the structured text/discourse). By emphasizing the functioning of public discourse, scholars of rhetoric have drawn attention to communicative acts that affected the entire community and are typically performed before the law courts, the legislative assemblies, and occasional gatherings of the citizens at large. The language of public discourse can thus be distinguished from the language of technical discourse addressed to specialized audiences and private discourse addressed to more personal audiences that did not directly affect the social and political community as a whole.

Rhetoric can also deal with the *language conflict*. There is an inherent conflict in communication through language. On the one hand, words can clarify, inspire, and articulate thoughts, feelings, and ideas. Thus, words can build bridges across chaos. On the other hand, they can oversimplify, conceal, and fail to communicate assumptions/presumptions or to convey intentions/emotions. Trying to understand how language works is a stimulating, and often rewarding, intellectual challenge. The pursuit of rhetorical studies presupposes and/or fosters a respect for language while it unveils its limitations: our words are sometimes interpreted as articulating more than we intended, and sometimes less.

SEE ALSO: ▶ Discourse ▶ Linguistic Pragmatics ▶ Linguistics ▶ Meaning ▶ Persuasion ▶ Rhetoric, Greek ▶ Rhetoric, Medieval ▶ Rhetoric and Philosophy ▶ Rhetoric and Politics ▶ Rhetoric, Roman ▶ Rhetoric in South Asia ▶ Rhetorical Studies ▶ Semiotics ▶ Style and Rhetoric

References and Suggested Readings

Barthes, R. (1988). The old rhetoric: An aide-mémoire. In *The semiotic challenge* (trans. R. Howard). New York: Hill, pp. 11–93. (English translation of "L'ancienne rhétorique: Aide-mémoire," Communications, 16 (1970), 172–223.)

Bitzer, L. F. (1968). The rhetorical situation. *Philosophy and Rhetoric*, 1, 1–14.

Chomsky, N. (1965). *Aspects of the theory of syntax*. Cambridge, MA: MIT Press.

Dodds, E. R. (ed.) (1959). *Gorgias: A revised text with introduction and commentary*. Oxford: Clarendon.

Dumarsais, C. (1825). *Des tropes ou des différents sens dans lesquels on peut penser un même mot dans une même langue*. Paris: Dabo-Butschert. (Original work published 1730).

Fontanier, P. (1968). *Les figures du discours*. Paris: Flammarion. (Original work published 1830).

Groupe μ [Dubois, J., Edeline, F., Klinkenberg, J. M., Minguet, Ph., Pire, F., & Trinon, H.] (1976). *Rhétorique générale*. Paris: Larousse. (Original work published 1970).

Halliday, M. A. K. (1978). *Language as a social semiotic: The social interpretation of language and meaning*. London: Edward Arnold.

Kennedy, G. A. (trans.) (1991). *Aristotle: On rhetoric: A theory of civic discourse*. Oxford: Oxford University Press.

Kennedy, G. A. (1998). *Comparative rhetoric: An historical and cross-cultural introduction*. New York: Oxford University Press.

Knoblauch, C. H. (1985). Modern rhetorical theory and its future directions. In B. W. McClelland & T. R. Donvan (eds.), *Perspectives on research and scholarship in composition*. New York: Modern Language Association, pp. 26–44.

Perelman, C., & Olbrechts-Tyteca, L. (1969). *The new rhetoric: A treatise on argumentation* (trans. J. Wilkinson & P. Weaver). Notre Dame: University of Notre Dame Press.

Sapir, E. (1921). *Language: An introduction to the study of speech*. New York: Harcourt Brace.

Saussure, F. de (1916). *Cours de linguistique generale* (ed. C. Bally and A. Sechehaye, with A. Reidlinger). Paris: Payot.

Whorf, B. (1956). *Language, thought and Reality*. Cambridge, MA: MIT Press.

Rhetoric and Logic

Hans V. Hansen

University of Windsor

Logic and rhetoric are such broad subjects that in order to profit from their comparison we must make at least one division in each field. Logic in the narrow sense is mainly concerned with the consequence relation ("following from"), and a well-documented tradition exists from Aristotle's *Prior analytics* to the present that explores this question. In a wider sense, logic includes the study and statement of the principles of good reasoning and may be seen as taking as its central problem the question of what makes for a good argument or a good inference. Developments of logic in the wide sense can be found as long ago as Aristotle's *Topics* and more recently in twentieth-century informal logic.

In the narrow sense, rhetoric deals with the study of persuasive discourse, especially argumentation. Aristotle's *Rhetoric* and Perelman's new rhetoric are prime examples of this (→ Logos and Rhetoric; Rhetorics: New Rhetorics). In a wider sense, rhetoric is the art of *making things matter* (Farrell's 1998 phrase), especially (but not only) through the effects of language, and includes poetry, drama, narratives, instructional discourse, and the like. It is only when we consider logic in the wide sense and rhetoric in the narrow that their domains can overlap, and that it may become difficult to tell logical and rhetorical considerations apart.

PLATO AND ARISTOTLE

In Plato we cannot identify any logic apart from what he calls dialectic, but many of the principles that can be extracted from what he says about dialectic also belong to logic in the wide sense. In the *Gorgias* Plato distinguishes dialectic and rhetoric on two related counts: (1) rhetoric is concerned with appearances and persuasion whereas dialectic is concerned with truth and justice; (2) dialectic is an art (or *technê*), meaning that it is a teachable and productive activity, and rhetoric is not (→ Rhetoric and Dialectic). At the outset of his later dialogue, *Phaedrus*, Plato again dismissed certain kinds of rhetoric on moral grounds. But he went on to outline a philosophical kind of rhetoric, which was a way of directing the soul toward knowledge by means of speech. Dialectic was still his preferred method, having the power of leading one to knowledge through its methods of division and collection; however, Plato allows that rhetoric could be based on dialectic when teaching another. It would then be an art because it would presuppose the speaker's acquaintance with the forms of knowledge and would additionally involve knowledge of the different kinds of souls and the kinds of speeches likely to affect them. The kind of rhetoric of which Plato approves, then, has only a narrow pedagogical range.

In Aristotle, in addition to logic in the wide sense that we see in the *Topics*, there is also logic in the narrow sense (in *Prior analytics*), rhetoric in the narrow sense (in *Rhetoric*), and rhetoric in the wide sense (in *Poetics*). In all four fields but the last, the concept of syllogism is central to the elaboration of the subjects. Near the beginnings of both *Prior analytics* and *Topics* Aristotle defines a syllogism as an argument in which the conclusion (1) follows necessarily from the premises, (2) is different from any of the premises, and (3) comes about because of the premises. (Notice that the extension of "syllogism" is thus much narrower than that of "valid argument.") In the *Prior analytics* syllogisms take first principles or their consequences for premises; dialectical employments of the syllogism, however, are identified as those that either are based on answers given to questions in discussions or are widely shared beliefs (*endoxa*). This last feature is shared with rhetorical uses of the syllogism (these Aristotle calls *enthymemes*) which are further distinguished by the fact that they do not require that conclusions should follow necessarily from their premises; that they follow for the most part suffices.

Aristotle identified three kinds of rhetoric, distinguishable by the nature of audiences: forensic rhetoric is addressed to courts and concerns events in the past; deliberative rhetoric is addressed to individuals or councils planning for the future; and ceremonial (*epideictic*) rhetoric is concerned with an audience's present attitudes or feelings about a person or event (→ Rhetoric, Epideictic; Rhetoric, Greek).

For Aristotle, rhetoric is the study of the various modes of persuasion and it is an art; he sees it as an outgrowth of both politics and dialectics. However, although he clearly gives an essential role to the *enthymeme* as being "the substance of rhetorical persuasion," it seems to play a significant role in only one of the three invented (or internal) modes of persuasion he identified, namely, *logos*. The other modes were *pathos* (the use of emotions) and *êthos* (display of character) (→ Ethos and Rhetoric; Pathos and Rhetoric). His conception of rhetoric in the narrow sense thus appears to be wider than that of logic in the wide sense since he recognizes that rhetoric as an instrument of persuasion will require knowledge of character, ethics, and the emotions, over and above knowledge of logical proofs.

WHATELY AND PERELMAN

Richard Whately in his *Elements of rhetoric* (1828) thought of rhetoric as the art of composing arguments. Logic, on the other hand, he took to be both a science that investigated the processes of the mind in reasoning and an art that furnished rules of reasoning to avoid erroneous deductions (see *Elements of logic* [1826]). He further distinguished inferring and proving. The former belongs to the search for truth and depends on logic, the latter is within the province of rhetoric and is concerned with establishing the truth to the satisfaction of another.

In the twentieth century Chaim Perelman worked to develop a rhetoric that would serve for philosophy as well as public discourse. This was largely in response to the dominance of the logical positivists who extended the innovations in logic in the narrow sense (originally wrought by Frege, Russell, and Wittgenstein to deal with uncertainties in the foundations of mathematics), to serve in the analysis of scientific discourse. But their methods being both formal and positivist were ill equipped to deal with either natural language arguments in public discourse or questions of value – issues that became of increasing concern after World War II. Perelman's response was to advocate a revival of the subject of argumentation and although it was inspired by both Aristotle's dialectical and rhetorical views, he referred to his approach as a *new rhetoric*. It is characterized by the marginalization of logic in the narrow sense as having no relevance to argumentation, and the broadening of the scope of rhetoric to include all natural language argumentation, not just the types that might be addressed to the three kinds of audiences posited by Aristotle.

Perelman saw logic as logic in the narrow sense: it was formal, demonstrative, concerned with truth and validity, and impersonal in its methods. Rhetoric, which he equated with argumentation, however, was concerned with reasonable and justifiable opinions rather than truth, and in contrast to logic, argumentation interacts with the minds of its audience, aiming to persuade or convince it. Arguments, rather than being valid or invalid as logic would have it, argumentation judges as more or less strong.

Perelman's rhetoric is a rhetoric in the narrow sense but it broadens Aristotle's approach by extending the object of discourse to any audience addressed (including oneself), and widening the subject of discourse to include the theoretical as well as the practical. He distinguished actual and particular audiences from the abstract universal audience. Actual audiences may be persuaded, but universal audiences – impartial and critical sounding boards constructed by the speaker – hold to a higher standard and will be convinced only by good argumentation.

In response to Perelman, Henry Johnstone, Jr. sought to distinguish philosophical method from rhetorical method. Since the purpose of rhetoric, even as refurbished by Perelman, was to gain assent to a thesis, Johnstone took the rhetor as having the overriding goal of getting his view accepted by his listener. But, Johnstone insists, if the listener is aware that rhetorical techniques are being employed against him, he will be resistant to persuasion. Thus rhetoric can succeed only when it conceals its methods. In contrast, philosophical argumentation must allow any technique used by an arguer to be equally available to her discussant.

RHETORICAL AND LOGICAL VALUES

Typically rhetoric exhibits its value in the analysis of speeches like Socrates' defence in Plato's *Apology* or Lincoln's "Gettysburg address," uncovering motivations and strategies and persuasive techniques. In contrast, logic paradigmatically seeks to display its excellence in the analysis of arguments such as Anselm's ontological argument or Hume's argument against miracles, identifying inferential structures, for example, and modal operators, and searching for ambiguities and missing or unsupported premises.

The central problem of logic in the wide sense is that of when one ought to accept a conclusion given certain reasons. The central problem of rhetoric in the narrow sense is how a set of ideas ought to be presented to an audience, how a presentation can come as close as possible to having its desired effect. Thus logic relies on semantic and epistemic considerations like truth and acceptability whereas rhetoric leans on social and psychological factors such as emotions, tradition and popularity. Accordingly, logic and rhetoric bring distinct sets of standards to argumentative discourse.

But whereas logic champions truth and consistency and puts persuasion at risk, and rhetoric prizes successful communication above logical excellence, neither the logician nor the rhetorician can escape logical or ethical responsibility for their discourses. Broadly speaking there are two kinds of responses to this situation. One is for each subject to incorporate items from the other's subject when they attempt a comprehensive theory for argument evaluation. Thus many elementary logic books include rhetorical maxims, and many rhetoric primers include a chapter on the elements of logic. Ralph Johnson, the informal logician, extends Johnstone's requirement for philosophical argumentation to rational persuasion in general: in addition to holding the three standards advocated by many other informal logicians (that the premisses should be acceptable, relevant and sufficient), Johnson stresses that argumentation must not be unilateral but that the argument presented to its addressee should be completely open, with all its features made plain and manifest. The reason for this is that the addressee's assent to the argument could be rational only if he or she has complete access to the same information and reasoning as the persuader. This awareness of and concern for the persuadee has not in the past been thought to belong to logic, even logic in the wide sense. It is therefore interesting that Johnson's concern for the epistemic welfare of his interlocutor is raised to the level of a right: the arguer has obligations to those whom he is trying to persuade. This is an example of logic treading on rhetoric's territory. The other response to the observation that we have both logical and rhetorical responsibilities is suggested by Joseph Wenzel. It is that logic, rhetoric and dialectic are in fact three distinct perspectives on argumentation, each having different scopes, resources and standards, and answering to different interests. Rhetoric, Wenzel maintains, deals with arguments as a process whereas logic treats them as a product. He considers rhetoric a resource to help communities find solutions to practical problems; but with the informal logicians, he sees good arguments as those that give acceptable, sufficient and relevant reasons for their conclusions. Tindale has gone a step further, agreeing with Wenzel that all three perspectives are necessary for a complete analysis of argumentative discourse, but adding also that rhetoric is the basic or most fundamental of the three components.

SEE ALSO: ▶ Ethos and Rhetoric ▶ Logos and Rhetoric ▶ Pathos and Rhetoric ▶ Rhetoric, Argument, and Persuasion ▶ Rhetoric and Dialectic ▶ Rhetoric, Epideictic ▶ Rhetoric, Greek ▶ Rhetoric and Philosophy ▶ Rhetorics: New Rhetorics

References and Suggested Readings

Farrell, T. B. (1998). Sizing things up: Colloquial reflection as practical wisdom. *Argumentation*, 12, 1–14.
Johnson, R. H. (2000). *Manifest rationality*. Mahwah, NJ: Lawrence Erlbaum.
Johnstone, H. W., Jr. (1965). Persuasion and validity in philosophy. In M. A. Natanson & H. W. Johnstone, Jr. (eds.), *Philosophy, rhetoric and argumentation*. University Park: Pennsylvania State University Press, pp. 138–148.
Perelman, C., & Olbrechts-Tyteca, L. (1969). *The new rhetoric*. Notre Dame, IN: University of Notre Dame Press.
Tindale, C. W. (1999). *Acts of arguing*. Albany, NY: SUNY Press.
Wenzel, J. (1990). Three perspectives on argument: Rhetoric, dialectic, logic. In R. Trapp & J. Schuetz (eds.), *Perspectives on argumentation*. Prospect Heights, IL: Waveland, pp. 9–26.

Rhetoric and Media Studies

Jay P. Childers
University of Kansas

Few would deny media's increasingly central role in the everyday lives of most individuals, particularly in first and second world countries. And increasingly, few would deny media's rhetorical influence in how people come to understand themselves and those around them. News media shape the way individuals see their communities as well as those on the other side of the planet (→ News). Television sitcoms offer representations of individual characters that frame how one sees others of differing national, ethnic, or economic backgrounds (→ Situation Comedies). Movies offer narratives filled with violence and crime, which often leads people to overestimate the occurrence of such acts in real life (→ Cultivation Effects). Media play a central role in shaping the way many people perceive themselves and the world around them (→ Media Effects; Media and Perceptions of Reality).

In → rhetorical studies, media have been most commonly understood as technologically mediated forms of communication. This way of defining media places an emphasis on media such as → photography, → radio, → television, film (→ Cinema), and the → Internet. The primary reason for these media being seen as differing from other types of media is the basic assumption that the technology somehow alters communication in fundamental ways, something that the German philosopher Walter Benjamin (1968) explored over 70 years ago. In his landmark essay, "The work of art in the age of mechanical reproduction," Benjamin argues that traditional forms of art are unique because of the sense of awe that the individual feels when he or she directly engages them, something he refers to as its aura. The use of mechanical reproduction, Benjamin suggests, destroys the aura as the mass audience takes the place of the individual. The recording of Mozart heard on the radio by millions of listeners is altogether different from the Vienna Philharmonic's live performance. Some may argue that it sounds the same, but few would agree that it does not feel different. Rhetorical studies have struggled to deal with these feelings created by media.

VISUAL RHETORIC

What makes media particularly unique for the field of rhetorical studies today, however, is its overwhelming emphasis on images. Rhetorical studies have long focused on the spoken and the written word. As technological advances made the production and reproduction of images easier, the symbolic force of pictures, both still and moving, became more salient for public communication. Rhetorical scholars, hitherto focused on public speaking and literature, have found this increasingly dominant form of communication troublesome to address, and long-held rhetorical assumptions dating back to Plato and Aristotle have been problematic. While rhetorical scholarship has begun to adapt to newer forms of communication, media studies have generated new conceptual distinctions.

Rhetoric has, of course, traditionally been rooted in the study of language and a rhetor's ability to persuade or influence his or her audience, regardless of whether the rhetor's authority was derived from → emotion, character, or logic (→ Rhetoric and Language; Persuasion). Media's reliance on imagery, according to some theorists, works outside these three basic rhetorical forms, something Aristotle's model could not have anticipated. Images function rhetorically in two basic ways (→ Rhetoric and Visuality; Visual Communication). First, every image is visually symbolic as it represents some original (→ Visual Representation). From the movies projected on screens to the pictures accompanying a news article, images present symbolic versions of reality. As a symbolic discourse, images belong (for some, naturally) to the realm of rhetoric. Second, people's reactions to images are not, by and large, the same as to words. Images, especially those that are mediated, function primarily through → aesthetics, calling forth pleasure or disgust, hope or fear. This privileging of the aesthetic, many suggest, requires new ways of employing → rhetorical criticism. While some scholars may work with both rhetorical functions of media images, the research that has emerged over the past few decades tends to fit into one of the two areas.

APPROACHES TO MEDIATED RHETORIC

Those who read mediated communication as a conventional text that relies, like human → discourse, on symbols, apply long-established rhetorical models (→ Text and Intertextuality). No one has been more influential in this area than Kenneth Burke. Burke understood rhetoric to be the study of symbols and their many functions, and many rhetorical critics have found it useful to adapt his critical concepts to more modern media. One such adaptation has been based on Burke's belief that the languages people use allow them to do and think certain things and, conversely, to hide alternatives, what he called *terministic screens*. Through these screens, → identifications with others are both created and stifled. In the aptly titled collection of essays *The terministic screen: Rhetorical perspectives on film*, David Blakesly notes the importance of the title when he argues that "film rhetoric – the visual and verbal signs and strategies that shape film experience – directs our attention in countless ways, but always with the aim of fostering identification and all that that complex phenomenon implies" (2003, 3). In addition, Burke's rhetorical pentad (act, agent, agency, scene, and purpose) as a way of critically engaging mediated texts, particularly those that are narrative in nature, has also proved invaluable to the study of media.

While Burke's pentad and other dramatistic tools are readily adaptable to media studies, other conventional rhetorical tools and methods have also been employed. Although primarily empirically based, Cappella & Jamieson's study (1997) has shown how underlying metaphors used by news media create what the title of their book makes clear, a "spiral of cynicism" for the American electorate. While the thrust of their research is empirical, its foundation is clearly rooted in metaphorical criticism. Using the classical notion of mimesis, Trevor Parry-Giles and Shawn Parry-Giles have turned to the popular television drama *The West Wing* to suggest that it teaches the American public about the presidency and the nation. Mimesis, as first explored by Plato and Aristotle, is rooted in the notion that through imitation or representation rhetorical work is being done.

Employing this concept, Parry-Giles & Parry-Giles argue that *The West Wing* presents a rhetorical representation of the presidency that works through approximating "a reality of the presidency that is persuasive and credible" (2006, 4).

In addition to these more traditional forms of rhetorical criticism of media, scholars have also begun to explore newer territory assuming that technologically mediated communication's reliance on the image requires new rhetorical approaches. The first of these approaches is rooted in *ideological criticism*, which explores and uncovers the media's reinforcement of hegemonic forces in society writ large (→ Critical Theory). Feminist scholar Bonnie Dow (1996) has, for instance, turned a rhetorical eye on the images of female identity created by media. Examining the way in which women have been portrayed in television shows in the United States such as *The Mary Tyler Moore Show* and *Doctor Quinn, Medicine Woman*, Dow uncovers a number of symbolic representations of women in popular media that offer mixed portrayals of feminist ideals (→ Feminist and Gender Studies).

Another, newer approach that applies rhetorical methods to media emphasizes the fact that visual media do *affect audiences at an emotional level*. Rhetorical critic Roderick Hart made just this argument when he turned to television. Taking a broad view of television – its role as a medium and its content – Hart argues that television reaches → audiences at the level of consciousness. To make sense of this aesthetic response, he uses a phenomeno-logical approach. Focusing on the level of emotional consciousness, → phenomenology walks a middle ground between the beliefs that people engage media as objective viewers or that visual media reach the individual at an unconscious level. In the end, such a rhetorical inquiry leads Hart to argue that "television makes us feel good about feeling bad about politics" (Hart 1999, 10).

The final dominant approach to understanding media rhetorically in recent years has been to dig deeply into a text to understand how its symbolic images impact audiences at the unconscious level. Such *psychoanalytic criticism* builds on Freud's original models to create a theory of how media construct the individual and collective personality or psyche. Janice Hocker Rushing was instrumental in pioneering this method in rhetorical studies. In just one of many examples, Rushing & Frentz (1995) examined the cyborg in a number of American films as a heroic reworking of the Western myth, suggesting that the cyborg represents a new, "transmodern," way of being that unites mind, body, and machine in one self. For Rushing & Frentz, the → cyborg becomes a rhetorical discourse that shows audiences, at an unconscious level, how to live with new technology.

The psychoanalytic approach to rhetoric and media also represents one of the current research trajectories that continues to open up possible understandings of how media influence the way people live with and through technologically reproduced communication. Incorporating the work of Jacques Lacan and others, rhetorical theorist Joshua Gunn has begun advancing new ways of using a psychoanalytic approach to mediated commu-nication. In one such instance, Gunn (2004) argues that a psychoanalytic understanding of fantasy offers a way to mediate the disjointed relationship between fragmented texts and de-centered subjects. Gunn's assertion is, put simply, that the media offers dominant portrayals of fantasy that causes one to desire and, ultimately, to repress such a desire. Psychoanalytic criticism, while not an uncontested rhetorical approach, continues to offer new ways of engaging media studies.

While Gunn's approach to rhetorical media studies seeks to penetrate media texts more deeply to see how they affect individual and collective psyches, another approach is to step back and look at the way in which media build on and work with other aspects of people's lived experiences. One way of doing this is for rhetorical scholars to incorporate the idea of *homologies*. In the sciences, things are said to be homologous when they share formal structures. Rhetorical and media scholar Barry Brummett (2004) has recently suggested that homologous patterns of discourse exist across communicative texts that work to structure lives through formal patterns. In his recent book, *Rhetorical homologies*, Brummett explores how films can present audiences with stories and images that are homologous to lived experience, additional mediated texts, and other, larger narratives. A rhetorical criticism built from an understanding of homologies offers the possibility of bringing media more directly into connection with other human communication.

FUTURE DIRECTIONS

One final note on rhetoric and media studies concerns the Internet. While the Internet incorporates many modes of communication (discussed above) with more traditional print-based media, how rhetorical scholarship might engage it theoretically or critically remains to be seen. This is not to suggest that it cannot. But to begin to understand how communities of individuals on Facebook "live" together or how virtual communities (e.g., Second Life) influence the way individuals see themselves and the physical world around them will require even newer ways of understanding the use of symbols through mediated channels toward further identifications.

SEE ALSO: ▶ Aesthetics ▶ Audience ▶ Cinema ▶ Critical Theory ▶ Cultivation Effects ▶ Cyborgs ▶ Discourse ▶ Emotion ▶ Feminist and Gender Studies ▶ Iconography ▶ Identification ▶ Internet ▶ Media Effects ▶ Media and Perceptions of Reality ▶ News ▶ Persuasion ▶ Phenomenology ▶ Photography ▶ Radio ▶ Rhetoric and Language ▶ Rhetoric and Visuality ▶ Rhetorical Criticism ▶ Rhetorical Studies ▶ Situation Comedies ▶ Television ▶ Text and Intertextuality ▶ Visual Communication ▶ Visual Representation

References and Suggested Readings

Benjamin, W. (1968). The work of art in the age of mechanical reproduction. In *Illuminations* (ed. H. Arendt; trans. H. Zohn). New York: Harcourt Brace Jovanovich, pp. 217–252. (Original work published 1936.)

Blakesly, D. (2003). *The terministic screen: Rhetorical perspectives on film*. Carbondale: Southern Illinois University Press.

Brummett, B. (2004). *Rhetorical homologies: Form, culture, experience*. Tuscaloosa: University of Alabama Press.

Burke, K. (1966). *Language as symbolic action: Essays on life, literature, and method*. Berkeley: University of California Press.

Burke, K. (1969). *A grammar of motives*. Berkeley: University of California Press.

Cappella, J. N., & Jamieson, K. H. (1997). *Spiral of cynicism: The press and the public good*. New York: Oxford University Press.

Dow, B. J. (1996). *Prime-time feminism: Television, media culture, and the women's movement since 1970*. Philadelphia: University of Pennsylvania Press.

Gunn, J. G. (2004). Refitting fantasy: Psychoanalysis, subjectivity, and talking to the dead. *Quarterly Journal of Speech*, 90, 1–23.

Hart, R. P. (1999). *Seducing America: How television charms the modern voter*. New York: Sage.

Parry-Giles, T., & Parry-Giles, S. J. (2006). *The prime-time presidency: The West Wing and U.S. nationalism*. Urbana: University of Illinois Press.

Rushing, J. H., & Frentz, T. S. (1995). *Projecting the shadow: The cyborg hero in American film*. Chicago: University of Chicago Press.

Rhetoric, Medieval

Beth S. Bennett

University of Alabama

As an area of investigation, "medieval rhetoric" refers to the discipline taught as rhetoric in the liberal arts curriculum of western Europe, as well as to how that art was adapted to communication practices for secular and ecclesiastical purposes, between the fifth and the fifteenth centuries. Study of medieval rhetoric includes examining the continuance of the classical rhetorical tradition, as it was transmitted from the ancient societies of Greece and Rome (→ Rhetoric, Greek; Rhetoric, Roman), along with the development of rhetorical education and pedagogical practices in composition that fostered the emergence of distinctive medieval discursive genres, which persisted even into the Renaissance (→ Rhetoric, European Renaissance). In its scope, medieval rhetoric is necessarily complex and only truly began to be studied on its own terms in the twentieth century, as medieval Latin texts were discovered and made accessible for close examination by scholars investigating the history of rhetoric.

DEVELOPMENT OF SCHOLARLY VIEWS TOWARD MEDIEVAL RHETORIC

The study of medieval rhetoric originated in the second half of the nineteenth century with publication of collections of medieval Latin texts not easily classifiable as literary but which shared recognizable rhetorical features (Bennett & Leff 1995, 5). These texts offered evidence of how rhetoric had been taught in the Middle Ages, as part of the trivium of verbal arts that included grammar and dialectic, and how its precepts had been adapted to new communication needs in medieval society, particularly preaching, letter writing, and verse writing. As medieval rhetorical texts were identified, examined, and translated, scholarly views toward medieval rhetoric developed, helping to reveal how the continuity of rhetorical teaching in the Middle Ages had provided a type of cultural coherence in the longest era in the western tradition (Woods 1990, 80).

Early twentieth-century scholarship took its direction from Baldwin's survey (1928), which represented such texts as blurred with grammar and the art of poetics, and viewed medieval rhetoric merely as instruction in the techniques of stylistic elaboration and ornamentation ($\rightarrow$ Rhetoric and Poetics; Style and Rhetoric). Baldwin differentiated it from Aristotelian rhetoric, which he characterized as imparting effectiveness to truth, and labeled it sophistic rhetoric, imparting effectiveness to the speaker ($\rightarrow$ Rhetoric of the Second Sophistic). Baldwin concluded that medieval rhetoricians did not advance rhetoric as an art but allowed its classical function of invention to be assimilated into dialectic ($\rightarrow$ Invention and Rhetoric). For the first half of the twentieth century, Baldwin's work focused scholarly attention on texts that evidenced this view of medieval rhetoric as sophistic and connected with poetics.

Offering a different view of medieval rhetoric was an important but difficult essay by Richard McKeon (1942). Motivated by an interest in rehabilitating historical connections between rhetoric and philosophy, McKeon considered how medieval rhetoricians conceptualized their art and influenced intellectual developments in logic and theology ($\rightarrow$ Rhetoric and Dialectic; Rhetoric and Philosophy). According to Bennett and Leff (1995), he identified *three lines of conceptualization*: rhetorical, based on the works of Cicero and Quintilian; philosophical-theological, based on Augustine; and logical, derived from Aristotle through the work of Boethius.

McKeon traced the development of these conceptualizations across four eras in the history of medieval logic: fifth to tenth centuries (handbooks on dialectic), late tenth to twelfth centuries ("Old Logic"), twelfth through thirteenth centuries ("New Logic"), and late thirteenth through fourteenth centuries (scholastic treatises). Though limited in its treatment of the traditional conceptualization of rhetoric, McKeon's essay demonstrated the need for a wider scope of investigation of medieval rhetoric and justified a more thorough examination of extant texts.

MEDIEVAL RHETORIC AND CICERONIAN RHETORIC

The impulse for a more thorough investigation of medieval rhetoric was generated by research published in the 1970s by James J. Murphy. Murphy (1974) offered a new approach, one that combined the disciplinary tradition of rhetoric, the rhetorical educational program inherited from Rome, with an expanded, flexible exploration of the manifestation of that tradition in the Middle Ages. Murphy argued that the Roman educational program outlasted the culture that created it and transmitted rhetoric into the Middle Ages as a living tradition of precepts for pragmatic application. From Murphy's view, rather than a fragmented or degenerative version of the classical tradition, medieval rhetoric demonstrates how its teachers and practitioners adapted the tradition to their own specific discursive or communicative needs, implicitly lending their assent to Cicero's dictum: "Eloquence is one . . . regardless of the regions of discourse it is diverted into" (Murphy 1974, 363).

Based on the foundation established by Murphy, medieval rhetoric is recognized as essentially Ciceronian in nature. The dominant sources of classical rhetorical precepts were Cicero's treatise on invention, *De inventione*, and the anonymous rhetoric to Herennius, *Rhetorica ad Herennium*, which was attributed to Cicero, along with fragments from Quintilian. Cicero's treatise on logical topics for arguments, *Topica*, and Aristotle's logical works were also influential. In the fourth century, Ciceronian rhetoric of pagan Rome was still widely popular in practice, but by the fifth century, the cultural dominance of Christianity threatened the survival of that tradition. Murphy (1974) marks the beginning of medieval rhetoric in the fifth century with the appearance of two works that secured the continuance of the rhetorical tradition but in different ways.

Writing at the start of the fifth century, St Augustine's *On Christian doctrine* argued that defenders of Christianity need rhetorical skill. Illustrating that even Jesus and Paul had used eloquence, he suggested that combining rhetorical eloquence with scriptural authority would better equip preachers to serve the church. The appropriation of Ciceronian rhetoric to the needs of the church assured the preservation of rhetorical texts and established grounds for medieval preaching theory (e.g., in works by Gregory the Great, Rabanus Maurus, and Walafrid Strabo).

Also written at the beginning of the fifth century was the allegorical treatise *On the marriage of Philology and Mercury* by Martianus Capella. In that work, Capella personified liberal arts from the Roman curriculum as handmaidens for the bride Philology. The first three dealt with words (grammar, dialectic, rhetoric), and the second four with numbers (geometry, arithmetic, astronomy, music). Lady Rhetoric is portrayed as a warrior-queen, resplendent in her adornment and armament, wielding power over people and armies alike. The popularity of Capella's work in the Middle Ages preserved the pagan tradition of rhetoric as an art and firmly established its dominance in the medieval liberal arts curriculum. Pedagogical practices continued to include both grammatical training in composition and rhetorical practice in declamation and disputation.

Systematic investigation of medieval rhetoric generally acknowledges two periods of development: an early period of transition (400–1050) and a second, known as the "High Middle Ages" (1050–1400). Works from the transitional period display a shared concern for preserving traditional rhetorical knowledge and typically appear as commentaries (Victorinus, Grillius), as encyclopedic compendia (Cassiodorus Senator, Isidore of Seville), or as treatises rehabilitating traditional precepts for current needs (works by Notker Labeo and Anselm de Besate). The High Middle Ages produced works that exhibit conscious efforts to adapt rhetorical precepts, such as those treating order or arrangement, linguistic correctness and the use of figures, or textual interpretation and elaboration, to medieval problems of composition and disputation (→ Arrangement and Rhetoric).

By mid-eleventh century, the rhetorical tradition gave rise to three medieval discursive arts. Communication needs for composing official letters were met with a new art of letter writing (*ars dictaminis*), for composing sermons, an art of preaching (*ars praedicandi*), and for composing verse and didactic literature, an art of poetic (*ars poetriae*). By the start of the twelfth century, numerous treatises appeared in each of these new rhetorical genres: *Ars dictaminis* (Hugh of Bologne, Guido Faba, Boncompagno da Signa), *ars praedicandi* (Alain de Lille, Robert of Basevorn), and *ars poetriae* (Matthew of Vendome, Geoffrey of Vinsauf, John of Garland, Gervase of Melkley).

As medieval educational practices developed under the dominance of the church, an intellectual movement known as scholasticism also emerged, which Christian scholars found useful for advancing and refuting competing theological arguments. Derived from traditional rhetorical declamatory practice but informed by the logical works of Cicero, Boethius, and Aristotle, scholasticism approached disputation as syllogistic demonstration based upon authoritative scripture or texts. Thus, scholastics tended to place dialectic or logic, used to demonstrate truth, above rhetoric or eloquence, regarded as popularizing ignorance.

CURRENT ISSUES IN THE STUDY OF MEDIEVAL RHETORIC

Despite the growth in scholarship since Murphy's work, many areas of study remain incomplete, such as the continuous tradition of commentary on Ciceronian rhetorical texts (Ward 1995), and medieval rhetoric still tends to be marginalized as a field of study in the history of rhetoric by communication scholars. One reason is the difficulty in working with medieval Latin texts. The other is the tendency to judge medieval rhetoric against an arbitrary classical rhetorical paradigm. Brian Vickers (1988), invoking Baldwin's earlier view, devoted a whole chapter to a discussion of "medieval fragmentation," in which medieval rhetoric is judged as fragments of "the genuine classical tradition." Martin Camargo (2003) has argued that Vickers' judgment relies upon several mistaken assumptions, the most significant of which accepts as fact only one authentic rhetorical tradition.

George Kennedy (1999) has asserted that throughout its history, rhetoric moves from its primary form to secondary ones, that is, to rhetorical techniques that contribute to the purpose of the speaker or the writer but only indirectly. By his description, most of medieval rhetoric becomes secondary. Marjorie Curry Woods (1990) has demonstrated the problems with Kennedy's distinction, and argues that the medieval tradition of pedagogical rhetoric offers a new foundation for assessing the western rhetorical tradition as a whole.

SEE ALSO: ▶ Arrangement and Rhetoric ▶ Invention and Rhetoric ▶ Logos and Rhetoric ▶ Memory and Rhetoric ▶ Rhetoric and Dialectic ▶ Rhetoric, European Renaissance ▶ Rhetoric, Greek ▶ Rhetoric and Logic ▶ Rhetoric and Philosophy ▶ Rhetoric and Poetics ▶ Rhetoric, Pre-Socratic ▶ Rhetoric, Roman ▶ Rhetoric of the Second Sophistic ▶ Style and Rhetoric

References and Suggested Readings

Baldwin, C. S. (1928). *Medieval rhetoric and poetics to 1400: Interpreted from representative works.* New York: Macmillan.

Bennett, B. S., & Leff, M. (1995). Introduction: James J. Murphy and the rhetorical tradition. In W. B. Horner & M. Leff (eds.), *Rhetoric and pedagogy: Its history, philosophy, and practice.* Mahwah, NJ: Lawrence Erlbaum, pp. 1–16.

Camargo, M. (2003). Defining medieval rhetoric. In C. J. Mews, C. J. Nederman, & R. M. Thomson (eds.), *Rhetoric and renewal in the Latin west 1100–1540: Essays in honour of John O. Ward.* Turnhout: Brepols, pp. 21–34.

Kennedy, G. A. (1999). *Classical rhetoric and its Christian and secular tradition from ancient to modern times,* 2nd edn. Chapel Hill, NC: University of North Carolina Press.

McKeon, R. (1942). Rhetoric in the middle ages. *Speculum,* 17, 1–32.

Murphy, J. J. (1974). *Rhetoric in the Middle Ages: A history of rhetorical theory from St Augustine to the Renaissance.* Berkeley, CA: University of California Press.

Murphy, J. J. (ed.) (1978). *Medieval eloquence: Studies in the theory and practice of medieval rhetoric.* Berkeley, CA: University of California Press.

Murphy, J. J. (1989). *Medieval rhetoric: A select bibliography,* 2nd edn. Toronto: University of Toronto Press.

Vickers, B. (1988). *In defence of rhetoric.* Oxford: Clarendon.

Ward, J. O. (1995). *Ciceronian rhetoric in treatise, scholion and commentary.* Turnhout: Brepols.

Woods, M. C. (1990). The teaching of writing in medieval Europe. In J. J. Murphy (ed.), *A short history of writing instruction from ancient Greece to twentieth-century America*. Davis, CA: Hermagoras, pp. 77–94.

Rhetoric in the Middle East

David A. Frank

University of Oregon

An overview of rhetoric in the Middle East should begin with the recognition that the terms "rhetoric" and the "Middle East" are not neutral, as they reflect the ideological and cultural values of the Occident. There is a general consensus that the notion of rhetoric, coined by Plato in the fourth century BCE to define the art of public → discourse and oratory practiced in ancient Greece and the western tradition, should be challenged for its Hellenocentrism. Western scholars of rhetoric have moved beyond the belief that those outside the constellations of Occidental thought lack a "rhetorical consciousness." The ancient Africans, Egyptians, Hebrews, and Chinese reflected on the role of symbols and argument (→ Rhetoric in Africa; Rhetoric in East Asia: China and Japan; Rhetorical Studies). Western rhetoric owes a deep dept to the Arab world, which preserved and translated the classical rhetorical texts of Greece and Rome during the Islamic world's renaissance in the ninth and tenth centuries CE, a period in which Athens yielded to Baghdad as the center of humanistic scholarship. Between 711 and 1492, the art of rhetoric flourished in Spain during the period known as *La Convinencia* ("the coexistence") as Muslims, Jews, and Christians lived in a cosmopolitan community (→ Rhetoric in Western Europe: Spain). The discourse of and in the modern Middle East is a tangle of religious, national, and sectarian myths and arguments, often prompted by traumas (e.g., the crusades, Muslim expansion, the rise of the Ottoman empire, colonialism, the Israeli–Palestinian conflict, 9/11, etc.) that are the result of conflict between the west and the Middle East.

The Middle East is the geographical descriptor used in the modern west to name the region of predominantly Arab and Muslim peoples who, from the vantage point of Europe and the west, live in lands that are to the east. The symbolic construction of the Middle East and its people by those in the Occident is often expressed as one part of a much larger reductive narrative about the east, which Edward Said (1978) termed "Orientalism." According to Said, western speakers, writers, artists, and media depict the Orient, Arabs, and Islam in essentialist terms.

The peoples of the Middle East (the term *Mashriq* is used by Arab language speakers to describe the region) have an understanding of symbols and discourse (the Arabic term *balagha* is closely related to the meaning of rhetoric) and are prompted to discourse by the exigencies of the region. Their view of the Occident is not immaculate as the symbolic construction of the west in this region clusters around a series of interpretations that Ian Buruma and Avishai Margalit call "Occidentalism" (2004). According to this frame, the west celebrates the sloth of the sinful city over the grounded rural; favors the economic over the heroic; values matter over spirit; and endorses the wicked and evil. Accordingly, the scholarship on rhetoric/*balagha* in and about the Middle East/*Mashriq* can be organized around three notions: Orientalism, Occidentalism, and cosmopolitanism.

ORIENTALISM

Arabs are often depicted in the west as fundamentally inhuman, warlike, emotional, and barbaric. Such essentializations, Said argued, reduce Arabs and Islam to an ideology of Orientalism, one that is both ahistorical and reductive (→ Postcolonial Theory). Many in the west reduce Islam to *jihad* or holy war, and the violence of some Muslims in the name of their religion is seen as representing the main rather than the marginal tenets of a faith held by over a billion people. A recent Pew report explains this view with data unveiling a significant "attitudinal divide" between the west and the Muslim world; many in the United States believe Muslims are fanatical, violent, and arrogant.

Said's Orientalism argument has been heavily criticized, but the scholarly consensus is that he captured a previously unrecognized dichotomy in western thought, one that defined the Orient against the Occident. This dichotomy extends into western literature and philosophy, as Martin Bernal documents in his *Black Athena* (1987). Bernal's argument, which is also contested in the literature, corroborates Said's thesis by setting forth evidence that the west has demonized the Orient, suppressing evidence that the Egyptians (a "Middle Eastern" people) provided the philosophical touchstones of western civilization. Bernal provides ample evidence that the Orient and the Occident were in relationship during the axial age.

OCCIDENTALISM

Occidentalism is the ideological frame of the west used by many residents of the Middle East, one that shares with Orientalism a commitment to an essentialist and bipolar vision of the social cosmos. A prime illustration of Occidentalism is the response of Palestinian Arabs to Zionism. The conflict between the Zionists and Palestinians was, in part, a clash between Orientalism and Occidentalism. Many Zionists brought with them colonial and Orientalist attitudes, viewing their mission as bringing civilization to a barren land and its backward people in need of enlightenment. The Palestinians saw the Zionists as invaders, a disease upon the Arab nation. They were foreign, with evil intention, bent on destroying Islam and the mosques of Palestine. The European Jews were viewed as communist, seeking to impose the material values of western civilizations on the land of Palestine and the indigenous Arab people.

The conflict between Zionism/Israel and Palestinian nationalism has often served as the primary exigency of discourse in the Middle East. Zionism and the creation of Israel, for example, are rarely placed in context by those in the region. Even those European Jews who did not yearn to return to an ancient homeland did so because their choices were severely restricted. The leading historian of Palestinian identity, Rashid Khalidi (1997), historizes Zionism and notes that Jews fleeing the Nazis and the Holocaust were barred from entering most western countries, and, irrespective of a commitment to the "land of Israel" ideology, had nowhere else to go. Tragically, these refugees from Europe, with a historical connection to the land of Palestine, participated in the dispersion of 800,000 Palestinian Arabs (the *Necba*), who also had deep religious and secular connections to the land. Edward Said was highly critical of Israel for its treatment of Palestinians, but he also condemned the Palestinian leadership for its failure to understand the "many wests" and its reliance on stereotypes of the Occident.

COSMOPOLITANISM

Cosmopolitanism, an ideology affirming cultural and identity change due to contact with others, an inclusive universalism, and a commitment to conversation and argument, has been offered by some as a third perspective. From this perspective, those who subscribe to the ancient hatreds theory of conflict in the Middle East (e.g., "Jews and Arabs have and always will hate each other"), or believe the conflict is an expression of a "clash of civilizations" often fail to contextualize the evidence justifying their beliefs and fall prey to a fatalism that is not supported by history. This history includes religious texts that are open to rhetorical interpretations and periods in history in which Jews, Arabs, and Muslims lived in creative harmony.

The alternative to Orientalism, accordingly, is to view Arabism and Islam as diverse, heterogeneous movements, rooted in rhetorical situations that host demanding exigencies. Not all Arabs are religious Muslims and not all Muslims are Arab. The notion of Arabism is largely secular, and is expressed in the communal connection felt by those who speak Arabic and share a narrative of common origins. In the twentieth century, Arabism was closely linked to the nation-state, introduced into the region by the Europeans. The most compelling exigency of the twentieth century for the people in the region was colonialism – the British and French divided the Middle East as the reward for their victory in World War II. They created the modern map of the region, and twentieth-century rhetoric from the region has featured calls for decolonization and national unity. Arabism has not prevented conflict and war between and among Arab states. For example, there are profound cultural differences between Gulf Arabs and those of the Levant, reflecting religion, class, and societal structure.

Islam, which is often intertwined with Arabism, lends itself to a host of different and sometimes competing interpretations of the Koran (the central religious text of Islam) and its expressions. A number of Arab scholars have approached the study of the Koran as a rhetorical document, seeking to provide exegesis that displays how the text invents and persuades. Modern scholars illustrate the Koran's commitment to reason; rhetorical interpretations place the text in its context, rejecting apodictic or literal understanding of its language. For example, the claims made by some that the Koran mandates jihad or suicide bombing or anti-Semitism are tempered and contextualized when the relevant texts are placed in their context. There are, of course, those who seek literal interpretations of the Koran, and derive from them fundamentalist principles dictating purity and cathartic violence, but they deviate significantly from normative Islam (→ Communication Modes, Muslim).

Orientalism yields in the face of experience that Arabism and Islam are contested notions, that self and group identity are in process, and, as Bernard Lewis has written, that the Middle East is a region of multiple and conflicted identities. Edwin Black, in his

Rhetorical questions, provides the ideal frame for an understanding of the discourse of this region. As Black observes, human identity is mutable and open to revision and change. Although there may be a diachronic or historical continuity in identity, the notion of identity itself is plastic, altered by the physical and symbolic forces that confront it.

A rhetoric of cosmopolitanism, which many scholars have advocated, features the need for people to narrate in the context of competing narratives about identity and place. Two key works of scholarship are important in gaining an appreciation of this alternative. The nature of a cosmopolitan rhetoric is what Chaïm Perelman and his colleague Lucie Olbrechts-Tyteca develop in the most important and influential philosophical rhetoric of the twentieth century, the *New rhetoric* (1969; → Rhetoric, Argument, and Persuasion; Rhetorics: New Rhetorics). Their work deals with confused identities and value conflicts, and has its roots in the writings of the ancient Hebrews. Perelman saw great value in the Talmudic holding that multiple truths could coexist and that human argument rather than divine revelation should yield humane judgments. Scholars have used their work to highlight the use of argumentative reason in the Torah, the Christian Bible, and the Koran. In turn, Marc Gopin, in his *Holy war, holy peace* (2002), draws on this shared sense of reason expressed in the Abrahamic faiths to identify the touchstones necessary for rapprochement between Israelis and Palestinians. These religious texts, he argues, can yield points of convergence and myths needed to create a new reality in the region.

SEE ALSO: ▶ Communication Modes, Muslim   ▶ Discourse   ▶ Postcolonial Theory   ▶ Rhetoric in Africa   ▶ Rhetoric, Argument, and Persuasion   ▶ Rhetoric in East Asia: China and Japan   ▶ Rhetoric in Western Europe: Spain   ▶ Rhetorical Studies   ▶ Rhetorics: New Rhetorics

References and Suggested Readings

Bernal, M. (1987). *Black Athena: The Afroasiatic roots of classical civilization*. New Brunswick, NJ: Rutgers University Press.

Black, E. (1992). *Rhetorical questions: Studies of public discourse*. Chicago, IL: University of Chicago Press.

Buruma, I., & Margalit, A. (2004). *Occidentalism: The west in the eyes of its enemies*. New York: Penguin.

Gopin, M. (2002). *Holy war, holy peace: How religion can bring peace to the Middle East*. New York: Oxford University Press.

Khalidi, R. (1997). *Palestinian identity: The construction of modern national consciousness*. New York: Columbia University Press.

Lewis, B. (1998). *The multiple identities of the Middle East*. London: Weidenfeld and Nicolson.

Perelman, C., & Olbrechts-Tyteca, L. (1969). *The new rhetoric: A treatise on argumentation* (trans. J. Wilkinson & P. Weaver). Notre Dame, IN: University of Notre Dame Press.

Roland, R. C., & Frank, D. A. (2002). *Shared land/conflicting identity: Trajectories of Israeli and Palestinian symbol use*. East Lansing, MI: Michigan State University Press.

Said, E. W. (1978). *Orientalism*. New York: Pantheon.

Rhetoric and Narrativity

Lisa Gring-Pemble
New Century College

For centuries, rhetoricians, communication scholars, and practitioners have recognized narrative's rich descriptive and persuasive appeal. Numerous essays, books, and monographs address the nature and functions of narrative in disciplines as varied as rhetoric and communication, biology and anthropology, psychology and sociology, political science and public policy, and theology and philosophy.

Throughout rhetorical history, narrative has assumed many roles from a rhetorical trope or figure, to a part of speech, to a paradigm that explains how humans make sense of their world. Such diverse roles reflect the varying levels of privilege theorists have accorded to narrative at any given point in time.

Discussions of *narrative in classical times* emphasize narrative's role as a part of speech and a form of proof. Rhetorical handbooks dating back to the fifth century BCE catalog narration (*narratio* or *diēgēsis*) as a formal part of speech. Handbooks were an important resource for citizens of democratic Athens. Male citizens, who were expected to speak on their own behalf in Athenian law courts, outlined the particulars of their case in the narration (Kennedy 1999, 21). In his *Art of rhetoric*, Aristotle conceived of narrative as a form of artistic proof. He outlined proof by example, noting that examples could arise from historical accounts as well as invented parables and fables. Cicero expanded the discussion of narrative further, attending to both fictitious and historical narratives in *De inventione* (→ Rhetoric, Greek; Rhetoric, Roman).

Narrative in all its forms (e.g., anecdotes, examples, allegories, fables, parables, stories) was a popular, if sometimes suspect, type of persuasion and instruction from classical Greco-Roman times through the establishment of the early Christian church and the *Middle Ages* (→ Rhetoric, Medieval). Surviving *progymnasmata* or handbooks of teaching exercises include sections on anecdotes, fables, and narratives among others (Kennedy 1999, 27, 205). Wary of narrative's appeal, some scholars questioned narrative's validity and truth value. Unlike scientific discourse and formal logical proofs, which resulted in certain knowledge, rhetoric yielded only probable knowledge. As unproved suppositions that could be imagined and falsified, narratives frequently prompted skeptical audience responses (→ Rhetoric and Logic; Rhetoric, Argument, and Persuasion).

Nevertheless, narrative persisted in rhetorical treatises, handbooks, and theories, receiving some of its most significant attention in recent years. *Contemporary rhetorical treatments* have produced a richer understanding of narrative's nature, scope, and function. Some theorists have explored the role of narrative in politics, the legislature, and judiciary while others have attended to the function of scientific narrative (Bennett & Edelman 1985; Jorgensen-Earp & Jorgensen 2002). Rhetorical discussions also include the role of narrative in social change, in health communication, and in professional communication.

Narrative's influence in rhetoric is magnified by the number of theories and methods that rely on principles of narrativity. For example, rhetorical-critical theories and methods such as depiction, fantasy-theme analysis, metaphoric criticism, and dramatistic criticism all draw on narrative concepts such as characters, examples, and stories (→ Rhetorical Criticism).

Much of the contemporary research on narrative draws on Walter Fisher's *theory of the narrative paradigm*. Outlining arguably the most comprehensive account, Fisher contends that narration is the dominant mode of human communication: humans are storytellers who create and communicate stories that form understanding, guide collective reasoning, and shape behavior. Contrasting his narrative approach with the formal logic associated with traditional argument, Fisher points out that the narrative paradigm has several advantages. In particular, because all humans have innate storytelling abilities, the narrative paradigm is democratic; that is, all people, not just experts, are qualified to render judgments. In addition, Fisher claims that the narrative paradigm promotes just decision-making based on good reasons (Fisher 1984, 1985).

Narrative theory and especially Fisher's narrative paradigm have been the subject of many *critiques*. Some critics argue that the narrative paradigm may not engender critical thinking since people will likely accept stories that reinforce beliefs they already hold even if those pre-existing beliefs are flawed. Others are troubled by Fisher's tendency to dichotomize traditional argument and narrative argument. Still others question the democratic and participatory nature of narratives (Gring-Pemble 2001; Rowland 1989; Warnick 1987).

In spite of the critiques, scholars recognize the value of narrative as both theory and method. Since rhetoric's inception, rhetoricians have valued narrative's capacity to help audiences "see" through vivid imagery, memorable characters, and unforgettable stories. Through narratives, people can celebrate common values, strengthen community, and assess the strengths and limitations of potential scenarios. As a heuristic, narrative theory will, no doubt, be strengthened as scholars attend to its many critiques. One especially fruitful line of inquiry that extends narrative's classical roots centers on narrative as a "rhetoric of possibility," a way of exposing alternatives and guiding people to moral judgment and action (Kirkwood 1992).

SEE ALSO: ▶ Rhetoric, Argument, and Persuasion ▶ Rhetoric, Greek ▶ Rhetoric and History ▶ Rhetoric and Logic ▶ Rhetoric, Medieval ▶ Rhetoric and Philosophy ▶ Rhetoric and Politics ▶ Rhetoric, Roman ▶ Rhetorical Criticism

References and Suggested Readings

Bennett, W. L., & Edelman, M. (1985). Toward a new political narrative. *Journal of Communication*, 35(4), 156–171.

Fisher, W. R. (1984). Narration as a human communication paradigm: The case of public moral argument. *Communication Monographs*, 51, 1–22.

Fisher, W. R. (1985). The narrative paradigm: In the beginning. *Journal of Communication*, 35(4), 74–89.

Gring-Pemble, L. (2001). "Are we going to now govern by anecdote?" Rhetorical constructions of welfare recipients in congressional hearings, debates, and legislation, 1992–1996. *Quarterly Journal of Speech*, 87, 341–365.

Jorgensen-Earp, C. R., & Jorgensen, D. D. (2002). "Miracle from mouldy cheese": Chronological versus thematic self-narratives in the discovery of penicillin. *Quarterly Journal of Speech*, 88, 69–90.

Kennedy, G. A. (1999). *Classical rhetoric and its Christian and secular tradition from ancient to modern times*, 2nd edn. Chapel Hill, NC: University of North Carolina Press.

Kirkwood, W. G. (1992). Narrative and the rhetoric of possibility. *Communication Monographs*, 59, 30–47.

Rowland, R. (1989). On limiting the narrative paradigm: Three case studies. *Communication Monographs*, 56, 39–54.

Warnick, B. (1987). The narrative paradigm: Another story. *Quarterly Journal of Speech*, 73, 172–182.

Rhetoric, Nonverbal

Mark L. Knapp

University of Texas at Austin

The word "nonverbal" is used to describe the many ways human beings communicate without overtly using words. Typically, this encompasses body movements (gestures, facial expressions, eye behavior, touching); body positioning (posture, distance from and alignment to others); and vocal behavior (rate, pitch, intensity). Sometimes physical (appearance) and environmental (architecture, design) features are also included.

HISTORY

The modern study of nonverbal communication has its roots in the second half of the twentieth century, but Greek rhetoricians discussed the use of body movements in persuasive speaking as far back as the fifth century BCE (→ Nonverbal Signals, Effects of; Rhetoric, Greek; Rhetoric, Pre-Socratic). These ideas were refined and expanded in the writings of Roman rhetorical theorists and practitioners (→ Rhetoric, Roman). This interest in the appropriateness and effectiveness of bodily behavior in the speech-making process waned during the Middle Ages and Renaissance (→ Rhetoric, European Renaissance; Rhetoric, Medieval), but re-emerged as the heart of the elocution movement. From the middle of the eighteenth century to the early twentieth century, elocutionists emphasized what they considered to be the proper use of the body in delivering speeches. They had little concern for studying naturally occurring behavior. Instead, they offered prescriptions for successful body movement and voice in speech-making, which led to more stylized and formal behavioral enactments (→ Delivery and Rhetoric).

Two landmark studies of spontaneous nonverbal behavior were completed during the ninteenth century – de Jorio's descriptions of Neapolitan gestures and Darwin's observations on facial expressions linked to emotional states (→ Facial Expressions; Gestures and Kinesics). But it was not until the 1950s that the phrase "nonverbal communication" appeared in a book title, and several ongoing developments came together to forge the foundation for nonverbal studies as we know it today. In the decades preceding the 1950s, scholars from many disciplines developed an interest in the scientific study of communication (→ Communication as a Field and Discipline; Communication and

Media Studies, History to 1968). There was also a growing desire to understand the nuances of natural, face-to-face interaction, and the technology for recording and analyzing those behavioral nuances was becoming increasingly sophisticated (→ Language and Social Interaction). The convergence of these factors resulted in numerous theoretical perspectives and research programs. Birdwhistell explored the possibility that body movement had a structure that paralleled the structure of spoken language; Hall began mapping the organization and effects of space on human interaction; Rosenthal viewed nonverbal signals as a source of unconscious influence in various contexts; others were interested in nonverbal behavior as an outward manifestation of psychological states. Scholars also began to look for similarities in nonverbal behavior across cultures and species (e.g., nonhuman primates; → Nonverbal Communication and Culture). Two broad approaches emerged from these early explorations and they remain with us today: one approach describes how nonverbal behavior manifests itself in the structure and organization of human interaction (→ Interpersonal Communication); the other manipulates selected behaviors (nonverbal and/or psychological) and observes the effects on human transactions. In both approaches, it is clear that nonverbal and verbal behavior are not separate entities, but co-acting units of a comprehensive communication system governing human transactions.

INTERRELATIONSHIPS WITH VERBAL BEHAVIOR

Verbal and nonverbal behavior interact and support one another in various ways. For example, the words "go north" can be reinforced and *repeated* with a pointing gesture that co-occurs or follows the verbalization.

Nonverbal behavior may also *complement* what is said verbally – e.g., a job interviewee who verbally expresses a desire to work for a company may also show his or her interest through positive facial and vocal expressions accompanied by an attentive, forward-leaning posture. When verbal and nonverbal behavior complement one another, this increases the possibility that a communicator's intended message will be decoded accurately.

There are, however, many times when verbal and nonverbal behavior do not complement one another. Instead, they appear to be *discrepant* or at odds with one another, communicating different meanings. Sometimes this discrepancy is intentionally performed in order to signal an alternative meaning for the verbal behavior – e.g., a sarcastic vocal tone indicating the verbal message is a sham or a smile that accompanies the phrase "you're a real loser," indicating the statement was made in the context of play and should not be taken seriously. Comedians use discrepant cues to get laughs and being coy requires displays of both approach and avoidance. Physicians and teachers can effectively communicate serious concern by combining positive verbal behavior with negative facial expressions. Discrepant verbal and nonverbal behavior may also occur when people try to hide or mask their true feelings or attitudes. In such cases, actual feelings may overpower the masks, and facial, vocal, and bodily behavior will signal just the opposite of "I had a nice time" or "Of course I love you." Because responses of this type can be ambiguous, there may be difficulty in accurately decoding. This can trigger a discrepant message in return. Sometimes discrepant messages are passed over or go unnoticed because the content is not perceived to be of great import. And sometimes subsequent conversation helps to resolve seemingly discordant behavior. Many of these discrepant messages occur during natural feelings of ambivalence – e.g., not being sure whether you like someone or not, or not wanting to tell the truth, but not wanting to lie either.

Typically, decoders tend to believe the meaning associated with signals perceived as harder to fake when choosing between discrepant verbal and nonverbal signals. Although verbal behavior is often perceived as easier to fake, those who are just beginning to learn a new language tend to give more credibility to the manifest verbal behavior.

Nonverbal behavior may also act as a *substitute* for verbal behavior. Without any verbal behavior, a person can signal a variety of short-term states (tired, playful, frustrated, sad, indifferent) and even some long-term conditions (gender, old age) with facial expressions and body movements.

The face, voice, and hands are particularly effective in *accenting and moderating* verbal behavior.

Nonverbal behavior also works with verbal behavior to coordinate and *regulate* interaction behavior. Speakers coordinate and organize the production of their own messages in a variety of ways – e.g., using gestural chops and pauses to demarcate a verbalized series of units. In addition, both interactants regulate the flow of interaction between them – coordinating greetings, goodbyes, and turns at talk. Nonverbal behavior, like verbal, is often reciprocated when it meets our relationship expectations and preferences and offset with counteracting behavior when it does not.

AWARENESS AND TRUST

Some nonverbal behavior is enacted without a great deal of conscious awareness, but this is not true of all nonverbal behavior. We may not be aware of certain nervous mannerisms we exhibit, some types of gestures we use, or the dilation of our pupils, but we are often very much aware of making gestures that are widely understood by our audience, many facial expressions of emotion, as well as the choosing of certain artifacts designed to affect our appearance. Our awareness of our interaction partner's nonverbal behavior also varies. If there is a reason to be particularly observant (e.g., suspected lying), our awareness of the other's nonverbal behavior is high; at other times our awareness of specific behaviors may be low even though the impression these behaviors collectively communicate is high – e.g., "It isn't anything you've said, but I feel like I can trust you." Nonverbal behavior plays a central role in judgments of another person's honesty, status, trustworthiness, liking, and competence (→ Attribution Processes). As a result, its influence in applied settings cannot be underestimated – e.g., demeanor in the courtroom, at security checkpoints, in political speeches, cross-cultural and classroom encounters, and in personal and work relationships.

ORIGINS

Our nonverbal behavior has both biological and cultural origins. For example, genes are responsible for how the facial muscles move when displaying various expressions of emotion, but culture teaches people whether and when to use certain facial displays, under what conditions they should be manifested, and how they should blend together

(Culture: Definitions and Concepts). Studies of twins and nonhuman primates suggest that we may be biologically predisposed to assume certain postures and possibly to enact whole sequences of movement behavior. Some aspects of nonverbal encoding and decoding skills may also have a genetic link. Tests repeatedly show females, as a group, to be somewhat more accurate encoders and decoders of nonverbal signals than males.

MEASUREMENT

Nonverbal behavior is typically measured in three ways: (1) with a specific instrument (e.g., machines that track eye movements or vocal variations; → Eye Behavior); (2) by observers who make detailed recordings of visible behavior or use an extant coding scheme (→ Gaze in Interaction); and (3) by observers who make judgments about the meaning of one or more nonverbal stimuli. Our knowledge and measurement of nonverbal behavior is becoming increasingly more precise, and computer-assisted analyses enable the processing of more → information in a shorter period of time. Recording equipment is increasingly portable and unobtrusive (→ Measurement Theory), providing an opportunity for a greater database of spontaneous nonverbal behavior in natural situations.

SEE ALSO: ▶ Attribution Processes ▶ Communication as a Field and Discipline ▶ Communication and Media Studies, History to 1968 ▶ Culture: Definitions and Concepts ▶ Delivery and Rhetoric ▶ Eye Behavior ▶ Facial Expressions ▶ Gaze in Interaction ▶ Gestures in Discourse ▶ Gestures and Kinesics ▶ Information ▶ Interpersonal Communication ▶ Language and Social Interaction ▶ Measurement Theory ▶ Nonverbal Communication and Culture ▶ Nonverbal Signals, Effects of ▶ Paralanguage ▶ Proxemics ▶ Rhetoric, European Renaissance ▶ Rhetoric, Greek ▶ Rhetoric, Medieval ▶ Rhetoric, Pre-Socratic ▶ Rhetoric, Roman

References and Suggested Readings

DePaulo, B. M., & Friedman, H. S. (1998). Nonverbal communication. In D. T. Gilbert, S. T. Fiske, & G. Lindzey (eds.), *The handbook of social psychology*, 4th edn, vol. 2. New York: McGraw-Hill.

Ekman, P., & Friesen, W. V. (1969). The repertoire of nonverbal behavior: Categories, origins, usage, and coding. *Semiotica*, 1, 49–98.

Ekman, P., & Rosenberg, E. (eds.) (1997). *What the face reveals: Basic and applied studies of spontaneous expression using the facial action coding system (FACS)*. New York: Oxford University Press.

Kendon, A. (1990). Some context for context analysis: A view of the origins of structural studies of face-to-face interaction. In A. Kendon, *Conducting interaction: Patterns of behavior in focused encounters*. New York: Cambridge University Press, pp. 15–49.

Kendon, A. (2004). *Gesture: Visible action as utterance*. New York: Cambridge University Press.

Knapp, M. L., & Hall, J. A. (2005). *Nonverbal communication in human interaction*, 6th edn. Belmont, CA: Wadsworth.

Manusov, V. (ed.) (2005). *The sourcebook of nonverbal measures*. Mahwah, NJ: Lawrence Erlbaum.

Manusov, V., & Patterson, M. L. (eds.) (2006). *Handbook of nonverbal communication*. Thousand Oaks, CA: Sage.

Riggio, R. E., & Feldman, R. S. (eds.) (2005). *Applications of nonverbal communication*. Mahwah, NJ: Lawrence Erlbaum.

Rhetoric in North America: Canada

Jennifer MacLennan

University of Saskatchewan

Rhetorical study in Canada resists neat categorization, in part because it is a relatively recent phenomenon characterized by a rich diversity of perspectives and approaches, and by a comparatively fluid conception of what it means to engage in scholarly activity in rhetoric. As an academic specialization, rhetoric emerged in Canada only in the last two decades of the twentieth century (→ Communication as an Academic Field: USA and Canada; Speech Communication, History of). Prior to the 1980s, the subject was not offered in Canadian universities; there were no communication departments where rhetoric might have been taught, and university literature departments, firmly in the belletristic tradition, disdained the teaching both of nonliterary works and of composition. However, despite the lack of institutional visibility and sanction, small numbers of individual rhetoricians found homes in professional colleges and in departments such as curriculum studies and political science, and – more rarely – in literature departments.

While most Canadian rhetoricians maintained memberships in American and international organizations, by the early 1980s they had gained sufficient confidence, if not prominence, to form three distinct scholarly organizations of their own. Though many rhetoricians belong to more than one, the three organizations are sufficiently diverse that they do not overlap completely in membership or activities. Because their differences provide a clear picture of the nature of rhetorical study in Canada, they are briefly profiled here.

The first to form was the *Canadian Society for the Study of Rhetoric* (CSSR; www.cssr-scer.ca), founded in 1980 as the Canadian Society for the History of Rhetoric. The name change, made formal in 1991, was intended to recognize the diversity of approaches (not just historical) that characterize Canadian scholarship in the field. Through its annual conference and its biennial peer-reviewed journal, this small society provides "a forum for the voices of scholars with a range of research interests and from a variety of disciplines, yet who share a passion for 'rhetoric' – in whatever terms that be defined" (Spoel 2007, 1). The CSSR is bilingual, with members presenting and publishing in both English and French. The society holds its annual conference in conjunction with the Congress of the Humanities and Social Sciences, a multidisciplinary gathering of scholars that is the largest academic conference in the country. The majority of papers presented at the annual conference and published in the society's electronic journal are concerned with rhetorical theory and with critical analyses of a range of objects (→ Rhetorical Criticism; Rhetorical Studies).

The *Canadian Association for the Study of Language and Learning* (CASLL) is the formal name of "Inkshed," a group founded in 1983 to "provide a forum and common context for discussion, collaboration, and reflective inquiry in discourse and pedagogy in the areas of writing, reading (including the reading of literature), rhetoric, and language" (CASLL, n.d.). The group maintains an active online discussion list and holds its own annual gathering separately from the Congress, where its focus is largely on the practice of "inkshedding," a collaborative process described by one of its originators as a "dialogically transactional" form of freewriting (Hunt, n.d.). Like CSSR, CASLL serves to provide common ground for a constellation of scholars, but it differs from CSSR by being far more centered on the practice and scholarship of writing and its instruction, and its members tend to be those who teach composition or are employed by university writing centers. Since 1994, CASLL has maintained a modest book publishing program featuring titles in the areas of composition and literacy. The few existing studies of the nature and scope of rhetorical study in Canada have been produced by this organization, though their coverage extends mainly to writing instruction and writing centers (Graves 1994; Smith 1999, 2005; Graves & Graves 2006).

Like the other organizations, the Canadian Association of Teachers of Technical Writing (CATTW; http://cattw-acprts.mcgill.ca) was established in the early 1980s. A bilingual organization, CATTW is somewhat larger than the other two groups, and proudly draws its members from professional schools like engineering, education, science, social work, and management, as well as from the public and private sectors. Its mandate focuses on examining the generation, interpretation, structure, and impact of nonliterary writing in the professions and in professional settings such as business, nonprofit organizations, and government. Like CSSR, CATTW meets annually in conjunction with the Congress of the Humanities and Social Sciences, and there is enough overlap in the two societies' interests and membership that they occasionally hold joint sessions. CATTW emphasizes collaboration and interdisciplinarity in research, reflecting the general state of rhetorical study in Canada. The association publishes two issues per year of its peer-reviewed journal, *Technostyle*, and maintains an active online discussion group.

The recent emergence of rhetoric as a field of academic specialization in Canada has *several implications*. First, rhetoric in the Canadian context remains a constellation of scholarly specialties and pedagogical interests rather than a unified disciplinary construct. Second, though the situation is gradually changing, rhetoric still suffers from a lack of institutionalized support, both within universities and in the national funding agencies. Third, since most Canadian rhetoricians were trained in the United States, a distinctly Canadian tradition in scholarship and theory has yet to fully emerge.

Nevertheless, the first decade of the twenty-first century has seen significant development in course offerings and programs, most of them in the contexts where Canadian rhetoricians have found homes: academic writing centers, professional schools, and departments of literature. The emergence and strengthening of graduate programs is one sign that the field is undergoing robust growth. Although Canada has thus far produced comparatively few theoretical advances (exceptions include Charland [1987] and Hunt), the eclectic and interdisciplinary nature of rhetorical study in Canada remains one of its strengths, providing opportunities for cross-fertilization of ideas and approaches. Theoretical innovation is likely to occur first in one of two areas: in writing practice and instruction, where Canadian rhetoricians have been most active, or – in keeping with Canada's central cultural preoccupation – in the rhetoric of identity formation (→ Identities and Discourse).

SEE ALSO: ▶ Communication as an Academic Field: USA and Canada   ▶ Communication as a Field and Discipline   ▶ Identities and Discourse   ▶ Rhetorical Criticism   ▶ Rhetorical Studies   ▶ Speech Communication, History of

References and Suggested Readings

Canadian Association for the Study of Language and Learning (n.d.). Constitution and by-laws. At www.stu.ca/inkshed/const.htm, accessed September 29, 2007.

Charland, M. (1987). Constitutive rhetoric: The case of *Peuple Québécois*. *Quarterly Journal of Speech*, 73, 133–150.

Graves, R. (1994). *Writing instruction in Canadian universities*. Winnipeg, MB: Inkshed.

Graves, R., & Graves, H. (2006). *Writing centres, writing seminars, writing culture: Writing instruction in Anglo-Canadian universities*. Winnipeg, MB: Inkshed.

Hunt, R. (n.d.). What is inkshedding? At www.stu.ca/~hunt/whatshed.htm, accessed September 29, 2007.

Smith, T. (1999). Recent trends in writing instruction and composition studies in Canadian Universities. At www.stthomasu.ca/inkshed/cdncomp.htm, accessed September 29, 2007.

Smith, T. (2005). How Canadian universities teach academic writing in credit courses. At www.ucalgary.ca/~smit/AcademicWritingCanadaU.htm, accessed September 29, 2007.

Spoel, P. (2007). Editor's introduction. *Rhetor*, 2(1). At http://uregina.ca/~rheaults/rhetor/2007/spoel-i.pdf, accessed September 29, 2007.

Rhetoric in North America: Mexico

Gerardo Ramírez Vidal

National Autonomous University of Mexico

Rhetorical practice and teaching existed in ancient native cultures in Mexico, mainly in the Aztec and Mayan civilizations (Beristáin & Ramírez Vidal 2005). Western rhetorical tradition was introduced into Mexico with the European conquest and Catholic evangelization: the triumph of the occidental civilization in the "new world" was due to the success of European rhetoric. During the sixteenth century, evangelization was founded on this rhetoric: the use of sermons was necessary to convert the inhabitants of the new world. In 1553 the Royal and Pontifical University of Mexico was erected; rhetoric was a mandatory course in the teaching program. The professors and the friars theorized on rhetoric and wrote many works about it (Osorio Romero 1980), such as the *Rhetorica Christiana* of the Franciscan missionary Fray Diego Valadés, published in Italy in 1579. In the seventeenth and eighteenth centuries there was an increase in teaching, practice, and theory of rhetoric, mainly because the Society of Jesus encouraged rhetorical studies in colonial Mexico. Rhetoric spread to other fields like poetry, as is shown in the work of Sor Juana Inés de la Cruz (Bizzell & Herzberg 2001, 780–787). The rhetorical development during the period of colonial domination has not been investigated comprehensively until now.

After the independence of Mexico (1810), internal wars and political and economic instability during the nineteenth century led to a decline in the teaching of rhetoric, it being restricted to religious colleges, a crisis that carried over into the next century. However, practice of rhetoric continued to be an important aspect of Mexican culture in the second half of the nineteenth century: debates and arguments in Congress and in newspapers were recurrent events. The Mexican revolution originated new rhetorical procedures that became controlled by the governing power. In Mexican universities courses on rhetoric had not been included in the curriculum until now. Isolated lectures and seminars had been given by Mexican and foreign experts (mainly from Spain) to familiarize students with this topic.

In 1941 and 1942, the Mexican essayist Alfonso Reyes dictated two courses about "The critic in the Athenian age" and "The ancient rhetoric" (later published; Reyes 1961), which point out *two main trends* of rhetorical studies in the second half of the twentieth century: first, the rhetorical analysis of literature, and second, research on the classical rhetorical tradition.

The spread of formalism, structuralism, and poetics, and the rise of attention to literary form, largely due to the works of Heinrich Lausberg and the "Group μ," stimulated *interest in textual analysis* in Mexican universities (→ Rhetoric and Poetics). Rhetoric and poetics were fused into one discipline for the study of literature, focusing mainly on literary figures, and to some measure on construction, characters, time, space, rhythm, verse structure, and so forth. In this field, prominent academics made important contributions, linked closely with → linguistics (→ Text and Intertextuality). Rhetoric is regarded as an essential characteristic of language.

On the other hand, Mexican researchers have *focused on the classical, medieval, and Renaissance rhetorical tradition* (→ Rhetoric, Medieval). Translations of Greek and Latin rhetorical treatises have been made in recent years: the fragments of Gorgias, the *Dialogues* of Plato, the *Rhetoric* of Aristotle, rhetorical works of Cicero, the *Dialogue on oratory* of Tacitus, the *Institutio oratoria* of Quintilian, and the *Poetria Nova* of Geoffrey of Vinsauf (→ Rhetoric, Roman; Rhetoric, Greek).

Scholars have studied and published about different rhetorical topics, periods, theorists, and authors: the Sophistic movement, the Attic orators (particularly Antiphon, Lysias, and Isocrates), Aristotle, the ancient Greek novel, Cicero, Quintilian, etc. Furthermore, the Middle Ages and the Renaissance have been the object of rhetorical studies. Mexican and foreign scholars have focused particular attention on rhetoric in colonial Mexico: history, preaching, teaching, and theory (Abbott 1996; Beuchot Puente 1996). Scholars in the US, Italy, Spain, and Mexico have largely studied the *Rhetorica Christiana* of Diego Valadés (1579).

Rhetoric is now being studied from *different orientations*, as seen in the recent organization in Mexico (by Helena Beristáin of the Institute of Philological Researches, UNAM) of two international congresses on rhetoric (1998 and 2004), the publication of the collection "Log of rhetoric" ("Bitácora de retorica"), and courses and seminars about rhetorical topics.

New trends of philosophical thinking from Europe and the US are opening new fields for the study of rhetoric in Mexico, particularly → semiotics and pragmatics, which have provided new instruments and theories (→ Linguistic Pragmatics; Rhetoric and Semiotics). Deconstructionism and → hermeneutics are promising domains for expansion of rhetorical studies. Furthermore, the modern disciplines on → discourse could be described as rhetorical, and some scholars consider argumentation as the main part of this discipline (→ Rhetoric, Argument, and Persuasion). Nevertheless, few researchers in Mexico are aware they are using rhetoric; this discipline is studied usually without being named as such.

Consequently, the future of rhetoric in Mexico depends on linking it more closely with the philosophical and textual disciplines, and on finding a particular development in the history of rhetoric.

SEE ALSO: ▶ Discourse ▶ Hermeneutics ▶ Linguistic Pragmatics ▶ Linguistics ▶ Rhetoric, Argument, and Persuasion ▶ Rhetoric in Central and South America ▶ Rhetoric, Greek ▶ Rhetoric, Medieval ▶ Rhetoric and Poetics ▶ Rhetoric, Roman ▶ Rhetoric and Semiotics ▶ Rhetorical Criticism ▶ Rhetorical Studies ▶ Semiotics ▶ Text and Intertextuality

References and Suggested Readings

Abbott, D. P. (1996). *Rhetoric in the new world: Rhetorical theory and practice in colonial Spanish America*. Columbia, SC: University of South Carolina.

Beuchot Puente, M. (1998). *Rhetoricos de la Nueva España*. México: Universidad Nacional Autónoma de México.

Beristáin, H. (1997). *Diccionario de retórica y poética*. México: Porrúa.

Beristáin, H., & Ramírez Vidal, G. (2004). *La palabra florida: la tradición retórica indígena y novohispana*. México: Universidad Nacional Autónoma de México.

Bizzell, P., & Herzberg, B. (eds.) (2001). *The rhetorical tradition*, 2nd edn. New York: Bedford/St Martin's.

Osorio Romero, I. (1980). *Floresta de gramática, poética y retórica en la Nueva España (1521–1767)*. México: Universidad Nacional Autónoma de México Ciudad Universitaria.

Reyes, A. (1961). *Obras completas XIII: "La crítica en la Edad Ateniense" y "La antigua retórica."* México: Fondo de Cultura Económica.

Rhetoric in North America: United States

James F. Klumpp

University of Maryland

The democratic ethic that has dominated the intellectual history of the United States has shaped a rhetorical practice driven by the socio-cultural influence of the word. The result has been a rich multiplicity of voices that defy generalization, yet define a complex texture. The first rhetorical period, approximately the first century and a quarter of the presence of British settlement in North America, was dominated by religious rhetoric and specifically by the *Puritans*. Puritan sermons were highly structured, linking lessons from biblical text to everyday life. Puritans respected reason and viewed it as a gift from God that opened human insight into God's structuring of the universe. The democratic content of Puritan rhetoric was constrained. Beneath God, the minister was separated from others in the community by his trained role as the interpreter of the Word. Men and women were similarly differentiated by the biblical separation of gender. And finally the elect of the Puritan community were separated from non-believers. Within that narrowed but still broad slice of Puritan life, democratic equality defined access to power (→ Rhetoric and Religion).

As the eighteenth century proceeded, *secular rhetorics* began to grow in importance. In these rhetorics can be heard two voices: democratic pragmatism and radical reform. Secular institutions of governance developed with an openness to public persuasion. Courts featured common law and self-representation for plaintiffs and defendants. Legislatures responded to petitions formulated at public meetings, most often requests for governmental attention to practical community problems. Beside the pragmatic secular rhetoric grew a more moralistic and spiritual religious rhetoric. The so-called *Great Awakening or New Light* preaching located spirituality and morality in the human heart. When joined with the Enlightenment's belief in the human capacity for reason, the result was a radical rhetoric of reform. The great rhetorical triumph of the eighteenth century, the American Revolution, was achieved with this combination of institutional pragmatism and reform.

With independence achieved, the dialectic tension between these two rhetorical forces grew. Adoption of the United States Constitution and similar state constitutions established forums for deliberation and → persuasion. The United States Senate, particularly, became a great deliberative body where the issues of the day were debated (→ Deliberativeness in Political Communication). Outside of the governmental forums, a high style of oratory, particularly prominent in great civic events, celebrated the nation and motivated the energy of expansion. The primacy of public rhetoric as the keystone of a democratic society was both a theme and the demonstrable commitment of this institutional discourse. Outside the government, through specialized newspapers, committed issue-interested organizations, the pulpit, and the lecture circuit, reformers called upon an idealistic moral rhetoric to resist injustice and motivate change. The energy of reform, and the failure of institutions such as the Senate to contain that energy, culminated in the collapse of rhetoric into the Civil War.

In the latter half of the nineteenth century, the balance of power between reform and institutional rhetoric shifted away from the institutions of government toward a more *public rhetoric*. The public was perceived as an agency of change and, as democracy diffused through broader notions of citizenship, the public became the dominant audience for rhetoric. The emergence of a more public rhetoric was exemplified most prominently in the great disputes about the impact of the new industrialization, the great immigration, and the emergence of urban poverty. Within the more conservative institutional venues the debate proceeded about poverty and its causes. Movements as diverse as social Darwinism, Christian socialism, and the gospel of wealth shaped public views on the responsibility of the poor for their own condition and the responsibility of the community to address poverty. But this intellectual exchange was in counterpoint with the great efforts of reformers among labor, African-Americans, women, farmers, and others to organize through direct action to alter the political and economic circumstances of ordinary citizens. The morality of reform was joined with the sense of democratic power that rhetorically motivated those affected to force change in their conditions.

The struggle between institutional voices and voices of reform culminated in the *progressive movement* by the turn of the twentieth century. Progressivism was more conservative than the reformist call for civil rights and economic conscience, but its agenda addressed the reformers' issues. Through its successful call for direct election of senators, recall, and referendum, progressivism expanded the institutional venues of a rhetorical public. But the most dramatic rhetorical change was the rhetorical presidency: presidents enhanced their power over other institutions of government by direct appeal to the public.

As the twentieth century proceeded, rhetoric's focus on the public audience was transformed by *technologies of communication*, including most prominently radio, television, and electronic augmentation of voice. Speakers could reach millions; millions could literally hear and later see their president and other leaders at the moment they spoke. Ironically, in the balance between institutional and reform voices, mass communication returned power to the institutions that controlled media. Yet, particularly in mid-century, reformers began to master techniques of mass communication and to activate civil rights movements for African-Americans, women, and other marginalized groups, as well as opposition to the Vietnam War. Even a more general counterculture rhetoric promoted a more libertine and free individualism. Popular conservative movements emerged late in the century, particularly from religious speakers who had mastered mass communication (→ Rhetoric and Technology).

At the start of the twenty-first century, the growth of the Internet promises to again transform the nature of rhetoric in the United States. The dominance of mass communication, where one addressing many dominated communicative technology, appears at an end. The connections of *virtual space* multiply the possibilities for voices to reach others. At the same time, the sheer proliferation of voices presents a problem of focus for those who attend to rhetoric. The model of citizenship developed within the context of mass communication must now adapt to new parameters created by the diffused Internet.

SEE ALSO: ▶ Deliberativeness in Political Communication ▶ Persuasion ▶ Religion and Popular Communication ▶ Rhetoric and Politics ▶ Rhetoric and Religion ▶ Rhetoric and Social Protest ▶ Rhetoric and Technology

References and Suggested Readings

Brigance, W. N., & Hochmuth, M. K. (eds.) (1943, 1955). *History and criticism of American public address*. 3 vols. New York: McGraw-Hill, Longman Green.

Eidenmuller, M. E. (comp.) (2006). American rhetoric. At www.americanrhetoric.com/, accessed December 4, 2006.

Reid, R. F., & Klumpp, J. F. (2005). *American rhetorical discourse*, 3rd edn. Long Grove, IL: Waveland.

Rhetoric in Northern and Central Asia

David Cratis Williams
Florida Atlantic University

Marilyn J. Young
Florida State University

Although the area of northern and central Asia is comprised of a large number of independent and sovereign nations, including the Russian Federation and the central Asian states of Kazakhstan, Kyrgyzstan, Tajikistan, Turkmenistan, and Uzbekistan, its recent history is dominated by the Union of Soviet Socialist Republics (USSR). For most of the twentieth century each of these now independent nations was a part of the USSR; since 1991, the central Asian states have struggled to survive in the shadow of the Russian Federation. The central story of rhetoric in this region in both modern history and contemporary times must therefore be framed in terms of the former USSR and its transformations in the continuing period of post-Soviet democratization, mock-democratization, and authoritarian reinstantiation (→ Rhetoric in Eastern Europe).

RHETORIC DURING THE SOVIET PERIOD

Rhetoric in the USSR was not at all times in all places the same, but certain general patterns were evident. Two dominant influences on Soviet rhetoric were the lack of strong rhetorical traditions from Tsarist times and the systematic suppression of the human rights vital to the flowering of rhetoric, such as freedoms of speech, press, and assembly, as well as most academic freedoms (→ Freedom of Communication; Freedom of the Press, Concept of). Soviet rhetoric was thereby constrained: inventional and deliberative attributes were systematically shorn from rhetoric in pedagogy, theory, and practice, leaving rhetoric as, primarily, a concern with either compositional stylistics or effective arrangement and presentation of pre-determined messages, following the "party line" (→ Invention and Rhetoric).

The study and practice of rhetoric was never vibrant under Tsarist regimes, nor did it prosper under the Soviets. Reuer (2000) surveys the historical study of rhetoric in Russia, finding little interest in it as a discipline. Although there were exceptions, interest and pedagogy in rhetoric were either for ceremonial purposes or limited to precepts for literary composition. Under the Soviets, the guiding principle of the curriculum was Marxism–Leninism, and there was no room for orientations that were rhetorical rather than material. In general, rhetorical pedagogy (although never by that name) within the Soviet academy emphasized style and presentation rather than invention and argumentation (→ Style and Rhetoric). The stylistic focus of rhetoric was indirectly reinforced during the Soviet period by state constraints on political and intellectual activities: both "subversive" activities and texts were suppressed. Just as dissident speech was not tolerated, neither were the texts that had the potential to equip readers in the arts of deliberative rhetoric. After all, such texts are designed to bring to public consideration possibilities of things being other than the way they are.

In a study of Soviet approaches to rhetorical education and practice during the 1950s and early 1960s, Butler found "a surprising amount of speech activity" that was "apparently grounded on classical rhetoric" (1964, 229). Butler focused much of his analysis of Soviet rhetorical pedagogy on a translation of *The art of oratory*, edited by A. Tolmachev (1959), which was one of only two Soviet texts on rhetoric that he located in the Library of Congress through 1963. Among venues for rhetorical practice, Butler found an abundance of "discussion clubs" as well as "groups, panels, committees, chapters, unions, directorates, and councils (the word soviet means council)." In all of these contexts, however, communication practices were "designed to express a single ideology," creating a "dominant 'downward' flow of communications": "Discussions are used for making decisions, but the answers sought are mainly the ways and means to implement an official policy decreed from above" (Butler 1964, 230).

The most prominent among forums for discussion were "study groups" to assist in "adult education." Although there were local groups in virtually every social entity, from schools to factories to collective farms, there was also an overarching national organization: the Znanie Society. The activities in these groups varied, ranging from indoctrination in Marxism–Leninism to the promotion of pragmatic government goals, such as increased production quotas. As Butler notes of Soviet speech situations generally, the "ends of speech," including "to inform, entertain, stimulate, and convince," were generally present, "but to the Soviets these are means to an end – that end being the building and perfecting of the Communist state" (1964, 238).

It follows that in public education, "speech skills" were "conceived of largely as a political instrument" (Butler 1964, 231), but one always in the service of "state-approved ideology" (238). Butler concludes that although the "standards of eloquence" that are "taught and practiced in the Soviet Union" include the basic "rhetorical elements" of speaker, subject matter, audience, and occasion, "the Soviets have added a fifth requisite – agitation and propaganda." Rhetoric was a mode of propagation, not a mode of inquiry: "Oratory is thereby reduced to an instrument for control over individuals, rather than for the development of individuals" (Butler 1964, 238; → Propaganda).

In restricting the role of rhetoric to propagation of Marxism–Leninism, as interpreted by Party leaders, the vitality and range of rhetoric was severely limited. The relative constancy of constriction of rhetorical topics during the Soviet period is evident in Hannah's (1965) content analysis of 120 speeches made by delegates from the Soviet Union to the UN Security Council over a period of roughly 15 years. Hannah concludes "on the basis of the evidence available that the Soviet delegates' formal political communications did not basically change during the years 1946–1960," although fluctuations were noted (Hannah 1965, 147).

The late Soviet period saw reforms under Gorbachev that loosened the ideological yoke on rhetorical practices, though education experienced little reform. Communication patterns remained predominantly "top-down," but under *perestroika* a "nascent Russian civil society" began to develop (Weigle 2000, 2), and with it came some grassroots political deliberation.

POST-SOVIET RHETORIC

The dissolution of the Soviet Union gave rise to 15 independent nations, including the Russian Federation and the five central Asian nations. The hegemony of the Soviet Union had broken asunder, and in many ways new and "open" societies were instantly born. But the old Soviet habits of life and attitudes toward authority did not simply vanish, and in many ways they merely reinstantiated themselves in "democratic" form (Williams 2007). There has not been a decisive shift from "closed" societies to "open" societies, nor has there been a consistent trajectory in this direction. Consequently, it might be more accurate to think of social and political regimes in northern and central Asia after the dissolution of the Soviet Union as "opening" and "closing" in varying degrees.

Curricular incorporation of rhetoric during the post-Soviet era has been spotty and ad hoc. In Russia itself, the curricula for both secondary and higher education are still centrally controlled: Moscow defines required courses of study as well as "majors" and areas of concentration. Neither rhetoric nor communication has gained national sanction, and although classes in various areas of communication (especially intercultural communication and public relations) are taught at several universities, they are generally taught as "electives" under the auspices of other approved programs of study such as foreign languages (especially programs in English and translation). They remain marginal to the primary curricula. Even so, occasional courses in rhetoric do now appear, as do classes in argumentation. Although most Russian approaches to argumentation remain primarily linguistic or philosophical, contemporary European perspectives on argumentation are gaining attention, notably the Amsterdam School's approach of pragma-dialectical analysis (van Eemeren et al. 1996, 353; → Rhetoric, Argument, and Persuasion). Some of the texts of the Amsterdam School are now translated into Russian.

A professional education organization, the Russian Communication Association (RCA), was formed in 2000; however, it does not have national NGO status under current Russian regulations. RCA functions primarily to promote the study of communication and as an information clearing house, facilitating course development, textbook acquisition, and pedagogical approaches for those who do teach courses in communication in various corners of the Russian curriculum. RCA, with support from the North American Russian Communication Association, has sponsored a biennial communication conference since 2002; rhetoric, argumentation, and political communication have been among program topics at these conferences. An affiliated NGO, "Metacommunication," associated with the Rostov Institute of Management, Business and Law, publishes an annual Bulletin of the RCA, *Vestnik*. Rhetoric, argumentation, persuasion, and public speaking are all categories included in its call for manuscripts. The first rhetorical journal in Russia, *Ritorika*, began publication in 1995, and a new *Russian Journal of Communication* will begin publication in the United States in 2008 in English (→ Communication as an Academic Field: Eastern Europe and Russia).

Although there are some initial efforts to begin a Kazakh Communication Association along the lines of RCA, that initiative is in its early phases. Despite the lack of professional organizations in central Asia to promote the study of rhetoric, international NGOs such as the International Debate Education Association (IDEA; www.idebate.org) have made great inroads throughout central Asia, and especially in Kazakhstan, in the promotion of debate training in secondary schools, institutions of higher learning, and civic organizations. IDEA incorporates into its debate training programs elements of argumentation and public speaking. IDEA is also active in Mongolia, again promoting debate as an agency of personal and political empowerment. Overall, since its inception in 1999, "IDEA has grown from a collection of debate clubs into the pre-eminent global debate organization, touching the lives of over 70,000 secondary school students, 15,000 university students . . . in 27 countries."

Rhetorical practices in the Russian Federation during the presidency of Boris Yeltsin were, relative to the darkest years of the Soviet Union, open and free: political parties with diverse ideological perspectives, political leaders with divergent styles and often dissident visions, as well as charismatic and demagogic leaders, all vied for public allegiance. Russian political space was opening at a rapid pace; however, it was not fully open, and Yeltsin continued throughout his presidency to resort to authoritative methods when more democratic ones became too cumbersome or unpredictable. Indeed, Russia's democratic "revolution" had a typically Soviet flavor to it: it was imposed and implemented in a "top-down" manner (Williams 2007).

Rhetorical analyses of Russian → political communication (Williams et al. 1997; Janack 2002) and transformations in Russian national identity (Ishiyama et al. 1997) have begun to appear in English-language journals, but few have appeared in Russian journals (an exception is Launer et al. 1997). From the perspective of rhetorical theory, the role of → memory in post-Soviet rhetoric is of increasing interest. The particular concern is with public memory, both relative to finding usable history from which to generate arguments for democratic actions and to reconciling with repressive and brutal dimensions of the Soviet legacy (→ Collective Memory and the Media; Memory and Rhetoric).

The central Asian nations did not open as radically after the dissolution of the Soviet Union as did the Russian Federation. Each retained strong elements of centralized, autocratic control, yet blended that control in different ways with democratic reforms. Under Vladimir Putin, Russia is now closing: media are centralized under government control, new laws greatly inhibit the development of civil society, and opposition political parties are de-registered and/or physically harassed (→ Russia: Media System). The dissolution of the Soviet Union created the political space for the cultivation of rhetoric in pedagogy, theory, and practice, and in the opening of the Russian Federation and the central Asian nations the seeds of rhetorical study were sown. As those nations, and particularly Russia, are now closing, it is not clear that rhetoric will come to a full flowering.

SEE ALSO: ▶ Collective Memory and the Media   ▶ Communication as an Academic Field: Eastern Europe and Russia   ▶ Freedom of Communication   ▶ Freedom of the Press, Concept of   ▶ Invention and Rhetoric   ▶ Memory   ▶ Memory and Rhetoric   ▶ Political Communication   ▶ Propaganda   ▶ Rhetoric, Argument, and Persuasion   ▶ Rhetoric in Eastern Europe   ▶ Russia: Media System   ▶ Style and Rhetoric

References and Suggested Readings

Butler, J. H. (1964). Russian rhetoric: A discipline manipulated by communism. *Quarterly Journal of Speech*, 50, 229–239.

Hannah, W. J. (1965). Environmental change and verbal stability. *Journal of Communication*, 15, 136–148.

Ishiyama, J. T., Launer, M. K., Likhachova, I. E., Williams, D. C., & Young, M. J. (1997). Russian electoral politics and the search for national identity. *Argumentation and Advocacy*, 34(2), 90–109.

Janack, J. A. (2002). We'll guarantee freedom when we can afford it: The free market, the Russian constitution, and the rhetoric of Boris Yeltsin. *Controversia*, 1, 57–74.

Launer, M. K., Young, M. J., Williams, D. C., Likhachova, I. E., & Ishiyama, J. T. (1997). Analysis of political argumentation and party campaigning prior to the 1993 and 1995 state Duma elections: Lessons learned and not learned. *Politia*, 2, 33–44 (in Russian).

Reuer, L. N. (2000). *The eighteenth-century Russian rhetorical tradition: V. K. Trediakovsky's career and rhetorical views*, doctoral dissertation, Purdue University, UMI no. 3033153.

van Eemeren, F. H., Grootendorst, R., Snoeck Henkemans, F., et al. (1996). *Fundamentals of argumentation theory: A handbook of historical backgrounds and contemporary developments*. Mahwah, NJ: Lawrence Erlbaum.

Weigle, M. A. (2000). *Russia's liberal project: State–society relations in the transition from communism*. University Park, PA: Pennsylvania State University Press.

Williams, D. C. (2007). Instant democracy: Rhetorical crises and the Russian Federation, 1991–2007. *Advances in the History of Rhetoric*, 9, 227–242.

Williams, D. C., Young, M. J., & Ishiyama, J. T. (1997). The role of public argument in emerging democracies: A case study of the 12 December 1993 elections in the Russian Federation. *Argumentation*, 11, 179–194.

Rhetoric and Orality-Literacy Theorems

Bruce E. Gronbeck

University of Iowa

Insofar as rhetorical practice travels through systems of symbolicity, so-called channels or modes of communication are the discursive spaces within which rhetoric operates. And insofar as rhetorical practice should culminate in some sort of adjustment or change in audiences', readers', or viewers' knowledges, feelings, self-identities, and/or behaviors, the ways in which those dimensions of individuals are accessed physiologically are central to rhetorical effectivity. Those two axioms comprise the grounds for rhetoricians' interest in the orality-literacy theorems.

The orality-literacy theorems grow out of studies of oral, literate, and electronic media of communication (→ Media History; Medium Theory). Milman Perry's work in the 1920s on rhythmic and syllabic patterns in Homer, arguing that oral rhetors could insert variously metered epithets – "pre-fabricated materials" (Ong 1982, 21) – from a stock list, showed us how grand epics could be presented without brute memorization; standardized forms plus commonplace epic themes could be woven endlessly into different-yet-coherent patterns in oral psychoculture. Psychocultural theorization, contrasting oral and literate cultures, had begun.

Here is a dual focus on both the ways in which whole societies are dominated by one or more of those media in any given epoch (*macro-theorems*) and the processes by which individuals come to process symbols delivered to them aurally, visually (via literate, pictorial, performed, or material symbols; → Visual Communication), and even tactilely, olfactorily, or gustatorily (*micro-theorems*). Theorems are understood broadly as propositions that are derived from axioms or other pre-existing formulae, as a logician might understand that notion, but also more narrowly as "more or less hypothetical statements" derived from observations of human communication practices (Ong 1982, 156). The observations come from combing historical accounts – epic oral/written poetry, early treatises, sacred and profane literature – in order to reconstruct communication practices that would be explained were the theorems accepted as true. The orality-literacy theorems, therefore, are largely post hoc explanations of the communication environments within which the human lifeworld operates and of the mental operations for perception, comprehension, understanding, and evaluation that are conditioned by different communication media (→ Rhetoric and History). After examining both the macro- and micro-theorems underlying interests in oral, literate, and electronic environments, this entry will relate them to a broader notion of → media ecology and to conceptions of rhetoric (→ Rhetorical Studies).

MACRO-THEORY: DOMINANT MEDIA IN SOCIETY

McLuhan first became known widely for writing about social structure, culture, and communication media (→ Culture: Definitions and Concepts; McLuhan, Marshall). Following other historians of technology and society, most notably Mumford (1934) and Innis (e.g., 1972), McLuhan's *The Gutenberg galaxy* (1962) was a study of the impact of mechanically reproduced literacy – the flood of publishing following the invention of the printing press (→ Printing, History of). "Technological environments are not merely passive containers of people," he argued (1962, 7), "but are active processes that reshape people and other technologies alike." McLuhan brought into focus the theorem that changes in dominant media of communication – oral to literate to electronic – rippled through the social, economic, political, and religious institutions of societies, altering them determinatively (→ Rhetoric and Media Studies; Rhetoric and Technology).

Oral culture: Havelock (1986) was concerned among other things with understanding how cultural frameworks – *nomoi* and *êthea* – were constructed, maintained, and transmitted in an *oral society*. Translating these words as *custom-laws* and *folk-ways*, respectively, he argued that orations and especially poems were the keys to managing life in pre-literate Greek society. Poetry embedded history and wisdom from the past, while orations contained the grand visions of the world and human beings' places within it at times of crisis and decision. Custom-laws were sayings or aphorisms that encapsulated the wisdom of one's ancestors in mnemonically memorable ways, while folk-ways were the accepted routines of doing everything from accomplishing everyday tasks to relating to other societies (→ Memory; Memory and Rhetoric).

Socialization and understanding of one's place in the collectivity were achieved through recitative educative processes, but more in the large on public occasions, festivals where the folk would gather to renew their collective commitments and have reinforced their individual and societal identities. The *nomoi* and *êthea* were captured in streams of sound from the poets, seers, priests, orators, and actors working amphitheater audiences, who in turn, with their clapping, singing, and recitations, legitimated cultural understandings. Together, they formed the *echo-principle*: the audience could follow celebrants, even join in repetitions of key notions or lessons, much as today's child reads a book over and over, finding joy in speaking the lines being read by a parent. Oral cultures thus live in an evolving present, grounded in traditions from the past that are echoed in public recountings of them, building futures molded out of tradition (→ Rhetoric, Greek).

Literate culture: McLuhan (1962) argued that the movement in the west from chirographic to *print literacy* conditioned European democratization, the Reformation, school teaching, and the scientific method. For Postman (1985), the west reached its zenith in the eighteenth and nineteenth centuries – the height to him of political writing, scientific advancement, school expansion, and public business. Deibert (1997) added that the mechanical-literate revolution represented by print radically changed modes of distributing knowledge and of thinking – social epistemology – and hence showed us that new media are environments rather than simply tools. Not only did societies' institutions change with the coming of new media, he argued, but so did the *mentalités collectives* – collective and individual consciousness.

Electronic culture: each new *electronic technology* – telegraph, telephone, silent then sound film, → radio, → television, computer-assisted communication (→ Cinema; Telegraph, History of) – deepened human beings' reliance upon "conveniences" in communication, work relationships, and entertainment, but, more than that, rewired the ways we talk in, interact with, access, and process the world. The electronic age, as well, became the age of → spectacle, where publicly shared images or sequences of (moving) images seized dominant places in western socio-political life, producing an *ocularcentric society*. If the electronic media gave us pictures that took the place of direct human encounter, computerization only accelerated reliance upon virtual interconnectivity, creating a *cyberworld* in which material spaces gave way to their pixilated representations and in which identities could be remanufactured at will (→ Digital Imagery; Digital Media, History of).

Overall, the social-historical shifts from oral to literate to electronic culture wrenched familial-institutional life and individuals' operations within it, producing new cultural rules and roles. Shifts in mediation were accompanied by wholesale revolution in human environments and the procedures needed to work within them.

MICRO-THEORY: ACOUSTIC CODING, LITERACY, AND VISUALITY

As already suggested, not only did the west witness fundamental changes in social-political-economic-religious institutions as orally based *monopolies of knowledge* yielded to literately and then electronically dispersed social epistemologies, but it has experienced shifts in mental operations accompanying alterations in human reliance upon acoustic, literate-symbolic, and visual-pictorial channels of communication. The orality-literacy theorems attempt to account for those shifts.

The acoustic world: with no inscription to record ideas, traditions, procedures, and marks of identity, how did oral (tribal) cultures socialize and grip their members? Through mnemonics and speech formulae with rhythm, balance, repetition, alliteration, and assonance, and proverbs that could be applied situationally, answer oralists. Ong (1982) inventoried characteristics of orally based thought and expression, suggesting among other things that acoustically circulated ideas were additive (not subordinate), aggregative and clichéd (not analytic), redundant (not sparse), conservative or traditionalist (without narrative originality), concrete or close to the lifeworld, agonistically toned (contrasting pieces of proverbial wisdom to solve specific problems), empathetic and participatory, homeostatic (seeking stable equilibria), and highly situational. One sees heroic achievement in oral cultures, but little in the way of individual identity; membership and totems define the self, acquired through recitation and ritual practice. The world and those dwelling in one's tribe are interiorized largely through sound.

The literate world: in the west, literacy spawned a very different consciousness. Writers and readers gained a sense of individual identity; places to read were built into living quarters, isolating self-consciousness. Writing separated ideas from those thinking them, even abstracting written philosophies and literatures that took on existences independent of authors. *Authorizing* could become a logical-rational, rule-based testing process rather than a matter of collective affirmation. Organized vocabularies representing community or national language practices and associated with discursive realms of life (economics, social relations, theological orientations), *grapholects*, grew strong enough to separate the knower from the known. From here, it was but a short journey to "typographical man" (McLuhan 1962), the "typographic mind" (Postman 1985), and even a new world, "typographic America" (Postman 1985) – modernism.

The electronic world: the theorems suggest that one should be able to trace the remanufacture of human subjectivity today. Assuming that westerners have been vision-biased since the beginning of cultural life, how might we pursue the impact of "new media" in our time? *Remediation* is a framing process, suggesting both that new media absorb and remake older channels/practices and that old media steal from the new to create *retrograde media* and hence adapt to new conditions. So, computer games draw on epic stories and film narratives, while both realistic films such as *Jurassic Park* and animated features such as *Shrek* work off digitized images, special effects, and editing. Waite (2003) goes further, arguing that the electronic screen arts, in particular, can alter humans' sense of duration and space, providing a *variable flex* orientation, constructing a new *communication matrix* within which we comprehend the external and our internal worlds through de-centered experiences. The medium is the message (McLuhan 1964), as well as the environment and the fundament of psychic life (→ Rhetoric and Visuality).

THE THEOREMS, MEDIA ECOLOGY, AND RHETORIC

If we assume that rhetoric is both a practice of figuration and means of → persuasion, then the internal-psychological figuration of the world via symbols and the external-social, public → discourses by which large groups of people are persuaded to experience that world both are significant rhetorical concerns. Rhetoric, like the orality-literacy theorems, must address means of treating issues of both consciousness and culture.

On the surface, the theorems account for the need of rhetorical theorists to remake the art of persuasion developed for oral societies – even those with writing available, as in fourth-century BCE Greece – into a *techne* more attuned to the formal characteristics of written language syntax and to the reasoning processes of emerging, formal logics in eras of literacy (→ Rhetoric and Logic). And, in our time, *visual rhetoric* explores the mechanisms by which images and their sequencing function discursively, creating persuasive texts. Most simply, the theorems magnify the importance of channel and coding in human communication; more profoundly, they undergird the proposition that oral, literate, and visual rhetorics are radically different processes of persuasion and identification because of their varied grounding in alternative subjectivities and cultural practices.

The orality-literacy theorems are being expanded and deepened today by *media ecology* studies. Starting with New York University's doctoral program fashioned by Postman in 1970, media ecology studies works from a broad base extruding the concepts underwriting the orality-literacy theorems: that media are sensorial *environments* (extending and emphasizing particular senses); symbolic environments (each governed by its own syntax, coding conventions, and social uses); and combined into multimediated environments (with varied avenues to communication available in industrial societies). And as well, environments are media, because architecture, urban and rural configurations of landscape, or nature itself, for example, can govern human interaction (see Lum 2005 for dilation of these claims).

Such propositions drive rhetoric to treat the materiality of the physical world, natural and social, as both figuration and a force in persuasion, and to consider environment not simply as context for communication, but integral to rhetorical effectivity. The orality-literacy theorems, especially as conceptualized in media ecology studies, radically expand rhetorical thinking about codes, symbolicity, and what counts as messages.

SEE ALSO: ▶ Cinema ▶ Culture: Definitions and Concepts ▶ Digital Imagery ▶ Digital Media, History of ▶ Discourse ▶ McLuhan, Marshall ▶ Media Ecology ▶ Media History ▶ Medium Theory ▶ Memory ▶ Memory and Rhetoric ▶ Persuasion ▶ Printing, History of ▶ Radio ▶ Rhetoric, Greek ▶ Rhetoric and History ▶ Rhetoric and Logic ▶ Rhetoric and Media Studies ▶ Rhetoric and Technology ▶ Rhetoric and Visuality ▶ Rhetorical Studies ▶ Spectacle ▶ Technology and Communication ▶ Telegraph, History of ▶ Television ▶ Visual Communication

References and Suggested Readings

Deibert, R. J. (1997). *Parchment, printing, and hypermedia: Communication in world order transformation.* New York: Columbia University Press.

Havelock, E. A. (1986). *The muse learns to write: Reflections on orality and literacy from antiquity to the present.* Princeton, NJ: Princeton University Press.

Innis, H. A. (1972). *Empire and communications.* Toronto: University of Toronto Press. (Original work published 1950).

Lum, C. M. K. (ed.) (2006). *Perspectives on culture, technology and communication: The media ecology tradition.* Cresskill, NJ: Hampton Press.

McLuhan, M. (1962). *The Gutenberg galaxy: The making of typographic man.* Toronto: University of Toronto Press.

McLuhan, M. (1964). *Understanding media: The extensions of man.* New York: McGraw-Hill.

Mumford, L. (1934). *Technics and civilization.* New York: Harcourt, Brace.

Ong, W. J. (1982). *Orality and literacy: The technologizing of the word.* New York: Methuen.

Postman, N. (1985). *Amusing ourselves to death: Public discourse in the age of show business.* New York: Viking.

Waite, C. K. (2003). *Mediation and the communication matrix.* New York: Peter Lang.

Rhetoric and Philosophy

Robert N. Gaines

University of Maryland

Interactions between rhetoric and philosophy have always been marked by concerns (and sometimes controversy) about the scope, status, and interdependence of the two disciplines. The reason is that while both disciplines are concerned with → discourse, their aims are different. Philosophy is chiefly concerned with discourse as a medium to express and test knowledge, whereas rhetoric is chiefly concerned with discourse as a medium of influence on minds of individuals and collectives. As a historical matter, contacts between rhetoric and philosophy have differed according to intellectual and cultural circumstances within the ancient, medieval, renaissance, modern, and contemporary eras.

ANCIENT ERA

The earliest relations between rhetoric and philosophy concerned whether principles of speaking constituted an art. Theoretical precepts about speech-making existed before mid-fifth century BCE, beginning evidently with Tisias (and possibly Corax) of Syracuse (→ Rhetoric, Pre-Socratic). By the early fourth century, a body of precepts had developed on public speaking that many conceived as an art. The status of the "art of speeches" was first questioned by Isocrates c. 390 BCE, when he insisted that speaking was not governed by an invariable, exact art, but rather a variable, productive art (*Against the sophists* 10–12). Shortly afterward, Plato enlarged the argument in his *Gorgias* (c. 387 BCE); rhetoric, he reasoned, did not possess knowledge of its object, the soul, could not explain its procedure, and aimed at pleasure – not benefit – of the soul; therefore, rhetoric was not an art (465). Plato later placed rhetoric on a philosophical foundation in *Phaedrus* (c. 367 BCE), where rhetoric was a soul-leading art dependent upon knowledge of soul types and the ability to adapt speeches to such types (261, 271).

Extending and responding to Plato, Aristotle's *On rhetoric* (c. 330 BCE) defended rhetoric as an art (1354a) and theorized artistic persuasion as deriving from rational arguments, the speaker's ethical influence, and emotional states of the audience (1355b–56a). Aristotle constructed rhetorical argumentation on analogy with dialectical argumentation (1354a). Accordingly, rhetoric received two logical instruments, enthymeme (rhetorical deduction) and example (rhetorical induction; 1356a–b); it was also furnished with general and particular heuristic topics (1358a). Concerning the scope of rhetoric, Aristotle constrained its application to settlement of matters falling outside the province of any art, especially matters that were deliberative, epideictic, and judicial (1357a; 1358a–75a; → Rhetoric, Epideictic).

Aristotle's *On rhetoric* combined philosophical conceptions of rhetoric with some preexisting doctrines to provide a fairly complete theory of the parts of rhetoric, including invention, expression (incorporating delivery), and arrangement of speech materials (→ Rhetoric, Greek). This theory facilitated further development, especially in the philosophical schools, for almost two centuries. However, around mid-second century BCE, renewed hostility arose toward rhetoric among philosophers. They argued that rhetoric was not an art because it dealt with uncertainties, did not reliably persuade, and was not useful, either to speakers or communities. They also complained about the scope of rhetoric. Hermagoras of Temnos' *Rhetorical arts* (plausibly c. 140–130 BCE) proposed that rhetoric was concerned with political questions of two sorts: particular questions (hypotheses) and general questions (theses). Philosophers argued that general questions were not the concern of rhetoric, because their treatment required knowledge that belonged to other arts (Cicero, *De oratore* 1.56, 85). Defenders of rhetoric denied that rhetoric was restricted to particular questions (Cicero, *De oratore* 1.47–57, 85–88); they also argued that philosophy had no practical use (implying it was not an art; e.g., Philodemus, *On rhetoric*, P. Herc. 1078/1080, fragments 13, 18; Sudhaus 1896, 154–55, 157).

Within this polemical context, Cicero composed *De oratore* (55 BCE), which reduced the dispute over rhetoric and art to a linguistic quibble (1.102–110) and required that any complete speaker know all important matters and arts (1.20). Cicero's requirement admitted the speaker's need to understand arts outside of rhetoric, but it also implied that speakers were superior to philosophers, because speakers added to philosophers' knowledge a capability for persuasive expression (3.143). Quintilian extended Cicero's view, claiming that rhetoric incorporated everything needed to educate a speaker, including all the philosophical arts (*Institutio oratoria* 1.pr.16–17, 2.21.13, c. 95 CE; → Rhetoric, Roman). Afterwards there were minor skirmishes between rhetoric and philosophy (see, e.g., Aristides, *To Plato on rhetoric*, 145–147 CE, and Sextus Empiricus, *Against the professors* 2, second–third century CE), but the two arts coexisted in a kind of intellectual détente through the remainder of antiquity (→ Rhetoric of the Second Sophistic).

MEDIEVAL ERA

During medieval times intellectual relations between rhetoric and philosophy were transacted chiefly in western Europe (→ Rhetoric, Medieval). Here rhetoric survived in three more or less philosophical venues – theology, logic, and the liberal arts – and its reception in these venues changed over time (cf. McKeon 1942). In relation to theology, rhetoric was initially theorized in Saint Augustine's *On Christian doctrine* (c. 425) as the instructional complement to scriptural interpretation in preaching. Within Augustine's theory, the materials of ecclesiastical speaking were to be discovered through semiotic interpretation of scripture, while the structure and expression of such materials was to be guided by rhetoric. Later preaching theorists embraced a broader range of rhetorical resources, including Thomas of Salisbury, whose *Principles of the art of preaching* (before 1230) exploited Roman principles concerning parts of rhetoric and parts of speeches.

Within the realm of logic, Boethius' *On topical distinctions* (before 523) conceived of rhetoric alongside dialectic as a means of argumentative invention – one of two parts of logic (the other part was judgment). This general conception, which subordinated rhetoric to logic, persisted throughout the medieval era, for example, in Isidore of Seville's *On distinctions of things* (before 636) and Hugh of St Victor's *Faculty of instruction* (around 1130). In the medieval tradition of liberal arts, rhetoric was treated as one of a family of arts, otherwise including grammar, dialectic, arithmetic, geometry, music, and astronomy. Our early sources for this tradition include Martianus Capella's *Marriage of*

Philology and Mercury (before 439) and Isidore of Seville's *Etymologies* (before 636); these works represented rhetoric as an autonomous art generally consonant with ancient theories. Still, the increasing stature of logical theory during medieval times eventually produced an erosion of this autonomy and a subjection of rhetoric to logic even in the context of liberal studies, for instance in John of Salisbury's *Metalogicon* (1159).

RENAISSANCE ERA

In the Renaissance, preaching theory and liberal studies persisted as venues in which rhetoric flourished; however, both were pursued along humanistic lines that showed significant independence from philosophy (→ Rhetoric, European Renaissance). In advanced education, the medieval *artes liberales* were largely supplanted by the *studia humanitatis* (grammar, rhetoric, poetic, history, moral philosophy), a course of study designed to inculcate an eloquent prose style. Likewise, innovation in preaching theory brought religious teaching in closer alignment with rhetorical concerns for discourse types, discourse parts, and eloquent style (e.g., in Hyperius' *On the composition of sacred sermons*, 1553). The principal site of interaction between rhetoric and philosophy was at the boundary between logic and rhetoric (→ Rhetoric and Dialectic). Along this frontier the competing claims of the two arts were prosecuted in a back-and-forth confrontation. The issue was joined first in Valla's *Recultivating dialectic and philosophy* (1439), which subordinated dialectical argument to rhetorical invention (Mack 1993).

This stance was countered in Agricola's *On dialectical invention* (1479), where Agricola added discourse arrangement and expression to invention and judgment as elements of the dialectical apparatus. Agricola's strategy was reversed by Melanchthon's *Principles of rhetoric* (1521); here, dialectical themes were added to the types of rhetorical speaking, and dialectical invention and judgment were integrated into the parts of rhetoric. Agricola received more positive response from Ramus, whose *Principles of dialectic* (1543) and *Criticisms of Aristotle* (1543) framed a critique of discourse arts that assigned dialectic the functions of invention and judgment (including arrangement) and allocated only style and delivery to rhetoric. Ramus's conception of the rhetorical art was soon realized in Talon's *Principles of oratory* (1545) and *Rhetoric* (1548), and this conception was influential for more a century throughout Europe and in North America. In this intellectual context it is not surprising that Bacon's *Advancement of learning* (1605) constricted rhetoric in favor of logic, reducing it to an illustrative function in discourses, the content and arrangement of which were supervised by logical arts.

MODERN ERA

Modern times brought a new alignment of rhetoric with philosophy, particularly through the attempt to reshape rhetoric in accord with philosophical conceptions of human nature. One of the most important of these conceptions was faculty psychology, or the theory that soul or mind is constituted by separate elements with characteristic faculties or capabilities. This theory was current in Renaissance philosophy, e.g., in Reisch's *The pearl of philosophy* (1503); however, in the modern era, rhetorical theorists increasingly conceptualized their art with special reference to its operation on mental faculties.

Pascal's *L'art de persuader* (1658) conceived of different means of persuasion for the understanding and will, and provided a method for achieving the former. So too, Fénelon's *Dialogues sur l'éloquence* (1717) presented the theory of eloquence as a set of precepts for proving to the understanding, portraying to the imagination, and moving the emotions. Such innovations popularized faculty psychology and encouraged its incorporation in more traditionally motivated rhetorics, for example, Gottsched's *Ausfürliche Redekunst* (1736) and Sheridan's *A course of lectures on elocution* (1762).

The flower of faculty psychology was realized in Campbell's *Philosophy of rhetoric* (1776), where a concern for the faculties of understanding, imagination, emotions, and will served as the basis for the definition of rhetoric, the distinction of types of discourse, and the central heuristic for the development of theoretical principles. Campbell intended that his account would reposition rhetoric among the arts, and his definition of eloquence as "that art or talent by which discourse is adapted to its end" included all the forms of purposive discourse – not least poetry. This extended the reach of rhetoric and provided a rationale for belletrism, a contemporary movement that subsumed rhetorical, poetical, and sometimes other forms of discourse under a general literary theory (as, for example, in Rollin's *De la manière d'enseigner et d'etudier les belles lettres*, 1726–1728). Although less programmatically inclined, Blair's *Lectures on rhetoric and belles lettres* (1783) and Whately's *Elements of rhetoric* (1828) both employed faculty psychology in explaining persuasion and its processes.

CONTEMPORARY ERA

In the twentieth century, rhetoric was most influenced by two philosophical trends, the linguistic turn and social materialism. The linguistic turn attempted to understand human nature and epistemology by focusing on semiotics, especially the reality-disclosing function of linguistic communication (→ Semiotics; Rhetoric and Semiotics). In the rhetorical discipline, this focus led at first to a narrow, communicative theory, where the subject of rhetoric became "misunderstanding and its remedies" (Richards 1936). However, later on it inspired a more expansive conception of rhetoric as a "symbolic means of inducing cooperation" (Burke 1950).

After mid-century, there was increasing philosophical support for the view that language constituted reality. This view heavily influenced theories of rhetorical criticism and eventually led to a new focus of the rhetorical discipline upon how rhetoric constitutes identities of individuals and communities (e.g., Charland 1987). A second and complementary trend was discursive materialism, or the philosophical view that the human condition is explicable through reference to its material basis in discourse. Consistent with this view, rhetoric came to be defined materially as "speech" (e.g., McGee 1982), and an immediate consequence was the identification of rhetorical theory with any systematic conceptualization of speech or situated discourse, including, for instance, discourse theories formulated by Toulmin, Foucault, and Habermas (see, for example, Foss et al. 1991).

SEE ALSO: ▶ Discourse ▶ Rhetoric and Dialectic ▶ Rhetoric, Epideictic ▶ Rhetoric, European Renaissance ▶ Rhetoric, Greek ▶ Rhetoric, Medieval ▶ Rhetoric, Pre-Socratic

▶ Rhetoric, Roman   ▶ Rhetoric of the Second Sophistic   ▶ Rhetoric and Semiotics ▶ Semiotics

References and Suggested Readings

Burke, K. (1950). *A rhetoric of motives*. New York: Prentice Hall.
Charland, M. (1987). Constitutive rhetoric: The case of the "Peuple Québécois." *Quarterly Journal of Speech*, 73, 133–150.
Foss, S. K., Foss, K. A., & Trapp, R. (1991). *Contemporary perspectives on rhetoric*. Prospect Heights, IL: Waveland.
Mack, P. (1993). *Renaissance argument: Valla and Agricola in the traditions of rhetoric and dialectic*. Leiden: Brill.
McGee, M. C. (1982). A materialist's conception of rhetoric. In R. E. McKerrow (ed.), *Explorations in rhetoric: Studies in honor of Douglas Ehninger*. Glenview, IL: Scott, Foresman, pp. 23–48.
McKeon, R. (1942). Rhetoric in the middle ages. *Speculum*, 17, 1–32.
Richards, I. A. (1936). *The philosophy of rhetoric*. New York: Oxford University Press.
Sudhaus, S. (1896). *Philodemi volumina rhetorica*, vol. 2. Leipzig: Teubner.

Rhetoric and Poetics

Jeffrey Walker

University of Texas at Austin

Any understanding of the relation between rhetoric and poetics will depend on how each category is conceived. The term "rhetoric" can mean "rhetorical discourse"; or the suasory practices observable in any given piece or kind of → discourse; or the *art* or *theory* of rhetorical performance. Further, "rhetorical discourse" may be defined narrowly or broadly – for example, as any discourse that intends or causes persuasion. "Persuasion" too may be defined narrowly, as the inducement of belief and the promotion of action; or broadly, as the production of any effect in an audience's psyche (→ Persuasion; Rhetoric, Argument, and Persuasion). Likewise, "poetics" can mean the *art* or *theory* of poetic discourse, while "poetic discourse" may mean anything from poetry to "literature" very generally conceived. Thus, any discussion of rhetoric and poetics is working with labile terms.

A persistent tradition in modern western culture tends to regard rhetorical and poetic discourse as *virtual opposites* that may, however, exert some influence on each other. This way of thinking played a formative role in the early twentieth-century revival of rhetoric as a modern academic discipline (→ Communication as a Field and Discipline; Rhetorical Studies). Scholars tended to conceptualize rhetoric as primarily an art of practical public discourse, and to regard the subject matters of rhetorical and literary studies as distinct. In North American universities, for example, rhetoric and literature were the provinces of Speech and English departments, respectively. At the same time, however, historians of rhetoric have become conscious of what Florescu (1971) has called *letteraturizzazione* –

the tendency of rhetorical forms to become or interpenetrate with literary forms – so that rhetoric becomes literary, and literature becomes rhetorical.

Another way of viewing the rhetoric–poetic relation is to regard rhetorical and poetic (or "literary") discourse as *intimately related* to each other, as sister arts, or even to view one as a subset of the other: poetic discourse as a particular type of rhetoric, or rhetoric as a particular ("applied") type of poetic discourse. Such views have both ancient and modern warrants. There are, for example, well-known connections between Aristotle's *Rhetoric* and *Poetics*, suggesting that he views them as "counterparts," just as he does rhetoric and dialectic – or, that he views rhetoric, dialectic, and poetics, along with other verbal arts (such as logic), as overlapping *genres* or sub-components of a more general art of discourse, each resembling (and differing from) the others in certain ways (→ Genre; Rhetoric and Dialectic; Rhetoric, Greek). Notably, Aristotle insists that poetry must represent a "plot" (*mythos*) that is a probable and logically coherent sequence of events – that is, a persuasive, cause-and-effect portrayal of how things probably would happen in a given set of circumstances – thereby revealing "universal" truths, leading the audience to insight, and provoking emotion (pity and fear, in tragedy). All of this is clearly related to his discussions of argument by example and the arousal of → emotion in the *Rhetoric* (→ Excitation and Arousal). Aristotle also says that the "speeches" in a drama (or, for that matter, in a novel, film, or short poem) belong to the art of rhetoric (→ Logos and Rhetoric; Pathos and Rhetoric).

There is a persistent tendency in ancient thought to divide the realm of rhetoric into *practical* and *epideictic* kinds, and to view poetic discourse as a type of *epideictic* rhetoric (Walker 2000; → Rhetoric, Epideictic). "Practical" rhetoric is typically represented as discourse of the law court and the forum, where juries or assemblymen vote, while "epideictic" ranges from civic celebration and commemoration to performance for the sake of entertainment, edification, philosophical reflection, praise/blame, and display. As early as the archaic poet Hesiod we find poetic "song" and civic "speech" portrayed as epideictic and practical types of eloquence, both derived from the same source (the Muses) and both exerting the same kind of persuasive, even hypnotic power. Indeed, for Hesiod, the civic orator is practicing an "applied" kind of poetic-epideictic discourse, transposed from verse to prose and serving the pragmatic purposes of everyday politics. Many early poets treat poetic discourse as a medium of epideictic persuasion and argumentation, and this idea recurs in the early sophists associated with the "birth" of rhetoric as an art, especially Gorgias and Isocrates (→ Rhetoric, Pre-Socratic). It persists as well into late antiquity: for example, Hermogenes of Tarsus, in his treatise *On types of style*, classifies poetry, along with history, philosophy, and civic ceremonial speech, as types of epideictic (or "panegyric") rhetoric.

Modern difficulties in following this ancient line of thought have much to do with a reticence to view poetic discourse as argumentative or persuasory (which is part of the general tendency to view rhetoric and poetics as opposites; → Argumentative Discourse). However, modern expansions of the idea of "rhetoric" have also made the ancient view more intelligible (→ Rhetorics: New Rhetorics). Richards' (1926, 1936) notion of the radically metaphorical nature of all language goes far toward breaking down that opposition, as does Burke's (1950) extension of the concept of persuasion to what he calls "identification." Indeed, with Burke all forms of discourse are rhetorical, from the classical oration to the inward workings of thought and ideology in individuals and whole societies (a view that puts Burke close to the perspective of the early sophists and Isocrates). If all forms of discourse are rhetorical, so must be poetic discourse too. Notably, Burke associates poetic (or "literary") discourse with what he calls "pure persuasion" – a kind of epideictic persuasion for persuasion's sake (and the unsettling of ossified ideologies). Richards' and Burke's thought is reflected in the important rhetorical-literary theorizing of Booth (1961), and other more recent scholars (e.g., Fish 1989). Finally, Perelman and Olbrechts-Tyteca (1958) have argued that epideictic discourse is not peripheral but central to the realm of rhetoric, insofar as epideictic serves to establish and sustain (or sometimes revise) the communal agreements about general values and beliefs that necessarily underlie judgment, motivation, agreement, and action in practical civic discourse. If that is so, and if poetic discourse is a type of epideictic, then poetic discourse must also be a "central" type of rhetoric.

SEE ALSO: ▶ Aesthetics ▶ Argumentative Discourse ▶ Communication as a Field and Discipline ▶ Discourse ▶ Emotion ▶ Excitation and Arousal ▶ Genre ▶ Logos and Rhetoric ▶ Pathos and Rhetoric ▶ Persuasion ▶ Rhetoric, Argument, and Persuasion ▶ Rhetoric and Dialectic ▶ Rhetoric, Epideictic ▶ Rhetoric, Greek ▶ Rhetoric, Pre-Socratic ▶ Rhetorical Studies ▶ Rhetorics: New Rhetorics ▶ Style and Rhetoric

References and Suggested Readings

Booth, W. (1961). *The rhetoric of fiction*. Chicago, IL: University of Chicago Press.
Burke, K. (1950). *A rhetoric of motives*. Berkeley, CA: University of California Press.
Fish, S. (1989). *Doing what comes naturally: Change, rhetoric, and the practice of theory in literary and legal studies*. Durham, NC: Duke University Press.
Florescu, V. (1971). *La retorica nel suo sviluppo storico*. Bologna: Il Mulino.
Perelman, C., & Olbrechts-Tyteca, L. (1958). *La nouvelle rhétorique: Traité de l'argumentation*. Paris: Presses Universitaires de France.
Richards, I. A. (1926). *Science and poetry*. New York: W. W. Norton.
Richards, I. A. (1936). *The philosophy of rhetoric*. New York: Oxford University Press.
Walker, J. (2000). *Rhetoric and poetics in antiquity*. New York: Oxford University Press.

Rhetoric and Politics

Shawn J. Parry-Giles

University of Maryland

The study of rhetoric and politics examines the role of → persuasion in the political process. The study of rhetoric most commonly begins with readings from ancient Greece and Aristotle's handbook, *On rhetoric*. Classical scholars conceived of rhetoric as a practical art involving the performance of public oratory in the contexts of politics, law, and ceremonial occasions, separated from the philosophy of knowledge. As Isocrates' words expressed during the classical period: "Speech is responsible for nearly all of invention. It legislated in matters of justice and injustice, in beauty and baselessness. . . . With speech we fight our contentious matters, and we investigate the unknown" (*Antidosis* 254–256, in Mirhady 2000; → Rhetoric, Greek; Rhetoric, Roman). While twentieth-century rhetorical scholars continued to address the role of persuasion in the → public sphere, its study has more recently expanded beyond public oratory to include other persuasive texts, including advertisements, autobiographies, → cartoons, films, manifestoes, memorials, photographs, → television and print news, and many other forms of → discourse circulating in public spaces (→ Advertising; Cinema; Newspaper; Photography). Rhetoricians of today also recognize the epistemological contributions of rhetoric, which accentuate its role in creating knowledge and constituting perceptions of political reality (→ Media and Perceptions of Reality; Rhetoric and Epistemology).

Scholarship that intersects rhetoric and politics includes not only the study of electoral politics, but other forms of political persuasion involving institutions (e.g., governments, corporations) and individuals and/or groups working to disrupt such institutional power (e.g., activist leaders and social movements; → Election Campaign Communication; Political Communication; Social Movements and Communication; Rhetoric and Social Protest). Such scholarship often relies on humanistic methodologies yet also utilizes social scientific measurements. The study of rhetoric and politics often centers on three broader areas of examination: the consideration of history in the study of rhetoric and politics, an examination of how political messages make meaning, and an assessment of message impact.

THE ROLE OF HISTORY AND POLITICAL RHETORIC

The study of rhetoric is often attuned to the history of ideas and how public texts contribute to the evolutionary understanding of political and cultural conflicts and norms. A public text, thus, functions as a historical artifact, which reflects the political and cultural ideas of the moment in which it was created. For some, an understanding of the historical and political context represents a necessary component in the comprehension of textual meaning. Of course, even as rhetoricians turn to history to inform rhetorical practice, rhetoricians also are mindful of rhetoric's role in creating historical narratives, which are likewise dependent on arguments and evidence (→ Argumentative Discourse).

Regardless of its rhetorical dimensions, history serves as a key component in the study of rhetoric and politics. Rhetorical analyses cognizant of history demonstrate how rhetoric helps enact, empower, and constrain human behavior over time, excavating the "rhetorical climate of an age" (Zarefsky 1998, 31; → Rhetoric and History). For some, understanding the relationship among history, rhetoric, and politics necessitates an examination of archival resources that inform the meanings of the public discourse, allowing for a more insightful and informed interrogation of text and context.

An appreciation of the generic features of political discourse represents one scholarly focus of those sensitive to the contributions of history to rhetoric and politics (→ Rhetorical Criticism). Campbell and Jamieson (1990, 8) explain that a generic approach to political discourse "emphasizes continuity within change" and assumes that "symbolic institutional needs" are integral to understanding "the force of events in shaping the rhetoric of any historical period."

Historically, the public speakers who attracted the attention of scholars of rhetoric and politics were white men in positions of political leadership. More recently, however, scholars have worked to expand the rhetorical canon by writing more leaders of *marginalized groups* into history. Zaeske (2003), for example, examines women's petitions housed in the Library of Congress to exhibit the role of women's signatures as expressions of their political participation during the US antislavery debates (→ Rhetoric and Gender). Focusing on issues of race and politics during the historical era of Reconstruction, Wilson (2002, xvii) illuminates the "social meanings of race and civil rights as these concepts were negotiated by the period's national politicians," revealing the gradual erosion of equality (→ Rhetoric and Race). Such scholarship often requires the use of archival depositories to uncover seldom studied political texts and to gain a greater appreciation of the political context in which the texts were produced.

While political texts often feature an examination of the written or spoken word, an exploration of the *visual turn* in rhetoric is gaining widespread scholarly attention (→ Rhetoric and Visuality). Olson (2004, 16–17) argues that more traditional forms of discourse are insufficient for capturing the historical political climate as "those without political power and economic privilege often resorted to types of rhetorical appeals in various mundane objects ... used for persuasion in public life." Recognizing that such visual images are historically situated, such scholars presume that visual meanings are complex and variable yet have held significant rhetorical power throughout history.

While some of the historically minded rhetorical research is concerned with broader theoretical issues, much of the scholarship is classified as *theory grounded in practice*, where the particulars of the case inductively invoke general theoretical principles that transcend the case. As David Zarefsky (1998, 25) explains, isolated case studies "suggest models, norms, or exemplars ... and they sometimes yield a 'theory of the case.'" Other rhetorical scholars, however, question such grounded theorizing, expressing concern that the particulars of the historical and the individual inhibit a more theoretical examination of the political persuasion process. Such differing views reveal the pluralism at work in the scholarship of rhetoric and politics, which also attends to the ways that messages create → meaning.

POLITICAL MESSAGES AND THE CREATION OF MEANING

Rhetorical scholars attending to political messages often rely on social scientific and critical-historical perspectives in their scholarship (→ Political Persuasion). Utilizing *social scientific methods*, Hart (2000), for example, demonstrates his concern for broader theoretical conclusions about political messages with his creation of a computer program, DICTION, which examines the "unconscious language choices people use when talking to one another" (Hart 2000, 4). Beginning with US political messages from the 1948 presidential election, Hart and his researchers downloaded over 20,000 public texts into DICTION in order to draw more general conclusions about political discourse through an analysis of variance (ANOVA) study. The data revealed, Hart contends, that political campaigns ideally reinvigorate the country, involving a "conversation" among candidates, the media, and the public. Citizens also typically look for a "middle ground" and dislike the negativity of campaigns. In the end, Hart offers an optimistic assessment of campaigning and its democratizing tendencies.

Other scholars of rhetoric and politics, however, opt to forgo social scientific methods and interrogate instead the nuances of meanings, utilizing, among others, rhetorical, political, and media theories as critical lenses by which to analyze public discourse. With such *critical perspectives*, objectivity is often shunned in favor of a rhetorical critic's insights that offer new and provocative ways in which to understand the meanings expressed in discourse. Many rhetorical critics assume, as Medhurst (1996, 219) explains, that "the truly important questions in life seldom lend themselves to clear-cut answers that can be held with absolute certainty," especially in a political world full of volatility, change, and conflict.

Questions of ideology and thus *power* are often foundational to rhetorical studies focused on political meaning. McGee (1980, 5), for example, argued that "ideology in practice is a political language, preserved in rhetorical documents, with a capacity to dictate decision and control public belief and behavior." Such a perspective views rhetoric as a "theory of social and political power" that can help unite or divide communities (Lucaites & Condit 1990, 24; → Rhetoric and Social Thought).

Ideologically grounded studies often are foundational to the examination of media texts (→ Rhetoric and Media Studies). *Popular culture* in particular is attracting increased attention by researchers interested in the political meanings created by fictionalized discourse. Dow (1996) explains that → popular culture completes "some of the cultural work" previously produced by public oratory; television works "rhetorically to negotiate social issues: to define them, to represent them, and ultimately, to offer visions of their meanings and implications" (Dow 1996, xv). For postmodern scholars, the lines between reality and → fiction are blurred, especially in a mediated world, which draws attention to the ideological struggles over issues of gender, race, and class more so than questions of truth (→ Postmodernism and Communication).

The *news media* are also, of course, the target of many scholars' critical interrogations (→ Journalism; News). Framing theories are commonly used to examine the news. Press frames, Jamieson and Waldman (2003, xii–xiii) explain, "shape what citizens know, understand, and believe about the world" as conceptions of truth and falsehood "pass through news frames," featuring particular journalistic interpretations. In the process, certain information is included while other details are excluded because of the "fixed borders" of press frames (Jamieson & Waldman 2003, xiii). More specifically, press frames group important words, phrases, and visual images to emphasize particular interpretations of political history, events, or people. While journalistic coverage can certainly provide alternative perspectives, often such frames inspire more stereotypical coverage, particularly of marginalized groups and individuals (→ Framing Effects; Framing of the News).

Even though attention to mediated texts is a popular focus for scholars of rhetoric and politics, other researchers, however, continue to examine the meanings created in *public speeches*, with some focused on the discourse of institutional leaders. The connection between the discourse of governmental officials and *theories of nationalism* is becoming increasingly popular. Such political discourse, Beasley (2004, 3–4) maintains, helps foster "feelings of shared national identity within a wildly diverse democracy." Depictions of citizenship are commonly featured; political discourse often renders visible or invisible those groups that are privileged or marginalized in a political culture.

Other scholars, however, are more concerned with those who combat institutional forces to effect political change. Morris and Browne (2006, 1) contend that *social protest* scholars "understand that *words* are *deeds*, that language has force and effect in the world." The social movement scholar generally eludes the focus on the single text and single leader in favor of a diversity of textual forms produced by multiple members of a movement. Such texts include the written and spoken words (e.g., speeches, songs, manifestoes, poems, autobiographies), the nonverbal symbols of a movement (e.g., gestures, emblems, signs), and different types of mediation (e.g., → Internet, marches, performances) used by leaders and members (→ Rhetoric, Vernacular). The focus, though, is often centered on questions of meaning regarding the discursive action of social protest – meanings that invoke questions of effectiveness for scholars of rhetoric and politics.

AN ASSESSMENT OF RHETORICAL IMPACT

One of the more contentious issues involving political rhetoric over the past few decades evolves around questions of effect. Instigating a debate, political scientist Edwards (1996, 214) asserted: "we do not know nearly enough about the impact of rhetoric, and we should not assume its importance" without the presence of "systematic evidence" often omitted from rhetorical analyses (217). In response to Edwards' charge, Medhurst (1996) explained that rhetoricians and social scientists often ask different research questions, with scholars of rhetoric concerned about matters of stylistic eloquence, source intent, rhetorical strategy and meaning, and argument, which often defy the measurement of hypothesis testing.

Regardless of the dispute, notions of effect are often categorized as more instrumental or constitutive by rhetorical scholars. An instrumental approach locates the scope of effect in the immediate context and assesses the text's impact on the intended audience. A constitutive approach, however, suggests that "discursive action constitutes the concepts that shape a social world so as to enable and constrain subsequent thought and action" (Jasinski 1998, 80). Such discourse, though, is viewed as one component of a much larger mosaic of political discourse that collectively creates or erodes a sense of community. Instrumental notions of effect, thus, are viewed more causally; constitutive notions of impact, rather, are viewed as reflective of, and contributing to, the rhetorical culture in which the texts circulate in more abstract ways.

The role of → *public opinion polling* is often viewed as a more instrumental assessment of effect, whose history is rooted in the nineteenth century (→ Polls and the Media). Such polling, though, has received considerable critical attention from scholars of rhetoric and politics. Hauser (1999, 5) is skeptical of the news media's reporting of public opinion polling because it typically "creates the impression of 'the public' as an anonymous assemblage given to volatile mood swings likely to dissipate into apathy and from which we personally are disengaged." The result, Hauser contends, is that individuals "seldom experience" such polling data as reflective of their own opinions, exacerbating feelings of alienation (Hauser 1999, 5).

The tendency of polling to reduce the individual to an aggregate leads other scholars to rely on *focus groups* to assess questions of impact. Some of the more robust focus group research in rhetoric and politics relates to the longitudinal research of DebateWatch, a program directed by Diana B. Carlin from the University of Kansas and sponsored by the Commission on Presidential Debates. Initiated in 1996, DebateWatch brings together citizens to watch the presidential debates and answer specific questions about those debates in small groups. Based on such research, Levasseur and Carlin (2001) note the importance of talking to "ordinary citizens" about politics, shifting attention toward what the American people have to say instead of attending to the words of the nation's political leaders or the percentages of their responses. Such studies, though, occasionally provide less favorable impressions of the electorate than anticipated. Reporting on the 1996 DebateWatch data, for example, Levasseur and Carlin (2001, 408–409) report that the electorate was more focused on "egocentric arguments," where "personal concerns" were assumed to represent "common affairs."

Such attention to issues of civic engagement represents for many the foremost outcome of scholarship associated with the study of rhetoric and politics. Scholars often return to rhetoric's roots when detailing notions of civic engagement, recognizing the contributions of Aristotle and Cicero, in particular, to notions of citizenship and rhetorical practice (Gronbeck 2004). In part, scholars write and teach about exemplars of civic engagement whose political involvement altered political practices in substantive ways. The scholarship in turn is designed to help promulgate civic engagement ends among citizens, particularly students in the earliest stages of civic consciousness, strengthening the relationship between democratic practice and rhetorical principles.

SEE ALSO: ▶ Advertising ▶ Argumentative Discourse ▶ Cartoons ▶ Cinema ▶ Discourse ▶ Election Campaign Communication ▶ Fiction ▶ Framing Effects ▶ Framing of the News ▶ Internet ▶ Journalism ▶ Meaning ▶ Media and Perceptions of Reality ▶ News ▶ Newspaper ▶ Persuasion ▶ Photography ▶ Political Communication ▶ Political Persuasion ▶ Polls and the Media ▶ Popular Culture ▶ Postmodernism and Communication ▶ Public Opinion Polling ▶ Public Sphere ▶ Rhetoric and Epistemology ▶ Rhetoric and Gender ▶ Rhetoric, Greek ▶ Rhetoric and History ▶ Rhetoric and Media Studies ▶ Rhetoric and Race ▶ Rhetoric, Roman ▶ Rhetoric and Social Protest ▶ Rhetoric and Social Thought ▶ Rhetoric, Vernacular ▶ Rhetoric and Visuality ▶ Rhetorical Criticism ▶ Social Movements and Communication ▶ Television

References and Suggested Readings

Beasley, V. B. (2004). *You, the people: American national identity in presidential rhetoric.* College Station, TX: Texas A&M University Press.

Campbell, K. K., & Jamieson, K. H. (1990). *Deeds done in words: Presidential rhetoric and the genres of governance.* Chicago, IL: University of Chicago Press.

Dow, B. J. (1996). *Prime-time feminism: Television, media culture, and the women's movement since 1970.* Philadelphia, PA: University of Pennsylvania Press.

Edwards, G. C., III (1996). Presidential rhetoric: What difference does it make? In M. J. Medhurst (ed.), *Beyond the rhetorical presidency.* College Station, TX: Texas A&M University Press, pp. 218–226.

Gronbeck, B. E. (2004). Citizen voices in cyberpolitical culture. In G. A. Hauser & A. Grim (eds.), *Rhetorical democracy: Discursive practices of civic engagement*. Mahwah, NJ: Lawrence Erlbaum, pp. 17–32.

Hart, R. P. (2000). *Campaign talk: Why elections are good for us*. Princeton, NJ: Princeton University Press.

Hauser, G. A. (1999). *Vernacular voices: The rhetoric of publics and public spheres*. Columbia, SC: University of South Carolina Press.

Jamieson, K. H., & Waldman, P. (2003). *The press effect: Politicians, journalists, and the stories that shape the political world*. New York: Oxford University Press.

Jasinski, J. (1998). A constitutive framework for rhetorical historiography: Toward an understanding of the discursive (re)constitution of "Constitution" in *The Federalist Papers*. In K. J. Turner (ed.), *Doing rhetorical history: Concepts and cases*. Tuscaloosa, AL: University of Alabama Press, pp. 72–92.

Levasseur, D. G., & Carlin, D. B. (2001). Egocentric argument and the public sphere: Citizen deliberations on public policy and policymakers. *Rhetoric and Public Affairs*, 4, 407–431.

Lucaites, J. L., & Condit, C. M. (1990). Reconstructing "equality": Culturetypal and countercultural rhetorics in the martyred black vision. *Communication Monographs*, 57, 5–24.

Lucas, S. E. (1988). The renaissance of American public address: Text and context in rhetorical criticism. *Quarterly Journal of Speech*, 74, 241–260.

McGee, M. C. (1980). The "ideograph": A link between rhetoric and ideology. *Quarterly Journal of Speech*, 66, 1–16.

Medhurst, M. J. (1996). Afterword: The ways of rhetoric. In M. J. Medhurst (ed.), *Beyond the rhetorical presidency*. College Station, TX: Texas A&M University, pp. 218–226.

Mirhady, D. C. (trans.) (2000). *Antidosis*, by Isocrates. In *Isocrates I*. Austin, TX: University of Texas Press.

Morris, C. E., III, & Browne, S. H. (eds.) (2006). *Readings on the rhetoric of social protest*, 2nd edn. State College, PA: Strata.

Olson, L. C. (2004). *Benjamin Franklin's vision of American community: A study in rhetorical iconology*. Columbia, SC: University of South Carolina Press.

Wilson, K. H. (2002). *The Reconstruction desegregation debate: The politics of equality and the rhetoric of place, 1870–1875*. East Lansing, MI: Michigan State University Press.

Zaeske, S. (2003). *Signatures of citizenship: Petitioning, antislavery, and women's political identity*. Chapel Hill, NC: University of North Carolina.

Zarefsky, D. (1998). Four senses of rhetorical history. In K. J. Turner (ed.), *Doing rhetorical history: Concepts and cases*. Tuscaloosa, AL: University of Alabama Press, pp. 19–32.

Rhetoric, Postmodern

Gary E. Aylesworth

Eastern Illinois University

Postmodern rhetoric is a set of discursive and critical practices that diverge from → persuasion by means of *ethos*, *pathos*, and *logos* (→ Rhetoric, Greek). Where classical rhetoric addresses a known and identifiable → audience, postmodern rhetoric puts into question the identities of the speaker, the audience, and the messages that pass between them, interrupting and displacing senders, receivers, and messages by realigning the networks through which they pass (→ Postmodernism and Communication).

PRECURSORS OF POSTMODERN RHETORIC

The most important precursors to postmodern rhetoric are Friedrich Nietzsche and Martin Heidegger. *Nietzsche* proposed that language is the result of a series of transformations, where bodily mechanisms are transformed into sensations and feelings that we express in sounds. Sounds become words when they designate things that are similar in certain respects, and they communicate the perspective of a community as if they referred to an independently existing reality (→ Realism). Logical categories are the result of equivocation and synecdoche, since they posit identities where there are only similarities, and they take as universal what is only a partial view. "*Language is rhetoric*," says Nietzsche, "because it desires to convey only a *doxa* [opinion] not an *epistêmê* [knowledge]" (Nietzsche 1989, 23; → Rhetoric and Epistemology; Rhetorics: New Rhetorics).

Heidegger, by contrast, takes rhetoric to be a matter of discourse rather than language, and discourse is rooted in shared moods (*pathe*), practices, and institutions. For him, rhetoric is originally an art of listening because speaking is a response to what has already moved us, and, as the capacity for being moved, *pathos* plays the leading role (Heidegger 2002; → Pathos and Rhetoric). Furthermore, Heidegger (2002) says *pathos* is ontological, for it reveals the being of beings in their totality. In *Being and time*, he declares Aristotle's rhetoric to be "the first systematic hermeneutic of the everydayness of Being with one another" (1962, 178; → Hermeneutics), and he emphasizes the *pathos* of anxiety in the ontology of human experience. In developing this ontology, Heidegger introduces many neologisms and unusually literal interpretations of keywords (e.g., *Dasein* as "being there"), because, he says, when it comes to grasping being "we lack not only most of the words, but, above all, the 'grammar'" (1962, 63). Traditional grammar, which privileges declarative statements about entities, cannot disclose being itself because being is articulated in the totality of relations entities have with one another, particularly in relation to the human being. Hence, there is an inherent strangeness to his discourse, which attempts to disclose relational totalities rather than to objectify entities as subjects and predicates in grammatical propositions.

POSTMODERN THINKING

Lyotard

Jean-François Lyotard develops an explicitly postmodern account of language and discourse in *The postmodern condition* (1984). Although influenced by Heidegger, Lyotard stresses the heterogeneity and multiplicity of discourses. For him, the relational totalities within which statements or phrases occur are not subject to any overriding unity or ontological reference. The *pathos* of this condition is not anxiety but something akin to the sublime described by Immanuel Kant, where the imagination is overwhelmed with intuitions that cannot be presented as a whole. The postmodern sublime is the sense that discourse is irreducibly and unpresentably multiple. Taking concepts from speech act theory (→ Linguistic Pragmatics) and from the later Wittgenstein (see Wittgenstein 1958), Lyotard portrays language as a plurality of → genres, where senders, addressees, and referents shift as we move from one genre to another. Since all statements are acts, however, genres are types of linguistic performance specified by differences in their pragmatic rules. However, since there is no rule for linguistic performance per se, it is always possible to invent new messages and new genres of discourse, as is evident in the new codes and statements at the leading edge of science and technology. Lyotard valorizes this inventiveness as *paralogy*, which he advocates as a strategy of resistance against the demand for communicative totality animating the flow of capital (information) in the postmodern age.

In *The differend* (1988), Lyotard addresses the absence of a common idiom for settling disputes between genres and phrases. A "differend" occurs when there is no rule according to which such disputes can be settled. While the situation may seem to call for persuasion tailored to each particular case, a differend demands something else. Here, the disputants are not human subjects but phrases and genres of discourse, which, says Lyotard, "are strategies – of no-one" (1988, 137). On this account, a phrase "happens" and must be linked onto by another phrase, even if in silence. Lyotard bears witness to differends by finding idioms for them, but these idioms keep open the question of linkage so that any final phrase is infinitely deferred. To bear witness to the differend is not to communicate a message, but to evoke the feeling that something incommunicable (the multiplicity of phrases) demands to be said (1988, xvi, 13).

Foucault

Michel Foucault also focuses upon → discourse as a set of concepts and practices that are not reducible to systems of signs or rules of grammar. In *The archeology of knowledge* (1972), Foucault notes that discourse neither expresses the intentions of a subject nor extends the contents of a concept nor designates objects already given. Instead, discourse consists of statements, and "a statement is always an event that neither the language (*langue*) nor the meaning can exhaust" (1972, 28). Furthermore, the unity of discourse is historical rather than logical, rhetorical, or conceptual, and its history is marked by breaks and discontinuities, as illustrated in the *History of madness* (2006).

In his studies of discursive formations, Foucault uses a genealogical method modeled after Nietzsche. "What is found at the historical beginning of things," he declares, "is not the inviolable identity of their origin; it is the dissension of other things. It is disparity" (1977, 142). In the *History of madness*, he shows that the concept of madness as mental illness can be traced back to the transitional period between the Middle Ages and modernity, where the mad were first allowed to roam free, then deported aboard ships, and finally confined in lazar houses after leprosy disappeared from Europe. By showing current concepts and practices to be the result of historical accidents and contingencies, Foucault reveals their lack of necessity or inevitability, and shows that we do not have to accept their objectionable consequences. This critical function of genealogy and archeology opens the way for new possibilities for "subjectivation," as he remarks in *The history of sexuality* (1985). Here, he studies "the games of truth in the relationship of self with self and the forming of oneself as a subject" (1985, 6). In this respect, he valorizes a freedom of invention similar to that in Lyotard, although for Foucault it is a freedom to constitute and empower ourselves as subjects rather than to invent new discourses in which subjects are shifted, dissolved, and displaced. Nevertheless, both find a precedent in Nietzsche, who saw subjectivity as a grammatical-social construction and as a dimension of transformative power.

Derrida

In his deconstructive writings, Jacques Derrida dismantles the notion that communication is primarily a transmission of → meaning between speaking subjects, particularly as conceived in speech act theory. In *Limited Inc.* (1988), for example, Derrida challenges J. L. Austin's assumption that speech acts are fully determinable by context, and that nonconventional speech is parasitical upon conventional norms (Austin 1975). Derrida protests that "a context is never absolutely determinable" (1988, 3) due to the structure of the sign, which characterizes all language. By virtue of its iterability, says Derrida, every sign presupposes a certain absence, since it functions in the absence of senders and addressees. In writing, for example, a mark is infinitely repeatable beyond the moment of its inscription; it is a "machine" functioning independently of the author (1988, 18). The context of such marks is a text without specifiable boundaries, for signs function only in relation to one another and generate their own difference (*différance*), which shifts them out of any limited context, e.g., through self-reference, or citation.

Derrida notes that Austin's distinction between serious and non-serious speech cannot be finalized because speech acts asserting this distinction are subject to citational doubling, which interrupts and displaces their intentional aim and opens them to "non-serious" uses they would presume to exclude. For Derrida, any theorizing about language or communication must itself be stated in language, and therefore cannot perform the theoretical gesture of a science, since the theory itself would be part of the field it investigates. In *The philosophical discourse of modernity* (1987), → Jürgen Habermas accuses Derrida of reducing critical discourse to (mere) rhetoric by denying its contextual limits. However, Derrida replies that he is not making such a reduction, a position he criticizes as "rhetoricism" (1988, 156), but is demonstrating a structural necessity of signs, which defers final separation between the rhetorical and nonrhetorical functions of language.

Vattimo and Perniola

In contrast to their French counterparts, Italian postmodernists emphasize aesthetic, rhetorical, and historical continuity in their work. Gianni Vattimo and Mario Perniola, for example, characterize the postmodern as a dissolution of progressive history, where past and present are contemporaneous as simulacra produced and reproduced by the media. As a result, advanced cultures experience a dissolution of their identity and foundations, in which their differences with what is "other" are suspended in a repetitive passage of "the same." For Vattimo, interpreting this experience requires a narrative in which Nietzsche's overturning of foundations is joined to Heidegger's destruction of the history of ontology (Vattimo 1988). Such a narrative distorts or twists the tradition back upon itself, so that being becomes a moment in which all of its interpretations are present at once. This marks the end of the concept of progress, since technological advancement has created conditions in which only "further progress" is possible, much like the state of contemporary art (1988, 101). Perniola, on the other hand, stresses the absence of a message in the communication of networks and contacts the new technology is spreading around the globe. For him, postmodern experience is best interpreted in terms of the Italian baroque, or the enigma of a passage into a realm between life and death, spirit and body, subject and object (Perniola 1995). He takes this movement as a kind of persuasion (*peitho*), which he interprets to mean trust in the present, without anticipating a future that will give it meaning and without reference to an origin in the past. Persuasion, then, has nothing to do with convincing someone of something, but is a way of living completely in the present, a passage through the intermediary spaces of communicative networks, where identities and differences are suspended in the passage itself.

Hence, where French postmodernists tend to characterize these networks as spaces of difference and alterity, the Italians, by contrast, characterize them as spaces of "sameness" and continuity in both the spatial and temporal senses. However, sameness is not identity, but a passage between identity and difference, and in this respect there is agreement on both sides as to the active non-identity at work in postmodern discourse. Rhetorically, this requires strategies of displacement, interruption, and delay in the transmission of messages between speaking subjects. Such strategies, both would agree, are afforded by the technological and linguistic mechanisms already at work in the postmodern world.

SEE ALSO: ▶ Audience ▶ Discourse ▶ Genre ▶ Habermas, Jürgen ▶ Hermeneutics ▶ Language and Social Interaction ▶ Linguistic Pragmatics ▶ Linguistics ▶ Meaning ▶ Pathos and Rhetoric ▶ Persuasion ▶ Postmodernism and Communication ▶ Realism ▶ Rhetoric and Epistemology ▶ Rhetoric, Greek ▶ Rhetoric and Semiotics ▶ Rhetorics: New Rhetorics ▶ Semiotics

References and Suggested Readings

Austin, J. L. (1975). *How to do things with words*, 2nd edn. (eds. J. O. Urmson & M. Sbisà). Cambridge, MA: Harvard University Press.

Derrida, J. (1988). *Limited Inc.* (ed. G. Graff). Evanston, IL: Northwestern University Press.

Derrida, J. (1997). *Of grammatology*, corr. edn. (trans. G. C. Spivak). Baltimore, MD: Johns Hopkins University Press.

Foucault, M. (1972). *The archaeology of knowledge* (trans. A. M. Sheridan Smith). New York: Harper and Row.

Foucault, M. (1977). Nietzsche, genealogy, history. In D. F. Bouchard (ed.), *Language, counter-memory, practice: Selected essays and interviews*. Ithaca, NY: Cornell University Press, pp. 139–164.

Foucault, M. (1985). *The history of sexuality* (trans. R. Hurley), vol. 2. New York: Random House.

Foucault, M. (2006). *History of madness* (trans. J. Murphy & J. Khalfa; ed. J. Khalfa). London: Routledge.

Habermas, J. (1987). *The philosophical discourse of modernity* (trans. R. Hurley). New York: Random House.

Heidegger, M. (1962). *Being and time* (trans. J. Macquarrie & E. Robinson). San Francisco, CA: HarperCollins.

Heidegger, M. (2002). *Grundbegriffe der aristotelischen Philosophie: Marburger Vorlesung Sommer Semester 1924* (ed. M. Michalski), GA vol. 18. Frankfurt: Klostermann.

Lyotard, J.-F. (1984). *The postmodern condition* (trans. G. Bennington & B. Massumi). Minneapolis, MN: University of Minnesota Press.

Lyotard, J.-F. (1988). *The differend: Phrases in dispute* (trans. G. Van Den Abbeele). Minneapolis, MN: University of Minnesota Press.

Nietzsche, F. (1989). *Friedrich Nietzsche on rhetoric and language* (ed. S. L. Gilman, C. Blair, & D. J. Parent). Oxford: Oxford University Press.

Perniola, M. (1995). Enigmas of Italian sensibility. In *Enigmas: The Egyptian moment in society and art* (trans. C. Woodall). London: Verso, pp. 141–153.

Vattimo, G. (1988). *The end of modernity* (trans. J. R. Snyder). Baltimore, MD: Johns Hopkins University Press.

Wittgenstein, L. (1958). *Philosophical investigations* (ed. G. E. M. Anscombe). London: Blackwell.

Rhetoric, Pre-Socratic

Richard Leo Enos

Texas Christian University

Pre-Socratic rhetoric is an overarching concept that captures not only the traits of Hellenic rhetoric that were demonstrated by the sophists who immediately preceded Socrates, but also the antecedent forces that shaped sophistic views on thought and its relationship to expression. The dialogues of Plato and the development of the Socratic movement have often been considered the seminal events in recognizing rhetoric as a formal discipline or *technê* (→ Rhetoric, Greek). Yet, the dramatic date of these dialogues – particularly such dialogues as Plato's *Gorgias* and his later *Phaedrus* – reveal that sophists were already established and teaching rhetoric within and throughout Hellenic culture well before Plato (apparently) abstracted and coined "rhetoric" as a discipline worthy of scrutiny. Gorgias, a sophist who was clearly older than Plato's mentor and primary dialogue-character, Socrates, professed to be an established teacher of rhetoric, claiming a pedagogical ancestry dating back to his fellow Sicilians Corax and Tisias. Of course, the debates over the "founding" of rhetoric, whether abstracted as a discipline or long practiced as a craft, continue even today. Yet, what is clear is that several forces were at work prior to the sophists and Plato, which contributed greatly to rhetoric's evolution into a discipline, regardless of when historians of rhetoric wish to select the moment when rhetoric became recognized as an area of study.

While we may not resolve with certainty the disagreement over rhetoric's origin, we can both appreciate and (better) evaluate characterizations of rhetoric's origin if we consider the confluence of forces that contributed to the nascent features of rhetoric's evolution into a discipline. That is, we are aided in understanding the emergence of rhetoric as a discipline by considering long-established social and intellectual forces. There is, of course, little doubt that the synthesis of these forces came about during the early decades of the fifth century BCE, in what is commonly called the pre-Socratic period of rhetoric, but our understanding of the development of pre-Socratic rhetoric will be better realized if we are sensitive to such forces and their history. The four primary forces shaping pre-Socratic rhetoric are: the Homeric tradition, the rise of logography, the emergence of pre-Socratic philosophy, and the evolution of the *polis* or Hellenic city-state. From this perspective, the emergence of Gorgias and his fellow sophists in Plato's dialogues is not the beginning, but rather the consequence, of important developments in Greek thought and expression.

HOMERIC ANTECEDENTS

The *Iliad* and *Odyssey* represent the earliest body of sustained Hellenic discourse. Now recognized as inscribed oral discourse, *Homerica* reveal emerging notions of rhetoric in two dimensions. The composition patterns of the *Iliad* and the *Odyssey* reveal systemic formulae that served as both an aid to memory for early bards (*aoidoi*) and later for the more formal guild of rhapsodes (*Homeridae*). Research on the composing processes of Homeric discourse done by Milman Parry, Albert B. Lord, and others reveals that such patterned heuristics demonstrate a consciousness about thought and its relationship to expression. Further, an internal examination of the works of Homer reveals that the characters themselves demonstrate techniques of persuasion and the manipulation of language that would one day be formalized by sophists and theorized by rhetoricians. The wily exploits of Odysseus to trick the cyclops Polyphemus in book 9 of the *Odyssey*, for example, reveal deliberate attempts to persuade and deceive through carefully crafted speech. Odysseus may have had little or no awareness of rhetoric as it was later understood by fifth-century BCE sophists, but the conscious awareness of structuring language for persuasive effect is unmistakably present among Homer's characters.

THE RISE OF LOGOGRAPHY

Greece's evolution in writing from Bronze Age syllabaries to an alphabet provided a technology both for preserving the spoken word that was much more efficient than the heuristics of oral composition and, eventually, for facilitating abstract thought and prose composition. The rhythmical structure of oral poetry offered a technology for preserving discourse by stable patterns of cadence. Writing made such a technology unnecessary, freeing discourse from the necessity of mnemonic devices for rhythmical meaning and allowing for unfettered prose composition. That is, just as writing mathematics – as opposed to doing such problem-solving orally – greatly facilitates abstract thought with the manipulation of numbers, so also does writing prose stabilize narrative (*logoi*) in a manner that facilitates abstract thought and makes the need for rhyming and poetic composition obsolete (→ Medium Theory; Rhetoric and Orality-Literacy Theorems).

As writing grew in popularity to the extent that a city such as Athens could be literate, the shift in composition from poetry to prose, particularly the use of writing for functional civic purposes, became clear. The multiple benefits of prose writing (logography) became readily apparent, extending this new art far beyond a recording device to a facilitator of abstract thinking. Logography branched out from the mere recording of speech to more specialized sub-genres of history and forensic argument; this shift from exclusively oral (momentary) communication to oral *and* literate communication enabled rhetors not only to freeze discourse but also to reflect on stable communication. Many scholars, such as Eric Havelock, believe this ability to freeze words helped to nurture abstract thought and philosophical inquiry.

THE EMERGENCE OF PRE-SOCRATIC PHILOSOPHY

Another pre-Socratic source contributing to the development of rhetoric was the early development of philosophy. Pre-Socratic thinkers such as Empedocles began to reflect not only on the nature and function of the universe, but also on human understanding and expression. Fragments of their work reveal the belief that knowledge was constrained by the limitations of our own sense perceptions and that inferences that could be advanced were both probable and interpretive. In addition to Empedocles, other pre-Socratic philosophers of the Eleatic school – such as Parmenides and Zeno – viewed concepts in antithetical and dissociative syntactic constructs (*dissoi logoi*).

Structuring knowledge on a polar continuum reflects itself in not only a correlative balancing of style and cadence but an epistemology of degree and relativism. That is, concepts such as *dissoi logoi* have obvious stylistic and syntactic patterns that make them attractive features in euphonic composition, but they also echo epistemologies that nurture a balancing of perspectives that result in probability as a dominant model of thought and expression. Pre-Socratic thinkers such as Empedocles stressed human understanding and probability over earlier Homeric notions of divine inspiration and myth, marking a departure from the Homeric tradition. The insights of pre-Socratic philosophy provided a foundation for sophistic rhetoric that would be based on opposi-tional thought, sense perception, relativism and opinion (*doxa*), formulaic composition, and the power of literacy in moving discourse from momentary expression to stabilized communication that facilitates abstract thinking. It is little wonder that, when we trace the rhetorical genealogy of sophists, we see direct and indirect relationships with pre-Socratic philosophers (→ Rhetoric and Philosophy).

THE RISE OF CIVIC ACTIVITY

The emergence of the *polis* has long been recognized as an important feature in Greek history. Focus on the rise of the city in Hellenic culture has centered on the development of imperialism, the enhanced activity of commerce and trade, as well as the political dynamics that resulted in the exposure to, and interaction with, rival Hellenic cultures. The rise of the Greek city also played an important role in the emergence of rhetoric, particularly pre-Socratic rhetoric. The archaic and classical periods of Greece witnessed the emergence of powerful political city-states, which aggressively promoted their hegemony through kinship ties and military conquest. In all such cities, rhetoric was an active and dynamic feature of civic operations (→ Rhetoric and Politics). One of the most important features of pre-Socratic rhetoric is that judgments about the validity of discourse were adjudicated by listeners and readers. That is, pre-Socratic rhetoric has the consistent feature of being constructed toward, and evaluated by, audiences.

Effective communication in a *polis* – democratic or otherwise – is directed to and judged by audiences. Having the validity of discourse based on the audience was a powerful force contributing to sophistic rhetoric, because effective discourse became a pragmatic and powerful civic force. As the *polis* developed, the role of effective expression increased in importance – whether that rhetoric was received by a tyrant or a democrat. What was reasonable and/or desirable became the standard for attaining agreement. Relative judgments of value and preference were made by the audience, which meant that effective methods of establishing what was most desirable varied according to the circumstances and wishes of the time. Pre-Socratic thinkers refined methods of probabilities, and these heuristics lent themselves well to the pragmatics of daily social problems that could be resolved by argument that stressed warrants for expressed values and opinions (→ Logos and Rhetoric).

In a democracy such as Athens, where securing conviction from the (male) populace determined policy and judgment, rhetoric would be a source of civic power. Yet, in other city-states, ones that had political systems rivaling Athens, rhetoric also was active, albeit that activity was manifested in different ways. In tyrannies such as Syracuse, rhetoric was often demonstrated in the arts of aesthetic performance, as well as with rhetors who functioned as formal representatives or *presbyters* of their rulers. Even in Sparta, famous for its militaristic orientation and (alleged) nonliterate bias, systems of effective communication were imperative for effective civic government. Sophists throughout Greece provided approaches to rhetoric in virtually every type of government, which variously treated rhetoric as an art, an ambassadorial function, a topic for advanced education, and (of course) for political and jurisprudential deliberation.

Pre-Socratic rhetoric thrived throughout Hellenic culture because the malleability of its systems and the range of its benefits cut across and met virtually every sort of orientation that required effective communication. Rhetoric's plasticity made it a pervasive and powerful force and a rival paradigm to Socratic thought. The fact that rhetoric adapted to existing conditions as it evolved through the classical and Hellenistic periods and into the Roman empire is testimony to the attractiveness of rhetoric, which is present in even its nascent, pre-Socratic forms (→ Rhetoric, Roman).

SEE ALSO: ▶ Logos and Rhetoric ▶ Medium Theory ▶ Memory and Rhetoric ▶ Persuasion ▶ Rhetoric and Epistemology ▶ Rhetoric, Greek ▶ Rhetoric and Orality-Literacy Theorems ▶ Rhetoric and Philosophy ▶ Rhetoric and Poetics ▶ Rhetoric and Politics ▶ Rhetoric, Roman ▶ Rhetorical Studies

References and Suggested Readings

Cole, T. (1991). *The origins of rhetoric in ancient Greece.* Baltimore, MD: Johns Hopkins University Press.

Diels, H., & Kranz, W. (eds.) (1951). *Die Fragmente der Vorsokratiker,* 3 vols. Berlin: Weidmann.

Enos, R. L. (1993). *Greek rhetoric before Aristotle.* Prospect Heights, IL: Waveland.

Freeman, K. (1966). *The pre-Socratic philosophers: A companion to Diels, "Fragmente der Vorsokratiker",* 2nd edn. Oxford: Blackwell.

Freeman, K. (1971). *Ancilla to the pre-Socratic philosophers: A complete translation of the fragments in Diels, "Fragmente der Vorsokratiker".* Oxford: Blackwell.

Havelock, E. A. (1963). *Preface to Plato*. Cambridge, MA: Belknap Press.

Havelock, E. A. (1983). The linguistic task of the Presocratics. In K. Robb (ed.), *Language and thought in early Greek philosophy*. LaSalle, IL: Monist Library of Philosophy, pp. 7–82.

Kennedy, G. A. (1994). *A new history of classical rhetoric*. Princeton, NJ: Princeton University Press.

Kirk, G. S., & Raven, J. E. (eds.) (1957). *The presocratic philosophers*. Cambridge: Cambridge University Press.

Lord, A. B. (1976). *The singer of tales*. New York: Atheneum.

Parry, M. (1980). *The making of Homeric verse* (ed. A. Parry). New York: Arno.

Pernot, L. (2005). *Rhetoric in antiquity* (trans. W. E. Higgins). Washington, DC: Catholic University of America Press.

Schiappa, E. (1999). *The beginnings of rhetorical theory in classical Greece*. New Haven, CT: Yale University Press.

Rhetoric and Psychology

Herbert W. Simons

Temple University

This entry examines the fields of rhetoric and psychology, each from the perspective of the other, and both from the meta-perspective of a psychologist-turned-rhetorician who retains equal measures of respect (and disrespect) for both. Rhetoric and psychology each study → persuasion but from radically different approaches that reflect their contrasting origins in the humanistic and scientific traditions of communication studies (→ Communication Theory and Philosophy). With a view toward advancing consideration of the issues that divide rhetoric and psychology, we can imagine their representatives as engaged in a conversation of sorts on questions of relative worth to their students, to the general advancement of knowledge, and to each other (→ Psychology in Communication Processes; Rhetorical Studies).

PSYCHOLOGIST: I don't know what I'm doing here. You're not even an academic discipline.

RHETORICIAN: What's that you say?

PSYCHOLOGIST: To qualify as an academic discipline requires a clearly defined and distinctive area of inquiry, and a method or methods capable of adding to the stock of knowledge. You fail on all these counts, and I'll sit with you just long enough to tell you why (→ Communication as a Field and Discipline).

RHETORICIAN: I'm all ears. Indeed, I'm honored that you've taken the time from your busy schedule to converse with me.

PSYCHOLOGIST: Busy indeed! These days we psychologists are active on many disciplinary fronts, both pure and applied. And that leads me to my critique of rhetoric as something less than a discipline. I'll start with the related problems of incoherence and lack of distinctiveness. From reading Kenneth Burke's "Traditional principles of rhetoric," I gather that rhetoric has accrued a great many meanings over the centuries, from the clearly self-celebrative to the pejorative, including among the latter the "art of proving opposites." Applied to itself, this definition is potentially self-damning. Assuming a reasonable definition of "proving" as demonstrating that something is the case, rhetoric would forever be undermining its own truth claims. What could possibly be the value of that?

RHETORICIAN: Interesting that you lead with so misleading a definition. But perhaps we can profit from it nonetheless. Let me ask you, are there not issues on which reasonable individuals might legitimately differ?

PSYCHOLOGIST: Of course. But . . .

RHETORICIAN: And are there not disputes within your own hallowed discipline of psychology on which even the experts take opposing views? Don't you psychologists continue to argue over the very definition of psychology, for example – without consensus as to whether psychology is the study of mind or of behavior?

PSYCHOLOGIST: I'll concede the point for now. But . . .

RHETORICIAN: My larger point is that not all differences can be resolved, even in your own field, by way of appeal to pure logic or indisputable fact. Indeed, the most interesting questions are of this sort, are they not?

PSYCHOLOGIST: I suppose.

RHETORICIAN: I could go on with this line of questioning, but I think I've said enough to suggest that continuing controversy is not necessarily a bad thing, nor premature consensus a good; furthermore, that not all issues, even scientific issues, lend themselves to demonstrative proofs, if by "demonstration" is meant proof beyond a shadow of the doubt.

PSYCHOLOGIST: Are you saying, then, that you rhetoricians don't really "prove opposites"?

RHETORICIAN: Yes and no. Rhetoric isn't about issues of pure fact or pure logic. Its concerns are with issues of judgment rather than certainty, and on these issues it offers instruction in how to argue opposing views, much of it time-tested and richly illustrated by way of critical accounts of rhetorical practices. It's in this sense that rhetoric "proves opposites," providing thereby wonderful preparation for law, politics, and for analysis of persuasion in the guise of objectivity in such fields as your own. That is surely one of our distinctive contributions. Rhetorical proofs are different from demonstrative proofs; they are extra-factual and extra-logical, but not necessarily counter-factual or illogical. And while rhetoric is an advantage-seeking art, it needn't disadvantage those persuaded by it. Over the centuries, we rhetoricians have learned a good deal about how to persuade and also about how to defend against the con artists who sully our good name. If we had time, I'd "prove" to you how precisely these sorts of proofs are used by psychologists when they are not preoccupied with proving what is trivially true (→ Logos and Rhetoric; Rhetoric and Epistemology; Rhetoric and Logic).

PSYCHOLOGIST: I think you've spoken long enough. Indeed, until now I barely have been able to get a word in edgewise. You've said that you rhetoricians have learned a good deal about how to persuade. I'm willing to go toe to toe with you on that issue, pitting what meager tools you rhetoricians use for accumulating knowledge about persuasion against those in our scientific arsenal. Won't you concede that even your own field's textbooks on persuasion borrow heavily from social psychological theory and research? Applied fields of persuasion such as → advertising, → public relations, → marketing, and political consulting do likewise (→ Political Consultant). They turn to us because our methods are scientific, enabling us psychologists to develop falsifiable theories of persuasion and to exercise controls over potential sources of error in research, such that we can be surprised by our data. That's the defining feature of a modern discipline; its hallmark is objectivity (→ Objectivity in Science). Some say that you rhetoricians are too wedded to the theorizing of the ancients; others that you are congenitally ill disposed to generalizing, preferring to wallow in the idiosyncratic particulars of every new case. You had a promising beginning back in Aristotle's day, but you haven't advanced very far since. Aristotle put forward some interesting hypotheses – about the effects of demographic variables in the use of emotional appeals, for example. We've tested them. You haven't!

RHETORICIAN: For a psychologist you aren't too bad at persuasion, albeit the sophistic persuasion of hyperbole. I take it that you haven't read our research on forms and genres of persuasion and on the situations that give rise to them (→ Rhetorical Criticism). That scholarship surely moves beyond "idiosyncratic particulars," as you put it. But it is true that we rhetoricians tend to prefer "muddleheaded anecdotalism" over "simpleminded empiricism," the former case-driven and storied in its telling; the latter typified by a "variable-effects" approach to the study of persuasion (→ Idiographic vs Nomothetic Science). If we had more time, I'd love to tell you more about it.

PSYCHOLOGIST: Since you rhetoricians are so good at proving opposites, perhaps the next time we meet you'll do a better job of representing my views.

SEE ALSO: ► Advertising   ► Communication as a Field and Discipline   ► Communication Theory and Philosophy   ► Discursive Psychology   ► Idiographic vs Nomothetic Science   ► Logos and Rhetoric   ► Marketing   ► Objectivity in Science   ► Persuasion ► Political Consultant   ► Psychology in Communication Processes   ► Public Relations ► Rhetoric and Epistemology   ► Rhetoric and Logic   ► Rhetoric and Narrativity   ► Rhetoric and Philosophy   ► Rhetoric of Science   ► Rhetorical Criticism   ► Rhetorical Studies

References and Suggested Readings

Billig, M. (1996). *Arguing and thinking: A rhetorical approach to social psychology*. Cambridge: Cambridge University Press.
Burke, K. (1969). *A rhetoric of motives*. Berkeley, CA: University of California Press.
Burke, K. (1969). Traditional principles of rhetoric. In *A rhetoric of motives*. Berkeley, CA: University of California Press, pp. 49–180.
Simons, H. W. (1978). In praise of muddleheaded anecdotalism. *Western Journal of Communication*, 42, 21–28.

Rhetoric and Race

Mark Lawrence McPhail

Southern Methodist University

One of the most persistent problems of → persuasion in the modern era has been the domination and subordination of racial "others," yet race has received little attention from rhetoricians until relatively recently (→ Rhetorical Studies). Not until the second half of the twentieth century were sustained explorations of race and racism pursued by rhetorical scholars in either Speech or English departments. Since 1999, however, numerous studies that link rhetoric and race have emerged, not only in the fields of communication and composition, but also in a variety of other areas of social and symbolic action and significance. While it would be impossible to consider all of this research in the limited space of this entry, an overview of those studies that link rhetoric and race reveals a powerfully interdisciplinary field of inquiry.

Early studies of race and rhetoric focused on literary and → discourse analyses and tended to emphasize black communication (→ Rhetorical Criticism). Over time, research on rhetoric and race expanded to address gender and sexuality, white power and privilege, and → cultural studies. Rhetorical studies of race and racism offer important opportunities for examining the symbolic and social dimensions of identification and division, and, perhaps most importantly, the potential for discourse to promote social transformation and change. Rhetorical studies of race and racism pose provocative challenges to a society that has struggled throughout its history to overcome what W. E. B. Du Bois presciently coined "the problem of the color line," the struggle for racial equality and social justice.

RHETORIC AND RACE IN BLACK AND WHITE

Before the 1960s, few studies in either composition or communication addressed issues of race either directly or indirectly, with the exception of Kenneth Burke's considerations of race in several of his early works (Crable 2003). Discussions of rhetoric and race were "an unlikely tandem" in composition studies (Campbell 1999), and in speech communication scholarship before the 1950s, much of the research that appeared in print focused mainly on "Negro" language practices. In the 1960s, both European and African-American scholars began to focus their research efforts on the relationship between rhetoric and race, and in doing so, they began to transform the ways in which language and social identity were understood and conceptualized.

During the 1960s, numerous essays and books appeared that examined and explicated rhetorics of black protest. By the 1970s, scholars began to question the efficacy of rhetoric for addressing racial issues, and theorized the need to reconceptualize and redefine rhetoric's traditional preoccupation with persuasion and argumentation (Asante 1971; → Communication Modes, African). This redefinition called for an enlarged and enhanced understanding of discourse that addressed the social realities of racial difference and identity in the United States, and would be echoed later by other scholars, who hoped to establish less oppositional rhetorical theories and practices in the areas of gender, composition, and other realms of social and symbolic action.

The *1980s* witnessed a continued expansion of research extending rhetoric and race beyond traditional critical analyses of African-American discourse and public address, and shifting to descriptive studies of the language of oppression as well as more theoretically complex explorations of the language of white racism (van Dijk 1987, 1993). This expansion continued into the 1990s, during which discourse studies and research influenced by symbolic and modern racism scholarship became much more prevalent. The focus on white identity and privilege continued to increase in the 1990s, as research began to attend to issues of power, ideology, and domination in areas such as critical legal studies, critical race studies, and media studies (Olmstead 1998). These studies signaled a shift toward enlarged conceptualization of rhetoric and race that would influence significantly the shape and trajectory of scholarship at the end of the twentieth century and into the twenty-first.

BEYOND BINARIES: RETHINKING RHETORIC AND RACE

In the 1980s and 1990s, researchers began to take rhetoric and race in new critical and theoretical directions. In areas where little research had been conducted, such as diversity studies (Fernandez & Davis 1999) and composition (Gilyard 1999), relationships between race and rhetoric became central concerns. Studies in the social construction of equality (Condit & Lucaites 1993), commemorative discourse (Browne 1999), and civil rights rhetoric (Jensen & Hammerback 1994) revealed an expansion of traditional critical approaches, and rhetorical theorists increasingly recognized race as a collaboratively constructed rhetorical phenomenon (McPhail 1994; Gresson 1995). Scholars also began to offer theoretically driven examinations of the *social and symbolic construction of whiteness and racial privilege* (Nakayama & Martin 1999). The momentum established at the end of the twentieth century, which saw a rethinking of rhetoric informed by emerging ideological and epistemological concerns, invigorated thinking about rhetoric and race as the twenty-first century began.

Indeed, since 2000, intellectual currents in the study of rhetoric and race have both returned to their roots and also moved in powerful and provocative new directions. While studies of black nationalism and black identity have returned the discussion of race and rhetoric to the early emphasis on African-American discourse (Gordon 2003; Terrill 2004), emerging explorations of the rhetorics of whiteness and anti-racism have established fertile new grounds for addressing the problems and possibilities of racial reconciliation (Watts 2005). Race remains central to discussions of political rhetoric (Frank & McPhail 2005; → Rhetoric and Politics), and has emerged as well in studies of visual rhetoric (Gallagher & Zagacki 2005). Rhetorical scholars have expanded the conceptualization of race well *beyond the boundaries of black and white identity*, and connections between race, class, gender, and sexuality continue to enlarge the terrains upon which issues of discourse and identity can be explored (→ Identities and Discourse; Rhetoric and Class; Rhetoric and Gender).

Rethinking the relationship between rhetoric and race has returned researchers to one of the earliest questions raised by scholars: whether or not racial conflict and division are, in fact, problems that can be remedied by rhetoric. *Two areas of inquiry* in which this question has become a central consideration are studies of reparations and reconciliation. Research on reparations questions the potential of rhetoric to erase the color line (Bacon 2003), while scholarship on reconciliation continues to look to the promise of rhetoric to bring about significant social transformations in the area of race relations (Hatch 2006). John Hatch's hopeful conclusions provide a salient representative anecdote for the future study of rhetoric and race: "The tragic reality of unequal and conflictual race relations might have to go from bad to worse before reconciliation's call to atonement becomes compelling" (2006, 271). Hatch's observation offers a guardedly optimistic assessment of the potential of rhetoric to reconcile what Ashley Montague (1964) over 40 years ago described as "man's greatest myth: the fallacy of race."

SEE ALSO: ▶ Civil Rights Movement and the Media ▶ Communication Modes, African ▶ Cultural Studies ▶ Discourse Analysis ▶ Identities and Discourse ▶ Media and Group Representations ▶ Persuasion ▶ Power and Discourse ▶ Rhetoric and Class ▶ Rhetoric and Gender ▶ Rhetoric in North America: United States ▶ Rhetoric and Politics ▶ Rhetoric and Social Protest ▶ Rhetorical Criticism ▶ Rhetorical Studies ▶ Symbolic Annihilation

References and Suggested Readings

Asante, M. (1971). Markings of an African concept of rhetoric. *Today's Speech*, 19, 3–18.

Bacon, J. (2003). Reading the reparations debate. *Quarterly Journal of Speech*, 89, 171–195.

Browne, S. (1999). Remembering Crispus Attucks: Race, rhetoric, and the politics of commemoration. *Quarterly Journal of Speech*, 85, 169–187.

Campbell, K. (1999). Race and rhetoric: An unlikely tandem? In J. Swearingen & D. Pruett (eds.), *Rhetoric, the polis, and the global village*. Mahwah, NJ: Lawrence Erlbaum, pp. 11–14.

Condit, C., & Lucaites, J. (1993). *Crafting equality: America's Anglo-African word*. Chicago, IL: University of Chicago Press.

Crable, B. (2003). Race and a rhetoric of motives: Kenneth Burke's dialogue with Ralph Ellison. *Rhetoric Society Quarterly*, 33, 5–25.

Frank, D., & McPhail, M. (2005). Barack Obama's address to the 2004 Democratic National Convention: Trauma, compromise, consilience, and the (im)possibility of racial reconciliation. *Rhetoric and Public Affairs*, 8, 571–594.

Fernandez, J., & Davis, J. (1999). *Race, gender, and rhetoric: The true state of race and gender relations in corporate America*. New York: McGraw-Hill.

Gallagher, V. (1999). Memory and reconciliation in the Birmingham Civil Rights Institute. *Rhetoric and Public Affairs*, 2, 303–320.

Gallagher, V., & Zagacki, K. S. (2005). Visibility and rhetoric: The power of visual images in Norman Rockwell's depictions of civil rights. *Quarterly Journal of Speech*, 91(2), 175–200.

Gilyard, K. (ed.) (1999). *Race, rhetoric, and composition*. Portsmouth, NH: Heinemann.

Gordon, D. (2003). *Black identity: Rhetoric, ideology, and nineteenth-century black nationalism*. Carbondale, IL: University of Southern Illinois Press.

Gresson, A. (1995). *The recovery of race in America*. Minneapolis, MN: University of Minnesota Press.

Hatch, J. (2006). The hope of reconciliation: Continuing the conversation. *Rhetoric and Public Affairs*, 9, 259–278.

Jensen, R., & Hammerback, J. (1994). Robert Parris Moses. In Leeman, R. (ed.), *African American orators: A bio-critical sourcebook*. Westport, CT: Greenwood.

McPhail, M. (1994). *The rhetoric of racism*. Lanham, MD: University Press of America.

McPhail, M. (2002). *The rhetoric of racism revisited: Reparations or separation?* Lanham, MD: Rowman and Littlefield.

Montague, A. (1964). *Man's greatest myth: The fallacy of race.* Cleveland, OH: World.

Nakayama, T., & Martin, J. (eds.) (1999). *Whiteness: The communication of social identity.* Beverly Hills, CA: Sage.

Olmstead, A. (1998). Words are acts: Critical race theory as a rhetorical construct. *Howard Journal of Communications, 9*, 323–331.

Terrill, R. (2004). *Malcolm X: Inventing radical judgment.* East Lansing, MI: Michigan State University Press.

van Dijk, T. (1987). *Communicating racism: Ethnic prejudice in thought and talk.* Newbury Park, CA: Sage.

van Dijk, T. (1993). *Elite discourse and racism.* Newbury Park, CA: Sage.

Watts, E. (2005). Border patrolling and passing in Eminem's *8 Mile. Critical Studies in Media Communication, 22*, 187–206.

Rhetoric and Religion

Kristy Maddux

University of Maryland

The relationship between rhetoric and religion is fourfold: (1) rhetoric is a tool used by religious groups; (2) political rhetoric draws upon religious language; (3) religious systems contribute to the discursive constructions of their adherents' worldviews; and (4) religious traditions contribute to rhetorical theory and practice.

Religious systems use *rhetoric as a tool* for interfacing with outside groups and communicating with adherents. Interfacing with outsiders includes efforts to share the message of the faith but also to create relationships with other groups. In the case of Christianity, the imperative to evangelize is especially strong, and Christian groups have been innovative in their rhetorical practices. Long a staple of Christian rhetoric, the sermonic → genre has become indispensable in the American context – used by the evangelists of the First and Second Great Awakenings, including Jonathan Edwards and Charles Finney, as well as twentieth-century evangelists, such as Aimee Semple McPherson, Oral Roberts, and Jimmy Swaggart. These twentieth-century preachers were among the first to appropriate media technologies – film, → radio, → television, and the → Internet – for religious purposes (→ Cinema). In the Catholic church, the pastoral letter remains an important tool for communicating with believers, and Carol Jablonsky (1989) explains that American bishops have used these letters to instruct members in the doctrine and practices of the faith.

Rhetoric and religion interact in the political context as *political leaders draw upon religious language*, but also as religious leaders assert influence over public policy matters (→ Rhetoric and Politics). Roderick Hart (1977) has argued that in the United States, church and state have arrived at an implicit contract, which he calls "civic piety," that is held stable by rhetorical practice. Civic piety rhetoric calls upon a nonsectarian God who watches over the United States, but it otherwise maintains a distinction between church and state. Presidential inaugurals typically demonstrate civic piety, such as Franklin Roosevelt's use of religious language calling for a "holy war" against recession and John F. Kennedy's statement that "on Earth, God's work must truly be our own." Steve Goldzwig (1987) has countered that in addition to this "official" civic piety, there are "unofficial" public theologies that explicitly use the language, imagery, and values of specific religious traditions to influence public policy. He cites Jerry Falwell and Archbishop Oscar Romero as examples, but that list could also include William Wilberforce, Dorothy Day, Martin Luther King, Jr, and Caesar Chavez (→ Rhetoric and Social Protest). Similarly, Erik Doxtader (2001) claims that Christian rhetoric, specifically the *Kairos Document*, contributed to bringing about the reconciliation that ended the system of apartheid in South Africa.

Religious systems also have rhetorical value as they *discursively constitute worldviews* for their adherents. Kenneth Burke (1961) notes that because words for the natural world are commonly used to explain the supernatural and because the reverse is also true, the ways that we see our natural world are always influenced by our theologies. For instance, Burke argues that the cycle of guilt, sacrifice, and redemption that is central to the Christian Bible also inheres in our discourse. The existence of the hortatory negative in language (the "thou-shalt-not") makes sin possible, which leads to guilt and the need for redemption and sacrifice. In their analysis of Hindu nationalism in India, Roy and Rowland (2003) suggest that this type of mythic structure is not unique to cultures influenced by Christianity. They note how Hindu nationalist identity is premised on a mythic structure that pits the great heroes of that tradition against the evils it identifies as inherent to Islam.

Finally, *religious traditions contribute to rhetorical theory* and practice. Rhetorical critics have acknowledged the contributions made by the scriptures themselves, as well as the writings of religious thinkers such as St Augustine, St Anselm, Søren Kierkegaard, and Dietrich Bonhoffer. James Darsey (1997), for instance, argues that the practice of radical rhetoric in the United States has been influenced by the prophetic tradition. The prophets of the Hebrew scriptures and contemporary radicals share a sense of mission, an attempt to hold listeners to a sacred principle, and an uncompromising posture. In a related vein, scholars have noted the persistence of the "jeremiad" in the tradition of American public address. The contemporary political jeremiad, which is heir to Puritan preaching as well as the prophetic tradition, holds up principles that are sacred to the community, expresses disappointment in the community's failure to live according to these principles, and then calls audience members to return to principled living (Murphy 1990; → Religion and Popular Communication; Rhetorical Criticism). Rhetoric scholars have primarily attended to the contributions that the Jewish and Christian traditions make to rhetorical theory, but other religions have much to offer as well.

SEE ALSO: ► Cinema ► Genre ► Internet ► Radio ► Religion and Popular Communication ► Rhetoric and Politics ► Rhetoric and Social Protest ► Rhetorical Criticism ► Rhetorical Studies ► Television

References and Suggested Readings

Burke, K. (1961). *The rhetoric of religion*. Boston, MA: Beacon Press.
Darsey, J. (1997). *The prophetic tradition and radical rhetoric in America*. New York: New York University Press.

Doxtader, E. (2001). Making rhetorical history in a time of transition: The occasion, constitution, and representation of South African reconciliation. *Rhetoric and Public Affairs*, 4, 223–260.

Goldzwig, S. (1987). A rhetoric of public theology: The religious rhetor and public policy. *Southern Speech Communication Journal*, 52, 128–150.

Hart, R. P. (1977). *The political pulpit*. West Lafayette, IN: Purdue University Press.

Hart, R. P., & Pauley, J. L., II (2005). *The political pulpit revisited*. West Lafayette, IN: Purdue University Press.

Jablonsky, C. J. (1989). *Aggiornamento* and the American Catholic bishops: A rhetoric of institutional continuity and change. *Quarterly Journal of Speech*, 75, 416–432.

Medhurst, M. J. (1991). Rhetorical dimensions in Biblical criticism: Beyond style and genre. *Quarterly Journal of Speech*, 77, 214–250.

Murphy, J. M. (1990). "A time of shame and sorrow": Robert F. Kennedy and the American jeremiad. *Quarterly Journal of Speech*, 76, 401–414.

O'Leary, S. D. (1994). *Arguing the apocalypse: A theory of millennial rhetoric*. New York: Oxford University Press.

Roy, A., & Rowland, R. C. (2003). The rhetoric of Hindu nationalism: A narrative of mythic redefinition. *Western Journal of Communication*, 67, 225–248.

Rhetoric, Roman

Jon Hall

University of Otago

Roman rhetoric aims to present practical and theoretical guidelines for effective verbal → persuasion. In ancient Rome such precepts found an application most regularly in speeches made in the criminal and civil courts, but they were relevant also to debates on political policy in the senate and at popular assemblies. All of these oratorical activities were traditionally restricted in ancient Rome to men of the elite classes. The main principles of Roman rhetoric derive largely from earlier Greek rhetorical theory, which achieved impressive levels of sophistication during the fourth century BCE, and which formed the major focus of formal education in the Hellenistic world (→ Rhetoric, Greek). As these Greek-speaking communities were gradually incorporated into the Roman Empire from the second century BCE onwards, the value of rhetorical training came to be appreciated by members of the ruling elite, although the process of acceptance and integration took considerable time. The first teachers of rhetoric in Rome essentially reproduced the existing Greek system; it is not until 92 BCE that we hear of Latin being used as a language of rhetorical instruction in the city. Over the next 50 years or so, formal training in rhetoric finally became established as a central feature of upper-class Roman education.

RHETORICA AD HERENNIUM

The three most influential works of Roman rhetoric are *Rhetorica ad Herennium* ("Rhetorical precepts addressed to Herennius," author unknown), Cicero's *De Oratore* ("On the orator"), and Quintilian's *Institutio Oratoria* ("The education of the orator"). The first takes the form of an instructional manual or handbook, probably written sometime between 88 and 82 BCE, and presents many of the conventional tenets of ancient rhetoric (Gaines 2007). Oratory is thus divided into three broad types (1.2): legal (*iudiciale*), deliberative (*deliberativum*), and epideictic (*demonstrativum*). Similarly the orator's job is viewed as consisting of five main tasks (*officia*; 1.3): deciding on the most appropriate arguments and subject matter (*inventio*); arranging these arguments effectively (*dispositio/ordo*); casting them in a suitable linguistic style (*elocutio*); memorization of the final text (*memoria*); and finally the persuasive delivery of the speech (*pronuntiatio/actio*; → Arrangement and Rhetoric; Delivery and Rhetoric; Invention and Rhetoric; Memory and Rhetoric; Style and Rhetoric). Some of these aspects receive greater emphasis than others. Greek intellectuals had been particularly interested in analyzing and categorizing types of argument, especially those applicable in legal contexts, and the *Rhetorica ad Herennium* reproduces this bias (see 2.1; → Logos and Rhetoric). Similarly, linguistic style is discussed in great detail, with some 80 stylistic devices (such as anaphora, tricolon, metaphor, and so on) catalogued, defined, and illustrated by example (4.19–4.46).

As a whole, the work is closely modeled on contemporary Greek works, although it does demonstrate the advances made in forging a new Latin terminology to match the technical vocabulary of Greek rhetoric (see, e.g., Pernot 2005, 102–104). Such handbooks placed a strong emphasis on systematization and practical utility, and the work illustrates well the main methodological hallmark of ancient rhetoric: the extensive use of categorization and taxonomy. (See, for example, the discussion at 1.8 of the four possible ways of gaining a jury's goodwill.) This kind of approach has the pedagogical virtues of clarity and order, and introduces into the study of persuasion an impressive logical rigor. Indeed, at its best, this form of analysis represents one of the most remarkable intellectual achievements of Greek and Roman scholars. It can also, however, encourage a rather formulaic approach to speech-making. As successful practitioners of oratory such as Cicero recognized, these "rules" of rhetoric offered only an initial framework for a speaker's attempts at persuasion. The realities of each specific rhetorical challenge usually called for some adaptation or variation to be introduced. As Cicero stresses, rhetorical precepts should be viewed primarily as a codification of oratorical "best practice" rather than an infallible and sacrosanct intellectual system (see *De Oratore* 1.146; 2.81–2.84; 2.131).

CICERO

Cicero's *De Oratore* (written in 55 BCE) is a more complex and ambitious work that combines features of the standard rhetorical handbook with elements of the Platonic and Aristotelian philosophical dialogue. Especially noteworthy is Cicero's attempt to raise the social and intellectual prestige of rhetoric. A longstanding challenge to the discipline was that it presented little more than a slick system of verbal tricks to be cynically applied by the orator for often immoral ends (Wisse 2002; the criticisms derive largely from Plato's *Gorgias* and *Phaedrus*). Cicero responds by asserting that a training in rhetoric ideally provides a well-rounded education, in which the orator learns to analyze and debate a wide range of subjects and gains a deep understanding of the world through the accompanying study of law, literature, and philosophy (*De Oratore* 1.72–1.73; 2.68; 3.143). This argument has its own biases and self-interested elements, but no less so perhaps than Plato's (Vickers 1988, 83–147). This controversy over rhetoric's ethical status was to be rehearsed in various forms in the Renaissance and beyond (Vickers 1988, 178–213; → Rhetoric and Ethics; Rhetoric and Philosophy).

De Oratore also reasserts the importance of the orator's exploitation of *ethos* (character) and *pathos* (strong emotion), aspects given prominence by Aristotle but often underplayed by the standard handbooks (Wisse 1989; → Ethos and Rhetoric; Pathos and Rhetoric). Cicero's own oratorical practices, which made considerable use of emotional pleas, may have been a further factor in his decision to stress these aspects (Hall 2007). *De Oratore* expands the traditional horizons of Roman rhetorical handbooks in another way too, through its inclusion of an analysis of oratorical humor (2.217–2.290). Although earlier Greek treatises on wit and humor existed, Cicero's incorporation of the topic into his framework of rhetorical theory seems to be an innovative step (Rabbie 2007). His discussion of the subject was influential enough to convince Quintilian to include humor as a topic for analysis in his own treatise written over a century later.

QUINTILIAN

Quintilian's treatise, a massive undertaking that took several years to complete (c. 93–95 CE), is the most comprehensive and detailed discussion of rhetoric to come down to us from the ancient world (Fernández López 2007). The work addresses all the features regularly found in the handbooks, and extends its discussion to include the very earliest stages of the orator's training (Book 1). Its level of scholarship is impressive: Quintilian frequently summarizes the contrasting views expressed on a topic over the centuries by various (often otherwise unknown) rhetoricians and displays sound judgment in his handling of them. He seizes shrewdly on the decisive issues that bear upon a particular debate and cuts through fussy, over-complicated elaborations of theory. He also presents sensible, humane views on the challenges of educating and motivating young students.

In many ways, Quintilian serves as an authoritative guide to virtually every issue in Roman rhetoric. He is more, however, than just a synthesizer of earlier scholars' views. His discussion of oratorical delivery in particular seems to have addressed the subject with far more rigor and detail than earlier treatments. Rhetorical theory had previously shown only limited interest in the performative elements of oratory such as hand gestures and facial expression; Quintilian by contrast treats the subject in considerable detail, documenting some 30 or so hand gestures available for use by the orator (*Institutio Oratoria* 10.3; Hall 2004). This discussion influenced Andrea de Jorio's pioneering study of nonverbal communication in eighteenth- and nineteenth-century Naples (de Jorio 2000), and thus has in turn influenced more recent analyses of body language (e.g., Kendon 1986). Quintilian's observations regarding the orator's need for careful image management also anticipates several other lines of approach in modern social studies. He urges the speaker, for example, to pay attention to his gait, dress, and overall bearing (or, to use Bourdieu's term, *habitus*); and several modern studies have identified ways in which Roman rhetoric's precepts regarding self-presentation and image management encode societal norms of masculinity (e.g., Gleason 1995; Richlin 1997; → Rhetoric, Nonverbal).

Quintilian's treatise as a whole demonstrates the extent to which rhetoric by this time had been embraced by the Roman elite as a central part of the educational system. (Suetonius' work *De Grammaticis et Rhetoribus* ["On grammarians and rhetoricians"] provides brief biographies of some of the renowned teachers of this period.) It was to retain this place until the fragmentation of the Roman Empire around the fifth century CE, and, during the Renaissance, rhetorical handbooks such as *Rhetorica ad Herennium* enjoyed a renewed prominence as they came to form the basic educational texts of the elite classes learning Latin for both administrative and broader cultural purposes (Ward 2007).

THE LITERATURE ON ROMAN RHETORIC

Several other discussions of Roman rhetoric survive from the classical period: Cicero's *De Inventione, Brutus, Orator, De Partitione Oratoria, De Optimo Genere Oratorum,* and *Topica* (written between 91 and 44 BCE); Tacitus' *Dialogus de Oratoribus* (c. 96–102 CE); and Iulius Victor's *Ars Rhetorica* (probably fourth century CE). Also extant are some 50 speeches by Cicero from legal trials, senatorial debates, and political assemblies, which provide illuminating examples of rhetorical theory put into practice.

Useful surveys of the main features of Roman rhetoric and its historical development can be found in Kennedy (1972), Clarke (1996), and Pernot (2005). Lausberg (1998) presents a compendious treatment of the technical elements of Greek and Roman rhetoric. Dugan (2007) provides an excellent synopsis of recent scholarly trends in the study of Roman rhetoric. These range from analyses of the influence of rhetorical training on Roman poets and historians, to the role played by educational declamatory exercises (such as the *suasoria* and *controversia*) in shaping upper-class social attitudes and ideals. All these approaches testify to the tremendous impact of rhetoric on the lives of the Roman elite. By the first century CE, the young men of this class were highly trained in analyzing moral, legal, and political issues from an essentially rhetorical perspective, and could deploy with great facility a formidable arsenal of persuasive techniques.

SEE ALSO: ► Arrangement and Rhetoric ► Delivery and Rhetoric ► Ethos and Rhetoric ► Invention and Rhetoric ► Logos and Rhetoric ► Memory and Rhetoric ► Pathos and Rhetoric ► Persuasion ► Rhetoric, Argument, and Persuasion ► Rhetoric, Epideictic ► Rhetoric and Ethics ► Rhetoric, European Renaissance ► Rhetoric and Gender ► Rhetoric, Greek ► Rhetoric and Language ► Rhetoric, Medieval ► Rhetoric, Nonverbal ► Rhetoric and Philosophy ► Rhetoric and Poetics ► Rhetorical Studies ► Style and Rhetoric

References and Suggested Readings

Clarke, M. L. (1996). *Rhetoric at Rome: A historical survey* (rev. D. H. Berry), 3rd edn. London: Routledge.
de Jorio, A. (2000). *Gesture in Naples and gesture in classical antiquity* (trans. A. Kendon). Bloomington, IN: Indiana University Press. (Original work published 1832).
Dominik, W., & Hall, J. (eds.) (2007). *Blackwell companion to Roman rhetoric.* Oxford: Blackwell.
Dugan, J. (2007). Modern critical approaches to Roman rhetoric. In W. Dominik & J. Hall (eds.), *Blackwell companion to Roman rhetoric.* Oxford: Blackwell, pp. 9–22.
Fernández López, J. (2007). Quintilian as rhetorician and teacher. In W. Dominik & J. Hall (eds.), *Blackwell companion to Roman rhetoric.* Oxford: Blackwell, pp. 307–322.

Gaines, R. N. (2007). Roman rhetorical handbooks. In W. Dominik & J. Hall (eds.), *Blackwell companion to Roman rhetoric*. Oxford: Blackwell, pp. 163–180.

Gleason, M. W. (1995). *Making men: Sophists and self-presentation in ancient Rome*. Princeton, NJ: Princeton University Press.

Habinek, T. (2005). *Ancient rhetoric and oratory*. Oxford: Blackwell.

Hall, J. (2004). Cicero and Quintilian on the oratorical use of hand gestures. *Classical Quarterly*, 54, 143–160.

Hall, J. (2007). Oratorical delivery and the emotions: Theory and practice. In W. Dominik & J. Hall (eds.), *Blackwell companion to Roman rhetoric*. Oxford: Blackwell, pp. 218–234.

Kendon, A. (1986). Some reasons for studying gesture. *Semiotica*, 62, 3–28.

Kennedy, G. (1972). *The art of rhetoric in the Roman world 300 BC–AD 300*. Princeton, NJ: Princeton University Press.

Lausberg, H. (1998). *Handbook of literary rhetoric: A foundation for literary study* (trans. M. Bliss, A. Jansen, & D. Orton; eds. D. Orton & R. D. Anderson). Leiden: Brill.

May, J. M., & Wisse, J. (2001). *Cicero on the ideal orator (De Oratore)*. Oxford: Oxford University Press.

Pernot, L. (2005). *Rhetoric in antiquity* (trans. W. Higgins). Washington, DC: Catholic University of America.

Rabbie, E. (2007). Wit and humor in Roman rhetoric. In W. Dominik & J. Hall (eds.), *Blackwell companion to Roman rhetoric*. Oxford: Blackwell, pp. 207–217.

Richlin, A. (1997). Gender and rhetoric: Producing manhood in the schools. In W. J. Dominik (ed.), *Roman eloquence: Rhetoric in society and literature*. London: Routledge, pp. 90–110.

Vickers, B. (1988). *In defence of rhetoric*. Oxford: Clarendon.

Ward, J. O. (2007). Roman rhetoric and its afterlife. In W. Dominik & J. Hall (eds.), *Blackwell companion to Roman rhetoric*. Oxford: Blackwell, pp. 254–266.

Wisse, J. (1989). *Ethos and pathos from Aristotle to Cicero*. Amsterdam: Hakkert.

Wisse, J. (2002). The intellectual background of Cicero's rhetorical works. In J. M. May (ed.), *Brill's companion to Cicero: Oratory and rhetoric*. Leiden: Brill, pp. 331–374.

Rhetoric of Science

Alan G. Gross

University of Minnesota

The rhetoric of science is the application of the resources of the rhetorical tradition to the texts, tables, and visuals of the sciences. It is a relatively new form of → rhetorical criticism that began over half a century ago with studies in science policy, shifted in the past quarter century to studies of science itself, and, in the past decade has evolved methodologically from case studies to forms more amenable to wide generalization.

PRECURSORS

Rhetoric of science begins with studies of science policy, an area that involves deliberative issues that fall readily within the traditional concerns of those trained in rhetorical analysis. Nevertheless, so strong was the traditional focus of the emerging discipline of speech on political oratory that the first rhetorical analysis of science policy was not made until 1953 (→ Rhetorical Studies; Speech Communication, History of). In this study, Richard Weaver is concerned with an early climax in a continuing conflict in American public education, the place of evolution in the public-school biology curriculum. The focus of Weaver's study is the Scopes trial. In that trial, he concludes, the prosecution and the defense argued at cross-purposes. The issue at hand was not the law against teaching evolution, but the legality of Scopes's conduct under the law. Given this issue, the scientific testimony in favor of evolution was irrelevant. Indeed, even in the legislature the question was not the truth of evolution but the right of the state to exclude from the curriculum what was, for the people of Tennessee, academic knowledge perhaps, but religious heresy certainly. This area of rhetoric of science has not remained dormant; it has been pursued, for example, by Jeanne Fahnestock, Alan Gross, John Lyne, Carolyn Miller, and Arthur Walzer.

A FIRST GENERATION OF STUDIES: EMERGING RHETORICAL CONSCIOUSNESS

The focus of rhetoricians on science itself rather than science policy, a focus initiated a quarter-century ago, represents a definite break with traditional rhetorical criticism. Among those who have devoted their attention to science itself are Charles Bazerman, Carol Berkenkotter, John Angus Campbell, Jeanne Fahnestock, Alan Gross, Randy Allen Harris, Greg Myers, Jean Dietz Moss, and Larry Prelli. From this group, I select Campbell as representative. In the study of science itself, he is the pioneer. Originally focused on the *Origin of species*, his work has since moved forward and backward in time, forward to Darwin on orchids, backward to Darwin's *Notebooks*. In all of his work, Campbell's message is the same: Darwin is the master rhetorician, willing even to distort and disguise his religious and scientific views if he believes that distortion and disguise will attain conviction on some issue central to evolutionary theory. Indeed, Darwin is a master rhetorician even in his *Notebooks*, whose audience is only Darwin himself. Campbell (1990) shows that these notebooks are a proving-ground for Darwin's theories, tested against the imaginary audience of such important potential objectors as his geological mentor and friend, Charles Lyell. Of the relationship between the *Origin* and the *Notebooks*, there is, Campbell says: "an unbroken continuity . . . From his jotting in his first notebook through the sixth and final edition of the *Origin*, scientific discovery and rhetorical invention, technical and social reason, so effectively unite in Darwin's thought that one can only say that each is an aspect of a single logic of inquiry and presentation" (1990, 86). While this conclusion shies away from implicating rhetoric in the content of science, it clearly asserts its integral relationship to scientific discovery.

In the 1990s, a new climate of opinion emerged, signaled by the linguistic turn in philosophy, exemplified by Ludwig Wittgenstein and John Austin, and popularized in 1979 by Richard Rorty's *Philosophy and the mirror of nature*. Accordingly, it is no accident that the 1980s, which saw the creation of rhetoric of science, also saw a rhetorical consciousness emerge in disciplines unconnected with the rhetorical tradition. Participating in this activity were the literary scholar Wilda Anderson; the economist Deirde (formerly Donald) McCloskey; the anthropologist Emily Martin; the philosophers Marcello Pera, Philip

Kitcher, and Ernan McMullin; the linguists John Swales, M. A. K. Halliday, and Ken Hyland; the historians Bruce Hunt and Evelyn Fox Keller; the sociologists Ricca Edmundson and Richard Harvey Brown; and the library scientists Bryce Allen, Jian Qin, and F. W. Lancaster. For illustration, I selected Allen, Qin, and Lancaster as representative of less radical and McCloskey as representative of more radical claims.

In Allen et al. (1994), the authors trace both the pattern and content of the citations in the *Philosophical Transactions*. The authors also infer from *citation analysis* that the primary medium of scientific communication shifted from books in the seventeenth and eighteenth centuries to journal articles in the nineteenth, and to journal articles, conference proceedings, and technical reports in the twentieth. The authors then trace the shift in scientific productivity from Europe to America, and track the rise of Soviet science. In addition, they follow the eighteenth-century shift in the language of science from Latin to the various vernaculars. In the latter part of the twentieth century, they note a further shift to English as the international language of science. Finally, and perhaps most importantly, by treating citations as rhetorical features, they are able to measure the rate of change of persuasive communities; slow in the seventeenth and eighteenth centuries and rapid in the nineteenth and twentieth. In connection with this trend, they venture a cautious prediction concerning the increased tendency toward obsolescence in scientific publications: "if the present trend continues, the median age of the persuasive community may overtake the time required for review and publication of traditional printed communications media. This would lead to increased pressure to adopt speedier means of formal communication in science" (1994, 304).

In a ground-breaking essay entitled "The rhetoric of scientism," McCloskey (1985) provides an example of her mastery of rhetorical technique. After a plain English summary of Muth's important article, McCloskey gives us parallel columns: in the left, she reproduces key sentences from his article, all written in the "scientistic" patois of economists; in the right, she *turns this patois into plain English*. It is a dazzling performance, demonstrating that nothing of substance is lost in the translation. Next, McCloskey infers that, if nothing of substance is lost, "the appeals to the methods of science are mainly matters of style, arising out of a modernist conversation" (97). Nonetheless, McCloskey avers, Muth *needs* these scientistic trappings: how else is he going to meet the expectations of economists, who would not be persuaded unless an argument is fitted out with appropriate jargon and decked out with appropriate mathematical formulae? In a finale to this fireworks display of rhetorical proficiency, McCloskey compares argument in economics with argument in three apparently disparate fields. Under their respective disciplinary skins, she finds, arguments in paleontology, mathematics, and literary history *parallel* those in economics. No interesting epistemological differences exist.

A SECOND GENERATION: NEW APPROACHES

In an attack on the positions represented by Campbell and McCloskey, Gaonkar (1993) contends that *rhetoric is constitutionally unsuited to the analysis of science*: it makes no sense to turn a system designed to teach oratory in ancient Greece and Rome into a system for the analysis of the texts produced by a social structure as complex as modern science.

Gaonkar's essay represents a reflective moment in which to meditate on the methodological limitations of the first generation of rhetoric of science, limitations that a second generation of scholarship will address: Jeanne Fahnestock, Leah Cecarelli, Celeste Condit, and Alan Gross, Joseph Harmon, and Michael Reidy.

Fahnestock (1999) undermines our comfortable sense that, aside from metaphor, the figures can be safely ignored by rhetorical critics, that the study of such schemes as *antithesis, incrementum, gradatio, antimetabole, ploche,* and *polyptoton* is the preserve only of pedants. She tells us why, while particular figures have been identified in great numbers over the centuries, a definition of figuration has eluded us. Her wide range of examples – from the Bible, from public address, and, most prominently, from science – suggest that the *figures exercise their powers* regardless of subject matter; the wide range of languages that are the origin of these sources – classical Greek, Latin, French, German, and English – suggest that they exercise their powers regardless of language (→ Style and Rhetoric). Most importantly, the attention she pays to the visual as well as the verbal strongly suggests that the figures are not linguistic, but conceptual, in nature, and that, as such, they can serve as a resource for invention and an index of conceptual change. This book also gives the lie to the pessimistic implication that many have drawn from Gaonkar's assertion that the rhetorical tradition lacks the hermeneutic wherewithal adequate to a robust criticism.

Ceccarelli (2001) is also innovative methodologically; she transforms three biological case studies – of Dobzhansky, Schrödinger, and Wilson – into an argument concerning the *effectiveness of interdisciplinary* → *persuasion* in the sciences. In Ceccarelli's view, Dobzhansky convinced geneticists and naturalists that they shared the same object of study; Schrödinger convinced physicists and biologists that their individual perspectives had a contribution to make to the study of the gene; Wilson, on the other hand, failed to persuade either scientists or humanists to embrace his reductionist vision. Ceccarelli thinks she can explain why. In her view, the two successful scientist-authors convince through intelligent rhetorical design that avoids confrontation. Wilson fails to persuade because he refuses the conciliatory gestures that come naturally to Dobzhansky and Schrödinger. Instead of promoting the language of compromise, Wilson gives us metaphors drawn from conquest. Instead of encouraging readings appropriate to each interest group, he clearly signals his intention to reduce the humanities and the sciences to a single material base subject to exceptionless laws.

While Fahnestock and Ceccarelli implicate rhetoric in the constitution of knowledge (→ Rhetoric and Epistemology), two other books – Condit (1999) and Gross et al. (2002) – do not engage epistemic issues. Each is innovative in its combination of rhetorical analysis with methods derived from the social sciences. Condit's intellectual quarry is the public perception of eugenics and genetics. But a successful hunt requires a *grounding in sampling and statistical techniques*: "the backbone of this study . . . consisted of 653 magazine articles drawn from the *Reader's Guide to Periodical Literature* from 1919 to 1995" (1999, 260; → Sampling, Nonrandom; Sampling, Random). The content of these – and of supplemental sources – was coded and analyzed (→ Content Analysis, Quantitative). In following these procedures, Condit is concerned with matters of statistical significance and inter-rater → reliability. But statistical analysis is not the end-point of her task. She also asks what her data mean, a task requiring both critical intelligence and rhetorical analysis. She makes her methodological claim explicit: "all critics can be assisted by → quantitative methodologies when those methodologies are understood as counting tools, embedded in the critical project, rather than as overarching frameworks that constrain critical thought within a hypothesis-testing method. It is possible to use numbers in a postpositivistic fashion" (Condit 1999, 257).

Gross et al. also combine rhetorical analysis with social science methods. Their goal is sweeping: to provide the reader with a *rhetorical history of the scientific article* from its seventeenth-century beginnings to their present. Accordingly, their generalizations are the result of "an analysis of 1,804 short passages for style and 430 whole articles for presentation and argument" selected randomly from three languages, English, French, and German (2002, viii). As with Condit, these texts are subjected both to statistical and rhetorical analysis. Gross et al. (2002) have two additional features of methodological interest: they expand the scope of text to include graphics, the tables, line graphs, photographs, and drawings that are so central to scientific communication and, in their final chapter, they sketch out an evolutionary theory of the rhetorical development of scientific prose and visuals (→ Rhetoric and Visuality).

SEE ALSO: ▶ Content Analysis, Quantitative ▶ Persuasion ▶ Quantitative Methodology ▶ Reliability ▶ Rhetoric and Epistemology ▶ Rhetoric and Visuality ▶ Rhetorical Criticism ▶ Rhetorical Studies ▶ Sampling, Nonrandom ▶ Sampling, Random ▶ Speech Communication, History of ▶ Style and Rhetoric

References and Suggested Readings

Allen, B., Qin, J., & Lancaster, F. W. (1994). Persuasive communities: A longitudinal analysis of references in the *Philosophical Transactions* of the Royal Society, 1666–1990. *Social Studies of Science*, 24, 279–310.

Campbell, J. A. (1990). Scientific discovery and rhetorical invention: The path to Darwin's *Origin*. In H. Simons (ed.), *The rhetorical turn: Invention and persuasion in the conduct of inquiry*. Chicago, IL: University of Chicago Press, pp. 58–90.

Ceccarelli, L. (2001). *Shaping science with rhetoric: The cases of Dobzhansky, Schrödinger, and Wilson*. Chicago, IL: University of Chicago Press.

Condit, C. (1999). *The meanings of the gene: Public debates about human heredity*. Madison, WI: University of Wisconsin Press.

Fahnestock, J. (1999). *Rhetorical figures in science*. New York: Oxford University Press.

Gaonkar, D. P. (1993). The idea of rhetoric in the rhetoric of science. *Southern Communication Journal*, 58, 258–295.

Gross, A. G. (2006). *Starring the text: The place of rhetoric in science studies*. Carbondale: Southern Illinois University Press.

Gross, A. G., Harmon, J. E., & Reidy, M. (2002). *Communicating science: The scientific article from the 17th century to the present*. Oxford: Oxford University Press.

McCloskey, D. N. (1985). The rhetoric of scientism: How John Muth persuades. In *The rhetoric of economics*. Madison, WI: University of Wisconsin Press, pp. 87–112.

Weaver, R. M. (1953). Dialectic and rhetoric at Dayton, Tennessee. In *The ethics of rhetoric*. Chicago, IL: Henry Regnery, pp. 27–54.

Rhetoric of the Second Sophistic

Tim Whitmarsh

Corpus Christi College, University of Oxford

"The Second Sophistic" is the name given by Flavius Philostratus (c. 170–245 CE) in his *Lives of the sophists* (481, 507) to the rhetorical style current in his day. The sophistic culture described by Philostratus involved highly educated members of the Greek elite improvising public declamations, often in the personae of famous figures from Greece's historical or mythological past. The primary emphasis was upon the re-enactment of key moments of military or political significance: most themes were drawn from the times of either imperial Athens (fifth century BCE) or the conquests of Philip and Alexander (fourth century BCE). This historical emphasis was matched at the level of diction, morphology, and style by the revival of the "Attic" dialect used by classical Athenian writers such as Thucydides, Plato, and Demosthenes (→ Rhetoric, Greek).

Modern scholars have taken over the phrase to encompass a number of broader phenomena (Whitmarsh 2005, 6–10). The term was revived in the nineteenth century by Nietzsche's friend Erwin Rohde (1876, 1886), who argued that *die zweite Sophistik* was a primarily linguistic phenomenon promoting Atticism at the expense of "Asianism," supposedly a more melodious style emanating from the Ionian Greek cities. Rohde based his arguments on the claims of an ancient author, Dionysius of Halicarnassus (writing in Rome at the turn of the millennium), who praised Roman conquest for its promotion of the "Attic muse" in response to "the other, who arrived yesterday or the day before from one of the pits of Asia" (*On the ancient orators*, 1). As was seen by the great Prussian scholar Ulrich von Wilamowitz-Möllendorff (1900), however, Dionysius' claims are motivated by the rhetorical (not to say xenophobic) need to promote Rome: there is no real evidence for an Asianist movement.

Wilamowitz-Möllendorff's weighty intervention deterred subsequent generations of scholars, who generally left the field alone, until the 1960s. In a more politically conscious era, Glen Bowersock (1969) turned the focus away from literary content, and onto the historical role of the orators (or "sophists") themselves, which he identified as one of mediation between the Greek elites who were politically dominant in the cities of the eastern Roman Empire and Rome itself. Against Bowersock's Rome-centered view, Ewen Bowie (1970) argued that the Second Sophistic – the term now extended to cover the wider phenomenon of the literary archaism practiced in most Greek literary composition in the first three centuries CE – was primarily a vehicle for the preservation of Greek cultural values in the face of Roman domination. This interest in relations between Greece and Rome was spurred on, from the 1990s onward, by → postcolonial theory: thus, for example, Simon Swain (1996) extends Bowie's ideas into a broad theory of Greek resistance to Roman occupation, and Tim Whitmarsh (2001) argues that Roman conquest forced Greeks to rethink their ways of understanding the nature of identity. The diverse range of interpretations can be sampled in a number of collections of essays (especially Goldhill 2001; Konstan & Saïd 2006).

While many use "the Second Sophistic" as a convenient label for Roman–Greek imperial literary production in general, the narrower phenomenon described by Philostratus has also received considerable attention. As a form of rarefied competition for elite status, sophistry was an important means of consolidating class hierarchies while allowing for a limited amount of mobility. Thomas Schmitz (1997) has helpfully cross-applied Pierre Bourdieu's theories of social distinction, built on the analysis of modern European educational structures. Bourdieu's ideas have also been used, along with those of the anthropologist Michael Herzfeld, by Maud Gleason (1995), who emphasizes the importance of sophistry as a forum for constructing and debating masculinity (→ Rhetoric and Gender). The self-conscious role-playing so central to the Second Sophistic (in the narrower sense) does indeed lend itself readily to discussion in terms of social constructionism, built around the idea of identity as performed rather than essentially inherent (→ Constructivism; Identities and Discourse). Such approaches have been further cultivated by postmodern interest in performativity and mimicry (e.g., Connolly 2001; Whitmarsh 2005; Webb 2006; → Postmodernism and Communication; Rhetoric, Postmodern).

SEE ALSO: ▶ Constructivism ▶ Identities and Discourse ▶ Postcolonial Theory ▶ Postmodernism and Communication ▶ Rhetoric and Gender ▶ Rhetoric, Greek ▶ Rhetoric, Postmodern ▶ Rhetoric, Roman

References and Suggested Readings

Bowersock, G. W. (1969). *Greek sophists in the Roman Empire*. Oxford: Oxford University Press.

Bowie, E. L. (1970). The Greeks and their past in the Second Sophistic. *Past and Present*, 46, 3–41.

Connolly, J. (2001). Reclaiming the theatrical in the second sophistic. *Helios*, 28, 75–96.

Gleason, M. (1995). *Making men: Sophists and self-presentation in ancient Rome*. Princeton, NJ: Princeton University Press.

Goldhill, S. D. (ed.) (2001). *Being Greek under Rome: The Second Sophistic, cultural conflict and the development of the Roman Empire*. Cambridge: Cambridge University Press.

Konstan, D., & Saïd, S. (eds.) (2006). *Greeks on Greekness: Viewing the Greek past under the Roman Empire*. Cambridge: Cambridge Philological Society.

Rohde, E. (1876). *Der griechische Roman und seine Vorläufer*. Leipzig: Breitkopf und Hartel.

Rohde, E. (1886). Die asianische Rhetorik und die zweite Sophistik. *Rheinisches Museum*, 41, 170–190.

Schmitz, T. (1997). *Bildung und Macht: Zur sozialen und politischen Funktion der zweiten Sophistik in der griechischen Welt der Kaiserzeit*. Munich: Beck.

Swain, S. (1996). *Hellenism and empire: Language, classicism, and power in the Greek world, AD 50–250*. Oxford: Oxford University Press.

Webb, R. (2006). Fiction, *mimesis* and the performance of the past in the Second Sophistic. In D. Konstan & S. Saïd (eds.), *Greeks on Greekness: Viewing the Greek past under the Roman Empire*. Cambridge: Cambridge Philological Society, pp. 27–46.

Wilamowitz-Möllendorff, U. von (1900). Asianismus und Atticismus. *Hermes*, 35, 1–52.

Whitmarsh, T. (2001). *Greek literature and the Roman Empire: The politics of imitation*. Oxford: Oxford University Press.

Whitmarsh, T. (2005). *The second sophistic*. Oxford: Oxford University Press.

Rhetoric and Semiotics

John Lyne

University of Pittsburgh

Semiotics is the study of → signs and signification, including both linguistic and non-linguistic signs (→ Linguistics; Semiotics; Sign Systems). The American philosopher Charles Sanders Peirce (1839–1914), who coined the term and did innovative work in the area, regarded it as the study of that which supports inferences; that is to say, of how signs enable interpretive inference to other signs. Peirce held that all we know or experience comes to us through the mediation of signs. He did not hold that all signification is solely the product of social convention or of language proper, maintaining that signs serve as tools for scientific investigation as well as for the exploration of human creations (→ Language and Social Interaction). One consequence of this view is that all inquiry is semiotic inquiry. Another lineage of semiotics, usually designated by the term "semiology," grows out of a tradition of European → structuralism traced back to the Swiss linguist Ferdinand de Saussure, and carried forward by such writers as → Roland Barthes, Roman Jakobson, and the anthropologist Claude Lévi-Strauss. In this tradition, emphasis is placed on the social structuring of meaning and the rendering of cultural forms as texts. In contrast to Peirce, this tradition places emphasis on the arbitrariness of signs and on binary structures of meaning.

Umberto Eco has helped to bridge the gap between the two traditions, perhaps with incomplete success, by bringing the Peircean approach (and the term "semiotics") into a common theoretical frame with semiology. Like Peirce, he emphasizes the triadic structure of signs; and like Barthes, he accesses discursive domains through → codes. Codes make signs intelligible in linguistic communication, visual information, emotional expressions, color schemes, scientific discourse, social rituals, literary → genres, and so on (→ Visual Communication). There is some debate about whether the Peircean logic of signification can be explained as functioning purely as social conventions. To hold so would appear to put one at odds with a central feature of the Peircean theory, that is, the belief that as-yet unconventionalized signs break in unexpectedly, challenging established semiotic conventions from without, a feature especially important to scientific inquiry. Similarly, there are different understandings of whether Peirce's idea of "infinite semiosis" should be read against the grain of his professed → realism. Peirce saw movement toward the fixing of belief as a matter of acquiring interpretive habits within communities; but these habits had to accommodate the recalcitrance that creates doubt and requires new interpretations. This process may go on indefinitely, so long as the opinion of the community of inquiry remains unsettled.

In a general sense, much of the rhetorical tradition can be understood as defining a semiotic practice, not just in respect to the study of tropes and figures, but in respect to how inferences are produced, on the scaffolding of signs, in the minds of audiences and observers (→ Rhetorical Studies). This would also encompass rhetorical invention, which aligns rather well with Peirce's treatment of abduction. Semiotics was attractive to early film theorists, who were seeking vocabularies and tools for discussing the visual, linguistic, musical, and image editing occurring in films (→ Film Theory). It was also used as a strategy for reading a wide variety of social signifiers, from clothing fashion to the subject positions constituted within semiotic practices. The idea of "codes," along with Peirce's terms, "icon," "index," and "symbol," found their way into common usage in books on rhetoric and communication. During the heyday of structural semiotics in the 1980s and 1990s, Peirce's philosophical realism may have made his approach less attractive to those rhetorical theorists and critics who shared widely held assumptions about the social construction of reality (→ Constructivism). As theories of structural semiology have become less fashionable, perhaps a space has been cleared for the largely untaken Peircean option. Apart from some theoretical work dealing with Peirce's "speculative rhetoric" and some theoretical preparation of the ground for a Peircean approach to rhetoric, there has been little work in rhetorical criticism that takes the explicitly semiotic approach.

On the expansive view of semiotics, found in such writers as Eco and Julia Kristeva, "implicit" semiotic theories can be found in writings stretching from the pre-Socratics to Freud and picking up much in between, reminiscent of the expansive view of rhetoric that invites appropriation of figures such as → Habermas and Foucault as "implicit" theorists of rhetoric. One way to draw the distinction between rhetoric and semiotics is to say that semiotics is largely concerned with mapping out the codes, patterns, and conventions of signification, whereas rhetoric is concerned with how such codes, patterns, and conventions can be put to use in the processes of → persuasion, → identification, and articulation. This is a rough distinction, but it has the virtue of emphasizing the performative, addressive, and pragmatic aspects of the rhetorical tradition, while acknowledging that rhetoric takes flight only on the wings of signification.

SEE ALSO: ▶ Barthes, Roland ▶ Code ▶ Constructivism ▶ Film Theory ▶ Genre ▶ Habermas, Jürgen ▶ Identification ▶ Language and Social Interaction ▶ Linguistics ▶ Persuasion ▶ Pragmatism ▶ Realism ▶ Rhetorical Studies ▶ Semiotics ▶ Sign ▶ Sign Systems ▶ Structuralism ▶ Visual Communication

References and Suggested Readings

Barthes, R. (1957). *Mythologies*. Paris: Seuil.
Barthes, R. (1974). *S/Z* (trans. R. Miller). New York: Hill and Wang.
Barthes, R. (1993). *Image – music – text: Essays* (trans. S. Heath). London: Fontana.
Eco, U. (1976). *A theory of semiotics*. Bloomington, IN: Indiana University Press.
Eco, U. (1983). *Semiotics and the philosophy of language*. Bloomington, IN: Indiana University Press.
Eco, U. (1990). *The limits of interpretation*. Bloomington, IN: Indiana University Press.
Eco, U. (1999). *Kant and the platypus: Essays on language and cognition* (trans. A. McEwen). London: Secker and Warburg.
Jakobson, R., & Halle, M. (1956). *Fundamentals of language*. The Hague: Mouton.
Kristeva, J. (1984). *The revolution in poetic language*. New York: Columbia University Press.
Lévi-Strauss, C. (1978). *Myth and meaning*. London: Routledge and Kegan Paul.
Lyne, J. (1980). Rhetoric and semiotic in C. S. Peirce. *Quarterly Journal of Speech*, 66, 155–168.
Nesher, D. (2002). *On truth and the representation of reality: A collection of inquiries from a pragmatist point of view*. Lanham, MD: University Press of America.

Peirce, C. S. (1998). *Collected papers of Charles Sanders Peirce* (ed. C. Hartshorne & P. Weiss), vol. 5. Bristol: Thommes.

Saussure, F. de. (2006). *Writings in general linguistics.* Oxford: Oxford University Press.

Stam, R., & Miller, T. (2000). *Film and theory: An anthology.* Malden, MA: Blackwell.

Wiley, N. (1995). *The semiotic self.* Chicago, IL: University of Chicago Press.

Rhetoric and Social Protest

Charles J. Stewart

Purdue University

Research in rhetoric and social protest strives to discover how organized, uninstitutional forces use symbols and symbolic actions to promote or resist change in societal norms and values. Its focus ranges from interpersonal to mass communication, from the colonial period to the present, from moderate to radical elements, and from formal discourses to the rhetoric of the streets.

Until the latter half of the twentieth century, research in the rhetoric of social protest lay dormant in the field of communication, while rhetorical scholars pursued traditional studies of great men speaking well in times of crisis (→ Rhetorical Studies). However, studies of protest rhetoric developed rapidly in the late 1960s with the rise of the civil rights movement in the US, threats of confrontational "black power" advocates, and widespread protests opposing the war in Vietnam (→ Civil Rights Movement and the Media). Rhetorical scholars could no longer ignore threatening protestors, who were in their streets, on their campuses, and in their classrooms. Researchers, at first, viewed conflict and confrontation with its attendant strident rhetoric as problems to be avoided or resolved through reasoning and locating common ground (→ Conflict Resolution; Social Conflict and Communication). Problems (controversies rather than conflicts) were perceived as communication breakdowns or failures to communicate.

THEORETICAL CONCEPTS

Simons (1972) was the first to challenge the "establishment bias" of rhetorical studies of social protest. He and others argued that while many questioned the rhetorical strategies and tactics of social protest, the protestors themselves faced nearly impossible rhetorical situations in which they were viewed as illegitimate, systematically denied access to normal channels and procedures, had virtually no powers of reward and punishment, and enjoyed neither legislative nor enforcement powers. Simons argued that methods of influence appropriate for "drawing room controversies" were ineffective in resolving conflicts in which neither party was willing or able to compromise. Confrontations were inevitable because they were clashes in which one party's relative gain was the other's relative loss. Simons described the essential nature of protest rhetoric as "coercive persuasion" designed to make institutions pay attention, address issues, and consider change. Both Simons and Burgess (1973) claimed that coercive persuasion was inherently rhetorical because protestors had to persuade target audiences that dire consequences were likely, if not certain, before they would feel forced to comply, and that audiences must become convinced of the coercer's probable capacity and intent to follow through with the threatened action.

When scholars began to study social protest rhetoric in earnest, doubts arose about the theoretical bases of such studies. After studying US president Johnson's "war on poverty" as three establishment movements, Zarefsky (1977) questioned whether the life cycle and strategies being attributed to the rhetoric of social movements were unique to social protest or common to most campaigns and movements. He claimed that Johnson's war on poverty followed the same cycle and employed the same strategies scholars claimed to be unique to non-establishment movements. McGee (1980) argued that the notion of a social movement was more → "meaning" than "phenomenon" and concluded that the study of social movements, and therefore social protest, might become a theory of human consciousness but not a rhetorical theory.

Lucas (1980) challenged these criticisms by claiming that the roles of rhetoric in social protest could not be understood by merely looking at the formal properties of protest discourse or by applying self-evident propositions to the role of rhetoric in constructing social reality, but only by carefully analyzing the interaction of discourses with other social and situational factors that influence the process of protest rhetoric within social movements. Simons (1980) took a similar position, noting that strategies and life cycle were not the definitive characteristics of social movements. He traced situational theory to classical Greek rhetorical theory and identified common situational factors with which protestors must contend in their efforts to bring about or resist change (→ Rhetoric, Greek). These factors made their rhetorical efforts unique, set them apart from establishment movements, and made them worthy of study. The emphasis on unique situational variables and the interaction of situational forces has significantly influenced the study of social protest rhetoric since the early 1980s.

RHETORIC AND SOCIAL CONFLICT

Rhetorical scholars have claimed that confrontational strategies in social protest are not only inevitable but essential to successful outcomes. Cathcart (1978) claimed that protestors must use such strategies to produce a *dialectical tension growing out of moral conflict* that provokes a clash with institutions and institutional leaders. The struggle becomes a moral battle for power and legitimacy to define and control the social order. To attain legitimacy in this moral struggle, protestors must strip institutions and their leaders of legitimacy by provoking confrontations that show how ugly institutions really are. The need to create this dialectical tension explains the use of symbolic actions and language strategies (vilification, obscenity, scapegoating, and polarization) to provoke repressive and sometimes violent reactions by institutional agents and agencies.

Researchers have also argued that conflict and controversy should not be avoided or stifled because both are critical to the development and improvement of society. Griffin (1969) employed the theories of Kenneth Burke when writing that to study social protests is to study strivings for salvation, perfection, and progress, rather than efforts to disrupt, do harm, or destroy. Stewart et al. (2007) have advocated an interpretive systems approach that sees the potential of conflict to create opportunities for societal growth and progress, adaptation and evolution. These notions have led to studies aimed at understanding the rationales and purposes of extremist rhetoric, violence, riots, terrorism, and disruptive acts such as sit-ins and boycotts.

Since confrontations inherently involve two or more adversaries, researchers have studied the rhetorical strategies and tactics of institutions and counter-movements – a rhetoric of control – created to resist or stifle protest rhetoric in moral struggles for right and wrong, good and evil (Bowers et al. 1993). They have studied institutional efforts to control language, media, channels, information, expertise, and agendas, and strategies such as evasion, counterpersuasion (framing issues, enhancing fear appeals, challenging motives, denigrating the opposition), coercive persuasion (expulsion, restrictive laws, harassment, arrests), and adjustment. Some researchers have focused on the internal conflicts among individuals and groups fighting for essentially the same causes, including competing labor unions and moderate to radical organizations struggling for women's rights, to preserve the environment, or to protect animals.

FUNCTIONAL APPROACHES

Studies from the 1950s to the 1990s often focused on the life cycle of social movements, many based on the research of sociologists and social psychologists. While usually avoiding the notion that social protest follows a linear life cycle, moving inevitably from one stage to another, researchers have attempted to discover recurring and changing rhetorical purposes, strategies, and ever-changing relationships. Recent efforts have focused on similarities and differences between first, second, and third wave feminism and environmentalism and how the perspectives of protestors are shaped and changed over time, for example, in the gay liberation and civil rights movements (Darsey 1991; Stewart 1997).

Rhetorical researchers have also conducted *leader-centered studies*. Simons' (1970) classic essay has had profound effects on the study of protest rhetoric. He identified the requirements, problems, and dilemmas leaders must resolve through rhetorical strategies, and concluded that, while protestors are denied the controls enjoyed by institutional leaders and are harassed from outside, they must perform the same functions while trying to adapt to the external system (→ Leadership in Organizations). Leaders of social protests must continually balance inherently conflicting demands on their positions and organizations. Stewart et al. (2007) studied the roles of protest leaders (organizers, decision-makers, and symbols), fundamental leadership characteristics based on Max Weber's work (charisma, prophecy, and pragmatism), and how they sustain their leadership. Other researchers have focused on the rhetoric of individual leaders, including their use of narratives, the jeremiad, a feminine style, dialectic, argument from transcendence, perspective by incongruity, and framing. They have analyzed efforts to adapt to generic and situational constraints and to use what they have, including family, position, personal sufferings, and personal testimony.

Theorists have long advocated a functional approach to understanding social protest rhetoric and to *constructing generalizations* that apply to past and future protest activities

($\rightarrow$ Functional Analysis; Generalizability). This approach sees rhetoric as the agency through which protestors perform necessary functions (indispensable processes) that enable organized efforts to come into existence, to meet oppositions, and perhaps to succeed in bringing about or resisting change (Stewart 1980). Researchers have developed schemes of functions and identified which might be most prevalent during differing phases of social protest. Simons (1970) identified three general functions or requirements: attracting, maintaining and molding believers into effective organizations; securing adoption of their ideology by established institutions; and reacting to resistance from within and without. Stewart et al. (2007) have identified six critical functions: transforming perceptions of social reality, altering self-perceptions, legitimizing the protest effort, prescribing courses of action, mobilizing for action, and sustaining the effort. Gregg's (1971) early functional study of ego enhancement has had major impact on research in social protest. He claimed that protest rhetoric was primarily self-directed because protestors must recognize and proclaim to self and others that their ego had been ignored or harmed to the point of disenfranchisement.

Many researchers have studied the *channels protestors have used* to transmit messages to believers, nonbelievers, and the opposition and to sustain their efforts. Such studies include artillery election sermons as a prelude to the American fight for independence, pamphleteering of anti-British colonialists, the radio addresses of the Rev. Charles Coughlin in the 1930s, the eulogies of Cesar Chavez, television coverage of feminism's Strike for Equality, and video documentaries opposing abortion. Several studies addressed the rhetorical characteristics, purposes, strategies, and impact of the Rev. Martin Luther King, Jr's "Letter from Birmingham Jail." Other research has focused on songs, slogans, the Internet, autobiographies, and memorials that recruit, celebrate, and recall past struggles to bring about change and equality and to sustain the struggles and gains of past protestors.

SEE ALSO: ▶ Civil Rights Movement and the Media ▶ Conflict Resolution ▶ Crisis Communication ▶ Functional Analysis ▶ Generalizability ▶ Leadership in Organizations ▶ Meaning ▶ Rhetoric and Class ▶ Rhetoric and Gender ▶ Rhetoric, Greek ▶ Rhetoric in North America: United States ▶ Rhetoric and Race ▶ Rhetorical Studies ▶ Social Conflict and Communication ▶ Social Movements and Communication ▶ Women's Movement and the Media

References and Suggested Readings

Bowers, J., Ochs, D., & Jensen, R. (1993). *The rhetoric of agitation and control*. Prospect Heights, IL: Waveland.

Burgess, P. (1973). Crisis rhetoric: Coercion vs force. *Quarterly Journal of Speech*, 59, 61–73.

Cathcart, R. (1978). Movements: Confrontation as rhetorical form. *Southern Speech Communication Journal*, 43, 233–247.

Darsey, J. (1991). From "gay is good" to the scourge of AIDS: The evolution of gay liberation rhetoric: 1977–1990. *Communication Studies*, 42, 43–66.

Gregg, R. (1971). The ego-function of the rhetoric of protest. *Philosophy and Rhetoric*, 4, 71–91.

Griffin, L. (1969). A dramatistic theory of the rhetoric of movements. In W. Rueckert (ed.), *Critical responses to Kenneth Burke*. Minneapolis, MN: University of Minnesota Press, pp. 456–478.

Lucas, S. (1980). Coming to terms with movement studies. *Central States Speech Journal*, 31, 255–266.

McGee, M. (1980). Social movement: Phenomenon or meaning. *Central States Speech Journal*, 31, 233–244.

Morris, C., & Browne, S. (eds.) (2006). *Readings on the rhetoric of social protest*. State College, PA: Strata.

Simons, H. (1970). Requirements, problems, and strategies: A theory of persuasion for social movements. *Quarterly Journal of Speech*, 56, 1–11.

Simons, H. (1972). Persuasion in social conflicts: A critique of prevailing conceptions and a framework for future research. *Speech Monographs*, 39, 227–247.

Simons, H. (1980). On terms, definitions and theoretical distinctiveness: Comments on papers by McGee and Zarefsky. *Central States Speech Journal*, 31, 306–315.

Simons, H., Mechling, E., & Schreier, H. (1984). Functions of communication in mobilizing for action from the bottom up: The rhetoric of social movements. In C. Arnold & J. Bowers (eds.), *Handbook on rhetorical and communication theory*. Boston, MA: Allyn and Bacon, pp. 792–867.

Stewart, C. (1980). A functional approach to the rhetoric of social movements. *Central States Speech Journal*, 31, 298–305.

Stewart, C. (1997). The evolution of a revolution: Stokely Carmichael and the rhetoric of black power. *Quarterly Journal of Speech*, 83, 429–446.

Stewart, C., Smith, C. A., & Denton, R. (2007). *Persuasion and social movements*, 5th edn. Long Grove, IL: Waveland.

Zarefsky, D. (1977). President Johnson's war on poverty: The rhetoric of three "establishment" movements. *Communication Monographs*, 44, 352–373.

Zarefsky, D. (1980). A skeptical view of social movements. *Central States Speech Journal*, 31, 245–254.

Rhetoric and Social Thought

Maurice Charland

Concordia University

Aristotle defines rhetoric as the art of determining the available means of persuasion in a particular case. This can be interpreted in a number of ways. When considered narrowly, the study of rhetoric can be equated with the psychology of → persuasion or with informal logic. However, when that definition is read along with the rest of the *Rhetoric*, as well as the *Ethics* and the *Politics*, and in the context of the rhetorical instruction given by the Sophists and Isocrates, rhetoric is better understood as the theory and practice of civic → discourse (→ Rhetoric, Greek).

This civic orientation is, at least among American scholars working in communication departments, usually associated with the study of political oratory, or what is called public address (→ Rhetoric and History; Rhetoric and Politics). While studies of public address in the early to mid-twentieth century were often primarily descriptive or appreciative, the last three decades of that century saw the development of a systematic attempt to link rhetorical theory and the study of public address to the literature on political and social theory. This was anticipated in the work of Kenneth Burke, which was heavily influenced by Marx and Freud, in books such as *Counter-statement* (1931), *A grammar of motives* (1945), and *A rhetoric of motives* (1950). Burke offered a philosophically rich account of the political and social implications of the human use of symbols. Rhetoric and social theory developed in the context of the "linguistic turn," the resurgence of French and German social philosophy, and the consolidation of → cultural studies in the humanities (→ Rhetoric and Philosophy). Rather than focusing on the artfulness or effect of particular speeches, rhetoric and social theory sought to identify the role that public discourse plays in social, cultural, and political processes (→ Rhetorics: New Rhetorics).

As a project, rhetoric and social theory has three trajectories. The first trajectory is *analytic and descriptive*, and directed toward properly identifying the manner in which public discourse mediates the development of politics and culture (→ Culture: Definitions and Concepts). The second trajectory is *critical*, and aims to identify the systematic distortions, biases, or interests produced or served by public discourse. These first two trajectories, when linked to a discussion of power, are often subsumed under the category of "critical rhetoric," a term coined by Raymie McKerrow (1989). Finally, the third trajectory is to *contribute to normative political philosophy* by developing norms for democratic public communication.

The most influential American rhetorical scholars in the development of rhetoric and social theory in the late twentieth century include Michael Calvin McGee and Thomas B. Farrell, both because of their authorship of heavily cited essays in the *Quarterly Journal of Speech*, and because of their formative effect on doctoral students at the University of Iowa and Northwestern University, respectively. While they did not collaborate and their work is in many respects incompatible, it in large measure defined the boundaries of work that would follow. McGee, an anti-foundationalist, argued that rhetoric rather than philosophy was the source of political values such as "liberty" and "equality." His work thus emphasized rhetoric's ontological power. Farrell, a neo-Aristotelean, looked to Aristotle's *Rhetoric* to develop an alternative to normative models of democratic communication developed by German political philosopher → Jürgen Habermas, the best-known heir to the "Frankfurt School" of → critical theory. Farrell, as such, emphasized rhetoric's power to create social knowledge.

The rhetoric and social theory project was in large part successful, in that contemporary rhetorical studies is written in the context of and responds to German critical theory, cultural studies, feminism, poststructualism, and postmodernism (→ Feminist and Gender Studies; Postmodernism and Communication; Rhetoric, Postmodern).

SEE ALSO: ▶ Critical Theory ▶ Cultural Studies ▶ Culture: Definitions and Concepts ▶ Discourse ▶ Feminist and Gender Studies ▶ Habermas, Jürgen ▶ Persuasion ▶ Postmodernism and Communication ▶ Rhetoric, Greek ▶ Rhetoric and History ▶ Rhetoric and Philosophy ▶ Rhetoric and Politics ▶ Rhetoric, Postmodern ▶ Rhetorics: New Rhetorics

References and Suggested Readings

Burke, K. (1931). *Counter-statement*. New York: Harcourt.
Burke, K. (1945). *A grammar of motives*. New York: Prentice Hall.

Burke, K. (1950). *A rhetoric of motives*. New York: Prentice Hall.
Farrell, T. B. (1976). Knowledge, consensus, and rhetorical theory. *Quarterly Journal of Speech*, 62, 1–14.
McGee, M. C. (1980). The "ideograph": A link between rhetoric and ideology. *Quarterly Journal of Speech*, 64, 1–16.
McKerrow, R. E. (1989). Critical rhetoric: Theory and praxis. *Communication Monographs*, 56, 91–111.

Rhetoric in South Asia

Amitava Chakraborty

University of Delhi

South Asia usually refers to the geo-cultural area traditionally known as the Indian subcontinent and consists of contemporary Afghanistan, Bangladesh, Bhutan, India, Nepal, Pakistan, Sri Lanka, Tibet, and the Maldives. The region has a rich tradition of conceptualization of the arts of argumentation, oration, and literary embellishment, marked by a flair for categorizing even the subtlest features.

In ancient India, the understanding of various forms of rhetoric practice was necessitated by cultural practices, including public deliberations in Vedic assemblies and post-Vedic republics, urban leisure cultures' adulation of oratory (*vacanam*) and the aesthetic, the tradition of public debates to establish and defend academic and religious thoughts, and well-organized judicial and political systems (→ Rhetorical Studies).

Comprehensive theorizations of scholarly argumentation were reached at in logic (*Nyāya*) and other disciplines (→ Argumentative Discourse; Rhetoric, Argument, and Persuasion). Caraka (400 BCE), in his treatise on medicine, classifies debate into two types: friendly discussion between two scholars (*Sandhāya sambhāṣā*) and argumentation of two hostile scholars (*Vigraha*). Gautama (c. 200 CE), the founder of *Nyāya*, however, classifies argumentation (*Kathā*) into three categories: discussion for truth without fear of losing (*Vāda*), a debate where the debater censures the opponent's thesis without establishing any counter-position (*Vitaṇḍā*), and debate for victory without care for the truth (*Jalpa*). Sanatni (c. 1000 CE) denies *Vitaṇḍā* any independent existence; Dharmakirti rejects all forms of debate except the *Vāda*. Gautama categorizes quibble (*Chala*) and false parity of reasoning (*Jāti*), the tricks used for victory in lieu of fair argumentation, and sub-varieties of these features. Gautama also identifies 22 categories of censuring a debate (*Nigrahasthāna*). Caraka and Maitreya (400 CE) prescribed some context-sensitive nonverbal strategies for public argumentation.

Emperor Ashoka (200 CE) proclaimed mutual tolerance, restraint of speech, and respect for the truth in each system as the basic principles of religious argumentation. Mughal Emperor Akbar (1500–1600 BCE) conceptualized "the path of reason" (*Rah-I-Akl*) as the guiding principle of interreligious dialogue.

Judicial argumentation was discussed in *Dharmaśāstras*, the Hindu treatises on law (200 BCE onwards), and *Arthaśāstra*, a treatise on polity by Kautilya (300 BCE). As testimonies were accorded importance, more than even divine tests, technical discussion on forms, qualities, and defects of legal argumentations (*Vāda*) are aplenty. Concise, relevant, reasonable, unambiguous, capable of proof, understandable without an explanation, consistent, and nonfigurative submissions (*Vākya*) are considered as ideal.

Arthaśāstra discusses the political rhetoric (→ Rhetoric and Politics). Persuasive verbal strategies used by spies and the composition of royal writs were discussed by Kautilya. He categorizes the qualities of royal writs as arrangement of the content (*arthakarma*), relevance (*samvandha*), completeness (*paripurnatā*), sweetness (*mādhurya*), dignity (*audārya*), and lucidity (*spastatva*).

Caraka, Kautilya, and Sushruta detailed a comprehensive system of technical textual composition (*Tantra-yukti*) having more than 30 clearly explained and categorized stylistic and logical devices (*Tantra*), including content (*vidhāna*), quotation (*apadeśa*), doubt (*samasyā*), derivation (*nirvacana*), and exception (*apavarga*) (→ Invention and Rhetoric; Style and Rhetoric).

Sanskrit aestheticians' endeavors in understanding the sources of literary persuasiveness focused on rhetoric figures. Bharata (c. 200 BCE), in *Nātyaśāstra*, the most ancient available treatise on poetics, identifies four literary figures –*Upamā*, *Rūpaka*, *Dīpaka*, and *Yamaka* (simile, metaphor, zeugma, and homophony). Later theoreticians' insistence on categorizing finer differences of rhetoric strategies proliferated figures and sub-figures. With the contributions of generations of scholars through the centuries, the number of figures had risen to 136 by the thirteenth century (in Appayadikshita's *Chitramimāṃsā*). However, the search for broader categories to understand the general ornamentality of literary writings also led to the concepts of *Soundrya* (beauty) and *Vakratva* (deviance) being propounded as defining categories of literary writings (→ Rhetoric and Poetics).

Aestheticians of other languages of the region also show comparable engagement with literary rhetoric. Though ancient Tamil aestheticians did not invest in subtle details, the *Tolka:ppiyam*, the earliest available Tamil treatise on poetics (c. 100 BCE), recognizes simile (*Uvamam* or *Uvamai*) as the most important literary technique and dedicates one full chapter to the subject. *Siyabaslakara* (c. 900 CE), the oldest prose work in Sinhalese, the Sri Lankan language, is a treatise on rhetoric. Other important works like *Dandyālaṃkara sama* and *Siyabās Lakuṇa* (c. 1200–1300 CE) continue the engagement. These works in general share close affinity with Sanskrit aestheticians' understanding of rhetoric, *Dandyālaṃkara sama* being itself a commentary on Dandi's work, the *Kāvyādarśa*.

With the spread of Muslim education during the medieval period, classical Arabic and Persian thinking became, and continued to be, an indispensable part of the south Asian knowledge system (→ Communication Modes, Muslim). Though some insights are offered on the art of oratory, as in the *Bayān-wa-al-Tabyīn* of Jahiz, classical Arabic and Persian thinking accords much importance to rhetorical aspects of literary works. Led by scholars like Al-Mubarad, Ibn-al-Mutaz, Qudama-bin-Jafar, Rashid al-Din Vatvat, Qays al-Razi, and Sad al-Din Taftazani, the tradition offers multidimensional understanding of the nature and categories of rhetoric figures and composition styles.

During the past two centuries, elements of western rhetoric have been incorporated into the south Asian knowledge system. However, the idea of rhetoric as a discipline covering areas other than literary figures has failed to gain circulation. In the west, Oliver (1971) and Kennedy (1998) have offered brief introductions to rhetorical practices of ancient India within a comparative framework. Though constrained by lack of access to important primary sources, these works take into account various areas of rhetorical practices other than the literary. In south Asia, however, non-innovative exposition of classical rhetoric figures in contemporary literary contexts has become predominant with a few comparative and interactive exceptions. Chakraborty (1988) offers valuable insights on possible interaction between western and Sanskrit rhetoric figures by identifying examples of western figures like asyndeton, anticlimax, etc. in contemporary Bengali literature and simultaneously noting how the finer peculiarities of various types of comparison-based rhetoric practices of the western literatures, overlooked by the western system, can be effectively categorized under the Sanskrit figures. Karickam (1999) provides a comprehensive comparative analysis of the Indian (Dravidian and Sanskrit) and western rhetoric figures, preparing the base for further interactivity.

SEE ALSO: ▶ Argumentative Discourse ▶ Communication Modes, Muslim ▶ Invention and Rhetoric ▶ Rhetoric, Argument, and Persuasion ▶ Rhetoric in the Middle East ▶ Rhetoric and Poetics ▶ Rhetoric and Politics ▶ Rhetorical Studies ▶ Style and Rhetoric

References and Suggested Readings

Chakraborty, S. (1988). *Alamkārchandrikā* [Treatise on rhetoric]. Kolkata: Kritanjali.
Karickam, A. (1999). *Rhetoric figures: Indian and western tradition*. Kerala: Comparative Literature Research and Study Center.
Kennedy, G. A. (1998). *Comparative rhetoric: An historical and cross-cultural introduction*. New York: Oxford University Press.
Oliver, R. T. (1971). *Communication and culture in ancient India and China*. Syracuse, NY: Syracuse University Press.

Rhetoric in the South Pacific

Susan Thomas
University of Sydney

Since the "new rhetorical" movement of the 1960s, the definition of rhetoric has expanded to encompass a variety of theories and movements, technologies and innovations, thereby raising the question of how rhetoric is understood and employed in the twenty-first century (→ Rhetorics: New Rhetorics). While its rich connection with composition studies has increased the profile, popularity, and applications of rhetoric in North America, the emphasis on composition or academic writing as a mainstay of tertiary education is not nearly so widespread in the South Pacific. As a result, the term "rhetoric" is regarded dubiously.

Popular uses of the word as a term of denigration, such as "rhetoric of the media," "just rhetoric," "empty rhetoric," and "political rhetoric," have propagated images of trickery, deception, or simply the antithesis of reality. In academic circles, "rhetoric" is too often perceived as synonymous with remedial, with "fixing up" bad writing, with teaching grammar, and with decorating language (→ Style and Rhetoric). However, progressive programs in the region reject these narrow definitions of rhetoric and see it instead as a valuable element of new textual cultures, particularly digital cultures. The five canons of classical rhetoric (invention, arrangement, style, memory, and delivery) have enjoyed a revival in everyday written and oral communication as a direct result of the information age. Particularly in online environments, critical applications of rhetoric are vital for managing, interpreting, and processing data (→ Technology and Communication; Rhetoric and Technology).

When considered in light of Andrea Lunsford's definition of rhetoric as the study of human communication, the South Pacific region becomes a rich environment for "communication studies." Claire Woods, Director of International Programs for the School of Communication, Information, and New Media at the University of South Australia, argues that rhetoric is central to a critical understanding of textual culture, to developing "an understanding of the theoretical and applied work involved in the *tekhne* of text production as readers, writers, makers and receivers of multi-genre textual forms" (2007; → Text and Intertextuality).

The English Department at the University of Auckland, New Zealand, offers a curriculum that features classical rhetoric and "writing studies" in much the same tradition as North American universities. This department is a leader in rhetorical studies in the region, and is one of very few to include courses in "rhetoric" alongside more mainstream degree requirements.

The emphasis on communication studies, however, is perhaps best demonstrated by the region's ever-evolving understanding of and increasing appreciation for its indigenous people. Studies of Aboriginal life writing have grown in popularity over recent decades and have awakened the region to its earliest histories of communication, in written, oral, and graphic forms. In *Writing never arrives naked* (2006), Penny van Toorn explores the involvement of Indigenous Australians in the colonizers' paper culture, and describes how Aboriginal people used the written word, creatively and resourcefully, for self-empowerment and survival (→ Culture and Communication, Ethnographic Perspectives on).

In *Comparative rhetoric*, George Kennedy writes that "evidence for traditional aboriginal rhetoric comes from an extensive body of prose myths and religious and secular song, which can be classified as epideictic in that its primary function was the transmission and reaffirmation of the beliefs and values of the community" (1998, 60; → Rhetoric, Epideictic).

As Edward Corbett, widely regarded as an unassuming giant of twentieth-century rhetoric, described it, rhetoric is the "enabling discipline" that crosses cultures and blurs boundaries. Though not always referred to as "rhetoric," this classical art is ever present in the South Pacific and remains a pillar of ethical and meaningful human communication.

SEE ALSO: ▶ Culture and Communication, Ethnographic Perspectives on ▶ Rhetoric, Epideictic ▶ Rhetoric and Technology ▶ Rhetorical Studies ▶ Rhetorics: New Rhetorics ▶ Style and Rhetoric ▶ Technology and Communication ▶ Text and Intertextuality

References and Suggested Readings

Dixon, R. M. W. (1980). *The language of Australia*. Cambridge: Cambridge University Press.
Kennedy, G. A. (1994). *A new history of classical rhetoric*. Princeton: Princeton University Press.

Kennedy, G. A. (1998). *Comparative rhetoric: An historical and cross-cultural introduction*. Oxford: Oxford University Press.

Lunsford, A. A., & Ouzgane, L. (eds.) (2004). *Crossing borderlands: Composition and postcolonial studies*. Pittsburgh, PA: University of Pittsburgh Press.

Van Toorn, P. (2006). *Writing never arrives naked*. Canberra: Aboriginal Studies Press.

Woods, C. (2007). Rhetoric and textual culture: Constructing a textual space in the curriculum. In S. Thomas (ed.), *What is the new rhetoric?* Newcastle upon Tyne: Cambridge Scholars.

Rhetoric and Technology

Barbara Warnick

University of Pittsburgh

Rhetoric as the study of forms of self-expression has many meanings depending on the context in which it is used. For theorists and practitioners of public speech, it is concerned primarily with the study of persuasion (→ Rhetoric, Argument, and Persuasion). For those interested in cultivation of effective expression, rhetoric concerns the use of style and development of polished writing and speaking (→ Style and Rhetoric). Rhetoric has been the subject of scholarly theory and analysis in education since at least the fourth century BCE, when Aristotle developed his theories of artistic proof and stylistic expression in *On rhetoric* (Aristotle 1991; → Rhetoric, Greek; Rhetorical Studies).

INFLUENCE OF TECHNOLOGY ON RHETORIC

Aristotle's On rhetoric exemplifies the ways in which technology has influenced rhetoric. The advent of writing in Greek culture meant that public oratory would be influenced by technical developments in inscribed expression. The adoption of writing in a previously oral culture precipitated interest in sequential logic and prescribed forms of organization. As Walter J. Ong (1982, 9) noted, "writing from the beginning did not reduce orality but enhanced it, making it possible to organize the 'principles' or constituents of oratory into a scientific 'art,' a sequentially ordered body of explanation that showed how and why oratory achieved and could be made to achieve its various specific effects." Pursuing this same line of work, Ong traced the work of Ramus, a sixteenth-century educator who developed pedagogical theories during the shift from oral to print culture and literacy. Ramus produced grand display schematics that "proceeded by cold-blooded definitions and divisions, until every last particle of the subject had been dissected and disposed of" (Ong 1982, 134). Ramus's visual displays and diagrams were remarkably well suited to dissemination in the new medium of print (→ Media History; Medium Theory; Rhetoric and Orality-Literacy Theorems).

The digitization of print technologies in the late twentieth century has further influenced the nature and form of rhetoric (→ Digitization and Media Convergence; Printing, History of). Early affordances introduced by digitization included use of new fonts and hypertext commentary on primary texts (Lanham 1993). Further development of hypertext markup language (HTML) in the 1990s provided enhanced possibilities for rhetorical expression that included embedded supporting hyperlinks, producers' ability to track users' movements through sites, automated personalization of messages delivered to users, and interactive user interfaces. These technical capacities of the new medium have been also combined with persuasive appeals in the form of animations and multimedia content to create online platforms that are highly effective for rhetorical expression (Farkas & Farkas 2002; Burnett & Marshall 2003).

The distinction between expressive forms seen in earlier media contexts and those associated with new media has been clarified by Lev Manovich (2001). He observed that an important difference between prior media and new media is that the latter are computerized. Whether it be a text or visual → image, the new media object originates on computers and is comprised of digital code and subject to algorithmic manipulation (→ Digital Imagery). Because it has been converted using mathematical functions, digital text is modular and is comprised of independent, separate elements such as pixels, hyperlinks, gif and jpeg elements, and media clips. These elements can be disaggregated, rearranged, and re-presented through automated processes. Thus, a good deal of digital media content is produced through the cooperation of multiple agents who produce variable texts that can be tailored to individual users, rather than unified, stable texts designed for mass audiences. As Manovich noted, another dimension of the digitally constituted text is its variability. Instead of a master text or copy that is created and stored, a digital text may give way to many versions as the text is altered automatically through periodic updates and processually through actions taken by users. This process has been termed "co-production" and viewed as a collaborative constitution of the text, in which content is jointly produced by authors and users (→ Text and Intertextuality).

THEORETICAL CONCEPTS

The need to study and analyze co-produced texts has led some scholars in the humanities to turn to the work of prominent theorists such as → Roland Barthes (1977) and → Mikhail Bakhtin (1981). Barthes' work shifted the critic's focus from the author as sole producer of an oral or written message to the reader or consumer of the text. Barthes believed that an author-centered orientation worked from the perspective of the "readerly text" – a finished work that views the author as the center of meaning production. This is in contrast to what Barthes labeled the "writerly text" – one which is incomplete, plural, and indeterminate, thus calling upon the reader to supply or fill in meaning. Barthes' view of text as a network in which meaning emerges along a horizon of possible significations aligns well with digital expression as experienced in contemporary media environments, where texts are produced through corporate authorship, constantly revised, often borrowed, and frequently parasitic on the other texts to which they are linked. Analysts and critics of rhetorical expression working from Barthes' framework often consider the range of possible meanings and construals of a persuasive message and how it might be taken up, rather than emphasizing the purported intention of its author in interpreting its meaning. (→ Rhetoric and Semiotics; Semiotics).

Because Bakhtin viewed artistic expression as seen in novelistic prose as interweaving the speech of the author, the characters, the various forms of expression in the host culture, and what is said in other texts, his theories have also been quite pertinent to study of rhetorical expression in certain current media forums. For example, the world wide web is host to many forms of heteroglossic speech, such as multiply authored sites, intertextual satire, parody, group discussion and deliberation, and other contexts where many voices blend and clash (→ Internet). In such an environment, it is useful to consider persuasion in multiply authored sites as an expression of orientations that evolve from multiple forms of expression and points of view.

METHODS AND STUDIES

The study of online persuasion has included various methods of analysis and criticism. For example, Laura Gurak's (1997) study of text-based discussion in listservs, newsgroups, and email used a → *case study method* to examine persuasion practices among people protesting actions that they considered to be a threat to online privacy. Gurak considered participants' use of form letters, petitions, and the patterns of their dissemination as well as the content of the messages circulated to explain why the agents against whom they were protesting acceded to their demands. In a later study of web-based protest, Gurak and her co-author John Logie (2003) considered member protest against online service provider Yahoo! in 1999 by using a comparative case study method. They demonstrated that the structure of hypertext discourse on the web enabled actions that would not have been possible in earlier text-based communication. These included defacement of existing websites, redirection of users to alternate sites, and use of notices and site placement to establish a single website as a central node in the protest action. These two studies indicate how the rapid grow of the web and its associated technologies changed the form and effectiveness of online protest over time (→ Rhetoric and Social Protest).

A second line of research on rhetorical discourse in new media environments is from a *critical perspective*. For example, Susan Herring studied the roles and nature of online communication involving women for over 15 years. In a 2001 retrospective of trends relating to gender, she used → discourse analysis to trace the ways in which gender differences emerged in control of online interaction and nature of online messages (→ Mediated Social Interaction). In the Internet's early days, when women were a small minority of Internet users, they were often harassed or dismissed by participants in online discussions. The advent of the web brought with it online pornography, which objectified women and exploited their representations for personal gain (→ Sex and Pornography Online). By the 2000s, online content came to be dominated by commercialized represent-ations that positioned women as having a need to please others and improve themselves. Herring's current work has considered practices of self-representation produced by women in personal home pages, online meeting sites, and on webcams to describe the ways in which online gender representation has continued to be stereotypical (→ Stereotypes).

Rhetorical criticism, a method of analysis that focuses on text-based persuasive strategies and how they function to influence users, has also been used to study online discourse (→ Rhetorical Criticism). This mode of criticism closely examines uses of expressive form, placement, genre, argument, visual image, and other means of symbolic representation that are used to persuade audiences. For example, a rhetorical criticism of web-based discourse would consider site layout, the link structure, ease of use, and the means by which site design is planned to encourage repeat visitors and increase site usability. Such an approach might also examine site elements such as interactivity and intertextuality as they are used to promote user involvement with site content, as well as the means by which site authors seek to establish their ethos, or credibility, with audiences (Warnick 2007; → Ethos and Rhetoric).

As communication and information technologies develop, the means used to persuade audiences are likely to change as well (→ Technology and Communication). During the classical period, additional logical forms emerged and exposition became increasingly linear. In the late nineteenth century in the United States, training in oratory emphasized dramatic use of the voice and elaborate gestures to convey content to large audiences in the absence of devices for oral projection of the voice. By the early twenty-first century, the Internet made possible new forms of immediate and highly visual persuasive expression. In each case, rhetoric has adapted to the communication contexts in which it has been used, and there is every reason to believe that this trend will continue in the future.

SEE ALSO: ▶ Bakhtin, Mikhail ▶ Barthes, Roland ▶ Case Studies ▶ Digital Imagery ▶ Digitization and Media Convergence ▶ Discourse Analysis ▶ Ethos and Rhetoric ▶ Image ▶ Internet ▶ Media History ▶ Mediated Social Interaction ▶ Medium Theory ▶ Printing, History of ▶ Rhetoric, Argument, and Persuasion ▶ Rhetoric and Gender ▶ Rhetoric, Greek ▶ Rhetoric and Orality-Literacy Theorems ▶ Rhetoric and Semiotics ▶ Rhetoric and Social Protest ▶ Rhetoric and Visuality ▶ Rhetorical Criticism ▶ Rhetorical Studies ▶ Semiotics ▶ Sex and Pornography Online ▶ Stereotypes ▶ Style and Rhetoric ▶ Technologically Mediated Discourse ▶ Technology and Communication ▶ Text and Intertextuality

References and Suggested Readings

Aristotle (1991). *On rhetoric: A theory of civic discourse.* (trans. G. A. Kennedy). Oxford: Oxford University Press.

Bakhtin, M. M. (1981). *The dialogic imagination: Four essays* (trans. C. Emerson & M. Holquist). Austin, TX: University of Texas Press.

Barthes, R. (1977). *Image – music – text: Essays* (trans. S. Heath). New York: Noonday.

Burnett, R., & Marshall, P. D. (2003). *Web theory: An introduction.* London: Routledge.

Farkas, D. K., & Farkas, J. B. (2002). *Principles of web design.* New York: Longman.

Gurak, L. J. (1997). *Persuasion and privacy in cyberspace.* New Haven, CT: Yale University Press.

Gurak, L. J., & Logie, J. (2003). Internet protests: From text to web. In M. McCaughey & M. D. Ayers (eds.). *Cyberactivism: Online activism in theory and practice.* New York: Routledge, pp. 25–46.

Herring, S. C. (2001). Gender and power in online communication, Center for Social Informatics working paper WP-01-05. At http://rkcsi.indiana.edu/archive/CSI/WP/WP01–05B.html, accessed September 23, 2007.

Lanham, R. A. (1993). *The electronic word: Democracy, technology, and the arts.* Chicago, IL: University of Chicago Press.

Manovich, L. (2001). *The language of new media.* Cambridge, MA: MIT Press.

Ong, W. J. (1982). *Orality and literacy: The technologizing of the word.* London: Methuen.

Warnick, B. (2007). *Rhetoric online: Persuasion and politics on the world wide web.* New York: Peter Lang.

Rhetoric, Vernacular

Gerard A. Hauser

University of Colorado at Boulder

The rhetorical tradition began with, and has remained linked to, the public discourse of official forums. Aristotle named these deliberative, forensic, and epideictic rhetoric (→ Rhetoric, Greek). Although these first appeared as genres and later included additional forms of address, such as the sermon and the essay, the distinctive focus of rhetorical theory and criticism into the mid-twentieth century remained on speaking and writing. With some notable exceptions, these genres were typically delivered in an official site, such as a legislative chamber, or by a person who was in a position of power, such as the leader of a movement. They are captured by the category of "public address." From the mid-1960s this category was challenged on a number of fronts, such as its inability to account for protest rhetoric, the rhetoric of new media, or that of marginalized groups, which became subjects of inquiry among rhetoricians (→ Rhetoric and Social Protest). In the mid-1990s, this challenge was extended theoretically and critically to reconsider excluded voices without access to official sites, voices that are not in positions of leadership, or whose modes of expression do not take the form of public address or formal essay, by considering them as they were manifested in vernacular exchanges, or *vernacular rhetoric*.

Vernacular rhetoric is variously understood as deliberation and opinion formation reflecting the rhetoric of the everyday (Hauser 1999), rhetoric of the people (McGee 1975), mundane rhetorical performances within a culture that shape it as a culture (Ono & Sloop 1995), and a critique of culture and a mode of resistance that makes power relations visible (Calafell & Delgado 2004; Hauser 2006; Holling 2006; Ono & Sloop 1995; Sloop & Ono 1997). Irrespective of these differences, those who study vernacular rhetoric examine "texts" that are outside power, and often as they interact with power. They contain the voices of citizens who do not hold office, do not have access to official forums, and whose expression of opinions and sentiments exerts influence more through its logic of circulation than as a significant official statement.

Usually vernacular rhetoric consists of → discourses that circulate within a particular group or community, such as a street gang. It may also include the range of expression outside power directed to pervasive concerns and issues or signal events, such as how lay people discuss euthanasia. And it may include artistic expression and images that reflect commitments and sentiments of some identifiable social unit, such as an identity group, a social movement, or a significant cross-section of a nation as these are expressed in the → *public sphere* (Finnegan & Kang 2004).

Study of vernacular modes of expression has opened rhetoric studies to areas heretofore ignored by the discipline. Vernacular rhetoric does not necessarily frame issues in the same way as authority, often uses different topoi, and is commonly expressed through alternative media, such as the Internet (Holling 2006), visual images (Calafell & Delgado 2004), the body (Hauser 2006), or other means of materiality to make different arguments from those expressed in official public spheres by the elite voices of the empowered. These differences are important for what they reveal about dimensions of human experience; invention and expression of community, subjectivity, and identity; and resistance and aspiration as they are expressed by people in their everyday lives, often in hush harbors, sometimes under conditions of overt oppression, but always drawn from the community. Sometimes they may reflect and circulate the ideas of authority figures, sometimes they may influence the expression of authority figures (Hauser 1999), but sometimes the ideas and sentiments circulating in everyday discourse may frame life's realities in ways that are quite different from, and are a critique of, those of authority (Sloop and Ono 1997). Regardless of how they relate to official expressions, they are an essential voice in a social dialogue that shapes a human world of values, ideas, beliefs, emotions, celebrations, and actions.

Within this frame, studies of vernacular rhetoric are an extension of the mid-twentieth century shift in rhetoric study's focus from producing influential communication to *exploring rhetoric as a social practice* (Burke 1969; → Rhetorics: New Rhetorics). This line of thought argued that society could not be understood without taking into account how humans use symbols – speaking and writing primarily but not exclusively – to shape social realities, which, in turn, constitute a human world. Because the rhetorical perspective toward language use always considers it as addressed, theorizing rhetoric as a social practice means it must be regarded as a performance that is always enacted ensemble.

The shift from production to social performance has had the significant consequence of decentering the privileged position of the speech or the essay as the focus of rhetoric scholars. In this respect, those who study vernacular rhetoric join a number of other schools within the discipline in addressing major questions now to the fore in rhetoric studies: how do we establish social identification through our modes of social discourse; what do our modes of rhetorical exchange reveal about a shared sense of identity and a shared reality; how does ensemble performance, which shifts from "an audience" addressed to "a public" that forms through networks of everyday rhetorical exchanges, challenge the definition and locus of agency, subjectivity, public memory, identity, and epistemology?

In addition to these questions, there are *major challenges* facing the study of vernacular rhetoric that are, to some degree, *sui generis*. How is a text constructed when the discourse, unlike a speech or a diary, is not continuous? The evidence of vernacular rhetoric is often like archeological shards that must be pieced together from fragments of significant symbolic performances. Does vernacular rhetoric have a logic or multiple logics of circulation? Must such logic(s) necessarily challenge those of official voices? This question is central to critique of vernacular rhetoric, since some, following Ono and Sloop (1997), always regard it as already "outlaw" rhetoric, while others, following Hauser (1999), regard it as an exchange out of power that, while constitutive of community, is often a mode of citizen deliberation that is not necessarily a mode of resistance.

Finally, what are the *methodological implications* that accompany studying vernacular rhetoric? The humanities have traditionally deployed methodologies suited to textual analysis of specific artifacts, such as the painting, the drama, or the public address. Although vernacular rhetoric may take these forms, it is more commonly found in everyday exchanges that require participant observation if not ethnographic methods (→ Rhetoric and Ethnography). Combining non-traditional methods with traditional methods poses intellectual challenges, but also opens an avenue to bringing the humanities to the street.

SEE ALSO: ▶ Discourse ▶ Public Sphere ▶ Rhetoric and Ethnography ▶ Rhetoric, Greek ▶ Rhetoric and Social Protest ▶ Rhetoric and Technology ▶ Rhetoric and Visuality ▶ Rhetorics: New Rhetorics

References and Suggested Readings

Burke, K. (1969). *A rhetoric of motives*. Berkeley, CA: University of California Press.

Calafell, B. M., & Delgado, F. (2004). Reading Latino/a images: Interrogating *Americanos. Critical Studies in Media Communication*, 21, 1–21.

Finnegan, C., & Kang, J. (2004). "Sighting" the public: Iconoclasm and public sphere theory. *Quarterly Journal of Speech*, 90, 377–402.

Hauser, G. A. (1999). *Vernacular voices: The rhetoric of publics and public spheres*. Columbia: University of South Carolina Press.

Hauser, G. A. (2006). Demonstrative displays of dissident rhetoric: The case of Prisoner 885/63. In L. Prelli (ed.), *The rhetoric of display*. Columbia: University of South Carolina Press, pp. 229–254.

Holling, M. A. (2006). Forming oppositional social concord to California's Proposition 187 and squelching social discord in the vernacular space of CHICLE. *Communication and Critical Cultural Studies*, 3, 202–222.

McGee, M. C. (1975). In search of "the people": A rhetorical alternative. *Quarterly Journal of Speech*, 61, 235–249.

Ono, K. A., & Sloop, J. M. (1995). The critique of vernacular discourse. *Communication Monographs*, 62, 19–46.

Sloop, J. M., & Ono, K. A. (1997). Out-law discourse: The critical politics of material judgment. *Philosophy and Rhetoric*, 30, 50–69.

Rhetoric and Visuality

Cara A. Finnegan
University of Illinois at Urbana-Champaign

If visuality is understood broadly as the practices, performances, and configurations of the appearances, then the relationship between rhetoric and visuality is as old as the art of rhetoric itself. The ancients tied rhetoric to the world of *mimesis*, or the appearances, rather than to the realm of philosophical truth; this relationship has often unfairly relegated both rhetoric and the visual to subordinate status in the Platonic regime of knowledge (Kennedy 2001). Yet in the ancient tradition the visual is constitutive of rhetoric in a number of ways (→ Rhetoric, Greek). The canon of delivery references visuality in its emphasis on gesture, movement, and performance (Kjeldsen 2003; → Delivery and Rhetoric; Gestures in Discourse). The trope of *ekphrasis* (literally "bringing-before-the-eyes") and Aristotle's notion of *phantasia* reference the ability of rhetoric to create → images in the mind and cultivate affective grounds for judgment (O'Gorman 2005; → Pathos and Rhetoric; Rhetoric, Epideictic). Sight is framed as a powerful influence on persuasion by Quintilian, who divided images into the categories of pictorial images and mental images, and argued that the best orators created visions (*visiones*) in their listeners' minds (Scholz 2001; Kjeldsen 2003; → Rhetoric, Roman).

A contemporary discussion of the relationship of rhetoric to visuality would position itself in relation to the rise of visual culture studies in the late 1980s and early 1990s. The concept of visuality emerged in the 1980s as a key term of the poststructuralist turn in art history (→ Art as Communication; Visual Culture). Hal Foster's germinal collection, *Vision and visuality* (1988), which featured the work of scholars such as Jonathan Crary and Martin Jay, notably framed visuality as the recognition that vision is socially constructed and historically constrained; how we see is not natural but tied to the historically specific ways that we learn to see. Jay (1996) usefully lists a range of concepts and theorists associated with the study of visuality, most importantly *the gaze* (Laura Mulvey), *surveillance* and *panopticism* (Michel Foucault), → *spectacle* (Guy Debord), → *scopic regime* (Christian Metz and Martin Jay), the *mirror stage* (Jacques Lacan), and the *pictorial turn* (W. J. T. Mitchell; → Spectator Gaze). The concept of the pictorial turn has been of particular interest to rhetorical scholars because it encourages scholars to revisit relationships between image and text, and marks a growing recognition that the visual is not reducible to the operations of language or text (Mitchell 1994).

In the field of communication, scholars' attention to the rhetorical aspects of visuality in this poststructuralist sense is relatively recent, though attention to the rhetoric of visual artifacts goes back several decades. The 1971 Wingspread Conference "Report of the Committee on the Advancement and Refinement of Rhetorical Criticism" famously argued that rhetorical critics should pay increased attention to visual artifacts, performances, and media (→ Rhetorical Criticism). While scholars after Kenneth Burke accepted the notion that rhetoric was best conceived broadly as symbolic action of all kinds, it was not until the 1970s and 1980s that a critical mass of scholars began conducting → case studies of visual artifacts such as murals, → posters, → documentary film, → television, political → prints, and memorials; their interests are reflected in Martin J. Medhurst and Thomas Benson's (1984) edited collection, *Rhetorical dimensions in media* (→ Rhetoric and Media Studies). Partly as a result of the growing disciplinary acceptance of rhetorical analysis of visual artifacts, and partly as a result of the rise of attention to visuality in the humanities more generally, by the late 1990s what was coming to be called "visual rhetoric" had begun to coalesce into a recognizable sub-field of rhetorical studies in communication departments. Scholars not only continued their decades-long interest in exploring the rhetorical aspects of historical and contemporary visual artifacts, they also began to attend to issues of visuality more explicitly. Today, communication scholars working at the intersection of rhetoric and visuality concern themselves with a wide variety of theoretical, critical, and historical questions, including the practices of visibility and invisibility, the role of spectacle in the → public sphere, rhetorical histories of viewing, the role of image appropriation and circulation in public culture, and the complex relationships among rhetoric, the body, and cultural performance (Prelli 2006; Olson et al. 2008).

SEE ALSO: ▶ Art as Communication ▶ Case Studies ▶ Delivery and Rhetoric ▶ Documentary Film ▶ Gestures in Discourse ▶ Image ▶ Nonverbal Communication and Culture ▶ Pathos and Rhetoric ▶ Poster ▶ Prints ▶ Public Sphere ▶ Rhetoric, Epideictic ▶ Rhetoric, Greek ▶ Rhetoric and Media Studies ▶ Rhetoric, Nonverbal

▶ Rhetoric and Poetics ▶ Rhetoric, Roman ▶ Rhetoric and Semiotics ▶ Rhetorical Criticism ▶ Scopic Regime ▶ Spectacle ▶ Spectator Gaze ▶ Television ▶ Visual Communication ▶ Visual Culture ▶ Visual Representation

References and Suggested Readings

Foster, H. (ed.) (1988). *Vision and visuality*. New York: New Press.

Jay, M. (1996). Vision in context: Reflections and refractions. In T. Brennan & M. Jay (eds.), *Vision in context: Historical and contemporary perspectives on sight*. New York: Routledge, pp. 3–12.

Kennedy, G. A. (2001). Imitation. In T. O. Sloane (ed.), *Encyclopedia of rhetoric*. Oxford: Oxford University Press, pp. 381–384.

Kjeldsen, J. E. (2003). Talking to the eye: Visuality in ancient rhetoric. *Word and Image*, 19(3), 133–137.

Medhurst, M. J., & Benson, T. W. (eds.) (1984). *Rhetorical dimensions in media: A critical casebook*. Dubuque, IA: Kendall/Hunt.

Mitchell, W. J. T. (1994). *Picture theory: Essays on verbal and visual representation*. Chicago, IL: University of Chicago Press.

O'Gorman, N. (2005). Aristotle's *phantasia* in the *Rhetoric: Lexis*, appearance, and the epideictic function of discourse. *Philosophy and Rhetoric*, 38, 16–40.

Olson, L. C., Finnegan, C. A., & Hope, D. S. (eds.) (2008). *Visual rhetoric: A reader in communication and American culture*. Thousand Oaks, CA: Sage.

Prelli, L. J. (ed.) (2006). *Rhetorics of display*. Columbia, SC: University of South Carolina Press.

Scholz, B. F. (2001). Art. In T. O. Sloane (ed.), *Encyclopedia of rhetoric*. Oxford: Oxford University Press, pp. 52–57.

Rhetoric in Western Europe: Britain

Sean Patrick O'Rourke

Furman University

The tradition of rhetorical theory and practice in Britain is longstanding and vibrant. In the Middle Ages, Britain produced important contributions to rhetorical theory. The Venerable Bede (c. 672/73–735), for instance, provided a treatment of the stylistic aspects of discourse in his *De schematibus et tropis*, and Alcuin (c. 735–804), the British-born tutor of and advisor to Charlemagne, left us his *Disputatio de rhetorica et de virtutibus*, a dialogue in which emperor and teacher explore the theoretical underpinnings of civic discourse in the Ciceronian tradition (→ Rhetoric, Medieval). While the practice of public address was quite limited during the period, British rhetorics explored the persuasive elements of verse, and monastic libraries in the British Isles preserved manuscripts of some of the key rhetorical texts of late antiquity.

While the Renaissance came relatively late to Britain, it brought continental influence to the rhetorics Britain produced (→ Rhetoric, European Renaissance). Humanist texts such as Leonard Cox's *Arte or crafte of rethoryke* (1530) and Thomas Wilson's *Arte of rhetorique* (1553) had a decidedly Ciceronian flavor. Cox treated invention (the ancient canon of discovering ideas or developing lines of argument) by drawing upon Roman theories of the *loci communes* (argumentative commonplaces; → Invention and Rhetoric). Wilson offered a full-blown treatment of all five *officia* of Ciceronian rhetoric (invention, arrangement, style, memory, and delivery) and adapted them to the needs of a Tudor audience. Both of these works were heavily influenced by the theories of Philipp Melanchthon (1497–1560), the German humanist theologian, whose *Institutiones rhetoricae* (1521) provided a four-fold division of the art (judgment, invention, disposition, elocution) compatible with both antiquity and Protestant Christianity.

Britain also produced stylistic and Ramistic rhetorics in the sixteenth century. Richard Sherry's *Treatise of schemes and tropes* (1550) and Henry Peacham's *Garden of eloquence* (1577) treated expression, the stylistic aspect of rhetoric (→ Style and Rhetoric). John Jewell (*Oratio contra rhetoricam*, 1548), Gabriel Harvey (*Rhetor*, 1575; *Ciceronianus*, 1576), and Douglas Fenner (*The Artes of Logicke and Rhetorike*, 1584) all gave voice to different aspects of Ramus's attack on Ciceronian rhetoric (→ Rhetoric and Dialectic).

In terms of diversity and innovation, rhetoric reached its zenith in Britain during the Enlightenment. Rhetorical theories developed along five broad lines of inquiry. The first of these is the neo-classical or neo-Ciceronian. In John Holmes' *Art of rhetoric made easy* (1755), John Lawson's *Lectures concerning oratory* (1758), and especially John Ward's *System of oratory* (1759), British writers crafted theories of rhetoric that adapted the broadly classical concerns of the orator in public controversy to the somewhat changed environment of Enlightenment Britain. These theories considered the civic goals of rhetorical discourse, the orator's argumentative resources, and the situations or causes (legal, political, occasional, and religious) he might confront.

A second and related line of inquiry considered rhetoric as an art of criticism and conversation. This line, the belletristic, expanded rhetoric to include literature, historical writing, and even epic poetry. Concerned largely with matters of taste, style, and sublimity, belletristic rhetoric shifted attention from the production of discourse to its reception. In his *Elements of criticism* (1762), Henry Home, Lord Kames, offered a nearly pure form of belletristic rhetoric, while Adam Smith's *Lectures on rhetoric and belles lettres* (delivered 1762–1763) and Hugh Blair's *Lectures on rhetoric and belles lettres* (1783) created rhetorics that combined neo-classical and belletristic concerns.

A third line of theory might broadly be called the philosophical, for it resulted from the quest to explain persuasion in light of contemporary advances in psychology and philosophy of mind. George Campbell, in his *Philosophy of rhetoric* (1776), drew upon both Thomas Reid's commonsense philosophy and David Hume's radically different conceptions of human thought and crafted a rhetoric rooted in faculty psychology, inductive processes, and the passions and judgments of the audience (→ Rhetoric and Philosophy). Hume himself, in his essays on eloquence, taste, and essay writing, assessed contemporary eloquence in light of the ancients and also suggested that women be included in the sphere of intelligent discourse.

Students were exposed most directly to a fourth kind of rhetoric, the lectures provided in the schools and universities. Robert Watson, George Jardine, William Greenfield, William Leechman, Archibald Arthur, and many others toiled in near obscurity but provided students with a version of rhetoric that was situated in the moral philosophy course. They taught students that rhetoric was best considered in its relationship to other moral studies, including what today would be called theology, psychology, philosophy of mind, ethics, jurisprudence, and logic. These teachers tended to make rhetoric subordinate to logic and limited to matters of style, taste, and criticism.

One final type of rhetoric, the elocutionary, focused almost exclusively on delivery of the speech (→ Delivery and Rhetoric). Thomas Sheridan, in his *Course of lectures on elocution* (1762), argued that a correct and powerful speaking voice would improve not only the speech but also the moral character of the individual and the institutions about which he spoke. Elocutionary theories tended to de-emphasize the inventional or substantive aspects of the art.

The eighteenth century also saw a dramatic increase in the quality and quantity of oratorical discourse. Preachers in the pulpits of the Scottish Kirk and the Anglican Church, advocates and barristers in the courts, and MPs in parliament made public discourse a central part of civic life, and illegal reports of political orations fed the public's growing appetite for speech texts. Political discourse of the period is best exemplified by the epic battles between Pitt the Elder and Horatio Walpole and the speeches of Burke and Pitt the Younger on the French and American revolutions.

SEE ALSO: ▶ Delivery and Rhetoric ▶ Invention and Rhetoric ▶ Rhetoric and Dialectic ▶ Rhetoric, European Renaissance ▶ Rhetoric, Medieval ▶ Rhetoric and Philosophy ▶ Style and Rhetoric

References and Suggested Readings

Gaillet, L. L. (ed.) (1998). *Scottish rhetoric and its influences.* Davis, CA: Hermagoras.

Howell, W. S. (1956). *Logic and rhetoric in England, 1500–1700.* Princeton, NJ: Princeton University Press.

Howell, W. S. (1971). *Eighteenth-century British logic and rhetoric.* Princeton, NJ: Princeton University Press.

Miller, T. P. (1997). *The formation of college English: Rhetoric and belles lettres in the British cultural provinces.* Pittsburgh, PA: University of Pittsburgh.

Oliver, R. T. (1986). *The influence of rhetoric in the shaping of Great Britain: From the Roman invasion to the early nineteenth century.* Newark, DE: University of Delaware Press.

Potkay, A. (1994). *The fate of eloquence in the age of Hume.* Ithaca, NY: Cornell University Press.